COMMUNICATION:
Foundations, Skills, and Applications

THIRD EDITION

WILLIAM J. SEILER
University of Nebraska at Lincoln

HarperCollins*CollegePublishers*

Acquisitions Editor: Cynthia Biron
Development Editor: Dawn Groundwater
Cover Design: Ruttle Graphics, Inc.
Compositor: Ruttle Graphics, Inc.
Electronic Production Manager: Angel Gonzalez Jr.
Publishing Services: Ruttle Graphics, Inc.
Printer and Binder: R. R. Donnelley & Sons Company
Cover Printer: The Lehigh Press, Inc.

ACKNOWLEDGMENTS: Unless otherwise acknowledged, all photographs are the property of Scott, Foresman and Company. Page abbreviations are as follows: (T) top, (C) center, (B) bottom, (L) left, (R) right.

COMMUNICATION: Foundations, Skills, and Applications
Third Edition

Library of Congress Cataloging-in-Publication Data
Seiler, William J.
    Communication: foundations, skills, and applications / William J. Seiler.—3rd ed.
        p.   cm.
    Rev. ed. of: Introduction to speech communication.   1992.
    Includes index.
    ISBN 0-673-99375-2
    1. Oral communication.   I. Seiler, William J.   Introduction to speech
    communication.   II. Title.
  P95.S45   1996
302.2'242—dc20   94-29862
                                     CIP

95 96 97 9 8 7 6 5 4 3 2 1

CONTENTS

Chapter 2

Perception and Human Communication 37

Chapter 3

Self-Concept In Human Communication 63

Chapter 4

Verbal Communication 84

Chapter 5

Nonverbal Communication 114

Chapter 6

Listening 144

PART II

Chapter 7

Selecting a Topic and Relating to the Audience 168

Chapter 8

Chapter 9

Chapter 10

Managing Anxiety and Delivering Your Speech 278

Chapter 11

Chapter 12

PART III

Chapter 13

Chapter 14

Chapter 15

Chapter 16

Employment Interviewing: Preparing for Your Future

PREFACE

The third edition, like the first and second editions, is designed to help all who wish to improve their understanding of and abilities in communicating with others. To reflect the book's content and its purpose more accurately, we have given the book a new title *Communication: Foundations, Skills, and Applications.* The text was written for college students who are taking an introductory communication course to help them learn about communication principles, public speaking, and interpersonal and group communication. It is our hope by providing a sound foundation for the understanding of communication along with information to develop and improve skills as well as how communication is applied in various contexts that students will become more competent communicators.

Goal

The goal of the third edition is the same as that of the first two editions: *To provide students with a comprehensive, practical, readable, enjoyable, and, most important, intellectually sound book from which to learn about communication.* As a result, *Communication: Foundations, Skills, and Applications, Third Edition* is adaptable to the teaching styles of experienced teachers, who will complement its content with their personal knowledge and experience, and to beginning instructors, who will be assisted by its thoroughness, pertinent examples, and well-organized pedagogy.

Changes in the Third Edition

Most books are not perfect for everyone or for every possible learning situation—thus, authors like myself and publishers like HarperCollins are always striving to make their books better and ultimately more useful and easier for students and instructors. This is our goal in the third edition. We think we have accomplished that goal.

The result I believe, is a text that truly represents input from many, many talented and helpful individuals. In my view, it is this commitment of listening to you and others in the field that accounts for the fact that you are now reading the third edition of my text.

The following list highlights some of the changes that were made in this edition, taking into account the input of students, instructors, colleagues, and reviewers:

- **A new four-color design makes the book more appealing and readable.** New photos and cartoons were added to provide more relevant and contemporary examples of communication situations. All visual materials are more integrated with the text and directly related to the content, making the graphics more closely integrated.

- **A sensitivity to gender and cultural differences encourages better communication.** Every attempt was made to ensure sensitivity to individuals from differing backgrounds, making it as meaningful as possible when applying and using communication in the United States.

- **Additional coverage on gender differences, cultural diversity, and critical thinking is included throughout the book.** There are specific sections on each in many of the chapters. Examples include a new section on how communication shapes the global village; expanded sections on cultural, racial, and gender differences related to perception and communication; more on gender and self-concept; a new section on gender-inclusive language; more gender and cultural-diversity examples related to nonverbal communication; a new section on critical thinking and listening; more thorough treatment of cultural diversity and relating to one's audience; more extensive coverage of gender, culture, and ethical issues in interpersonal contexts; an expanded section on gender difference in group participation; and a new section on gender differences and leadership style. Finally, to encourage critical thinking, questions and exercises have been integrated into the text for students to think about and respond to.

- **A new chapter on Developing Relationships complements the chapter on interpersonal communication.** This new chapter provides information on how we interact, handle conflict, and develop and end relationships.

- **A new transactional model of communication** is included in Chapter 1. The model helps explain and define what communication is and illustrates the key components.

- **Expanded coverage of public communication** includes more student-oriented examples, more information on topic selection, and a broader emphasis on organization and outlining. Also, there is more information on the use of computer searches to obtain information; an expanded discussion of vocal delivery; and additional material on speech anxiety and how to eliminate it. Finally, new examples from student speeches are provided to aid students in developing their own speeches and a new section on fallacies is included.

- **Updated text with the most recent research and examples.** When appropriate, actual research studies have been used to help students understand the relationship between content and the research it supports.

- **Condensed discussion of small-group communication is now covered in one rather than two chapters.** The material was condensed for clarity's sake, and now includes gender and cultural issues related to small-group communication. In addition, there is more coverage of critical thinking as it applies to small-group communication.

- **Many new chapter openings and scenarios.** These student oriented scenarios grab the reader's attention and make the chapter more meaningful by showing the relevance of communication to their everyday lives.

- **Updated and revised "Think About It" and Mini-Exercises.** These will help students develop critical thinking skills and to become competent communicators.

Features

Effectiveness in speech communication is an acquired skill. Although natural speaking ability is an asset, any person's capabilities in communication can be improved through (1) an understanding of communicative theories and principles, (2) training in the basic principles, and (3) practice. This book meets students' needs in all three areas by providing:

- Simply stated and specific learning objectives at the beginning of each chapter

- Thorough and systematic explanations of basic principles

- Clear, concrete, student-oriented examples, photos, cartoons, and other visual materials that support and expand on key concepts

- Thought-provoking "Think About It" probes and exercises that encourage students' active involvement throughout each chapter

- Review sections that highlight key information

- Lists of down-to-earth hints and guidelines that help students transform theory into practice

- Thorough end-of-chapter summaries that review key terms and concepts

- Discussion questions at the end of each chapter

- Chapter-by-chapter glossaries of key terms plus a complete glossary at the end of the text

Organization

The chapters are organized to provide a practical and workable approach to teaching the fundamentals of communication. Part I: "Foundations of Communication" provides the necessary background and basic principles for all communication. Part II: "Public Communication" helps students to develop their speaking skills as they learn to select a topic, analyze an audience, gather and use supporting and clarifying materials, organize and outline speech material, deliver a speech with confidence, and effectively inform and persuade an audience. Part III: "Interpersonal Communication" describes communication in relationships, in small groups, and on the employment interview.

Public communication skills are discussed early, before interpersonal communication, because I believe that they are fundamental to all communication. All communication is goal-oriented. Therefore, in order to communicate effectively throughout life—whether socially or on the job, in one-to-one situations, in small groups, or before an audience—a person must be able to communicate with confidence; support and clarify his or her thoughts; organize information; analyze those with whom he or she is communicating; and inform and persuade effectively. Moreover, in life after college, students will discover that purposeful, career-related communication relies more on the preparedness underlying public communication than it does on the empathy of self-disclosure found at the heart of interpersonal communication.

This sequence of presentation is also based on the recognition that students in an introductory communication course must master a great deal of basic information before they give a speech, yet because of time constraints, they need to begin preparing and presenting speeches as early in the term as possible. Introducing public speaking skills first provides a more even balance between speech presentations and other activities and alleviates the tendency to focus on speechmaking exclusively at the end of the term.

Considerable demands are placed on those who teach the introductory communication course, and as a result, there is a wide variety of ways to teach the course—for example, emphasis on interpersonal communication, emphasis on public speaking, or equal emphasis on all types of communication. To meet these differing needs, each chapter is completely self-contained so that an instructor can easily arrange the sequence to meet the demands of the specific teaching situation.

The Instructor's Manual

The Instructor's Manual is authored by Mary Bort and has been revised to reflect the changes included in the third edition. It provides nuts-and-bolts information about designing and developing a fundamental communication course and offers suggestions for aiding instruction. The manual includes methods for managing and organizing the basic course, and provides classroom as well as outside-of-classroom exercises and assignments;

resources for instruction including additional readings, games, simulations, and films; a section on evaluating speeches; a complete test file, including multiple-choice, true-false, and short-answer questions; a section on training and working with part-time instructors and graduate teaching assistants; and finally, a section on the Personalized System of Instruction, which is a method for teaching the basic course.

Other Supplements

Test Bank contains multiple-choice, true-false, and short-answer questions for each chapter. All questions are referenced to text chapter and page number.

TestMaster, also by Mary Bort, is an ideal test-generation system that features all test items in the Test Bank, with answers keyed to the text. Users can easily mix, scramble, or edit the supplied questions, or create questions of their own.

HarperCollins Video Library includes a collection of videotapes highlighting a vast array of communication topics such as public speaking, group problem solving, listening, persuasive speaking, and interviewing.

Instructional Tape is a collection of student speeches and evaluations developed by students for students. To acquire this training tape, send a blank VHS video tape to Bill Seiler, Department of Communication Studies, University of Nebraska-Lincoln, Lincoln, Nebraska 68588-0329 or call 402-472-2069. The E-mail address is BSEILER @ UNLINFO.UNL.EDU

PSI-Study Guide Manual is a manual that provides students with questions and exercises to aid them in studying. The manual was designed for use at the University of Nebraska, but could be modified or changed to meet different uses. For a sample manual, contact Bill Seiler, at the address listed above.

About the Author

William J. Seiler is currently Professor and Chair of the Department of Communication Studies, University of Nebraska at Lincoln, where he has taught since 1972. He received his doctorate from Purdue University and has an adjunct appointment in Teachers College as a professor of Curriculum and Instruction. Professionally trained in the areas of business and organizational communication, instructional communication, psycholinguistics, statistics, and speech communication, Dr. Seiler is an experienced educator, consultant, researcher, and author. He has published numerous monographs, articles, and educational materials in the field of communication.

In addition, Dr. Seiler has presented lectures and speeches throughout the midwest. As an author, he has published two other textbooks: *Communication in Business and Professional Organizations* and *Communication for the Contemporary Classroom.* He has also served on editorial boards for several of his discipline's major research journals and has held a variety of offices in professional associations.

Dr. Seiler has been honored as an Outstanding Educator of America, and as an Outstanding University and College Teacher by the Nebraska Communication Association. He is the only person in the university's history to receive both the Outstanding Young Alumni and Distinguished Alumni Awards from the University of Wisconsin at Whitewater. He is also listed in the *International Who's Who in Education.*

Dr. Seiler is also the director of the introductory communication course at the University of Nebraska at Lincoln. He has been directing the course since his arrival there some 23 years ago. Dr. Seiler was one of the first people in the nation to use a Personalized System of Instruction (PSI) in a large, multiple-section basic communication course. Presently, the University of Nebraska teaches more than a thousand students a year using the PSI method.

Acknowledgments

Numerous individuals have contributed to this and previous editions of this book. First and foremost are the students who have shared their time and learning experiences with me. I would also like to acknowledge the instructors who patiently taught me about communication and life, the colleagues who have shared their expertise with me, the many graduate students who have worked in our introductory communication course over the past 23 years, and the hundreds of undergraduate assistants and assistant supervisory instructors who have worked in our Personalized System of Instruction introductory communication course during the past 14 years.

With any project of this proportion, there are many to thank who helped make this edition possible. I would like to especially thank Dr. Diane Badzinski of the Department of Communication Studies at the University of Nebraska for reviewing the Verbal, Nonverbal and Interpersonal Communication chapters and making many excellent suggestions, and Dr. Larry Routh, the Director of Career Planning and Placement at the University of Nebraska, for his review and guidance in the writing of the Employment Interview chapter.

Special thanks are also extended to Linda Bornholdt Dickmeyer, Associate Director of our introductory communication course and graduate teaching assistant in our doctoral program. Linda reviewed first and second drafts of the third edition, made numerous suggestions for changes, wrote examples, provided resources, and was a sounding board for many of the new examples, sections, and ideas included in this edition. I am deeply indebted to her for her willingness to give her time and her superb editorial skills. Additional special thanks also goes to Mary Bort, a graduate student, instructor, and past Associate Director of our introductory communication course, who reviewed this edition and provided suggestions for change as well as the resource materials which helped me in revising this edition of the book. Finally, a thanks to all the other graduate students in our department and to the forensics students who provided resources and examples.

I am also grateful to Dawn Groundwater, HarperCollins Publishers, for her guidance, editing and developmental skills. It was Dawn, more than any other individual, who made the third edition come together. Thanks are also extended to Cynthia Biron, the Speech Communication editor at HarperCollins, for her willingness to take on this project in midstream.

The publishing of any book requires people dedicated to quality, and this book is no exception. I would also like to thank all those who participated in the review process of the first and second editions of the book:

Philip M. Backlund, Central Washington University
Barbara L. Breaclen, Lane Community College
Allan R. Broadhurst, Cape Cod Community College
Patricia Comeaux, University of North Carolina at Wilmington
Skip Eno, University of Texas at San Antonio
Mary C. Forestieri, Lane Community College
Anne Grissom, Mountain View College
Donald L. Loeffler, Western Carolina University
Richard G. Rea, University of Arkansas
Marc E. Routhier, Frostburg State College
Colleen Hogan-Taylor, University of Washington
Kathie A. Webster, Northwest Missouri State University.
Larry A. Weiss, University of Wisconsin at Oshkosh

Finally, I would like to thank those who provided analysis of the second edition, suggested changes, and reviewed the third edition:

William Patrick Barlow, Madison Area Technical College
Jeanine Fassl, University of Wisconsin at Whitewater
Ted Hindermarsh, Brigham Young University
Mary Lee Hummert, University of Kansas
Karla Kay Jensen, University of Kansas
Catherine Egley Waggoner, Ohio State University

Sincerely,

Bill Seiler
Department of Communication Studies
University of Nebraska-Lincoln,
Lincoln, Nebraska 68588-0329
402-472-2069
E-mail address—BSEILER @ UNLINFO.UNL.EDU

FOUNDATIONS OF HUMAN COMMUNICATION

Chapter 1

Human Communication

LEARNING OBJECTIVES

After studying this chapter, you should be able to:

1. Explain what speech communication is and what it involves.

2. Demonstrate the importance of having effective oral communication skills by citing examples from history and the business world.

3. Use the four fundamental principles of communication to illustrate the complex nature of communication.

4. Describe the functions and inter-relationships of the eight essential components of communication.

5. Describe the types of communication and the contexts in which they occur.

6. Identify four common misconceptions about communication and tell why they are incorrect.

J oey (age 4 months) is sitting on his mother's lap, facing her. She looks at him intently but with no expression, as if she were absorbed in thought elsewhere. For a long moment, they remain locked in a silent mutual gaze. She finally breaks it by easing into a slight smile. Joey quickly leans forward and they trade smiles.

Then Joey's mother's expression turns to exaggerated surprise and she leans all the way forward and touches her nose to his, smiling and making bubbling sounds. With the second nose touch, his smile freezes. His expression moves back and forth between pleasure and fear. After another suspenseful pause, Joey's mother makes a third approach at an even higher level of hilarity, and lets out a rousing "oooOH!" Joey's face tightens.

Joey has entered a short but extraordinary epoch of his life. Beginning between 8 and 12 weeks, he undergoes a dramatic leap in development. Capacities for interaction blossom: The social smile emerges, he begins to vocalize and he makes long eye-to-eye contact. Almost overnight, he has become truly social. Still, his most intense social interactions are immediate, limited to the face-to-face and the "here and now, between us." In its undiluted form, this intense social world will last until he is about 6 months old. As a way of interacting with others and reading their behavior, it will last all his life.

Excerpt from *Diary of a Baby* by Daniel N. Stern. Copyright © 1990 by Daniel N. Stern, M.D. Reprinted by permission of Basic Books, a division of HarperCollins Publishers, Inc.

Joey's communicative exchanges as described are relatively innocent, but they will become more varied and integral as he develops and interacts with others. Through his communication with others, Joey will establish perceptions about himself, others and the world around him. He will quickly learn that every time he communicates he is revealing who he is to others. He will also discover who he is, based on how others communicate with him (see Figure 1.1). Like Joey, no matter who you are, there is one thing you share with other humans, and that is the need to communicate. Not only do you have a need to communicate with others, but in today's complex society you also need to be an effective and proficient communicator in order to help ensure your success.

Although by our very nature we are communicative beings, we are not automatically effective or proficient communicators. Think about people you know who are successful in their family, social, and professional relationships, and ask yourself why they excel. Of course, you can name many factors, but the ability to communicate effectively will probably head your list as a key factor. Clearly, communication is one of the crucial skills that successful people possess, yet most of us do little, if any, thinking about it. Do you communicate effectively with others? Even if you answer *yes* to this question, you probably will have to admit that whether you are

Figure 1.1:

Learning to communicate is a lifelong process that begins with our very first communication exchanges. We also learn how to communicate early and understand how others perceive our communication which, in turn, determines who we become and our successes as a person.

18 or 60, female or male, shy or outgoing, working or unemployed, there is always room to improve your ability to communicate.

A recent research study questioned 344 students at a large public university during the last week of their communication class. The students perceived themselves to be more competent communicators than when they entered the course.[1] Specifically, the students reported that they were significantly better in group communication, interviewing, public speaking, and interpersonal communication. Probably the most exciting finding of the study was that the students also felt their self-confidence had improved significantly as a result of their communication course. The implication of the study is clear—you *can* improve your communication.

Our ability to communicate, like that of Joey in the opening scenario, is something most of us are born with. However, our ability to communicate effectively and proficiently is learned. Improving our communication competence requires ambition, hard work, and an appropriate learning environment. This book cannot be a substitute for those basic requirements, but it can serve as a foundation and a catalyst for developing your communication effectiveness. The goal of this book and of your communication course is to supply you with the essential information you need to become a more effective and more competent communicator.

What do we mean when we say that communication has taken place? How do we know we have communicated effectively? Can we send what we believe is a perfectly clear message, yet not be understood by those for whom the message was intended? Does the relationship of the people communicating with each other influence the outcome? How do electronic media influence what and how we communicate with each other? Why is it that some people know what to say, how to say it, and when to say it, and others do not? What does it mean to be politically correct or inclusive in our communication?

Answering these questions requires an understanding of the communication process and of the requirements for successful interaction. This chapter presents the underlying principles of effective communication in everyday life. In particular, you will examine what the communication discipline is, the importance of effective communication, and what communication is—its essential components and principles, misconceptions about it, types of communication, and contexts in which communication occurs.

COMMUNICATION DISCIPLINE

The word *speech* evokes a range of interpretations and reactions among individuals, but most people would agree that the ability to communicate effectively and efficiently with others is one of the most important abilities a person in our society can possess. At the present time, our discipline has no uniform or universally accepted label. For example, some scholars refer to the discipline as "Speech Communication" while others use "Communication" or "Communication Studies":

People who underestimate the value of communication usually do so because they think of it as merely the giving of speeches, which is only one aspect of the discipline. "Speech Communication" for some is a misleading description of the current approach to the study of communication. As the discipline has evolved in the '60s, '70s, '80s, and '90s, "Speech Communication" has become a limiting and increasingly narrowing term leading those outside the discipline to conclude that the discipline is defined only as the skill training of speech givers. The Association for Communication Administrators defines the **speech communication** discipline as:

> a humanistic and scientific field of study, research, and application. Its focus is upon how, why, and with what effects people communicate through spoken language and associated nonverbal messages. Just as political scientists are concerned with political behavior and economists with economic behavior, the student of speech communication is concerned with communicative behavior.[2]

According to this definition, communication involves a range of behaviors and occurs in a variety of situations: private and public, business and social, home and school, informal and formal. These diverse situations are all brought together by one common thread—human symbolic interaction. In reading this text, you will learn about human symbolic interaction as it applies within and among individuals, groups, organizations, and cultures. In the process, you will learn about the nature of human communication—listening; public speaking; and interpersonal communication, which includes small group communication and interviewing. By studying and practicing the principles and strategies of communication, you will improve your competency as a communicator.

"To succeed in college, undergraduates should be able to write and speak with clarity, and to read and listen with comprehension."
E. L. Boyer (1987). *College: The Undergraduate Experience.* New York: HarperCollins, 73.

How would you assess the effectiveness of your communication skills? What concerns do you have about your ability to communicate effectively?

What are doing to ensure you are able to do what Boyer suggests is necessary to be successful in college?

IMPORTANCE OF EFFECTIVE COMMUNICATION

Boyer's statement is not surprising, nor is it anything that most of us do not already know, but it *is* important for us to think about our communication abilities and about how we can improve them to ensure our success. To better understand why studying and practicing speech communication is so important, just examine the impact it has on you every day. In our society, it is not uncommon to find ourselves in competition with others who are both competent and skilled as communicators. Some people claim that our ability to communicate may well determine our position and success in life. These are strong statements, you say; but they are nevertheless true. Stop and think. How does communication affect you personally? How does it affect your family, friends, education, job, community, country, and world? Have you ever thought about ways to improve your communication with a roommate, a friend, a lover, a family member, an instructor, a boss, or a person from another culture? How effective are you as a communicator? Today more than ever, communication is what shapes our lives and our relationships with others[3] (See Figure 1.2).

As a college student, your ability to communicate will be one of the determining factors of your success both in and out of college. Your desire to influence others to keep the noise level down so that you can study, to convince an instructor that your research topic is appropriate for an assignment, to persuade a fellow student to work out with you, or to get two friends interested in one another are examples of situations in which it would be a value to be a more competent communicator. The most important reasons for being an effective communicator include saving time, making life more enjoyable, and allowing us to establish relationships and accomplish our goals. There is a definite link between the quality of our communication and the quality of our lives.

Figure 1.2:

Communication allows us to have relationships with others. Our ability to communicate effectively with others will ultimately determine our success in our chosen career.

David R. Frazier/Photolibrary

Communication Shapes History

There are also ways in which communication helps shape the world we live in. For example, read the following excerpt from a special issue of *Time* magazine about communication:

The early '80s welcomed Reagan to the White House, the hostages home, Diana to the Family and Andropov to the Kremlin. It was the start of a decade characterized by crisis and revelation that checked the collective directions of the nation and the world. The President, the Pope and John Lennon were targets of a wave of senseless violence, leaving Americans doubly disillusioned during the longest recession since the 1930s. The economy reeled in the 1980s, beset by chronic budget deficits and double-digit rates of inflation and interest. The energy crisis lingered on, although small cracks appeared in OPEC's unified oil pricing. Nagging unemployment in the "rust belt" was blamed on a wave of imports that jeopardized old-line American industries. For the first time since the Great Depression, most Americans foresaw falling standards of living for future generations. Mount St. Helens overflowed, and the *Challenger* went up in smoke. Chernobyl suffered a massive meltdown. Western Europe was beset by terrorism. Apartheid weighed heavily on the people of South Africa. Around the world, the visions of the women's movement were realized in the milestone strides of Sandra Day O'Connor, Margaret Thatcher, Geraldine Ferraro and Cory Aquino, while Jim and Tammy Baker, Gary Hart, Ivan Boesky, Ollie North, Jimmy Swaggart and Leona Helmsley tested the moral structure of America in a sudden ethical upheaval that shook the nation. The threat of AIDS, the shock of the crash and the promise of glasnost brought Reagan's second term in office to a close, while the massacre in Beijing, the reshaping of Roe V. Wade and the ramifications of democracy and capitalism among the Eastern bloc countries ushered in Bush and his Administration.

Time Magazine special issue *Communication 1923–1989, Retrospective (1991)*, 57. Reprinted by permission of HarperCollins College Publishers.

The *Time* magazine story illustrate the importance of communication and the roles it plays in keeping us informed about the critical events that occur in our society and the world around us. The role of communication is also prominent in events of the '90s. For example, President Clinton, in his first year in office, nominated several individuals for important government positions but withdrew the nominations before the confirmation hearings, because the nominees had written on controversial social or political issues, thus making it unlikely that they would receive congressional confirmation.

Although the significant impact of written communication cannot be denied, oral communication has had more direct effects on a greater number of people. Karl Marx's *Communist Manifesto,* as a written document, influenced large numbers of individuals, but it was the oral communication of Marx's writings that affected the masses and eventually spread the philosophy of communism throughout the world. Adolph Hitler's *Mein Kampf,* as a written document, records Hitler's struggle to attain power, but it was his oratory that established his political dominance during the 1930s and 1940s. Oral communication provides the basis and means for all political systems to exist. The successes of world leaders have generally been attributed to their ability to speak effectively. Consider, for example, the well-honed speaking skills of Winston Churchill, Franklin D. Roosevelt, Golda Meir, John F. Kennedy, Martin Luther King, Jr., Barbara Jordan, Billy Graham, Bella Abzug, Pope John Paul II, and Ronald Reagan. These individuals' oral communication competence and style has led them to prominent positions of leadership and influence. Those who study speech communication have always been concerned about the power of the spoken word and the role it plays in our lives.

Today's world leaders are instantaneously heard throughout the world via electronic media. Thus, those in prominent positions of leadership must recognize that what they say and how they say it have significant effects not only for the long term but instantaneously as well. As a college student, you may not be a world leader, but nevertheless, it is important that you recognize that what you say and how you say it can have both positive and negative consequences. Communication and how we use it does play a significant role in shaping our future. So, the more we understand about communication and the better we know how to effectively use it, the better our chances for success.

Communication Shapes the Global Village

Our society is at the center of what is referred to as an emerging global village—a village that is interconnected as a result of improvements in transportation technology, communication technology, globalization of the economy, and changes in immigration patterns. Each of the above factors has contributed to our need for a better understanding of people from various racial, ethnic, and cultural backgrounds. Today, technology has literally shrunk the world and has made it possible through communication satellites, digital switches, and fax machines to exchange information almost instantly with people anywhere in the world.

Within our own country, cultural diversity is something that we can no longer ignore. To see the importance of understanding diversity and communication in our society, we need only examine the change in student populations and the increase in the number of children traditionally considered members of ethnic, national, or racial minority groups. In 1976, for example, 24 percent of the total enrollment in U. S. schools was nonwhite. By the year 2000, one-third of all students enrolled in public schools will be people of color,[4] and it is projected that by 2020, 46 percent will be people of color. The changes in diversity are already occurring throughout the country. For example, students from so-called minority cultural groups compose 50 percent of the school populations in California, Arizona, New Mexico, Texas, and Colorado.[5]

Along with ethnic and racial diversity often comes communication diversity. For example, many of the young people entering school from minority backgrounds have little or no competence in the English language. Although Spanish is the predominant first language of many of the young people, there is also an increasing number of new students who speak Arabic, Chinese, Hmong, Khmer, Lao, Thai, and Vietnamese.[6] Because a person's language structures have symbolic meanings that are important to understanding the world, people whose symbol systems differ from those of the dominant group in a society require patience and understanding. The same would be true for any of us who were entering into a different culture. The ways in which people communicate, the circumstances of communication, the language and language style people use, and nonverbal behaviors are all primarily functions of culture. Thus, as cultures differ from one another, the communication practices and behaviors of people from those cultures will also be different. Do differences in the way two people communicate mean that either person's communication is inappropriate or wrong?

Communication Shapes Careers

Even though most of us may not aspire to national or international leadership, we do aspire to success in a career. Ample evidence supports the effect of communication on career success. In a study of 84 personnel officers from major companies throughout the United States, 85 percent indicated that communication skills in comparison to other abilities are "very important," and 95 percent indicated that when they hire someone, it is because of good communication skills.[7]

Surveys as early as the 1960s asked public leaders to rank six college curriculums—physical sciences, biological sciences, social sciences, communication skills, specialized or technical skills, and humanities—according to their importance in obtaining an executive position after graduation. Of the 217 surveyed, 45 percent ranked communication skills highest, and 95 percent ranked communication skills within the three most important curriculums.[8] No matter which curriculum or major you are in, you will find that more students are required to take courses in speech communication than any others offered. As Lee Iacocca, past president of Chrysler Motors, explains, "You can have brilliant ideas, but if you can't get them across, your brains won't get you anywhere."[9]

A 1980 review of 25 studies designed to examine communication skills that students will need in their careers found that listening, writing, oral reporting, motivating and persuading, interpersonal relations skills, informational interviewing, and small-group problem solving are the communication skills most often required and important for success.[10]

In a study of 1,000 personnel managers representing corporate, service, financial, government, insurance, retail, and wholesale organizations they were asked which skills are the most important in helping graduating college students obtain employment. The three skills named most often were oral (speaking) communication, listening ability, and enthusiasm.

The same personnel managers were asked what are the important skills for successful job performance. The top-ranked skills included: interpersonal relations skills, oral (speaking) communication skills, persistence and determination, enthusiasm, personality, dress and grooming, poise, and interviewing skills.

The survey of personnel managers also indicated that the abilities a young manager needs to advance within an organization include:

- to work well with others one-on-one
- to gather accurate information from others to make a decision
- to work well in small groups
- to listen effectively and give counsel
- to give effective feedback (appraisal)[11]

Ruth Kay, a communication scholar, conducted a survey of 1,800 college graduates employed in a wide variety of careers. The survey's results identify the following five communication skills as being important for a successful career:

- listening
- relationship building
- advising
- routine information exchange
- motivation[12]

All of these skills are discussed either directly or indirectly in this book.

Despite what many may think, communicating effectively is not easy; it does not occur automatically or by chance. It takes time, energy, desire, instruction, and practice—the same basic requirements needed for success in anything. To become effective communicators, we must know and understand exactly what it means to communicate.

Effective communication simply means that a message is received as intended by its creator. It does not automatically mean that the communicator's purpose is virtuous. For example, if one person persuades another to do something morally wrong, the communication is effective but not virtuous. Deliberate lying can certainly achieve a person's goal, but an unethical communication should not be condoned or accepted merely because it communicates effectively. A receiver of messages cannot be passive.

EXERCISE

Interview someone in the field of medicine, business, education, government, or your chosen career to learn more about the importance of communication. Ask questions such as the following:

1. **How important is effective communication in the field? Why?**
2. **What specific communication skills are required by people entering the field?**
3. **What advice would you give to someone entering the field about the importance of being an effective communicator?**

Compare your findings to those of others in your class, and discuss. What did you learn about the importance of communication within career fields?

WHAT IS COMMUNICATION?

Com-mu'-ni-ca'-tion 1. the act or process of communicating. 2. the imparting or interchange of thoughts, opinion, or information by speech, writing, etc. 3. something imparted, interchanged, or transmitted. 4. a document or message imparting information, opinion, etc.[13]

In this dictionary definition, as in most definitions of communication, you will find certain terms either used or implied: *process, transmit, impart, transfer,* and *transact.* Communication is considered a process because it is an active and changing event or set of behaviors. It is not an object that we can hold, but rather an activity in which we participate.

The terms *transmit* and *impart* suggest that something is sent. But if a message is sent, does that mean that communication has occurred? If a person yells "Help!" and is not heard, has communication occurred? The crowd at a basketball game boos a call made by an official, but the official ignores them. The crowd is transmitting sound, but is the crowd communicating? The professor tells her students that their term papers are due the next class period. She certainly has imparted information, but if students do not turn in their papers on time, has the professor communicated? When does communication take place?

In considering these situations, you might ask if information has been transferred. There is no question that something has been sent in all three, but has it been transferred? The crowd noise may or may not have been heard by the official, but regardless, if no action is taken by the official to change the original call, what has been transferred? If no one responds to the professor's deadline by meeting it, has anything been transferred? Has communication taken place?

To transact means "to make an exchange." *Transaction* means "a message has been sent and a message was returned." The situations above can illustrate what *transaction* implies when we communicate with others. For example, if the person's yell for help is heard by another person and the hearer responds with, "How can I help you?" and the first person then states what help is needed, a transaction has taken place. If the crowd boos the official and the official doesn't change the call but reacts to the crowd by smiling at them, is this a transaction? Has communication occurred?

A review of speech communication textbooks quickly shows the lack of a universally accepted definition of communication. Definitions can be long and complex, or they can be brief. They may take the view of the initiator, the receiver, or both. Our purpose is not to argue whether one definition is better than another, but to provide a common starting point for understanding communication. For these reasons, we will define **communication** as *the simultaneous sharing and creating of meaning through human symbolic action.* Each term in this definition will be explained in more detail later in the book.

EXERCISE

In your opinion, are the following statements true or false? Justify your answers.

1. **Communication can solve all of our problems.**
2. **The more we communicate, the better.**
3. **Communication can break down.**
4. **Meanings are in words.**
5. **Communication is a natural ability.**

Read pages 30–32 for answers.

Communication is a complex phenomenon. If it were simple, we would have no difficulty in communicating with one another. To understand the true nature of communication, we must know its principles, essential components, and types, and avoid common misconceptions about it.

PRINCIPLES OF COMMUNICATION

To appreciate the true nature of communication, it is important to understand four fundamental principles: (1) communication is a process, (2) communication is a system, (3) communication is both interactional and transactional, and (4) communication can be intentional or unintentional.

Communication as a Process

Communication is considered a **process** because it is a series of actions that have no beginning or end and are constantly changing.[14] It is not an object that you can hold to examine or dissect. It is more like the weather, which is made up of a variety of complex variables and changes constantly.[15] Sometimes the weather is warm, sunny, and dry, and at other times it is cold, cloudy, and wet. The weather at a given moment is a result of complex interrelationships among variables that can never be duplicated. The interrelationships among such variables as high- and low-pressure systems, the position of the earth, and ocean currents, among a whole host of other factors, determine the weather that we experience on any given day.

Communication, too, also involves variables that can never be duplicated. The interrelationships among people are affected by such variables as environments, skills, attitudes, status, experiences, and feelings. Each of these influences our communication at any given moment. Think about a relationship you developed with someone recently. How did it occur? It may have happened by chance (striking up a conversation with someone you met while walking to class), or it may have been a prearranged meeting (a blind date set up by your roommate). No two relationships are developed in the same way, nor is the communication that allows them to occur the same. And like the weather, some relationships are warm and others cold.

Not only is communication an ever-changing process, but it can effect change. Saying something that you wish you hadn't said is an excellent example of this principle. No matter how hard you try to take back your comment, you can't. It has made its impact and has, in all likelihood, affected your relationship with another person in some way. The change may not be immediate or significant, but it does take place as a result of your communication.

Furthermore, all events that occur in your life are, at some point, related to some act of communication. The communication and the changes it produces may not have a clearly identifiable beginning or end. For example, someone might say that communication in this course began the moment you stepped into the classroom, but the reason you came was to learn, and you probably made that decision before you even registered. Although specific situations may have definite beginnings and endings, the events leading to them and the resulting effects might not. If you were to stop reading this book, it would not be the end of its effect on you. You would carry away some new information, or at least a general impression, whether positive or negative. If you can accept the idea that communication is a process, you will view events and relationships around you as constantly changing and as having continuity.

Communication as a System

Simply stated, a **system** is a combination of parts interdependently acting to form a whole. The human body is an excellent example of a system. All parts of the body are interdependent and work together as parts of one complex system. If something is not functioning correctly, some response usually occurs either to correct what has gone wrong or to warn that something is going wrong.

In a similar sense, the communication process is a system that occurs only when the necessary components interact. If any of the components necessary for communication malfunctions or is not present, communication is prevented or made less effective.

Interactional and Transactional Communication

The interactional and transactional aspects of communication are closely related and should be considered together. **Interaction** is an exchange of communication in which people take turns sending and receiving messages. It is similar to playing catch. Someone throws a ball. The other person catches it and then throws it back. Each throw and each catch is a separate action. It is, however, necessary for the ball to get to the other person before he or she can throw it back, and so on. Figure 1.3 illustrates interaction in which Person A at time 1 sends a message to Person B, and then Person B, after receiving Person A's message, at time 2 responds to Person A. In interaction, there is a distinct time delay before each message is sent. An example of communication as an interaction is a phone conversation between two people. In order for the phone conversation to be an interaction, Person A speaks and Person B listens; then Person B speaks and Person A listens, and so on. Each message is a separate action. Even though there is a reaction to each message being sent, the reaction occurs subsequent to, not simultaneous with, the sending of the message.

Communication as Interaction

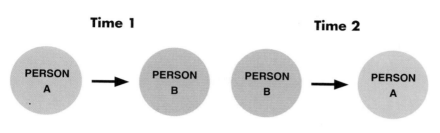

Figure 1.3:

This figure illustrates the notion of interaction as a seies of distinctly separate actions, or turn taking. That is, Person A communicates to Person B, then B communicates to A, then A communicates to B, and so on.

Most face-to-face communication does not occur as a series of distinctly separate actions. Thus, the term **transaction** is used to extend the concept of interaction to allow us to view communication as simultaneous actions; that is, the persons involved in the communication process engage in sending and receiving messages at the same time (see Figure 1.4). For example, when teachers communicate to their students, they not only send information, but also receive information at the same time. The teacher and students are sending and receiving messages simultaneously. This does not necessarily mean they are talking at the same time; it does mean, however, that two-way communication is taking place. Communication could be in the form of posture, facial expression, and other nonverbal communications while the other person is talking. Your handshake communicates a message that the other person interprets at the same time that you are receiving and interpreting the message in the handshake that you are receiving. In addition, both of you are simultaneously receiving feedback about your own message from the handshake you are giving.

Without simultaneous actions, face-to-face communication would be impossible or extremely limited—for example, sending a letter to someone

Communication as Transaction

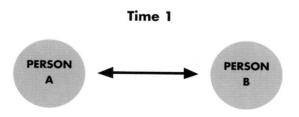

Figure 1.4:

Transaction is communication which occurs simultaneously. That is, both Person A and Person B are communicating at the same time. This does not mean that they are both speaking at the same time. Rather, they are aware of each other and are reacting to one another simultaneously.

and then having to wait a week or two for a response. In face-to-face communication, each person affects the other and shares in the process simultaneously. Thus, communication transaction can be seen as the simultaneous exchange by which we share our reality with others. The principle of transaction is more fully depicted in Figure 1.

Intentional and Unintentional Communication

Communication can occur whether it is intended or not. Generally, when one person communicates with another, he or she intends that specific messages with specific purposes and meanings be received. **Intentional communication** is a message that is purposely sent to a specific receiver. **Unintentional communication** is a message that either was not intended to be sent or was not intended for the individual who received it. Based on intent or the lack of intent, four possible communication situations can occur, as shown in Figure 1.5. Arrow 2 indicates a situation in which a person unintentionally communicates something to someone who is intentionally trying to receive a message or messages. This situation arises every time someone reads more into a communication than was intended by the source. For example, when a student in a quiet classroom gets up to sharpen a pencil, the eyes of the other students immediately focus on the moving student, who may have no specific intention of communicating

Intentional and Unintentional Communication

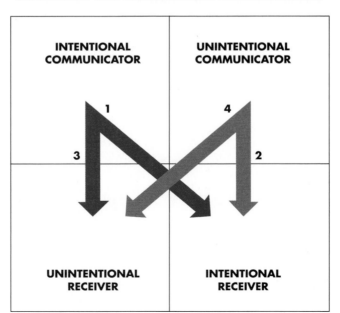

Figure 1.5:

Communication occurs both intentionally and unintentionally. Thus, we must be aware that even when we do not intend to communicate to others, communication can occur. Can you recall any instances where you unintentionally communicated to another person?

anything. The mere movement, however, provides an opportunity for many messages to be received by the observers. If the pencil-sharpening student is attractive, many different messages might be created unintentionally but received intentionally. For instance, one observer may believe that the moving student is trying to flirt with her, another may think that he's trying to call attention to his attractiveness, and the instructor may think that he is trying to disrupt the others' concentration. Despite the student's lack of intention to communicate anything, others have read meaning into his movement, and in one way or another, he may have to contend with their interpretations.

Arrow 3 illustrates the opposite situation. Here the source intends to send a message but the person for whom the message is intended is not consciously receiving it or is intentionally not receiving it. Such a situation arises when a parent tries to communicate to a child who intentionally does not want to hear. It also happens in the classroom when students daydream while the instructor is lecturing.

Arrow 4 shows that communication can be unintentional for both the source and the receiver and can occur without anyone's intentionally sending or receiving a message. Communication that is not intended, or that is at least not consciously sent and received, is usually nonverbal. **Nonverbal communication** is any information that is expressed without words. For example, the clothing a person wears might not be worn to communicate any specific message, and persons observing the clothing might not intentionally or consciously receive any message through it, but they do see it and may subconsciously receive a message from it; e.g., if Person A sees that Person B is sloppily dressed every time they meet, even without explicity noticing it Person A may subconsciously form the opinion that Person B has a poor self-image. Thus, communication occurs even though neither the person nor the observer has any intention of communicating.

ESSENTIAL COMPONENTS OF COMMUNICATION

How might you list and describe the components of communication? What would you include? Your response could be as simple as listing and describing only a speaker, a message, and a listener. Or your response could be technical and complex, listing and describing the components of computer language. Although there may be no all-inclusive list of the components of communication, you can begin to understand the nature of the process if you are familiar with eight of its most basic elements. The most often listed components of communication are:

1. Source
2. Message

3. Interference
4. Channel
5. Receiver
6. Feedback
7. Environment
8. Context

Figure 1.6 illustrates how the essential components relate to one another by depicting two people communicating. The limitation of the schematic model and of the components as illustrated is that it is not possible to show their movement and interdependence. In fact, if it were possible to illustrate communication as it occurs, the components would appear to be constantly moving and their relationships to one another would be changing and reacting to each other. Thus, the model would illustrate the principles of process, system, interaction and transaction, and intentional and unintentional communication all at one time. As you examine the components depicted in the model, keep in mind that you are looking at them in an artificial and stagnant state. Thus, in order to visualize the components as they engage in an ongoing communicative event, you must use your imag-

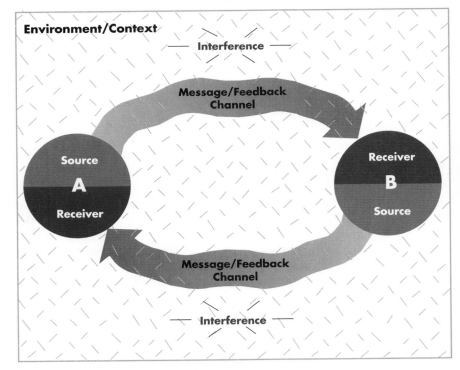

Schematic Model of the Essential Components of Communication

Figure 1.6:

This model displays the essential components of the communication process. The components are constantly changing, ongoing, and dynamic, and they affect one another as they illustrate the notions of process and transaction.

A = Person #1
B = Person #2

ination to allow the components to move and change constantly as each reacts to the other.

Source

The **source,** or Person A depicted in the model, is the creator of the message. In other words, the prime function of the communication source is to initiate the message. Because communication usually involves more than one person, there is always the potential for more than one source of communication to exist at a time. For example, both the teacher and the students in a classroom can function as sources, sending messages simultaneously to one another—teacher to students, students to teacher, and students to students.

The communication source has four roles: to determine the meaning of what is to be communicated, to encode the meaning into a message, to send the message, and to perceive and react to a listener's response to the message. Person A, in fulfilling the role of the source, also has communicative skills, knowledge, attitudes, and a cultural/social background which make him or her a unique individual. No two communicators are identical in their abilities to communicate, nor do they see other people, events, or situations in exactly the same way. Thus, it is important that we learn to respect others' views, especially when they differ from our own. This does not mean that we have to agree with those views, but it does imply that we should respect differences. So the greater the differences between Person A and Person B, the more effort and skill it will take for Person A to be an effective communicator to Person B.

Determining Meanings   A source has many decisions to make in creating a message. The first is to determine the meaning of what is to be sent. The meaning of some communication messages is relatively simple, but others can be extremely complex and difficult. For example, telling someone about a high grade you received on a recent speech entails making a decision about the meaning you wish to convey. Do you want the other person to know that this is the highest grade you've ever gotten on a speech, or merely that you got a high grade? Do you want the person to know what you did to get the high grade? Do you want the person to know how you felt about receiving the grade?

Before one speaks, meaning of the message is partially controlled by the source's ability to process information. The way information is processed internally and the decision about what is to be communicated determine the source's meaning for a message. For example, when we act as a communication source, we must transfer our feelings, thoughts, and experiences into language so that we can communicate them to others. Because we are all individuals, we have varying experiences, varying levels of ability, and varying willingness to express our thoughts and feelings. These factors contribute to how each of us determines the meaning of a message that we intend to send.

Encoding   Once a source has chosen a meaning, he or she encodes it. In other words, **encoding** occurs when a source translates the thoughts or feelings into the words, sounds, and physical expressions, which make up the actual message that is to be sent.

Sending   The source then sends the message. Sending involves the source's ability to communicate overtly, that is, to use voice and body to express the intended meaning accurately. For example, if your internal meaning is to tell the other person how pleased you are to receive a high grade on your speech, then you must use words and actions to illustrate what you are feeling and thinking.

Reacting   Finally, a source must interpret a receiver's response to the message. A source's perception of a receiver's response in most communication situations is simultaneous with the response. For example, the person you are telling about the high grade will be sending you messages (smiles, nods of the head, eye contact) as you speak, to indicate both his or her attention and his or her reaction to what you are saying. If you interpret that response as positive, you will probably continue talking about your high grade.

Message

A **message** is the stimulus that is produced by the source. It consists of words, grammar, organization, appearance, body movement, voice, personality, self-concept, style, environment, and noise. Any stimulus that affects a receiver is a message, whether it is intended or not. Hence, the teacher whose words tell a student that everything appears to be fine, but whose face shows deep concern, might be communicating more to the student than intended, especially if the concern on the teacher's face has nothing to do with the student.

Remember, communication is a process that is constantly changing. Thus, each message that is created differs from all other messages. Even if the same message were created over and over, it would be different because a message cannot be received more than once in exactly the same way. To illustrate this, imagine reading the headline "The World Has Been Invaded by Small Green People!" in a comic book and then in your local newspaper. Although the words might be the same, the messages would be quite different.

Interference

Anything that changes the meaning of an intended message is called **interference.** It is included in our model because it is present, to one degree or another, in every communication environment.

Interference can be external, or physical, such as the slamming of a door, the blasting of a stereo, or the sudden and unexpected movement of an object. Other examples of external interference include smoky air in the room; a room temperature that is too cool or too hot; an odor, such as the overuse of a strong perfume; or a speaker who wears too much makeup, has a speech impediment, talks too fast or too slow, mumbles, or wears unusual clothing.

Interference can also be internal or psychological. For example, thoughts going through a person's mind can interfere with the reception or creation of a message. Consider the ways in which a person who speaks in a loud voice to get someone's attention may create both physical and psychological interference. If the receiver perceives the loudness as anger, the loud voice creates not only a distraction from attending but also a distortion of interpretation. If the receiver responds accordingly, the sender may be quite surprised.

Essentially, interference is anything that reduces or distorts the clarity, accuracy, meaning, understanding, or retention of a message. This may include a speaker's annoying vocal habits or physical movements, inadequate lighting, an inappropriate seating arrangement, or perceptual inaccuracies or a physical hearing impairment on the part of the receiver.

THINK ABOUT IT

In what ways could each of the following factors interfere with communication?

Chewing gum	*Sunglasses*
A hot, sticky room	*The playing of a stereo*
Shyness	*An inappropriate choice of words*
A cold	*An accent*
A personal bias	*Cultural background*

Channel

A **channel** is the route by which messages flow between a source and a receiver. The usual communication channels are light waves and sound waves; that is, we see and hear one another's communications. The medium through which the light and sound waves travel, however, may differ. For example, when two people are talking face to face, light and sound waves in the air serve as the channels. If a letter is sent from one person to another, light waves serve as the channel, but the paper and the writing itself serve as the means by which the message is conveyed. Books, films, videotapes, television sets, computers, radios, magazines, newspapers, and pictures are all media through which messages may be conveyed.

We also receive communication by smelling, touching, and tasting. We sometimes take these senses for granted, but imagine walking into a bakery and not being able to smell the aroma or taste the flavors. All you have to do is hug someone you care about to recognize how important touch is as a means of communicating. All five of our senses, therefore, allow communication to exist.

Receiver

A **receiver,** Person B depicted in the model, analyzes and interprets messages, both intended and unintended. *You are simultaneously a receiver and a source.* As you listen to another person's message, you react with body movements and facial expressions, and the person, as he or she is sending the message, receives the information conveyed by your physical reactions. Like the source, a receiver has several roles: to receive (listen, see, touch, smell, or taste) the message; to attend to the message; to interpret and analyze the message; to store and recall the message; and to respond to the source, message, channel, environment, and interference. In addition, Person B definitely has communication skills, knowledge, attitudes, and a cultural/social background different from those of Person A. The greater the differences between Person A and Person B, the more effort Person B must make in order to be a competent receiver.

Receiving   A receiver must be an able and willing participant, or communication will be difficult at best. Willingness to receive a message does not guarantee an accurate interpretation, however. It means merely that a person is open to a communication message and will attend to it.

Attending   Receivers also have a responsibility to attend to messages intended for them. This is not easy, because many stimuli are begging for a receiver's attention at one time. Effective receivers must learn to concentrate on specific stimuli and to eliminate extraneous stimuli (noise) that can interfere with the reception and interpretation of a message. This ability takes effort, but can be learned.

Interpreting and Analyzing   The receiver must not only attend to messages, but also interpret and analyze them. Accurate interpretation requires an ability to understand an intended meaning. This process of translating a message into the thoughts and feelings that were sent is called **decoding.** On the surface decoding may seem rather easy, but because messages consist of symbols and signs that are transmitted through a channel, the possibility of a misunderstanding always exists. For example, if I say to you as we stand together by an open door, "Please close the door," the message is simple and leaves little room for misunderstanding, but is the intention of the message clear? Why did I tell you to close the door when I could have closed it myself? The intention might be clearer if my hands are full of books. But assume that I have nothing in my hands and that you see no reason why I cannot close the door myself. In that case, there are a number of possible intended messages. For instance, I might be lazy and using you to do something that is work for me, or I might be testing my authority by seeing if you will close the door when I tell you to do so. Although there is only one basic meaning to the sentence "Please close the door," the message might be open to different interpretations when the intention of the sender is taken into account.

The responsibility to convey clearly the intention of a message is the sender's, unless he or she deliberately intends to be unclear. But it is also the receiver's responsibility to determine the intention and meaning of the sender's message.

The receiver must analyze and evaluate each message. Does the message mean what the receiver thinks it means? Is the message ethical? Is the received message the one that was intended? Many other questions need to be considered to ensure clear and accurate understanding, and the process of analyzing and evaluating these questions and their answers will vary from source to source, message to message, situation to situation, and receiver to receiver. Despite this complexity, a receiver is responsible for making sure the received message is the one intended.

Storing and Recalling   The topic of storing and recalling messages is too complex to be discussed fully in this book. Suffice it to say, however, that the ability to store messages varies from individual to individual. Let's assume, for example, that your roommate asks you to pick up some groceries on your way back from class. Not everyone will store and recall messages in the same way. Some will remember the grocery list without any addtional cues. Some who are poor at remembering such lists may write each item down or use a memory trick. For example, if the items you were to get at the grocery store were hamburger, eggs, lettuce, and pop you might use the word *help* to represent *h*amburger, *e*ggs, *l*ettuce, and *p*op. Receivers cannot decode, analyze, or respond to a message unless they can receive and store it.

Responding   The final role of the receiver is to respond to the communication source. **Responding** may be simply a nod of the head or a comment indicating that the message was received and understood, or it may be a request for more information. A response makes the receiver a source of information to the sender. Note that a receiver's failure to react or respond is also considered a response, and is itself a message that may be received and interpreted.

Feedback

Another component in the communication process is **feedback,** the response reaction that a receiver gives to a source. Feedback enables the sender to determine whether the communication has been received and understood as intended. If communication is sharing meaning accurately, then some way of correcting faulty messages, misconceptions, missed meanings, and incorrect responses is necessary.

EXERCISE

Ask a friend to listen carefully as you read the following story aloud. Use a monotone voice and do not vary your speaking rate.

> **Homer Garrison, a school teacher, unexpectedly inherited $60,000. He decided that he would invest his money in a restaurant.**
> **He spent $18,000 for a down payment on an old house in his hometown of Greenwood. He did not want a showplace, just a nice family-style restaurant. He used the remaining portion of the money to purchase equipment and to convert the house. Soon his restaurant became the talk of the small town.**

When you have finished, ask your listener to repeat the story.
How much detail did the person remember? Why did the person remember some things and forget others? What could you as a speaker do to help the listener to recall the information? What could the listener do to improve his or her memory?

Feedback is a natural extension of effective receiving. Receivers have the responsibility of attending to messages, decoding them, and determining their intended meaning. The next logical step by the receiver is to respond or react (feedback) to the sender's message. The feedback can be facial expressions, gestures, body movement, words or any combination of these or it can be no response or reaction. It is then up to the sender to decide if the feedback provides enough information to judge whether the receiver accurately interpreted the message. In this way, feedback serves as a kind of control mechanism in the communication process. Unfortunately, we too often fail to monitor our own communication and—more important—

others' reactions to it, so we are misunderstood or not heard. To imagine the consequences, consider what would happen to the temperature in a room if the heater and the thermostat acted independently of each other.

Feedback is an essential component of the communication process, because it is not only a corrective device but also a means by which we learn about ourselves. It allows us to function better by adjusting to others and to our surroundings. Feedback from others helps us to assess ourselves—to determine our personalities and individual needs. Giving feedback to others is just as important as receiving it, because it makes the communication process more personal.

Feedback has other advantages. A classic study found that when feedback is increased, the reception of information becomes more accurate.[16] The experiment required students to construct geometric patterns that were described by a teacher under these conditions: (1) zero feedback—the teacher's back was turned to the students, and students were not allowed to ask questions or make noise; (2) visible audience—the students could see the teacher's face, but could not ask questions; (3) limited verbal feedback—the students were allowed to ask the teacher questions, but the teacher could respond only with *yes* or *no;* (4) free feedback—all channels of communication were open, with no limits placed on the type of questions asked of the teacher or the depth of response the teacher could provide. Two important findings from this study are that as the amount of feedback increases, so does the accuracy of communication, and as the amount of feedback increases, so does the confidence about performance.

Costs of Feedback   To enhance accuracy and confidence in communication, we must provide and monitor feedback. This takes time and effort and entails potential and actual costs. For example, the study on feedback shows that the time used for gaining accuracy and creating confidence can be costly in terms of getting things done. A free-feedback condition takes much longer—from three to ten times longer—than the zero-feedback condition. Time wasted or used excessively to get a message across can be as costly as mistakes.

On the other hand, the extra time may be well spent. A large manufacturing company, after making changes in its production process, found that many misunderstandings occurred, which resulted in breakdowns in the system and low worker morale. After the production managers increased the opportunity for feedback, there were fewer misunderstandings, fewer breakdowns, and more satisfaction among workers. In this situation, the additional time spent on increased opportunity for feedback paid off.

Besides requiring time, increased feedback may entail costs at a personal level. Feedback responses may diminish the sender's or self-concept. For instance, if someone tells you don't understand something or you're not making yourself understood, you may feel hurt. You can probably recall situations in your life in which feedback seemed too threatening. At times, preventing or ignoring feedback might be easier than running the risk of negative reactions.

Although most of us would rather receive positive feedback, negative feedback, if given and taken in the right perspective, can be helpful and productive. For example, if your professor says, "Your term paper was interesting, but you had several spelling errors," the feedback is both positive and negative and potentially constructive. Her comments may encourage you to be more careful in your future writing. On the other hand, if your professor says, "This is the worst paper I've ever read. You sure have a lot to learn," her feedback is belittling and potentially destructive. It may destroy your confidence and perhaps make you want to quit. Feedback, like all messages, should be carefully chosen and treated as an important aspect of the communication process.

Environment

The **environment**, or atmosphere, is the psychological and physical surroundings in which communication occurs. The environment encompasses the attitudes, feelings, perceptions, and relationships of the communicators as well as the characteristics of the location in which communication takes place; for example, the size, color, arrangement, decoration, and temperature of the room.

The environment affects the nature and quality of the communication. For example, it is much easier to carry on an intimate conversation in a private, quiet, and comfortable setting than in a public, noisy, and uncomfortable setting. Most of us find it easier to communicate with someone we know than with someone we do not know. Some environments appear to foster communication, while others seem to inhibit it. Consider these contrasting environments:

> The room is clean, painted light blue, and has quiet music playing in the background. Two people, seated in soft, comfortable chairs, are facing each other, smiling, and one is gently touching the other. They show genuine concern for each other. Their communication is open and caring.

> The room is dirty, painted dark brown, and has loud music playing in the background. Two people, seated ten feet apart on folding chairs, are staring at each other. They show little respect or concern for each other. Their communication is guarded.

Both effective and ineffective communication are, in part, the results of their environments. Effective communication can occur anywhere and under most circumstances, but pleasing, comfortable environments along with open, trusting relationships are more likely to produce positive exchanges (see Figure 1.7).

The characteristics of communication environments are usually discussed in terms of positive and negative poles: supportive–defensive, open–closed, confident–uncertain, accepting–rejecting, trusting–suspicious, orderly–chaotic, friendly–unfriendly. Climates that are positive tend to en-

Figure 1.7:

Environment and setting influence our communication. The setting and atmosphere in which communication occurs can help to foster more positive outcomes or at least improve the chances for a thorough exchange between the participants.

Ed Wheeler/The Stock Market

hance communication. A study of the characteristics of supportive versus defensive climates in business and industrial organizations revealed that people in defensive climates frequently believed they were being evaluated, manipulated, criticized, and subjected to too many rules and procedures.[17] Supervisors seemed indifferent, cold, and condescending. The supportive climate encouraged openness, trust, and confidence. People were more involved with one another and were more likely to seek out the causes of difficulties rather than rely on rules.

In a supportive climate, people describe events and behaviors; in a defensive climate, people judge events and behaviors. In a supportive climate, people show **empathy** toward one another, that is, they identify with others or vicariously experience their feelings, thoughts, and attitudes. People in a defensive climate show no outward concern or feelings for one another. For example, in a supportive climate, a comment like the following is apt to be heard: "Dave, you really spoke well during the first part of your speech. It had a lot of good examples and was clearly organized. The last part didn't seem to have as many examples as the first, but your delivery had good vocal variety throughout." In a defensive climate, similar thoughts might be expressed like this: "Dave, the first part of your speech was OK and the last part was not very good. You sure didn't do well." What we say and how we react to others help to determine the environment in which communication takes place. People who are always talked down to, evaluated, or governed by strict rules will tend to become distant and therefore less open in their communication.

Context

The **context** is the circumstances or situation in which communication occurs. Communication does not occur in a vacuum. Communication occurs in informal and formal settings with family members, friends, classmates, instructors, and business acquaintances, and takes place in a context. For example, some common contexts in which our communication takes place are business and professional organizations, homes, schools, government agencies, health organizations, local clubs, malls, and so on. Each context affects what we say and how we say it and also determines the type of communication we use. The context and the type of communication are not inseparable, and the distinctions between them are not always clear-cut. The following discussion offers some information that should help you understand the various applications of the different types of communication as they are presented through this book.

TYPES OF COMMUNICATION

Three types of communication are discussed in this text: intrapersonal, interpersonal, and public. The type of communication is usually distinguished by the number of people involved, by the purpose of the communication, and by the degree of formality of the situation in which it occurs. As with contexts, each type of communication has certain expected communicative behaviors—that is, certain verbal and nonverbal behaviors that are considered appropriate.

Intrapersonal Communication

To communicate with others, we must first understand how we communicate with ourselves. The process of understanding information within oneself is called **intrapersonal communication**. As we mature, we learn a lot about ourselves and our surroundings. Much of what we learn, we learn from our own experiences. Even though there are many things we are taught by others, there are many other things we must learn through our own experiences and can learn no other way. For example, the first time you experience the sensation of warmth coming over your chilled body is a form of intrapersonal communication. If the warmth is coming from a fire, the fire is the source of heat, but that heat is not really known to you until it is felt by your body and is eventually registered in your brain. Your skin senses the heated air and transmits the sensation through your central nervous system to your brain, which records it as warmth. In this sense you are communicating within yourself.

Intrapersonal communication also occurs anytime we evaluate or attempt to understand the interaction that occurs between us and anything that communicates a message to us. We are involved in intrapersonal communication whenever we receive, attend to, interpret and analyze, store and recall, or respond in some fashion to any message. Thus, communication between two individuals is far more complex than it appears on the surface, because within each of the individuals a great deal of intrapersonal communication is also taking place.

Intrapersonal communication includes such diverse internal activities as thinking, problem-solving, conflict resolution, planning, emotion, stress, evaluation, and relationship development. All messages that we create first occur within us. This makes communication a personal event, because we can never divorce ourselves from our interaction with others, no matter how neutral or empathetic we may think we are. We say to someone, "I understand your feelings," but we understand another's feelings only after they are filtered through our own feelings and perceptions. Ultimately, all communication takes place within each of us as we react to communication cues. Intrapersonal communication may occur without the presence of any other type of communication, but no other type of communication can occur without it. In fact, intrapersonal communication is almost always occurring, yet we don't often think of it as a type of communication. (Intrapersonal communication is discussed further in Chapter 13.)

Interpersonal Communication

Interpersonal communication is the informal exchange of information between two or more people. Interpersonal communication is similar to intrapersonal communication in that it helps us to share information, solve problems, resolve conflicts, understand our perception of self and others, and establish relationships with others. (In Chapters 13 and 14, interpersonal relationships and our relationships with friends and family members are discussed in more detail.)

A subcomponent of interpersonal communication is dyadic communication. **Dyadic communication** is defined simply as an exchange of information between two people. It includes informal conversations, such as talks with a parent, spouse, child, friend, acquaintance, or stranger, and more formal conversations, such as interviews. An **interview** is a carefully planned and executed question-and-answer session designed to exchange desired information between two parties. (Two types of interviews are discussed: the information-gathering interview in Chapter 8 and the employment interview in Chapter 16).

Another subcomponent of interpersonal communication is **small group communication,** which is an exchange of information among a relatively small number of persons who share a common purpose. A small group is usually considered to include from 3 to 13 individuals. Small group communication occurs in a variety of contexts for a variety of purposes, such as solving problems, making decisions, and doing a job. (Chapter 15 discusses the purposes and characteristics of small group communication, including leadership, participation, decision-making, problem-solving, and evaluation.)

Public Communication

Public communication is the transmission of a message from one person who speaks to a number of individuals who listen. The most widely used form of public communication is the public speech. We find ourselves on the listening end of a public speech in lecture classes and at political rallies, meetings, convocations, and religious services.

Although there are many similarities between public speaking and other types of communication, there are also some differences. Public speaking is almost always more highly structured than other types of communication. If it is to be done well, it demands much detailed planning and preparation by the speaker. Listeners to a public speech, unlike participants in other types of communication, do not usually interrupt the speaker with questions or comments. It is the responsibility of the public speaker to anticipate what questions listeners may have and to attempt to answer any that are asked in a formal question-and-answer session.

Public speaking almost always requires a more formal use of language and a more formal delivery style than other types of communication. The use of jargon, poor grammar, or slang is usually not accepted or tolerated in public speeches. The public speaker must use language more precisely and must adjust the delivery in order to be heard clearly throughout the audience. Public speaking may also require the speaker to eliminate distracting vocal and physical mannerisms that might be tolerated in other types of communication.

Public speeches are most often presented for three purposes: to inform, to persuade, and to entertain. They are also presented to introduce, to pay tribute to, or to welcome someone. (Chapters 7 through 12 discuss public speaking in detail.)

MISCONCEPTIONS ABOUT COMMUNICATION

Several misconceptions keep many of us from examining our own communication more closely.[18] Notice the words *our own!* Most of us who have problems communicating tend to look for the fault in places other than ourselves. Becoming aware that misconceptions exist and that many people accept them as truths should help us to understand why the study of communication is necessary. Here are some of the most common myths that interfere with people's ability to improve their own communication skills.

Communication as Cure-All

The first misconception is the notion that communication has the magical power to solve all of our problems. The act of communicating with others does not carry any guarantees. Obviously, without communication we cannot solve our problems, but sometimes communication can create more problems than it solves. In this regard, a personal experience comes to mind. During an annual review of a colleague, I remarked that the student evaluations for one of his courses appeared to be rather negative. He immediately launched into a long and bitter defense of his teaching ability, telling me in no uncertain terms that I was being unfair because I was looking only at his negative evaluations and not at his positive ones. What I thought was a simple descriptive statement created a significant problem between us. What should I have done differently to have prevented the problem?

Communication can help to eliminate or reduce our problems, but it is not a panacea. Communicating does not make the difference; what is communicated does.

Quantity for Quality

Most of us assume that the more we communicate, the better off we will be. Within limits, people who communicate a great deal are often perceived to be more friendly, more competent, and more powerful and to have more leadership potential than those who do not. However, quantity of communication is not the same as quality. In the discussion I had with my colleague about his negative student evaluations, the more we talked, the more we disagreed and the more negative our discussion became. Hence, as with the first misconception, it isn't the act or the amount of communication, but the content of communication that makes the difference.

Meanings in Words

If I tell you that I don't feel well, what does that mean to you? That I am ill? That I have a cold? That I have an upset stomach? That my feelings have been hurt? It could mean any number of things. Without context and more information, the statement is not clear. If I tell you that I have a cold and I don't feel well, would that be clear? Well, at least it would narrow the choices a little. Confusion may arise because the statement "I don't feel well" is relative; that is, it may not mean the same thing to you that it does to me. You may seldom get a cold, but when you do, it is a bad one. On the other hand, because I get colds all the time and have hay fever, my not feeling well means merely that I have a stuffy nose and a sinus headache. Thus, MEANINGS ARE IN PEOPLE AND NOT IN THE WORDS WE USE.

The notion that words contain meanings is probably the most serious misconception of all. Words have meaning only when we give them meanings. "No two people share the same meanings for all words, because no two people completely share the same background and experiences."[19] Thus the meaning of a word cannot be separated from the person using it. For you to know how I feel when I say that I have a cold and don't feel well, you have to know me and the degree to which I suffer from colds and hay fever. Now that you have read about the misconceptions regarding communication return to the Exercise on page 12. Would you change any of your answers? Which ones? Why?

Natural Ability to Communicate

Many people believe that because we are born with the physical and mental equipment needed to communicate, communication must be a natural ability. This simply is not true. The ability to communicate, like almost everything we do, is learned. Most of us are born with the physical ability to tie our shoes, but we still have to learn how the strings go together. Similarly, most of us are born with the ability to see, but that does not make us able to read. Reading requires knowledge of the alphabet, the acquisition of vocabulary, and practice. The ability to communicate requires not only that we be capable, but also that we understand how human communication works and that we have an opportunity to use that knowledge.

SUMMARY

The discipline of *speech communication* is a humanistic and scientific field of study that focuses on how, why, and with what effects people communicate through spoken language and associated nonverbal messages. Communication shapes our everyday lives, our careers, human history, and the global village.

Communication is defined as the simultaneous sharing and creating of meaning through human symbolic action—as the process by which verbal and nonverbal symbols are sent, received, and given meaning. There are seven components of communication: source, message, channel, receiver, feedback, environment, and interference. Each is an integral part of communication. The *source* (creator of messages) uses *encoding* (the process of changing thoughts or feelings into words that become the *message*, or *stimulus*). The *channel* is the route that allows messages to flow between source and receiver. The *receiver*, after obtaining the message, uses *decoding* (the process of translating the message into thoughts and feelings). The receiver then gives positive or negative *feedback*, indicating his or her reaction to the message. Although it takes time and effort to provide and receive feedback, the result is usually that communication is more effective. The *environment* is the physical and psychological climate in which communication occurs. Environments can be described as supportive, in which case the communicators show *empathy* (identification with another person) toward one another, or they can be defensive, in which case the communicators show no outward mutual concern. Interference is always present to one degree or another. *Interference* is anything that changes the meaning of a message.

Communication is described as a *process*, because it is dynamic and has no specific beginning or end. Communication is also a *system*, because it is made up of several interdependent components. Communication may be *interactional* or *transactional* and *intentional* or *unintentional*. *Interaction* is an exchange of communication in which communicators take turns sending and receiving messages; *transaction* is the simultaneous sending and receiving of messages. *Intentional communication* is purposely sent to a specific receiver, while *unintentional communication* is a message that either was not intended to be sent or was not intended for the individual who received it. A message received that is not intended is often sent unconsciously and is usually *nonverbal* (information expressed without words). Communication, whether it is intended or not, always takes place in a *context* (circumstances or situation in which communication occurs).

Three types of communication are discussed in this text. *Intrapersonal communication* is the process of understanding oneself. It is necessary for all other forms of communication to occur. *Interpersonal communication* is the informal exchange of information between two or more people, and it includes *dyadic communication* (exchanges between two people), the *interview* (planned question-and-answer session where information is exchanged between two parties), and *small group communication* (exchange of information among a relatively small number of persons sharing a common purpose, such as a job or solving a problem). *Public communication* is the transmission of a message from one person who speaks to a number of individuals who listen.

Some common misconceptions keep many of us from examining and improving our own communication, which cannot solve all of our problems, but when it is ineffective can create more problems than it solves. Merely increasing the quantity of communication cannot improve relationships or solve problems, but it may engender more confusion and misunderstandings. Problems stem from communicators, not from communication. Communication is a tool; it is how we use communication that makes it either effective or ineffective.

KEY TERMS

Channel: Route by which messages flow between the source and the receiver; for example, light waves and sound waves.

Communication: The simultaneous creating and sharing of meaning through human symbolic action.

Context: Circumstances or situation in which communication occurs.

Decoding: Process of translating a message into the thoughts or feelings that were communicated.

Dyadic Communication: Exchange of information between two people.

Empathy: Identification with another person, or vicarious experiencing of his or her feelings, thoughts, and attitudes.

Encoding: Process by which the source changes thoughts or feelings into the words, sounds, and physical expressions that make up the actual message to be sent.

Environment: Psychological and physical surroundings in which communication occurs, encompassing the attitudes, feelings, perceptions, and relationships of the communicators as well as the characteristics of the location in which communication takes place.

Feedback: Response or reaction that the receiver gives to a source's message.

Intentional Communication: Message that is purposely sent to a specific receiver.

Interaction: Exchange of communication in which communicators take turns sending and receiving messages.

Interference: Anything that changes the meaning of an intended message.

Interpersonal Communication: Informal exchange of information between two or more people.

Interview: Carefully planned and executed question-and-answer session designed to exchange desired information between two parties.

Intrapersonal Communication: Process of understanding information within oneself.

Message: Stimulus that is produced by the source.

Nonverbal Communication: Any information that is expressed without words.

Process: Series of actions that has no beginning or end and is constantly changing.

Public Communication: Transmission of a message from one person who speaks to a number of individuals who listen.

Receiver: Individual who analyzes and interprets the message.

Small Group Communication: Exchange of information among a relatively small number of persons, usually between 3 and 13 in number, who share a common purpose, such as doing a job or solving a problem.

Source: Creator of messages.

Speech Communication: A humanistic and scientific field of study, research, and application, focusing on how, why, and with what effects people communicate through language and nonverbal behaviors.

System: Combination of parts interdependently acting to form a whole.

Transaction: Exchange of communication in which the communicators engage in actions simultaneously; that is, encoding and decoding go on at the same time.

Unintentional Communication: Message that is not intended to be sent or not intended for the person who receives it.

DISCUSSION STARTERS

1. Why is it so difficult to agree on a single definition of communication?
2. What current national leader do you believe to be the most effective oral communicator? Why?
3. What distinguishes an effective communicator from an ineffective communicator?
4. Why is our society so dependent on communication?
5. Explain how communication can be both a process and a system at the same time.
6. Who is responsible for effective oral communication—the source or the receiver? Why?
7. What would happen to our communication if there were no feedback?
8. Drawing on your own experiences, describe how feedback can be both a motivator and an inhibitor of behavior.
9. In what ways can the environment hinder communication and help communication?
10. Explain the difference between interaction and transaction. Why do you think communication scholars disagree about these two terms?
11. Why is it helpful to understand that communication is a transaction?
12. Which misconception about communication do you think can cause us the most difficulty when communicating with others?
13. How well did this chapter meet its purpose of introducing you to the underlying principles of effective communication?

NOTES

1. W. S. Zabava Ford and A. D. Wolvin, "The Differential Impact of a Basic Communication Course on Perceived Communication Competencies in Class, Work, and Social Contexts," *Communication Education* 42 (1993): 215–223.
2. *Communication Careers* (Falls Church, Va: Association for Communication Administrators, 1981).
3. Stephen W. Littlejohn, *Theories of Human Communication,* 4th ed. (Belmont, CA.: Wadsworth Publishing Company, 1992): 3–4.
4. H. L. Hodgkinson, *All One System: Demographics of Education—Kindergarten Through Graduate School* (Washington, DC: Institute for Educational Leadership, 1985).
5. *From Minority to Majority: Education and the Future of the Southwest* (Boulder, Colorado: WICHE, Western Interstate Compact for Higher Education, 1988).
6. R. Oxford-Carpenter, L. Pol, M. Gendell, and S. Peng, *Demographic Projections of Non-English-Background and Limited-English-Proficient Persons in the United States to the Year 2000 by State, Age, and Language Group* (Washington, DC: National Clearinghouse for Bilingual Education, InterAmerican Research Associates, 1984).

7. J. Belohlov, P. Popp, and M. Porte, "Communication: A View from the Inside of Business," *Journal of Business Communication* 11 (1974): 53–59.

8. "1963 Public Leaders' Conference—State of Washington" (unpublished report).

9. *L. Iacocca, An Autobiography* (New York: Bantam, 1984); 16.

10. V. S. Di Salvo, "A Summary of Current Research Identifying Communication Skills in Various Organizations," *Communication Education* 29 (1980): 283–390.

11. D. B. Curtis, J. L. Winsor, and R. D. Stephens, "National Preferences in Business and Communication Education," *Communication Education* 38 (1989): 6–14.

12. Ruth E. Kay, "Identification of CORE and Unique Communication Skills and Problems Found in Organization Related Careers," unpublished M.A. Thesis, University of Nebraska, 1987.

13. *The American Heritage Dictionary of the English Language* (Boston: American Heritage and Houghton Mifflin, 1973).

14. D. K. Berlo, *The Process of Communication* (New York: Holt, Rinehart & Winston, 1960): 23.

15. John T. Masterson, S. A. Beebe, and N. H. Watson, *Speech Communication Theory and Practice* (New York: Holt, Rinehart & Winston, 1983): 6–7.

16. H. J. Leavitt and R. Mueller, "Some Effects of Feedback on Communication," *Human Relations* 4 (1951): 401–410.

17. J. Gibb, "Defensive Communication," *Journal of Communication* 11 (1961): 141–148.

18. The misconceptions described here are for the most part taken from J. McCroskey and L. R. Wheeless, *Introduction to Human Communication* (Boston: Allyn & Bacon, 1976): 3–10.

19. Ibid., 9.

Chapter 2

Perception and Human Communication

LEARNING OBJECTIVES

After studying this chapter, you should be able to:

1. Describe the relationship between perception and communication competence.

2. Discuss what perception is and how it functions.

3. Explain why perception differs from one person to another.

4. Suggest ways to alter and improve perception as well as communication competence.

> *Tommie:* (walking out of his Psychology class after the first day, with fear showing on his face) Man, I'm dropping Psych. It's too hard; the prof's a geek and she thinks I am a screw-up.
>
> *Maria:* You said that about the last Psych class, and you aced it. Besides, I think the prof is cool. You can't drop. It's a required course, and its not going to be that hard. Besides, the prof doesn't even know you yet. So, hang in there.
>
> *Tommie:* I don't know. Its the way she looks at me. And she knows that I'm a jock. It's pretty clear she doesn't like jocks.
>
> *Maria:* She never said anything about sports or jocks. What makes you think she's going to give you a hard time?
>
> *Tommie:* It's the way she talks and looks at me—as if I am nothing.

The preceding conversation illustrates the influence perception has on our communication. **Perception** is the process of selecting, organizing, and interpreting information in order to give it personal meaning. What we perceive about ourselves, others, objects, and events around us gives meanings to our experiences, and it is these meanings that we communicate to others. Differences in perception create differences in what individuals see, hear, smell, taste, and feel. The meanings we give to our experiences are in us, not in the experiences themselves. For this reason, no two people have identical meanings for the same words, messages, or experiences. Communication is indeed personal! In this chapter we discuss perception as it relates to communication; in Chapter 3 we focus on self-perception.

The brief incident given above illustrates how perceptions influence our thoughts and how different people communicate differently about events and people. Tommie perceived that the psychology professor was going to discriminate against him because he was an athlete. Yet Maria thought Tommie was overreacting and didn't understand how he could have interpreted what the instructor said in the way in which he did. This type of exchange is not uncommon, because it is the perception of what takes place that leads us to either similar or different interpretations about people, events, and objects. Which interpretation is correct? Why doesn't Maria's perception of the classroom interaction agree with Tommie's?

"Did you see what I saw?"

"I thought you said. . . "
"I didn't say that at all."

"I am so shy."
"I don't think you are."

"Miguel is handsome."
"I don't think he is."

"That perfume she has on smells good."
"It does?"

Person 1: "Officer, the blue Trans Am caused the accident."
Person 2: "No, it was the red Chevy van."
Person 3: "No, it was the yellow Sunbird."

Perception is at the heart of communication. Our perceptions make events, people, ideas, and objects become real to us, but what is perceived by one person is not always perceived by another in the same way. A difference between two perceptions does not necessarily mean that the perception of one person is more correct or accurate than that of the other. It does, however, mean that communication between individuals who see things differently may require more understanding, negotiation, persuasion, and tolerance of those differences. Perception, like communication, is a complex phenomenon. (See Figure 2.1.)

In Chapter 1, we discussed intrapersonal communication and indicated that to communicate with others, we must first understand how we communicate with ourselves. Whenever we receive messages either internally or externally, we are using perception. Thus, any time we receive, attend to, interpret, analyze, store, recall, or respond to a message, we are using communication. When someone says to another person, "I understand your feelings," the statement is based on the perceptions that the person who made the statement has of the other person's feelings. Because there is no way in which one person can actually feel what another person feels, we perceive those feelings by selecting, organizing, and interpreting

Figure 2.1:

Some individuals and groups see things differently than we might. When people see things and issues differently, it requires understanding, negotiating, and persuading as well as tolerance of those differences.

Paul Conklin/Photo Edit

the information cues that are received. This is why we say that, ultimately, all communication takes place within each of us as we react to communication cues and our perceptions of those cues.

THE PERCEPTION PROCESS

Many people imagine the brain to be similar in operation to a camera or tape recorder; information enters through the eyes or ears and is stored in the brain. Actually there exists far too much information for our brains to absorb at once, and most of it is not relevant to our immediate needs, so the brain ignores it. The brain reduces the amount of information it accepts and organizes the incoming information into meaningful patterns. The amount of information discarded is tremendous. Much of what we know about perception and the way we perceive events, objects, and people seems to center around how we select, organize, and interpret information. All of this happens in milliseconds.

Selection

It is impossible to attend to, sense, perceive, retain, and give meaning to every stimulus we encounter, so we narrow our focus. A **stimulus** incites or quickens action, feeling, or thought. Although the eye can see millions of bits of stimuli, or data, at one time, the mind can process only a small fraction of those stimuli. On both the unconscious level of the nervous system and the conscious level of directing attention, **selection** is the sorting of one stimulus from another.

There are two kinds of selectivity: selective attention and selective retention. To respond appropriately to a given situation, we must constantly select and attend to stimuli relevant to that situation and ignore the others. Focusing on specific stimuli while ignoring or downplaying other stimuli is called **selective attention.** That is, your concentration is such that you eliminate or reduce all other stimuli in the situation so as to focus your attention. This task is sometimes easier said than done. Paying attention to something usually requires that we decide to make the effort and concentrate, but sometimes our attention may be distracted. For example, a book dropped in a quiet classroom, a loud sneeze, a siren, a baby's cry, a call for help, an odor, or a movement can distract our attention from the original stimuli. Continuing to attend to the original stimuli eventually requires some deliberate effort. Similarly, when we converse with someone in a crowded lounge with loud music playing in the background, we focus on each other's words and ignore the other sounds. This blocking out of all extraneous stimuli to concentrate on the other person is an instance of selective attention. To make sense out of the multitude of stimuli that surround us, we learn to focus our senses on a few stimuli at a time.

Because we cannot possibly remember all the stimuli we encounter, we also select the information we will retain. **Selective retention** occurs when we process, store, and retrieve information that we have already selected, organized, and interpreted. We are more likely to remember information that is in agreement with our views and selectively forget information that is not in agreement with our views. Also, after perceiving and choosing certain stimuli, we may retain only parts of them. For example, how many times have you listened to someone tell you how to do a task, and later, after thinking that you had done everything, found that you had done only a portion of it? Chances are that you had retained the pleasant parts of the task and forgotten the not-so-pleasant parts. Selectivity plays an important role in what, why, and how we communicate.

THINK ABOUT IT ▮▮▮▮▮▮

How does selectivity affect your communication?

In what ways has selectivity created a barrier between you and others who are different from you?

As a college student, how do selective attention and selective retention affect you in the classroom?

Organization

The categorizing of stimuli in our environment in order to make sense of them, known as **organization,** plays an important role in how we perceive and communicate about events, objects, and people. Probably the most common way to organize stimuli is to distinguish between figure and ground. **Figure-and-ground organization** is the ordering of perceptions so that some stimuli are in focus and others become the background. Examine Figure 2.2. You may see a Native American *Eskimo* or you may see a Native American *Indian*. People who see an Eskimo identify the middle of the drawing as the figure, and the sides, or dark area, as the ground. They see the dark area on the right as an opening of an igloo with the Eskimo looking out into a snowy night. Alternatively, the dark area can be seen as an Indian's headdress. The Eskimo's right arm is the Indian's ear, and the Eskimo's legs are the Indian's neck. This is a good example of figure-and-ground perception, because the two interpretations of the lines and shading are equally good. After you have seen both figures—the Eskimo and the Indian's head—it is impossible for you to focus only on one and not eventually focus on the other. Try it! Look only at the Indian. It is impossible to do it. Why do you think this is so?

Figure 2.3 is another example of a figure-and-ground perception. Look at the figure. What do you see? It may not be immediately apparent, but Figure 2.3 is a map. When we look at a map, we usually consider the water area to be the background for the land. However, many nautical maps convey just the opposite. In Figure 2.3 the black area (the figure) represents water—the Mediterranean Sea. The boot shape is Italy. Once we

Figure and Ground: Eskimo or Native American

Figure 2.2:

It is difficult to focus on one of the images without ignoring the other image because both figures compete for our attention. Thus, organizing and selectively attending to one image is difficult.

J. R. Block and H. E. Yuker, *Can You Believe Your Eyes?* New York; Gardner Press, 1989.

Figure and Ground: Water or Land?

Figure 2.3:

Once we recognize that the white represents the land (or figure) and the dark represents the water (or ground), the figure becomes dominant. Thus, our understanding of what is represented in the figure helps us to organize our perception of it. How is communication influenced by how we organize our perceptions and views of events?

J. R. Block and H. E. Yuker, *Can You Believe Your Eyes?* New York: Gardner Press, 1989.

have associated what we see with something we are familiar with, it is difficult to shift figure and ground to perceive something else. Our first perception of the illustration will not persist after we recognize the Mediterranean Sea. How and why does this differ from what happens when we look at Figure 2.2?

Figure-and-ground organization helps to illustrate how our perceptions influence what we hear and communicate. For example, a student who was unhappy about a grade on an assignment asked how to earn a higher grade. As the professor, I began to discuss ways for the student to improve on the next assignment. The student, however, didn't really want to talk about improvement, but wanted a higher grade on the assignment. For the student, the grade was the figure and improvement was the ground. For me (the instructor), the student improving on the next assignment was the figure and the grade was the ground. Each of our communication messages was influenced by how we organized our thoughts regarding the importance of improving the grade.

Another way we organize the stimuli around us is to fill in missing pieces and to extend lines to finish or complete figures. This completion process is called **closure.** In Figure 2.4 we see a figure—a tree—that doesn't really exist in the printed material. This occurs because we are always trying to make meaningless material meaningful. The tree is seen by mentally connecting the white spaces. Interestingly, the illusory figure is often seen in front of the figures that make them up and thus appears closer to the viewer than the paper on which the figures are printed.

Filling in the blank spaces or missing information helps us to categorize, label, and make sense of the things we see and hear. We sometimes do the same thing with people as well. For example, if we don't know someone or the person is from a different ethnic or cultural background, we

Closure: Tree or Incomplete Circles?

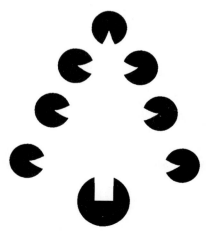

Figure 2.4:

The order of the lines and the need to fill-in the missing lines leads us to organize the drawing so that we can make sense of it. This, in turn, allows us to give it meaning.

J. R. Block and
H. E. Yuker,
*Can You Believe
Your Eyes?*
New York:
Gardner Press,
1989.

sometimes fill in unknown details in order to make sense of the person. Unfortunately, what we fill in may be based on biases and ignorance. When filling in the missing information, we must remain aware that we are doing so and at the same time distinguish between what we know and what we don't know. If we don't do this, we are increasing our chances of forming the wrong perceptions, or at least an inaccurate perception, of who the person really is.

Two additional aspects of organizing stimuli are proximity and similarity. **Proximity** is the grouping of two or more things that are close to one another. Proximity assumes that because objects or people appear together, they are basically the same. This, of course, is not always true. For example, people who live close to each other do not also behave the same, and to assume that they do is wrong.

Similarity is the grouping of stimuli that resemble one another in size, shape, color, or other traits. For example, Shelly, who like baseball, might believe that others who enjoy baseball resemble her in other ways as well. That is, if Shelly likes both baseball and opera, she might assume that others who like baseball will also like opera. Of course, this may be wishful thinking on her part, but just because two people are similar in one attribute, that doesn't automatically mean they are similar in another. Perceptual assumptions like Shelly's sometimes occur when we encounter people from different cultures, there is a tendency to assume that because people are similar in appearance, they must behave similarly as well.

To help you understand how we organize stimuli and organization's affects on communication, consider what happens when you walk into a room filled with people. When you first walk into the room, you begin to sort and organize people into groups, or categories. Chances are good that first you will begin to look for people whom you know. By doing this, you are sorting the people in the room into two categories: those you know (figure) and those you don't know (ground). People whom you know and who happen to be nearest to you (proximity) are those whom you will likely visit with first. It is also likely that you will spend more time with those whom you perceive to be like you (similarity) than with those who are not.

In the crowd, a woman spots a man she has been interested in but whom she has had the chance to meet only briefly at another gathering. As she moves through the crowd toward him, another woman moves next to the man and places her arm around him. He also places his arm around her, and they engage in what the woman perceives to be intimate conversation (closure). She quickly moves back into the crowd so as not be noticed by him, and begins talking with another friend, but her mind is still concentrating on the image of the man and the woman. Her thoughts drift off as she tries to involve herself in conversation with her friend. It is clear that organizing the stimuli around us affects with whom we communicate, what we communicate, how we communicate, and why we communicate with others.

Interpretation

Our interpretations of the stimuli around us depend on our past experiences. **Interpretation** is the assigning of meaning to stimuli. The more familiar you are with objects, events, and people, the less ambiguous are your interpretations of them. For example, when you first arrived on campus, you probably either had help or consulted a map in order to locate various buildings and classrooms. Your perception of campus locations was a bit unclear. With each passing day, however, you probably found it much easier to get around and probably even discovered shortcuts from one place to another. In similar ways, all of our experiences provide contexts that help us to make sense of the world around us. Figure 2.5 demonstrates the relationship between perception and interpretation. The figure also illustrates how our perceptions guide our interpretations of what we believe reality to be and how we communicate that reality. Look at drawing A and describe what you see. Do you see a person? If so, what sex is the person? How old is the person? What is the person wearing? How easy would it be to communicate with the person you see? Did you see a young woman in the picture, an old woman, or both? If you saw only one woman, look again until you see both the young woman (drawing B) and the old woman (drawing C) in drawing A. Although drawing A is designed to create an illusion, it does point out how easy it is for us to misinterpret what we see and to assume that what we see is the only thing to be seen. If you were shown only drawing B or only drawing C before you saw drawing A, you would probably see the image you were exposed to first in your first look at the ambiguous drawing A.

Good communicators understand that others may not always agree with their view or perception of events. They know that most issues have

Interpreting Perception: Young Woman or Old Woman?

(a)   (b)   (c)

Figure 2.5:

There is a distinct relationship between our perceptions and communication. This figure points out the importance of validating our perceptions and the experiences in which our perceptions are based before we communicate them to someone else. There may be more than one way to look at something and thus more than one interpretation of it.

many sides and that if they don't want to be misunderstood, they must be careful to examine an issue from as many angles as possible before they try to pass their views about it on to others. They also know that jumping to conclusions can be a useless exercise, especially if those conclusions are not based on fact.

While past experiences become a basis for our interpretations of stimuli, we must be careful not to let these experiences interfere with our ability to find fresh meanings in new situations or events. For example, having an experience with an incompatible roomate does not automatically mean that your next roomate experience will be the same. It is important to recognize that sometimes our past experiences can create blinders and thus produce inaccurate perceptions.

Often people think that information is by itself communication. It is not unusual to hear people say, "The truth doesn't lie," "Seeing is believing," or "The facts speak for themselves." This approach to communication is unfounded. Any information, regardless of the form in which it is received, must always be interpreted to be meaningful. Since interpretation is based on the experiences of the person who is receiving the information, it is not unusual for different people to receive exactly the same information and disagree about what it means, what it entails, or what conclusions can be drawn from it.

Each of us perceives the world through our own set of "lenses." We can never see the same river, tree, mountain, person, or event or receive the same message as others do because we are different from them. The examples in the beginning of this chapter illustrate how we interpret information differently from one another. One interpretation is not necessarily more correct than the other, but it is important to recognize the differences in our perceptions and how we communicate those perceptions.

Our perceptions are often altered or influenced by how and what others communicate to us. Much of what we learn about our world comes from magazines, newspapers, and television. It is through these media that our perceptions of reality are formed. Often the world we know is shaped and created for us by the perceptions others have formed about the world they see.

A few years ago Washington, D.C., had several major snowstorms. The headlines in two different newspapers read "Blizzard Paralyzes Capital" and "Snow Gives 300,000 Day Off in D.C." Both headlines are factually correct, but as you can see, they give quite different interpretations to the same event. If you read the first headline, you would get one impression of the storm; if you read the second headline, you would get an entirely different picture. Thus, the perceptions and experiences of the authors of the headlines would determine your understanding of the snowstorm's effects on the city. Which is the correct perception? Which represents reality? Which communicates most accurately the impact the snowstorm actually had?

PERCEPTUAL DIFFERENCES

Because communication takes place within each of us and because each of us is different, it is important that we understand that perceptions of incoming messages are often different from what others perceive. Sometimes those differences are small and have no appreciable effect on the meaning of the message as we understand it. In some situations, however, the differences between individuals and the circumstances in which they receive the message can actually reverse the meaning or alter it in such a way as to create distortions in the message being received. If you took a poll of your friends on any important social issue such as date rape, abortion, AIDS, health care, gays in the military, college athletics, or the environment, you would find some agreement and some disagreement. When senders and receivers are different in gender, cultural background, age, or health, these differences can create additional problems in how messages are received and understood.

Our perceptions are affected by age, sex, race, ethnic group, association with religious, social, or professional groups, values, beliefs, and attitudes. The differences in our perceptions occur because we are all psychologically and physically different from one another, and our experiences are not identical, even if we participate in the same events. In addition, each individual perceives things differently when he or she is sick or well, tired or rested, and when he or she is feeling strong emotions such as depression, loneliness, love, anger, or hate. Our physical and psychological makeup, our current physical and psychological state, and our past experiences determine what we perceive, how we interpret, evaluate, and organize our perceptions, and what actions we might take in response to them. The following sections discuss how our perceptions are influenced by physical characteristics, psychological state, cultural background, gender, media, and perceptual set.

Physical Characteristics

A person's weight, height, body shape, health, strength, and ability to use his or her five senses account for perceptual differences. For example, a visually impaired person experiences the world in ways that a sighted person finds difficult to comprehend or even imagine.

Short persons sometimes perceive events differently from the way tall persons do. Consider this situation. Two young boys were walking to a neighborhood store when two older boys threatened them with a knife and demanded their money. Afterward, the police asked the victims to describe their assailants. One boy gave the robbers' heights as about 5'6" and 5'10" and estimated their ages to be about 16 and 20. The other boy described them as about 5'10" and 6'2" and guessed their ages to be about 20 and 27. The first boy was 9 years old and 5' tall; the other was 6 years old and 4'1" tall. Of course, the smaller boy perceived the robbers as much taller and older.[1]

The cartoon in Figure 2.6 depicts much the same situation. Whose perception is right? This kind of situation has probably happened to each of us. Our perceptions usually change with experience; it is difficult for us to see a situation through someone else's eyes, even if we were once in the very same position. Our experiences can help us solve problems or see things more clearly, but they can also limit our view of events and people, hinder us in solving problems, and create barriers to effective communication.

Psychological State

Our state of mind can influence or alter our perceptions of people, events, and things. All information that we receive goes through various filters and screens, which tend to sort and color what we receive and how we perceive it. When everything is going well and we are in a positive mind set, things, events, and people are viewed much more positively than when we are not in a positive mind set. When we are under a great deal of stress or if we have a low image of ourselves, for example, there is going to be difference in how we perceive the world around us. Sometimes this distortion is small and has no appreciable effect on the intended message. At other times, our state of mind can actually reverse the meaning or alter the message in such

Figure 2.6:

While not all experiences are so dramatic in difference as those shown here, the age and physical height differences between the son and the father clearly affects their perception of the snow depth.

a way that it changes how we select, organize, and interpret it. It is undeniable that our psychological disposition can color or alter our perceptions. Think about when you are upset, angry, or frustrated with someone or something and when you are not, how your attitude affects your perception of that person or thing. It is clear that we perceive differently depending on our state of mind and how we see ourselves. In the next chapter self-concept and perception will be discussed in more detail.

Cultural Background

When the sender and receiver are from different cultural backgrounds, this can affect communication. Culture is explained by some as a status issue concerning manners, music, art, and types of food. To some historians, sociologists, archaeologists, or anthropologists, culture is a term used to describe objects and artifacts of an early civilization. **Culture** is defined as patterns of values and traditions which are symbolically communicated through objects, behaviors, and utterances. We acquire culture through our interaction with others. Gage and Berliner, two educational psychologists, suggest that individuals' differences include such factors as intelligence, cognitive development, personality, and sex roles, which are defined in the context of culture. Culture, according to Gage and Berliner, is powerful because it influences all of us in ways that we are often unaware of.[2] Take a moment and think about how you use personal space and what is a comfortable distance when talking to another person. Most North Americans prefer to be no closer than an arm's length. Latin Americans and many Mediterranean peoples prefer standing closer than an arm's length. If a North American and a Latin American were talking to each other, what do you think would happen? The North American would probably try to keep back or maintain an arm's length distance, while the Latin American would try to move closer. Each of these behaviors is a result of the influence of culture. If you didn't know that Latin Americans like to be close when they communicate, how would you interpret their behavior? You, like many North Americans, might interpret the moving closer as being pushy, disrespectful, or as a sexual advance. On the other hand, the Latin American is likely to interpret the pulling away behavior of North Americans as being aloof or unfriendly.[3] Which intepretation is accurate—the North American or the Latin American?

Culture is an integral part of each of us and to a large extent determines our individual differences. Culture identifies us as being members of a particular group, shapes our values, and leads to our biases. Much of this occurs without us realizing what has happened, because so much of our behavior is unconsciously conditioned by our culture. The way we greet others, the way we use language, our opinions about what and when to eat, and many of our personal preferences are all culturally conditioned.[4]

The link between culture and communication is crucial to understanding communication because it is through the influence of culture that we learn to communicate, according to Richard Porter and Larry Samovar, two intercultural communication scholars. For example, a Korean, an Egyptian, or an American learns to communicate like other Koreans, Egyptians, or Americans. Each knows that certain behaviors convey meaning because they are learned and shared in their respective cultures.[5] Since people behave differently, they also perceive and organize their values differently as products of their culture (see Figure 2.7).

The study of communication between different cultures is referred to as **intercultural communication.** Intercultural communication "occurs whenever a message is produced by a member of one culture for the consumption by a member of another culture."[6] Because we communicate from our experiences and because our experiences exist within a culture, people who come from different cultural backgrounds bring a variety of perspectives and world views to their interactions with others. If there is a common or shared set of experiences between people, there is a likelihood that words and other meanings are likely to be similar. However, when experiences are different, as they often are in different cultures, then it is likely the meanings are also different, making communication more difficult and less shared.

Some cultural differences in perception are so deeply rooted that they are reflected in the language. The Navaho Indian language, for example,

Figure 2.7:

Cultural background can affect perceptions and interactions. When people come from different cultural backgrounds, they often behave, perceive, and organize their values differently.

Robert Brenner/Photo Edit

has words for white, red, and yellow but none for gray, brown, blue, or green. The language does have two terms that correspond to black—one denoting the black of darkness and the other the black of objects such as coal. The Navaho vocabulary reflects how the culture divides the color spectrum. This does not imply that the Navahos are incapable of making color distinctions or that they suffer from some form of color blindness. It only means that their vocabulary does not take certain color differences into account. In their culture, there is little or no need to make further distinctions. How would this lack of color differentiation affect the way they view the world around them?

Culture not only influences our own perceptions; it also influences others' perceptions of us. People with differing backgrounds may not see things in the same way we do, and sometimes those differences create barriers to effective communication. Effective communication between people of diverse backgrounds can be limited or impossible because of an unwillingness of some to recognize there may be more than one correct way to view the world around us.

When we focus on our own cultural background and automatically assume our view is superior to any other culture's view, we are ethnocentric. **Ethnocentric** persons go beyond pride in their heritage or background to the conviction that they know more and are better than those who are different from themselves. If we have not had sufficient interaction or contact with other cultures, it is sometimes hard to understand that other cultures and their practices may be as acceptable as our own. Even if we know of weaknesses in our own culture (too competitive, too materialistic, too informal, and so on), we are unlikely to criticize our culture when comparing it to others. Why is it so difficult to be critical of one's own culture?

Gender

Communication between men and women is sometimes described as if men and women are automatically different because of their sex. Unlike biological sex, **gender** is a social construct related to masculine and feminine behaviors which are learned. It is believed by some that women and men learn to perceive the world around them differently, resulting in different ways of communicating. One explanation for these differences can be found in social cognitive theory.[7] **Social cognitive theory** suggests that our initial behaviors are learned from same-sex models and serve as foundations for other types of behavior, including the way we communicate. Social-cognitive learning theorists further claim that differences between male and female perceptions are based on rewards received for appropriate sex-role behaviors and punishments received for inappropriate behaviors. For example, playing with dolls may be seen as appropriate behavior for girls and inappropriate for boys. The appropriateness or inappropriateness of the behavior is usually reinforced by societal norms and expectations. Social cognitive theory is useful in that it does help to explain how people develop their sex role identity, but it really doesn't explain the communicative differences between men and women or masculine and feminine persons.[8]

Identification theory is another explanation of the differences between men's and women's behaviors.[9] **Identification theory** asserts that children learn their sex role and behaviors through the intimate and ongoing interaction with a parent or caretaker. Many psychologists assume most children of either sex identify most strongly with their mother early in life. This relationship to the mother is one of nurturance and dependence, which is more likely to continue with girls than with boys over time. Boys, after a period, begin to identify with their fathers, who are generally more aggressive, and tend to take on the behaviors of their fathers. Thus, identification theory is one attempt at explaining why males are often considered more assertive than females. The theory, however, assumes that children are almost always reared in two-parent homes where the female is the primary caretaker during the first years of life. The theory also assumes that all mothers are passive and the primary caretakers, while all fathers are assertive and are not the primary caretakers of their children. Although identification theory, like social learning theory, may give partial explanation as to why males and females often *behave* differently, neither one explains why men and women *communicate* differently, if indeed they do in the first place.[10]

It has been shown in groups containing both females and males that males tend to talk for longer periods of time, take more turns at speaking, exert more control over the topic of conversation, and interrupt females more frequently than females interrupt males. Also, what males say appears to be given more weight than what females say.[11] These communication differences may occur because of how females and males perceive their roles and also how the roles are defined in a culture. The differences that have been described in the above research may account for some of the differences in how females and males perceive their surroundings and ultimately how they communicate with each other.

There is still much confusion about the role of men and women in our society. We are told about "the gender gap" and that men and women don't understand each other or speak the same language. Men are often confused when women want to continue to talk about something that in their minds has been settled; women often find themselves frustrated when men don't seem to listen or respond to what they say. Thus, the perceptions that men and women have of each other and themselves are not always clear. Men are no longer the sole breadwinners, nor are women soley responsible for taking care of the home as traditional views once held. Most of us today believe that there is no reason why both men and women can't pursue careers or that both can't be involved in homemaking and child care. Americans as a group have to some extent enlarged their perspectives on the roles and abilities of both men and women.

THINK ABOUT IT ▮▮▮▮▮▮

Many men honestly do not know what women want, and women honestly do not know why men find what they want so hard to comprehend and deliver.

Do you agree with the above statement? Why?

What will have to happen in order for men and women to better understand each other?

D. Tannen, *You Just Don't Understand: Women and Men in Conversation* (New York: Morrow, 1990), 81.

Media

Sometimes our perceptions are influenced by others deliberately. Advertisers, government leaders, political advocates, and many others attempt to shape our images of the world around us. Advertisers have mastered techniques for influencing us to think and behave in desired ways. Think about this situation. Bob, a photographer, is hired to create a positive image for a motel in a large city. His job is to take photographs that will make the motel appear to be attractive for a brochure. Bob discovers quickly that the motel is located in an undesirable part of town, parking is difficult, and there are few other attractions nearby. Thus, he does not take any shots that show the motel's surroundings. He photographs a model dressed to look like a distinguished businessperson approaching the newly remodeled entrance. He takes photos of a few attractive models in the pool. He takes a shot of one of the rooms using a wide-angle lens to give the illusion of spaciousness. Thus, Bob creates the impression that the motel attracts businesspeople, its customers are attractive, and its rooms are spacious. Bob's brochure is successful in influencing our perceptions of the motel. But did Bob capture the real motel? The assumption that "pictures don't lie" allows us to accept Bob's interpretation of what the motel is. If Bob had taken his photographs without the attractive models, shown more of the surrounding area, and not used a wide-angle lens, would we have gotten the same image of the motel?

Have you ever wondered how much the media influence our perceptions? In recent elections, candidates have hired people often referred to as "handlers." The handlers' job is to create a positive image of the candidates and to protect them from any exposure that might create a negative image.

What about the shows we watch on television? Do they create or alter our perceptions? The family sitcoms, for example, present families that are considered by many to be atypical of most families regardless of race or ethnic background, but the image presented influences our image of families. Network news shows select events from all the reports they receive and present them to us in a half-hour broadcast which, when the commercials are removed, amounts to approximately 24 minutes of actual news.

The information we see is not only limited, but it is specifically selected, forming our perceptions of the world around us.

In the above examples the media are molding our perceptions. You may think there is nothing wrong with this, but think about how dependent we are on the media for information and how literally so many people accept what is presented to them. There can be a great deal of difference between what is real and what is presented to us.

Perceptual Set

When we ignore information and maintain fixed, previously determined views of events, objects, and people, we are using a **perceptual set.**[12] A perceptual set allows our past experiences to control or focus our perceptions so that we eliminate information that is different or has changed about the event, object, or person. It is a form of stereotyping. **Stereotyping** is the categorizing of events, objects, and people without regard to unique individual characteristics and qualities. Perceptual set and stereotyping are similar in that they both involve selective attention and selective retention. The difference between stereotype and perceptual set is that stereotyping uses categories and perceptual set does not. See Chapter 4 for more on stereotyping. To illustrate perceptual set, quickly read the statements inside the triangles in Figure 2.8. Look again. Did you notice two *a*'s and two *the*'s in the statements the first time you read them? If you didn't, you are not alone. Most people don't notice these extra words for several reasons: (1) the statements are familiar and common, (2) most of us have learned to read groups of words rather than each individual word, (3) the words are placed in an unusual setting and in an unusual arrangement, and (4) we have been conditioned to ignore certain types of errors for speed and efficiency in processing information. The problem with perceptual set is that it can interfere

Perceptual Set

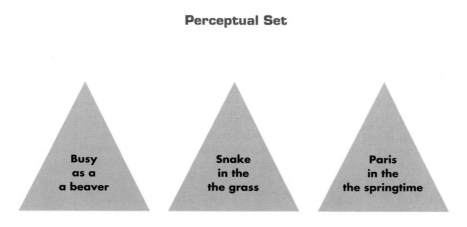

Figure 2.8:

Sometimes we see only what we want to see. Once we are familiar with something, we tend not to look closely enough to see if it is different from what we expect to see. How is this true with this Perceptual Set?

with our communication. For example, some parents communicate with their children as if they were still children even though they are adults. The perceptual set held by the parents is "those are our children, and they will always be our children." Therefore, the parents communicate with them as children and are unwilling to communicate with them as adults.

Perceptual set may prevent us from seeing things that are different from what we expect to see and from seeing changes in things we know have changed. Many of us, for one reason or another, refuse to accept change in others, particularly when we have lost trust in them. We become accustomed to seeing things that are familiar to us in certain ways and we assume that they will always remain the same. For example, prison officials would probably find it difficult to believe that a repeat offender would ever be completely rehabilitated.

EXERCISE

Use a sheet of paper to cover the numbers listed below. Move the paper slowly downward to reveal one number at a time, and add the numbers aloud as they appear: for example, "one thousand, two thousand, two thousand twenty," and so on.

1,000

1,000

20

1,000

40

1,000

30

1,000

10

What did you get for a total? 6,000? 6,100?, 5,010?, 6,010? If you did, you are wrong! The correct answer and explanation can be found on page 62.

J. Wenberg and W. Wilmot, *The Personal Communication Process* (New York: Wiley, 1973), 115. The "counting game" was adapted by Wenburg and Wilmot from an exercise used in AIDS Communication Seminars, Michigan State University.

Perceptual sets do not always limit or hinder us. Sometimes they help us to make decisions more efficiently. We could not make sense of the world around us without perceptual sets. They provide us with expectations of how things, events, or people should be, and they enable us to compare our expectations with the reality of the moment and respond accordingly. The key is to avoid the assumption that perceptual sets will always be accurate. Many scholars in communication believe that one of the, if not the, "greatest single problem with human communication is the assumption that our perceptions are always correct.[13] The fact is, people do not always act in prescribed ways in similar situations. Thus, it is necessary for us to adapt to each individual circumstance.

THINK ABOUT IT

An attractive young man, aged 17, came to the attention of a certain clinic as a voluntary case. For several years his parents had been concerned over the abnormal shyness which he exhibited in the presence of young women or girls. In the presence of members of the opposite sex he would blush violently and lapse into a nervous silence after a few stammered remarks. His behavior was arrogant when he was with guys his own age, and at least confident in the presence of adult men.

The medical findings were negative . . . The social investigation revealed nothing in the home environment at the moment which would seem to be responsible for his mental condition. But social investigation did yield the significant fact that his shyness had developed quite suddenly three years before. The parents had no explanation to offer as to the possible cause of the condition.

The psychologist talked with the young man in a friendly and informal manner. In the course of the conversation it was observed that, while he discussed sports and school activities quite freely, he would invariably become emotional when the subject of girls was mentioned . . .

Little by little the following story came out: Three years before at a party the boy had been playing with some girls. In some manner he caught his fingers in a door when it was slammed shut. This caused the boy such extreme pain that he became ill and vomited. The incident was quickly forgotten by everybody but the young man himself, to whom it remained a crushing misfortune. Although he tried not to think of it, the bitter memory was always there to be reinstated by the presence of girls!

This case clearly points out how events in our past influence our perceptions and how those perceptions can be transferred to future communication with others.

> *How do perceptual sets influence the way we communicate with others?*
> *Describe some perceptual sets that have affected you recently.*
> *How might you train yourself to avoid using perceptual sets inappropriately?*

Case adapted from *Psychology and Life*, 3rd ed. (F. L. Ruch. Copyright © 1948). Reprinted by permission of HarperCollins College Publishers.

IMPROVING PERCEPTION

In order to be competent communicators, we must understand the impact that perceptions have on us, on how we communicate with others, and on what we accept as reality through the communication we receive. We tend to take our perceptions for granted and fail to look beneath the surface. If we look at our personal experiences, though, we can begin to recognize and identify the misperceptions that create problems for us.

Knowing that our perceptions can be wrong is the first sign of a competent communicator. Our perceptions should be verified whenever possible, especially when the accuracy of our communication is important. We must always acknowledge to ourselves and to others that our perception may be limited or incomplete. This acknowledgement is especially true when we are forming new relationships or experiencing something for the first time. It is not unusual, for example, for students to form a favorable or unfavorable impression of a teacher on the basis of what they have heard from others or on the basis of the first few minutes of class. There is nothing wrong with forming such an impression, as long as we remain open to more information which may in fact contradict what we expected. Many of us often assume that our first impression is correct, even though it is based on limited information. Most of us do too little, if any, checking of our perceptions to determine their accuracy.

Because so many factors are involved in perception, making the process of perceiving so complex, there are no simple rules to follow to improve our perceptions. However, there are several things we can do. First, we must be *active* as perceivers. We must be willing to seek out as much information as possible about a given person, subject, event, or situation. The more information we obtain, the deeper our understanding and the more accurate our perceptions will be. We must question our perceptions to determine how accurate they are. By considering the possibility that we may have misinterpreted the information we received, we are telling ourselves that more information may be needed in order to draw an accurate conclusion. Taking the time to gather more information and to recheck the accuracy of our perceptions often is well worth the effort.

A second way we can improve our perceptions is by recognizing the uniqueness of our own frame of reference. We must remember that our view of things may be only one of many views. Each of us has a unique window to the world, as well as a unique system of understanding and storing things. Some of us make judgments about people based on appearance, while others base their judgments on ability, income, education, gender, ethnicity or other factors. The variety of approaches means that all of us operate on different systems, and it is wrong to assume that one system is better than another.

A third way to improve our perceptions and their interpretations is to recognize the fact that people, objects, and situations change. We must, therefore, be prepared to evaluate our own perceptions. We cannot assume that an accurate perception will remain accurate over time.

As communicators we need to be aware of the role that perceptions play in our communication, take others' perceptions into account, and avoid the tendency to assume too much about what we perceive. To make the most of the information that we receive, we must first evaluate it. We should check the source of the information and the context in which the information was acquired. We should make sure we are not reading too much into the information. To help ensure that our perceptions are accurate, we should ask questions and use feedback whenever possible. There is really no way to determine whether our perceptions are accurate or not except to test them.

Checking our perceptions requires that we keep an open mind and remind ourselves that our perceptions may not be complete or totally accurate. Thus, we must continue to observe for more information, be willing to describe what we observe mentally and out loud, state what the observation means to us, and put our perceptions into words to verify their accuracy. Here are two common situations to illustrate how you might check your perceptions.

> Sue runs into the room crying. She can barely speak, but there is anger written all over her. Sam, her boyfriend, knows from past experiences that when Sue behaves this way, he should leave her alone. However, he asks her, "What's wrong? Are you upset with me? Is there anything I can do?"
>
> Bob's eyes begin to drift over to Joan's paper. He begins to appear self-conscious and a little suspicious in his behaviors. The teacher observes Bob and begins to question Bob's honesty. But before the teacher draws any final conclusion, she continues to watch Bob and asks him, "Do you need any help? Is there something I can do?"

In both situations, there is the possibility that an initial perception is wrong. The questions being asked are not judgmental, nor do they assume any particular interpretation of what was observed.

CHECKING YOUR PERCEPTIONS ▰▰▰▰

Keep the following in mind when monitoring your perceptions:

> *Learn to separate facts from assumptions.*
>
> *Hold evaluation until you have ample information.*
>
> *Remember that perceptions, especially first impressions, are not always accurate.*
>
> *Learn to recognize your personal biases.*
>
> *Recognize that people from different cultural backgrounds do not always share the same meanings of events, objects, and people.*
>
> *Remember that perceptions are a function of the perceiver, the perceived, and the situation in which the perception occurs.*

Recognize that people, events, and places change over time.
Be willing to change your misperceptions.

SUMMARY

Perception is the process of selecting, organizing, and interpreting information in order to give it personal meaning. It lies at the heart of the communication process. Our perceptions of events, people, ideas, and things become our reality.

Selection is the sorting of one *stimulus* (incites or quickens action, feeling, or thought) from another. We use two kinds of selection—*selective attention* and *selective retention*—to focus on some stimuli and ignore or downplay other stimuli, and to process, store, and retrieve information that we have already selected, organized, and interpreted.

Organization is the categorizing of stimuli so that we can make sense of them. *Figure and ground* (focusing in on stimuli while other stimuli become the background), *closure* (the filling in of details), *proximity* (grouping of stimuli that are physically close to another), and *similarity* (grouping of stimuli that resemble one another in size, shape, color, space, or another trait) are all ways in which we organize our perceptions.

Interpretation is the assigning of meaning to stimuli. The meanings we choose are usually based on our past experiences. We must therefore take care that our past experiences do not create blinders that distort our perceptions.

Differences in people's perceptions result from each individual's state of mind, physiological makeup, cultural background, gender, and media exposure. These differences occur because we are all psychologically and physically different, and our experiences are not identical, even if we participate in the same events. When the sender and receiver are from different cultural backgrounds, this can affect communication. *Culture* is defined as patterns of values and traditions which are symbolically communicated through objects, behaviors, and utterances. Since people behave differently, they also perceive and organize their values differently. The study of communication between different cultures is *intercultural communication,* and a person who notices differences that go beyond pride in his or her heritage or background to the conviction that he or she knows more and is better than others is *ethnocentric.*

Communication between men and women is also culturally related. Unlike biological sex, *gender* is a social construct related to masculine and feminine behaviors which are learned. One explanation for these differences between the way men and women communicate can be found in *social cognitive theory,* which suggests that our initial behaviors are learned from same-sex models and serve as foundations for other types of behavior, including the way we communicate. Another explanation of the differences between men's and women's behaviors is *Identification theory,* which asserts that children learn their sex role and behaviors through the intimate and ongoing interaction with a parent or caretaker.

Because we communicate from our experiences and because our experiences exist within a culture, people who come from different cultural backgrounds bring a variety of perspectives and world views to their interactions with others. If there is a common or shared set of experiences between people, there is a likelihood that words and other meanings are likely to be similar. People tend to believe that their own perception of the world is the only correct one. This, of course, is not so. Because perception is so subjective, one person's perception of a situation is no more correct than another's.

A common phenomenon that can distort our perception of reality is a perceptual set. A *perceptual set* is a fixed, previously determined view of people, things, or events. People tend to see things they expect to see and to look on people, things, and events as if they never change. Perceptual set is a form of stereotyping. *Stereotyping* is the categorizing of events, objects, and people without regard to their unique individual characteristics and qualities.

To improve our communication, we must constantly remember that no one way of perceiving anything can be considered right or wrong; perceptions reflect how we have learned to view the world and ourselves.

KEY TERMS

Closure: Filling in of details by a perceiver so that whatever is perceived appears to be complete.

Culture: Patterns of values and traditions which are symbolically communicated through objects, behaviors, and utterances.

Ethnocentric: Term describing a person who notices differences that go beyond pride in his or her heritage or background to the conviction that he or she knows more and is better than those who are different.

Figure and Ground Organization: Ordering of perceptions so that some stimuli are in focus and others become the background.

Gender: a social construct related to masculine and feminine behaviors.

Identification Theory: Theory that asserts that a child learns his or her sex role and behaviors through the intimate and ongoing interaction with a parent or caretaker.

Intercultural Communication: The study of communication between different cultures.

Interpretation: Assigning of meaning to stimuli.

Organization: Categorizing of stimuli in our environment in order to make sense of them.

Perception: Process of selecting, organizing, and interpreting information in order to give it personal meaning.

Perceptual Set: Fixed, predetermined view of events, objects, or people.

Proximity: Grouping of stimuli that are physically close to one another.

Selection: Sorting of one stimulus from another.

Selective Attention: Focusing on specific stimuli while ignoring or downplaying other stimuli.

Selective Retention: Processing, storage, and retrieval of information that we have already selected, organized, and interpreted.

Similarity: Grouping of stimuli that resemble one another in size, shape, color, or another trait.

Social-cognitive Theory: Theory that early behaviors are learned from same-sex models and serve as foundations for other types of behavior.

Stereotyping: Categorizing of events, objects, and people without regard to unique individual characteristics and qualities.

Stimulus: Something that incites or quickens action, feeling, or thought.

DISCUSSION STARTERS

1. Define *perception* in your own words.
2. How does understanding perception's role in communication help you to be a more effective communicator? Provide specific examples.
3. Describe the role you think perception has in determining whether a person is a competent communicator or not.
4. What advice would you give to people who have not read Chapter 2 about the role perception plays in communication? Be descriptive of specific behaviors or skills.
5. What is the difference between selectivity and perception?
6. Why do people from differing backgrounds see things in differing ways? Cite an example from your experience.
7. How do you think men and women differ in the way they communicate?
8. What is the basis of your values, beliefs, and attitudes?
9. How can perceptual sets interfere with communication? How can they aid in communication?
10. In what way do the media control our perceptions of the world around us?
11. Suggest ways to improve or alter perceptions when communicating with others in addition to those listed in the text.
12. What was the most important principle, idea, or concept that you learned from having read Chapter 2?

NOTES

1. J. Pearson and P. Nelson, *Understanding and Sharing: An Introduction to Speech Communication,* 3rd ed. (Dubuque, Iowa: Brown, 1985): 27.
2. N. L. Gage and D. C. Berliner, *Educational Psychology,* 5th ed. (Boston: Houghton Mifflin, 1992): 167.
3. Ibid, 167.
4. Ibid, 167.
5. R. E. Porter and L. A. Samovar, "An Introduction to Intercultural Communication," *Intercultural Communication: A Reader,* 7th ed., edited by L. A. Samovar and R. E. Porter (Belmont, CA: Wadsworth, 1994): 19
6. L. A. Samovar and R. E. Porter, *Communication Between Cultures* (Belmont, CA: Wadsworth, 1991): 70.
7. A. Bandura, "Social Cognitive Theory of Self-Regulation," *Organizational Behavior and Human Decision Processes,* 50 (1991): 248–287.
8. D. J. Canary and K. S. Hause, "Is There Any Reason to Research Sex Differences in Communication?" *Communication Quarterly,* 41 (Spring 1993): 129–144.
9. P. H. Early, "Sex Role Development," in D. A. Goalin (ed.), *Handbook of Socialization Theory and Research.* (Chicago: Rand McNally, 1969).
10. D. J. Canary and K. S. Hause, 139.
11. L. P. Stewart, A. D. Stewart, S. A. Friedley, and P. J. Cooper, *Communication Between the Sexes,* 2nd ed. (Scottsdale, Ariz: Gorsuch Scarisbrick, 1990): 23–26.
12. W. V. Haney, *Communication and Organizational Behavior: Text and Cases,* 3rd ed. (Homewood, Ill.: Irwin, 1973): 289–408.
13. C. Stewart and W. Cash, *Interviewing: Principles and Practices,* 7th ed. (Dubuque, Iowa: Brown, 1994): 4.

Answer and Explanation for Exercise on page 55   The correct answer is 5,100. How is it possible to have obtained anything other than 5,100? The error is probably because of perceptual set. Since grade school, you have been taught to add one column at a time and carry the remainder to the next column. This time you were asked to move the paper down the numbers, which changed your perception and may have led you to obtain an incorrect total.

Chapter 3

Self-Concept in Human Communication

LEARNING OBJECTIVES

After studying this chapter, you should be able to:

1. Characterize the relationship between self-concept and perception.

2. Describe how self-concept is developed.

3. Explain how gender affects self-concept.

4. Discuss how style of communication relates to self-concept.

5. Suggest ways to improve self-concept.

*S*cott is thinking to himself—I've got to see Professor Jackson about cutting class last week. I know she thinks I'm a loser, especially because I am in a fraternity. She probably thinks all guys are screw-ups. How can I convince her than I'm not a screw-up? I didn't blow off her class and I'm definitely not a screw-up. She'll never believe me.

In order to become a competent communicator, we must understand that our image of self plays a significant role in how we communicate with others, and therefore we must understand what a self-concept is.

Who is the real me? This is a question that people ask themselves, but seldom can they find a complete or entirely accurate answer. Our parents tell us we are hardworking and talented, our friends tell us we are too serious, and our major advisor tells us we are overcommitted to our goals. Is who we are who we think we are or who others think we are? In the opening paragraph, Scott sees himself as responsible, confident, and as a good student. However, he is concerned that his action of missing class may have created another impression with his professor. Thus, Scott is telling us how *he* sees himself, how he thinks the *professor* might see him, and how *he* wants to be seen. This example does not, however, illustrate how Professor Jackson, from her point of view, sees Scott and what her perceptions are of him. Perception, as defined in Chapter 2, is the process of sensing, selecting, and interpreting the world around us. Scott is acting on what he believes Professor Jackson's perceptions are of him. His perceptions, whether accurate or not, will help him determine who he his and what he is going to say to Professor Jackson to explain his absences or tiredness in class. Unfortunately, we often weigh negative information about ourselves more heavily than positive. Thus, negative information or beliefs about self will influence our perceptions of self much more than positive information.

Each of us is an extremely complex human being. Many psychologists believe there are many selves—a social self, a psychological self, a physical self. Each of these aspects of self contributes to a generalized view of self. Each aspect of self is discussed in more detail in this chapter.

Who then are you? How would you describe yourself? Would you say that you are an effective speaker, a good listener, well organized, a good writer, happy, outgoing, responsible, lovable, attractive, warm, sensitive, caring, tall, thin, intelligent, and interesting? Or would you choose other adjectives to describe yourself? The next question is: What makes you think your description actually describes the real you?

EXERCISE

Write a brief response to the following questions. Your answers should address appearance, personality, ability, and intelligence.

1. **How do you see yourself as a student, a friend, a son or daughter, a parent, a communicator?**
2. **How do you believe others see you in the same roles?**

Ask a friend to write a brief response indicating his or her perceptions of you based on the same questions. Compare your friend's response to yours. What did you learn about yourself? Does your friend see you as you see yourself? If there are differences, why do you think your friend sees you differently?

SELF-CONCEPT AND ITS RELATIONSHIP TO COMMUNICATION

Our **self-concept** is what we perceive ourselves to be, our mental picture and evaluation of our physical, social, and psychological attributes. Self-concept is determined by our experiences and communication with others, the roles and values we have selected for ourselves, and our perception of how others see us. Self-concept consists of two components: **self-image,** the person we perceive ourselves to be, and **self-esteem,** our feelings and attitudes toward ourselves (See Figure 3.1.)

Self-concept, self-image, self-esteem, and perception are very closely related, so it is difficult to separate them. They constantly interact with one another. For example, what you think about yourself shapes, and in many ways determines, what you do and say. What you think about yourself is influenced by the information you receive from others, which helps you create an image of who you are. If you think of yourself as a good piano player, you would take positive comments made about your piano playing

Figure 3.1:

Self-concept is our perception of self. We see ourselves as we think others see us and those perceptions are based on our interaction with others and determine our self-image and self-esteem.

Jon Feingersh/The Stock Market

as affirmation of your ability and skill as a piano player. If, however, some-one made a disparaging comment, you probably would dismiss the comment as not reflecting your notion of how well you play the piano. In fact, you musn't interpret the comment as a sign of jealousy or humor, or simply decide that the person who made the comment just doesn't know you.

The messages that we communicate, intentionally or unintentionally, relate directly to the way we feel about and view ourselves. Who and what we perceive ourselves to be influence how we present ourselves to others. What and how we communicate with others and the reactions of others toward us help develop our self-image and self-esteem, both of which ultimately make up our self-concept. Each of us has a unique identity and a special sense of who we are. Why is it important for us to understand self-concept? Think about this and read on for an answer to the question.

Self-Concept as a Process

We described communication as a process because it has no beginning or end and is constantly changing. In the same sense, self-concept is also a process. Self-perceptions, and the perceptions others have of us, differ from time to time, from situation to situation, and from person to person. For example, your view of yourself may vary somewhat according to how you feel about yourself at any given time. If you receive a high grade in a difficult class, you might feel good about yourself, or at least about your effectiveness as a student. Your view of yourself might be different if you receive a low grade. In addition, the perception you have of yourself as a student is probably different from the one you have of yourself at work, at church, or at home.

The notion that self-concept is a process is illustrated by how others view us and how we view ourselves. In the opening scenario, the professor's view of Scott and Scott's view of himself are not the only perceptions that exist. Scott's parents view him as a caring, loving, and hardworking kid. Scott's friends see him as outgoing, the life of the party, a guy who loves to have a good time. Scott's boss describes him as unreliable and not very ambitious, but a nice guy. Scott's coach sees him as tough, a team leader, a guy who has great talent on the football field. Scott's girlfriend describes him as good looking, warm, great personality, and an excellent student. Who is Scott? (See Figure 3.2.)

Is Scott the person others perceive him to be, or is he the person he perceives himself to be? In reality, Scott may not be any of the persons described, including his own description of himself. The perceptions, however, whether accurate or inaccurate, become *Scott the person* as seen through others and himself. Scott's self-concept consists of his and others' perceptions and is determined by the beliefs he holds about those perceptions. Perceptions of Scott by others may not be accurate or even known to him, but nevertheless, he must deal with them.

The perceptions others have of us affect their communication with us and ultimately affect the way they perceive our responses to their commu-

Figure 3.2:

Who are we? What are we really like? There are many perceptions that contribute to one's self-concept. The perceptions are almost always different, depending on the relationship and experiences people have had with each other.

Mitch Kezar/Tony Stone Images

nication, and vice versa. It is equally important to understand that our view of ourselves also influences how we communicate with others. Communication and self-concept are inseparable and both involve process—continuous change with no beginning or end.

Development of Self-Concept

As children, our first communication involves the sensing of our environment—all the sights, sounds, tastes, and odors that surround us. We learn about ourselves as others touch and speak to us. Their responses to us help determine how we view ourselves. Parental communication, both verbal and nonverbal, generally has an extremely strong impact on the initial development of self-concept. For example, the clothes and toys they give us and what and how they communicate to us all affect who we become in some way. As we expand our environment and relationships, the communication of others may reinforce or alter our perceptions of self.

THINK ABOUT IT

"You're pathetic. You can't do anything right! Get outta here! I'm sick of looking at your face. You're more trouble than you're worth. I wish you'd never been born."

"You're so talented. You do everything so well! I enjoy having you around! Your smile makes me feel good. You're so helpful and easy to love. I am glad you are here."

People often believe what others tell them. Stop and listen to what you're saying. You might be surprised at some of the messages you've been sending.

In what way does our communication help form others' concept of themselves? In what way does our communication reflect who we are?

Social psychologist Daryl Bem believes that sometimes we don't know our own attitudes, feelings, or emotions directly. We therefore focus on others for such information.[1] Bem does, however, indicate that we learn a great deal about ourselves by observing our own behaviors. He suggests that what we do or act like is a guide to how we feel about ourselves and what is happening inside us. Further, according to Bem, we draw inferences about ourselves in the same manner that we do about others. Thus, the process through which we come to know ourselves is very similar to the process in which we come to know others.

Our self-concept, which develops through an extremely complex process, usually consists of many images that we place on a continuum from negative to positive. There is no way to predict which image will dominate, because our view of ourselves is a composite of all the self-images that interact within our mind at any moment. Our self-concept is affected not only by how we look at ourselves, but also by how we look at others, how others look at us, and how we think others see us. In effect, our self-concept is based on both past and present experiences, which affect how we will see ourselves in the future. Our self-concept is determined by the values, attitudes, and beliefs we possess, by how we attribute these qualities to others, and by how they attribute them to us.

Values   General, relatively long-lasting ideals that guide our behavior are called **values.** Values can be classified into broad categories, such as aesthetic, religious, humanitarian, intellectual, and material. Each category determines our behavior as well as our communication and is reflected in our self-concept. For example, if material things are important to us, we tend to judge ourselves by what we do or do not possess. A desire to have the finer things in life is not unusual, at least not in our society, but the strength of the desire can greatly affect our behavior. Possessions can become so important for some people that they ignore other concerns. They may pursue high income at the expense of job satisfaction, family life, leisure time, and personal health. Thus values can have both positive and negative influences on how we behave and communicate.

Attitudes   Evaluative dispositions, feelings, or positions about oneself, others, events, ideas, or objects are called **attitudes.** Our attitudes help to determine our self-concept, but unlike values, they are more narrowly defined. In addition, the relationship between values and attitudes is close because our values are reflected in our attitudes. For example, your attitude might be that the federal government is spending too much money on defense, especially at the expense of social programs. Your attitude says something about your value system; in other words, you value helping those in need above building a strong military.

Beliefs   Closely related to attitudes are beliefs. A **belief** is a conviction or confidence in the truth of something that is not based on absolute proof. We have, for example, beliefs about history, religion, schools, events, people, and ourselves. We say, "Space exploration is helpful to humanity," "God is good to us," "Speech class is important," "We will win the Orange Bowl game," "I know Sally loves me," or "I am going to get a high grade on my next speech." These statements and hundreds of similar statements that we make daily could begin with the words *I believe* or *There is evidence that.*

Our beliefs, like our attitudes and values, have a hierarchy of importance. That is, some are much more important than others. Our most important beliefs, such as those about religion, education, and family life, do not change easily, but our less important beliefs, such as those about today's weather or the outcome of a sports event, are only momentary.

Making clear and absolute distinctions among values, attitudes, and beliefs is difficult because they are interrelated. Consider, for example, the close relationship among the following three statements:

Value (ideal): People should love one another.

Attitude (feeling or position): Love is good.

Belief (conviction): Love is important in our lives.

Attitudes differ from beliefs in that attitudes include an evaluation of whether someone or something is good or bad. Beliefs, in turn, reflect the perception of whether something is true or false. Your attitudes and beliefs about love may change as a result of your experiences, but the value you place on love endures. The following chart provides a review of values, attitudes and beliefs. After you have finished reviewing it, create your own example for each.

Values, Attitudes, and Beliefs		
	Definition	**Example**
Values	Broad-based ideals that are relatively long lasting.	Everyone should have an education.
Attitudes	Evaluate dispositions, feelings, or positions about ourselves, other persons, events, ideas, or objects.	Our education system, as it operates today, is too costly.
Beliefs	Convictions or confidence in the truth of something that lacks absolute proof.	Even though it has its faults, our educational system is the best in world.

Hierarchy of Self-Concept

Like the beliefs we hold, the components of our self-concept may be organized into a hierarchy, as shown in Figure 3.3. At the highest level is our general self-concept, a set of beliefs we hold about ourselves. These beliefs are well established and relatively difficult to change or modify. At the second level are the principal components of self-concept—self-esteem and

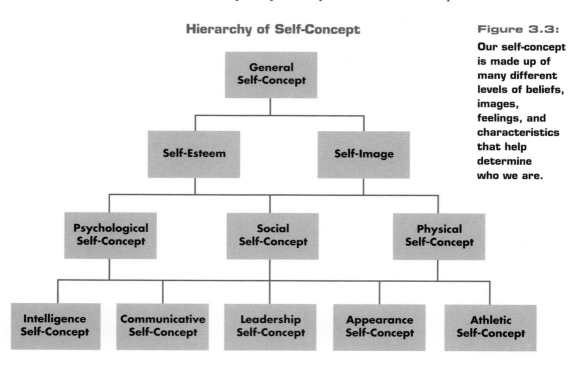

Hierarchy of Self-Concept

Figure 3.3:

Our self-concept is made up of many different levels of beliefs, images, feelings, and characteristics that help determine who we are.

self-image. The next level consists of the elements that form our self-esteem and self-image—psychological self-concept, social self-concept, and physical self-concept. On the lowest level are self-concepts of specific characteristics, such as intelligence, communication skills, leadership, appearance, and athletic ability.

The further we travel down the hierarchy, the more specific and the more susceptible to change the elements become. On the lowest level, the elements are not only susceptible to change but often do change from situation to situation and from time to time. For example, the academic self-concept of my youngest daughter (presently a high school junior) is heavily based on her grades and the teacher feedback she receives about her work and attitude in school. Her athletic self-concept is heavily dependent upon her play during a given game, how the coach and her friends react to that play, and her perceptions of her own play. During the past two years, her self-concept regarding her academic ability has changed dramatically from modestly positive to extremely positive. Her perception of her intelligence and academic ability seems to vary from one day to the next. On the other hand, her success on the volleyball and basketball courts has brought her self-confidence and respect from her peers and coaches. Her athletic self-concept is quite positive and remains that way from day to day.

Communication and Self-Concept

A reciprocal relationship seems to exist between our self-concept and the way we communicate: Communication affects our self-concept and our self-concept affects how and what we communicate. A model developed by social psychologist John Kinch demonstrates this relationship.[2] (See Figure 3.4.) Our perceptions of how others see us (P) affect our self-concept (S). Our self-concept affects how we behave (B). Our behavior is directly related to how others react to our behavior (A). The actual responses of others relate to our perceptions of others' responses (P), and so we have come full circle.

According to Bill Wilmot, a leading communication scholar, "Each person's view of himself affects his as well as his partner's behavior."[3] What this means is that each person's self-concept is influenced by the interaction with the other person. How we perceive the communication that we receive from others has a direct impact on our self-concept and our subsequent communication. For example, people who have a weak self-concept are more likely to be depressed, less certain of their self-worth, and more affected by and concerned with derogating sources of negative feedback. Individuals with a strong self-concept are usually the opposite in their behaviors. They are more likely to adjust to the situation. Generally, those with high self-esteem function better in social situations than those with weak self-esteem.

Expectations others have of us play an important role in determining our self-concept because others often behave and communicate with us

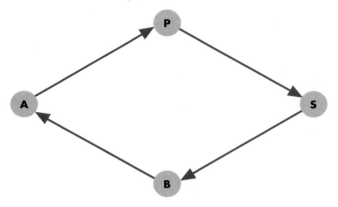

Kinch's Model of the Relationship Between Self-Concept and Communication

P = Perception of other's responses
S = Self-Concept
B = Behavior
A = Actual responses of others

Figure 3.4:

Kinch illustrates in his model the relationship between self-concept and communication. Our self-concept is based on our communication with others.

J. Kinch, "A Formalized Theory of the Self-concept," American Journal of Sociology 68 (January 1963): 481-486.

based upon their expectations. Thus, our self-concept is formed, to a large extent, by the communication we receive from others.

Self-Fulfilling Prophecy

In addition to values, attitudes, and beliefs, expectations determine how we behave, who we eventually become, and what we communicate to ourselves and others. Our own expectations and those of others influence our perceptions and behavior. Thus, our self-concept is affected by our past experiences, our interactions with others, and the expectations others have of us.

Expectations help to create the conditions that lead us to act in predicted ways. If we act in those predicted ways, we will, indeed, satisfy those expectations, so what was expected does happen. The expectations become a **self-fulfilling prophecy.**[4] Attitude can affect our communication effectiveness, which means we can create a positive outcome.

We are more likely to succeed if we believe that we have the potential for success. By the same token, we are more likely to fail if we believe ourselves to be failures. For example, students sometimes believe that they aren't good at speaking before groups. These students often do poorly on their public speaking assignments. Thus, to some extent, their expectations are based on past behavior. Their expectation of not succeeding becomes reality and reinforces their negative self-concept. The pattern of expectation of failure and actual failure becomes difficult to break. On the other hand, a person with a strong self-concept will react differently, and may make an opposite prophecy by saying, "I can present a good speech."

Culture and Self-Concept

There is general consensus that culture is a broad and encompassing aspect of each of us. Self-concept involves our perception of self, our culture, our perception of our culture, and other's perception of us and our culture. These views, in some combination, determine our self-concept. The development of self-concept varies from one culture to another and is determined by a specific combination of norms and behaviors within the culture in which we are nurtured. Within a culture, the construction and maintenance of social, institutional, and personal norms and beliefs related to self-concept are considered universal. This is especially true when two people from the same culture communicate within the context of their own culture. For instance, a white Anglo-Saxon Protestant in American society or a Japanese in Japanese society would have a stable self-concept with relatively few problems. Our self-concept in today's global village is established through continued social interaction with others both in and outside of our culture.

When individuals are taken out of the context of their own culture and placed in a totally different society and culture, problems can arise. These problems develop because views and expectations of self no longer "fit" the new culture. For example, if two people are communicating and they have high "cultural identities" with different cultural backgrounds, then they each will have different expectations regarding the other. To survive in this situation, the individuals must draw from their own culture and apply it to the other culture through their communication. This situation can create a cultural conflict and may lead to a redefining of one's self-concept which then allows the person to function in the new culture. Being able to communicate with individuals from different cultural backgrounds requires an understanding of their culture and culture's influence on self-concept and the ability to adapt communication to accommodate those differences in cultural background.

Gender and Self-Concept

From the moment of birth, no other characteristic slants the treatment we receive more directly than our biological sex. The behavior of children begins to be shaped by their very first pink or blue blanket. It appears that these initial influences placed on children lead to gender stereotypes and expectations which strongly influence a person's self-concept.

Gender Stereotypes Even though our society has taken great strides to reduce stereotypical thinking about males and females, the stereotypes and narrowly defined role expectations are still accepted by many in our culture and even more so in other cultures. These stereotypes affect communication behavior. There are many similarities in the communication behaviors of men and women. For example, there are men who are soft-spoken and women who are verbally aggressive; many men discuss their families and friends, and many women discuss sports and investments. It is, however, commonly accepted in our society that men and women communicate differently. In addition, there are situations where men and women are expected to communicate differently because of the imposed cultural norms of our society.

Females have often been the object of stronger and more persistent stereotypes than males. That is not to say that there are no stereotypes assigned to males because they, too, are perceived as being "all alike" in their possession of certain traits. Female stereotypes, however, are often more negative in content than those of males. In some cultures, males are assumed to possess desirable traits such as decisiveness, aggressiveness, ambition, and logical thought patterns. In comparison, stereotypes for females include less desirable characteristics such as submissiveness, high emotionality, passivity, and indecisiveness.[5] The positive stereotypes for feminine behaviors include such characteristics as nurturance, sensitivity, and personal warmth. The traits assigned to female behaviors are seen by some to be less desirable and less suited for valued roles of leadership and authority than the gender stereotype for males.[6]

Are the stereotypes about males and females accurate? Are the traits assigned to feminine behaviors less desirable than those assigned to masculine behaviors? Do men and women really differ in ways the stereotypes suggest? The answers to these questions are complex, for such differences between males and females, even if observed, may be based more on the perceived stereotype itself than actual differences between men and women. The research does seems to imply that when there are observed differences between sexes, those differences are often overstated. Overall, it is concluded that the magnitude of such differences is far less than the implication of the prevailing stereotypes attributed to both females and males.

Gender Expectations An overwhelming body of evidence demonstrates that sex differences in communication are the result of gender expectations. According to psycholinguist Deborah Tannen, men and women do see themselves as different, and as a result, communicate differently. She says, "In this world [the man's] conversations are negotiations in which people try to achieve and maintain the upper hand if they can and protect themselves from others' attempts to put them down and push them around. Life, then, is a contest, a struggle to preserve independence and avoid failure." The man's world is a hierarchical social order in which people are either one-up or one-down. In the women's world, according to Tannen, "Conversations are negotiations for closeness in which people try to seek and give confirmation and support and to reach consensus. They try to protect themselves from others' attempts to push them away. Life, then, is a community, a struggle to preserve intimacy and avoid isolation."

The women's world is also hierarchical, but the order is related more to friendship than to power and accomplishment.[7] Are we really different?

When asked to describe themselves, males and females do differ in their descriptions. Males mention qualities such as ambition, energy, power, initiative, instrumentality, and control over external events. They are likely to discuss their success in sports and with females. Females, on the other hand, list qualities such as generosity, sensitivity, considerateness, and concern for others.[8] Males, it seems, are expected to be powerful and authoritative, while females are expected to be concerned with relationships and expressiveness. Figure 3.5 illustrates the differences in how men and women communicate and negotiate differences with each other.

In our culture masculinity is described by such terms as *aggression, self-confidence, forcefulness, toughness, strength, dominance, frankness, and industriousness,* whereas femininity is described by *appreciativeness, cooperativeness, modesty, emotionality, warmth, frivolousness, sympathy, submissiveness,* and *friendliness.*[9] Males seem to learn that they are expected to control and manipulate their environments and the people around them. In addition, they are expected to be competitive, solve problems, and take risks. Females, on the other hand, seem to learn that they are expected to be dependent, passive, sociable, conforming, and accommodating to the needs of others.[10]

Although the research is not conclusive, it does appear that women in our society are more likely to report lower self-esteem than men. The tendency of women in our culture is the expectation that they be feminine, which may lead or cause them to report lower self-esteem than men do.

Figure 3.5:

Men and women negotiate differently. Men usually are more competitive while women generally seek out consensus and agreement. Do you find this to be true in your own interpersonal communications? Why or why not?

There are some studies which suggest that there is little difference between how men and women perceive themselves.[11] Most, however, indicate that women, for whatever reason, tend to rate themselves lower in self-esteem than men.[12] This is generally understood to be the result of the expectations placed on females and their roles in our society.

Today, even though there have been some strides toward equality of the sexes, there is still a cultural bias in favor of masculinity. Since communication behaviors are learned and are culturally defined, they can be unlearned and changed over time. The roles women play today are significantly different from their roles a few decades ago. For a time in our society, women expected and were expected to stay home and rear their children, while men were to be breadwinners. Today, it is estimated that somewhere between 70 and 80 percent of married women work outside the home. The U.S. Women's Bureau predicts that by the end of the century, two out of every three jobs will be filled by women. There is also a significant population of single parents who work outside the home. Along with these changes in roles and responsibilities come changes in the way we communicate with one another.

Psychologists indicate that women and men who are **androgynous**— have both male and female traits—are more likely to be successful in their interactions and careers than people who are totally masculine or feminine in their behaviors. For example, as you move from interactions with co-workers to interactions with your family, you may move from more "masculine" behaviors to more "feminine" behaviors. If you are a manager or owner of a business, you are expected to be assertive or task-oriented, but if you are taking care of your children, you are expected to be patient and loving.

In spite of these changes in sex roles, there are still many communication behaviors that are considered more appropriate and expected from one sex than the other. For example, the research suggests that women in our society learn to talk more about their relationships with others, while men learn to talk about sports and finances. Women learn to express their emotions, while men learn to repress them. Women learn to be patient and wait for promotions, while men are expected to be more assertive in their careers.[13] If men and women are to break the stereotypes and expectations attributed to them, we must avoid categorizing behaviors as exclusively male or female.

EFFECTS OF SELF-CONCEPT ON COMMUNICATION

Our self-concept affects everything we do, especially our communication with others. Think for a moment about how you communicate with others. Do you see yourself as outgoing, relaxed, open, friendly, quiet, reserved, argumentative? Each of these is a style of communication. **Style of commu-**

nication is the way a person interacts verbally and nonverbally with others or how individuals portray themselves through their communication. The following are some different styles of communication.

The *dominant* communicator talks frequently, takes charge in a social situation, and controls informal conversations.

The *dramatic* communicator manipulates with exaggerations, fantasies, stories, metaphors, rhythm, voice, and other stylistic devices to highlight or understate content.

The *contentious* communicator is argumentative.

The *animated* communicator provides frequent and sustained eye contact, uses many facial expressions, and gestures often.

The *impression-leaving* communicator tends to be remembered because of the emphatic stimuli he or she projects.

The *relaxed* communicator is calm, is not tense under pressure, and does not show nervous mannerisms.

The *attentive* communicator listens to people, shows interest in what they are saying, and deliberately reacts in such a way that people know they are being listened to.

The *open* communicator reveals personal things, expresses feelings and emotions, and tends to be unreserved and somewhat frank.

The *friendly* communicator encourages people, acknowledges others' contributions, openly expresses admiration, and tends to be tactful.

The *precise* communicator tries to be accurate, prefers well-defined arguments, and likes proof or documentation for statements.[14]

THINK ABOUT IT

Of your friends and acquaintances, how would you describe each using the communicator style labels listed above?

How would you describe yourself?

Personality theorists, such as the late Carl Rogers, believe that our self-concept is the single most important aspect of our personality. It is our image of self that determines our personality, which in turn determines our style of communication. It is generally agreed upon by scholars that those with high self-concepts function better in interpersonal situations than do those with low self-concepts. In other words, our view of self determines our communication style as seen by others and internalized by us, which in turn affects how we communicate with others.

There is some evidence that how others see us relates to our style of communication, which in turn is a reflection of our self-concept. One study examining the relationship between preschool children's style of communication and their perceived attractiveness by their teachers and peers found that the higher children were rated on each style, the more attractive they were to others. Those who were rated as less attractive were seen as having lower "communicator image," that is, were less open, dramatic, contentious, animated, or impression leaving."[15]

Also relevant to style of communication is the notion of communication apprehension, which also relates directly to self-concept. **Communication apprehension** is "an anxiety syndrome associated with either real or anticipated communication with another person or persons."[16] Fear of communicating with others is a learned behavior usually based on how we think others will respond to us and our communication. Communication apprehension can involve a fear not only of public speaking, but of any form of communication. Some highly apprehensive people avoid talking, but others talk incessantly or inappropriately because of their nervousness. In either case, the apprehension can ultimately lead to an inability to communicate effectively. (Other impacts of communication apprehension are discussed in Chapter 10.)

IMPROVING SELF-CONCEPT

Changing a self-concept is not easy. It usually begins with a concentrated effort to change behavior. Sometimes, dramatic events may force a change in behavior and thus alter the self-concept. For example, getting married or having a first child may drastically change people's behavior, thus affecting their self-concept. Or, that change in situation may change their view of roles, thus affecting their behavior.

To alter the self-concept requires a strong desire to change and a belief that you can succeed. A defeatist attitude diminishes anyone's chances for improvement. You must make the self-fulfilling prophecy work in your favor. Just thinking about success won't make you successful; you must take action. Anytime you act, you run the risk of failure, but successful people learn how to learn from failure and to avoid similar defeats in the future. When you understand your shortcomings, learn how to deal with them, and believe that you can succeed, you will begin to see yourself in a more positive light.

Here are several specific things you can do to help improve your self-concept.

1. *Decide what it is that you would like to change about yourself.* In order to begin the process of improvement, you must know what needs changing. Describe, as accurately and specifically as you can, what you are unhappy about or what you don't like about yourself.

2. *Describe why you feel the way you do about yourself.* Is your problem brought on by yourself or by others? Many students, for example, do not really want to be in college. They are there because their parents or their friends put pressure on them. Although they'd rather be doing something

else, they are afraid to take a stand. Before they can begin to feel better about themselves, they must recognize why they are unhappy and who is contributing to their problem. You may feel that you are not capable of earning good grades in a certain subject or that you are too shy to make friends easily. Ask yourself why you feel that way. Are you living out a self-fulfilling prophecy?

3. *Decide that you are going to do something to change your feelings about yourself.* If you can describe your problem, you can almost always find a solution, that is, if you want to find one. If you are unhappy about your appearance, make plans to change it. If you feel inadequate about meeting people, plan some ways to build your confidence. Nothing will ever change unless you want it to change.

4. *Set reasonable goals for yourself.* You must be reasonable in setting your goals. You may be able to change some things overnight, but other things may require long-term effort. For example, you may decide that you are going to improve your grades by studying for several hours every night. You can begin your new study schedule immediately, but actually raising your grades may take much longer.

Sometimes a problem becomes more manageable if it is solved step by step. For example, you may feel hesitant to visit your professor in his or her office. Why not start by speaking briefly with your professor before or after class? You might begin by asking a question about your progress. Once you begin to feel comfortable, ask for an appointment or stop in to visit during office hours. If you pursue such visits, you will gradually gain more confidence in yourself.

5. *Associate with people who will support and help you.* Try to surround yourself with people you like and trust. That will make it much easier to discuss your problems and ask for support. When others know what you are trying to do and how you need help, they can provide support to make your behavioral changes easier (see Figure 3.6).

Figure 3.6:

When good things happen, self-concept improves. It is important to associate with those individuals who will reinforce our successes and help us when we are having difficulty. Support from others helps us become more positive about ourselves.

Robert McElroy/Woodfin Camp, Inc.

EXERCISE

Based on your perceptions of what you believe an ideal communicator should be, mark the scales below.

Expert	__	__	__	__	__	__	Incompetent
Intelligent	__	__	__	__	__	__	Unintelligent
Qualified	__	__	__	__	__	__	Unqualified
Interesting	__	__	__	__	__	__	Boring
Nervous	__	__	__	__	__	__	Poised
Calm	__	__	__	__	__	__	Anxious
Honest	__	__	__	__	__	__	Dishonest
Kind	__	__	__	__	__	__	Cruel
Undependable	__	__	__	__	__	__	Dependable
Powerful	__	__	__	__	__	__	Powerless
Bold	__	__	__	__	__	__	Timid
Silent	__	__	__	__	__	__	Talkative
Aggressive	__	__	__	__	__	__	Meek
Organized	__	__	__	__	__	__	Disorganized
Unpleasant	__	__	__	__	__	__	Pleasant
Irritable	__	__	__	__	__	__	Good-natured
Cheerful	__	__	__	__	__	__	Gloomy

Now mark the form as you perceive yourself. Compare the results. Discuss in small groups what you have learned.

Adapted from *Speech Communication for the Classroom Teacher,* 4th ed, by Pamela J. Cooper, © 1991 by Gorsuch Scarisbrick, Publishers, (Scottsdale, Arizona), Reprinted with permission.

SUMMARY

Our self-concept is made up of our perceptions of our physical, social, and psychological selves. *Self-concept* consists of our *self-image,* the mental picture we have of ourselves, and our *self-esteem,* our feelings and attitudes toward ourselves. Self-concepts are affected by how we look at ourselves, how we look at others, how others look at us, and how we think others see us. Like communication, self-concept is a process that has no beginning or end and is constantly changing. Self-perception and other people's perceptions of us change from time to time, from situation to situation, and from person to person.

Our self-concept is based on our values, attitudes, and beliefs. *Values* are general ideas that are relatively stable over time; *attitudes* are evaluative dispositions or feelings that relate to ourselves, others, events, or objects; and *beliefs* are convictions about the truth of something.

The components of self-concept may be organized into a hierarchy. The lower in the hierarchy a particular component is, the easier it is to change. Gender in our society plays a significant role in determining our self-concept and how we communicate with others. Even though our society has taken great strides to reduce stereotypical thinking about males and females, the stereotypes and narrowly defined role expectations are still accepted. Gender stereotypes affect communication behavior of both males and females. Expectations can become *self-fulfilling prophecies* that determine how we behave, who we eventually become, and what we communicate to ourselves and others. People who have both male and female traits are referred to as *androgynous.* They are more likely to be successful in their interactions and careers than people who are totally masculine or feminine in their behaviors. *Style of communication* is the way a person interacts verbally and nonverbally with others. Our style of communication reflects our self-concept. *Communication apprehension* is anxiety associated with either real or anticipated communication with another person or persons and directly relates to our self-concept.

Although it is not easy to alter our self-concept, we can achieve some progress through hard work, a desire to improve, and the belief that we are and will be successful. Specific steps we can take to help ourselves are:

1.   decide what we want to change,
2.   describe why we feel the way we do,
3.   decide that we are going to do something to change,
4.   set reasonable goals for ourselves, and
5.   surround ourselves with supportive people.

KEY TERMS

Androgynous: Term describing a person with both masculine and feminine traits.

Attitude: Evaluative disposition, feeling, or position about oneself, others, events, ideas, or objects.

Belief: Conviction or confidence in the truth of something that is not based on absolute proof.

Communication Apprehension: Anxiety associated with real or anticipated communication with other persons.

Self-concept: Person's mental picture and evaluation of his or her physical, social, and psychological attributes.

Self-esteem: Person's feelings and attitudes toward himself or herself.

Self-fulfilling Prophecy: Molding of behavior by expectations so that what was expected does indeed happen.

Self-image: Person's mental picture of himself or herself.

Style of Communication: Way a person interacts verbally and nonverbally with others.

Value: General, relatively long-lasting ideal that guides behavior.

DISCUSSION STARTERS

1. How does self-concept affect communication? Give both a positive and a negative example.
2. How is self-concept determined?
3. How do expectations influence self-concept and ultimately communication? How have your expectations helped or hindered you?
4. How does gender affect self-concept?
5. What role does style of communication have in determining self-concept?
6. What can a person do to alter his or her self-concept?
7. How can a person help to change another person's self-concept?
8. What is the most important thing you learned in this chapter about communication, perception, and self?

NOTES

1. D. J. Bem, "Self-Perception Theory," in L. Berkowitz (ed.), *Advances in Experimental Social Psychology* (New York: Academic Press, 1972): Vol. 6.
2. J. W. Kinch, "A Formalized Theory of Self-Concept," *American Journal of Sociology 68* (January 1963): 481–486.
3. W. W. Wilmot, *Dyadic Communication,* 3rd ed. (New York: Random House, 1987): 61.
4. R. Rosenthal and L. Jacobson, *Pygmalion in the Classroom: Teacher Expectation and Pupils' Intellectual Development* (New York: Holt, Rinehart & Winston, 1968): vii; and T. Good and J. Brophy, *Looking in Classrooms*, 4th ed. (New York: HarperCollins, 1987).
5. K. Deaux and L. L. Lewis, "The Structure of Gender Stereotypes: Interrelationships Among Components and Gender Label," *Journal of Personality and Social Psychology 46* (1984): 991–1004.
6. M. E. Heilman, R. F. Martell, and M. C. Simon, "The Vagaries of Sex Bias: Conditions Regulating the Underevaluation, Equivaluation, and Overevaluation of Female Job Applicants," *Organizational Behavior and Human Decision Processes 41* (1988): 98–110.
7. D. Tannen, *You Just Don't Understand: Women and Men in Conversation* (New York: Morrow, 1990): 24–25.
8. J. H. Block, "Differential Premises Arising from Differential Socialization of the Sexes: Some Conjectures," *Child Development 54* (1983): 1335–1354; J. T. Spence and R. L. Helmreich, *Masculinity and Femininity: Their Psychological Dimension and Antecedents* (Austin: University of Texas Press, 1978).
9. A. B. Beilbrun, "Measurement of Masculine and Feminine Sex Role Identities as Independent Dimensions," *Journal of Consulting and Clinical Psychology 44* (1974): 155–162.

10. I. Karre, "Stereotyped Sex Roles and Self-Concept: Strategies for Liberating the Sexes," *Communication Education* 25 (January 1976): 43–52.

11. D. J. Canary and K. S. Hause, "Is There Any Reason to Research Sex Differences in Communication," *Communication Quarterly* 41 (Spring 1993): 129–144; and D. M. Zuckerman, "Self-Esteem, Self Concept and the Life Goals and Sex-Role Attitudes of College Students," *Journal of Personality* 48 (1980): 149–-62.

12. A. R. Gold, L. R. Brush, and E. R. Sprotzer, "Developmental Changes in Self-Perceptions of Intelligence and Self-Confidence," *Psychology of Women Quarterly* 5 (1980): 231–39.

13. L. P. Stewart, A. D. Stewart, S. A. Friedley, and P. J. Cooper, *Communication Between the Sexes,* 2d ed. (Scottsdale, Ariz.: Gorsuch Scarisbrick, 1990): 23–38.

14. R. W. Norton, "Teacher Effectiveness as a Function of Communicator Style," in *Communication Yearbook I,* an annual review published by the International Communication Association (New Brunswick, N. J.: Transaction Books, Rutgers—The State University, 1977): 523–541.

15. C. Stohl, "Perceptions of Social Attractiveness and Communicator Style: A Developmental Study of Preschool Children," *Communication Education* 30 (1981): 367–376.

16. J. C. McCroskey, "Classroom Consequences of Communication Apprehension," *Communication Education* 26 (1977): 27–33.

Chapter 4

Verbal Communication

LEARNING OBJECTIVES

After studying this chapter, you should be able to:

1. Define language and discuss its role in the communication process.

2. Describe the four key elements of language.

3. Identify three language-based barriers to communication and suggest how they can be overcome.

4. Discuss gender-inclusive language, the effects of sexist language and how to avoid it.

5. Explain how accuracy, vividness, verbal immediacy appropriateness, and the use of metaphors contribute to a speaker's effectiveness.

Like, I don't even know where to start, you know? Melissa and I are at the mall the other day, you know, and here comes Krissie, and she goes, "It passed! It passed!" Like you know what she's talking about.

So anyway, Melissa goes, "What passed?" and Krissie goes, "The referendum!" And I look at Melissa and Melissa looks at me, and we both, like, crack up, you know? And we go, "What referendum?"

So Krissie goes, "The English language referendum that was on the California ballot to make English the official language. I'm wrapped about the whole thing—like who cares, you know?"

Krissie looks at me like I'm a total jel, you know? Then she goes, "What language do you speak, Tamara?"

I go, "English."

Then she goes, "And what's California's official language going to be?" And I go, "English."

Then she goes, "And who speaks 'official languages'?" And I go, "Politicians?"

"Who else?"

"TEACHERS?!!"

She goes, "Fer sure."

"Gag me with a spoon! You mean, every one of those geeks at school will be, you know, talking just the way we do?"

So now Melissa and I are thinking of learning Chinese.

Bummer.

Adapted from Rich Horowitz, "English Language, It's Like, you know, Truly Tubular," *Chicago Tribune,* 23 November 1986, Sec 5,3.

"Don't zone out, all you kens, herbs and chips heads! Get stoked for a cholo blizz of news writing."[1]

How we use language tells a lot about us. The two examples above illustrate how language may be acceptable to those using it with their peers. However, it would be assessed quite differently if the same language were used in a business conversation or in other more formal situations. Because the language we use is a message in itself, its use can influence our image positively or it can damage and degrade ourselves and others. We live in an English-speaking culture, and even though there are many subcultures within our society, educated individuals need to know which form of English is expected and appropriate for different settings. For example, in a college classroom, business meeting, network news program, or national political speech, a certain language use is dominant and expected, while in other settings, different forms of language may be expected. Your task is to determine which form of language is appropriate for different situations and which is not.

Because how we use language is so important to communication, in this chapter we will examine what language is, some common barriers to effective language use, gender-inclusive language, and how we can use language more effectively.

EXERCISE

State Workers Learning Words Can Be Harmful

Too often language is viewed as being innocent. But it can get you into trouble. . . . Wop, chili belly and Kike. Polack jokes. And black "Over the Hill" balloons for 40th birthday celebrations—are all off limits in Nebraska state agency offices. Too often language is viewed as being innocent. But it can get you into trouble. (*The Lincoln Star,* 1989 June 21, 1.)

Discuss the following question in class: How can we balance our right to free speech with our obligation to avoid language that is disrespectful or harmful to others?

IMPORTANCE OF LANGUAGE

Language is a structured system of signs, sounds, gestures, or marks that are used and understood to express ideas and feelings among people within a community, nation, geographical area, or cultural tradition. (See Figure 4.1.) Without language, there would be little or no human communication as we now know it. Language allows us to encounter our world in a meaningful way because it allows us to share meaning with others. Can you imagine what it would be like not to be able to tell someone what you know or think or feel? Language is a powerful tool! As a tool, language is neither good nor bad, and it is only as effective and efficient as the person or persons using it.

Power of Language

We depend not only on our own experiences for information, but also on those of people we know and people we do not know. Because we use language and are able to communicate, we are not limited to just our own personal experiences and knowledge. We can learn by talking with others, taking courses, watching television, and reading newspapers, magazines, and books.

Figure 4.1:

Signing is the language of the hearing impaired. These individuals use symbols and gestures which allow them to communicate. In order for the signs to be interpreted as language they must be structured and have meaning within a community or cultural tradition. Signing allows for shared meaning.

Michael Newman/Photo Edit

Language allows us to change, to cooperate, to create, and to resolve conflicts. It can prevent wars or start them, create friends or enemies, and change our behavior or the behavior of others. Yet most of us take language for granted and ignore its potential effects. We regard language as a "mere matter of words," forgetting that words have the power to affect our mind, feelings, thoughts, will, actions, and being. Successful communicators respect language and have learned how to use it.

Language and Thought

Consider the following excerpt from an article about how thought might influence what we say:

We're constantly at war with our tongues. Who hasn't tried to say something, then startled himself by saying something else?

And who hasn't occasionally wondered if a verbal gaffe is more than a mere mistake, a faint signal from our subconscious, perhaps a reminder of long-suppressed feelings and desires?

Many psychologists regard slips as "information processing" errors, brief breakdowns in the neural machinery that controls speech.

But many also follow Sigmund Freud's belief that slips are clues to a person's most intimate and repressed feelings.

Researcher Bernard J. Baars, seeking to assess Freud's ideas in the lab, developed a technique to induce volunteers to commit slips and another to affect the content of the slips by changing the context of the experiment.

Baar tries to "prime" a volunteer to think about a particular subject. The goal is to see how the "priming" will affect the content of the slips.

In one experiment, male subjects were divided into three groups. The first was run by an attractive female experimenter, who volunteered to dress in a sexually spectacular fashion; the second group was told they might receive an electric shock during the experiment, and was shown some impressive-looking equipment (no shock was given); and the third group received neither of these treatments.

The results were dramatic. Subjects were given different word pairs such as "lice legs" and "shad bok."

When exposed to the lovely female experimenter, they were more than twice as likely to mess up "lice legs" by saying "nice legs."

When threatened with a shock, they more than doubled their rate of saying "bad shock" instead of "shad bok."

Adapted from Keay Davidson, "Programmed Loose Lips Think Slips," *San Francisco Examiner.*

Why is it so difficult for the subjects in the above experiment to say what they were asked to say? Did the subjects' thoughts control their language, or was it the other way around? The misuse of language is more than the mere misuse of words. Misused language also affects our ability to think. Thought and language are inseparable. But which comes first? As with the chicken and the egg, the answer is debatable, but most scholars agree that words help us to form thoughts. For example, at times we may think we know what we want to say, but find that we don't know how to say it. However, the fact is that if we really knew what we wanted to say, we would probably have no trouble expressing it. There are other times when we speak and later realize we didn't say what we meant. This usually occurs because we didn't think about what we were saying.

Erasing the effect of something you said is extremely difficult. You can correct or retract a statement, and you can even apologize for saying it, but you cannot eliminate the fact that you said it.

Politicians, for example, often try to assess how each word they speak might be interpreted by others. They do this because they know that what they say not only places them in an awkward position, but it may also cost them an election or jeopardize national security. One such incident occurred in the 1992 Presidential campaign when candidate Ross Perot used the expression "you people" while speaking to group of prominent Africian Americans. His language choice brought about a great deal of comment about his insensitivity to his audience and to Africian Americans in general. No matter how Perot tried to clarify what he meant, he could not overcome the stigma his statement created. Although Perot's choice of words did not eliminate him as a candidate,it did create an uproar that may have cost him votes and loss of respect from some people.

When we communicate, we first form thoughts and then decide how we are going to express them. The experiment by Baars described above clearly indicates that the thoughts of the subjects influenced what they said. To be an effective communicator we must be thinking clearly, and we must know what language is and how to use it.

ELEMENTS OF LANGUAGE

Language, speech, and communication are three different, but related, phenomena. **Language** is a structured system of symbols that allows people to express ideas and feelings to others; **speech** is one vehicle used to transmit language; and **communication** is the exchange of meanings. Language is one means by which we communicate, and speech is one way in which we use language. The fact that we process language does not automatically mean that we can communicate, but we cannot communicate without language, and language would be useless if it did not convey meanings.

To clarify the relationship among language, speech, and communication, consider the fact that you can indicate an affirmative response to a question by nodding your head, thus using a sign to communicate without speech. You can also indicate the same response by writing the word *yes*, thus using writing instead of speech as the vehicle to transmit language. If you were traveling in a foreign country and said "yes," you might use language and speech without communicating.

The goal is to get language and speech working together to produce effective communication, which is the transfer of meaning as intended. You can learn more about language by examining four of its key elements: sounds, words, grammar, and meaning.

Sounds

Language must be spoken before it can be written. Most of us are born with the physical mechanisms for making the speech sounds that are essential to create language. However, we do not all learn to produce the sounds in exactly the same way. Hence, languages and dialects sound strange or different to outsiders.

The **International Phonetic Alphabet (IPA)** was devised as a consistent and universal system for transcribing the speech sounds of all languages.[2] We cannot rely on the letters of our alphabet or spelling system because neither completely represents the sounds of our language. For example, the same letter may be pronounced in different ways (*g* in *go* and *gin*; *th* in *thin* and *then*) and different letters may represent the same sound (*c* in *cat* and *k* in *kite*; *c* in *cite* and *s* in *sight*).

The smallest functional unit of sound in a language is called a **phoneme**. In the English language there are thirty-nine phonemes. Each phoneme is different enough from other phonemes to be useful in distinguishing meaning. If, for example, the vowel sound in *get* is distorted, the word could sound like *gate*. The two different vowel phonemes make it possible to distinguish one word from the other.

For language to exist, a series of sounds must be produced by successive movements of the speech organs. When we sound out a word, for example, [k myoo n ka' sh n], we reduce the word into the sounds that compose it. When we successively put the sounds together, the parts form the word *communication.*

Words

Words are symbols that stand for the objects and concepts that they name. A word can represent an object, as the word *chair* represents an actual piece of furniture, or it can represent an abstract concept, as *freedom* represents the intangible qualities of self-determination and civil and political liberty.

Words are agreed-upon sound combinations within a language community. For example, the sounds in the word *help* constitute a word because English speakers agree that they do. On the other hand, *zelp,* while consisting of common sounds in our language, is not a word because this combination of sounds does not have an agreed-upon meaning.

Grammar

Just as language has rules that govern how sounds may be joined into words, it also has rules that govern how words may be joined into phrases and sentences. This second set of rules is **grammar.** For example, the English grammar system requires that singular nouns take singular verbs and plural nouns take plural verbs. (table *is,* tables *are.*)

As we join sounds together to form words and join words together to form phrases, sentences, and paragraphs, we use language's sound and grammar systems simultaneously. The ability to use sounds and grammar correctly is crucial to efficient and effective communication. Grammar enables us to make up complete sentences and to understand the sentences of others.

Despite the many rules that govern language, there is virtually no limit to the number of different messages that can be created. It has been estimated that in the English language, there is the possibility of 10 quintillion twenty-word sentences.[3] This does not include sentences either shorter or longer than twenty words. Thus, the number is infinite.

Meaning

The study of meaning, or the association of words with ideas, feelings, and contexts, is called **semantics.** If language did not have meaning, it would serve little or no purpose. Because words and word patterns can be repeated from person to person and from generation to generation, language becomes meaningful and useful as a tool for communication.

We tend to associate language with specific meanings and to take that relationship for granted. But it is important to understand that, in fact, language is arbitrary and by itself has no meaning. This notion may seem to contradict our entire discussion so far. You may wonder how language can be a system with rules and meanings and still be arbitrary. Language is arbitrary because it uses words, and words are symbols that merely represent people, objects, concepts, and events. The relationships between words and things are not always logical or consistent. Why? Because the word is not actually the person, object, concept, or event. For example, *chair, car, snake, communication, tall, black, money,* and *freedom* are merely words and not the entities they symbolize. Even though they are not the entities, scream "Spider!" in front of someone who dislikes spiders and you will quickly see how words cause reactions—as if they were the actual thing! Words and meanings exist only in people's minds. (See Figure 4.2.)

Meanings are in People

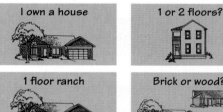

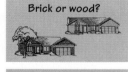

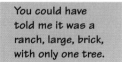

Figure 4.2:

Meanings are in people. The message sent may not be the message received because the words we use are symbols which represent people, objects, events, and situations.

MEANINGS ARE NOT IN WORDS BUT IN PEOPLE. To illustrate this notion, read the following scene from Lewis Carroll's *Through the Looking Glass*. Humpty Dumpty and Alice become involved in an argument about language and meaning:

"I don't know what you mean by 'glory,'" Alice said.

Humpty Dumpty smiled contemptuously. "Of course you don't—till I tell you. I meant there's a nice knock-down argument for you!"

"But 'glory' doesn't mean 'a nice knock-down argument'," Alice objected.

"When I use a word," Humpty Dumpty said, in a rather scornful tone, "it means just what I choose it to mean—neither more nor less."

"The question is," said Alice, "whether you can make words mean so many different things."

"The question is," said Humpty Dumpty, "which is to be master— that's all."[4]

Which is the master—you, words, or the meaning you give words? The answer is you. You control which words you use, what meaning you wish to give them, and the reactions to them. You must also realize that everyone has this same control over words and their meanings. Thus, a sender may have one meaning for a message, but the receiver can unintentionally or intentionally give the message a different meaning. Missed meaning between a sender and receiver may be more of a problem when the sender and receiver have different cultural backgrounds and experiences.

THINK ABOUT IT

"When people talk to each other, the actual meanings of the words stated convey a very small part of the meaning of the conversation."

Deborah Tannen, psycholinguist and author

What is Dr. Tannen implying in the above quotation?

If someone were to say, "I hope you have a *twif* day," you would not know what he meant. However, if that person were to explain that when he says *"twif"* he means "nice," you would understand what he meant, even though you might think he was a little strange. If every time he saw you, he used the word *twif* instead of *nice,* you would eventually associate *twif* with *nice* and automatically know exactly what he meant.

The point is that *twif,* the word (or symbol), is arbitrary because it does not mean anything until people give it meaning. Words have no direct relationship to the person, object, concept, or event they represent. Thus, the message sent may not be the message received.

Concreteness and Abstractness   The meanings of words can be classified as either: concrete/abstract or denotative/connotative. **Concrete words** are symbols for specific things that can be pointed to or physically experienced (seen or touched). For example, words such as *car, book, keys,* and *dog* are concrete words. They represent specific, tangible objects. Because they are specific, their meanings are usually quite clear. Consequently, communication based on concrete words leaves little room for misunderstanding, and any disagreement can be resolved by referring to the objects themselves.

Abstract words, on the other hand, are symbols for ideas, qualities, and relationships. Because they represent intangible things, their meanings depend on the experiences and intentions of the persons using them. For instance, words such as *right, freedom, truth,* and *trust* stand for ideas that mean different things to different people. Thus, the use of abstract words can easily lead to misunderstandings and result in ineffective communication, as illustrated by the following conversation:

Student: Your tests are unfair.
Instructor: Why do you say that?
Student: They're unfair and it's impossible to get a high grade on them.
Instructor: Do they include material that wasn't covered in class or in our readings?
Student: No.
Instructor: Do you mean the wording is too ambiguous for you to understand?
Student: No.
Instructor: What's unfair about them?

The problem here is that the student (speaker) expects the instructor to understand what the speaker meant by the word *unfair,* but because *unfair* is an abstract word, its meaning can vary greatly from person to person and from situation to situation. To clarify what the speaker means by *unfair,* the student needs to use more concrete language, for instance, "Your tests are unfair because they contain too many items to complete in the time allotted." It is always a good idea to define or illustrate any abstract word that may be misunderstood.

Figure 4.3 illustrates varying degrees of concreteness. *Cynthia* is the most tangible word because it refers to a specific individual named Cynthia. As you can see, as the words move from concrete to abstract, they become less specific and more intangible.

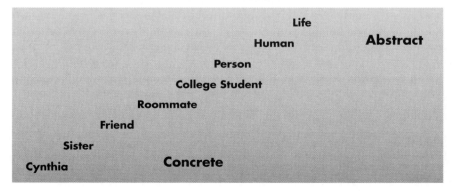

Concrete to Abstract

Life
Human   **Abstract**
Person
College Student
Roommate
Friend
Sister
Cynthia   **Concrete**

Figure 4.3:

Word meanings become more concrete when they refer to a specific person, place, or thing. Concrete language helps reduce the number of interpretations for that which is intended by the sender, leaving less chance for misunderstanding.

Denotation is the core meaning of a word, its standard dictionary definition. Denotative meanings are usually understood and exchanged by many people, whereas connotative meanings can be limited to a single person or group of people, depending on the understanding of and familiarity with those meanings. Many people use words as if they had only a denotative or specific meaning. There are commonly understood dictionary definitions (denotative meanings), but when we communicate, we usually use words connotatively.

Connotation is the subjective meaning of a word, what a word suggests because of feelings or associations it evokes. The connotative meaning is based on the context, how the meaning is expressed verbally, and the understanding of the person who is receiving it. The competent communicator knows that the meaning communicated may not be the dictionary meaning of the word. Connotative meanings may be generally accepted by most of the people who use the language or by people within a particular group, or they may be quite individual. For example, to one city person, the word *farm* may mean a place where crops are grown and animals are kept, but to a particular rural person, *farm* may represent a livelihood, a workplace, or a home.

The more communicators have in common in terms of background, experience, and attitudes, the more likely they are to have similar meanings for the words they exchange. However, competent communicators do not assume too much about how others will interpret their messages; they are always seeking and refining messages based on the feedback they receive. Consider the following situation:

> Jill and her parents are discussing college. When the subject switches to Jill's boyfriend and the word *sex* is mentioned, Jill immediately stops the discussion because she knows her parents' views on sex are much different from her own. The word simply has different meanings for Jill and her parents.

Jill cannot talk about sex with her parents because their differing connotations of the word result in misinterpretation and distrust. What can be done to prevent this kind of obstacle to communication? Who is at fault? Why?

Different experiences, backgrounds, and ages of the communicators as well as their relationship to one another can influence the choices of words used and their meanings. Jill, in the above example, knows that her parents have a different meaning for sex, so she chooses to avoid communication with them on that subject. The word "sex" as used by Jill and her parents exemplifies the connotative meanings each has attached to the word. Yet the denonative meaning is something entirely different from either Jill's, her parents', or for that matter your interpretation of it.

The meanings of words, like the words themselves, change from time to time and from place to place. It is easy for us to forget that the meaning we have for a word may not be the same meaning others have for the same word. For example, ask a person over 60 what these words mean: *grass, geek, speed, pot, joint, gay, high,* or *stoned.* What words do you use now that might change in the next 20 years? We also are constantly adding words to our language. This is especially true with the invention of new technologies, for example, fax, compact disc, cellular phone, ATM, and so on.

Not only do word meanings change over time, but they also change from one region of the country to another. For example, where I was brought up in Wisconsin, *pop* meant "soda" and *bubbler* meant "drinking fountain." Regional word usage can lead to misunderstandings, and thus we must be sensitive and aware of potential differences in how words are used. Words can also take on different meanings to people from different cultural backgrounds. For example, *very dear* connotes to most Americans something that is highly valued or loved, while in Ireland *very dear* means "very expensive" and has nothing to with value or love.

Word meanings also vary based on experience and direct relationship of those experiences to the word being used. For example, the term *heart attack* has a denotative meaning which almost everyone understands as a serious health problem related to the heart. However, a doctor, a patient, a relative of a patient, and a statistician in a hospital will understand it quite differently from one another. The doctor thinks of what procedures need to be taken to help the patient; the patient thinks "Will I live or die?" The family members ask "What can I do?", and the statistician sees it as a probability related to life and death. Their connotative meanings are based on experience, emotion, and relation to the situation.

Words also take on connotative meanings when subpopulations of a language community use words in special ways so as to make their use unique to a particular group (see Figure 4.4.) When language is used

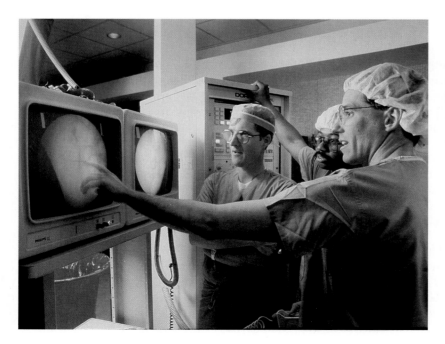

Figure 4.4:

Some language, such as that used by those in the medical profession, can be very specialized, technical and difficult to understand for those outside the field. Why is jargon important?

Andrew Sacks/Tony Stone Images

differently from the general population of a culture, it is refered to as slang or jargon. For example, language used by people selling cars includes such terms as "flea" for a person who is out to get a great bargain, a prisoner refers to a knife or to stabbing with a knife as "shank," or a real estate agent might use the term "handyman's special" to refer to a house which is in need of repair.[5] *Merriam-Webster Collegiate Dictionary* conducted an unscientific poll on 23 campuses nationwide, in which they asked 460 students to name the five hottest words on campus and to define them. Some of the words were:

Zone out—to lose concentration

Phat—very cool

Herb—geek

Homeskillet—good friend

Reality-impaired—unintelligent

Cholo—macho

Boot—to get sick from drinking

Circle of death—lousy pizza[6]

The list of slang terms is endless and the groups using them vary from professional groups to college students, to ethnic groups to gangs, and so on.[7]

It is important to analyze how others might interpret what we say, and we must always make sure the context in which meanings are exchanged is clear. If we do not take these differences into account, there are bound to be differences between what a speaker intends to say and what a listener receives.

Language That Obscures Meanings Language is used to share meaning, but it is also can be used to obscure, distort, or hide meaning. One way we use language to obscure meaning is the euphemism. A **euphemism** is the use of an inoffensive or mild expression for one that may offend, cause embarrassment, or suggest something unpleasant. Our society also uses euphemism to avoid taboo subjects or negative emotionally charged words, thereby making them less controversial. For example, when a person has died, we use an euphemism such as "passed away." Using the words "passed away" seems to soften the emotions of the situation.

Euphemisms can also be used to enhance or make something seem a little more glamorous than it actually is. In our society, we have become so concerned with labels that we have essentially renamed many things in order to make them sound more important. For example, we no longer refer to a person as a salesman, because *salesman* is not only sexist, but it also conjures negative connotations due to media influence and people's personal experiences. Thus, we refer to a person who sells merchandise as a salesperson, sales associate, sales consultant, sales representative, and so on. Similarly, the term *trash collector* or *garbage man* has been relabeled by some as "sanitation engineer," which conveys a different message, making the job seem more attractive than the connotations of previous labels.

Language can also be used to create deliberately ambiguous messages. Professor William Lutz, a professor at Rutgers University, says he can live with ordinary euphemisms, but he says his teeth gnash when a worker is told he has been "dehired" because the firm is experiencing "negative employee retention." The employee has been fired, according to Lutz, in a layoff. But no one is willing to say so, laments Lutz, who has written *Doublespeak* a book denouncing the use of words to conceal meaning. **Doublespeak** is the deliberate misuse of language to distort meaning.

> . . . [I]t is going just too far, says Lutz, when the Pentagon refers to bombs that accidentally kill civilians as "incontinent ordinance" or when lawyers write off a plane crash as "the involuntary conversion of a 727." That, he says, is language "designed to distort reality and corrupt thought."[8]

Lutz thinks the practice is disgraceful, dangerous to democracy, perverse, and pervasive. It's hard work, too. Doublespeak isn't just the natural work product of the bureaucratic mind, he says; it is invented painstakingly by committees laboring to cloak what the words aren't permitted to say. Doublespeak is not a slip of the tongue or language use out of ignorance, but is instead a very conscious use of language as a weapon or tool by those in power to achieve their ends at our expense.

According to Lutz and other scholars, doublespeak is particularly harmful when it distorts or hides meaning by making something that would be considered inappropriate or negative appear to be appropriate or positive. Thus, language and meaning are inseparable if communication is to occur. Unfortunately, communication can occur without correct understanding.

LANGUAGE-BASED BARRIERS TO COMMUNICATION

Although it takes little physical effort to say something to someone, it does take mental effort to ensure that what we say conveys our intentions. Even if we create what we *think* is the perfect message, the possibility always exists that the receiver will misinterpret the message or find it ambiguous. Thus, the receiver must also make an effort to ensure that he or she receives the intended message.

According to three educational and cultural scholars, Kenneth Cushner, Averil McClelland, and Philip Safford, "There are over 300 different languages in everday use in the United States. This number includes over 200 Native American languages, the languages of the colonizers (English, French, and Spanish), languages of immigrants—both old and new—and a variety of dialects spoken in various regions of the country."[9] We, therefore, must recognize that communication is a symbolic interaction, and because of its symbolic nature, there will always be the potential for misunderstanding. Within the communication process there are numerous physical, mental, and cultural reasons for misunderstandings to occur, and our use of language is one. Among the most common language-based barriers to effective communication are bypassing, indiscrimination, and polarization.[10]

Bypassing

What is *meant* by a speaker and what is *heard* and *understood* by the listener are often different. Such misunderstanding between a sender and a receiver is called **bypassing.** How many times have we said to someone, "But that's not what I meant?" The problem is that we forget that language is symbolic. The words we speak or write are not the actual objects, ideas, or feelings, but merely symbols that represent them. Here is a classic illustration of bypassing:

> A motorist was driving down a highway when her engine suddenly stalled. She quickly determined that her battery was dead and managed to stop another driver, who consented to push her car to get it started.
>
> "My car has an automatic transmission," she explained to the other driver, "so you'll have to get up to 15 to 20 miles per hour to get me started."
>
> The man smiled and walked back to his car. The motorist climbed into her own and waited for him to line up his car behind hers. She waited—and waited. Finally, she turned around to see what was wrong. There was the man—coming at her car at 15 to 20 miles per hour!
>
> The damage to her car amounted to over $1,000![11]

That end result could not have been anticipated by either driver, given each one's understanding of the message. The driver of the stalled vehicle thought she knew exactly what she had asked of the other driver, but the meanings of the message sent and the message received obviously were different. Bypassing took place.

Bypassing is usually the result of the false belief that each word has only one meaning and that words have meaning in themselves. A glimpse at our everyday language quickly illustrates that most words have multiple uses and meanings. For example, the *Random House Dictionary of the English Language* provides 60 different definitions for the word *call,* 30 for *fast,* 22 for *seat,* 29 for *see,* and 96 for *turn.* Words acquire these many uses and meanings because they change over time, vary from one culture or region to another, and vary with the knowledge and situation of the user. Thus, it is crucial that all of us as communicators, both senders and receivers, stay alert to the fact that words can be interpreted differently by different people.

The interpretations of words is even more complex when people from diferent cultures exchange everyday communication. The problem is magnified when someone uses common phrases that are unfamiliar to non-native speakers of English. For example, "Won't you have some tea?" The non-native speaker of English listens to the literal meaning of the question and answers "no," meaning "Yes, I *would* have some tea." But we in the United States ignore the double negative because of common usage, and the non-native speaker gets no tea. Here the word *no* means *yes*. Unfortunately, sometimes even when native speakers of the English language say "no," it can be interpreted by the receiver to mean "yes," though the person saying "no" really means "yes." In the first situation bypassing occurred unintentially by both parties involved because of their cultural differences.[12] In the second situation the receiver chose to intentionally disregard the meaning of the sender—is this bypassing?

The belief that words have meaning in themselves is widespread. During the past four or five years I have asked students in my beginning communication classes to tell me if words have meaning. The data, though not scientifically collected, suggest that better than 75 percent of my students believe words do have meaning. But the simple fact is that words do NOT contain meanings by themselves. They only acquire meaning through the context in which they are used and are given meaning by those who use them.

The fact that some speakers and listeners bypass deliberately when using euphemisms or doublespeak language to soften or distort meanings should not be overlooked. For example, politicians sometimes will say one thing in order to get people to believe or accept something else. When this occurs, there are ethical considerations that message senders and receivers should take into account. The issue of what is right or wrong and what is beneficial or harmful must rest with the norms of society and one's own conscience.

The following techniques should help you to reduce the frequency of bypassing when speaking and listening. Bear in mind that the most these techniques will do is help, because there is little chance that bypassing will ever be completely eliminated.

1. BE PERSON-MINDED, NOT WORD-MINDED. Think not only of the words and their meanings, but also of the persons using the words and of the meanings they give to those words. Constantly question your interpretation: "This is what the word means to me, but what does it mean to the other person or persons?"

2. QUERY AND PARAPHRASE. Ask questions and paraphrase whenever there is a potential for misunderstanding that results from differences in background, age, gender, occupation, attitudes, knowledge, and perceptions. If you don't understand something or if you feel uncertain about what people mean, ask them to explain. Restating a message in your own words gives you and the sender a chance to check that you received the message as it was intended. As the importance and complexity of a message increases, so does the need for asking questions and paraphrasing.

3. BE APPROACHABLE. Encourage open and free communication. The most frequent barrier to effective communication is an unwillingness to listen to others. Allow others to question and paraphrase, and show respect for what they say. Being receptive to others is not always easy, but make the effort to ensure a clear exchange of information.

4. BE SENSITIVE TO CONTEXTS. Take into account the verbal and situational contexts in which communication occurs. The meaning of a word can be more precisely interpreted by considering the words, sentences, and paragraphs that precede and follow it and the setting in which communication takes place.

Indiscrimination

Indiscrimination is the neglect of individual differences and the overemphasis of similarities. Indiscrimination is a form of perceptual set (see Chapter 2) in which a person chooses to ignore differences and change in events, things, and people. Language plays a significant role in our tendency to see similarities even when they don't exist. Categorizing nouns *(teenager, divorce, student, professor, black, southerner, liberal, friend, government, politician, salesperson)* encourage us to focus on similarities. Statements such as "Politicians are crooks" and "Students cheat in school" come to mean all politicians and all students instead of some politicians and some students. They fail to distinguish between individuals. Such categorization often results in stereotyping.

A **stereotype,** as defined in Chapter 2, is a categorizing of events, objects, and people without regard to unique individual characteristics and qualities. Stereotypes are often negative, but they may also be positive, for example, "All liberals are hard-working," "All conservatives want peace," "All teachers are dedicated professionals," "All environmentalists are concerned citizens." Whether the stereotype is negative or positive, the problem is the same: Individual qualities are ignored. Stereotyping is quick and easy to do because it does not require analysis, investigation, or thought. By precluding distinctions, stereotypes give us neat, oversimplified categories that facilitate our evaluation of people, situations, and events.

There are ways in which we can reduce the frequency of indiscimination in our communication. **Indexing** is a technique to sort out differences among various members of a group and thus reduce indiscrimination. Indexing is identifying what specific person, idea, event, or object a statement refers to. When you hear someone say "Politicians are corrupt," "College men are oversexed," "Athletes are dumb," or any statement that lumps persons, ideas, events, or objects into a single category, immediately ask, "Which ones are you talking about?" No matter what people may think, not all politicians are corrupt. Politician A is different from Politician B, and Politician B is different from Politician C. The same is true of college men and athletes. They may belong to a class or group that has an identity and whose members have similar interests, but the group is composed of individuals, each different from the other.

Dating, another technique for reducing indiscrimination, is a form of indexing that sorts people, ideas, events, and objects according to time. By telling when something occurred, we acknowledge that things change over time and add specificity to a statement. For example, indicate the year in which each of the following news bulletins was probably made:

POPE CONDEMNS USE OF NEW "HORROR" WEAPONS
Vatican City—Prompted by widespread fears that new weapons of mass destruction might wipe out Western civilization, the Pope today issued a bulletin forbidding the use of these weapons by any Christian state against another, whatever the provocation.

MORAL ROT ENDANGERS LAND, WARNS GENERAL
Boston—The head of the country's armed forces declared here today that if he had known the depth of America's moral decay, he would never have accepted his command. "Such a dearth of public spirit," he asserted, "and want of virtue, and fertility in all the low arts to obtain advantages of one kind or another, I never saw before and hope I may never be witness to again."[13]

The thoughts expressed in these two paragraphs could easily apply to what is happening today, but in fact, the first paragraph pertains to a statement made by Pope Innocent II in 1139 and the second quotes a comment made by George Washington in 1775.

Did you think that the above news bulletins referred to recent events? If so, you fell victim to indiscrimination. Why do such errors occur in our language? How we can avoid or prevent them? For example, the contexts of the statements in the above news bulletins could be greatly clarified merely by adding dates: Vatican City, 1139, and Boston, 1775. Dating gives listeners valuable information that can increase their understanding of the intended message.

Polarization

Polarization is the tendency to view things in terms of extremes—rich or poor, beautiful or ugly, large or small, high or low, good or bad, intelligent or stupid—even though most things exist somewhere in between. This either-or black-or-white way of thinking is aggravated by language.

Supply the polar extreme for each of the following words:

	none	some
all		
high		
fat		
happy		
correct		

Now try to think of a word that would describe the middle ground between each pair of extremes. Which task was easier? Why?

Finding a word to express a polar extreme is fairly simple in most cases. Coming up with a word that describes the middle ground between a pair of opposites often takes some thought; it may be necessary to use more than one word. In addition, people are less likely to agree on what actually constitutes the middle ground.

The most destructive consequence of polarization is the escalating conflict that results from the use of polar terms to describe and defend our perceptions of reality. This is referred to as the **pendulum effect.** The pendulum represents a person's reality, which includes feelings, attitudes, opinions, and value judgments about the surrounding world. When the pendulum is hanging in the center, a person's perception is considered to be realistic, virtuous, intelligent, sane, honest, and honorable. Of course, most of us believe that most of the time our pendulums are at or near the center. When two individuals disagree in their perceptions of reality, their pendulums begin to move in opposite directions. The distance the pendulum swings represents their differences and the convictions expressed by their language. As the conversation intensifies, each remark provokes a stronger and stronger reaction until both parties are driven to opposite extremes. For example, when two roommates argue over whose turn it is to clean, one may begin by saying, "It's your turn. I did it the last time." The other is likely to respond, "No, I did it the last time. Now it's your turn." If the disagreement continues and no solution is found, both will become firmer in their positions, and their comments may turn into personal attacks: "You're always so messy and lazy." "And you're always so picky and critical." Eventually the situation may degenerate to the point where one or the other threatens to move out. Such an extreme outcome is typical of a discussion driven by the pendulum effect. Emotions may eventually run so high that the differences between the parties may seem insurmountable and a mutually agreeable settlement may seem unattainable.

Speakers can avoid the dangers of polarization by recognizing the potential for misunderstanding and by specifying degrees between extremes. For example, a statement such as "Nebraska is hot in the summer" is not as meaningful as it could be because the word *hot* is a generalized extreme. To avoid confusion, further information is necessary: What is the basis of comparison (Florida or Minnesota)? Are Nebraska summers all the same or do they vary from year to year? Is a Nebraska summer the same in all parts of the state or does it vary from north to south? What is the average summer temperature? The problem of polarization is solved by stating, "Nebraska summers can be hot. The average temperature is 85 degrees Fahrenheit, with lows around 74 degrees and highs around 105 degrees." It may take more words and time, but the risk of misunderstanding is substantially reduced.

Gender-Inclusive Language

There is a difference in how men and women may use language and converse with one another (as indicated in Chapter 3). Deborah Tannen, for example, suggests men use language to create status while women use language to establish and maintain social relationships.[14] Tannen goes on to say that rather than using language to dominate another, women will use it to establish closeness and support. Men, on the other hand, use language to dominate or compete. The result, according to Tannen, is that the game of communication for men and women is the same, but the rules are different. When men and women communicate with each other, there is the potential for clash and conflict because of different language use. The problem is magnified when sexist language is used either consciously or unconsciously. Our goal should be to use **gender-inclusive language**—language that does not discriminate against males or females.

Unfortunately, the English language is structured to have an inherent bias toward men. There are, for example, no non-gender pronouns in the English language that refer to both men and women. Thus, the tendency has been to use the masculine pronoun *(he, him, his)* even if the referent could be a male or a female. Using the masculine pronoun is not incorrect grammatically, but its use in generic situations is a social issue. Language sets expectations that at times discriminates against and stereotypes women. The tendency has been to use the masculine pronoun, giving the impression that men hold important roles while women do not. Thus, the expectation created by our language is that males are active and have important roles while females are inactive and do not hold important roles in our society.

When sexual stereotypes or the superiority of one gender over another is expressed, the language used is **sexist.** In our society, sexist language is as much an attitude as it is the use of specific words. Words that are used to describe males acquire positive connotations—*independent, logical, strong, confident, aggressive;* words associated with females have negative connotations—*dependent, illogical, weak, gullible, timid.* Sexist language suggests that men are more important than and superior to women. Language, when used to discriminate against women, can also be subtle.[15] For example, someone might say "She is president of the company and she's a woman" or "Wanda got that position because she's a woman." These types of statements describe women who have risen to high authority positions, but they also imply that women do not typically hold these positions, or that the only reason Wanda got the position was because she's a woman. In another words, the implication is that women are less qualified then men.

Stereotypes do not occur in a social vacuum. On the contrary, they often exert powerful effects on how judgments and evaluations are made on those who are stereotyped. Gender stereotypes, of course, are no exception—they influence perceptions and behaviors of both men and women. In the case of women, the impact of such stereotypes is much more negative than on men. The above examples of women holding positions of authority and the remarks made about them is a clear indication of the type of insensitive use of language that can occur. In general, the traits assumed to be necessary for success in leadership or positions of authority are much closer to the content of male gender stereotypes than female gender stereotypes.

Metaphors to describe how society views men and women in our culture are often sexist. A **metaphor** is a figure of speech in which a word or phrase compares two ideas that are not commonly linked together. Using animal metaphors, for example, men are likely to be described as aggressive (wolf, tomcat, stud) and women as harmless pets (kitten, lamb, chick) or as unattractive barnyard animals (cow, pig, dog). Language usage is a reflection of the society in which we live, and as long as our society treats men and women in terms of sex-role stereotypes, the use of language to exploit those differences will persist.

Here are some suggestions to help avoid sexism and to make your language more gender-inclusive:

1. Commit yourself to remove sexism from your communication.

2. Practice and reinforce nonsexist communication patterns until they become habitual. The ultimate test is your ability to carry on nonsexist private conversation and to think in nonsexist terms.

3. Use familiar idiom whenever possible, but if you must choose between sexism and the unfamiliar, use the unfamiliar until it becomes familiar.

4. Take care not to arouse negativism in the receiver by using awkward, cumbersome, highly repetitious, or unnecessary rewording. There are so many graceful and controlled ways to rewrite that you need not use bland or offensive constructions.

5. Check roots and meanings of words to be sure that the words need to be changed before changing them.

6. Check every outgoing message—written, oral, and nonverbal—for sexism before sending it.[16]

It is important that the language we use be inclusive and not discriminating or demeaning to any group of individuals. Language influences how we see others around us. If language is used inappropriately, it will cause perceptual and social problems which should not be tolerated in our society.

EXERCISE

Change the following words into gender-inclusive language. The first one is done for you.

workmen	workers
policeman	
stewardess	
salesmen	
cameraman	
mankind	
waitress	

HOW TO USE LANGUAGE MORE EFFECTIVELY

People of all ages, cultures, and educational levels use language every day. Nevertheless, the ability to use language effectively requires years of practice and study. While many variables enter into the effectiveness of language, five variables play key roles and merit special attention. They are accuracy, vividness, verbal immediacy, appropriateness, and metaphorical language.

Accuracy

Using accurate language is as critical to a speaker as giving accurate navigational directions is to an air controller. Choosing a wrong word can distort your intended message, misguide your receiver, and undermine your credibility. When you speak, your goal should be precision. Don't leave room for misinterpretation. You should constantly ask yourself, "What do I want to say?" and "What do I mean?" When necessary, consult a dictionary to be sure you have chosen the correct word to express yourself.

The more words you can use accurately, the better the chance that you can find the one you need to make your meaning clear. You must expand your vocabulary. Two of the best ways to do this are listening to others and reading. Pay attention to words that you don't understand. Whenever you run into an unfamiliar word, determine the context in which it is used and consult a dictionary for its meaning. Once you have learned a new word, try to put it to use. Words that are not used are likely to be forgotten. Expanding your vocabulary takes effort and time, but with practice, it can become part of your daily routine.

One word of warning, however: As you develop your vocabulary, avoid the temptation to use long or little-known words when short or common words would serve the purpose. Also be sure you know the shades of meaning and connotations of new words before you use them.

Remember that words may have different meanings for different people. Sometimes when our meaning is unclear, it is because we did not structure our statement effectively. For example, classified advertisers in newspapers frequently condense the content of their ads so much that their intended meaning becomes distorted or obscured. The result may be "1979 Cadillac hearse for sale. Body in good condition" or "Wanted to Rent— Four-room apartment by careful couple. No children." Obviously, these advertisers knew what they intended to communicate, but their failure to phrase their messages accurately interfered with their intended meaning.

When conversing, we can easily clear up misunderstandings caused by scrambled sentence structure or poor word choice. But it is our responsibility to be aware of our listeners' reactions to what we are saying. If they appear confused or ask a question, we should rephrase our message more clearly.

Effective speakers do not assume that what is clear to them is necessarily going to be clear to their listeners. They are especially aware of this problem in situations such as public speeches during which it may not be possible or appropriate for listeners to ask questions. To avoid problems, the speakers strive to make their meaning so clear that there is little chance of misunderstanding. They try to ensure comprehension by, among other things, using familiar and concrete rather than abstract language, and by being aware of the connotations and changing meanings of words.

THINK ABOUT IT

"I see one-third of a nation ill-housed, ill-clad, ill-nourished."

Compare the above statement, by Franklin Delano Roosevelt, to one author's version of it.

It is evident that a substantial number of persons within the continental boundaries of the United States have inadequate financial resources with which to purchase the products of agricultural communities and industrial establishments. It would appear that for a considerable segment of the population, perhaps as much as 33.333 percent of the total, there are inadequate housing facilities, and an equally significant proportion is deprived of the proper types of clothing and nourishment.

How do these speakers differ in their choice of words? How do their choices affect your emotions and your impression of them as speakers?

Excerpt from "Gobbledygook" in *Power of Words,* copyright © 1954, 1953 and renewed 1982, 1981 by Stuart Chase, reprinted by permission of Harcourt Brace & Company.

EXERCISE

Change the following phrases and statements to make them more accurate and less likely to be misunderstood. The first one is done for you.

fresh fruit   **an apple picked this morning**
a cold day
a high evaluation
a losing team
She hit him several times.
They made a lot of money.

Vividness

To communicate your message more effectively, make what you say seem alive, animated, and interesting. Active, direct, and fresh language can bring a sense of excitement, urgency, and forcefulness to what you say. Such **vividness** tells your audience that they had better listen because what you have to say is important.

For example, suppose an organization is trying to raise money for the homeless. It could take one of two approaches in seeking a donation from you: present statistics to illustrate the numbers that are believed to be homeless in our society, or present cases of actual individuals who are homeless, including children and their families. The first approach is rational, informative, abstract, and distant. The second approach is emotional, urgent, concrete, and forceful. Also, the vividness of the second approach is likely to at least get your attention and perhaps get you to contribute.

According to social psychologists, vivid language affects us in several ways. For example, vivid language is more persuasive than pallid information because it is more memorable. Vivid messages are more likely to create mental images that are readily retained and recalled. Vivid language is more persuasive also because it has an emotional impact on us. Finally, it is clear that people tend to listen to vivid messages more attentively than they do to uninspiring or uninteresting messages.[17]

To increase vividness, fill in details about the event taking place: "They had realized their most cherished dream; they discovered the actual tomb of the Egyptian king they had sought for so long" is a sentence that shows action and excitement. Note how much more animated and energetic it is than the dry and passive statement, "The old tomb was found by the explorers."

You should also avoid using clichés such as "happy as a lark," "blind as a bat," and "fit as a fiddle." Such overused and unimaginative phrases lack impact. You will be more likely to get and hold your audience's attention if you use fresh language to present your ideas in a new and exciting way.

Verbal Immediacy

Verbal immediacy helps identify and project the speakers' feelings and makes the message more relevant to the listener. Immediacy indicates a speaker's commitment to the topic and a direct relationship between the speaker and the topic. To illustrate, the statements below are listed in descending order of verbal immediacy. The first displays strong verbal immediacy and the last weak verbal immediacy:

1. We certainly will enjoy the baseball game.
2. You and I will enjoy the baseball game.

3. I think you and I may enjoy baseball.

4. People often enjoy baseball games.

The first statement is directly related to the speaker, the listener, and the situation. It is assertive and the speaker makes a close association with the listener. In each successive statement, the speaker decreases his or her association with the listener and the event. The language becomes less immediate.

   The use of verbal immediacy also helps create the image of being a relaxed, confident, competent, and effective speaker. Language that is immediate will produce messages that receivers see as similar to their own beliefs more readily than language that is not related to the speaker, topic, or receiver.[18]

Appropriateness

Each time you speak, your listeners have specific expectations about the kind of language you will use. The kind of language that is appropriate varies from situation to situation. For example, the language you would use in addressing the president of your college or university would be much more formal than the language you would use when chatting with friends. You would be unlikely to call the president by a nickname and you would be equally unlikely to call a friend Dr. or Mr. or Ms. except in jest.

   If the language you use is inappropriate for the situation, your credibility will suffer and your message may be misinterpreted or disregarded. It is therefore crucial to assess each speaking situation and adjust your language accordingly. In public situations, profanity, improper grammar, and slang are always inappropriate.

Metaphorical Language

According to some language scholars, our way of looking at the world around us is fundamentally metaphorical in nature. Metaphors help us to structure what we think, how we perceive, and what we do. Metaphorical language pervades our everyday language and our thoughts. A **metaphor** is a figure of speech in which a word or phrase relates one object or idea to another object or idea that it is not commonly linked with. The metaphor is used to make the object or idea more clear and vivid. Sports terms are often used as metaphors, for example, "Wow! Was I thrown a curve" or "She's a real team player."

   Metaphors can help the speaker make a specific point more meaningful. Jesse Jackson, for example, at the 1988 Democratic National Convention, used a quilt metaphor to make his point that America is made up of many different people, ideas, and lifestyles. Jackson said:

America's not a blanket woven from one thread, one color, one cloth. When I was a child, growing up in Greenville, South Carolina, and grandmother could not afford a blanket, she didn't complain and we did not freeze. Instead, she took pieces of old cloth—patches, wool, silk, gabardine—barely good enough to wipe off your shoes with.

But they didn't stay that way very long. With sturdy hands and a strong cord, she sewed them together into a quilt, a thing of beauty and power and culture.

Now, Democrats, we must build such a quilt.

J. Jackson, "Common Ground and Common Sense," *Vital Speeches of the Day 54* (1988): 649–653.

Metaphorical language is culture-bound, and most metaphors have meaning only within a specific language community. Thus, you should be sure that your receivers can identify with any metaphors you use, or they will be meaningless to the receivers. As a student you probably can think of many metaphors that describe your college experiences. For example, some students have said that college life like a roller coaster ride. There are many ups and downs as well as turns. You probably can think of many metaphors that describe your experiences and thus make them more meaningful to others.

SUMMARY

Learning how to use language is important for effective communication in any situation. Our ability to use language determines our success, makes communication personal, and allows us to translate our thoughts, feelings, and experiences into messages.

Language is a structured system of signs, sounds, gestures, and marks used and understood to express ideas and feelings. It allows us to progress, to cooperate, and to create and resolve conflict.

The misuse of language is more than just a matter of misusing words; it also affects our ability to think. Thought and language, according to most scholars, are inseparable. When we cannot find the words to express a thought, perhaps the thinking is not clear. If our thoughts are not expressed clearly and accurately, misunderstanding is inevitable.

Language is made up of four key elements: sounds, words, grammar, and meaning. Sound allows us to have language. The *International Phonetic Alphabet* is a system for transcribing the speech sounds of all languages. The *phoneme* is the smallest distinctive and functional unit of sound in a language.

When sounds are joined together in agreed-upon combinations, they form *words*, symbols that stand for the objects and concepts they name. Words, in turn, can be joined together to form phrases and sentences. The rules that govern how phrases and sentences must be constructed form a language's *grammar*. A language's sound and grammar systems work simultaneously to ensure effective and efficient communication.

The goal of communication is to exchange meanings. The study of meaning, or the association of words with ideas, feelings, and contexts, is called *semantics*. If language did not have meaning, it would serve little or no purpose.

We tend to associate words with specific meanings and to take that relationship for granted, but in reality language is arbitrary because language users arbitrarily pair words with meanings. Words are not actual objects or ideas, but symbols that represent them. Meanings, therefore, are not in words but in people. Words can be *concrete* (specific) or they can be *abstract* (general). Words have a *denotative* meaning (dictionary definition) and a *connotative* meaning (social or personal definition).

Language can also obscure, distort, or hide meaning. A *euphemism* is the use of an inoffensive or mild expression for one that may offend, cause embarrassment, or suggest something unpleasant. *Doublespeak* is the deliberate misuse of language to distort meaning.

Three common barriers to effective communication are bypassing, indiscrimination, and polarization. *Bypassing* is the misunderstanding that occurs between a sender and a receiver. It usually occurs as a result of the belief that a word has only one meaning and that words have meaning in themselves. To reduce the frequency of bypassing, we should be person-minded, approachable, and sensitive to contexts, and we should query and paraphrase.

Indiscrimination is the neglect of individual differences and the overemphasis of similarities. Indiscrimination can lead to *stereotyping*, which is a fixed mental picture of a group that is attributed to an individual member of the group without regard to his or her unique characteristics and qualities. To help reduce the misunderstandings due to indiscrimination, we can use *dating* (sorting people, events, and objects according to time) and *indexing* (technique to reduce indiscrimination) to add distinguishing detail.

Polarization is the tendency to view things in terms of extremes. Polarizations can give rise to the *pendulum effect,* escalating conflict between people that stems from their use of polar terms to describe and defend their perceptions of reality.

Gender-inclusive language is language that does not discriminate against males or females. Unfortunately, the English language is structured to have an inherent bias toward men. When sexual stereotypes or the superiority of one gender over another is expressed, the language used is *sexist.*

Effective use of language requires practice and study. Among the most important areas to address when attempting to improve language effectiveness are accuracy, vividness, verbal immediacy, appropriateness, and metaphorical language. Accuracy reduces room for misinterpretation. *Vividness* makes messages come alive and grabs listeners' attention. *Verbal immediacy* helps identify and project the speakers' feelings and makes the message more relevant to the listener. Appropriateness ensures that a speaker's choice of words and manner of speaking suits the situation. A *metaphor* is a figure of speech in which a word or phrase relates one object or idea to another object or idea that it is not commonly linked with, which makes ideas and points clearer and more meaningful.

KEY TERMS

Abstract Word: Symbol for an idea, quality, or relationship.

Bypassing: Misunderstanding that occurs between a sender and a receiver because of the symbolic nature of language.

Concrete Word: Symbol for a specific thing that can be pointed to or physically experienced (seen or touched).

Connotation: Subjective meaning of a word; what a word suggests because of feelings or associations it evokes.

Dating: Form of indexing that sorts people, events, ideas, and objects according to time.

Denotation: Objective meaning of a word, or standard dictionary definition.

Doublespeak: Deliberate misuse of language to distort meaning.

Euphemism: Use of an inoffensive or mild expression for one that may offend, cause embarrassment, or suggest something unpleasant.

Gender-Inclusive Language: Language that does not discriminate against males or females.

Grammar: Rules that govern how words are put together to form phrases and sentences.

Indexing: Technique to reduce indiscrimination by identifying the specific persons, ideas, events, or objects a statement refers to.

Indiscrimination: Neglect of individual differences and overemphasis of similarities.

International Phonetic Alphabet (IPA): Alphabet of sounds devised to provide a consistent and universal system for transcribing speech sounds of all languages.

Language: Structured system of signs, sounds, gestures, and marks used and understood to express ideas and feelings among people within a community, nation, geographical area, or cultural tradition.

Metaphor: Figure of speech in which a word or phrase relates one object or idea to another object or idea that it is not commonly linked with.

Pendulum Effect: Escalating conflict between two persons or groups that results from their use of polar terms to describe and defend their perceptions of reality.

Phoneme: Smallest distinctive and functional unit of sound in a language.

Polarization: Tendency to view things in terms of extremes.

Semantics: The study of meaning, or the association of words with ideas, feelings, and contexts.

Sexist Language: Language that creates sexual stereotypes or implies that one gender is superior to the other.

Verbal Immediacy: Use of language that identifies and projects the
speaker's feelings and makes the message more relevant to the listener.
Vividness: Use of active, direct, and fresh language that brings a sense of
excitement and urgency to a message.
Word: Symbol that stands for the object or concept that it names.

DISCUSSION STARTERS

1. Why is language so powerful?
2. How are thought and language related?
3. Why are language and communication not synonymous?
4. How is it possible that language can have rules and still be arbitrary?
5. The notion that meanings are in people is extremely important to the understanding of how we use language. Why is this so?
6. Which of the language barriers discussed in this chapter is the most likely to occur in everyday conversations? Why?
7. What advice would you give to someone about indexing and dating their communications?
8. How can language increase or reduce credibility?
9. What does it mean to say that you use language effectively?

NOTES

1. "Collegespeak Interpreted for Un-phat," *Lincoln Journal-Star,* 19 October 1993, 3.
2. R. R. Leutenegger, *The Sound of American English: An Introduction to Phonetics* (Glenview, Ill.: Scott, Foresman, 1963).
3. G. A. Miller, *The Psychology of Communication* (Baltimore: Penguin, 1967).
4. Lewis Carroll, *Alice's Adventures in Wonderland, Through the Looking Glass, and The Hunting of the Smark* (New York: Modern Library, 1925): 246–247.
5. P. Dickson, *Slang!* (New York: Pocket Books, 1990).
6. "The Hottest Words," *Parade Magazine,* 2 January 1994, 8.
7. Ibid, P. Dickson.
8. W. Lutz, *Doublespeak: From "Revenue Enhancement" to "Terminal Living": How Government, Business, Advertisers, and Others Use Language to Deceive You* (New York: HarperCollins 1987).
9. K. Cushner, A. McClelland, and P. Safford, *Human Diversity in Education: An Integrative Approach* (New York: McGraw-Hill, 1992): 159.
10. Adapted from W. V. Haney, *Communication and Organizational Behavior,* 3rd ed. (Homewood, Ill.: Irwin, 1973): 211–330; and *Communication and Interpersonal Relations,* 5th ed. (Homewood, Ill.: Irwin, 1986): 213–405.
11. W. V. Haney, *Communication and Organizational Behavior,* 246.

12. L. M. Barna, "Stumbling Blocks in Intercultural Communication," in *Intercultural Communication: A Reader,* 7th ed., edited by L. A. Samovar and R. E. Porter (Belmont, CA.: Wadsworth Publishing, 1994): 340.

13. News bulletins from W. R. Espy, "Say When," *This Week,* 13 July 1952, quoted in W. V. Haney, *Communication and Organizational Behavior,* 3rd ed. (Homewood, Ill.: Irwin, 1973): 396.

14. D. Tannen, *You Just Don't Understand* (New York: Morrow, 1990).

15. C. Miller and K. Swift, *The Handbook on Nonsexist Writing,* 2d ed. (New York: HarperCollins, 1988).

16. Adapted from B. D. Sorrels, *Nonsexist Communicator: Solving the Problem of Gender and Awkwardness in Modern English* (Englewood Cliffs, N.J.: Prentice-Hall, 1983): 17.

17. S. T. Fiske and S. E. Taylor, *Social Cognition* (Reading, Mass.: Addison-Wesley, 1984): 190–194.

18. J. J. Bradac, J. W. Bowers, and J. A. Courtright, "Three Language Variables in Communication Research: Intensity, Immediacy, and Diversity," *Human Communication Research* 5 (1979): 257–269.

Chapter 5

Nonverbal Communication

LEARNING OBJECTIVES

After studying this chapter, you should be able to:

1. Describe eight forms of nonverbal communication and their relationship to culture and gender.

2. Cite five common uses of nonverbal communication.

3. Tell why the four basic characteristics are crucial to using and interpreting nonverbal communication.

4. Explain why nonverbal communication is difficult to interpret and understand.

5. Suggest ways to improve both the interpretation and use of nonverbal communication.

"Hi, did you see the game last night? I'm done—it's your turn to speak."
"No, but I did go to the dance recital. Your turn—I am done."
"Thanks, the game was really great. Dana was really hot. She must have made . . ."
"Do you mind? I'd like to say something."
"Oh! You want to talk about the recital some more—sure, go ahead."

Unusual conversation, you say, but is it? Actually, if our conversations did not include nonverbal communication, this is very similar to what they would be like. Keep in mind that we would have no vocal or bodily cues to help express ourselves and there would be no way of knowing when one person was done speaking and the other should start. In other words, our communication would be verbal only and monotone in sound. It would be very difficult at best for us to carry on a conversation without nonverbal communication.

Nonverbal communication is any information that is expressed without words. Nonverbal communication includes tone of voice, facial expressions, postures, gestures, and appearance, all of which are used to communicate messages. Nonverbal communication, however, supplements words, such as when tone of voice, volume, or facial expression is used to add emphasis to the meaning of a word. Nonverbal communication can complement our messages by helping to make our messages clearer and more effective. Unfortunately, nonverbal communication can also change the intended meaning of a message or make it confusing and unclear.

The inclusion of nonverbal behavior in the study of communication is relatively recent. We tend to take nonverbal communication for granted because it is so basic, but its importance is unmistakable. Research indicates that in most situations, we spend more of our time communicating nonverbally than verbally and that our nonverbal messages carry more meaning than our verbal messages. Studies have estimated, for example, that the average person speaks for only 10 to 11 minutes per day, and that the average spoken sentence spans about 2.5 seconds. In a normal two-person conversation, 60 to 93 percent of communicative meaning is transmitted through nonverbal behaviors.[1] Most research comparing nonverbal and verbal communication points to the general superiority of nonverbal over verbal information.

A review by Knapp and Hall of nonverbal research concluded that some people depend more heavily on verbal messages, while others seem to rely more on nonverbal.[2] Argyle, Alkema, and Gilmour in their research found that nonverbal behaviors were 12 to 13 times more powerful in their impact compared to the accompanying verbal message.[3] This indicates the importance and impact that nonverbal behaviors have and shows that communication must be viewed as a whole and not just as verbal or nonverbal messages. What is your preference—nonverbal or verbal? Why?

Without realizing it, you often use nonverbal communication as the basis for many daily decisions. For example, whether or not you approach your professor about turning in an overdue paper might depend on your perception of his or her nonverbal behavior. If he or she has an open office door and is smiling, you would probably conclude that the professor is friendly and approachable at the moment and that this would be an appropriate time to discuss your late paper.

Even though our culture is highly speech-oriented, more and more scholars and teachers are recognizing the significant contribution of nonverbal behavior to the communication process. In this chapter we examine nonverbal forms, functions, characteristics, and interpretation, as well as how individuals can improve their nonverbal communication.

THINK ABOUT IT

What role does nonverbal communication have in your everyday communication?

How and with what effect do you communicate nonverbally?

FORMS OF NONVERBAL COMMUNICATION

Have you ever dressed up for a meeting, smiled at someone, sat in a specific seat in class, used your hands while talking, played with a pen or pencil while listening, dimmed the lights to create a romantic atmosphere, played music loudly, looked someone directly in the eyes, or burned incense to create a pleasant odor? If so, you have communicated nonverbally. Every day we perform a wide range of nonverbal behaviors without even thinking about many of them, yet such behaviors convey definite messages to others. Because nonverbal communication is so diverse, common, and informative, we need to be more sensitive to its many manifestations. In the following section, we will examine some of the more significant forms of nonverbal communication, including body motions, physical characteristics, touch, space, time, paralanguage, artifacts, and environment.

Body Motions

We can use body motions to create an infinite number of nonverbal messages. For our purposes, a **body motion** is any movement of the face or body that communicates a message. One particularly significant category of body motions is **facial expressions,** configurations of the face that can reflect, augment, contradict, or be unrelated to a speaker's vocal delivery (see Figure 5.1).

A major aspect of facial expression is eye movement. According to some researchers, eye movement is the first and primary characteristic noticed by people. The researchers found that during interactions people spend about 45 percent of the time looking at each other's eyes.[4] The primary function of the eyes is to establish relationships with others. Eyes also convey a variety of other important messages. We notice a speaker's eye contact, share mutual glances with friends, feel uncomfortable when stared at. The eyes are a significant part of our facial expressions.

Essentially, we communicate by trading visual information through the use of our eyes which allows us to use facial expressions as a means of communicating our feelings and emotions. For example, after studying numerous videotapes of couples fighting, psychologists Robert Levenson of the University of California and John Gottman of the University of Washington concluded that facial expressions of fear and disgust during marital conflicts seemed to indicate the union would fail within four years.[5]

The key, explained Levenson, is that facial expressions associated with emotional distance—fear and disgust—seem to predict marital failure. The role facial expressions have in communication and relationships is extremely powerful. It is clear that of the body motions, facial expressions convey the most information about people to others. The face is one of the most important sources of emotional information. Even though there are specific emotions that observers are able to judge with high accuracy, facial expressions cannot always be interpreted from one culture to another. For example, the expressions of happiness or sadness are judged quite accurately as to their intensity and meaning by observers from differing cultural

Figure 5.1:

Body motions send many messages which can reflect, augment, contradict, or be unrelated to what is being said.

Jon Feingersh/The Stock Market

backgrounds, but other facial expressions are not interpreted in a similar manner.[6] One reason for the differences is that interpretation of emotions is learned and usually conforms to specific cultural expectations. When observing facial expressions from one culture to another, we must remember that there may be cultural differences in the circumstances that produce an emotion, the effect of the emotion, and the rules that govern the use of a particular facial expression in a specific social situation.

The fact that facial expressions do indeed reflect our feelings raises an interesting question: Are some facial expressions universal? If you were to travel to other parts of the world and visit an unfamiliar culture, would people's facial expressions in various situations be similar to your own? Would they smile when happy, frown when unhappy, and so on? Would their facial expressions be identifiable as signs of these emotions? The answer to all of the above questions appears to be *yes.* People throughout the world do seem to use similar facial expressions in similar emotion-creating situations (see Figure 5.2). Not only do they use similar facial expressions, but they are also able to recognize these expressions fairly accurately in others.[7] This universal use and recognition is only true for our basic emotions as described above.

However, no matter what the cultural rules are, our faces do often communicate feelings and emotions spontaneously in reaction to a situation. For example, you open the door to your house, a group of your friends hiding in the dark turn on the lights and yell "Congratulations!" Your face

Figure 5.2:

Some facial expressions can be universally understood. In most instances, our basic facial expressions communicate the same message no matter where we are or regardless of cultural differences. Facial expressions often communicate feelings and emotions spontaneously and with little or no control. What emotion is being communicated with this facial expression?

Wolfgang Kaehler

will probably automatically and unconsciously express surprise. If you open the door and they yell "Boo," your face will probably show fear or anxiousness.

Although many of our facial expressions are unconscious and involuntary reactions to certain stimuli, researchers have found that facial cues may be only partially reliable in terms of what they express. Mike Motely, a communication researcher, in a recent study confirms that facial expressions are often ambiguous and may be only relevant and interpretable as they relate to the conversation and context in which they occur.[8] In addition, people learn to conceal their real feelings.[9] They learn to control their facial muscles in order to hide inappropriate or unacceptable responses. Such controlling behaviors are referred to as **facial management techniques.** Facial management techniques may be used to intensify, deintensify, neutralize, or mask a felt emotion.[10]

Intensifying is a facial behavior response that exaggerates facial expressions to meet the expectation of others. If someone gives you a gift, whether you like the gift or not, you are likely to try to look completely surprised, excited, and delighted. We exaggerate our facial behaviors to meet the expectations of others, to avoid giving offense, and to maintain a positive relationship with them.

Deintensifying is a facial behavior response that understates reactions in order to maintain favorable relationships with others. For example, you and your roommate each give a speech in the same class. You get an A and your roommate gets a C. You tend to tone down your elation, just in case your roommate feels bad about receiving a lower grade.

Neutralizing is the avoidance of any emotional expression in a situation, in other words, maintaining a "poker face" or nonexpressive facial behavior. Men and women may differ in the emotional reactions they neutralize because of cultural norms. In the United States, for example, fear and sadness are considered to be less than manly, so some men may try to neutralize facial displays that express those responses, even when the men are actually experiencing the responses.

Masking is the replacing of one expression of an emotion with another thought to be more appropriate for the situation. We have all seen the moment in beauty contests on television in which the winner is announced and all the other contestants smile and hug the winner. We know that the other contestants are not happy, but are masking their real emotions.

Categories of Body Motions   To make sense of thousands of different body motions, Paul Ekman and Wallace Friesen devised a classification system based on the origins, functions, and coding of nonverbal behavior.[11] Their system divides body motions into five categories based on the way the human body functions: emblems, illustrators, regulators, affect displays, and adaptors. Because there are so many body motions, many of which are interdependent of one another, it is important to understand that the categories are not always independent or mutually exclusive of one another. Therefore, some body motions may be classified under more than one category.

Body motions that can be directly translated into words or phrases are called **emblems.** They include the hand signs for "OK," "I want a ride," peace, power, and the many other signs that we use as substitutes for specific words or phrases. The meanings of emblems are like the meanings of words in that they are arbitrary, subject to change with time, learned, and culturally determined.

Body motions that accent, reinforce, or emphasize an accompanying verbal message are **illustrators.** An instructor who underlines a word on the chalkboard to emphasize it, a child who indicates how tall he is by holding his hand up, a softball player who swings her arms while describing a hit, children who use their thumbs and fingers as if they were guns—all these people are using illustrators.

Body motions that control, monitor, or maintain the back-and-forth interaction between speakers and listeners are **regulators.** Regulators include eye contact, shifts in posture, nodding of the head, and looking at a clock or wristwatch. These cues tell us when to stop, continue, repeat, hurry, elaborate, make things more interesting, or let someone else speak. The opening scenario in this chapter illustrates the importance of regulators.

Body motions that express emotions and feelings are **affect displays.** Although your face is the primary means of displaying affect, your body may also be used. For example, you may slouch when you are sad, slam your fist on a table whey you are angry, and jump up and down when you are excited. Affect displays communicate messages that may repeat, contradict, supplement, replace, or not even relate to verbal messages.

Body motions that help us to feel at ease in communication situations are **adaptors.** They are the most difficult nonverbal signals to interpret because interpreting them requires the most speculation. Scratching, playing with a pencil, sitting straight in a chair, grooming motions, and smoking are adaptors. People are especially likely to engage in such actions in stressful situations such as those that involve trying to satisfy needs, manage emotions, or develop social contacts.

Adaptors fall into three categories:

1. **Self-adaptors** are generally not directed at others but serve some personal need. They include such common actions as scratching, smoothing hair, and straightening clothes.

2. **Object-adaptors** involve the use of an object, such as a pencil, paper clip, coin, cigarette, or jewelry, for a purpose other than its intended function. Most object-adaptor behaviors are unconscious. They help to release excess energy and tend to occur only when people are nervous or anxious.

3. **Alter-adaptors** are body motions directed at others that are learned from past experiences and from the manipulation of objects. They include gestures used to protect yourself from others, such as putting

your hands in front of your face; movements to attack others, such as assuming a fighting position; actions to establish intimacy with others, such as moving closer to someone; and actions to withdraw from a conversation, such as moving toward a door. Several authors of books on body language contend that alter-adaptors are performed unconsciously and reveal hidden desires or tendencies. For example, the way a person crosses his or her legs may indicate sexual invitation, introversion, or aggressiveness. To date, however, there is not sufficient proof to support these claims.

Categories of Body Movements and Facial Expressions

Category	Key Characteristics	Examples
Emblems	Translate directly into words	Extended thumb of a hitchhiker
Illustrators	Accent, reinforce, or emphasize a verbal message	A child holding up his hands to indicate how tall he is while saying "I'm a big boy"
Regulators	Control, monitor, or maintain interaction	Eye contact, shift in posture, nod of head
Affect displays	Express emotion and feelings	Sad face, slouching, jumping up and down
Adaptors	Help one feel at ease in communication situations	Scratching, playing with coins, moving toward someone

Physical Characteristics

While body movements and facial expressions change quickly and can be controlled to some extent, physical characteristics, such as body type, attractiveness, height, weight, hair color, and skin tone, are fairly constant and more difficult to control, especially in the course of a single interaction.

Physical appearance and condition play a significant role in communication and relationships. In recent years, segments of our society have become obsessed with physical appearance and general health, spending billions of dollars each year on modifying, preserving, and decorating their bodies. One of the reasons for this concern with appearance is that we have acquired some stereotypes about body shapes that seem to influence how we react to and interact with each other. In one research study, participants were asked to rate silhouettes of people with three different body shapes—overweight, athletic, and thin—that were all the same height. The subjects consistently rated the overweight people as older, shorter, more old-fashioned, less attractive, more talkative, more warm-hearted and sympathetic, more good-natured and agreeable, more dependent, and more trusting of others. They rated athletic people as stronger, younger, taller, more masculine, better looking, more adventurous, more mature in behavior, and more self-reliant. They rated thin people as younger, taller, more ambitious, more suspicious of others, more tense and nervous, less masculine, more stubborn and inclined to be difficult, more pessimistic, and quieter.[12]

Although this research suggests people tend to make judgments about personality and behavior characteristics based on body shape, there is little proof that such judgments are accurate. As you learned in Chapter 4, operating on the basis of such stereotypes can lead to serious misunderstandings.

Physical attractiveness has an extremely powerful influence on everyday communication. In our society, attractive people are generally treated more positively than those who are not. It appears that both males and females are strongly influenced by attractiveness, though males seem to be more responsive to appearance than do females.[13] Numerous research studies have indicated that attractive people, when compared to unattractive people, are perceived to be more popular, successful, sociable, persuasive, sensual, and happy. Attractiveness affects credibility and plays a strong role in a person's ability to persuade others, to get a job, and to gain a higher salary. Handsome males are perceived as more masculine, while beautiful females are seen as more feminine, in comparison to those perceived as less attractive.[14]

THINK ABOUT IT

Attractiveness Discovered to Be Average Quality

Alluring eyes and sunny smile are not enough. If you want to find an attractive face, a new high-tech study suggests, look for one that is basically average. A computer was used to construct faces that blended facial features of up to 32 people, averaging out such features as nose length and chin prominence. In this way, the more faces that went into a composite, the more it represented an average face.

Although other factors may contribute to making movie stars handsome or beautiful, Judith Langlois of the University of Texas at Austin states, "I'll bet their faces have the fundamental attributes of averageness, and without that they would not be very attractive."

In a few situations, attractiveness can also be a disadvantage. Although attractiveness was found to be an asset for men throughout their executive careers, one research study found that being attractive can be a liability for women managers. Even when such women had reached top executive levels, their success was attributed to their looks rather than to their abilities, and they were consistently judged less capable than unattractive women managers.[15] Attractive females, in comparison to other women, are judged by some to be more vain, more materialistic, and less faithful to their husbands.[16] Regardless if you are male or female, attractiveness is assumed to result in status and success—people feel that attractiveness is the reason for these rewards, not because the person has earned it.[17]

We know that our society places a great deal of value on physical appearance, but do attractive individuals differ in their behavior from others who are less attractive? The answer is basically *no.* In fact, attractive people do *not* seem to fit the stereotypes associated with how they appear.[18] Surprisingly, self-esteem is not consistently high for those who are considered the most attractive. This could be due to the feeling that they are rewarded not for what they have done, but because of how they look, thus diminishing their self-worth.[19]

THINK ABOUT IT

Babies who are held are more alert, healthier. But without hugs and caresses, people of all ages can sicken and grow touch-starved.

Touch is stronger than verbal or emotional contact. It affects nearly everything we do.

What would it be like to not experience touch?

Are you someone who likes or dislikes to be touched? Why?

D. Ackerman, *Parade Magazine*, March 25, 1990, 4.

Touch

"Reach out and touch someone" is a slogan used by a national phone company. Although the company's ads suggest touching in an abstract sense, the idea behind the ads is that touch is a personal and powerful means of communication. As one of our most primitive and yet sensitive ways of relating to others, touch is a critical aspect of our communication. It plays a significant role in giving encouragement, expressing tenderness, and showing emotional support, and it can be more powerful than words. For example, when you've just received some bad news, a pat on the shoulder from a friend can be far more reassuring than many attempted words of understanding.

The kind and amount of touching that is appropriate varies with the individuals, their relationship with each other, and the situation. Some researchers have set up categories to describe these variations. The categories are functional-professional, social-polite, friendship-warmth, love-intimacy, and sexual-arousal.[20]

Functional-professional touch is an unsympathetic, impersonal, cold, or businesslike touch. For example, a doctor's touch during a physical examination or an athletic trainer's touch of an injured athlete serves a purely medical, functional purpose. A tailor who takes customers' measurements is another example of functional-professional touching. The person being touched is usually treated as an object or nonperson in order to prevent any other messages from being implied.

Social-polite touch is touch that acknowledges another person according to the norms or rules of a society. In our society, the handshake is the most predominant form of polite recognition of another. In many European countries, a kiss is used in place of the handshake to acknowledge another.

Friendship-warmth touch expresses an appreciation of the special attributes of others. Friendship-warmth touch is also the most misinterpreted type of touching behavior because it can be mixed or confused with touching related to sex. For example, you see two men meet in an airport, hug, and walk off with their arms around one another. Although another kind of relationship could potentially be inferred, these two men may in fact be close relatives or friends who have not seen each other for a while. Their touching conforms to social expectations about how friends behave in a public context. Their behavior expresses and reinforces the warm feelings they have for one another.

Love-intimacy touch usually occurs in romantic relationships between lovers and spouses. It includes caressing, hugging, embracing, kissing, and many other forms of intimate touch. It is highly communicative. Usually this form of touch requires agreement between both parties, although love-intimacy touch can be initiated by one person and may not always be reciprocated by the person being touched.

Intimate touch conveys strong caring, devoted, enamored, and loving interpersonal messages. It also complements and validates verbal messages such as "I love you" or "You are someone special in my life." Intimate touch does not necessarily imply sexual involvement. Sometimes confusion between intimate and sexual touch leads to dissatisfaction in some couples' special relationships.

Sexual-arousal touch is the most intimate level of personal contact with another. Sexual touch behavior, if agreed on, is an extremely pleasurable form of touch to most people, but it can also produce fear and anxiety.

Touch in this category is primarily an expression of the physical attraction that occurs between two consenting individuals.

The meaning of a particular touch depends on the type of touch, the situation in which the touch occurs, who is doing the touching, and the cultural background of those involved. Some cultures are more prone to touching behavior than others. Research has found that people in the United States are less touch-oriented than persons in other cultures. For example, a study examining touching behavior during a one-hour period in a coffee shop found that people in San Juan, Puerto Rico, touched 180 times in an hour, those in Paris, France, touched 110 times, while those in Gainesville, Florida, touched only 2 times.[21]

Gender differences in touching behavior are also interesting to note. Men tend to touch more than women, women tend to be touched more often than men, and women seem to value touch more than do men. Gender differences in touching behavior may be partially attributed to men's sexual aggressiveness in our culture and their expression of power and dominance. According to Nancy Henley, men have access to women's bodies, but women do not have the same access to men's bodies. This, according to the research, may be man's way of exerting power because touch represents an invasion of another's personal space.[22]

THINK ABOUT IT

When the boss places an arm around the secretary, does that mean something different than when the secretary places an arm around the boss?

When a teacher places a hand on a student's shoulder, does that mean something different than when a student places a hand on a teacher's shoulder?

When a doctor touches a patient, does that mean something different than when a patient touches the doctor?

Space

Statements such as "Give me some room to operate," signs such as "Keep Out," and the bumper sticker that reads "Keep Off My" followed by a picture of a donkey all are attempts to regulate the distance between people. Such behaviors are of special interest to researchers in **proxemics,** the study of how we use space and the distance we place between ourselves and others when communicating.

The need for us to identify certain amounts of space as our own is an aspect of proxemics called **territoriality.** We often position markers such as books, coats, pencils, papers, and other objects to declare our space. Some students become upset when someone else sits in a seat they usually occupy, even though seating is not assigned. This uneasiness stems from a strong desire to stake out and protect a territory. Similar reactions occur when someone enters a room without knocking or tailgates when driving—it's our territory and thus someone else requires our permission to enter.

We usually give little conscious attention to the role of space in our communication, yet the way others use space gives us strong clues to what they are thinking and how they are reacting to us. Three variables—status, culture, and context—influence our use of space when communicating.

Status affects the distance that is maintained between communicators. Research shows that people of different status levels tend to stay farther apart than do individuals of equal status. Furthermore, people of higher status tend to close the distance between themselves and people of lower status, but seldom do people of lower status move to close the distance between themselves and a person of higher status.

Culture creates a wealth of differences in the way individuals use distance for communication. For example, people from the United States tend to stand farther apart during conversations than do people from many European and Middle Eastern cultures. Arabs, for example, consider it polite to stand close to the person with whom they are communicating. There are as many culture-based differences as there are cultures, and it is not unusual for one group to be perceived as cold and unfriendly and another as pushy and forward as a result of their use of space. The important thing is to recognize that not all cultures view distance in the same way.

Context also influences the space that is maintained between individuals. For example, people in line at an automated teller machine usually stand back far enough to give the person using the machine the feeling that his or her transaction is not being observed. But passengers waiting to board a bus ordinarily stand close together to avoid losing their places.

Time

Chronemics is the study of how people perceive time and structure, and how they use time as communication.[23] People in our society are preoccupied with time. Everything seems to have a starting time and an ending time. We worry about how long we have to wait for something, how long it takes to do something. We even go so far as to say time is money. Because we place such a high value on time, it plays a significant role in our nonverbal communication. We are particularly sensitive to people and events that waste or make exceptional demands on our time. Consider your reaction, for instance, when your date keeps you waiting, when an instructor continues to lecture after the bell has signaled the end of class, or when you are given only one day's notice about an upcoming test. Your feelings may range from confusion to indignation to outrage, but you will almost certainly not be neutral. To some extent, your reaction will depend on who the other person is. You will probably be more tolerant if the offending party is a friend or someone who has great power over you. Thus, if a blind date keeps you waiting too long, you may decide to leave, but if your professor is late for an office appointment, you will probably suffer in silence and continue to wait for his or her arrival.

We tend to have many expectations about how time should be used, and we often judge people by their use of time. For example, students are expected to be on time for class. Thus, students who are punctual are more likely to create a positive impression, while students who are consistently late may be perceived as irresponsible, lazy, or uninterested. Thus, we must be constantly aware of the message we send through our use (and misuse) of time.

Individuals can differ in their approaches to time. For example, some people are always looking to the future, others long for the past, and still others live for the moment. Each approach communicates something about people and the ways they use time to communicate who they are. Each culture teaches its members about time expectations, and these expectations vary. In some cultures being punctual is expected, while in others, being punctual is not important and, in fact, people are expected to be late. In American culture, for example, guests are expected to be on time for a dinner party, but up to twenty minutes late is socially accepted and still considered on time. In some European countries, showing up late to a dinner party is considered an insult. Time communicates messages about us, and it is important that we adhere to cultural norms.

Paralanguage

Paralanguage is the study of all cues, which include sound or silence, other than the content of words themselves. Paralanguage includes not only speech sounds, but also speech rate, accents, articulation, pronunciation, and silence. Sounds such as groans, yawns, coughs, laughter, crying, and yelping, which are nonsymbolic but can communicate very specific messages, are also included. Words such as "um," "uh-huh," "you know," "like," and "OK" are referred to as vocal fillers and are considered paralanguage. Vocal fillers are often interspersed in conversations without thought or a set order. They may be used due to nervousness, as part of a sub-culture, or from habit. In any case, the use of vocal fillers can influence our image positively or it can damage and degrade ourselves and others.

The content of words is verbal communication, while the sounds that create the words are nonverbal communication. We often rely more on paralanguage than on the words themselves when interpreting another person's message.

Note how the meaning of a sentence may vary according to the word that is emphasized:

1. JANE'S taking Tom out for pizza tonight. (not Hilary or Dana)
2. Jane's taking TOM out for pizza tonight. (not Bill or Dave)

3. Jane's taking Tom OUT for pizza tonight. (not staying home)

4. Jane's taking Tom out for PIZZA tonight. (not seafood or hamburgers)

5. Jane's taking Tom out for pizza TONIGHT. (not tomorrow or next weekend)[24]

Even though the words are identical, each sentence creates an entirely different message, distinguished solely by the emphasis placed on specific words.

Paralanguage includes pitch (how high or low the voice is), vocal force (intensity or loudness of the voice), rate (speed), quality (overall impression of the voice), and pauses or silence. The way we vary our voices conveys different meanings to our receivers. For example, a person who speaks quickly may communicate a message that is different from a person who speaks slowly. Even when the words are the same, if the rate, force, pitch, and quality differ, the receiver's interpretations will differ. Researchers estimate that approximately 38 percent of the meaning of oral communication is affected by our use of voice, by *the way* something is said rather than by *what* is said.[25]

On the basis of paralanguage, we make many judgments about what is being said, the person saying it, the speaking and listening roles, and the credibility of the message. Of course, judgments about people based on paralanguage can be just as unreliable as judgments based on body type. We must, therefore, recognize the effect that paralanguage can have on our communication and adjust accordingly.

Silence or vocal pauses are very communicative and are part of the paralinguistic features of our communication. Vocal pauses or hesitation are usually short in duration, while silence is usually for extended periods of time. Vocal pauses can be used to emphasize a word or a thought, or to make a point. Hesitations are usually the result of gathering thought or nervousness. Silence is sometimes expected due to the context, for example, a funeral or a speech presentation, or is self-imposed in order to think or do nothing at all. Silence has many possible meanings, and it would be absurd to attempt to provide a list of all of them here. The next time a good friend says "Hi," pause for five to ten seconds before reacting. You will quickly learn the effect silence can have as a message.

EXERCISE

I really love you.

Read the above statement aloud four different ways:

1. with no expression at all,
2. as if you really do love the other person,
3. as if you actually despise the other person,
4. as if you are desperate because the other person is leaving you.

Note how you can change your meaning without changing the words. In what way does your voice change the meaning? What

else do you notice about yourself each time you try to create a different meaning?

Artifacts

Artifacts are personal adornments or possessions that communicate information about a person. They include clothes, perfume, makeup, eyeglasses, hairstyles, beards, automobiles, briefcases, and the many hundreds of other material cues that we use to communicate our age, gender, status, role, class, group membership, personality, and relation to others.

Effective communicators learn to adapt their use of artifacts to the specific situation. In that way, they try to ensure that the message conveyed by the artifacts will be consistent with and reinforce their intended message and that the artifacts used will not contradict or distract from the intended message. For example, dressing in a suit, dress, or other conservative clothing would be appropriate for a job interview in order to give the impression that you are a serious applicant.

Environment

Environment, as discussed in Chapter 1, is the physical and psychological surroundings in which communication occurs, including the furniture, architectural design, lighting conditions, temperature, smells, colors, and sounds of the location and the attitudes, feelings, perceptions, and relationships of the participants. The impact of the environment has a lot to do with the individuals, their backgrounds, and their perceptions of what is important to them at the time of the interaction. The best environment allows a speaker's intended message to be delivered accurately. Thus, soft background music, dim lights, a log burning in a fireplace, a tray of hors d'oeuvres, and two glasses of wine would create the perfect environment for a romantic encounter, but would fail to create the proper atmosphere for a pre-game pep really.

USES OF NONVERBAL COMMUNICATION

Nonverbal communication adds life to our exchanges by complementing, repeating, regulating, and substituting for our words. In addition, sometimes we even use it to deceive others.

Complementing Verbal Behavior

Nonverbal cues can be used to complete, describe, or accent verbal cues. This use is called **complementing.** For example, a golfer, after shooting a chip shot from about 75 yards, tells her partner that she missed the cup by inches and uses her thumb and index finger to show the distance. When saying hello to a friend, you show your genuine interest by displaying a warm smile, maintaining steady eye contact, and holding the friend's hand.

We use complementary nonverbal cues to accent verbal behavior by emphasizing or punctuating our spoken words. For example, if a husband wants sympathy from his wife when he's not feeling well, he may tell her, in a weak voice, that he feels sick and give her a look that implies he is about to collapse. We often use our voices to highlight or accentuate what we are saying. A student trying to get his roommates to quiet down may say quietly, "Will you guys please keep it down." If that doesn't work and the noise is really bothering him, he may raise his voice to indicate that he wants quiet immediately.

People who are excited or enthusiastic are more likely to use nonverbal cues for accenting than are people who are restrained, are having a difficult time expressing themselves, are not paying attention, or are not understanding what is being said. If used correctly in a public speech, that is, if accenting gestures and changes in tone of voice appear natural and flow smoothly with the message, they can be especially effective ways of making a point clearer to an audience.

Repeating Verbal Behavior

While complementing behaviors help to modify or elaborate verbal messages, repeating behavior express the same message as the verbal. For example, a father attempting to keep his child quiet at an adult gathering may place his index finger to his lips while saying "Shush!" A speaker stating that she has two points to make may hold up two fingers. The nonverbal actions of the father and the speaker are called **repeating** because they convey the same meaning as the verbal message.

Such repetition is especially common in sports. For instance, the referee on a basketball court shouts "Traveling" while rolling her arms in a circular motion, and the baseball umpire cries "Strike" while raising his right arm. These repeating nonverbal signals are deliberately planned so that all players and spectators will know the official's call, but most repeating messages are sent without much thought. They are simply a natural part of our communicative behavior.

Regulating Verbal Behavior

Nonverbal cues can also be used for controlling the flow of communication, a behavior known as **regulating.** For example, we frequently use nonverbal signals to indicate that we want to talk, to stop another person from interrupting us when we are talking, or to show that we are finished talking and that the other person may take a turn. When we are listening, we may nod our head rapidly to suggest that the speaker hurry up and finish, or we may nod slowly to show that we want to hear more.

Senders may not even realize that they are sending regulating cues, but receivers are usually aware of such signals. In class, for example, a professor receives a clear message when students put on their coats or close their notebooks to indicate that class is over. While the students are merely recognizing that it is time for them to leave, the message the professor receives is quite different.

Substituting Verbal Behavior

We often use nonverbal messages in place of verbal messages (see Figure 5.3). Such **substituting** is common when speaking is impossible, undesirable, or inappropriate. For example, ramp controllers at airports use hand signals to guide planes to their unloading positions because the noise level is too high for spoken communication; friends will often exchange knowing looks when they want to say something behind another person's back; the hearing-impaired use a sophisticated formal sign language in place of the spoken word.

Figure 5.3:

Nonverbal messages can substitute for verbal ones when it is impossible or undesirable to speak and still allow communication to occur.

Michael Newman/Photo Edit

Deceiving Nonverbal Behavior

Deceiving others is when we purposely mislead them by using nonverbal cues to create false impressions or to convey incorrect information. Among the most common of such nonverbal behaviors is the poker face we assume when playing cards. Masking is a form of deceiving. We may try to appear calm when we are really nervous or upset, and we often act surprised, alert, or happy when in fact we are feeling quite the opposite. In addition, we consciously try to manage our nonverbal behavior when we give a speech or attend a job interview in order to disguise our true purpose or emotions.

Detecting which nonverbal cues are used to determine when others are being truthful and when they are trying to mislead us is a part of our social behavior. Research indicates that determining whether someone is telling the truth or not relies heavily on nonverbal cues. In general, we are fairly good at successfully recognizing deception when we encounter it. There are certain cues that we rely on. For example, fleeting facial expressions lasting only a few tenths of a second, changes in voice (pitch of voice often rises when a person is lying), pauses or hesitations (see Figure 5.4), eye shifting or blinking, or hand movement can all be used to help us detect deception.

Although all of the above may be clues to deception, there is no research to support that these types of cues automatically mean you are being deceived. They are simply clues which can raise question as to whether a person is telling the truth or not, but they are not in themselves proof of either truth or lying.

Uses of Nonverbal Communication

Category	Key Characteristics	Examples
Complementing	Completes, describes, accents verbal message	A person needs help immediately, so he yells as loud as he can.
Repeating	Express identical message to the verbal	A person says yes and shakes her head up and down.
Regulating	Control flow of communication	A person shakes his head up and down to indicate "I am interested in what you are saying" implying "tell me more."

| Substituting | Replaces verbal message with nonverbal signals to exchange thoughts | Two people use hand signals to communicate because it is too loud to hear each other's voices. |
| Deceiving | Purposely disguises or misleads to create false impression | A doctor examining a patient discovers a serious problem, but facial expressions remain neutral so as not to alarm the patient. |

CHARACTERISTICS OF NONVERBAL COMMUNICATION

We can better interpret and use nonverbal communication if we understand its basic characteristics. Think, for example, of the far-reaching implications of the fact that through our nonverbal behavior, we are always communicating something, whether we intend to or not. We must also consider that the interpretation of nonverbal cues depends on the context, that nonverbal communication is more believable than verbal communication, and that nonverbal communication is our primary way of expressing our feelings and attitudes toward others. The four basic nonverbal communication characteristics are (1) it is constantly occurring, (2) it is dependent on context, (3) it is more believable than verbal communication, and (4) it is a primary means of expression.

Constantly Occurring: Intentionally or Unintentionally

Whenever another person is present, you have to communicate. Whether you make eye contact, smile, frown, or try to ignore the other person totally,

Figure 5.4:

Nonverbal messages unrelated to the verbal message are sometimes helpful in identifying deception.

By permission of Mell Lazarus and of Creators Syndicate, Inc.

you are communicating something. Sometimes it is not what is said that is important, but what is not said. For example, not attending a meeting at which you were expected, coming late to an employment interview, wearing jeans when you were expected to dress more formally, wearing a suit when jeans were expected, talking about a sad situation with a smirk on your face, and speaking to someone but never looking him or her in the eye, all convey strong messages. We all believe we can tell a great deal about people based on their facial expression, appearance (sex, race, physique), clothing, willingness to make eye contact, body movements, and posture.

To illustrate that we are always communicating, whether intentionally or unintentionally, consider the following example. Jack is always perfectly groomed and smells of expensive aftershave lotion. George has shoulder-length hair and always wears sweat shirts and jeans. By just looking, we cannot really tell what the two men actually intend to communicate. Jack may simply be neat and use aftershave lotion because it feels good, or he may really want to communicate that designer clothes and expensive aftershave lotion are important to him. Similarly, George may simply like to dress comfortably, or he may be attempting to communicate that he disdains society's seeming obsession with outward appearances. Ultimately, it's not so much what Jack and George intend to communicate as what others perceive. Both students, whether they want to or not, are communicating something about themselves through their appearance.

Dependent on Context

The context in which nonverbal communication occurs plays a crucial role in its interpretation. Pounding on a table to make a point during a speech means something entirely different from pounding on the table in response to someone's calling you a liar. Direct eye contact with a stranger can mean something entirely different from direct eye contact with a close friend.

When you communicate, your nonverbal and verbal cues usually supplement and support each other. Your appearance, tone of voice, eye movement, posture, and facial expression provide cues about the communication relationship. For example, when you talk to a friend, your relaxed tone of voice, eye contact, and posture reveal much about your friendship. Your nonverbal cues can tell your friend how much you value him or her, how comfortable you feel, and how intimate your relationship has become. Such nonverbal communication is interpreted within the context of your friendship and is complemented by casual and personal conversation.

Without an understanding of the context in which communication occurs, it is almost impossible to tell what specific nonverbal behavior may mean, and there are no guarantees that misunderstanding will not occur even when the context is fully understood. That is why we must think twice about our interpretation of others' nonverbal behavior and their possible interpretations of ours.

More Believable than Verbal Communication

Most of us tend to believe nonverbal communication, even when it contradicts the accompanying verbal message. Consider, for example, the case of a student who tried to persuade his professor that he had a valid reason for not turning in a required paper. He explained that he had been working on the paper for several weeks and only had to finish typing it when his computer broke down. Throughout the conversation, the student appeared nervous, made little, if any, direct eye contact, and smiled at the wrong times. Based on this behavior, the professor decided that the student was lying and thus refused to accept the story. She found that the student's nonverbal message was more convincing than his verbal one.

Primary Means of Expression

We can often detect other people's feelings of frustration, anger, sadness, resentment, or anxiety without their actually saying anything. Our ability to detect other's emotions exists because nonverbal communication is so powerful. Almost all of our feelings and attitudes are expressed through our nonverbal behavior. For example, at a graduation party attended by many young children, one little girl entered with her parents and spotted a neighbor. She turned up her nose and walked away. Her mother, running after her, asked why she had suddenly left, to which the girl replied, "I don't like that girl over there." The nonverbal communication really didn't need much explanation—it was obvious what the little girl was saying through her actions, whether intentional or unintentional.

INTERPRETING NONVERBAL COMMUNICATION

If nonverbal communication is so credible and prowerful and if we are able to define, categorize, describe, and observe nonverbal communication, why do we still have difficulty interpreting it? There seem to be at least three good reasons.

Multiple Meanings for the Same Nonverbal Cue

Nonverbal communication is difficult to understand because a single behavior may have many different meanings. For example, a frown may indicate unhappiness, sadness, anger, pain, thought, aggressiveness, disapproval, dejection, fear, fatigue, discouragement, disapproval, or a combination of these. Unlike words, most nonverbal cues lack acceptable dictionary definitions.

Interpretations are unreliable because they depend so heavily on perceptions. Suppose, for example, that you have just walked out of a sad movie when you see a friend with tears in her eyes talking to her sister. She might be reacting to the movie, or her crying could stem from breaking up with her boyfriend, hurting herself, or hearing about a death in the family. Her tears could even stem from laughing hard at something that occurred after the movie. Of course, some nonverbal behaviors, such as nodding the head for yes and shaking it for no (in our society), are consistent in both their meaning and their interpretation, but unfortunately, they are the exception rather than the rule.

Interdependence of Nonverbal Cues

The meaning of one nonverbal cue often depends on the correct interpretation of several other, simultaneous cues. For example, when we see someone enter a room, we begin to select certain cues about him or her, such as gender, physical traits, facial expressions, voice characteristics, and clothing. Each cue depends on the others and tends to add to the total picture. This interdependence of nonverbal behaviors and our inability to perceive all aspects of any one nonverbal communication makes interpretation risky.

Looking for meaning by using more than one nonverbal message at a time is called the **functional approach.** The functional approach examines nonverbal behavior not by isolating nonverbal cues, but by seeing how each cue interacts and works with the others to perform various communicative functions.

Subtlety of Cues

Many nonverbal behaviors are subtle and difficult to observe. A cue that one person notices immediately may be overlooked by another person, and thus multiple interpretations may be made in the same situation. For example, a friend tells you that a person whom you are interested in getting to know has been looking at you, but you haven't noticed the glances or you see the eye contact as more accidental than a deliberate message of interest in you.

IMPROVING INTERPRETATION OF NONVERBAL COMMUNICATION

Nonverbal communication is complex, but there are some things that you can do to interpret it better. First, be observant of and sensitive to the nonverbal messages that you receive. Second, verify nonverbal messages that you are not sure of or that are inconsistent with other cues. Assume, for example, that a friend who used to visit regularly hasn't come over in several weeks. It might seem logical to conclude that she doesn't want to see you anymore, but then again, she may have gotten wrapped up in her studies, taken a part-time job, or fallen ill. To ensure an accurate interpretation of her behavior, it is crucial to consider all the possibilities and avoid jumping to conclusions. Because it is so tempting to make inferences based on nonverbal behavior, it is important to remember not to go beyond actual observations.

One method that can help you to determine the true meaning of a nonverbal message is **descriptive feedback,** or checking your understanding of another person's nonverbal behavior by describing your interpretation of it. The other person can then clarify his or her intended meaning. Descriptive feedback is not always necessary, but when a message is inconsistent with the situation or other behaviors, or when you're not sure you have accurately interpreted an important message, you should verify your perceptions with the other person. When using descriptive feedback, do not express agreement or disagreement or draw conclusions; simply describe the message you believe was communicated. For example, if you think someone's behavior seems to indicate that he is uncomfortable around you, but you're not sure, don't ask, "Why are you so nervous when I'm around?" Rather, describe the situation nonjudgmentally: "Jim, I get the impression that you may not be comfortable around me. Is that the case?" This allows the other person to explain without feeling defensive, and it enables you to avoid inaccurate interpretations.

IMPROVING NONVERBAL COMMUNICATION

We must be aware of the nonverbal messages we send to others. Fortunately, most of us do a good job of communicating nonverbally and thus do not need to make dramatic changes in the way we behave. Nonetheless, we cannot afford to ignore the effects of our nonverbal behavior or to allow the nonverbal messages that we send to go unexamined. If you find that others often misunderstand your intended meaning, you might want to look at how you communicate nonverbally.

There is no question that our nonverbal messages greatly influence how others perceive us and our communication. For example, an extremely bright and talented student was constantly being turned down for jobs that he should have been getting. When I asked why he thought this was happening, he replied that he had no idea. To find out, friends videotaped a mock interview in which he was interviewed by another student. When he reviewed the tape, he immediately noticed that he never looked at the interviewer. Instead, his gaze wandered about the room. The lack of direct eye contact by the student gave the impression that he lacked confidence and that he might not be totally candid in what he was saying. Once he knew why he was being rejected, he could try to change his behavior. To help him practice, his friends videotaped another interview session. This time, he was reminded to look at the interviewer each time his gaze wandered. After several such sessions, he grew relaxed about looking at the interviewer and consequently appeared more confident and truthful in his communication.

Although changing your nonverbal behavior is not simple, it can be done with a little effort and desire. The key is to examine conscientiously how your nonverbal cues may be undermining your intended message. If you realize that you have distracting mannerisms, such as smirking, playing with coins, twisting your hair, shuffling your feet, or saying "you know" or "OK" too much, you can ask others to call your attention to these things when you do them so that you can make a conscious effort to change.

SUMMARY

Nonverbal communication encompasses everything that we communicate to others without using words. It is not what we say, but how we say it with our tone of voice, body movements, appearance, and use of space, touch, and time.

There are eight categories of nonverbal communication behaviors: body motions, physical characteristics, touch, proxemics, chronemics, paralanguage, artifacts, and environments. All are interdependent and, together with verbal communication, contribute to the total communication process. A *body motion* is any movement of the face, hands, feet, trunk, or other parts of the body that communicates a message. *Facial expressions* are configurations of the face that can repeat, augment, contradict, or be unrelated to a speaker's vocal delivery. One major aspect of our facial expression is eye movement. The eyes, through eye contact with others, have the primary function of establishing relationships.

There are *facial management techniques* that we use to conceal inappropriate or unacceptable responses to others. The techniques are *intensifying* (responses that exaggerate expressions to meet expectations of others), *deintensifying* (responses that underestimate reactions and emotions), *neutralizing* (responses that avoid showing any emotional expression), and *masking* (responses that replace an expression of emotion with another thought).

Body motions may be classified as *emblems* (translated directly into words or phrases), *illustrators* (accents, reinforces, or emphasizes an accompanying verbal message), *regulators* (controls, monitors, or maintains the interaction), *affect displays* (expresses emotions and feelings), and *adaptors* (increases feeling at ease in communication situations).

Physical characteristics (appearance) play significant roles in the way we interact with one another. Physical attractiveness is an influential variable in everyday communication.

Touch is one of the most personal and powerful means of communicating with others. The kind and amount of touching that is appropriate varies greatly from one situation to another and depends on the individuals and their relationship. Touch has been categorized as follows: *functional-professional touch,* an unsympathetic, impersonal, cold, or businesslike form of touch; *social-polite touch,* touch that acknowledges another according to the rules of a society; *friendship-warmth touch,* touch to express appreciation of the special attributes of others; *love-intimacy touch,* a variety of different forms of touch including personal stroking and the holding of another person; *sexual-arousal touch,* the most intimate level of personal contact with another. Research has found that generally men touch more and women are touched more often than men. Touching behaviors differ from one culture to another.

Proxemics is the study of the way we use space and the amount of distance we place between ourselves and others gives strong clues about our thoughts and reactions. Researchers in proxemics are especially interested in territoriality, the need to identify certain areas of space as our own. Status, culture, and context all influence our use of space when communicating.

Chronemics is the study of how people perceive time and structure and how they use time as communication. Because we place such a high value on time, it plays a significant role in our nonverbal communication. We often judge people by their use of time.

Verbal communication is our use of words to convey a message, and *paralanguage* is the way we say those words. We often rely more on paralanguage than on the words themselves when interpreting another person's message.

Artifacts are material cues, such as adornments and possessions, that we use to communicate information about our age, gender, status, personality, and relation to others. To ensure clear understanding, effective communicators learn to adapt their use of artifacts to the specific situation.

The impact of the *environment* in which communication takes place has to do with the individuals, their backgrounds, and their perception of what is important to them at the time of the interaction. The best environment is one that allows an intended message to be communicated accurately.

Nonverbal communication adds life to our exchanges by *complementing* (cues to complete, describe, or accent verbal cues), *repeating* (cues to repeat what is expressed verbally), *regulating* (cues to control the flow of communication), and *substituting* (cues in place of verbal messages). We sometimes use nonverbal communication for *deceiving* (cues to present a false appearance or incorrect information to mislead) others.

We are always communicating something through our nonverbal behavior, whether we intend to or not. The interpretation of nonverbal cues depends on their context. Nonverbal communication is more believable than verbal communication. Nonverbal communication is our primary way of expressing our feelings and attitudes toward others.

Nonverbal behavior may be interpreted differently by different people because each cue has multiple meanings; the meaning of a nonverbal cue often depends on the correct interpretation of several other, simultaneous cues; and some nonverbal cues are so subtle they may be difficult to detect. The *functional approach* examines nonverbal behaviors by seeing how each cue interacts with others to perform various communicative functions. To avoid misinterpretation, we must be observant of and sensitive to the nonverbal messages we receive, consider all their possible meanings, and avoid jumping to conclusions. The surest way to determine the true meaning of a nonverbal message is to use *descriptive feedback.*

We must also be aware of the nonverbal messages we send to others. It is important to recognize that our nonverbal messages strongly influence how others perceive us. We should ask others for help in changing any distracting nonverbal behaviors we may have.

KEY TERMS

Adaptor: Body motion to increase feeling at ease in communication situations.

Affect Display: Body motion that expresses emotions and feelings.

Alter-Adaptors: Body motion directed at others that is learned from past experience and from the manipulation of objects.

Artifact: Ornament or possession that communicates information about a person.

Body Motion: Any movement of the face or body that communicates a message.

Chronemics: Study of how people perceive time and how they structure and use time as communication.

Complementing: Use of nonverbal cues to complete, describe, or accent verbal cues.

Deceiving: Use of nonverbal cues to present a false appearance or incorrect information in order to mislead others.

Deintensifying: Facial behavior response that understates reactions and emotions in order to create or maintain a favorable relationship with another person.

Descriptive feedback: Receiver's checking of his or her understanding of a sender's nonverbal behavior by describing his or her interpretation of it to the sender.

Emblem: Body motion that can be translated directly into words or phrases.

Environment: Psychological and physical surroundings in which communication occurs, encompassing the attitudes, feelings, perceptions, and relationships of the communicators and the characteristics of the location.

Facial Expression: Configuration of the face that can reflect, augment, contradict, or be unrelated to a speaker's vocal delivery.

Facial Management Techniques: Control of facial muscles in order to conceal inappropriate or unacceptable responses.

Friendship-warmth touch: Touch that communicates appreciation of the special attributes of another person.

Functional Approach: Examination of nonverbal behavior not by looking at each nonverbal cue separately, but by looking at how they all interact to perform various communicative functions.

Functional-professional touch: Unsympathetic, impersonal, cold, or businesslike touch.

Illustrator: Body motion that accents, reinforces, or emphasizes an accompanying verbal message.

Intensifying: Facial behavior response that exaggerates expressions in order to meet the expectation of others.

Love-intimacy Touch: Touch usually occurring in romantic relationships which includes kissing, stroking, and other forms of highly communicative touch.

Masking: Facial behavior response that replaces an expression of emotion with another thought to be more appropriate for the situation.

Neutralizing: Facial behavior response that avoids showing any emotional expression in a given situation.

Nonverbal Communication: Any information that is expressed without words.

Object-Adaptor: Body motion that involves the use of an object, such as a pencil, a paper clip, or keys, for something other than its intended function.

Paralanguage: The way we vocalize, or say, the words we speak, rather than the words themselves.

Proxemics: Study of the use of space and of distance between individuals when they are communicating.

Regulating: Use of nonverbal cues to control the flow of communication.

Regulator: Body motion that controls, monitors, or maintains the interaction between speaker and listener.

Repeating: Use of nonverbal cues to repeat what is expressed verbally.

Self-Adaptor: Body motion that is not directed at others but serves some personal need.

Sexual-Arousal Touch: Most intimate level of personal contact with another.

Social-polite touch: Touch that acknowledges another person according to the norms or rules of a society.

Substituting: Use of nonverbal cues in place of verbal messages when speaking is impossible, undesirable, or inappropriate.

Territoriality: Need to identify certain areas of space as our own.

DISCUSSION STARTERS

1. What is nonverbal communication?
2. Why do you think that nonverbal communication was not seriously studied until recently?
3. How does eye contact serve to develop relationships?
4. Do you agree or disagree with the notion that you cannot not communicate? Explain your response.

5. Which nonverbal function do you think contributes the most to your understanding of a message? Why?
6. What is paralanguage?
7. In what ways do vocal cues help us to make judgments about others?
8. Why do you think that nonverbal communication is more believable than verbal communication?
9. What does it mean to say that the interpretation of nonverbal communication depends on the context in which it occurs?
10. How can we become more accurate in our interpretations of the nonverbal messages that we receive?

NOTES

1. M. L. Hickson III and D. W. Stacks, *Nonverbal Communication: Studies and Applications*, 3rd ed., (Dubuque, IA: Brown & Benchmark, 1993): 4; A. Mehrabian, *Silent Messages: Implicit Communication of Emotions and Attitudes*, 2nd ed. (Belmont, CA.: Wadsworth, 1981): 77; R. L. Birdwhistell, *Kinesics and Context: Essays on Body Motion* (Philadelphia: University of Pennsylvania Press, 1970): 158; R. L. Birdwhistell, "Background to Kinesics," *ETC* 13 (1955): 10–18; A. Mehrabian and S. R. Ferris, "Inference of Attitudes from Nonverbal Communication in Two Channels," *Journal of Consulting Psychology* 31 (1967):24–252.
2. M. L. Knapp and J. Hall, *Nonverbal Communication in Human Interaction*, 3rd ed. (New York: Harcourt Brace 1992):22.
3. M. Argyle, F. Alkema, and R. Gilmour, "The Communication of Friendly and Hostile Attitudes by Verbal and Nonverbal Signals," *European Journal of Social Psychology* 1 (1971): 385–402.
4. S. W. Janik, A. R. Wellens, J. L. Goldberg, and L. F. Dell'osso, "Eyes as the Center of Focus in the Visual Examination of Human Faces," *Perceptual and Motor Skills* 4 (1978): 857–858.
5. Cox News Service, *Lincoln Journal Star,* 16 October 1990, 10.
6. P. Ekman and H. Oster, "Review and Prospect," in *Emotion in the Human Face,* 2nd ed., ed. P. Ekman (Cambridge: Cambridge University Press, 1982): 148.
7. P. Ekman and W. V. Friesen, *Unmasking the Face* (Englewood Cliffs, N.J.: Prentice-Hall, 1975).
8. M. T. Motely, "Facial Affect and Verbal Context in Conversation: Facial Expression as Interjection," *Human Communication Research* 20 (1993): 3–40.
9. M. Zukerman, D. T. Larrance, N. H. Spiegel, and R. Klorman, "Controlling Nonverbal Displays: Facial Expressions and Tone of Voice," *Journal of Experimental Social Psychology* 17 (1981): 506–524.
10. P. Ekman, W. V. Friesen, and P. Ellsworth, "Methodolocial Decisions," in *Emotion in the Human Face,* 2nd ed., ed. P. Ekman (Cambridge: Cambridge University Press, 1982): 7–21.

11. P. Ekman and W. V. Friesen, "The Repertoire of Nonverbal Behavior: Categories, Origins, Usage, and Coding," *Semiotica* 1 (1969): 49–98.

12. W. Wells and B. Siegel, "Stereotyped Somatypes," *Psychological Reports* 8 (1961): 77–78.

13. T. F. Cash and R. N. Kilcullen, "The Eye of the Beholder: Susceptibility to Sexism and Beautyism in the Evaluation of Managerial Applicants," *Journal of Applied Social Pyschology,* 15 (1985): 591–605; A. Feingold, "Good-looking People Are Not What We Think: An Integration of the Experimental Literature on Physical Attractiveness," Unpublished Manuscript, Yale University, New Haven, CT; V.S. Folkes, "Forming Relationships and the Matching Hypothesis," *Journal of Personality and Social Pyschology* 8 (1982): 631–636; and E. Hatfield and S. Sprecher, *Mirror, Mirror . . . The Importance of Looks in Everyday Life* (Albany, NY: SUNY Press, 1986).

14. B. Gillen, "Physical Attractiveness: A Determinant of Two Types of Goodness," *Personality and Social Psychology Bulletin* 7 (1981): 277–281.

15. "When Beauty Can Be Beastly," *Chicago Tribune* (21 October 1986): 26a.

16. T. F. Cash and N. C. Duncan, "Physical Attractiveness Stereotyping Among Black College Students," *Journal of Social Psychology* 122 (1984): 71–77.

17. S. M. Kalick, "Physical Attractiveness as a Status Cue," *Journal of Experimental Social Pyschology* 24 (1988): 469–489.

18. A. Feingold, "Gender Differences in Effects of Physical Attractiveness on Romantic Attraction: A Comparison Across Five Research Paradigms," *Journal of Personality and Social Pyschology* 59 (1990): 981–994.

19. G. Maruyama and N. Miller, "Physical Attractiveness and Personality," ed. B. Maher, *Advances in Experimental Research in Personality* (New York: Academic Press, 1981), and B. Major, P. I. Carrington, and P. J. D. Carnevale, "Physical Attractiveness and Self-Esteem: Attbributions for Praise From an Other-Sex Evaluator," *Personality and Social Psychology Bulletin* 10 (1984): 43–50.

20. R. Heslin and T. Alper, "Touch: A Bonding Gesture," in *Nonverbal Interaction,* ed. J. M. Wiemann and R. P. Harrison (Beverly Hills, Calif: Sage, 1983): 47–75.

21. S. M. Jourard, *Disclosing Man to Himself* (Princeton, N. J.: Van Nostrand, 1968).

22. N. Henley, "Power, Sex, and Noverbal Communication," *Berkeley Journal of Sociology* 18 (1973–1974): 10–11.

23. J. K. Burgoon, D. B. Buller, and W. G. Woodall, *Nonverbal Communication: The Unspoken Dialogue* (New York: HarperCollins, 1989): 139.

24. B. E. Gronbeck, R. E. McKerrow, D. Ehringer, and A. H. Monroe, Principles and Types of Speech Communication, 11th ed. (Glenview, Ill.: Scott Foresman, 1990): 325.

25. M. L. Knapp, Essentials of Nonverbal Communication (New York: Holt, Rinehart & Winston, 1980):7.

Chapter 6

Listening

LEARNING OBJECTIVES

After studying this chapter, you should be able to:

1. Explain why it is important to develop skills in listening.

2. Distinguish between hearing and listening.

3. Outline the six stages in the listening process.

4. Explain the role of feedback in listening.

5. Define and illustrate the four functions of listening.

6. Identify six common barriers to effective listening.

7. Discuss two activities involved in listening with a critical ear.

8. Suggest specific guidelines for becoming a more effective listener.

Joe:	*Hi, Dionne.*
Dionne:	*Hi.*
Joe:	*How are you?*
Dionne:	*OK, but I'm in big trouble.*
Joe:	*I'm OK, too, but I've really been busy. It seems as if every professor has doubled the homework.*
Dionne:	*It looks as if I'm going to flunk calculus. My parents are going to kill me.*
Joe:	*Oh! I know calc can be pretty rough. I've been so involved with my job that I've fallen way behind in my studies.*
Dionne:	*Well, I better go to class.*
Joe:	*What kind of a problem are you having?*
Dionne:	*Never mind. I'll tell you later.*

Are Joe and Dionne listening to each other? The answer to this question is yes and no. They may be hearing each other, but they are not actively listening to one another. Listening requires effort and concentration, and it is difficult to know when someone is listening and when they are not. In the above conversation, Dionne and Joe appear to be listening to one another, but really they are not. Both are deeply involved in their own thoughts and personal concerns. The conversation moves from one topic to the next and the result is that neither is tuning in to what the other is saying. The problem of not actively listening usually occurs when we are not ready to listen or when we have competing thoughts that interfere with our ability to listen.

About six years ago, a major manufacturing corporation spent more than $4 million on a year-long television and print advertising campaign to build its image as a company that listens to its customers. Their slogan states: "Sperry . . . We Understand How Important It Is to Listen." Sperry is not the first company to emphasize listening skills. Many companies acknowledge the importance of listening in both consumer relations and communication within the workplace. Senior executives of major corporations are often appalled by the ineptness of their workers, especially young, new employees, in their ability to listen. This should come as no surprise considering that listening, analyzing, processing, and recording information are often neglected during formal education.

If you are a typical college student, you have had course work in reading, writing, and speaking, but did any of your teachers ever present a systematic course in how to listen? You probably never received any formal training and little, if any, informal training in how to listen more effectively. The purpose of this chapter is to help you become a more effective listener and, as a result, a more effective respondent. To enhance your listening competence, you will need to understand the importance of effective listening, the elements of listening, the functions of listening, the most common barriers to listening, how to analyze and evaluate what you listen to, and specific steps you can take to improve your listening.

IMPORTANCE OF EFFECTIVE LISTENING

Most of the misunderstandings that arise in our daily lives, such as with the conversation between Joe and Dionne in the opening of the chapter, are due to poor listening habits. Poor listening skills can create serious personal, professional, and financial problems. For students, poor listening can result in incorrectly done assignments, missed appointments, misunderstood directions, lower grades, and lost job opportunities.

It may surprise you to realize how much of your day you spend listening, but think about it—when you are not talking or reading, you are probably listening to something or someone. Larry Barker, a communication scholar, and several colleagues found that college students spend 42 to 53 percent of their communication time listening, 30 to 32 percent speaking, 15 to 17 percent reading, and 11 to 14 percent writing (Figure 6.1).[1] Hargie, Saunders, and Dickson, in a more recent study, found similar results.[2] If, as we said in Chapter 5, the average person spends about 10 minutes each day speaking, you can see just how much time is left for listening to others, to television, to radio, to records, and to thousands of other sounds. If so much of our time is spent listening, then why is listening such a problem?

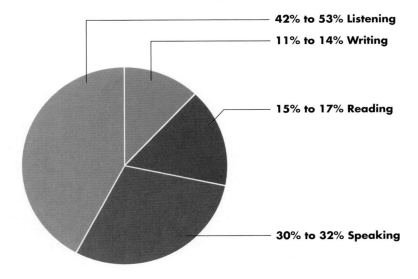

Proportional Time Spent by College Students in Communication Activities

42% to 53% Listening

11% to 14% Writing

15% to 17% Reading

30% to 32% Speaking

Figure 6.1:

The graph is an indication of how the typical college student spends his or her waking time. The proportions given in this graph are averages and, of course, can vary dramatically from person to person and situation to situation.

L.Barker, R. Edwards, C. Gaines, et al., *The Journal of Applied Communication Research* Volume 8, 1980, pages 101-109. Copyright by the Speech Communication Association. Used by permission of the Speech Communication Association.

From the time we get up in the morning to the time we end our day, we are constantly listening to something. Yet most of us give little thought to the role that listening plays in our everyday experiences. Parents say of their children, "They don't listen to me," and children say, "My parents never seem to listen to me." We hear the same from husbands and wives, workers and bosses, teachers and students. You may even have heard a friend say to you, "You really ought to listen to yourself." As simple as listening appears to be, most of us are not effective as listeners.

When surveyed, graduates from a major university who were professionals and businesspeople all wished they had more training in listening, since effective listening is the communication skill that they believed contributes most to job success.[3] A study surveying 457 members of the Academy of Certified Administrative Managers found that of 73 skills, listening ranked as the number one "supercritical" competency for being a successful manager. Further, the top four supercritical competencies were all related to communicating and working with people.[4] There is little doubt about the significant role communicating, and in particular listening, plays in society.[5]

LISTENING AND HEARING: A DIFFERENCE?

Because most of us take listening for granted, we tend to think of it as a simple task. However, listening is actually quite complex. In fact, scholars still are not sure what listening is or what it involves. They do agree that hearing and listening are not the same. It is impossible to listen to sounds without first hearing them, but it is possible to hear sounds without listening to them. What is the difference between listening and hearing? The opening conversation between Joe and Dionne is a good example of the difference. They both certainly heard each other, but they weren't listening to each other.

The greatest difference is that *listening* is active, whereas *hearing* is passive.[6] **Listening** is an active process of receiving aural stimuli by hearing, selecting, attending, understanding, evaluating, and remembering. Listening takes energy and desire. **Hearing** is a physiological passive process in which sound is received by the ear. The major difference between listening and hearing is the word *active*. You must get involved and take action in order to listen (See Figure 6.2). It doesn't just happen; we must make it happen. Hearing, on the other hand, occurs with little or no effort when sound waves reach our ears. Thus, a person can have excellent hearing (the physical ability to hear sounds), but be a terrible listener.

STAGES OF EFFECTIVE LISTENING

The listening process involves six stages: hearing, selecting, attending, understanding, evaluating, and remembering. Connected to these six stages is the final action of responding (See Figure 6.3).

Figure 6.2:

Effective listening requires energy and desire. Listening means involvement and being active—it doesn't just happen, it requires effort to make it happen.

Michael Newman/Photo Edit

Hearing   Hearing is the passive registering of sounds. You may sense the sounds, but you do not allow them to penetrate beyond a superficial level. For example, when you play the radio while studying, you hear the music, but are you really listening to it? The radio provides background sounds, but you may not remember what you heard.

Selecting   As mentioned in Chapter 2, we are constantly bombarded with more stimuli than we can decipher at one time. To make sense out of our environment, we must choose which stimuli we will listen to and which we will ignore. This process is called **selecting.** For example, at a party a friend may be talking to you, there may be loud music playing, and other people may be talking. In order to listen to the friend speak, you select his or her voice and ignore other sounds and stimuli.

   Stop reading for a moment and listen to the sounds around you. Notice that while you were reading, you might not have been registering traffic noises, the ticking of a clock, the hum of the refrigerator motor, the sound of someone's stereo. Selecting one source of sound does not necessarily mean that you are listening, but at least you are in a position to begin the listening process.

Attending   Not only must you select what you are going to listen to, but you must also attend to it. **Attending** is the mental process of focusing on specific stimuli while ignoring or downplaying other internal or external stimuli. Your attention span can be only a few seconds or much longer. The more things you notice around you, the less able you are to concentrate on any single thing, and the less able you are to listen effectively. Thus, it is

Stages of the Listening Process

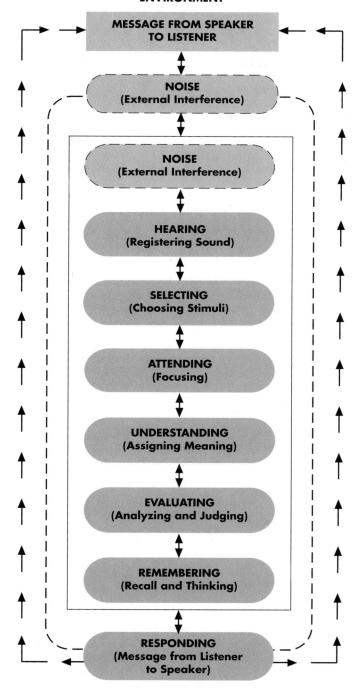

Figure 6.3:

Listening is a very complex process and involves more than just the hearing of sounds. It also requires selecting, attending, understanding, evaluating, and remembering the message of the sender.

ENVIRONMENT

MESSAGE FROM SPEAKER TO LISTENER

NOISE
(External Interference)

NOISE
(External Interference)

HEARING
(Registering Sound)

SELECTING
(Choosing Stimuli)

ATTENDING
(Focusing)

UNDERSTANDING
(Assigning Meaning)

EVALUATING
(Analyzing and Judging)

REMEMBERING
(Recall and Thinking)

RESPONDING
(Message from Listener to Speaker)

important that you attend to the specific stimuli (messages, sounds) that you want to listen to. Attending to something does take effort and concentration, but this alone does not mean that you are listening.[7] You must also understand the message in order to be listening.

Understanding   The main difference between hearing and listening is **understanding.** Once you have heard, selected, and attended to sounds, you assign meaning to them. Although there is no commonly accepted explanation of how understanding occurs, it is known that past experiences play an important role and that you relate and compare new sounds to those you have heard in the past. To learn calculus, for example, you must first learn algebra. Thus, if you walk into a calculus class unprepared, you can select and attend to what the teacher is saying. But because you are unable to interpret the teacher's message, you will not understand the material being presented. So, even though you may be hearing, selecting, and attending to what the calculus teacher is saying, you are not prepared to understand what is being said. The inability to understand reduces your listening effectiveness and the meaning of the what the teacher is communicating.

Evaluating   In the **evaluation** stage, the listener analyzes evidence, sorts fact from opinion, determines the intent of the speaker, judges the accuracy of the speaker's statements and conclusions, and judges the accuracy of his or her own conclusions. Once we begin to assess the message that has been received and understood, we may no longer hear and attend to other incoming messages. Analyzing and evaluating messages will be further discussed.

Remembering   When you say you are listening to someone, you usually mean that you are paying attention to what is being said. You are not indicating, however, that you understand the message or that you will remember it. **Remembering** is thinking of something again. The last stage in the complete listening process is being able to recall what was said to you.

Unfortunately, many of us do not remember information for very long. Why we remember some things and not others is not completely clear.

EXERCISE

A simple experiment can illustrate what people tend to remember and for how long. Read a two- or three-minute newspaper or magazine article to a friend, and then ask him or her to repeat the key information. Do the same with several other friends. Most people will be able to report only about 50 percent of what they've heard. Then, wait 24 hours and ask each person to repeat the information again.

Discuss in class what you learned from the exercise. Did some people do better than others? If so, why do you think they did?

Certain evidence suggests that we remember approximately half of newly heard information (assuming that it is meaningful), but that after a month we forget more than half of what we remembered.[8] Just as our understanding depends on the selecting and attending stages, so too does our memory. Present facts on listening suggest that 25 percent of what most people listen to can be recalled. Of that 25 percent recalled by the receiver, 80 percent is distorted or not received accurately, leaving only 5 percent of the total message as being accurately received.[9] Of course, this is all relevant to the length of the message and how complex the message is for the receiver. All too often we select, attend to, and therefore remember only information that supports our views, and tend to forget information that does not.

Responding   A receiver who has listened to a message can verbally or nonverbally verify its reception or indicate a lack of reception to the sender. The verification by the receiver is referred to as responding or feedback. **Responding** is the listener's overt behavior that indicates to the speaker what has and has not been received. Examples of such behaviors are total silence (didn't hear the message, ignoring the message, or angry about what the message says), smiling or frowning (agreeing or disagreeing with the message), and asking for clarification of what was received.

Feedback is an important part of being an effective listener. Feedback was defined in Chapter 1 as the response to a message that a receiver sends back to a source. Our use of feedback helps to ensure understanding and also helps speakers determine if they have been successful in communicating with us. Feedback should be appropriate to the situation, deliberate, and thoughtful to communicate clearly your impressions of the message. When it is important that you grasp every detail of a message, you should paraphrase or repeat the information for the sender in order to verify your reception, understanding, and recall of it. This also indicates to the sender that you are actively listening and are committed to receiving the message as it was intended.

As students, you are always providing your instructors with feedback, both consciously and unconsciously. Some of you, however, may not always be completely honest in your response. For example, even though you may be totally confused, you may indicate through verbal and nonverbal cues that you are listening to, understand, and agree with everything being said. This behavior, unfortunately, may lead to more unclear messages and further confusion. If, however, those who are confused admit their confusion, their instructors are more likely to improve their presentations. Active listeners are always trying to get the most out of the message by making sure that they have received it accurately and completely.

As you can see, listening is not just a matter of paying attention. Listening is an extremely active and complex process that involves hearing, selecting, attending, understanding, evaluating, and remembering. Although we have discussed the stages of the process separately, all six are interdependent. That is, active listening requires all six stages in order for optimum listening to occur.

Effective listeners check their attention periodically. In other words, they ask themselves, "Am I paying attention?" Asking this question can be a distraction, but not asking it can create more of a problem. When listeners realize that they are not paying attention, they can tune themselves back in to the message.

Effective listeners adopt behaviors that support their listening effectiveness. They demonstrate active nonverbal behaviors in that they maintain eye contact and lean forward, preparing themselves to receive the message. Ineffective listeners, on the other hand, employ passive behaviors such as not facing the person they are communicating with, adopting a defensive, tense posture, and avoiding direct eye contact.

FUNCTIONS OF LISTENING

You wake in the morning to the sound of an alarm clock, or your roommate moving around in the next room, or the ring of a telephone. While you get dressed, some students talk outside your door, a fire engine wails in the street, you turn on your stereo. At breakfast you join in a heated discussion about the new dormitory visitation rule. Then you rush off to the last lecture before an upcoming exam. In the evening you go to a rock concert. After the concert you meet a good friend, who is really upset over receiving a low grade on a test.

Throughout this day you have listened to many different people and things for a variety of purposes. You listened to the alarm clock to know that it was time to get up; you listened to your friends' opinions to evaluate the new dorm policy; you listened to your professor to get information about a subject; you listened to the rock concert for enjoyment; you listened to your troubled friend to understand his feelings. In each case, listening served a different function and involved different skills.

Let's look at each of these functions in greater detail and the listening skills that each requires.

Listening for Information

You probably spend most of your listening time **listening for information,** that is, listening to gain comprehension. You listen to your speech communication teacher discuss process, perception, nonverbal and verbal communication, famous speakers, and similar topics in order to learn about speech skills. Each day you listen for such information as news, weather forecasts, sports scores, directions, orders, assignments, names, and locations.

Evaluative Listening

Evaluative listening is listening to judge or to analyze information. For example, a car owner who hears a squeak coming from the front end rolls down the window and does some evaluative listening. That is, the owner tries to pinpoint the exact location and cause of the bothersome noise. A speech communication teacher listens to students' speeches to discriminate between good and poor presentations and to assign grades. In most situations we should listen critically. We should constantly judge evidence, arguments, facts, and values. We are bombarded by messages asking us to believe, accept, or buy things. For our own protection, we must evaluate everything we listen to. (Later in this chapter, specific guidelines are presented for evaluating what we hear.)

Empathic Listening

Empathic listening is listening to learn what someone else is experiencing and to understand that person's thoughts and feelings. Most of us find it difficult to avoid making judgments when we listen to someone else's problems, but that is exactly what we must do if we hope to listen with empathy. Experiencing emphatic listening can be a healing and soothing process. Empathic listening indicates that we are aware, appreciative, and understanding of another person's feelings.

Caring about someone requires a great deal of sensitivity as well as the ability to communicate that sensitivity. It is not easy to listen; it is even more difficult to listen with empathy. If, however, we fail to empathize with others, we also fail to understand them. No two people can experience the same event in exactly the same way. Yet, for some reason, most of us believe that other people should perceive things just as we do. Only when we accept the great differences in people's perceptions can we understand them.

Listening for Enjoyment

When we listen purely for pleasure, personal satisfaction, and appreciation, we **listen for enjoyment.** We usually listen to music, for example, simply because we enjoy it. The same is true when we watch a "sitcom" or go to a movie.

Listening for enjoyment involves more than merely sitting back and letting sounds enter our ears. To enjoy listening to something, we must also understand it and be able to evaluate it. Thus, even when we listen for enjoyment, we are busy selecting, attending, understanding, evaluating, and remembering.

BARRIERS TO EFFECTIVE LISTENING

Why are most people poor listeners? The answer to this question is surprisingly complex. The quality of our listening changes from time to time and from situation to situation. A number of barriers contribute to our ineffectiveness as listeners. The relative importance and contribution of each barrier to our ineffectiveness can vary dramatically. Also, some of the barriers that reduce our listening effectiveness are under our control and others are not. The following six barriers to effective listening are particularly significant.[10] Although these six barriers are the most common, they are not the only ones. Fortunately, because listening is a learned behavior, we can learn to overcome the obstacles that interfere with our listening effectiveness.

Calling the Topic or Speaker Uninteresting or Boring

The level of interest and the amount of importance we place on a subject or speaker usually govern how much effort is put into listening. The decision that a subject or person is uninteresting or boring often carries with it the conclusion that the information is not important. However, this is not necessarily true. What appears to be dull or insignificant may very well be vital for passing an exam, doing an assignment correctly, and learning something. In other words, a good listener keeps an open mind.

Perhaps we are indifferent because we have heard the person speak before or have had some experience with the topic. We think we know what the speaker is going to say and that there is nothing for us to learn. Such an attitude usually stems from not understanding the topic. We leave the situation complaining that we were bored stiff, never realizing, or learning only later, that we missed something worthwhile.

By deciding not to listen we may not only miss something of value, but we also waste our own time and energy as well as the speaker's. Furthermore, poor listening behavior can be costly in terms of lost friendship, opportunities, and more. We may think that the time spent ignoring or blocking out a speaker can be used for better things. Occasionally we may be right, but a more creative approach is to consider how we can use the information that seems boring at the time. The key point to remember is that subjects are not interesting or uninteresting by themselves; our own active investigation and consideration of every idea presented to us finally determines a subject's suitability, application, and acceptability. (See Figure 6.4.)

Figure 6.4:

Effective listening requires an interest in what the speaker has to say.

Comstock Inc.

Criticizing the Speaker Instead of the Message

How many times have you judged a speech by the number of "ahs" and "ums" the speaker used? How many times has your opinion been influenced by a speaker's volume, mispronunciations, or accent? Have you ever missed a message because you were focusing on a mismatched shirt and tie, bizarre earrings, or distracting facial expressions?

Of course, when possible, speakers should do everything in their power to eliminate personal quirks that may distract attention from their message, but listeners must share the responsibility. An effective listener must be able to overlook the superficial elements of a person's delivery style or appearance in order to concentrate on the substance of the presentation. In other words, you must stay involved.

Concentrating on Details, Not Main Ideas

Most of us listen for specific facts, such as dates, names, definitions, figures, and locations, assuming that they are the important things to know. But are they? Specific facts are needed in some situations, but often we focus too much on details. As a result, we walk away with too many disjointed details to remember and no idea how they relate to each other and to the total picture. When we listen only for facts, we often forget to analyze and evaluate the message. All stages of the listening process are affected adversely when we forget that general ideas may be more significant than the details that surround them.

Analyze a situation to determine what kind of information it requires. If you decide that specific facts are important, you should listen for them. If, however, it is more important to assess the speaker's general message, focus on the ideas rather than the individual facts. As a result, you will not only have a better understanding, but you will also find it easier to remember details and understand how they relate to one another.

Avoiding Difficult Listening Situations

Most of us find it difficult to keep up with the vast amount and increasing technical complexity of the information that confronts us each day. At times we tend to deal with a complex listening situation by giving up and ignoring what is being presented.

A great deal of concentration and energy is needed to overcome the tendency to ignore or avoid what may appear to be difficult and confusing. The best approach is usually to ask questions, even though it may seem inconvenient, inappropriate, or embarrassing. For example, physicians often use complex medical terminology when talking to patients, but patients can take the responsibility for gaining understanding. They can ask the physician to explain terms, to review procedures, to supply missing information. The same principles apply to the classroom. You should never hesitate to ask when you don't understand something, because without understanding, you cannot learn.

Sometimes you may not listen to new and difficult information because you lack motivation, but once again, the responsibility falls on you to make the effort to listen. Try consciously and continually to listen to such communication. Each time you are successful at staying tuned in, not only will you acquire some information, but your confidence and ability to cope with such situations will also improve. It is important to be both physically and mentally prepared to listen.

Tolerating or Failing to Adjust to Distractions

Distractions constantly arise to disrupt concentration. As listeners, we have the responsibility to adjust to, compensate for, or eliminate distractions and to focus on speakers and their messages.

There are some distractions that we can control. If, for example, noise from another room competes with the speaker, the listener should not think, "I can't hear, so the heck with it." Rather, the listener has the responsibility to close the door, ask the person who is creating the noise to be quiet, move closer to the speaker, or, as a last resort, ask the speaker to talk louder.

Some distractions must be overcome through mental rather than physical effort. A noise in the background can become a major distraction, or we can reduce it to a minor nuisance by forcing ourselves to listen more intently to the speaker. We know that the human ear is capable of hearing a coin hit the pavement on a crowded, noisy city street, but that doesn't mean that everyone in the vicinity stops and reacts to it. We must take advantage of our ability to filter out extraneous noise and distractions and focus on the sounds that are important to us (see Figure 6.5). If we cannot modify external noise, we must alter our internal listening behavior to understand the speaker's message.

Faking Attention

At one time or another everyone pretends to pay attention to something or someone. You appear to listen intently, but your mind is definitely somewhere else. You might even smile in agreement, when all you are really doing is maintaining eye contact. In class you may pretend to be taking notes, although your mind is not following what is being said.

Pretending to pay attention may become a habit. Without even realizing what you are doing, you may automatically tune out a speaker and let your mind wander. If, after a speech, you cannot recall the main purpose or the essential points presented by the speaker, you were probably faking attention. While it may seem harmless, such deceptive behavior can lead to

Figure 6.5:

Effective listeners adjust to distractions. Effective listeners ignore extraneous noise and distractions and focus on the sounds that are of importance to them.

Michael Newman/Photo Edit

misunderstandings and cause people to question your credibility and sincerity. The table below summarizes the differences between ineffective and effective listening habits.

Ineffective Versus Effective Listening Habits

Bad Listener	Good Listener
Thinks topic or speaker is of no interest	Finds areas of interest—keeps an open mind
Focuses on the speaker's appearance and delivery	Concentrates on the content of the presentation and overlooks speaker characteristics—stays involved
Listens only for details	Listens for ideas
Avoids difficult materials	Exercises mind—prepared to listen
Is easily distracted	Resists distractions
Fakes attention	Pays attention

CRITICAL LISTENING AND CRITICAL THINKING: ANALYZING AND EVALUATING MESSAGES

As listeners, our goal may be more than just understanding a message, but being critical listeners. **Critical listening** is when a person judges the accuracy of the information presented, determines the reasonableness of its conclusions, and evaluates its presenter. In other words, we must listen critically as well as think critically. Is the message true? Is it based on solid evidence? Is it complete? Is it logical? What is the speaker's motivation for presenting the message?

We are constantly confronted with many choices and decisions. For example, we are exposed to about 65 to 90 commercial messages each day in addition to all the interpersonal messages we receive at school, home, work, and recreation. Since we are limited in the amount of experience we can acquire on our own, we must depend on others for information and advice. Thus, we must evaluate and assess that information in order to make judgments about its value and utility. This requires us to be effective critical thinkers. **Critical thinking** is the ability to analyze and assess information.[11] Critical thinking is a skill that is important to us as students and will also continue to be important to us for the remainer of our lifes. There are many general principles employed in effective critical thinking. For example, critical thinkers are intellectually curious, flexible, objective, persistent, systematic, honest, and decisive. It is also important to understand that people who think critically love to explore issues and ideas, are skeptical, are open-minded, and respect other viewpoints. Listening with a critical ear involves two phases: (1) assessing the speaker's values and intent and (2) judging the accuracy of the speaker's conclusions.[12] Both of these phases require critical thinking.

Assessing the Speaker's Motivation

Assessing a speaker's motivation generally involves several stages of information processing: (1) making a judgment about the values of the speaker, (2) comparing our standards and those of the speaker, and (3) determining the appropriate response to the message based on our judgment of its worth as presented.

Values are central to the communication process and to each individual's perceptual system. They affect our perception and interpretation of both the messages we send and the messages we receive. The first consideration in listening, therefore, is to examine the message in order to determine the speaker's values. Critically think about what the speaker is saying and how it compares to your value system.

Of course, we should not automatically dismiss a message merely because the speaker's values conflict with our own. However, any time we are confronted with a message that differs from our own views—one that asks us to do something, buy something, or behave in a certain way—we should be aware of the purpose behind it.

The second consideration in listening is to ask what pressures are facing us to conform or to go against our principles or standards. Finally, we must consider how we are going to respond to the message. We must use critical thinking to recognize and understand the motivation behind the messages we receive.

Judging the Accuracy of the Speaker's Conclusions

In order to make accurate judgments and to think critically about important messages, you must ask the following questions.

- Is the speaker qualified to draw the conclusion?
- Has the speaker actually observed what he or she is talking about?

- Does the speaker have a vested interest in his or her message?
- Is there adequate evidence presented to support the conclusion?
- Is the evidence relevant to the conclusion?
- Is there contrary evidence to what has been presented?
- Does the message contain invalid or inadequate reasoning?

EXERCISE

How do you think the following people would rate you as a listener? Use a scale of 0 to 100, with 100 being the highest rating.

1. **Your best friend**
2. **Your boss or teacher**
3. **Your roommate or a coworker**
4. **Your parents**

After you have rated yourself, go to each person and ask him or her to rate you (without disclosing your rating, of course). Then compare the ratings. Were they the same? If not, why not?

IMPROVING LISTENING COMPETENCY

With appropriate knowledge and practice, all of us can become better listeners (See Figure 6.6). First, we must recognize the importance of listening effectively. Second, we must begin to think of listening as an *active* behavior that requires our conscious participation. Third, we must recognize that a willingness to work and a desire to improve are essential to increased listening effectiveness.

Passive listening is fine in some situations. For example, listening to the stereo while carrying on a casual conversation with a friend isn't likely

cathy®   **by Cathy Guisewite**

Figure 6.6:

In order to be an effective listener you must know what to do and how to do it. With a desire to learn and with practice you can improve your listening.

to create problems. However, we must be able to identify cases in which active listening is crucial. To listen more effectively, we must put energy and concentration into the process and constantly remind ourselves that listening is vital to communication. Here are some specific suggestions for improving your listening behavior.

Being Prepared to Listen

Although this suggestion may seem quite obvious, few people prepare themselves to listen. Many assume that listening is going to happen by itself and that no preparation is necessary. This assumption is wrong—hearing will happen by itself, but listening will not.

Conditioning yourself for listening is important. Your attention span, which is directly related to your ability to listen, depends on your physical and mental condition at a given moment. If you are tired, your capacity to listen actively is severely reduced.

Whenever possible, determine your goals in advance and prepare to listen accordingly. If you are able to plan ahead and know what you want to gain from a situation, you can motivate yourself to maintain the high energy level needed to listen effectively. Ask yourself, "Do I want to listen to what will be said?" If you answer yes, you need to behave like a good listener.

Behaving Like a Good Listener

Here are some guidelines for behavior to enhance listening effectiveness.

- **Stop talking.** You cannot listen while you are talking.
- **Do not interrupt.** Interrupting is not only rude, but also distracting to both the speaker and the listener.
- **Empathize with the other person.** Try to put yourself in the other person's position in order to understand what the communication means from his or her point of view.
- **Concentrate on what is being said.** Focus your attention on the message, the ideas, and the speaker's feelings toward the message.
- **React to the ideas expressed, not to the person talking.** It is difficult at times to separate the message from the speaker, but the message must take priority. If, for example, someone shouts that your dorm is on fire, you are not going to ignore the message because you dislike the person giving it. Effective listening requires the ability to evaluate the content of a message without regard for personal reactions to the source.
- **Look at the speaker.** Looking at the speaker enables you to compare his or her verbal and nonverbal messages. Observing the speaker's nonverbal communication can aid in your interpretation. Be careful, however,

not to be unduly influenced by the speaker's nonverbal messages. Looking at the speaker also helps you to concentrate and conveys your interest in the message. A speaker who senses audience interest tends to communicate with more enthusiasm, making the task of listening a little easier.

- **Ask questions.** If you do not understand something, need clarification, or want to show that you are listening, ask questions at appropriate times. This will help the speaker gauge the clarity of his or her message and ensure more accurate communication.

- **Be flexible in your views.** Even if you disagree, you must be receptive to others' opinions in order to gain new information. There is nothing wrong with questioning another's point of view, but you should at least listen. Then, if you disagree, you can either reject the information or rebut the speaker's viewpoint.

- **Listen for main ideas.** A key to good listening is to grasp the total picture. Facts are often important, but they are only one aspect of a message and are easy to forget. In many cases, it is better to concentrate on concepts and general ideas rather than on details. Most speakers are trying to make one or two significant points. They use details, but knowing them will do little good if you do not understand the main ideas.

- **Take notes.** Closely related to effective listening is note taking, an activity usually associated with, but not limited to, the classroom. In fact, it is wise to take notes in any lengthy and difficult listening situation.

Note Taking

Because note taking is a special skill, we will spend a little time describing the basic technique. First, decide whether notes are appropriate for the listening situation. Common sense will usually tell you whether to take notes or not. If you plan to use the information immediately and have a strong memory, notes may not be necessary. If you must retain the information for a long period of time or have a weak memory, notes may well be the appropriate solution.

Next, determine what kind of notes to take. Notes can be taken in several different formats. You may prefer to jot down key words, a partial outline, or a complete outline.

The key word format is best used to remember only the specific points in a message. For example, to remember the definition of the word *process* as it is used in communication, list such key words and phrases as *ongoing, changing,* and *no beginning or end.* You must choose highly descriptive words, and enough of them to make sense of your notes in the future.

In the partial outline format, you write key ideas in full, with only enough detail to help you remember the main concept. This format is most appropriate when there is no need to recall all the information, or when you are interested in only certain aspects of the message. A partial outline need not be formal. (See Appendix at the end of this chapter for an example of a partial outline.)

The problem with outlining is that some speakers' presentations will not be well organized, making it difficult to create a complete and systematic outline.

Whatever format you choose, here are a few suggestions.

- Do not try to write everything down.
- Keep your comments brief to give yourself time to study the speaker and think about what is being said.
- Write clearly so that you can read your notes later.
- Review your notes as soon after the speaking event as possible. Reviewing your notes will help you to recall and learn the information.
- Annotate, reorganize, or even rewrite your notes before filing them away for future reference.

Of course, care must always be taken to avoid getting so involved in note taking that effective listening is forgotten. Note taking should be used only as an aid to listening, never as a substitute for it.

SUMMARY

Until recently, the listening process was taken for granted primarily because it seemed so obvious. People are now recognizing that listening is a complex process that must be carefully cultivated because it is so crucial to effective communication.

Hearing is the physiological process in which sound is received by the ear. *Listening* is an active process, which requires energy, desire, and commitment, involves hearing, selecting, attending, understanding, evaluating, and remembering sounds. *Selecting* is choosing what we are going to listen to. *Attending* is focusing on specific stimuli while ignoring or downplaying others. *Understanding* is assigning meaning to the stimuli that we have selected and attended to. *Evaluating* is analyzing and judging the information received. *Remembering* is recalling something from memory, thinking of something again. *Responding* is providing feedback to the speaker.

Listening serves four principal functions: (1) *listening for information* enables us to gain comprehension; (2) *evaluative listening* enables us to judge or analyze information; (3) *empathic listening* seeks to understand what another person is thinking and feeling; and (4) *listening for enjoyment* creates pleasure, personal satisfaction, and appreciation.

Many obstacles prevent us from listening effectively. We may be indifferent to the topic or speaker, criticize the speaker instead of the message, concentrate on details rather than on main ideas, avoid difficult listening situations, permit distractions to interfere, or fake attention. Because listening is a learned behavior, we can learn to overcome some of these bad listening habits.

Critical listening is when a person judges the accuracy of the information presented, determines the reasonableness of its conclusions, and evaluates its presenter. To be effective critical listeners we must also be effective critical thinkers. *Critical thinking* is the ability to analyze and assess information. This involves assessing the values and intent of the speaker and judging the accuracy of the speaker's conclusions.

We can improve our listening ability by being mentally and physically prepared to listen and by behaving like a good listener. To be a good listener, we need to stop talking, avoid interrupting, empathize with the other person, concentrate on what is being said, react to the ideas and not to the person talking, ask questions when we do not understand something, be flexible in our views, listen for main ideas, and take notes.

KEY TERMS

Attending: Focusing on specific stimuli while ignoring or downplaying other stimuli.

Critical Listening: Listening that judges the accuracy of the information presented, determines the reasonableness of its conclusions, and evaluates its presenter.

Critical Thinking: The ability to analyze and assess information.

Empathic Listening: Listening to understand what another person is thinking and feeling.

Evaluative Listening: Listening to judge or analyze information.

Hearing: Passive physiological process in which sound is received by the ear.

Listening: Active process of receiving aural stimuli by hearing, selecting, attending, understanding, evaluating, and remembering.

Listening for Enjoyment: Listening for pleasure, personal satisfaction, or appreciation.

Listening for Information: Listening to gain comprehension.

Remembering: Recalling something from stored memory, thinking of something again.

Responding: Overt verbal and nonverbal behavior by the listener indicating to the speaker what has and has not been received by the listener.

Selecting: In the process of listening, the stage of choosing the stimuli that will be listened to.

Understanding: Assigning meaning to the stimuli that have been selected and attended to.

DISCUSSION STARTERS

1. Why do we take listening for granted?
2. What could you say to persuade someone of the importance of listening?

3. How would you go about teaching a person to be a more effective listener?
4. What are the differences between listening and hearing?
5. What makes listening so much more complicated than hearing?
6. What role does memory play in the listening process?
7. Why is it important to understand the different functions of listening?
8. What does it mean to listen with empathy?
9. Why don't we listen effectively?
10. What are the three most important things to remember about note taking?

NOTES

1. P. Rankin, "Listening Ability," *Proceedings of the Ohio State Educational Conference's Ninth Annual Session,* 1929; Larry Barker, R. Edwards, C. Gaines, et al., "An Investigation of Proportional Time Spent in Various Communication Activities by College Students," *Journal of Applied Communication Research* 8 (1980): 101–109.
2. O. Hargie, C. Saunders, and D. Dickson, *Social Skills in Interpersonal Communication* (Cambridge, MA: Brookline Books, 1987).
3. V. Di Salvo, "A Summary of Current Research Identifying Communication Skills in Various Organizational Contexts," *Communication Education* 29 (July 1980): 283–290; V. Di Salvo, D. C. Larsen, and W. J. Seiler, "Communication Skills Needed by People in Business," *Communication Education 25* (1976): 274.
4. H. T. Smith, "The 20% Activities That Bring 80% Payoff," *Training Today* (1978): 6.
5. S. S. Benoit and J. W. Lee, "Listening: It Can Be Taught," *Journal of Education for Business* 63 (1986): 229–232.
6. E. C. Glenn, "A Content Analysis of Fifty Definitions of Listening," *Journal of the International Listening Association* 3 (1989): 21–31.
7. T. G. Devine, "Listening Skills Schoolwide: Activities and Programs," Selected from *ERIC Clearinghouse on Reading and Communication Skills* (1982): ED 219–789.
8. A. G. Dietze and G. E. Jones, "Factual Memory of Secondary School Pupils for a Short Article Which They Read a Single Time," *Journal of Educational Psychology* 22 (1931): 586–598, 667–767.
9. Ibid, Benoit, 229–332.
10. R. Nichols, "Factors Accounting for Differences in Comprehension of Materials Presented Orally in the Classroom," (Doctoral dissertation, University of Iowa, Iowa City, 1948), R. O. Hirsch, *Listening: A Way to Process Information Aurally* (Dubuque, Iowa: Gorsuch Scarisbrick, 1979): 36–41.
11. R. H. Ennis, "A Concept of Critical Thinking," *Harvard Educational Review* 32 (1962): 83–84.

12. E. D'Angelo, *The Teaching of Critical Thinking* (Amsterdam, The Netherlands: B. R. Gruner, 1971): 7; and R. H. Ennis, "A Taxonomy of Critical Thinking Dispostions and Abilities," In *Teaching Thinking Skills: Theory and Practice,* eds. J. Baron and R. Sternberg (New York: Freeman, 1987).

APPENDIX: NOTE TAKING

A partial outline, for a speech about improving your diet, might look like the following:

Date: January 15, 1995
Topic: Improving diet and health
Speaker: Dr. Jane Smith, health expert from University of Nebraska
Purpose: To provide suggestions on improving students' eating habits and general health

   I.   Balanced diet is important to a healthy life.
      A.   Foods from all three groups: proteins, fats, and carbohydrates.
      B.   Meats, vegetables, and cereal.
  II.   Exercise with balanced diet is important.
      A.   Walk, swim, or do some other physical activity.
      B.   Exercise at least three times a week for approximately 15 minutes or more each time.

PUBLIC COMMUNICATION

Chapter 7

Selecting a Topic and Relating to the Audience

LEARNING OBJECTIVES

After studying this chapter, you should be able to:

1. Describe how to choose a topic for a speech.

2. Assess whether a topic is appropriate for a speaker, an audience, and a speaking situation.

3. Formulate the general and specific purposes of a speech.

4. Determine the relationship between the speaker, the speech, and the audience.

5. Explain what information a speaker should gather about an audience when preparing a speech.

6. Interpret data from an audience analysis and apply this data to a specific speaking situation.

Caller:	*My name is Jane Smith and I'm with the state retailers' association. We're having our annual conference in your city this year on Wednesday, April 20. You have a reputation as a fascinating speaker on the topic of communication, so we were wondering if you would be willing to speak at our conference.*
Speaker:	*Let me look at my calendar. Yes, I am available on that day.*
Caller:	*Good! We would like you to talk about the importance of communication to retailers. You would be speaking at approximately noon, during our luncheon. We would like you to speak about thirty to forty-five minutes and then allow about fifteen minutes for questions. Is that OK?*
Speaker:	*Yes, but I do have a few questions. How many people will be attending?*
Caller:	*About sixty-five to seventy-five.*
Speaker:	*Who will these people be?*
Caller:	*They are mainly retailers—people who either own their own small businesses or manage large stores.*
Speaker:	*Could you be more specific?*
Caller:	*Yes. The business owners tend to have small clothing stores or sporting goods stores, something like that. The managers are employed by supermarkets or stores like Sears or Target.*
Speaker:	*Can you be more specific about the topic you would like me to cover?*
Caller:	*I'll have Sue Jones, our president, call you. She can give you more details.*

You may be thinking to yourself, "What does that situation have to do with me?" The above scenario occurs more often than most people think. In fact, the high school one of my daughters attends held a career day to introduce sophomores to different career choices. The guidance counselor at the high school asked a medical doctor, a sales representative, a police officer, a physical therapist, an architect, an accountant, a small business owner, a teacher, a bank president, and a college professor (me), along with others, to talk about careers. Several presenters later told me they never thought they would be giving talks like this as a part of their present jobs. When I was a college student, I certainly didn't think that I would be giving as many talks to others as I do today.

Thus, it is not unusual for students to believe that they will never have to give a speech and that learning about speech making is a waste of their time. A survey of 202 randomly selected blue-collar workers in a medium-sized city, however, found that almost half had given speeches to ten or more people at least once during a previous two-year period. They spoke to community groups, church groups, students in courses they were taking, and members of their unions. The more education they had and the higher their economic status, the more likely they were to make speeches. The report observed that college graduates were more likely to give speeches than nongraduates.[1]

In another survey, 67 out of 71 top corporate executives in the United States stated that training or competence in public speaking was essential for a person in middle management.[2] While public speaking isn't the only skill required for a successful career, it is considered necessary for those who wish to reach the top (see Figure 7.1).

Even in your present situation you may be called upon to make speeches. Here are several examples of talks typical college students like yourself might be giving in addition to what you are doing in this class:

> Shawn is preparing a ten-minute oral report for his history class based on research he has done on the Vietnam War.
>
> Kelley, the volleyball team captain, has been asked to speak to the students at the local high school about the effects steroids have on young athletes.
>
> As a former member of Future Farmers of America, Mark will speak to a group of high school students about the importance of the organization and try to convince them to join.
>
> Megan, a student teacher, is about to present to a seventh-grade class her first lecture on how to use BASIC computer language.
>
> Lee, a volunteer at the Campus Multi-Cultural Center, gives several presentations and tours to incoming international students during orientation week.

Figure 7.1:

Survey data of top corporate executives clearly indicate the importance of public speaking competency. It is considered one of the necessary skills for top management positions, such as that of Bill Gates of Microsoft Corp.

Luc Novouitch/Gamma-Liaison

Each of these students is preparing for a public speaking event. Thus being able to give an effective speech presentation is also important while you are in college. For example, many of you will give presentations or reports in classes you are taking, dorm meetings, fraternity/sorority meetings, sports team meetings, student government campaigns, political demonstrations, or a variety of other events that take place on a college campus. **Public speaking** is the presentation of a speech, usually prepared in advance, during which the speaker is the central focus of an audience's attention. In Chapter 1, we stated that the ability to communicate is one of the most important skills a person can possess in our society, and speech making is a vital and significant form of communication.

You may have reasons for doubting the need to learn how to develop and present a speech, but whatever they are, you must be willing to set them aside. The two most frequent concerns of beginning speech makers are not having anything worthwhile to say and nervousness at speaking in front of others. Both of these concerns are addressed in detail in this part of the text. Learning about speech making will not only help you become a more effective speaker, but it will also help you develop your writing, listening, organizing, researching, and reasoning skills. This in turn will help develop your self-confidence.

THINK ABOUT IT

When Jim Wickless was in high school, he enrolled in a speech class largely against his will. "I would never have taken it if it hadn't been required," Wickless said. "But it turned out to be one of the most important courses I've ever had."

Wickless' public speaking ability has come in handy in his seven years on the Lincoln Board of Education. He speaks frequently to community groups, testifies before the state legislature, and in his spare time lectures on speech writing in a public speaking class at Southeast Community College.

Wickless tried to make speech a requirement for high school graduation but couldn't persuade the rest of the board to go along with him. In his reelection campaign he argued that Lincoln students need better training in three key areas: oral and written communication, critical thinking skills, and foreign languages. All three subjects, he said, are vital to students' future in a competitive society of changing careers and international markets.

Should a course in oral communication be required for high school graduation? Why or why not?

*Should a course in oral communication be required for college grad-
uation? Why or why not?*

*In what ways is oral communication "vital to students' future in a
competitive society of changing careers and international markets"?*

Excerpt from Bob Reeves, "Wickless Finds Speech Class Was Valuable Lifetime Lesson,"
The Lincoln Star, 21 April 1987, p. 8.

SELECTING A SPEECH TOPIC

Selecting a topic is the first step in preparing a speech. In these chapters on
public communication, you will read about topics that were presented in a
variety of classroom, business, and professional speaking situations. As illustrated by the brief scenario at the beginning of this chapter, the choice of
topics is often prompted by the situation itself, the needs of others, and the
position and qualifications of the speaker.

Similar circumstances accompany most invitations to speak. People,
whether well-known speakers or not, are usually asked to discuss a topic
within their area of expertise. For example, a teacher may be asked to speak
on computers in the classroom, a businessperson on the economy, and a
farmer on the high price of farm equipment.

Classroom speaking situations are in many ways similar to these examples except that the instructor is the person requesting the speech. A typical classroom speech assignment might be:

> Your first speech will be a five- to seven-minute informative presentation.
> You may choose your own topic as long as it is relevant to your audience.

In this assignment the instructor is telling the students that any topic is appropriate as long as it can be presented as an informative speech within a
five- to seven-minute time limit. There are several pieces of very helpful information contained in the above statement: (1) The time limit is specified. (2)
The speech purpose is to be informative. (3) You can choose your own topic.
Here are a few topics that students have chosen for a similar assignment.

College drug use	Dieting and its implications
Genetic cloning	NAFTA (North American Free Trade Agreement)
Agriculture in the year 2000	The cost of college texts
AIDS awareness	Is a college education worth it?
Cocaine: good or evil?	Martin Luther King, Jr.: a man of peace
Violence and our society	Dyslexia
Gangs and youth	Gun control
Jealousy	Jogging and your health

The stock market	Organ transplants
Steroids and athletes	Parking on campus
Date rape: a serious problem	Flooding: an economic disaster
Foreign vs. American cars	Animal rights
UFOs	College athletics
Pornography	Dreams
Microcomputers	Parenting: a difficult task
Lasers and our health	Single parents
MTV	Fast foods that are good for you
The ozone layer	*The Simpsons:* a TV phenomenon
Sex and television	Adoption: Do the laws work?

As you can see, the list has no specific direction and it covers a vast range of subjects. There are an infinite number of topics to choose from for most classroom speaking assignments. Selecting a good topic for you and for the speaking situation requires thought and a systematic approach to ensure that you make the appropriate topic choice.

Selecting the Appropriate Topic

Many factors contribute to an effective speech presentation, including research, organization, wording, and delivery, but none is more important than selecting an appropriate topic. The topic and your interest and motivation in developing and presenting it are vital to your success as a speaker. The topic that is best for your audience, the assignment, and you isn't always easy to determine.

Some beginning speech makers worry that they might not be able to think of something to talk about. This worry is simply unwarranted. If you read any newspaper or magazine or watch television, you will be exposed to a variety of stimulating and interesting topics ranging from "military involvement in foreign lands" to "health care." When a topic isn't given by the instructor, the trick is to identify a topic that matches your interests and qualifications, the interests and existing knowledge of your audience, and the requirements of the situation in which the speech is to be presented.

There are three guidelines you should consider in your search for an appropriate speech topic. FIRST, TRY TO CHOOSE A TOPIC THAT WILL ALLOW YOU TO CONVEY AN IMPORTANT THOUGHT TO YOUR AUDIENCE. The thought does not have to be of a matter of life and death to be considered important, but it should at least be relevant to your audience's interests, have some direct effect on them, or be something that you believe the audience should know. Ask yourself the following:

Will the audience want to learn more about the topic?

Will the audience see the topic as relevant?

Will the audience be affected in some way by the topic?

Will the audience benefit from listening to information on the topic?

Will the audience see you as a credible speaker on the topic?

If after you have selected a topic you can answer "yes" to each of the above questions, you are on your way to ensuring that the topic you have selected is appropriate.

SECOND, TRY TO CHOOSE A TOPIC THAT IS FAMILIAR AND INTERESTING TO YOU. Choosing a topic that is familiar and interesting to you helps make the development and delivery of your speech easier. It would certainly be easier to begin your research and development of a talk on laser disc technology if you have some knowledge of what a laser disc is and how it works. And it certainly makes the time you spend researching and developing a speech more enjoyable when you are interested in the topic. You may find it enjoyable to select a topic that you are interested in but know little about. For example, you may have heard of "*in vitro* fertilization" (fertilization in a test tube of an egg by a sperm) but not know about the exact procedure or issues surrounding it. Further, choosing a topic that you have an interest in can increase the likelihood of audience interest.

If you don't think that you know any subject well enough to present, consider the case of Hilary. She insisted that she wasn't familiar with any topic that would interest others. Because she was majoring in computer engineering, her instructor suggested that she think about the one aspect of her major that interested her most. As a result, Hilary presented a fascinating speech on the history and development of computer simulation. The depth of her knowledge and her enthusiasm for her subject impressed her classmates and held their interest throughout the presentation.

The more you know about a subject, the easier it is for you to speak about it. You must feel confident in your information and in your ability to understand and manage it. This does not mean that unfamiliar topics should be completely avoided. It merely means that if you either know something about a topic or have an interest in learning more about it, your job of developing and presenting the speech will be easier.

A general rule for any speaking situation, whether in class or outside, is that you should know more about the topic than most of your audience. This is not as difficult as it may seem; most people have only superficial knowledge of most topics, so any investigation of a subject is likely to give you more information than your audience has. Listed below are some topics based mostly on students' personal knowledge and experiences that were presented in class.

Misconceptions about farming	How to bow-hunt deer
Concern about AIDS	Buying a used car
Being a nontraditional student	Running a marathon
Being Hispanic in the United States	Importance of working out
Free fall—a sky diver's view	Value of an education
Satisfaction derived from gymnastics	

Third, try to choose a topic that has some meaning to you. The more meaningful a topic is to you, the more likely you are to put the necessary time and effort into researching and developing your speech. The stronger your commitment to a topic, the more enthusiastically you will present it. A speaker's commitment to a topic usually transfers to the audience members and encourages them to get involved. The involvement of the audience in a topic can be an effective gauge of your success as a speaker. After all, the reason for giving a speech (besides meeting your assignment) is to gain your listeners' attention, and this is more easily accomplished if you consider the topic to be important.

Techniques to Help Find a Topic

If you have difficulty thinking up interesting subjects to speak on, there are some techniques that might help you: self-inventory, brainstorming, and reviewing the current media. All three are designed to generate a wide range of possible topics from which you can then select the most appropriate.

Self-Inventory   A **self-inventory** is a list of subjects that you know about and find interesting. You might include books and newspaper articles you've read, television shows you watch, hobbies you enjoy, sports you participate in, and community, state, regional, national, or international issues that concern you. The following list gives some examples:

Books and Articles
The Closing of the American Mind
Swim with the Sharks
Dictionary of Cultural Literacy
Miniaturization of Machines
Chemical Weapons
Economic Illiteracy

Television Programs
Poverty in America
Money in America
The 21st Century

Hobbies
Beekeeping
Astrology
Taxidermy

Sports
Handball
Steroids
Stress

Community Issues
Drug abuse
Computerized traffic lights
Homelessness

State Issues
Improving education
Expanding the state prison
Water supplies

Regional Issues
Population density
Air pollution
Wind erosion

National Issues
Gun control
Open trade
Health care

International Issues
Terrorism
Protecting the ozone layer
Human rights

Another way of using a self-inventory is to list things and ideas as broad categories and then narrow them from the broad categories to specific areas, as in the following example:

Athletics

Drug use in athletics

Use of steroids in athletics

Effects of steroids on athletics

Effects of steroids on athletes

Effects of steroids on college athletes

The category "athletics" was narrowed to a specific area, "effects of steroids on college athletes," which is a possible speech topic. Anything or any idea can stimulate an appropriate topic for a speech.

EXERCISE

Complete the following self-inventory by supplying as many more items as you can for each category. Then examine each of the items to determine if it could be an appropriate topic for a speech.

BOOKS AND NEWSPAPERS
See, I Told You So

SPORTS
Volleyball

TELEVISION
Beavis and Butt-head

REGIONAL ISSUES
Flooding

HOBBIES
Gourmet cooking

COMMUNITY ISSUES
Gang violence

STATE ISSUES
Economic growth

NATIONAL ISSUES
Health insurance

INTERNATIONAL ISSUES
Free markets

PLACES
The new Russia

PEOPLE
Malcolm X

VALUES
Diversity on campus

PROBLEMS
Cheating on campus

ACTIVITIES
Student Spring Festival

Brainstorming If a self-inventory doesn't help you determine a topic, try brainstorming. **Brainstorming** is a technique used to generate as many ideas as possible in a given amount of time. Set aside a short period of time (two to five minutes) for intensive concentration, and write down all the ideas that come to mind as topics. To keep things simple, just write key words or phrases. Don't stop to think about whether the ideas are good or bad. The goal of brainstorming is to generate a lot of ideas, so no word or phrase is inappropriate. For example, you might produce the following list.

politics	energy	health	school
drugs	pets	justice	sex
radio	drinking	peace	computers
space	sports	food	business
imports	movies	video	vacations
dance	housing	technology	pollution
crime	fitness	agriculture	television
hate	education		

After listing as many thoughts as you can, select those that appeal to you and brainstorm on them. For example, the term *technology* could serve as the springboard for an entirely new list:

space travel	microwaves	robotics
satellite dishes	genetic engineering	lasers
organ transplants	microchips	medical research
computer imaging	x-rays	superconductor

With a little effort, brainstorming will help you generate a number of potential topics in a short time. And the process can be repeated over and over until a suitable topic is found. For example, you could take the subject "lasers" and generate another more specific list.

laser development	laser history	laser uses
laser surgery	laser beams	laser energy
laser communication	laser x-rays	laser graphics
lasers and space	laser benefits	laser weapons

Reviewing the Current Media   The last technique for generating topic ideas involves the popular media. The media are channels or means of communicating messages to the public, such as through newspapers, books, magazines, television, and movies. **Reviewing the current media** is a technique for developing a list of possible topics by looking at current publications, television, movies, and other forms of communicating to the public. Card catalogs and standard reference works summarize the print media. *The Readers' Guide to Periodical Literature* is a source of hundreds of up-to-date topics. For example, you will find listings of articles on athletics, education, government, finance, marketing, terrorism, crime, air safety, health, entertainment, and so on. Specialized indexes, such as those in the fields of agriculture and natural resources, business, economics and statistics, biology and life sciences, computers, education, and history, can provide thousands of suggestions. You can scan the headlines, the articles, and even the advertisements in any magazine or newspaper—*Time, Newsweek,*

Sports Illustrated, Consumer Reports, Money, Business Week, Wall Street Journal, USA Today, and your local newspaper. Another wealth of current topics lies in television documentaries, news, and regular programs. For example, a movie about Ryan White, a young AIDS victim, was televised. Ryan, a young boy who suffered from hemophilia (a tendency to bleed excessively), had contracted AIDS as a result of shots he had received to help him with his blood disorder. The film relates the story about him, his family, and the problems they encountered in a small town in Indiana. Ryan's story could lead to a speech topic on AIDS and society's reactions to the disease.

Even the dictionary can be an excellent source for speech topics. One student said she located a topic by picking a letter or page at random, reading entries, and writing down possible topics. For example, under *s* you might select:

salt	self-esteem	solar
Sanskrit	semiconductor	sports
Santa Claus	sex	Stalin
satellite	shark	star
Saturn	shroud	swastika
schizophrenia	sickle cell anemia	Switzerland
schooner	slang	

Each of these has potential to be an interesting speech topic if developed carefully. The possibilities are limitless and all you have to do is choose one that interests you.

There is one caution about using the current media to generate speech topics. Some beginning speakers have a tendency to rely on the media for their entire speech. A summary of an interesting article or movie is not acceptable for most classroom speaking assignments. The media are an excellent source for potential topics, but they are only a starting point from which to build. The speech must be adapted to you and your specific audience, and most classroom assignments call for more than one source of information. You should always bring something new to your topic, a fresh insight or an application that is suitable to the speaking situation.

How you find your topic is not the critical issue, but it is important that you begin looking as soon as possible. Over the years of talking with students who have been successful in selecting appropriate topics, one common factor emerges: They start looking for a topic immediately upon receiving their assignments. Those students who delay almost always have more difficulty in finding an appropriate topic. Begin your search as soon as you receive your assignment. Whenever you come across something that you think might be a good idea, write it down. The more ideas you can accumulate, the easier your job of selecting a good topic will become. Also, the earlier you choose your topic, the more time you will have to research, prepare, and practice your speech.

Use brainstorming to generate several topics you might use for your next speech. What criteria would you use to determine the best topic for your presentation? Using the criteria you have established, determine which topic you will use.

Assessing the Appropriateness of a Topic

Once you have identified a possible topic, the next step is to determine whether it is appropriate for you, your assignment, and your audience. Ask yourself these questions:

1. Does the topic merit the audience's attention?
2. Will the audience see a relationship between you and the topic and between the topic and themselves?
3. Will the topic meet the objectives of the assignment?
4. Does the audience have sufficient knowledge and background to understand the topic?
5. Can you make the topic understandable to everyone in the audience?
6. Is the topic of sufficient interest to you that you will be motivated to present it effectively?
7. Do you have adequate knowledge of the topic?
8. If you are not already familiar with the topic, will you be able to learn enough about it to give an informed speech?
9. Is the topic appropriate for the situation in which you will present it?

Narrowing the Topic

Once you have determined that your topic is appropriate to your audience and you, the next step is to decide whether it is narrow enough to meet the time limit and the goal of the assignment. This step can save you much time and trouble in the long run, because a topic that is well focused is much easier to research than one that is too general. For example, you could work for years on "the problems with American education" and still not cover all the information that is available. If you restrict the scope to problems with American education during the past five years, you begin to reduce your literature search. You could narrow the topic even further by focusing on a single problem with American education during the past five years, and so on. Each time you narrow your topic, you increase its potential depth.

The more abstract a topic, the more important narrowing becomes to meet the constraints of a speech situation. For example, a member of a university's speech and debate team started the process of selecting a topic for her ten-minute informative speech by expressing an interest in pop culture. To narrow the topic, she decided to examine only pop culture fads. As soon as she recognized the abundance of such fads, she began to focus on video games. While thinking about video games as a fad and as an element of pop culture, she decided to be even more specific and limited her attention to the effects of video games on children. This continual narrowing of the topic enabled the student to focus her research and content development on a single well-defined area of interest.

DETERMINING THE GENERAL PURPOSE, SPECIFIC PURPOSE, AND THESIS OF A SPEECH

General Purpose

The **general purpose,** or overall goal, of a speech is usually to perform one of three overlapping functions—to inform, to persuade, or to entertain. Rarely does a speech serve only one function. Even though most classroom speech assignments are intended to emphasize a single function, the speeches themselves may contain aspects of all three functions. For example, the speech about the effects of video games on children is meant to inform, but this does not mean that the speech cannot contain some persuasive and entertaining elements as well.

For classroom speaking assignments, your general purpose is usually specified by the instructor, but for speeches outside the classroom, the occasion, what the audience knows or doesn't know about your topic, and how you want the audience to respond will determine whether you speak primarily to inform, to persuade, or to entertain.

Notice that the three functions are stated as action verbs in the infinitive form: to inform, to persuade, to entertain. This suggests that the speaking goal is "to affect" the listeners in some purposeful way. The reaction of the listeners determines whether or not your speech accomplished its purpose successfully. (See Figure 7.2.)

Speeches That Inform   When the general purpose of your speech is to inform, you are expected to convey your knowledge of a particular subject. An **informative speech** enhances an audience's knowledge and understanding by explaining what something means, how something works, or

Figure 7.2:

In order to achieve success, a speaker must influence the listeners in some purposeful way. It is the audience's reactions that allow the speaker to determine whether the purpose of the speech was successful or not.

David R. Frazier/Photolibrary

how something is done. The goal is to present information clearly and accurately, while making the learning experience as enjoyable as possible for the audience.

If you describe how to protect yourself during an assault, discuss why small pickup trucks are dangerous, explain the important uses of an electromagnetic field, report how the university uses its parking fees, or demonstrate how computer word processing can save time and money, you should do it with the assumption that most of your audience does not already know the information you are planning to present. The content of the speech depends heavily on what you think the audience knows and on how much you know or are able to learn about the topic.

When a topic is controversial, for example, "using condoms as a means of preventing AIDS," speakers whose general purpose is to inform should not take sides. They should allow audience members to draw their own conclusions.

Speeches That Persuade   The goal of a **persuasive speech** is to change listeners' attitudes or behavior by advocating or gaining acceptance of a point of view. When speakers try to convince audience members to eat less sugar, to vote for a particular student candidate, to endorse the building of a new football stadium, to give blood at the local Red Cross, to ensure a safe campus by joining a volunteer patrol group, or to support the call for better financial aid programs for all students, they are attempting to persuade. The speakers must present evidence and arguments to justify their position in order to win their audience over to their point of view.

The difference between persuading and informing isn't always clear-cut. Convincing your parents to give you money to buy a car is, for example, a persuasive goal. There is, however, a difference between informing them of the circumstances in which you would use a car, convincing them that you need a car and that you need the money to buy it, and their actually giving you money to buy it. They may accept the reasons you present for needing a car and may even agree that you need the money, but they still may not give the money to you. In this example, the persuasive purpose is not only to inform your parents that you need a car and the money and convince them that this is so, but for them to give you the money you need in order to buy the car. Providing information is a necessary part of persuasion, but this speech goes further because its goal is action (in this case, a particular behavior). Once your parents give you the money, you have achieved your persuasive purpose.

Thus, while the focus of an informative speech is to convey information and understanding by explaining, reporting, or demonstrating your point of view, the purpose of a persuasive speech is action. That action may be to think, to respond, or to behave in a certain way. Thus, the purpose (direction or course of action) may be to change diet, to vote, to approve of a proposal, or to join a group. The request to take action differentiates the persuasive purpose from the informative.

The important and necessary ingredient that makes persuasion different from information is the action (to think, to respond, to behave) taken by the listener as a result of the message presented. The informative speech provides more knowledge about a topic, while the persuasive speech provides not only more information, but also a direction or course of action the listener is to take.

EXERCISE

Listed below are the titles of some informative speeches. Convert each one into a topic that would be appropriate for a persuasive speech. The first one is done for you.

INFORMATIVE	*PERSUASIVE*
Nine Steps to a Healthy Body	**Daily Exercise Will Save Your Life**
Understanding the Use of the Microcomputer	
Diversity in the Curriculum in the 21st Century	
Star Wars: The Defense System of the Future	
Health Care in the U.S.A.	
Defining Sexual Harrassment	

Speeches That Entertain   An **entertainment speech** provides enjoyment and amusement. Usually speeches that entertain are humorous in nature and occur at special occasions such as a dinner or a roast. The key qualities of a speech to entertain are lightness, originality, and appropriatess to the situation. For example, the speaker may use imaginative illustrations or figures of speech, twist meanings, tell amusing stories, create amusing character sketches, or tell jokes, all with the willing participation of the audience and in the spirit of the occasion. This does not mean, however, that an entertaining speech cannot be both informative and persuasive or that informative and persuasive speeches cannot be entertaining. The principal difference among these three kinds of speeches is the function (informing, persuading, entertaining) on which the speaker places the most emphasis. The entertaining speech should therefore leave the audience members feeling they were entertained as the primary function of the speech.

Specific Purpose

The general purpose of a speech provides direction for its content. In the classroom, a speech's general purpose is usually specified in the assignment. Outside the classroom, it may or may not be specified. When the general purpose is not identified, you must determine it for yourself. To be a successful speaker, you must know exactly what you plan to accomplish by speaking.

Once you have determined your general purpose (to inform, to persuade, or to entertain), you are ready to determine your specific purpose. A **specific purpose** defines precisely what you intend to accomplish in your speech. Recall the student who chose video games as her topic. Her specific purpose was "To inform my listeners about the three major effects of video games on children." This clear and concise statement tells exactly what the speaker intends to do and what she wants her audience to know.

An effective specific purpose identifies the general purpose of the speech, the audience, and the exact topic to be covered. These three pieces of information significantly help the speaker develop and deliver the speech. Note that in the video games example, the speaker's specific purpose cites the general purpose of the speech, which is to inform. The specific purpose also identifies the audience, which is important because different audiences may require different information. For example, if a speech is to be presented to children only, to adults only, or to both children and adults, the content will have to be adjusted to fit the group. Thus, even though the general and specific purposes are the same, the content of the speech will vary depending on the listeners' background, knowledge, and attitude toward the topic.

The careful writing of a specific purpose is important to all aspects of planning and developing a successful speech. The following guidelines will help you write an effective specific purpose.

1. The specific purpose should include a verb form that describes the general purpose of the speech. The inclusion of the verb form clarifies the action the speaker hopes to accomplish.

   INCORRECT   Video games and children

   CORRECT   To inform the audience of two effects of video games on children.

2. The specific purpose should be limited to one distinct thought or idea. The incorrect statement below is too long and contains more than one subject. In fact, an entire speech could be developed around either area. It is best to select only one idea and refine it as the purpose for the speech.

   INCORRECT   To inform the audience of the three effects of drugs and the four best ways to prevent alcohol abuse by teenagers.

   CORRECT   To inform the audience about the three most dangerous effects of drugs on teenagers.

                   or

                   To inform the audience about the four best ways to prevent alcohol abuse by teenagers.

3. The specific purpose should not be a question. While a question may indicate the topic, it is not a clear or complete specific purpose because it fails to specify the general purpose of the speech.

   INCORRECT   How does capital punishment affect society?

   CORRECT   To persuade the audience that capital punishment can be extremely harmful to society.

4. The specific purpose should be concise and carefully worded. The incorrect statement below tries to cover too much, is too general, and does not state clearly what is to be achieved by the speech.

   INCORRECT   The effects of a permissive society can be extremely harmful to children and can also create a society that eventually becomes desensitized to reality.

   CORRECT   To persuade the audience that a permissive society can lead to the breakdown of law and order.

EXERCISE

What is wrong with each of the following specific purposes? How would you correct them?

1. **What is euthanasia?**
2. **To inform the audience about sailing.**
3. **To persuade the audience that a need exists for quality education in our society.**
4. **Skydiving can be fun.**

Formulating your general and specific purposes makes it easier to develop your speech. These purposes will guide your thinking and planning. You should be ready to revise your specific purpose, however, throughout the development stages of the speech. As you research a topic, you may find additional information that leads you to revise your thinking, or you may learn something about your audience that will makes you want to revise your specific purpose.

WRITING AN EFFECTIVE SPECIFIC PURPOSE

A specific purpose should:

Include a descriptive verb	Use action verbs such as *explain, describe, demonstrate, motivate, change, persuade, convince, inform, give insight, and show.*
Be limited to one distinct thought	Do not confuse the audience by trying to convey too much information.
Not be stated in the form of a question	Use a simple, declarative phrase.
Be concise and carefully worded	Choose words that tell exactly what you plan to accomplish or the desired effect on the audience.

Thesis

The specific purpose states what you wish to accomplish or what effect you wish to have on your audience. It also serves as the foundation for the thesis of the speech. The **thesis** provides more detail and forecasts exactly what is going to be discussed in the speech. For example, the specific purpose "To explain to my audience four advantages of using computer-aided instruction" tells what the speaker wants to do, but it does not describe the content of the speech. A thesis would be "Computer-aided instruction saves time, allows for self-pacing, provides practice, and is enjoyable." This clearly worded statement tells exactly what the four advantages of computer-aided instruction are.

If the specific purpose is "To persuade the audience to contribute to the new football stadium fund," the thesis might be "The new football stadium will help the university attract better players, will generate more money through ticket sales, and will bring a renewed sense of pride to our university." The thesis gives the three main ideas that the speaker will discuss: (1) why a new stadium will attract better players, (2) why it will generate more money through ticket sales, and (3) why it will bring a renewed sense of pride to the university. The thesis should be expressed as a full sentence, should not be in the form of a question, and should be clearly and concisely worded.

The following two examples show the relationship of the topic, general purpose, specific purpose, and thesis.

TOPIC:	Energy of the future
GENERAL PURPOSE:	To inform
SPECIFIC PURPOSE:	To inform my audience of the four forms of energy to be used in the future.
THESIS:	The four forms of energy in our future are solar, wind, ethanol, and nuclear.

TOPIC:	Maps
GENERAL PURPOSE:	To inform
SPECIFIC PURPOSE:	To inform my audience about the development and use of maps.
THESIS:	Maps have a rich history, are used widely today, and are affected by advancements influencing the future.

You can see how the broad topic area is narrowed as the speaker moves from the topic to the thesis. This narrowing procedure is a crucial step in preparing a speech.

RELATING TO THE AUDIENCE

Selecting a topic, narrowing it, and wording its general purpose, specific purpose, and thesis require some understanding and knowledge of the target audience. Developing the content of the speech requires the same understanding and knowledge. Recall from the opening scenario that the speaker asked the caller several questions about the audience. Specifically, the speaker asked how many people would be attending and who the people would be." The speaker was asking this so she would be able to relate her topic to the audience. Because relating to the audience is so important to a speaker's success, the remainder of this chapter examines the audience's point of view, kinds of audience members, key information to learn about an audience, methods for researching audiences, and adapting a speech to an audience.

Audience analysis is the collection and interpretation of data about characteristics, attitudes, values, and beliefs of an audience. Analyzing the audience is an essential step in developing and delivering a speech. An audience becomes actively involved in a speech and reacts to the speaker, to the subject, to what is said, to how it is said, to other audience members, and to the situation. Thus, the more speakers know about the audience, the better they can adapt their speeches to them.

Why is it even more important today to know as much as you can about your audience make-up?

Understanding the Audience's Point of View

An **audience** is a collection of individuals who come together to watch or listen to someone or something; for our purposes here, the audience includes individuals who listen to a speech. The individuals may become part of the audience for many different reasons. Each individual may have several reasons for being present, and the individuals may come from many different backgrounds. Students, for example, come to class to listen to lectures because they are required to attend as part of their speech assignment.

The reason individuals come together to form an audience is an important point that every speaker should consider when planning a speech. If people join an audience because they wish to listen to a speech, then it is reasonable to assume that they also want to hear something that is meaningful to them. Most individuals ask the same basic questions about their involvement in an audience. What is in it for me? Why is this important to me? How will this affect me?

These questions suggest that your audience will be judging what they hear on the basis of their past experiences and the relevance of the information presented. The more you know about your audience's past experiences, knowledge of the subject, relation to the subject, and reason for being there, the easier it will be for you to develop a speech that is meaningful to them. For example, imagine that you are an expert on reading and have been asked to give a speech entitled "How to Teach Children to Be More Effective Readers." You have spent many hours getting ready for the speech and are now prepared to present it. But are you really prepared? Have you thought about the members of your audience? Who are they? What do they know about reading? What is their attitude toward reading?

Would you present the same information to professionals who teach reading as you would to parents who want their children to become better readers, to children who are indifferent about reading, or to a combination of all three groups? What results would you expect if you used the same approach for all three audiences? What results would you expect if you varied your approach? Knowing to ask the above questions and how to find answers to them is essential to an effective and successful presentation.

Captive Versus Voluntary Participants

Many kinds of people attend speeches for many reasons, but all are either captive or voluntary participants. Audience members required to listen to a particular speech are **captive participants.** They may happen to want to hear the speech, but they have no choice but to attend. Some people may resist participation more than others.

Even though few circumstances (at least in this country) force a person to be in an audience, some situations demand attendance to avoid a penalty. For example, a teacher requires attendance during speech presentations, an employer requires employees to attend new product demonstrations, or a military leader orders troops to attend lectures on military maneuvers. In such situations, audience members cannot be absent or cannot leave without being noticed or penalized for doing so. To be effective, a speaker must recognize when he or she is dealing with captive participants.

In contrast to captive participants, **voluntary participants** choose to hear a particular speech because of some interest or need. True volunteers attend only because of what they expect to hear. There is no other motivation or force behind their presence.

In practice, the difference between captive and voluntary participants is not always clear because many situations that appear to be voluntary may actually be captive. The reverse may also be true. The deciding factor is whether the participants are required to listen or not. For example, students may be required to attend a lecture and may also be tested on what the speaker says. They are definitely captive participants. On the other hand, children may be required to attend church with their parents, but may not be expected to listen to what's being said. They are voluntary participants, in the sense that they are voluntary listeners; whether or not they listen is up to them.

This distinction is important to recognize because your objective as a speaker is to get your audience to listen. Speakers addressing voluntary audiences have a definite advantage over those addressing captive audiences. They do not have to spend as much effort persuading their audiences to listen. Voluntary participants have already decided they want to listen to the speaker.

KEY AUDIENCE INFORMATION

Two kinds of information—demographic and psychological—should be gathered about an audience. The more you know about your audience members, the better able you will be to adjust to them and to relate your topic to them.

Demographic Analysis

The collection and interpretation of such basic information as age, gender, cultural or ethnic background, education, occupation, religion, geographical origins, and group membership is called **Demographic Analysis.** The more similar the demographic characteristics of an audience, the easier is it for a speaker to adapt to their needs and interests. For example, if an audience consists of only 17- and 18-year-olds, the speaker has only one age group to deal with. If audience members range from 15 to 65 years old, the speaker will have to take into account several age groups.

Age   Knowing that members of the audience differ in age can help the speaker select a range of appropriate examples and evidence. An age difference between the speaker and the audience can also alter messages and how they are expressed. Both the speaker's and the audience's experiences may play a critical role in how a subject is approached or perceived, and also the difficulty level of language chosen.

Gender   Gender is an important demographic characteristic that can present problems. Not only have the attitudes of each sex toward the other changed, but so have the attitudes of each sex toward itself. Women take a greater role in activities that were once exclusively male-dominated, and vice versa. Thus, speakers must always be sensitive to potential gender-based biases, for example, referring to women as passive or only in certain types of career fields such as nursing or teaching. Although some topics may still be more appropriate for one sex than the other, clear-cut distinctions are becoming increasingly rare.

Cultural or Ethnic Background   Cultural or ethnic background is often not considered as thoroughly as it should be, even though a tremendous diversity of backgrounds exists in our society. Speakers should be sensitive to the different groups that may be present. The following communication variables may be culturally determined and influence interactions between and among members of different ethnic and racial backgrounds.

Attitudes	Use of spatial relationships
Social status within the group	Meanings of words
Thought patterns	Time
Expected behaviors	Nonverbal expressions
Use of language	

Each of these variables determines and regulates how an individual creates and interprets messages. Although the list is not exhaustive of all variables, it gives you an idea of some of the important cultural/ethnic factors to consider. Speakers who do not take these factors into account may embarrass or insult an audience. Speakers may also need to adjust speech content so as not to offend the audience regarding values, customs, or beliefs. Race, for example, can alter speakers' topic choices or speech purposes. The point here is simple: speakers must be sensitive to cultural differences and avoid statements that offend or are insensitive to members of their audience.

Education   Although it may be impossible to find out exactly what an audience knows and understands about a specific topic, it is often possible to ascertain their general education level. Knowing whether most listeners have completed high school, college, or graduate school can help you to gauge their intellectual level and experience and to adapt your speech accordingly.

Occupation   Knowledge about audience members' occupations can also tell you something about possible interest in and familiarity with some subjects. For example, lawyers might be interested in topics related to the law or in legal aspects of some topics.

Religion   Speakers must be as sensitive to religion as they are to ethnicity. That is, they must recognize issues that touch on religious beliefs and treat them carefully. If you plan to speak on an issue that may have religious ramifications, you should evaluate how your message will affect audience members. Otherwise, you run a risk of offending or losing the attention of some or all of your audience. For example, our choice of evidence in support of a viewpoint to an Islamic audience might be more appropriate from the Koran than from the King James Version of the Bible.

Geographical Origins   Knowing the geographical origins of your audience can help you to adapt your speech to them. For example, people from rural communities are more likely to know and care more about agricultural topics than people from large urban areas. People from the South may not be interested in problems involving heating their homes, but if they live in an oil-producing state, they may be interested in the price of a barrel of oil.

Group Membership   A group is a collection of individuals who have joined together for some common cause or purpose that may be social, professional, recreational, or charitable. Recognizing that individuals in your audience come from groups with special interests can help you relate your speech directly to their needs and concerns. Of course, it isn't always possible to reach every group in your audience, but by appealing to the largest group, you can create strong attention and interest. For example, a student who belonged to a sorority decided to inform her audience about sorority and fraternity functions other than social activities. Three-quarters of her student audience were not affiliated with any Greek group. Knowing this, she began her speech by talking about her thoughts on Greek organizations before she became a member. By first pointing our her reservations about such groups, she created a common understanding between herself and her listeners. Had her audience been three-quarters sorority and fraternity members, that kind of introduction would have been unnecessary.

Psychological Analysis

Psychological analysis is the collection of data on audience members' values, attitudes, and beliefs. A psychological analysis seeks to determine how the audience will react to the speaker, the speaker's topic, and the surroundings in which the speech is presented. The size of the audience, the physical setting for the presentation, the knowledge level of the audience, and the attitude of the audience toward the speaker, the topic, and the situation all play vital roles in the planning, development, and delivery of a speech.

Size of Audience   The number of audience members has a considerable psychological effect on a speaking situation and strongly influences how a speech should be delivered. The larger the audience, the more difficult it is to use an informal, conversational speaking style. Size also affects the speaker's use of language, gestures, and visual aids. There is a difference between speaking to ten or thirty people, as in a typical classroom speech assignment, and speaking to several hundred people in an auditorium. (See Figure 7.3)

The size of an audience can also affect the psychological disposition of the audience members and their relationship to each other and the speaker. For example, each member of a small audience is aware of him- or herself as a unique member of the audience, and each feels a close, intimate relationship to the speaker. As the size of the audience increases, members will lose their sense of identity as unique individuals and thus feel more distanced from the speaker. Effective speakers know this and plan their presentations to meet the requirements of each situation.

Physical Setting   In evaluating the physical setting, consider such factors as room size, ventilation, seating arrangement, lighting, speaker's platform, and potential for using visual aids. Some professional speakers require specific settings and will refuse to give their presentations if their

Figure 7.3:

There is much to consider when speaking to different size audiences. For example, as the audience size increases, the more difficult it is to become intimate with the audience. Size impacts the use of language, gestures, and visual aids. Effective speakers take audience size into account in their speech development and preparation. How do you think this speaker prepared for her speech?

Bob Daemmrich/The Image Works

conditions can't be met. Unfortunately, you do not have that choice in a classroom assignment. You can, however, assess the physical setting and make sure to take full advantage of what is available to you.

The seating arrangement of your audience is often predetermined, as it is in classroom settings, but sometimes a slight modification may make your presentation more effective. For example, a speech professor was asked to address a group of thirty police officers. He purposely arrived early so he could see the room and assess the speaking conditions. The seats were arranged classroom-style. That is, the chairs were in uniform rows directly in front of a raised speaker's podium, on which stood a large wooden lectern with a microphone. The professor felt that the setting was organized too formally and would inhibit his presentation, so he quickly rearranged the room by placing the chairs in a semicircle and moving the speaker's podium off to one side. These simple changes gave his presentation a more casual feeling and encouraged audience involvement. The physical setting can also affect audience members' psychological disposition toward each other as well as the speaker. The more relaxed the physical setting, for example, the more open and comfortable audience members will be with each other and with the speaker.

Knowledge Level   The extent of an audience's knowledge about a topic has a tremendous effect on the outcome of a speech. If an audience has little or no background on a topic and the speaker does not realize this, both the audience and the speaker may become frustrated. When an audience isn't ready to receive information, or when the information is too technical for them to understand, the speaker must present the material in terms everyone can understand.

A speaker must also adjust his or her presentation to a knowledgeable audience. A physician addressing a medical conference would not waste his or her time and bore the audience by explaining familiar medical terms. Even though people are apt to be more interested in subjects they know something about, an audience does not want a rehash of familiar information; they want to hear a new twist and to add to their existing knowledge. For example, a student decided to present a four- to six-minute informative speech about the lead pencil. After interviewing his classmates, the speaker noted that they all had a similar response: "What can you say about a lead pencil other than that it is made of lead and wood and is used for writing?" Based on his analysis, the student developed a creative, fascinating speech. Using a casual and entertaining style, he provided detailed information about the history of the lead pencil and its effect on society. The speech was a great success.

Audience Relationship to the Speaker   The audience's knowledge of the speaker strongly influences how a speech should be developed and delivered. Two speech professors arrived late to a workshop they were offering on effective communication. Anxious to start, the professors said little about themselves and quickly launched into their main topic. Fifteen minutes into the presentation, they noticed that most of the participants were not paying attention and appeared confused. Finally, an audience member asked, "Who are you?" When the speakers replied that they were speech communication professors and listed their credentials and qualifications, the audience settled down and became attentive.

As this example illustrates, an audience's attitude toward a speaker can make the difference between success and failure. Audience members always formulate some attitude toward a speaker. Effective speakers recognize this fact and adjust their presentations accordingly.

Relation of Attitude/Values to the Topic   The audience's attitude and values as they relate to the topic are just as significant as their knowledge of the speaker. If audience members do not relate to a topic, the speaker will have a difficult time getting them to listen. For instance, a student chose to speak on individual retirement accounts for his persuasive speech. He researched the subject thoroughly, practiced his delivery, and presented the speech in an enthusiastic manner, but his audience remained cool and uninvolved. The problem was that the speaker failed to consider the attitude toward and value the audience placed on the topic, given the age of his audience. Saving for retirement is not high on the priority list of most college students. The speaker could have made the speech more relevant by discussing young people's indifference to retirement saving and convincing them that they should be concerned now.

Audience Attitude Toward the Situation   The speaker must also examine the audience's relation to the situation in which the speech is to be presented. Why has the audience gathered? The audience's expectations influence their attitude toward the situation, which in turn affects the speaker and the topic. For example, a speaker who talks about the high use of drugs among teenagers at a local high school where drugs are not a problem is speaking to the wrong audience. The students are less likely to listen to the speaker because they don't see the topic as relevant to their situation.

METHODS OF AUDIENCE RESEARCH

The three most common ways of gathering information about an audience are observation, survey interviews, and questionnaires.

Observation

Probably the easiest method of audience research is observation. **Observation** is a method of collecting information about an audience in which the speaker watches audience members and notes their behaviors and characteristics. The speaker draws on accumulated experience with a particular audience and with similar groups. He or she watches audience members and notes their behaviors and characteristics. Although this approach relies strictly on the speaker's subjective impressions, it can be useful. For example, when asked to give a presentation to the Home and School Association, a professor relied on her observations of previous meetings to determine the kinds of information her audience would like to know. Based on past audience behavior she had observed, she made inferences about the people likely to attend her presentation. She felt safe in assuming, for example, that men and women who attend Home and School Association meetings are interested in improving the quality of their children's education and in learning how to become better parents. Her observations were basically sound because she had made them over a two-year period.

No doubt you have already learned a great deal about your audience for classroom assignments. You already know the number of students, the number of males and females, and the approximate ages. Through introductions, general conversations, and other interactions, you have learned what subjects these students are majoring in, what campus groups they belong to, whether they hold jobs, whether they commute or live on campus, what their interests are, and so on. By listening carefully to the speeches your classmates have given and observing others' reactions, you have learned a great deal about your classmates' attitudes, interests, values, and knowledge. You know your instructor's views and expectations for your classroom performance. You also know the size of the classroom, the location of the speaker's podium (if there is one), the seating arrangement, the availability of audiovisual equipment, and other physical features of the environment. You have obtained all of this information by observation. List things that you have learned about your classmates by observing their behavior. What information would be especially helpful to you in choosing a topic and developing a speech to deliver to them?

Survey Interviews

A **survey interview** is a series of carefully planned and executed person-to-person, question-and-answer sessions during which the speaker tries to discover specific information that will help in the preparation of a speech. The interviews can be done in person or over the phone. The purpose of the survey is to establish a solid base of fact from which to draw conclusions, make interpretations, and determine future courses of action. This method of audience research can be highly productive. To be most useful, however, surveys require a great deal of planning, organization, time, and energy. (Specific interviewing skills are discussed in more detail in the next chapter.)

It is often impossible or impractical to survey every audience member. In such cases, you may prefer to use sampling. **Random sampling** is selecting a small group of interviewees from a larger group by a means that gives every individual an equal chance of being selected. For example, you might write each classmate's name on a piece of paper, place all the names in a box, and then draw out slips of paper equal to the number of students you wish to interview. If you have a truly random sample, the information you obtain should closely resemble the information you would have obtained if you had interviewed the entire audience. Of course, the outcome will depend on the number of people involved, how varied they are, and the suitability of the method of selection.

To be successful, the questions should be tested before the survey is conducted to make sure they will be understood and will yield the desired information. Here are some guidelines to help you get started.

1. Will the interviewees understand what is wanted and why?
2. Are the questions clear without further explanation?
3. Will the questions elicit the kind and amount of information desired?
4. How much probing will be necessary?
5. Will interviewees react negatively to any questions?
6. Are the answer categories adequate?
7. Do any of the questions reflect the interviewer's own biases?
8. Can the responses be tabulated easily and meaningfully?

After completing the survey, the interviewer usually codes the data, calculates totals, and tabulates percentages. The final stage is to analyze what the percentages mean and how they can be used in developing the speech's message.

Questionnaires

A **questionnaire** is a set of written questions that is distributed to respondents to gather desired information. The same techniques used in survey interviews are used in questionnaires. In some cases, questionnaires are more practical and take less time than interviews. They can be administered to relatively large groups of people at the same time. One advantage is that the respondents can remain anonymous, which often leads to greater honesty and openness.

Although learning to develop good questionnaires takes much time and practice, here are some simple guidelines to help you get started.

1. Decide exactly what information you want to gather.
2. Decide on the best method for making multiple copies of your questionnaire.
3. Decide when, where, and how to distribute the questionnaire.
4. Plan the introduction to the questionnaire. Will the respondent need specific instructions?
5. Make sure your questions are clear and understandable.

6. Limit the number of possible responses to each question.

7. Keep the questionnaire as brief as possible.

Figure 7.4 shows a typical questionnaire. Note that it provides simple instructions, it is brief, the questions are clear, and the number of possible responses is limited.

Among the methods of gathering information, the easiest way to find out about your audience is through observation. Your success with this method will depend on the amount of experience you have with your au-

---

Sample Questionnaire

Directions: Check the response that indicates how strongly you agree or disagree with each statement. Do not write your name on this questionnaire.

1. Date rape on campus is a serious problem.
   _____ Strongly agree
   _____ Slightly agree
   _____ Undecided
   _____ Slightly disagree
   _____ Strongly disagree

2. Victims of date rape usually are asking for it.
   _____ Strongly agree
   _____ Slightly agree
   _____ Undecided
   _____ Slightly disagree
   _____ Strongly disagree

3. There needs to be more definition and instruction on what is and what is not date rape.
   _____ Strongly agree
   _____ Slightly agree
   _____ Undecided
   _____ Slightly disagree
   _____ Strongly disagree

4. The students, faculty, and administrators must do more to provide a safe campus environment for all students.
   _____ Strongly agree
   _____ Slightly agree
   _____ Undecided
   _____ Slightly disagree
   _____ Strongly disagree

Figure 7.4:

Questionnaires are a set of written questions that serve as an excellent tool for gathering information quickly from large groups of people. If done effectively, they can be practical, take less time than interviews, and provide for the anonymity of the respondent.

dience and your ability to make accurate inferences. For most classroom situations, observation will yield adequate information, but if you seek more specific data, you may want to use a survey. A survey interview takes planning and time and is not very efficient, but it does provide an opportunity to get information in person and to probe when necessary. If you are dealing with a large group of people, you may decide to gather information by using a questionnaire. Although good questionnaires take time to write, they can be administered more quickly than interviews and often yield more candid responses, especially on sensitive topics.

Relating and Adapting to the Audience

The goal of observing, survey interviewing, and administering questionnaires is to gather information so that you can relate to and adapt your speech to those who make up your audience. Can you discern any patterns in the information you have gathered? What conclusions can you draw? How certain can you be of them? How can you use what you have learned to improve your speech? For example, suppose you surveyed a random sample of 25 female and 25 male students on your campus, using the questionnaire in Figure 7.4. You found that 75 percent of the women thought date rape was a serious problem, but only 30 percent of the men thought it was a serious problem. How could that information help you with a speech in which you want to convince your audience that date rape is a serious problem on your campus?

If your analysis is thorough and correct, you should have a fairly good picture of your audience—their relevant demographics, interests, knowledge levels, and attitudes toward the topic, the speaker, and the general situation. Although your findings will rarely be uniform, you should be able to reach some general conclusions. For example, you may find that 70 percent of your respondents strongly disagree that capital punishment should be used in our society, 15 percent have no opinion, and 15 percent strongly agree. If your purpose is to persuade them that capital punishment should be used in our society, you will need to adjust your speech to this audience. How will you get those who oppose you to listen to what you have to say? What can you say to include those who have no opinion or who strongly agree with you?

Although it is never easy to win over people who oppose your views, you can try by discussing their views first and then leading the audience into a discussion of your views. You should also use credible and unbiased sources that people are likely to accept. In addition, you should acknowledge that your listeners' views have as much merit as yours but assert that your views foretell a better solution.

If your research indicates that your audience has little or no opinion about the information you are presenting, you need to provoke their interest. Begin by telling why they should listen to what you have to say and by showing how the topic relates to them personally. Focus on helping them recognize the benefits and importance of your topic, and remember that clearly communicating your own enthusiasm can also help generate their interest.

Finally, when you are dealing with an audience that agrees with you and what you have to say, or knows a lot about your topic, you need to acknowledge what you share with them. For example, if you and your audience agree that a new auditorium should be built, note your shared agreement and then go on to talk about what can be done to get the new facility built. In the process, you might try to strengthen their beliefs about the need for the auditorium.

The crucial point is that no matter what your audience's position on your topic may be, your research enables you to identify it in advance. You can use this information to pursue your specific purpose and to adjust to your audience. Of course, the more information you have available to you, the better equipped you will be to adapt your speech to your audience's uniqueness.

EXERCISE

Your specific purpose is to persuade your classmates that a higher student fee is needed to support more student activities on campus. Your survey of the class indicates that 30 percent favor the increase, 50 percent are moderately opposed, 10 percent are strongly opposed, and 10 percent don't care one way or the other. Explain how you might plan your speech to address your audience's views.

SUMMARY

Public speaking is the presentation of a speech, usually prepared in advance, during which the speaker is the central focus of an audience's attention. The ability to speak in front of others will not only aid you in your career, but will also help you develop writing, listening, organizing, researching, and reasoning skills.

When selecting a topic, choose an area that you already know something about and that is of interest to you and your audience. Three methods of finding topics are *self-inventory*, listing your own interests; *brainstorming*, attempting to generate as many ideas as possible in a limited amount of time; and *reviewing the current media*, looking at current publications, television, movies, and so on. Once you have selected a subject, you must assess its appropriateness for you and your audience and narrow it to meet the situation and time requirements.

A speech should serve one of three *general purposes* (overall goal of a speech): to inform (*informative speech*), or enhance an audience's knowledge and understanding; to persuade (*persuasive speech*), or advocate or gain acceptance for a speaker's point of view; or to entertain (*entertainment speech*), or provide enjoyment and amusement. Rarely does a speech serve a single general purpose exclusively; more often, the three purposes overlap.

Part of the narrowing and focusing of a topic is the formulation of a *specific purpose*, a single phrase that defines precisely what is to be accomplished in a speech. The clearer the specific purpose, the easier it is to plan, research, and develop a successful speech. The *thesis* focuses the topic further by detailing and forecasting exactly what is to be discussed in the speech.

Effective speakers know that they must tailor their speeches to their audience. An *audience analysis* is a collection and interpretation of data on characteristics, attitudes, values, and beliefs of an audience. An audience analysis can provide the kind of basic information a speaker needs to ensure success. An *audience* is a collection of individuals who have come together to watch or listen to someone or something, such as a speech. The more speakers know about their audience's past experiences, knowledge, attitudes, and reasons for attendance, the easier it is to develop speeches that are meaningful and relevant.

Although audience members vary greatly in their personal traits and reasons for attendance, they can be divided into two basic categories based on the nature of their participation. *Captive participants* are audience members who are required to hear a particular speaker or speech, while *voluntary participants* are audience members who choose to hear a particular speaker or speech because of some personal interest or need.

To be fully prepared, a speaker needs to gather demographic and psychological information about an audience. *Demographic analysis* is the collection and interpretation of basic information such as age, gender, cultural and ethnic background, education, occupation, religion, geographical origins, and group membership. *Psychological analysis* is the collection and interpretation of information about values, knowledge, beliefs, and attitudes toward the speaker, the topic, and the surroundings in which the speech is presented. The size of the audience and the physical setting for the presentation also play roles in the planning, development, and delivery of a speech.

The three most common ways of gathering information about an audience are observation, survey interviews, and questionnaires. *Observation* relies on the speaker's perceptions of the audience's behaviors and characteristics. It is the easiest way to gather information about an audience, but its accuracy relies on the amount of experience a speaker has had with the audience and his or her ability to draw reliable conclusions. The *survey interview* is a series of carefully planned and executed person-to-person, question-and-answer sessions. Speakers may use *random sampling* to reduce the time that would be required to talk to every audience member. A *questionnaire* is a set of written questions. It is an efficient way to reach large numbers of people at one time.

No matter what information-gathering technique you use, you must analyze the results with the goal of understanding the audience and discovering any patterns that will help in the development of your speech. Once you have completed your analysis, you can use your findings to adapt your speech to the characteristics of your audience. As a result, your audience should have little difficulty answering the question "What's in it for me?"

KEY TERMS

Audience: Collection of individuals who have come together to watch or listen to someone or something, such as to listen a speech.

Audience Analysis: Collection and interpretation of data about characteristics, attitudes, values, and beliefs of an audience.

Brainstorming: Technique used to generate as many ideas as possible in a limited amount of time.

Captive Participant: Person who is required to hear a particular speech.

Demographic Analysis: Collection and interpretation of data on characteristics (age, gender, religion, occupation, and so on) of individuals, excluding values, attitudes, and beliefs.

Entertainment Speech: Speech that provides enjoyment and amusement.

General Purpose: Overall goal of a speech, usually one of three overlapping functions—to inform, to persuade, or to entertain.

Informative Speech: Speech that enhances an audience's knowledge and understanding by explaining what something means, how something works, or how something is done.

Observation: Method of collecting information about an audience in which the speaker watches audience members and notes their behaviors and characteristics.

Persuasive Speech: Speech that attempts to change listeners' attitudes or behaviors by advocating or trying to gain acceptance of the speaker's point of view.

Psychological Analysis: Collection and interpretation of data about audience members' values, attitudes, and beliefs.

Public Speaking: Presentation of a speech, usually prepared in advance, during which the speaker is the central focus of an audience's attention.

Questionnaire: Set of written questions that is distributed to respondents to gather desired information.

Random Sampling: Method of selecting a small number of interviewees from a arger group so that every individual has an equal chance of being elected.

Reviewing the Current Media: Technique for developing a list of possible topics by looking at current publications, television, movies, and other forms of communicating to the public.

Self-Inventory: Technique for developing a list of possible topics by listing one's own interests.

Specific Purpose: Single phrase that defines precisely what is to be accomplished in a speech.

Survey Interview: Series of carefully planned and executed person-to-person, question-and-answer sessions during which the speaker tries to discover specific information that will help in the preparation of a speech.

Thesis: Sentence that states specifically what is going to be discussed in a speech.

Voluntary Participant: Person who chooses to listen to a particular speech.

DISCUSSION STARTERS

1. How can becoming an effective public speaker influence your life?
2. Name three speakers you find especially effective. What contributes to their effectiveness?
3. Your best friend has been asked to give a speech, but the topic has been left open. What advice would you give him or her about choosing an appropriate topic?
4. Describe the criteria you would use to determine whether a speech topic is appropriate for you and your audience.
5. Why is it necessary to formulate a general purpose and a specific purpose to develop a speech?
6. In what ways can demographic analysis of your audience help you in the development and delivery of a speech?
7. Which audience, in your opinion, would be easiest to address: captive participants, voluntary participants, or a mixture of both?
8. How does audience members' self-interest affect their attitudes toward a speech? What can a speaker do to take this into account?
9. What information can a psychological analysis of your audience provide?
10. Why is it important to know your audience's attitudes toward you before you give a speech?
11. You are preparing to speak on the need for stricter laws governing illegal drugs and are uncertain of your audience's views. What should you know about your audience? How would you go about getting the information you need?

NOTES

1. K. K. Edgerton, "Do Real People Give Speeches?" *Central States Speech Journal* 25, no. 3 (Fall 1974): 233–235; R. L. Sorenson and J. C. Pearson, "Alumni Perspectives on Speech Communication Training: Implications for Communication Faculty," *Communication Education*

30 (1981): 299–307; V. Di Salvo and J. K. Larsen, "A Contingency Approach to Communication Skills Importance: The Impact of Occupation, Direction, and Position," *Journal of Business Communication* 24 (1987): 3–22; and V. Di Salvo and R. Kay, "An Identification of Core Communication Skills Found in Organization-Related Careers," unpublished paper (1988).

2. J. D. Trent and W. C. Redding, "A Survey of Communication Opinions of Executives in Large Corporations" (unpublished special report, no. 8, Purdue University, West Lafayette, Ind., September 1964); J. C. Benett and R. J. Olney, "Executive Priorities for Effective Communication in an Information Age," *Journal of Business Communication* 23 (1986): 13–22; and P. Freston and J. Lease, "Communication Skills Training for Selected Supervisors," *Training and Development Journal* (1987): 67–70.

Chapter 8

Gathering and Using Information

LEARNING OBJECTIVES

After studying this chapter, you should be able to:

1. Identify three principal sources of information about a speech topic and indicate how each contributes to the research process.

2. Determine when it is appropriate to use an interview for gathering information.

3. Construct interview questions that will elicit the information you seek.

4. Use the library to gather information for a speech.

5. Cite five guidelines that can make the research process more efficient and effective.

6. Explain how testimony, examples, definitions, and statistics can be used to support and clarify a speaker's message and enhance the impact of a speech.

Dana works part-time in the radiology lab at the local hospital. She knows from her work that lasers are becoming the technology of the future in health care. When she had to present an informative speech in her communication class, she decided to speak on the medical uses of the laser in the United States.

To prepare for her speech, Dana interviewed several radiologists and surgeons about their use of lasers and read several articles about the latest developments in laser technology. But when she sat down to outline her presentation, Dana realized that she still didn't have enough current information on laser technology. She decided to research her subject more thoroughly in the school library. There she found more than enough additional information to fulfill her assignment.

By the time Dana finished gathering information, she had drawn on her own experiences, spoken with other people, and read the most recent printed sources she could find. By being so thorough in gathering information, she had taken a crucial step toward developing a first-rate speech.

Gathering information takes time and effort, but as Dana found out in the above scenario, it is also one of the most rewarding aspects of developing a speech. Gathering information is rewarding because you learn from the information gathered and increase your chances of developing an interesting and effective speech. The more current the information you gather, the more likely you are to impress your audience. Because the information you gather becomes the backbone of your speech, the speech can only be as good as your information. This chapter focuses on researching and using the information you find to support and clarify what you want to say.

Professional speakers have said that every ten minutes of speaking time requires at least ten hours of research and preparation time. Each topic and speaking occasion will require a different amount of information, but there is no question that the more information you have, the better equipped you are to design and develop your presentation and adapt it to your audience. Of course, quality of information matters more than quantity, especially when your time is limited. That is why it is important to develop your research skills. The more skilled you become at doing research, the better use you will make of your time.

USING YOURSELF AS A SOURCE OF INFORMATION

If you want to make the best use of your time and gather the best information, where should you begin? The most often suggested answer is with yourself. You are one of the most valuable sources of information available.

Your experiences and knowledge can contribute to the content of your speech and give you some authority to speak on a subject. In our first example, Dana's experiences as a part-time lab assistant gave her information, helped her locate additional sources of information, gave her confidence in her ability to handle the subject, and gave her credibility as a speaker. Here is part of what she said:

New technology in the health profession is allowing life expectancy to increase by several months every year. My work in a local radiology lab has given me first-hand experience in working with some of the latest medical advances and technologies. Our office recently purchased a laser scanner, which has improved the doctors' ability to read x-rays reliably and accurately. All of the lab assistants have been instructed in the use and benefits of the scanner. Today, I would like to explain to you what a laser scanner is, its uses in reading x-rays, and its benefits in providing better health care for all of us.

By using her own experience and knowledge, Dana established her authority and competence with her classmates and a strong and positive relationship between herself and her topic.

Another example of this is an Asian student who used her experiences of growing up in another culture. She talked about her people, the educational traditions of her country, and some of the unique cultural differences between her country and the United States. Your job, special situations you have encountered, hobbies, causes, and other life experiences are valuable sources of information that can be used in your speeches. (See Figure 8.1.) Probing your own knowledge of a subject can also help you organize your thoughts, develop a research plan, and, eventually, save a great deal of time.

Figure 8.1:

Life experiences provide information. What you know is a valuable source of information and your experiences can assist you in developing your speech.

Alan Carey/The Image Works

THE INTERVIEW AS A SOURCE OF INFORMATION

Of course, for most topics your firsthand experience and knowledge will not be sufficient. The interview can be a valuable tool for gathering expert opinion and the most up-to-date information. A good interviewer can often discover information that could never be obtained through any other sources.

As we have said, an **interview** is a carefully planned, person-to-person question-and-answer session aimed at gathering information. An interview requires the constant exchange of messages, usually in the form of questions and answers, between two individuals. That is, both persons interchange roles of speaker and listener, as in a social conversation. Therefore, an interview calls for the same skills and insight as social conversation. The key difference between a social conversation and an interview is that the interview requires careful preparation, including a decision as to what information is desired and a clear, well-thought-out plan for obtaining that information.

You should consider using the interview as a means of researching your topic for several reasons. When you want up-to-date information, when the information might not be available elsewhere, when you have access to experts who are willing to share their knowledge with you, and when a person's point of view or opinion will make your speech more acceptable or interesting to your listeners are all appropriate times to use the interview.

After watching people who do interviews as part of their work, beginning students often assume that interview is simple. However, the interview, like most forms of communication, requires knowledge, skill, and practice. The best way to ensure an effective interview is to use common sense and prepare yourself as much as possible. The following will give you an idea of some of the things you need to consider in order to carry out a successful interview.

Establishing the Purpose of the Interview

You need to determine, based upon your existing knowledge of the subject, the specific purpose for doing an interview. Dana, in our opening example, observed the laser scanner being used and received some instruction in its use. However, she really didn't understand how the radiologists used it and what they thought about it. She decided that interviewing several radiologists would give her some of the information she lacked and would help her gain insight into their thoughts.

Choosing the Interviewee

Selecting the right persons to interview is essential to getting high-quality information. You should ask yourself:

What individuals have the information I need?

What are their credentials?

Are they willing to give information openly and honestly?

Are they accessible to me?

How many individuals do I need to interview to get accurate information?

Interviewees are usually selected because of their particular position or expertise. Dana, in the opening scenario, knew that she wanted to interview a radiologist. She knew that the head of the lab not only had the most information, but also loved to talk about the new laser scanner. Since the doctor had an extremely busy schedule, she asked for an appointment to be sure that she could conduct the interview. She felt that since the radiologist was so knowledgeable and her topic did not touch on any controversial issues, the one interviewee would be sufficient.

EXERCISE

List some people you would consider interviewing if you were planning to speak on the following topics.

SUBJECT AREA	INTERVIEWEE
High cost of auto insurance	Insurance agent, state director of insurance, several insurance policy holders
Air traffic safety	
Prison reform	
High cost of education	
Test-tube babies	
Corruption in athletics	

Which individuals would be most likely to give you unbiased information? Why?

Research Before the Interview

Before the interview, try to get as much background information as possible on both your topic and your interviewee. The more background information you have, the better equipped you will be to conduct the interview. You will ask better questions and understand the answers. Obtaining information about the topic or the person may require library work or may even involve interviewing others in preparation for the main interview.

Recording the Interview

To ensure that you accurately recall the information you obtain in an interview, you will need to record it. Most interviewers use either written notes or a tape recorder. Because your recording skills will greatly affect the outcome of your interview, choose the method that allows you the most freedom to interact with your interviewee.

Here are some guidelines for taking notes.

1. At the outset of the interview, ask permission to take notes and explain why note taking is necessary. To alleviate the interviewee's concern about being reported accurately, show the interviewee your notes occasionally or ask him or her to check them.

2. To encourage open and natural communication, maintain eye contact and take notes as inconspicuously as possible, using abbreviations or shorthand to speed the process.

3. Do not begin to take notes frantically during or immediately after an answer, but take them throughout the interview.

4. To gain trust, agree to follow any ground rules the interviewee may set up, explain how and when you will use the material, and, if necessary, agree to let him or her see the script of your speech before you deliver it.

5. To ensure accurate reporting from your notes, review them as soon after the interview as possible.

When you need an accurate record of a large amount of information, tape-recording may be more efficient than note taking. Here are some recommendations for using a tape recorder.

1. Be thoroughly confident and familiar with the tape recorder, so you can minimize the amount of time you spend operating it.

2. Select a machine that operates on batteries and has a built-in microphone.

3. Make sure that everything is operating correctly before the interview.

4. Know exactly how long the tape runs, and be prepared to switch quickly to the opposite side or to a new tape at the right time.

5. Make sure you have the volume set correctly.

6. Be sure to ask the interviewee for permission to tape-record the interview. Explain to the interviewee why you want to use the recorder. You might say, "I am interested in getting all the details in precisely our own words. Since I can't take shorthand and don't want a third person present, the best way is to let this machine do all the work." Or, "I always prefer to record an interview so that the information will be accurate. I transcribe the relevant material on paper so that the tape can be used over again."

7. If possible, arrange the physical setting so that the recorder is out of the interviewee's sight. Place the microphone so that it is inconspicuous and out of the direct line of sight as you and the interviewee face each other.

8. Once the interview begins, show no awareness of the recorder's presence.[1]

Preparing Questions

The underlying objective of any interview is to obtain reliable and valid information. **Reliability** (in reference to an interview) is the extent to which the same information could be obtained from the same interviewee. If an interviewer asks the same question twice and the interviewee answers similarly both times, the responses would be considered reliable.

Validity is the extent to which both the interviewer and the interviewee accomplish the purpose of the interview. For the interviewer, this means that each question or statement should lead to a related response. For example, if you ask "What's it like outside?" and the interviewee answers, "My car doesn't start in cold weather," the answer has not met your intent in asking the question. A question may fail to produce an appropriate response because of the way it is worded, the way the interviewer asks it, or the interviewee's misunderstanding of what's wanted, unwillingness to give the information wanted, or ignorance.

Although it is impossible to obtain perfect reliability and validity in all interview situations, you can do much to ensure getting reliable and valid information by preparing conscientiously. The keys to developing effective questions, which are the heart of the interview, are knowing the types of questions to ask and phrasing the questions appropriately. The first step is to identify the various forms of interview questions, their uses, and the kinds of responses they produce. Questions can be classified as either open or closed, primary or secondary, and neutral or leading.

Types of Questions

Open questions usually evoke responses of more than just a few words. They encourage the interviewee to talk. There are two subcategories of open questions. A *general* open question merely specifies a topic or asks the interviewee to tell what he or she knows. Some examples are:

1. Tell me about solar energy.
2. What do you like about the city's new crime prevention program?
3. Tell me about yourself.

A *direct* open question identifies or limits the topic and asks for a more specific reply. Some examples are:

1. How did your solar equipment perform?
2. What do you think are the main criticisms of the parking situation on campus?
3. Why do you believe the coach was fired?

Whether general or direct, the open question is extremely useful because it provides an opportunity for the interviewee to respond freely.

Closed questions call for a restricted or short response. Because such questions allow for only a limited number of acceptable, or responsive, answers, the answers are often predictable. A yes-no question, called a **bipolar question,** is the most extreme form of closed question, allowing no freedom of expression. Some closed questions are:

1. Do you know that we are harming the environment? (Bipolar)
2. Was there something else involved in the cost of the new mail? (Bipolar)
3. What brand comes to mind when you think of candy?
4. Who is your favorite professor?

Closed questions can be valuable for verifying information, probing a response for more information, and controlling the discussion. Closed questions can be answered quickly and require little effort from the interviewee. However, they do restrict communication and limit the interviewee's opportunities to volunteer information. Beginning interviewers often unknowingly overuse this form of question.

Primary questions introduce new topics or new areas within a topic. Primary questions can stand by themselves, meaning that even out of context, they would still make sense to the interviewee. For example:

1. Tell me how the supercomputer will affect our campus.
2. Why do you like your favorite sport?
3. How did you do on your last speech?

Secondary questions encourage the interviewee to expand on replies that may be incomplete, unresponsive, unclear, inaccurate, or superficial. Secondary questions are most commonly called **probing questions.** Unlike primary questions, secondary questions generally do not stand on their own. The purpose of secondary questions is to direct the interviewee to expand on or further explain what has been said or to move on to a deeper level of thinking. Secondary questions are follow-up questions to a superficial or incomplete response. Assume, for example, that the interviewer's primary question is "Tell me about yourself" and the interviewee's response is mainly demographic—she describes where she lived as a child and lives now, where she went to school, how old she is, and so forth. The interviewer might respond with a probing question, such as "That's interesting, but I would like to know more about what you are like and how you get along with people." A probe does not always start with "why" or "how" and needn't even be phrased as a question. It can be brief vocal sounds, such as "Oh" or "Uh-huh," or short phrases, such as "I see," "Please continue," and "Go on."

A probe can be introduced at any time during an interview. A probe may be interpreted by the interviewee as a sign of the interviewer's attentiveness and as encouragement to continue speaking. The probe serves two functions: it motivates further communication and it controls the interaction by providing direction.

Neutral questions avoid implying an expected or desired response. The wording of a neutral question does not push the interviewee to respond in any particular way. All of the sample questions in the previous sections are neutral questions. Even bipolar questions allow interviewees to choose their own responses, although there is only a choice between yes and no.

Leading questions implicitly or explicitly guide the interviewee to an expected or desired response. Look at the following examples of leading and neutral questions.

LEADING	NEUTRAL
You like speech class, don't you?	Do you like speech class?
The new field house isn't needed, is it?	Do you think we need a new field house?
Isn't the new bookstore easy to use?	Do you think the new bookstore is easy to use?

The use of leading questions can bias the information you receive, because interviewees may adapt their responses to match what they think you want to hear. Such questions may also suggest answers to respondents that they would not have thought of on their own. Consequently, if you wish to obtain valid and reliable information, it is crucial to avoid asking leading questions.

EXERCISE

Identify the following questions as open or closed, primary or secondary, and neutral or leading:

1. **What sport do you like best?**
2. **Do you like the new library building?**
3. **Tell me about yourself.**
4. **Your last term paper was well researched, wasn't it?**
5. **Let me see if I have this straight. Did you say that we are going to need more funds for the rally?**
6. **Go on.**
7. **You really like soccer, don't you?**

Phrasing Questions

The second concern in asking effective questions is phrasing. Questions that are wordy or grammatically incorrect will not be clear. Vague phrasing may fail to communicate the intent of the question to the interviewee. A vague question, such as "What about the new parking lot?" gives the interviewee little or no guidance about the kind of information the interviewer is seeking.

An effective question should contain only one thought or idea. Questions that are too complex should be avoided. Some examples of very complex questions are:

1. What causes the ailerons on airplane wings to move, and why do they move up and down when the plane is banking laterally in flight?
2. How, when, and why did pollution begin in our city?

Each question could be improved by dividing it into two or more separate questions that are clearer and shorter. Remember that poorly phrased questions hinder the interviewee's thought process and reduce the quality of his or her response.

EXERCISE

What's wrong with each of these questions?

1. **How does euthanasia affect our society?**
2. **What are your reactions to the new drug law that is going before Congress?**
3. **Would you say that the basketball coach is doing a good job, or could she do better?**
4. **What impact do you think the President's health care plan will have on our economy, on the poor, on the wealthy, and on states?**
5. **Have you stopped cheating on your taxes?**

Organizing the Interview

An interview usually has three identifiable segments—an opening, a body, and a closing. The length and content of each segment depend on you, your purpose, the interviewee, and the situation.

Opening   The opening can vary from a brief introduction to a lengthy explanation. During the opening you should try to put your interviewee at ease, state your purpose, and provide appropriate background information, if needed. A typical introduction might be:

Good morning, Dr. Kay. My name is Julie Smith and I'm a student at the university. I'm delighted that you're willing to visit with me. I know how busy you must be, so I'll take only about fifteen minutes of your time. As you know from our phone conversation, I'm interested in learning more about you and the new computer facilities. I'm taking a speech communication course and will be giving a speech on what the university computer can do for students. I'd like to tape-record the information because I'm not good at note taking and I want to make sure I get everything you say as accurately as possible. Do you mind? Good. Let's begin.

An opening may be much shorter than this example, but when you and the interviewee do not know each other, it is important to be as informative as possible. The success or failure of an interview is often determined by the way the opening is handled. Notice that the interviewer indicates that the interview will take approximately fifteen minutes. If you make this kind of statement, you should try to keep the interview within the time you specify.

Body   The body, or main part, of an interview consists of questions and answers. The questions may have no specific sequence, or they may follow a specific outline, with little or no flexibility. Within the general limitations of the purpose, the situation, and the persons involved, interviewing methods may vary widely. Some situations, such as an audience analysis, require a highly structured interview format to ensure that all interviewees are asked the same questions. In contrast, a news conference requires flexibility to adapt questions to the interviewee's responses. In more informal settings, nonscheduled and moderately scheduled formats are likely to be used.

In a **nonscheduled interview,** the interviewer keeps to a central objective or a list of possible topics and subtopics, but does not ask questions in any planned order; thus, there is no anticipated response. Most talk show interviews are nonscheduled interviews. The principal advantages of this format are its openness, which permits greater probing, and its flexibility, which allows changes in the direction of the discussion. The primary disadvantage is that the interviewer must be highly skilled.

In a **moderately scheduled interview,** the interviewer works from a prepared list of basic questions or topics and related possible probes. John is seeking information about a recent tuition hike and goes to the president of the university to discover her reasons for the increase and how it is going to affect the students' education. He might plan to ask questions with related probes in the following sequence:

1. Why was a tuition increase necessary, in your opinion?
2. How will it affect students?
   a. Will the tuition increase benefit all students?
   b. How will the tuition increase affect low-income students?
   c. How will the tuition increase bring more qualified instructors to the university?

The greatest advantage of the moderately scheduled interview, especially for the inexperienced interviewer, is that it is easy to use. The interviewer does not have to concentrate too much on the questions that need to be asked since they are planned, but at the same time he or she can probe and shift directions as necessary. In addition, this method shows the interviewee that the interviewer is well-prepared for the interview.

Closing As the interviewer, at some point you decide that you have obtained as much information as you need or recognize that you have used up your time. You must then be ready to conclude the interview, a step that can be one of the most awkward aspects of interviewing. The closing should be timed so that the meeting is not stopped too abruptly or prolonged unnecessarily.

The ability to end an interview effectively comes from experience and knowing how to control the direction of a conversation. In most instances, you can end an interview by expressing appreciation for the interviewee's cooperation and time and by summarizing the information you have learned. Do not close, however, until you have either reached your interview objective or accomplished as much of your objective as time will allow. If you have not achieved your purpose, indicate that you would like to schedule another meeting, but never overstay your welcome!

Other Considerations Factors such as dressing appropriately, being punctual, and listening attentively also contribute to the success of an interview. Think about how you want to be perceived by the interviewee when deciding what to wear. For example, presenting a businesslike appearance to a businessperson shows that you respect the person you are interviewing. (See Figure 8.2).

Being on time for an interview is essential. One of the most disrespectful things an interviewer can do is be late. Plan to be at least ten minutes early. If for some reason you will be late, call the interviewee as soon as possible to let him or her know. This is a must!

Always give the interviewee your undivided attention throughout the session. Finally, as soon after the interview as possible, review your

Figure 8.2:

Finding the right person to interview, such as the example of Dana in the chapter opening vignette, is important in getting quality information that will help in speech development.

Bob Daemmrich

notes and fill in details as much as possible. If any information you need is unclear or incomplete, call the interviewee as soon as possible, if necessary and appropriate to do so.

PREPARING AN INTERVIEW: A REVIEW

Determine the kind of information you are seeking.

Formulate a clear and concise general objective.

Select the right person for the interview.

Research the topic and the person before the interview.

Decide how you are going to record the information, and prepare your equipment.

Prepare questions and possible probes.

Organize the interview's opening, body, and closing.

Dress appropriately.

Be on time.

Give the interviewee your undivided attention.

Review your notes as soon as possible after the interview.

THE LIBRARY AS A SOURCE OF INFORMATION

After class one day, a student approached her professor and said, "I can't find enough information on my topic." "Oh?" the professor replied, in a tone of surprise, since the topic was space technology. "What did you find in the library?" The student quickly responded, "I didn't go to the library." The professor didn't know whether to laugh, cry, or just feel sorry for the student. How sad that this student had not considered the library as a resource for her speech.

Making use of the library does require some effort, but once you understand how the system works—and most libraries use essentially the same system—you will find that it is the most useful and beneficial resource for speech preparation. Libraries are becoming more user-friendly. Many libraries have invested great sums of money to install computerized systems so that researchers can find materials quickly and easily.

If you do not know how to locate material, now is the time to learn. A little time invested now will save you a great deal of time later, and you will find that the library is a convenient and pleasant place to locate the information. If you do not utilize the library, you will be at a disadvantage not only in your speech class, but in all your other classes as well.

Start by attending one of the tours or orientation sessions that many libraries offer. Some also provide educational packages with instructions on how to use the library. After your introduction to the system, you need to practice using the library. There are five principal sources of information in the library: yourself, the librarian, computer-assisted search programs, the card catalog, and the reference department.[2]

Yourself as Source

To create an effective speech, you must be willing to go to the library and put some effort into your research. You can save much time and work if you determine in advance what information you are seeking. For example, if your specific purpose is to inform your audience of the effects of pornography on society, you might begin your library search with the key terms *pornography, pornography effects,* and *pornography and society.* As you search the subject catalog, reference indexes, and computer data bases, you will probably find a number of terms related to your key terms, and you may discover that some of your key terms are not listed. You can then adjust your search and proceed. Knowing what you want, however, is still the best starting place for any library search.

Librarian

Librarians are exceptionally well trained to serve anyone who needs information. When you don't know how to find something, ask! Some students are afraid to request assistance, but even experienced library users frequently seek help from the librarian, an expert who is your most valuable resource when searching for information (see Figure 8.3).

Figure 8.3:

Librarians are experts at locating information that is relevant to your speech and are there to help you. Don't be afraid to ask for help.

David R. Frazier/Photolibrary

Computer Search

Most libraries have computer-assisted research systems, and each year these systems improve and become more user-friendly. You can do a search with little or no computer background. Even if you have an aversion to computers, find out about the services your library has available.

Many universities and colleges have network systems that allow you to enter the library indexes through home or on-campus computers. Once you learn the appropriate log-on procedures to access the library computer, you will be menu-guided by the computer through the steps you need to find what you want. You will learn where the materials are located and if they are available at your library.

There are also nationwide network systems that allow you to enter a variety of indexes. You don't have to be a computer expert, as most of these computer searches can be accessed only by a librarian. Make an appointment with a reference librarian. All you need to bring with you are the topics you wish to research and the key descriptors. The librarian can help you determine what to look for and how to limit your search. The librarian will also help you decide which data base (computer search) is best for your needs. The computer will provide a printout listing bibliographic citations for your topic. Some systems also provide a printout, which may be available immediately or may be mailed to you, listing and summarizing journal articles related to your topic.

The advantages of computer searches far outweigh the disadvantages. However, you should be aware of the disadvantages. Although most data bases are regularly added to and updated, many are not complete. For example, they may store information for limited periods of time and on a limited number of journals. Another disadvantage can be cost. Using a library's computer network is usually free, but searches through outside data bases usually cost from $10 to $20 and may run as high as $100. As the technology improves and the computer research services expand, these drawbacks may be reduced.

Card Catalog

The card catalog, an index to all the books in the library, is designed to be a quick and easy means of locating materials. The use of computer data bases is slowly but surely replacing the card catalog, but because not all libraries are completely computerized, you still need to understand how the card catalog works. Most card catalogs list books in three ways: by author's last name, by title, and by subject. Entries in the card catalog are arranged alphabetically.

Periodicals (magazines, professional journals, newspapers, and serials) are listed by title or may be listed by the name of the issuing body, such as Modern Language Association or American Council on the Teaching of Foreign Languages. To find a specific piece of information or magazine article, you must go to the reference department.

Reference Department

Most library research begins in the reference department, which contains all the books needed for easy access to specific subject areas, such as dictionaries, almanacs, biographical aids, encyclopedias, yearbooks, newspapers, atlases, bibliographies, indexes, and guides to periodical literature. If you are uncertain which to use or how to use them, ask the librarian.

There are specialized indexes for particular subjects, such as agriculture and natural resources; business, economics, and statistics; biology and life sciences; computers; education; and history. (See the Appendix at the end of this chapter for a more complete list.) But the index that is probably most widely used by beginning speech students is the *Readers' Guide to Periodical Literature.* This index lists articles from over 190 popular periodicals. Issues of the guide, published semimonthly or monthly, are bound separately for the latest publications and in volumes for publications that are a year or more old.

Entries in the Readers' Guide are listed alphabetically by author and subject. For example, if you are interested in the most recent information on computers, look in the latest issue of the Readers' Guide under the subject heading *Computers.* If *Computers* is not listed, keep searching earlier issues until you find it. Each article that has been written about computers is also listed alphabetically. The *Reader's Guide to Periodical Literature* also lists subheadings for special areas related to computers. A typical listing would look like this:

Subject heading:	College Graduates
Subheading:	Employment
Article:	Out of college—What's next? A. Farnham
	Fortune 28:58–61, Jul 12, '93

The citation includes the article's title, the author's name, the title of the periodical, the volume, the pages, and the date.

Finding materials in the library is usually quite simple, especially after you have familiarized yourself with its organization. Since most libraries have so many kinds of materials shelved in so many locations, they assign retrieval numbers and codes to tell you exactly where materials are located and in what form they can be found. If you have trouble locating any material, see the librarian.

Commonly Used Resources

Because magazines, research journals, and newspapers have the most recently available information on a subject, they are the resources most often used for speech writing. If you want to know the latest opinions and trends on almost any social, political, or economic issue, weekly magazines and newspapers will probably be your best resources. If you are looking for specific scientific research, research journals may be your best alternative.

Magazine and newspaper articles are usually brief and written for a general audience, so they are rich sources of basic information for speeches. Given their briefness, you can read several articles in order to gather differing points of view. In addition, libraries not only have local and state newspapers, but they usually have major newspapers from all over the world, which can provide you with an even broader perspective.

If you do not know what your library has to offer, take time to learn about it. The search for knowledge is never easy, but thought and preparation will enable you to find ample information about almost any speech topic.

SUGGESTIONS FOR DOING RESEARCH

There are no shortcuts to doing good research, but there are things that can make research more enjoyable and easier. Here are several suggestions:

1. STATE A CLEAR PURPOSE BEFORE STARTING YOUR RESEARCH. Knowing what you want to find makes the job of searching easier. If, for example, the purpose of your speech is to inform your audience about the importance of maintaining a good diet, the key term in your purpose statement would be *diet*. Your search for information should begin with *diet*, followed by *maintaining* and then *importance* of a good diet. Thinking of other key terms will help lead you to topics related to diet, such as *nutrition* and *health*. Considering all the possible areas of research in advance will get you started quickly and productively.

2. BEGIN YOUR RESEARCH EARLY. Because finding appropriate materials takes time, you should start your research as soon as possible. If you wait until the last minute, you may discover that the materials you need are unavailable or that it takes longer to find them than you anticipated.

3. USE COMPUTER SEARCHES WHEN POSSIBLE. The computer is one of the simplest means of obtaining lists of sources on any topic. If you are unfamiliar with your library's computer system, ask your librarian. He or she will gladly help you find what you need.

4. MAINTAIN A BIBLIOGRAPHY OF SOURCES. As you find sources in the card catalog and periodical guide, copy them in the same form onto a sheet of paper or index cards (3″ × 5″ or 4″ × 6″). The advantage of index cards is that you can sort them quickly either alphabetically or by importance to your speech. List each item separately and make notes about its importance to your speech presentation. Although this can be a rather tedious job, it is essential that you keep track of the materials you find.

5. TAKE NOTES. Efficient and accurate note taking is a must. Once you have located information, you must either record it by hand or photocopy it for later use. Whether you wish to quote a statement verbatim, summarize it, or paraphrase it, you must record the original information accurately and completely. Take plenty of notes and always make sure that the source is fully and accurately indicated, as in the sample note cards

in Figure 8.4. Nothing is more frustrating than having information and not being able to use it because you don't know its source and are not able to return for additional information. The more information you record, the better. You should always have more than you need to write your speech.

Sample Note Cards

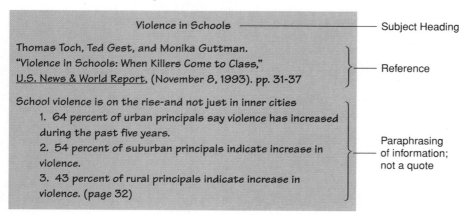

Violence in Schools ———————— Subject Heading

Thomas Toch, Ted Gest, and Monika Guttman.
"Violence in Schools: When Killers Come to Class,"
<u>U.S. News & World Report</u>, (November 8, 1993). pp. 31-37 ——— Reference

School violence is on the rise-and not just in inner cities
   1. 64 percent of urban principals say violence has increased during the past five years.
   2. 54 percent of suburban principals indicate increase in violence.
   3. 43 percent of rural principals indicate increase in violence. (page 32) ——— Paraphrasing of information; not a quote

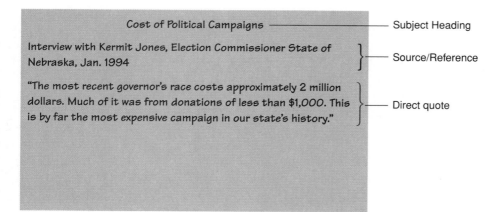

Cost of Political Campaigns ———————— Subject Heading

Interview with Kermit Jones, Election Commissioner State of Nebraska, Jan. 1994 ——— Source/Reference

"The most recent governor's race costs approximately 2 million dollars. Much of it was from donations of less than $1,000. This is by far the most expensive campaign in our state's history." ——— Direct quote

Figure 8.4:

Note taking, if done accurately and completely, can save you a great deal of time and effort. It is always best to take plenty of notes and to make sure you have the source of the notes recorded correctly.

EXERCISE

Before you reach for that keyboard to enter a computer search, take a few minutes. Analyze your topic and plan your approach. Warm up your brain.

One good way to begin is to see if you can break your topic down into component parts. Let's say you are interested in finding

out about Japanese management techniques, particularly those related to dealing with employees. One way to break this subject down is to list the key terms: *management, employees, Japan.* If you are looking for material about course content in Christian schools, you might break your subject down into *course content, schools, Christian religion.*

The next step is to expand your list of key terms to define your topic further. In the first example, you might choose *personnel management* and *employment policies.* In the second, you might add *curriculum, denominational schools, church-supported education, sectarian schools,* and *parochial schools.* This process allows you to clarify what you want before you begin the search process and helps you overcome one of the most common obstacles to good subject researching—a narrow view of the terminology needed to define a subject.

Now go to the library and do a search.

Adapted from J. E. Thornton-Jaringe, *Do You Ever Feel Confused About Where to Start Once You Get to the Library?* (Lincoln: University of Nebraska Libraries, 1983).

USING RESEARCH TO SUPPORT AND CLARIFY IDEAS

Over two thousand years ago, Aristotle, a famous Greek scholar, wrote that there are essentially two parts to every speech—a statement and its proof. Aristotle's description is still valid today. How a speaker clarifies and supports the ideas he or she presents determines the quality of the speech. For example, consider the following statement:

> Students of today are far more advanced than students of a decade ago. Today's students, for example, have access to computer technology, which has allowed them to advance at a much faster rate.

On the surface, the above statement seems to have validity, but is it accurate and will an audience accept it at face value?

Audiences generally accept information because of the perceived believability of the speaker or the information itself. Thus, the above statement would be more acceptable to audiences if it were made by a well-known educator and researcher than if it were made by a student. But, regardless of the source, most listeners require some proof or specific data before they completely accept a statement. Consequently, effective speakers justify each main idea in their speeches with a variety of supporting and clarifying materials.

Supporting and clarifying materials bring life to a speech. They can make the content of a speech appealing, vivid, exciting, meaningful, acceptable, and more useful to listeners. Compare these two paragraphs:

To what extent do males and females differ in the way they learn and communicate? The sexes are psychologically similar in many respects. Although some of the differences may have a biological basis, the existing evidence is conflicting.

To what extent do males and females differ in the way they learn and communicate? Eleanor Maccoby and Carol Jacklin, two widely respected psychologists and authors, report in their book, *The Psychology of Sex Differences,* that "the sexes are psychologically much alike in many respects." Although some of the differences in behavior—such as the superior verbal ability of girls and accelerated math skills of boys—may have a biological basis, a great deal of conflicting evidence surrounds such differences.

Which paragraph do you find to be more meaningful? More acceptable? More interesting? More useful? Why?

Consider the following statement a student made in a speech:

Exercise is the best means for losing weight. Although many people consider exercise to be hard work, it doesn't have to be. In fact, there are a number of exercise programs that are easy, and you don't even have to sweat to lose pounds.

This sounds great, but as they say, something that sounds too good to be true is probably not true, or in this case, not convincing. Most of us would question something that claims we are going to lose weight with little or no effort. The student must provide some evidence before his audience is going to accept what he is saying.

The quantity and quality of a speaker's supporting and clarifying materials, plus the speaker's ability to use them correctly, usually make the difference between a mediocre speech and a good one. Thus, in this section we will focus on the basic kinds of supporting and clarifying materials used in speeches: expert opinion, examples, definitions, and statistics.

Expert Opinion

The opinions, testimony, or conclusions of witnesses or recognized authorities are referred to as **expert opinion.** Speakers use expert opinion to support or reinforce points they want their audiences to accept. The value of the expert opinion is related both to the listeners' opinion of its acceptability and to the speaker who presents it. Consider this opening of a students' speech:

You try to stop yourself, but for some reason you can't! The child keeps on screaming, "Mommy, Mommy, please don't hit me anymore!" You've lost control and until your rage subsides, you can't stop, even though you know you should. Not until you are caught or you do something severely harmful is anything done about it. When it's all over, you have inflicted the worst kind of human atrocity on your own child. How do I know this? Because I used to beat my own child until I got help.

The young woman who gave this speech had her audience's attention not only because of the story she was recounting, but also because she had the courage to relate what she had done and how she had overcome it. Her abuse of her own child did not enhance her believability and create acceptance for what she was saying, but her willingness to admit that she was personally involved in her topic did.

The use of expert opinion usually adds trustworthiness to what a speaker says—a necessity for all speakers who are not yet established as experts on their chosen speech topic. The speaker's own experience can be an excellent form of testimony, as in the previous example. When the speaker's reputation and experience are insufficient, the use of a recognized and trusted authority can be invaluable in gaining listeners' acceptance.

Expert opinion can either support or clarify material, or both. Here is an example of testimony that does both.

> The following statement by the American Automobile Association sums up experiments too numerous to mention and represents the best current professional opinion on automotive safety: "We know that seat belts, if used properly and at all times, can save hundreds of lives each year. By 'used properly' we mean that both the shoulder and seat belts must be fastened."[3]

Here the speaker adds support by citing the American Automobile Association as a source of information and clarifies what seat belts can do and the meaning of "used properly."

Expert opinion can be either quoted directly or paraphrased. Paraphrasing is an effective method of condensing a long text or clarifying a passage that is too technical for audience members to understand. Sometimes audience members tune out speakers who use long and complex quotations. Restating long quotations in your own words makes the source's words fit the tone of your speech. If you paraphrase, make sure you do not violate the meaning of the original statement.

Certain statements are so well phrased that they could not be stated any better. An example is the forceful and unforgettable statement made by John F. Kennedy in his 1960 presidential inaugural address: "Ask not what your country can do for you. Ask what you can do for your country." Always quote such statements word for word. Misquoting someone can be embarrassing, and even worse, it can destroy your believability. Double-check every quotation for accuracy and source, and never use a quotation out of context.

Expert opinion should meet two essential tests: The person who is cited must be qualified by virtue of his or her skills, training, expertise, recognition, and reputation; and the expert's opinion must be acceptable and believable to your listeners.

The person you cite should be a qualified authority on the subject. For example, an athlete's endorsement of tennis shoes and a movie star's endorsement of cosmetics are fairly believable since they use such products in their work. But when celebrities advertise products completely unrelated to their expertise, their opinion becomes less believable. Avoid using celebrities' names solely because they are well known. The best testimony comes from a person whose expertise is related to the topic and who is recognized by your listeners.

For maximum believability, expert opinion should also come from objective sources. The objectivity and neutrality of authorities is particularly important when your subject is controversial. For example, in trying to persuade an audience that today's automobiles are safer than those of a decade ago, it is more convincing to quote the American Automobile Association or the National Safety Council than the president of an automotive company. Listeners tend to be suspicious of opinions from a biased or self-interested source.

USING EXPERT OPINION: SOME TIPS

- Use expert opinion when you need additional supporting or clarifying information for what you say.
- Cite sources completely and accurately.
- Paraphrase long and difficult quotations in your own words.
- Keep quotations short, accurate, and relevant to what you are saying.
- Use recognized, qualified, unbiased, and trusted authorities.

Examples

An **example** is a simple, representative incident or model that clarifies a point. Examples are useful when you are presenting complex information to listeners who are unfamiliar with a topic and when you are informing or instructing. Brief examples, illustrations, analogies, and restatements are four kinds of examples that help make things clearer for an audience.

Brief Examples   A **brief example** is a specific instance used to introduce a topic, drive home a point, or create a desired impression. The following brief example was used to introduce a subtopic related to the main topic of map making.

> In fact, the November 15, 1992, special series in the *New York Times* explains, "Maps have always been a means to influence, or distort, people's view of the world."

A series of brief examples can also be used to create a desired impression.

> In fact, the November 15, 1992, special series in the *New York Times* explains, "Maps have always been a means to influence, or distort, people's view of the world." Ask any Native American about the lasting effect of Amerigo Vespucci's depiction of North America as empty land. Modern history pro-

vides another example: The November 15, 1992, *New York Times* indicates, "Old Soviet maps displaced entire cities for military reasons and these towns have had to be shifted by Western map makers as the truth has emerged."

Illustrations An **illustration,** or extended example, is a narrative, case history, or anecdote that is striking and memorable. Illustrations often exemplify concepts, conditions, or circumstances, or they demonstrate the findings that have been obtained through the acceptance of a plan or proposal.

If an example is not fully explained or detailed but refers to a single aspect or event, it is an illustration. Because illustrations go into more detail than brief examples, they are useful in establishing proof. When the earlier examples regarding map making are put together, they form the following illustration.

> There has been no period in history when people of all nations have been more reliant on maps.
>
> In fact, the November 15, 1992, special series in the *New York Times* explains, "Maps have always been a means to influence, or distort, people's view of the world." Ask any Native American about the lasting effect of Amerigo Vespucci's depiction of North America as empty land.
>
> Modern history provides another example: The November 15, 1992, *New York Times* indicates, "Old Soviet maps displaced entire cities for military reasons and these towns have had to be shifted by Western map makers as the truth has emerged."
>
> The Library of Congress Geography and Map Reading Room alone contains a collection of more that four million maps, 54,000 atlases, and 300 globes from around the world.
>
> Despite the prevalence of all types of maps, American youths are geographically illiterate.[4]

An illustration provides depth and explanation to the point a speaker is trying to make. It also gives the information more meaning. An illustration may be either factual or hypothetical. A **factual illustration** tells what has actually happened; a **hypothetical illustration** tells what could or probably would happen given a specific set of circumstances.

A hypothetical illustration, because it is speculation, asks listeners to use their imaginations. Such examples are often short stories that relate to a general principle or concept. One instructor used the following hypothetical example to help her students envision how to use their voices when delivering an emotional speech.

> Imagine that an angry mob has accused your friend of a crime—a serious crime—and that they are going to hang him because they believe he is guilty, even though you know he isn't. Your only chance to save your friend is to persuade the unruly mob that he is innocent.

This hypothetical illustration demonstrates that people who are involved in serious situations must use their voices to make their point. The speech to the mob would have to be vivid, forceful, convincing, and highly emotional.

The use of a hypothetical illustration can be particularly effective when it involves the listeners. The illustration should create a vivid picture in the listeners' minds. The more realistic the situation, the more likely it is that the listeners will become involved. A speaker should always specify whether an illustration is factual or hypothetical.

Analogies   An **analogy** is a comparison of two things that are similar in certain essential characteristics. Analogies explain or prove the unknown by comparing it to the known.

There are two kinds of analogies. A **figurative analogy** draws comparisons between things in different categories. For example, the thermostat, whose workings are understood by most people, is commonly used to explain feedback. The thermostat reacts to the heat produced by the furnace and sends a message back to the furnace; the listener responds to the sender's message and sends a message to the sender. A **literal analogy** compares members of the same category and is a simple comparison. For example, it may compare two universities—Florida State University and University of Southern California, two cities—New York and Milwaukee, or two languages—Spanish and German.

Most speech topics offer many opportunities to use analogies. Generally, figurative analogies make ideas clear and vivid, while literal analogies supply evidence to prove points. Not only are analogies an effective and creative means of proving a point and clarifying information, but they are also efficient because they use fewer words to communicate information.

Restatements   A **restatement** is the expression of the same idea using different words. It may take the form of a summary, synonym, or rephrasing.

Restatement does not provide evidence, but if often has a persuasive effect. A well-planned use of restatement can add clarity, meaning, and dramatic rhythm to a message. Martin Luther King, Jr., in his famous "I Have a Dream" speech, used both repetition and restatement to make his point. (See Figure 8.5).

Figure 8.5:

Martin Luther King, Jr. civil rights leader in the 1960s and outstanding speaker, used repetition and restatement of the phrase "I have a dream" to make his point memorable and persuasive.

Reprinted by arrangement with The Heirs to the Estate of Martin Luther King, Jr., c/o Joan Daves Agency as agent for the proprietor. Copyright © 1963 by Martin Luther King, Jr., copyright renewed 1991 by Coretta Scott King.

Bob Adelman/Magnum Photos

> I say to you today, my friends, so even though we face the difficulties of today and tomorrow, I still have a dream. It is a dream deeply rooted in the American dream.
>
> I have a dream that one day this nation will rise up and live out the true meaning of its creed, "We hold these truths to be self-evident, that all men are created equal."
>
> I have a dream that one day on the red hills of Georgia the sons of former slaves and sons of former slave owners will be able to sit down together at the table of brotherhood . . . [5]

King repeated the phrase "I have a dream that one day" six times in the course of his speech, and each time he made the same point by using a different example to support the conclusion that one day all people will be treated equally.

Another example of restatement follows:

> During the last part of the season, our football team was inconsistent and often scored fewer points than our opponents. Putting it another way, our defense did not hold up through the last half of the season as well as our offense. In still a different sense, this means that if we are going to win the national championship, we must work together as a team and strengthen our weak areas.

The example above shows how restatement can be used to present an idea from several different perspectives.

USING EXAMPLES: SOME TIPS

- Use factual examples to add authenticity to your presentation. A factual example builds on the basic information presented and adds believability to both you and your speech.
- Use examples that are realistic and relate directly to your discussion. If you try to generalize from unusual or rare situations, you risk undermining believability.
- Use examples that are authentic, accurate, and verifiable. Always give credit to the source of an example so that your listeners can verify it.

Definitions

You must define all unfamiliar words and concepts, especially technical terms, if you want your listeners to understand and accept your speech. Nothing is more bothersome to listeners than a speaker who uses terminology they do not understand. In most cases, it is better to offer too much explanation than too little. On the other hand, you do not want to patronize your audience by explaining the obvious. You can use several different kinds of definitions to keep your audience's attention.

A **logical definition,** the most common form used by speakers, usually contains two parts: a term's dictionary definition and the characteristics that distinguish the term from other members of the same category. For example,

> *Sociology* is defined as an academic field of study—the science of society, social institutions, and social relationships. Its focus of study is the origin, development, organization, and function of human society.

The above definition states what sociology is and how it differs from other academic fields, such as communication, anthropology, biology, and chemistry.

An **operational definition** explains how an object or concept works, gives the steps that make up a process, or states how conceptual terms are measured.

> *Selective perception* is the choosing of stimuli we want to perceive and the ignoring of stimuli we do not want to perceive. The *mean* is the result of adding all the scores in a set of scores and dividing by the number of scores in the set.

> Sex is defined as the biological differences between males and females, whereas gender is defined as masculine and feminine traits displayed by either males or females. Thus, gender is characterized by traits a person displays and not by biological differences.

> A *communicative apprehensive* person is defined as a person who scores 90 or above on the Personal Report of Communication Apprehension Test.

A **definition by example** clarifies a term not by describing it or giving its meaning, but by mentioning or showing an example of it.

> When I speak about *large universities,* I mean institutions such as the Universities of Wisconsin, Southern California, or Minnesota, each of which has an enrollment of over thirty thousand students.

> A *scissors kick* is different from other swimming kicks in that you extend both legs and open sideways—then you cross and recross them, like scissors, alternating top leg. Here is what it looks like. (The speaker shows a diagram displaying the scissors kick.

USING DEFINITIONS: SOME TIPS

- Define a term or concept whenever you suspect your audience may not understand what you mean or that multiple interpretations are possible.
- Keep definitions short and to the point. Do not make your explanation more complex than necessary.
- Use clear and concise language that your audience can easily understand. Make your definitions come alive for your audience by providing examples.

Statistics

Numerical data that show relationships between and among phenomena or that summarize and interpret many examples are known as **statistics**. Every day we are confronted with numerical analyses. We read, for example, that the earth's population is over 5 billion; the gross national product increased by one-tenth of 1 percent; in the past two years, the enrollment at the university declined from 23,500 to 22,100; or 17 percent of all married couples prefer to have 1.7 children. Although statistics can point out some interesting information, they can be difficult to interpret.

Statistics enable speakers to summarize a large amount of data rapidly, to analyze specific occurrences or instances, to isolate trends, and to calculate probabilities of future events. They are used to clarify and support a speaker's position. For example, consider these two statements.

> Many women are growing increasingly dissatisfied with men.
> In 1970 two-thirds of the 3,000 women surveyed by the Roper organization, as reported on the AP wire service, indicated that "most men are basically kind, gentle, and thoughtful." Today, only one-half of 3,000 women surveyed agreed—a difference of almost 17 percent. (*Lincoln Journal Star,* 1993)

The first statement does not tell us what is meant by "many." The vagueness of the statement makes it weak and difficult to defend. The second statement, because it cites specific numbers, gives listeners a clearer picture of the situation and is thus more convincing. In addition, the second statement uses a source to add credence to the data.

Statistics can be used to emphasize the seriousness or magnitude of a particular issue, as seen in the following example:

Figure 8.6:

Statistics, if not too complex, can help point out interesting information about things around us. But they can also be boring and difficult to interpret if not used correctly.

Bruce Ayres/Tony Stone Images

The November 8, 1993, issue of *U. S. News & World Report* in its lead article "Violence in schools: When killers come to class" states that 64 percent of urban principals said violence has increased in their schools in the past five years; so did 54 percent of suburban principals and 43 percent of those in rural areas.[6]

Statistics can also be informative:

Dr. Roger Grooters, Director of Academic Programs at the University of Nebraska Athletic Department in an August 1993 report states:

Out of 1.5 million eligible high school athletes, only one in one hundred will recieve an athletic scholarship. Only one in 12,000 make it to a professional sport. The odds of a high school athlete are better at becoming a doctor or an attorney professional athlete. Of the more than one million young men who play high school and college football every year, fewer than 200 rookies make an NFL roster. This information indicates a strong need for the college bound student athlete to consider academics and career to ensure future success.[7]

Statistical Measure Statistics can be used in many ways to support or clarify your position on a given subject, but it is important to use them correctly. To use and understand statistical data accurately, you should know some basic statistical terminology. The four most commonly cited statistics are the mean, the median, the mode, and the range.

The **mean,** often referred to as the average, is an arithmetic value calculated by adding all the scores in a set of scores and dividing by the number of scores in the set. In the sample data provided in Table 8.1, to find the mean of the scores of all the students in group A, add their scores and divide the total (744) by the number of students in the group (9). The mean is 744 divided by 9 = 82.67. The mean for group B is calculated the same way: 811 divided by 10 = 81.10.

The **median** is the middle value in a series; that is, half the values are above it and half below it. In group A in Table 8.1, four scores are higher than 83 (90, 88, 86, 85) and four scores are lower (79, 79, 79, 75). Thus in group A the median is 83. In group B it is 79.5. If the number of scores is even, place all scores in an ordered array from lowest to highest, or vice versa. Assuming the distribution contains an odd number, as in Group B, order the numbers from lowest to highest or vice versa, total the number of scores in the distribution, add one, and divide by 2, thus, (n + 1)/2. For Group B the median is 79.5.

The **mode** is the most frequent value in a series of numbers. In Table 8.1 the most frequently received score in Group A is 79 (earned by three students), so 79 is the mode. The mode in group B is 87.

The **range** is the lowest to the highest or the highest to the lowest numbers in a series of numbers. In Table 8.1 the range for group A is 75 to 90 or 90 to 75 and for group B, 72 to 95 or 95 to 72.

Choosing the Best Statistics Knowing a set of data's mean, median, mode, and range is not enough. You must also know which data best repre-

Table 8.1

Group A Test Scores	Group B Test Scores
90	95
88	87
86	87
85	85
83	80
79	79
79	77
79	75
75	74
	72
774	811

	A	B
Mean (total divided by number in set)	82.67	81.10
Median (middle score)	83	79.5
Mode (most frequent score)	79	87
Range (highest to lowest number)	75 to 90 (90 to 75)	72 to 95 (95 to 72)

sent each group's scores. When comparing the two sets of scores, which data provide a better analysis? The answers to these two questions depend on the point you are trying to make and what you wish to compare. Selecting the most appropriate statistic is a matter of interpretation and emphasis, and it is here that statistics can be misleading.

Darrell Huff, in his book *How to Lie With Statistics,* illustrates how numbers can be manipulated and distorted.[8] The classic notion that "Numbers don't lie" has to be taken in the context of how they are used. Suppose, for example, the mean (average) salary of professional football players is $160,000.[9] Assuming that this figure is correct, does it reflect the actual salaries that football players make? Yes, to a degree it does, but let's look at the data from another perspective.

Suppose that the median salary of a professional football player is $105,000, that is, half the players make more and half make less than $105,000 a year. The mode, the most frequent salary, is $90,000, and the range of all football players' salaries runs from a low of $45,000 to a high of $1.5 million. Looking at all these data, we can see that there is a $70,000 difference between the average and the most frequently paid salary, and almost $1.5 million separates the lowest-paid player from the highest-paid.

How would a speaker use these statistics? That depends on the purpose of the speech. To report on professional football players' salaries, a speaker might use the mean or, looking at only a few superstars, might present calculations to show that some players earn as much as several thousand dollars an hour. But no single statistic by itself represents the true picture of what professional football players are paid. To present a more accurate picture, the speaker should cite several statistics. Listeners should ask questions about statistical data, especially when they are not given all the figures they need to form a clear and accurate interpretation of the actual situation.

Making the Most of Statistics   Following five simple guidelines will help you make the most of the statistics you've gathered.

1. MAKE SURE THAT THE STATISTICS YOU PRESENT IN YOUR SPEECH ARE FROM RELIABLE AND NEUTRAL SOURCES. The motives of the source of any statistics must be carefully assessed. For example, if you heard two sets of data on fuel economy per gallon of gasoline—one prepared by the Chrysler Corporation and the other by the Environmental Protection Agency—which would you expect to be more reliable? Although the Chrysler Corporation's data may be perfectly accurate, listeners would tend to believe that their data are biased. It would be to a speaker's advantage, therefore, to use the more neutral source, in this case, the Environmental Protection Agency.

   There are many times, however, when it may be difficult to identify the most neutral source. For example, whose statistics would you use if you wished to inform your audience about the United States' strength in nuclear weapons—the Department of Defense or the Americans for Peace? Here the choice is debatable unless you intend to take a position on the issue. Remember, statistics can be used in many different ways and can thus influence interpretations and outcomes.

2. TAKE TIME TO EXPLAIN THE STATISTICS YOU ARE USING. Interpret and relate your statistics to your listeners. Consider the following use of statistics.

   > The diameter of the sun is about 865,000 miles, about 109 times the diameter of the earth. Because the sun is about 93 million miles from the earth, it does not appear larger than the moon. But the sun's diameter is 400 times as large as that of the moon. The sun is also almost 400 times farther from the earth than is the moon.
   >
   > If the sun were the size of a skyscraper, the earth would be the size of a person. The moon would be the size of a cocker spaniel standing next to the person.[10]

   This explanation makes statistics meaningful by clearly comparing the size and distance of the sun and the moon. When using data that listeners may have difficulty understanding or visualizing, try to provide the appropriate comparisons in order to make the data more meaningful.

3. USE STATISTICS SPARINGLY. Statistics are difficult to comprehend, so if you use too many, you run a high risk of boring or confusing your audience. Use statistics only when necessary, and make sure they are easy to understand. The following example would be difficult for even the most attentive listener to comprehend.

> If my new proposal is accepted, we will have at least a 20 percent increase in production efficiency and at least a 50-cent-per-unit cost reduction, according to our 1999 projections. This, I might add, means a 10 percent, or minimum 35-cent-per-unit, cost reduction over the next five to six years. What this all adds up to is a 15 percent increase over this time period and an eventual profit of $110,000 per year. That will also give us a 6 percent depreciation allowance.

It would be much easier to understand if the data were presented as follows:

> The new proposal, if accepted, will increase production efficiency by 20 percent or 50 cents per unit, according to our 1999 projections. This would provide a minimum cost reduction of 35 cents per unit over the next five to six years and a $110,000 per year profit for a 15 percent increase over the time period.

4. ROUND OFF LARGE NUMBERS WHEN POSSIBLE. Listeners understand and remember figures better when they are not complicated. For example, it is easier to remember 10,000 than 9,987. While it's true that the Statue of Liberty's torch rises 305 feet and 1 inch, or 92.99 meters, above the base of the pedestal, it is less complicated to say that the torch rises 305 feet or 93 meters. Unless an exact figure is needed, round off most statistics to the nearest whole number.

5. USE VISUAL AIDS TO PRESENT STATISTICAL INFORMATION, IF APPROPRIATE AND POSSIBLE. Using visual aids saves explanation time and also makes statistics easier to understand. Compare the clarity of the following paragraph with Table 8.2. Note how all the words in the verbal presentation are summed up in a simple four-column display.

> The first quarter net sales were $44,000, which created a net earning of $2,900, thus producing a 10 cent dividend per share. The second quarter

Table 8.2

Dividends			
	Net Sales	**Net Earnings**	**Dividends Per Share**
1st quarter	$44,000	$2,900	$0.10
2nd quarter	50,000	3,500	0.15
3rd quarter	55,000	4,500	0.20
4th quarter	56,700	5,700	0.22
Total	$205,700	$15,900	$0.67

net sales were $50,000, leading to a net earning of $3,500 for a 15 cent dividend per share. The third quarter net sales of $55,000 created a net earning of $4,500 for a 20 cent dividend per share. And the fourth quarter net sales of $56,700 produced a net earning of $5,000, or a 22 cent dividend per share. The total net sales were $205,700, with a total net earning of $15,900 paying a total dividend per share of 67 cents.

Figure 8.7 presents another example of how complex data can be summarized and presented in an interesting way. Note how the graphic makes it much easier for the viewer to understand the comparisons of salaries. (Chapter 10 discusses in more detail the use of visual aids in a speech presentation.)

Visualizing Statistical Data

Figure 8.7:

Artwork can help summarize complex data and make it come alive and interesting to your audience.

USING STATISTICS: SOME TIPS

- Make sure that the statistics you use come from reliable and neutral sources.
- Take the time to explain the statistics you are using to your listeners.

- Use statistics sparingly.
- Display statistics visually whenever possible in order to save explanation time.

SUMMARY

Gathering information plays an essential role in the speech development process. Many resources are available to help you locate information. Begin with yourself. Even if you are not an expert on your topic, you probably have some knowledge of it. If your personal experiences do not suffice, you can obtain information from others and from the library.

Interviews can provide information that is more in-depth and up-to-date than that found in newspapers or magazine articles, information that is not covered in published materials, and the views of experts or others who have firsthand knowledge of the topic. An *interview* is a carefully planned, person-to-person question-and-answer session aimed at gathering information. The objective of any interview should be high *reliability* (the extent to which the same information could be obtained from the same interviewee) and high *validity* (the extent to which both the interviewer and interviewee accomplish the purpose of the interview).

Determine the specific purpose of your interview and then select the interviewees who will be most able to help you meet your purpose. To obtain the most accurate recall, record the interview either by taking notes or by using a tape recorder.

Match the type of questions you ask to the kind of information you desire. *Open questions* encourage the interviewee to talk. *Closed questions* limit or restrict the interviewee's response. The *bipolar question* (true-false, yes-no) is an extreme form of closed question that allows no freedom of response.

Primary questions introduce new topics. *Secondary* or probing questions encourage the interviewee to expand his or her answers or further explain a response. *Neutral questions* avoid implying an expected response. *Leading questions* encourage the interviewee to respond the way an interviewer wants him or her to respond. An interviewer should phrase questions clearly by avoiding wordiness, vagueness, and unnecessary complexity.

An interview has three identifiable segments: the opening, the body, and the closing. An informal information gathering session is usually organized as a *nonscheduled interview,* in which the interviewer follows a central objective or list of possible topics and subtopics, or as a *moderately scheduled interview,* in which the interviewer uses a prepared list of questions or topics and related secondary questions.

There are five principal sources of information in the library: yourself, the librarian, computer-assisted search, the card catalog, and the reference department. You should have a working knowledge of the library and know what you want to find before you begin your search. Trained librarians are available to help you find sources of information and locate the material. The card catalog, an alphabetical index to all the books in the library, is designed to be a quick and simple means of locating materials. Most card catalogs list books by author's last name, by title, and by subject. Periodicals are also listed by title or by name of issuing organization. Another means for locating library materials is the computer search. Relatively new, computer searches allow access to library indexes through home or campus computers. The reference department contains dictionaries, biographical aids, encyclopedias, yearbooks, atlases, indexes, and guides to periodical literature.

To simplify your research process, know what you want to find, begin early, record citations accurately and completely, and take clear notes of the information.

Although a speaker's believability and delivery are critically important to the success of a speech, how effectively he or she uses research to support and clarify main points usually makes the difference between a good speech and a poor one. The four basic kinds of supporting and clarifying materials used in speeches are expert opinion, examples, definitions, and statistics.

Expert opinion is the opinions or conclusions of witnesses or recognized authorities. Using expert opinion benefits student speakers who have not yet established themselves as experts on the topics they present. When presenting expert opinion, use short quotations, quote and paraphrase accurately, and use qualified and unbiased sources.

Examples are the most useful form of supporting and clarifying material. There are four kinds: the *brief example,* a specific instance used to introduce a new topic, drive home a point, or create a desired impression; the *illustration,* an extended *factual* or *hypothetical* example that is striking and memorable; the *analogy,* a *figurative* or *literal* comparison of two things that are similar in certain essential characteristics; and the *restatement,* an expression of the same idea using different words. When presenting examples, use factual cases whenever possible, relate them to the topic you are discussing, make them realistic and believable, provide verifiable sources, and give proper credit to the originator.

Speakers who are sensitive to their audiences realize the importance of defining unfamiliar terms. There are three basic forms of definitions. The *logical definition,* which is the most common, consists of a term's dictionary definition and a description of how the term differs from other members of the same category. The *operational definition* explains how an object or concept works. The *definition by example* explains terms and concepts through the use of verbal or actual examples. When using definitions, keep them short, use clear and concise language, explain every term that your audience might not understand or could misinterpret, and provide examples to clarify meanings.

Statistics enable speakers to summarize a large amount of data rapidly, to analyze specific occurrences or instances, to isolate trends, and to calculate probabilities of future events. The four most commonly cited statistics are the *mean* (average), *median* (middle value), *mode* (most frequent value), and *range* (lowest to highest numbers or vice versa). Statistics should be accurate, meaningful to your audience, used sparingly, representative of your claims, and taken from a reliable source.

KEY TERMS

Analogy: Comparison of two things that are similar in certain essential characteristics.

Bipolar Question: Question that demands a single-word answer (yes-no, true-false); extreme form of closed question that allows no freedom of expression.

Brief Example: Specific instance that is used to introduce a topic, drive home a point, or create a desired response.

Closed Question: Question that calls for a restricted or short response from the interviewee.

Definition by Example: Clarifying a term not by describing it or giving its meaning, but by describing or showing an example.

Example: Simple, representative incident or model that clarifies a point.

Expert Opinion: Opinions, testimony, or conclusions of witnesses or recognized authorities.

Factual Illustration: Report of something that exists or actually happened.

Figurative Analogy: Comparison of things in different categories.

Hypothetical Illustration: Report of something that could or probably would happen given a specific set of circumstances.

Illustration: Extended example, narrative, case history, or anecdote that is striking and memorable.

Interview: Carefully planned, person-to-person question-and-answer session aimed at gathering information.

Leading Question: Question that explicitly or implicitly guides the interviewee to an expected or desired response.

Literal Analogy: Comparison of members of the same category.

Logical Definition: Definition consisting of a term's dictionary definition and the characteristics that distinguish the term from other members of the same category.

Mean: Arithmetic value, often referred to as the average, that is the sum of all the values in a set divided by the number of values in the set.

Median: The middle value in a series of numbers, with half the values above it and half below it.

Mode: The most frequent value in a series of numbers.

Moderately Scheduled Interview: Interview format in which the interviewer follows a list of basic questions or topics and possible probes under each question or topic.

Neutral Question: Question that avoids implying an expected or desired response.

Nonscheduled Interview: Interview format in which the interviewer follows a central objective or a list of possible topics and subtopics, with no formalized order of questions and no anticipated responses.

Open Question: Question that evokes a response of more than just a few words.

Operational Definition: Definition that explains how an object or concept works or lists the steps that make up a process.

Primary Question: Question that introduces a new topic or a new area within a topic.

Range: The lowest to highest numbers, or vice versa, in a series of numbers.

Reliability: In relation to an interview, the extent to which the same information could be obtained from the same interviewee.

Restatement: Expression of the same idea using different words.

Secondary or Probing Question: Question used to encourage the interviewee to expand on replies that may have been incomplete, unresponsive, unclear, or inaccurate.

Statistics: Numerical data that show relationships, summarize, or interpret many instances.

Validity: In relation to an interview, extent to which both the interviewer and the interviewee accomplish the purpose of the interview.

DISCUSSION STARTERS

1. What advice would you give to a beginning speech student about gathering information for a speech?
2. Why is it important to examine what you know about a topic before you consult with others or use the library?
3. Why is an interview a particularly productive way of gathering information?
4. What advice would you give a person who has never conducted an interview? What would he or she need to know to be an effective interviewer?
5. You have just entered the library to research your speech topic, gun control. You want to learn as much as possible about this subject. Where would you begin?
6. How can the reference department in a library help a speaker to gather materials for a speech?
7. What advice would you give to a beginning speaker about using supporting and clarifying materials in a speech?

8. On what basis should you judge the effectiveness of a source of information in supporting a particular point of view?

9. If you were comparing the salaries of teachers, doctors, baseball players, and lawyers, which would provide the best comparisons—medians, modes, or means? Explain.

10. As a receiver of information, what cautions should you take when you hear someone using statistics?

NOTES

1. C. Steward and W. B. Cash, *Interviewing: Principles and Practices*, 7th ed. (Dubuque, Iowa: Brown, 1994):94–96 and 6th ed. (1991):85.

2. Information contained in this section was reviewed by Eva Sartori and Scott Stebeman of the University of Nebraska library staff.

3. *Buckle Up* (American Automobile Association, 1985).

4. Taken from a speech by Maran Schulte, a University of Nebraska student, with permission.

5. From "I Have a Dream" by Martin Luther King, Jr., Copyright 1963. Reprinted by permission of Joan Daves.

6. Thomas Toch, Ted Gest, and Monika Guttman,"Violence in Schools: When Killers Come to Class," *U.S. News & World Report*, 8 November 1993, 32.

7. Roger Grooters, "A Perspective on High School Athletics," *Patron Newsletter for Residents of School District 145*, August 1993, 1–2.

8. D. Huff, *How to Lie with Statistics* (New York: Norton, 1954).

9. The data are not actual salaries of professional football league players. The numbers were chosen to serve as an example only.

10. *World Book Encyclopedia*, 1984, 780.

APPENDIX: PERIODICAL INDEXES ARRANGED BY SUBJECT

I. General information indexes
   Alternative Press Index
   Magazine Index (reel-to-reel microfilm reader)
   Readers' Guide to Periodical Literature
II. General subject indexes
   A. Humanities, literature and history
      Arts & Humanities Citation Index
      British Humanities Index
      Humanities Index
   B. Social science
      Social Sciences Citation Index
      Social Sciences Index
      PAIS
   C. Science indexes
      General Science Index
      Science Citation Index
III. Specific subject indexes
IV. Agriculture and natural resources
   Bibliography of Agriculture

Biological & Agricultural Index
Selected Water Resources Abstracts
World Agriculture
Economics & Rural Sociology Abstracts

A. Anthropology
   Abstracts in Anthropology
   Anthropological Index
   Current Periodicals
   Anthropological Literature

B. Architecture
   Architectural Periodicals
   Index
   Art Index
   Avery Index to Periodicals

C. Art
   Art Index

D. Astronomy
   General Science Index
   Science Citation Index

E. Biology and life sciences
   Biological Abstracts
   Biological and Agricultural Index
   Ecology Abstracts
   Wildlife Review

F. Book review
   Book Review Digest
   Book Review Index
   Combined Retrospective
   Index to Book Reviews in: Humanities
      Journals, 1802–1974
   Scholarly Journals, 1886–1974
   An Index to Book
   Reviews in the Humanities

G. Business, economics, and
      statistics
   American Statistics Index
   Business Perodicals Index
   Business Index
   Index of Economic Articles
   Index to International Statistics
   Predicasts F & S Index: Europe
   Predicasts F & S Index: International
   Predicasts F & S Index: United States
   Statistical Theory & Method Abstracts
   Statistical Reference Index
   The Wall Street Journal Index
   Work Related Abstracts

V. Chemistry
   Chemical Abstracts

A. Computer
   ACM Guide to Computing Literature
   Computer and Control Abstracts
   Computer & Information Systems
      Abstracts
   Journal
   General Science Index

B. Criminal justice
   Criminal Justice
   Periodical Index
   Criminology & Penology Abstracts
   Social Sciences Index

C. Dissertations
   Comprehensive Dissertation Index
   Dissertaton Abstracts International

D. Education
   Business Education Index
   Current Index to Journals in Education
      (CIJE)
   Education Index
   Educational Administration
   Abstracts
   ERIC Indexes: see
   Current Index to Journals in Education
      and Resources in Education
   Exceptional Child
   Education Resources
   Multicultural Education
   Abstracts
   Resources in Education
   School Organization & Management Ab
      stracts

E. Engineering
   Applied Science and Technology
      Abstracts
   Engineering Index
   Ergonomics Abstracts

F. Film studies and media broadcasting
   Film Literature Index
   Magazine Index (reel-to-reel mircrofilm
      reader)
   Reader's Guide to Perodical Literature
      Topicator

G. Geography
   Geographical Abstracts:

Annual Index:
vol. 1, index to parts A, B, E, G—
   physical geography
vol. 2, index to parts C, D, F—
   social/economic geography
Social Services Citation Index
H. Geology
General Science Index
Science Citation Index
I. Government documents
American Statistics Index
CIS Annual: Index & Abstracts
*Cumulative Subject Index to the
   Monthly*
*Catalog of U.S. Government
   Publications: 1895–1899*
1900–1971
*Cumulative Title Index to United States
   Public Documents, 1789–1976*
Government Documents
Rollfiche Reader (reel-to-reel microfilm
   reader)
Index to U.S. Government Periodicals
*Monthly Catalog of U.S. Government
   Publications*
PAIS
J. Health, physical education,
   recreation, ad dance
*Behavior Medicine
Abstracts*
Index Medicus
Physical Education Index
Physical Fitness/Sports Medicine
Sports Bibliography
K. History
America: History and Life
Arts & Humanities Citation Index
Historical Abstracts
Humanities Index
L. Journalism
Communication Abstracts
PAIS
M. Linguistics, language, and literature
Arts & Humanities Citation Index
British Humanities Index
Essay and General Literature Index
Humanities Index

*Linguistics and Language Behavior
   Abstracts (LLBA)*
MLA Bibliography
N. Mathematics
General Science Index
Mathematical Review
Science Citation Index
O. Medicine, nursing, and hospital
Behavior Medicine Abstracts
*Cumulative Index to Nursing & Allied
   Health Literature*
Health Literature Index
Index Medicus
International Nursing Index
*Nutrition Abstracts & Reviews, Series A:
   Human & Experimental*
P. Muszi
Music Article Guide
Music Index
RILM Abstracts of Music Literature
Q. Newspaper
Chicago Tribune
Christian Science Monitor
Los Angeles Times
New York Times
Newsbank
The Times Index of London: 1790–1939
1940–present
R. Philosophy
Arts & Humanities Citation Index
British Humanities Index
Humanities Index
Philosopher's Index
S. Physics
Physics Abstracts
T. Political science
CIS Annual: Index & Abstract
*Combined Retrospective Index to
   Journals in Political Science
   1886–1974*
*International Bibliography of Political
   Science*
International Political Science Abstracts
PAIS
*Sage Public
Administration Abstracts*
Social Sciences Citation Index

U.S. Political Science Documents
U. Psychology
    *Child Development
    Abstracts & Bibliography
    Index to Perodical
    Literature on Aging
    Psychological Abstracts
    Psychological Documents
    Social Sciences Citation Index
    Social Sciences Index
    Women's Studies Abstracts*
V. Religion and theology
    *Religion Index One: Periodicals
    Religious and Theological
    Abstracts*
W. Sociology and social work
    Gerontological Abstracts

*Inventory of Marriage & Family Literature
Sage Race Relations Abstracts
Social Sciences Index
Social Work Research & Abstracts
Sociological Abstracts
Urban Affairs Abstracts
Women's Studies Abstracts*
X. United Nations
    United Nations Documents Index: vol.
       (1950)-vol. 24 (1973)
    Undex (UN Documents Index), series
       A, B, C (1970–1978)
    *Undoc (Current Index, UN Documents
    Index)*, 1 (1979 to the present)
    *U.N. Index to Proceedings of the General
    Assembly*
    (1950 to the present)

Chapter 9

Organizing and Outlining

LEARNING OBJECTIVES

After studying this chapter, you should be able to:

1. Identify the purposes and contents of the three main parts of a speech.

2. Select and appropriately state the main points of a speech.

3. Assess six patterns of organization and choose the one that best suits a speech's topic and purpose.

4. Use transitions, signposts, and internal summaries to connect the thoughts in a speech.

5. Compose an effective introduction and an effective conclusion for a speech.

6. Prepare a complete sequence of preliminary, full-content, and presentational outlines for a speech.

Turner, the recreational director for his dorm, is responsible for planning this year's spring break trip. He knows from his previous spring break trips that the key to a successful spring break is organization. Turner has to plan for over 100 students in terms of location, transportation, lodging, and many other miscellaneous considerations.

Turner, as the responsible person, will probably spend most of his time planning and organizing the trip. Turner also knows from his past experiences the importance of what he has to do to ensure a successful trip. There are very few things that we do that don't require some organization and planning. Even an activity such as such as baking a cake requires organization—if you want the cake to taste good, that is. The first step is to choose a recipe. This step is similar to selecting a topic for a speech. The second step is to assemble all the ingredients. This corresponds to a speaker's research. The third step is to combine the ingredients to make the batter in the order and manner prescribed by the recipe. If you randomly put ingredients in a cake pan and bake them, your chances of creating a delicious cake diminish dramatically. Correspondingly, if you randomly combine pieces of information, your chances of creating a meaningful and effective speech diminish dramatically. So, whether it is planning a fund drive, baking a cake, or developing a speech, success is more likely if you are organized.

We have discussed selecting a topic, stating the general purpose, specific purpose, and thesis, analyzing the audience, and gathering information. These are all crucial steps in the speech making process. But for a speech to make sense, it must be organized. In this chapter we will examine how to bring all the parts of your speech together through organizing and outlining (see Figure 9.1).

Figure 9.1:

Organizing. The thought and time you put into finding the most effective organization for your presentation will result in a speech that is interesting and that makes sense to your audience.

David R. Frazier/Photolibrary

ORGANIZING YOUR SPEECH

Organizing is the arranging of ideas or parts into a systematic and meaningful whole. Once you have thoroughly researched your topic, you can ease your writing task through careful organization. All speeches are organized into three main parts: introduction, body, and conclusion. At this point in your speech development, it is assumed you have determined your general and specific purposes and have begun to think about your thesis statement, which should help guide you in the organizing process. Since the body is the main part of any speech, we will examine it first.

Body

The **body** is the main section (the content) of a speech that fulfills the speaker's general and specific purposes as well as the thesis. To ensure that the body of your speech is well organized, your content must be divided into main points that are thoughtfully selected and stated, limited in number, and carefully ordered, connected, and supported.

Selecting and Stating Your Main Points   The principal subdivisions of your speech, or **main points,** are critical to the achievement of your thesis statement. Assume that the specific purpose of your speech is to inform your audience about the most significant causes of automobile accidents in the United States. To determine the main points as well as help to finalize your thesis, ask yourself three questions:

What are the causes of auto accidents?

Which causes contribute to the most significant accidents?

How is *significant* defined?

By asking these questions, assuming you have thoroughly researched your subject, you can begin to determine the main points of your speech. The following is a list of possibilities.

Specific Purpose: To inform my audience of the three major causes of auto accidents in the United States.

Main Points:
1. Manufacturing defects in automobiles are a significant cause.
2. Driving too fast for conditions is a significant cause.
3. Driving under the influence of alcohol is a significant cause.

These three main points, or causes, form the basic structure of the body of the speech. The main points are derived from the research on the causes of auto accidents. In the above example, the research indicated that there were three causes that contribute significantly to auto accidents. Each significant cause is an additional main point; the number found is the number of causes stated in the specific purpose and thesis. Thus, the specific purpose and thesis for the above example would be:

*Specific
Purpose:*   To inform the audience of the three major causes of auto accidents in the United States.

Thesis: Manufacturing defects, driving too fast, and alcohol are the major causes of auto accidents in the United States.

Relating the Main Points to Your Specific Purpose and Thesis
The main points of a speech usually relate to the general purpose and ultimately aid in specifying the specific purpose, thesis, and main points. As discussed in Chapter 7, the specific purpose and thesis statements should be carefully developed and written. For example, Nicki Schneider, a first-year student, stated her specific purpose as follows: "To inform the audience of the effects of speical interest groups on drinking and driving legislation." Nicki's thesis statement was "MADD (Mothers Against Drunk Drivers) is a drinking and driving awareness organization that has influenced our society, as evidenced through the organization's purpose (history), activities (functions), and effects (influences) on legislation." Nicki's purpose and thesis establish three main points: the purpose, activities, and impact of MADD. The speech would be organized as in the following example:

*Specific
Purpose:*   To inform the audience about the purpose, activities, and impact of MADD.

Thesis: MADD (Mothers Against Drunk Drivers) is a drinking and driving awareness organization that has influenced our society, as evidenced through the organization's purpose (history), activities (functions), and effects (influences) on legislation

Main Points: 1. MADD is an organization founded as a voice for victims of drunk driving accidents.
2. MADD is an organization with goals and activities that increase public awareness related to drinking and driving.
3. MADD has had a positive influence on legislation related to drinking and driving laws.

Let's start from another perspective. Assume you have been assigned to give a speech that will persuade your audience to adopt a particular point of view. From your research on computers and your belief that they are making our society impersonal, you decide to discuss the harmful effect computers have on interpersonal relationships. The main points for this speech do not evolve as readily as they did in the previous examples, but as you begin to think about and research your topic, you will also begin to refine your specific purpose. First, state your general purpose.

*General
Purpose:*   To persuade my audience that computers can be harmful to interpersonal relationships.

At this point you should ask the question "Why are computers harmful to interpersonal relationships?" As you generate answers, you begin to determine the main points of your speech. You conclude that two key reasons support your view: Computers are mere machines without the ability to react on their own, and computers limit the amount of personal contact people have with each other. At this point you should refine your specific purpose and state your thesis to match your main points.

Specific Purpose: To persuade my audience that there are two reasons why computers can be harmful to interpersonal relationship development.

Thesis: Computers are harmful to interpersonal relationship development because they are machines and because they limit contact with others.

Main Points:
1. Computers are harmful because they are machines that do not react on their own.
2. Computers are harmful because they limit personal contact with others.

Stating Your Main Points Carefully   Main points, like the specific purpose and thesis, should be carefully developed and written. They should also be specific, vivid, relevant, and parallel in structure.

BE SPECIFIC   The more specific the main points, the less confusion they will create and the more meaningful they will be to an audience. Each main point in a speech should be independent of the others and simple to understand. Compare the following:

Ineffective:
1. Nuclear power is the most efficient fuel in our society, but it has been historically misunderstood by most people.

Effective:
1. Nuclear power is the most efficient fuel in our society.
2. Nuclear power has been historically misunderstood by most people.

As you can see, the first example contains two ideas in one point, which makes it too complicated. The second example divides the two ideas into two separate points, thus making the main points easier to follow and understand.

BE VIVID   The more vivid the main points, the more likely they are to create interest. The main points should be thought provokers and attention grabbers that stand out from the supporting materials. Vivid phrasing should be realistic, not overstated, and appropriate to the ethical standards of the occasion. In the two examples that follow the first one is more vivid.

The proposed federal regulation regarding birth control for anyone under 18 would have a devastating effect on teenagers' lives!

The proposed federal regulation requiring family planning clinics that receive federal funds to notify parents of anyone under the age of 18 who wishes to use birth control devices would have a devastating effect on teenagers.

SHOW RELEVANCE   Main points that are relevant to the audience's immediate interests encourage greater involvement and empathy. For instance, instead of saying "air pollution has reached high levels," say "air pollution in our city has reached high levels." Using direct references to the audience whenever possible increases the link between you, what you are saying, and your audience. Audience members like to know how the speaker's subject relates to them and why they should listen (refer to Figure 9.2).

CREATE PARALLEL STRUCTURE   Main points should be parallel in structure, meaning that the same grammatical pattern and similar wording should be used when possible. For example:

Not Parallel:
1. Child pornography has been a serious problem in our community.
2. Our community is experiencing increased amounts of child pornography.
3. Child abuse has increased because of the pornography in our community.

Parallel:
1. Child pornography has been a serious problem in our community.
2. Child pornography has increased in our community.
3. Child pornography has caused an increase in child abuse in our community.

A consistent pattern makes material easier to work from and remember. Audiences usually have only one opportunity to hear a speech. Therefore, anything you can do to make the main points stand out from the rest of the content is to your benefit. In addition, the speaker relates to the audience by consistently using "our community" in each of the three main points.

Figure 9.2:

Relating to the audience. Using direction references to the audience helps link the audience to the speaker. It is important that audience members feel that the subject is relevant to them.

David R. Frazier/Photolibrary

Limiting the Number of Your Main Points   The number of main points in your speech will depend on at least three considerations:

1. The time available to deliver the speech
2. The content to be covered in the speech, especially the amount and complexity of the supporting materials required for each point
3. The amount of information that your audience can reasonably comprehend and remember from one speech

The time available for most classroom speech assignments is limited by practical considerations. As a result, most classroom speeches have no more than five main points, and the majority have two or three.

Try to balance the amount of time that you devote to each main point. For example, if you are assigned a five- to seven-minute speech, plan to allow about two minutes for the introduction and conclusion, with the remaining time equally distributed among the main points. Of course, this is just a guideline. It isn't always possible to balance the main points exactly, nor should you. The nature of some speech topics requires that some main points be emphasized more than others.

An audience should be able to sort out and recall each main point. This recall is impossible if there are too many points. Common sense tells us that three points are easier to remember than five or more. Thus, as a speaker, you must set reasonable expectations for both your listeners and yourself. If you have too many main points and a limited amount of time, you will be unable to develop each point thoroughly enough to make it clear, convincing, and memorable.

Ordering Your Main Points   Once you've identified your main points, you must decide their order of presentation. This ordering takes serious analysis, for the order determines your speech's structure and strategy. The most effective order of presentation depends on the topic, the purpose, and the audience. One of six basic patterns of presentation is used in most speeches: time-sequence, spatial, topical, problem-solution, cause-effect, or motivated sequence.

TIME-SEQUENCE PATTERN   The **time-sequence (or chronological) pattern** is an order of presentation that begins at a particular point in time and continues either forward or backward. The key is to follow a natural time sequence and avoid jumping haphazardly from one date to another. This pattern is especially useful for tracing the steps in a process, the relationships among a series of events, or the development of ideas. Topics such as the history of photographic technology, the steps in setting up an advertising display, and the development of the computer in today's society lend themselves to the time-sequence pattern. Here is an example of a time sequence that moves forward from a specific period of time.

Main Points: 1. In 1887 softball was developed as an indoor game.

2. In 1895 softball was adapted as an outdoor game.

3. In 1933 softball was sanctioned by the Amateur Softball Association of America.

4. In 1993 softball has become the largest recreational sport in America.

A reverse-order time sequence begins at a specific period of time and works chronologically backward. For example, a speech discussing advertising trends in the auto industry, organized in reverse-order time sequence, could start as follows:

Main Points:
1. In the 1990s advertisements emphasize safety.

2. In the 1980s advertisements emphasized fuel economy.

3. In the 1970s advertisements emphasized how well a car rode.

4. In the 1960s advertisements emphasized the size of the car.

The time-sequence pattern can also be used to explain a process. Such topics as the development of the space industry, how to make wine, how to use CPR in an emergency, and how to water-ski all have specific steps that must be presented in sequence if the result is to be successful.

SPATIAL PATTERN In a **spatial pattern** of presentation, the content of a speech is organized according to relationships in space. This method is especially appropriate for presentations that describe distances, directions, or physical surroundings. For example, a spatial pattern might be used to describe each area in a factory's floor plan, the floor-by-floor plans for a building, or how to get from one location to another by moving from east to west, north to south, center to outside, clockwise, and so on. A spatial pattern describes the relationships among all the main points. Here is an example of a speech's main points organized by spatial pattern.

Main Points:
1. The southeastern part of the country was devasted by Hurricane Andrew.

2. The midwestern part of the country was devasted by flooding.

3. The southwestern part of the country was devasted by wind and fire.

4. The northwestern part of the country was devasted by drought.

Both the time-sequence and the spatial patterns are well-suited for informative speeches.

TOPICAL PATTERN The **topical pattern** is an order of presentation in which the main topic is divided into a series of related subtopics. Each subtopic becomes a main point in the speech, and all main points are joined to form a coherent whole. In this way, the topical pattern is a unifying structure.

The topical pattern is most likely to be used when none of the other patterns of organization can be applied to the topic or purpose of a speech. Topics such as the advantages of running, study habits that can improve your grades, uses of the video camera, and barriers to effective listening can easily be organized using the topical pattern. Here is how the topical pattern could be used to organize a speech about the barriers to effective listening:

Main Points: 1. Language distractions are barriers to effective listening.

2. Factual distractions are barriers to effective listening.

3. Mental distractions are barriers to effective listening.

4. Physical distractions are barriers to effective listening.

When the topical pattern is used correctly, each main point is parallel and related to the others. Because the topical pattern is versatile, it can be adapted to most speech purposes.

PROBLEM-SOLUTION PATTERN   A speech that follows the **problem-solution pattern** is usually divided into two parts: the problem and the suggested solution. The problem is defined as a need, doubt, uncertainty, or difficulty, and the suggested solution remedies or eliminates the need, doubt, uncertainty, or difficulty without creating other problems. A problem-solution approach could be used to address such topics as the lack of a sufficient exercise facility for students, the discovery that the new water treatment plant is not working correctly, the fact that there is no way to be sure that the new crime stopper program will work, or the belief that the university has had a difficult time retaining quality faculty members.

The problem-solution pattern, if used correctly, should do more than just state a problem and a solution; it should help the audience to understand both the problem and the solution and why the solution will work. For example, a speech that advocates a change in the university's policies towards violence might follow this problem-solution pattern.

Problem: 1. The past two semesters have seen a significant increase in violent crimes against students on the campus.

Solution: 2. A volunteer security force must be instituted by students to help protect each other from violent crime on the campus.

The problem-solution pattern usually includes three to five of the following:

1. A *definition* and *description* of the problem, including its symptoms and size

2. A *critical analysis* of the problem, including causes, current actions, and requirements for a solution

3. *Suggestions of possible solutions,* including descriptions of each solution's strengths and weaknesses

4. A *recommendation of the best solution,* including a thorough justification of its superiority over other proposed solutions

5. A *discussion of the best solution put into operation,* including a description of how the plan can be implemented

CAUSE-EFFECT PATTERN   The **cause-effect pattern** is an order of presentation in which the speaker explains the causes of an event, problem, or issue and discusses its consequences. Causes and effects may be presented in two different sequences. A speaker may either describe certain forces or factors and then show the results that follow from them, or describe conditions or events and then point out the forces or factors that caused them.

Consider this example of using the cause-effect pattern to discuss the effects of computers on students' job placement. A speaker might begin by recounting recent developments in computer procedures that have led to a more accurate analysis of students' skills, and then show that as a result, the number of students who have obtained first jobs in their chosen fields has increased dramatically. Or, the speaker might reverse the process and first point out that the number of jobs that students are landing in their chosen fields is the result of more accurate computer analysis of their skills.

Regardless of the exact sequence, a speech organized by cause and effect has two main points—a description of the factors that are the *cause* and a prediction or identification of the subsequent *effect*. Such topics as eating disorders in young adults, television violence, heart disease, and new approaches to improving memory all lend themselves to the use of the cause-effect pattern.

Using the cause-effect pattern, a speech on the need to raise taxes to support education might be arranged in either of the following ways:

Cause: 1. School officials have planned poorly, overspent, and mismanaged tax dollars since 1991.

Effect: 2. Because of the mishandling of tax dollars, tuition was raised to compensate, in order to run the university.

Cause: 1. Without a tuition increase several programs will have to be cut from the university.

Effect: 2. Poor planning, overspending, and mismanagement of funds by school officials have been the primary contributors to the need for a tuition increase.

Because the cause-effect pattern can be used in a variety of ways, it is a useful format for either informative or persuasive speeches. As long as the cause can be directly related to the effect that you are trying to prove, this pattern can be an excellent choice for many different topics.

MOTIVATED SEQUENCE A widely used pattern of organization for the persuasive speech is the **motivated sequence,** developed by Professor Alan H. Monroe of Purdue University in the 1930s.[1] This pattern is specifically designed to help the speaker combine sound logic and practical psychology. The motivated sequence is particularly effective because it follows the human thinking process and motivates listeners to take action. The sequence has five steps: attention, need, satisfaction, visualization, and action.

1. *Attention.* In the first step, the persuader attempts to create an interest in the topic so that the audience will want to listen. This step takes place in the introduction and follows the guidelines for an effective presentation. The speaker is saying, "Pay attention. This is important to you."

2. ***Need.*** In the second step, the persuader focuses on the problem by analyzing the things that are wrong and relating them to the audience's interests, wants, or desires. At this point the speaker is saying, "Something is wrong and something must be done about it."

3. ***Satisfaction.*** In the third step, the persuader provides a solution or plan of action that will eliminate the problem and thus satisfy the audience's interests, wants, and desires. The speaker is saying, "What I have to offer is the way to solve the problem."

4. ***Visualization.*** In the fourth step, the persuader explains in detail how the solution will meet the audience's need. The speaker's message now becomes, "This is how my plan will work to solve the problem, and if you accept my solution, things will be much better."

5. ***Action.*** In the fifth and final step the persuader asks the audience for a commitment to put the proposed solution to work. The speaker closes by saying, "Take action!"

The following is an example of a motivated sequence outline:

Specific Purpose: To persuade my audience to accept the Personalized System of Instruction (PSI) as the best method of teaching.

Introduction

Attention:
1. A method of instruction now being used throughout the country makes learning much easier for most students and costs a lot less than traditional methods of instruction.

Body

Need:
2. We need a method of instruction that will increase students' competencies and at the same time reduce the costs of education.

Satisfaction N:
3. The only method that appears to accomplish both of these goals is the Personalized System of Instruction, which was created by Dr. Fred Keller.

Visualization:
4. We can count on PSI to meet our needs because this approach has been shown to boost competencies and reduce costs in thousands of schools across the country. In addition, students receive individual attention.

Action:
5. Observe courses that use the PSI method, talk to students who have been in PSI courses to learn their reaction to them, and finally request faculty in your major to consider offering more courses using the PSI method.

The motivated sequence is most often used in persuasion. It is commonly used by advertisers because it works well in "selling" ideas.

Choosing the Best Pattern of Organization   We have already emphasized the importance of matching your speech's pattern of organization to your topic, specific purpose, and thesis. You must also consider another key factor—your audience. The wise speaker anticipates responses from the audience. Thus, if your audience analysis indicates that important questions or objections are likely to be raised, you should arrange your main points to meet those objections. For example, if you are advocating that a lottery be legalized in your community and are certain that your audience is likely to ask whether a lottery will bring crime into the community, you might structure your presentation as follows:

Main Points:
1. Lotteries are one of the most economical ways to raise revenue.
2. Lotteries are cost-efficient.
3. Lotteries are crime-free.

No matter what pattern you select, you should be careful to use only that pattern when sequencing your main points. For example, do not organize some of your main points by time sequence and others by cause and effect.

Connecting the Main Points   A conversation can move from one unrelated topic to another without losing meaning or impact, but for a speaker to communicate effectively with an audience, the thoughts in his or her speech must be systematically connected. The most common connecting device that speakers use are transitions.

TRANSITIONS   **Transitions** are phrases and words used to link ideas. They form a bridge between what has already been presented and what will be presented next. Transitions are typically used between the introduction and the body of a speech, between main ideas, between supporting materials and visual aids, and between the body and the conclusion. A transition can review information that has already been presented, preview information to come, or summarize key thoughts. Here are some typical transition statements that might be made in a speech.

Let me move on to my next point . . .

Now that I have discussed the history of the Frisbee, I would like to talk about its uses . . .

Turning now . . .

The final point I would like to make is . . .

Another example might be . . .

Keeping in mind the four items I have discussed, we arrive at the following conclusion . . .

There are two specific forms of transitions: one lets the audience know where you are going, the tells where you have been.

Signposts are words, phrases, short statements or questions that let the audience know what is ahead, just as a traffic sign warns of a coming curve in the road. Some typical signposts are:

Let me first illustrate . . .

My second point is . . .

To recap . . .

As you look at my chart . . .

Next . . .

Finally . . .

Why does our tuition continue to increase?

What does this all mean for us?

How can we solve this problem?

Who, then, is responsible?

Such questions draw the audience's attention to a forthcoming answer.

A signpost not only prepares an audience for what to expect next, but also alerts the audience that the upcoming information is important. For example:

The most essential aspect of this is . . .

Let's look at possible solutions to . . .

The only thing you need to know is . . .

An **internal summary** is a short review statement given at the end of a main point. Internal summaries are extremely useful in helping the audience to follow along when a presentation is lengthy or complex. For example:

Let me briefly summarize what I have said so far. Inflation is the number one factor contributing to our rising costs. For every percent that inflation increases, we must raise tuition by four percent. The problem of inflation must be solved . . .

Connecting Thoughts: A Recap	
Transitions:	Phrases and words used to link ideas
Signposts:	Words, phrases, and short statements that let the audience know what is ahead
Internal summaries:	Short reviews of key information made after main points

Supporting the Main Points   Main points by themselves are nothing more than assertions. An audience needs supporting and clarifying materials in order to accept what a speaker says. Therefore, it is imperative that each main point be supported and that the support be relevant and logically organized.

Your supporting materials should be clearly related to the specific purpose, thesis, and main points of your speech.

When supporting materials are included, the body of a speech expands to look like this:

Main Point: I. Japan is experiencing trouble in its auto industry.

Support and   A. Sales for the Japanese auto industry are down.
Clarifying
Material:

             1. According to *Time*, January 11, 1993, sales are down 13 percent from 1990.

             2. Sales for the five biggest car makers—Toyota, Nissan, Honda, Mitsubishi, and Mazda—are off 64 percent from 1990, explains *Time*, January 11, 1993.

             3. Car sales constitute 10 percent of japan's economy.[2]

Introduction

Experienced speakers usually develop their introduction after, not before, the body of their speech. An **introduction** includes opening statements that serve two important functions: motivating the audience to listen and orienting them to the subject. Thus, your introduction should prepare your audience for the body of your speech by setting the stage for the topic.

Your introduction should be based on the information you gathered in your audience analysis. If your analysis was accurate and thorough, you should have a pretty good understanding of your audience's frame of reference and how it might differ from your own. Your introduction should include:

I. Orienting the audience to the topic

    A. Get attention and arouse interest

    B. Give specific purpose and thesis statement

    C. Define terms (if necessary)

II. Motivating the audience to listen

    A. Be relevant

    B. Establish credibility

Orienting the Audience to the Topic Base your background information on what your audience knows or does not know about your subject. This is the appropriate time to gain attention, state specific purpose and thesis, and define terms.

Several approaches can be used to gain attention and arouse the interest of your audience, including referring to the subject or occasion, using personal references or narratives, asking rhetorical questions, presenting a startling statement, using humor, or using quotations.

1. REFERRING TO THE SUBJECT OR OCCASION. You may be asked to speak on a special occasion such as a holiday, founders' day, graduation, or anniversary. Here is a sample attention-getter related to an occasion.

> I am honored to have been asked to give a speech in celebration of Public Education Week. This is truly a special occasion because our public educational system has made this community what it is today.

2. USING PERSONAL REFERENCES OR NARRATIVES. Whenever you can relate your own experience to a speech, do so. Personal experiences make your speech more meaningful to your audience and show them that you know what you are talking about. Here is how a speaker used a personal experience to introduce his speech on convenience food packaging.

> In a recent investigation of my wastebasket, I discovered an empty yogurt container, a cup of microwavable Cheeze Whiz, a hand pack of Teddy Grahams, a V-8 sip box and a single-serving box of raisins. It appears that I, like many Americans, have fallen into the ocean of garbage created in our society by convenience foods and their plastic packaging.[3]

3. ASKING RHETORICAL QUESTIONS. A *rhetorical question* is a question for which no answer is expected. Asking rhetorical questions in an introduction usually encourages an audience to become intellectually involved. Such questions can also be used to create suspense. Here is how one student used rhetorical questions to involve her audience in a speech about sleep deprivation.

> Do you ever go through the day feeling like you're missing something? Well, what would you do if I said each one of you probably suffers directly from a deficit every day that you might not even realize? A loss that, according to the May 15, 1990, issue of the *New York Times*, affects 100 million Americans and causes 200 billion dollars a year in lost creativity and business productivity, industrial and vehicular accidents, and medical costs. This loss is not our deprivation of national dollars, but a loss concerning deprivation of sleep.[4]

4. PRESENTING A STARTLING STATEMENT. A startling statement can be used when you want to shock or surprise your audience. Startling statements are extremely effective at attention getting, as shown by the following example.

> Big Dan's Tavern certainly didn't appear to be anything special to the mother of two who crossed its threshold for the first time to make a simple purchase. Try as she may, though, she will never forget the barroom, because when the youthful mother entered it—her nightmare began. She endured more shame and terror that night than most of us probably will ever have to face. She was stripped, assaulted, and raped by four men for over an hour. She pleaded for mercy or aid and yet more than 15 other bar patrons simply stood and watched the spectacle. One man brushed aside her pleading hands as he moved out of the way. Another helped hold her on the pool table for the convenience of the attackers. Many cheered and applauded, but no one called the police.[5]

5. USING HUMOR. A funny story or relevant joke can not only gain the attention of your audience, but also get them to relax. One speaker began his talk as follows.

> The last time I gave a speech to this large a group, an audience member raised his hand in the back row and shouted, "I can't hear you." Immediately, a hand went up in the front row and the person asked, "Can I move back there?" Now I know all of you want to hear me, so I'll try to speak loud enough, and if I don't, I'll know why some of you are moving to the back row.

6. USING QUOTATIONS. Sometimes a quotation can grab your audience's attention, and if cited accurately, it can also add to your speech's believability. A student talking about the future started her speech as follows.

> Lew Lehr, the former president of the 3M Company, one of the companies cited in the popular best seller *In Search of Excellence*, wrote, "The future belongs to those who see opportunity where others see only problems." The future is ours, but we must see it as an opportunity to excel. Our college education equips us for this opportunity. Today, I want to talk to you about what the twenty-first century will bring to each of us.

Whatever you choose to gain attention and maintain interest in your introduction, it should be relevant and orient the audience to the topic. (See Figure 9.3).

After getting your audience's attention, you need to state the specific purpose and thesis of your speech. Both the specific purpose and thesis statement were discussed in detail in Chapter 8. Sometimes the specific purpose and thesis statement are together; sometimes it is appropriate to state the specific purpose toward the beginning of the introduction and the thesis toward the end, where it serves as a preview of the speech. By stating the specific purpose or thesis, you are orienting your audience to the topic and giving them a clear indication of where you are headed with your speech.

Motivating the Audience to Listen   Design your introductory comments to gain the attention and interest of your audience. You must hold their interest and attention throughout your entire presentation, but that task will be easier if you can capture them by making the topic significant and important to the audience (relevancy) and by establishing your credibility.

A standard way of making your topic relevant is simply to point out the reasons for presenting your speech. It is important that the audience find a reason to listen to the speech as soon as possible. Besides orienting your audience to the topic and motivating them to listen, you should also consider whether it is necessary to establish your credibility in regard to the topic you have selected.

Credibility is a speaker's believability based on the audience's evaluation of the speaker's competence, knowledge, experience, and character. If, for example, Madonna (entertainer) wanted to speak on health care or violence in our society, she would have to establish her credibility on the subject by relating the subject to herself and by indicating how she became an

THE FAR SIDE   By GARY LARSON

Figure 9.3:

Attention getting. Using attention getting devices should be relevant to the speech and interest arousing at the same time.

The class was quietly doing its lesson when Russell, suffering from problems at home, prepared to employ an attention-getting device.

expert. Let's take a look at some sample introductions. The following portion of an introduction shows you how the two purposes fit together.

Orienting Material

"When I was a kid," recalls author and columnist Pete Hamill, "the library gave us the world. My brother and I would get up early on Saturday mornings and wait on the library steps to be the first ones in the building."

Today our nation boasts of 100,000 public, university, and community libraries which circulate over one billion books each year. It is safe to say that each one of us has shared and enjoyed the adventure, excitement, and knowledge that our libraries offer through their collections of books, periodicals, and other materials.

Motivating Material:

But in spite of their contributions to each one of us, the library systems of the United States are in the midst of

a quiet, but serious, crisis. With obstacles to funding, inflation, rising book costs, thefts, and mounting expenses, our libraries are in serious trouble. . . . Because of its importance to
all of us, it is necessary for us to examine this problem.[6]

Can you label the specific parts of the above introduction? Now look at the
following example. The specific parts are labelled for you.

Orienting Material *Attention-Getter*	Twenty-five-year-old Scott Wilson, a gardener at a Florida condominium, accidentally sprayed the herbicide he was using on his face and hands. He had used chemicals many times in the past, and that's why he simply washed his face and hands and returned to work—even though his shirt was still dripping wet. Five days later, Scott Wilson was rushed to the hospital barely breathing.
Motivating Material: *Definition of Term* *Significance of Topic*	Paraquat, the herbicide that Wilson was using, kills plants within hours by disrupting the photosynthetic process, causing individual cells to collapse. Paraquat, in diluted form, is also a herbicide of choice for thousands of home gardeners. Its brand name is Ortho Spot Weed and Grass Control.[7]

The next introduction accomplishes several functions at one time—it gets
the audience's attention, it relates the topic directly to them and to the
speaker, it establishes the speaker's credibility on the topic, and it tells the
audience what the main points of the speech are.

Rhetorical Questions and Relating *Topic to Audience* *Citing a Source to Establish* *Credibility* *Establishing Credibility* *Trrough Experience* *Thesis*	If you were asked what you feared the most, what would *you* respond? A survey conducted and reported in the Nation's Business Magazine found that Americans' greatest fears were accidents, deaths, and heights, but over 50 percent of those polled listed speaking in public as their greatest fear. Many people, including me and possibly some of you, would probably agree with this finding. Speaking in public is never easy, and yet through my experiences with 4-H and this class, I have developed self-confidence as well as public speaking skills. The number one fear of most people is not accidents, deaths, or heights—it is the fear of speaking in front of others, or speech anxiety. I am going to define speech anxiety, its causes, its effects, and finally how it can be controlled or reduced.[8]

Suggestions for Developing Your Introduction

1. Keep the introduction relatively brief, between 5 and 10 percent of your
   total content.

2. Allow plenty of time to prepare the introduction carefully. Because it is
   critical to the success of your speech, it should not be rushed or written
   at the last minute.

3. Make the introduction creative and interesting. To accomplish this, think of several possible introductions and choose the most effective one.

4. As you research your speech, watch for material to use in the introduction. Keep a notebook or file of interesting quotations, stories, humorous statements, and other items that might liven up your opening. But remember that one key to a successful introduction is making it relevant to the speech topic.

5. Develop the introduction after you have completed the main part of your speech. Relevant introductions are easier to create after you have determined the content and direction of the body.

6. Write out the introduction word for word. This section is too important to improvise or leave to chance. In addition, writing it out will give you confidence and help you get off to a strong start.

A Sample Introduction

The following introduction was part of a college student's award-winning speech:

Background and Attention Getter

One year ago two of my professors, Steve and Mary, were involved in a head-on collision with a drunk driver. Steve was killed instantly. Mary was critically injured and was not expected to live. The case was especially tragic because Steve and Mary had two young daughters and no will. Without a will, the state was required to take possession of the children, despite the fact that friends and family were more than willing to raise them.

Reason to Listen

Significance of Topic

Relevancy

Specific Purpose and Thesis

Over 60 percent of all Americans die without a will, and most of us don't even consider writing a will until relatively late in life. To those of us in the prime of our lives, the thought of writing a will of our own seems morbid and unnecessary. That simply isn't true. The fact is that each of us needs some kind of will, and most of us don't have the least idea of how to go about writing one. My purpose today is to convince each of you that having a will is important. I will discuss what a will is and why a will is necessary, the reasons people avoid writing a will, and finally, how to obtain a will.[9]

EXERCISE

Here are three speech topics. Select one of the following topics and either alone or in a group assigned by your instructor develop in writing a complete introduction for the topic selected. Your instructor

may ask you to share and discuss your's or your group's introduction in class.

   Importance of Mammograms
   Pet Population
   Rap Music

Conclusion

Your **conclusion** should focus your audience's thoughts on the specific purpose of your speech and bring your most important points together in a condensed and uniform way. You may also use your conclusion to spell out the action or policies you recommend to solve a problem. In every case, your conclusion should reinforce what you want your audience to remember. Because your conclusion is as important as any other part of your presentation, you should give it the same amount of attention. Be especially careful to avoid using it to add new information. Instead, use your conclusion to:

1. Reinforce your purpose by reviewing your main points
2. End with a memorable thought

Reviewing the Main Points   Repeating the main points of a speech is particularly helpful in informative speeches or any time you want your audience to remember your main points. For example, the speaker who informed her audience about barriers to effective listening concluded her speech as follows:

> Let me review the barriers that have the most impact on our listening. They are language, factual, mental, and physical distractions. If you remember these and how they affect listening, you will be a more effective listener.

In addition to helping the audience remember your content, reveiwing the speech reinforces the thesis statement.

Ending with a Memorable Thought   A memorable thought may include referring back to an attention-getting device, citing a quotation, or issuing a challenge or appeal. Citing a memorable quotation can be a good way to leave a lasting impression on your audience. When it is relevant and reinforces your thesis statement, a quotation can give your speech additional authority and help to increase your credibility. It is crucial that you always cite the source of all quoted information or any information that is not your own. The importance and responsibilities of a speaker to cite sources are discussed in Chapter 10. A student speaking on the right to die with dignity concluded her speech as follows:

> If we can adopt these two requirements, we can forever banish death as a grim reaper. As former New York Senator Jacob Javits said shortly before his death, "The right to die with dignity is profound, moral, and essential."[10]

If your speech purpose is to persuade, the conclusion may also include a challenge or appeal to action. The following conclusion was used in a persuasive speech on how to eliminate illiteracy in our society.

> Finally, our involvement must begin from the very simplest of tasks. We must observe our own friends, students, and classmates. It isn't easy for an adult to admit he or she can't read. If you suspect someone is having difficulties, tactfully encourage him or her to take advantage of the literacy programs that exist. A little compassion and understanding can make the difference between the number of those that do participate and those that don't.[11]

Signal your audience that your speech is nearing its end by using such phrases as "Today, we have examined," "In the past minutes we have examined," "Finally, let me say," "In closing," or "My purpose has been." Each of these prepares your audience for your concluding remarks.

Suggestions for Developing Your Conclusion

The following hints should help you develop a strong conclusion for any speech.

1. The conclusion should be brief and should end with a definite summarizing statement. The conclusion should account for between 5 and 15 percent of the content of your speech.
2. The conclusion should not contain information that was not already mentioned in either the introduction or the body of your speech.
3. The preparation of the conclusion should not be rushed. Allow plenty of time to develop and write it carefully.
4. Leave your audience with an impact that will make your speech memorable. Think of several possible endings and choose the one that best serves the purpose of your speech.
5. Write out the conclusion word for word. Then learn it well so that you can end your speech smoothly and confidently.

A Sample Conclusion

The following conclusion was part of a college students' award-winning speech.

Signal of Speech's End
Summary of Main Points

I have attempted to give you some of the reasons why art should be such a vital part of the curriculum of our schools. We, as concerned citizens, need to appeal to the large number of well-intentioned citizens who are not aware of the consequences of their actions against the arts. In some areas parents are forming boosters for the arts, which are similar to

Appeal for Action

athletic boosters. This is something perhaps you could start in your own community. Also, plans are now afoot for the launching of a National Association for Education in the Arts, which could form the spearhead of a movement to exert pressure on policy makers.

Memorable Final Thought

We all understand that a germinating seed needs the right surroundings to grow. If the environment becomes sterile, the plant will cease to grow or, if it does survive, will not be healthy. We, as gardeners for our lawns, provide the proper environment for those lawns. Are we willing to accept less for children? True, the damage to a crop or lawn without proper care is obvious, but the damage to the independence and creative thinking of our children, while less obvious, is a loss to us all.[12]

OUTLINING YOUR SPEECH

Outlining is one of the most difficult (and therefore mistakenly avoided) steps in preparing a speech. Outlining and organizing are similar terms. Both steps involve the arranging of information to form a meaningful sequence, but outlining is a more rigorous, written process. **Outlining** is arranging the entire contents of a speech in a logical sequence and writing out that sequence in a standardized form. The outline is often referred to as the blueprint or skeleton of a speech.

Because outlining is more detailed than organizing, an outline helps to unify and clarify thinking, make relationships clear, and provide the proper balance and emphasis to each point as it relates to the specific purpose. Outlining also helps ensure that information is both accurate and relevant.

As you prepare your outline, you will gain an overview of your entire presentation. Developing an outline should help you to gauge the amount of support you have for each of your main points and identify any points that need further development.

The actual process of outlining usually requires three steps:

1. Create a preliminary outline that identifies the topic and the main points to be covered in the speech.

2. Expand the preliminary outline into a full-content outline that clearly and fully develops the speech's content.

3. Condense the full-content outline into a presentational outline to aid in delivery.

EXERCISE

For a speech entitled "Making Reading Your Hobby," rearrange the following sentences in proper outline form for the body. This exercise should help you arrange content into a logical sequence. Place the number of each sentence in the proper place in the outline. (See the end of the chapter to verify your answers.)

I.
   A.
   B.
II.
   A.
   B.
III.
   A.
   B.

1. **Low cost rental libraries are numerous.**
2. **Reading is enjoyable.**
3. **Reading may lead to advancement in one's job.**
4. **Books contain exciting tales of love and adventure.**
5. **Many paperback books cost only .95 to $1.25.**
6. **People who read books are most successful socially.**
7. **Reading is profitable.**
8. **One meets many interesting characters in books.**
9. **Reading is inexpensive.**

Preliminary Outline

A **preliminary outline** is a list of all the points that may be used in a speech. Suppose you are preparing a four- to six-minute persuasive speech on safety requirements for compact trucks and passenger vehicles.[13] Because of the limited amount of time, you know you cannot possibly cover everything related to the topic. And because your general purpose is to persuade, you need to focus your speech's content in that direction. So, recalling what you have already read about topic selection, analyzing your audience, gathering information, and using supporting and clarifying materials, you determine your specific purpose: "To persuade my audience that safety standards should be established for compact/light trucks and passenger vehicles." Based on this specific purpose, you can prepare a preliminary outline of possible main points, as shown in the following Sample

Preliminary Outline. Once your possible main points are arranged in this way, you will find it easier to analyze your thoughts. You can then decide exactly which main thoughts to include in your speech and choose the best order for presenting them.

Sample Preliminary Outline

Topic: Safety regulations for compact/light trucks and passenger vehicles.

General Purpose   To persuade

Specific Purpose: To persuade my audience that safety regulations should be adopted for light/compact trucks and passenger vehicles.

Possible Main   1. Existing safety regulations for light/compact trucks and passenger
Points: vehicles
                           2. Production standards for light/compact trucks and passenger vehicles
                           3. Need for additional safety regulations for light/compact trucks and passenger vehicles
                           4. Growing popularity of light/compact trucks and passenger vehicles
                           5. Recent improvements in safety standards for automobiles
                           6. Why safety standards haven't been adopted for light/compact trucks and passenger vehicles
                           7. Effects that the lack of safety regulations for light/compact trucks can have on society

Full-Content Outline

A **full-content outline** is an expansion of the main points selected from the preliminary outline. The full-content outline is a detailed skeleton of a speech with all main and secondary points written in complete sentences. A full-content outline helps a speaker clarify and polish his or her thoughts because:

1. A major point that cannot be written in a complete sentence is probably weak or invalid and does not belong in the speech.
2. Writing a complete sentence for each point requires thought.
3. The outline shows the flow of the speech and whether the sequence is logical and effective.
4. The outline illustrates the relationship of each point to the specific purpose and enables the speaker to analyze how each point contributes to the total presentation.
5. The outline is a form of communication in itself that serves as an excellent summary of the text and can be used by others to see the main points of the presentation.

6. The outline helps to make each topic sentence clear and shows transitions from point to point.

The full-content outline should close with a bibliography that lists all the sources used in preparing the speech. The bibliography includes books, magazines, interviews—any source that either the speaker or the listener might want to refer to in order to learn more about the subject.

Because it serves so many purposes, a full-content outline is an essential part of planning any speech. Writing a full-content outline is not necessarily an easy task. But once the job is completed, the outline makes the rest of the preparation and delivery of a speech much easier. The full-content outline of the speech on safety regulations shows the complete introduction and conclusion and the fully developed main and secondary points and uses a problem-solution pattern of organization.

Guidelines for Writing A Full-Content Outline

1. Cover the three main parts of your speech in your outline— introduction, body, and conclusion—with appropriate transitions.
2. Identify each main point in your speech with a Roman numeral (I, II, etc.). Identify subpoints with capital letters, and successive levels of subpoints with Arabic numerals and lowercase letters.
3. Follow standard outline style to ensure consistency in symbols and indentation.
4. Use only one idea per symbol.
5. State each main point as a single sentence.
6. All main points (Roman numerals) should have subpoints (capital letters). All main points and subpoints in a full-content outline should have at least two parts. That is, there should be no I without a II, no A without a B, no 1 without a 2, and so on.
7. The body will usually contain two, three, or four Roman numerals.
8. Be sure the outline makes sense from one symbol to the next.

Sample Full-Content Outline

Title:	A Cruel Hoax
Topic:	Safety regulations for light/compact trucks and passenger vehicles
General Purpose:	To persuade
Specific Purpose:	To persuade the audience that safety regulations should be adopted for light/compact trucks and passenger vehicles

Thesis:

The lack of safety standards, the cost to each of us, and the reasons for the inadequate safety standards all suggest why safety regulations should be adopted for light/compact trucks and passenger vehicles.

Introduction

Attention Getting and Orienting Definition

It isn't surprising that a consumer culture which eats light food, drinks light beer, and performs light aerobics also drives, in ever increasing numbers, light/compact vehicles. Light/compact vehicles include pickups, minivans, jeeps, sport utility vehicles, and station wagons built on truck chassis.

The truth is that light cuisine frequently isn't, light beer frequently isn't, and light aerobics are still a sweaty proposition. As for light/compact vehicles . . . Well, Diana Richards saw the light by accident.

Story

Startling Statement

Diana Richards, a 36-year-old credit manager, was driving her pickup home after a hard day at work when she was sideswiped by a car. Knocked unconscious, she awoke to the horrifying discovery that her foot was missing. Later, most of her lower leg was amputated. Ms. Richards described the sense of betrayal she felt: "I always thought that a truck had more protection. I couldn't believe how it crumbled. It was as if someone took aluminum foil and just wadded it up. And it crumbled so bad—and then when I saw the other people's car and how it was hardly even hurt, I kept asking, why did ours fall apart?"

Quotation
Analogy

Significance of Topic

Thesis

Diana Richards' case, as presented on the June 10 television show "Newsmagazine, 1986," is not unique. Each year, thousands of Americans are tragically maimed or killed as a result of light/compact vehicle accidents. Many lives could be spared if it weren't for a lethal combination of legislative perversity and manufacturers' callousness. The lack of safety standards also suggests why safety regulations should be adopted for light/compact trucks and passenger ehicles. I will begin by talking about the lack of safety standards.

Signpost

Body

Main Point

I. Light/compact vehicles are dangerous due to the lack of safety regulations.

Identification of Problem

   A. Light/compact vehicles are exceedingly popular.

      1. Ford Motor Company expects to sell 4.4 million this year alone.

Supporting Material

      2. People are buying them because of their near carlike comfort, according to the *Wall Street Journal*.

   B. Light/compact vehicles are exceedingly dangerous.

      1. Max Bramble is just one example of the danger of driving a compact vehicle.

        a.   His pickup was hit from behind with such force it was crushed.

        b.   Max suffered brain damage and died.

   2.   Each year thousands of people die or sustain serious injuries as a result of driving compact vehicles.

        a.   Between 1982 and 1984 the number of deaths related to driving compact vehicles nearly doubled.

        b.   There are 35 deaths for every 100,000 compact pickups registered, compared to 21 per 100,000 for all cars registered.

Internal Summary Transition	So far I have shown you how dangerous light/compact vehicles are by providing specific examples and statistics. They are not only dangerous, but they also cost society money.
Main Point	II. Light/compact vehicles, because they are not regulated, cost each one of us money.
Supporting Materials	A. Unregulated light/compact vehicles cost us in terms of higher health care, lost wages, and increased insurance premiums.
	B. The cost of unregulated light/compact vehicles to society as a whole, according to the National Safety Council, was $1 billion last year.
Internal Summary Transition	There is a tremendous cost to each of us—in both dollars and lives—because there are no regulations. Why isn't something being done?
Main Point	III. Two reasons are often cited for the lack of safety standards for light/compact vehicles.
Supporting Materials	A. Manufacturers assert that light/compact vehicles are safer than other vehicles because they are manufactured to meet other car standards and thus should be safe.
	B. Manufacturers claim that most accidents are the driver's fault and that no number of standards will change that.
Internal Summary Transition	It is clear that the manufacturers do not see safety standards as the solution to the problem—they blame the driver. What is the solution?
Main Point	IV. There are two solutions to the problem of light/compact vehicle safety regulations.
Suggested Solutions	A. We must take action to protect ourselves when we buy light/compact vehicles.
	1. Purchase light/compact vehicles that have safety features such as steel-reinforced beams.

2. Wear a seat belt at all times while driving or riding in a light/compact vehicle.

B. Congress must do something to pass legislation to improve the standards of light/compact vehicles.

Internal Summary

We must help ourselves and get Congress to pass legislation if we are going to improve the safety standards of these vehicles.

Conclusion

Transition

Summary

Appeal

After examining the absence of light/compact vehicle standards, the cost to each of us, the reasons for the absence of standards, and the appropriate corrective measures, the choice is clear. Either we can adopt and enforce simple safety standards that ensure adequate protection to those involved in accidents with light/compact vehicles, or we can ignore the carnage that is visiting our nation's highways, and like Diana Richards and Max Bramble, risk "seeing the light . . . by accident."

Bibliography

General Accounting Office, Report to the Congress, 6 July 1978.

Landis, David. "Big Deals About Small Trucks," USA Today, 1 February 1987, 10E.

Levin, Doron P. "As Small Trucks Gain in Popularity, Questions Arise About Their Safety," Wall Street Journal, 20 March 1986, 33.

National Safety Council Report Transcript from television show, "Newsmagazine, 1986," 10 June 1986, vol. 1, no. 1.

Presentational Outline

A **presentational outline** is a condensation of the full-content outline in which detail is minimized and key words and phrases replace full sentences. This is the outline that you will work from when you present your speech. The advantages of the presentational outline as an aid to delivery are that it is concise, requires little space, and is comprehensible at a glance.

Your presentational outline should include your main points and sufficient clarifying and supporting material to aid you in your presentation. The outline may also include your complete introduction and conclusion, although the choice is up to you. Key words and phrases are important to use in a presentational outline because they will remind you of the points you want to make. Some speakers use codes, symbols, or even colors to remind them of key points, vocal pauses, changes in rate of speaking, and so on. But remember, if your presentational outline is too long, complex, or detailed, you can easily get too involved in your notes and lose contact with your audience.

The presentational outline can be easily transferred onto note cards. Some speakers prefer to use note cards, and in many classroom situations students are required to use them. The number of note cards and their use should be kept to a minimum. Classroom assignments sometimes specify that you use only one side of only two or three cards. When this is the case, you need to adjust the amount and type of information that you include to aid you in remembering key information. The advantage to using note cards is that they are easier to handle than full sheets of paper and usually require only one hand, thus freeing the hands for gestures.

Sample Presentational Outline

Topic:

Safety Regulations for light/Compact trucks and Passenger Vehicles

General Purpose:

To persuade

Specific Purpose:

To persuade my audience that safety regulations should be adopted for light/compact trucks and passenger vehicles.

Thesis:

The lack of safety standards, the cost to each of us, and the reasons for the inadequate safety standards suggest why safety regulations should be adopted for light/compact trucks and passenger vehicles.

Reminders About Delivery

DON'T READ NOTES
SLOW DOWN—LOOK AT AUDIENCE—PAUSE

Introduction

I. Consumer culture—light foods, light beer, light aerobics, also light/compact vehicles.
    A. List types of vehicles
    B. Diana Richards story
       1. 36-year-old credit manager
       2. Lost foot
       3. 1,000 Americans—"Newsmagazine 1986" television show

BRIEF PAUSE

Thesis

II. Safety regulations should be adopted
    A. Costs to each of us
    B. Lack of safety standards
    C. Reason for lack of standards
    D. Solution to problem

Body

Signal that Body and Main Points are Coming

I. Light/compact vehicles are dangerous
    A. Exceedingly popular
       1. Ford/4.4 million vehicles

Source Noted to Help Speaker Remember and to Quote Report Data Accurately

  2. Buying because of comfort—*Wall Street Journal*
 B. Exceedingly dangerous
  1. Max Bramble story
  2. Thousands die or sustain serious injuries
   a. 1982—84 deaths doubles
   b. 35/100,000 pickups; 21/100,000 cars

Reminder of Internal Summary and Transition

(I've shown danger by providing examples and statistics. . . .)

Reminders of Key Terms and Sources

II. Not regulated—cost everyone money
 A. Higher health care, lost wages, increased insurance
 B. National Safety Council—$1 billion last year

Internal Summary and Transition

(Tremendous cost to each—Why isn't something done?)
III. Two reasons
 A. Manufacturers—safe enough
 B. Manufacturers—drivers at fault

Internal Summary and Transition
Pause to Highlight Key Point

(Manufacturers don't see problem. What is the solution?)
                                             PAUSE
IV. Two solutions
 A. Protect ourselves
 B. Congress must act

Internal Summary and Transition
Reminder to Speak Slowly
Signal that Conclusion is Coming

(Must help ourselves and get Congress to pass legislation)
                                    SLOW DOWN
                                     Conclusion
I. Absence of light/compact standards
II. We can adopt and enforce safety standards . . . or we can ignore the carnage.
 A. Diana Richards and Max Bramble
 B. "Seeing the light . . . by accident."

Suggestions for Using Presentational Note Cards

1. Use as few note cards as possible.
2. Number note cards so if they get out of order, you can reorder them.
3. Write on only one side of the card.
4. Use abbreviations as much as possible.
5. Do not write out your speech—use an outline format.
6. If you prefer, write out the introduction and conclusion in their entirety.
7. List only the main points and subpoints on the cards.
8. If necessary, write out quotes, statistical data, and other information that must be cited accurately. (See Figure 9.4 for sample note cards.)

```
                        A CRUEL HOAX
        Pause-Slow
It isn't surprising that a consumer culture that eats light food,
drinks light beer, and performs light aerobics also drives, in ever-
increasing numbers, light/compact vehicles. Light/compact vehicles
include pickups, mini vans, jeeps, sport utility vehicles, and station
wagons built on truck chassis.
        The truth is that light cuisine frequently isn't light beer,
and light aerobics are still a sweaty proposition. As for
light/compact vehicles...Well, Diana Richards saw the light by
accident.
        Diana Richards-- (tells her story)
Today, I would like to tell you why safety regulations should be
adopted for light/compact trucks and passenger vehicles.
        I will examine--lack of safety standards. Costs to us, reasons
for lack of standards, and solutions to problem.
        I will begin
```

```
        I. Light/compact vehicles are dangerous
           A. Exceedingly popular
              1. Ford/4.4 million vehicles
              2. Buying because of comfort--Wall Street J.
           B. Exceedingly dangerous
              1. Max Bramble story
              2. Thousands die or sustain serious injuries
                 a. 1982-84 deaths double
                 b. 21/100,000 cars
           So far I have shown...
       II. Not regulated--cost everyone money
           A. High health care, lost wages, increased insurance
           B. National Safety Council--$1 Billion last year
```

```
      III. Two reasons
           A. Manufacturers-safe enough
           B. Manufacturers at fault
           (Manufacturers don't see problem. What is the
           solution)
       IV. Two solutions
           A. Protect ourselves
           B. Congress must act
    (Must help ourselves and get Congress to pass legislation)
        V. Absence of light/compact standards
       VI. We can adopt and enforce safety standards...or we
           ignore the carnage.
           A. Diana Richards and Max Bramble
           B. "Seeing the light by accident"
```

Figure 9.4

Presentational note cards can be either handwritten or keyboarded on a computer. In either form, note cards should be easy to read and use. They should be there to help you quickly recall information and remind you of key ideas in your speech.

SUMMARY

Organizing is the arranging of ideas and elements into a systematic and meaningful whole. Organizing requires planning, time, and know-how. Most speeches are organized into three main parts: introduction, body, and conclusion.

The *body*, which is the main content of a speech, develops the speaker's general and specific purposes as well as the thesis. The body consists of the main points of a speech plus the supporting and clarifying materials. The *main points,* which are the principal subdivisions of a speech, are critical to the accomplishment of a speaker's specific purpose. Main points should relate to the specific purpose and thesis, be stated carefully, and be limited in number.

One of five basic patterns is used in most speeches. The *time-sequence pattern* begins at a particular point in time and continues either forward or backward. The *spatial pattern* organizes the main points according to their relationship in space. The *topical pattern* divides a speech topic into a series of related subtopics. The *problem-solution pattern* first discusses a problem and then suggests solutions. The *cause-effect pattern* illustrates logical relationships between the cause of something and its subsequent effect. The *motivated sequence pattern* combines logic and practical psychology; it involves five steps: attention, need, satisfaction, visualization, and action. The pattern of presentation should match the topic and the speaker's specific purpose.

The main points of a speech connected to one another by transitions, signposts, and internal summa *Transitions* are words and phrases used to link idea *Signposts* are words, phrases, and short statements that let an audience know what is coming. *Internal summaries* are short reviews of what was said under each main point. Main points cannot stand alone; they must be supported and clarified.

The principal functions of the *introduction* (opening statements) are to orient the audience to the topic and to motivate them to listen. Besides orienting and motivating an audience, it is also important in the introduction to establish *credibility* (believability based on the audience's evaluation of the speaker's competence, knowledge, experience, and character). The main functions of the *conclusion* (closing statements) are to focus the audience's thoughts on the specific purpose and to bring together the most important points in a condensed and uniform way.

Outlining provides a written account of the main features and ideas of a speech that can then serve as a blueprint or skeleton. The *preliminary outline* lists all possible main points and forms the basis for early decisions about a speech's content and direction. A *full-content outline* gives all the main and secondary points in full-sentence form. A *presentational outline* condenses the full-content outline into key words and phrases that will aid the speaker in delivering the speech. When you have completed the outlining process, you should have an extremely clear picture of exactly what you will say and how you will say it.

KEY TERMS

Body: Main section of a speech that develops the speaker's general and specific purposes.

Cause-Effect Pattern: Order of presentation in which the speaker first explains the causes of an event, problem, or issue and then discusses their consequences.

Conclusion: Closing statements that focus the audience's thoughts on the specific purpose of a speech and bring the most important points together in a condensed and uniform way.

Credibility: Speaker's believability based on the audience's evaluation of the speaker's competence, knowledge, experience, and character.

Full-Content Outline: Detailed skeleton of a speech with all main and secondary points written in complete sentences.

Internal Summary: Short review statement given at the end of a main point.

Introduction: Opening statement that orients the audience to the subject and motivates them to listen.

Main Points: Principal subdivisions of a speech.

Motivated Sequence: Pattern of organization specifically developed for persuasive speaking that combines logic and practical psychology. Five steps are involved: attention, need, satisfaction, visualization, and action.

Organizing: Arranging of ideas and elements into a systematic and meaningful whole.

Outlining: Arranging materials in a logical sequence, often referred to as the blueprint or skeleton of a speech, and writing out that sequence in a standardized form.

Preliminary Outline: List of all the main points that may be used in a speech.

Presentational Outline: Condensation of the full-content outline that aids delivery by minimizing detail and listing key words and phrases in place of full sentences.

Problem-Solution Pattern: Order of presentation that first discusses a problem and then suggests solutions.

Signpost: Word, phrase, or short statement that indicates to an audience the direction a speaker will take next.

Spatial Pattern: Order of presentation in which the content of a speech is organized according to relationships in space.

Time-Sequence (Chronological) Pattern: Order of presentation that begins at a particular point in time and continues either forward or backward.

Topical Pattern: Order of presentation in which the main topic is divided into a series of related subtopics.

Transition: Phrase or word used to link ideas.

DISCUSSION STARTERS

1. How can a speech's organization affect an audience?
2. Why should the main points of a speech be carefully developed and written?
3. What usually determines the number of main points in a speech?
4. What should be done to make a speech's main points more meaningful to an audience?
5. Why is it important for a speaker to understand the different patterns for ordering the main points in a speech?
6. Why is the introduction so important to a speech's overall effectiveness?
7. What should the introduction of a speech accomplish?
8. What suggestions would you give beginning speakers about how to develop the introduction of a speech?
9. What should the conclusion of a speech accomplish?
10. What suggestions would you give beginning speakers about how to develop the conclusion of a speech?
11. How do the three kinds of outlines differ?

NOTES

1. B. E. Gronbeck, R. E. McKerrow, D. Ehninger, and A. H. Monroe, *Principles and Types of Speech Communication*, 11th ed. (Glenview, Ill.: Scott, Foresman/Little, Brown Higher Education, 1990): 180–203.
2. M. Schulte, "United States Automobile Industry," (University of Nebraska—Lincoln student speech, 1993). With permission.
3. P. K. Epp, "Convenience Food Packaging," *Winning Orations* (Mankato, Minn.: Interstate Oratorical Association, 1991): 66.
4. P. K. Pankow, "Hours to Go Before I Sleep," *Winning Orations* (Mankato, Minn.: Interstate Oratorical Association, 1991): 123.
5. B. Randles, "My Brother's Keeper," *Winning Orations* (Mankato, Minn.: Interstate Oratorical Association, 1984): 70.
6. D. J. Edwards, "Dewey or Don't We? Saving Our Libraries," *Winning Orations* (Mankato, Minn.: Interstate Oratorical Association, 1984): 70.
7. M. Blashfield, "The Paradox of Paraquat," *Winning Orations* (Mankato, Minn.: Interstate Oratorical Association, 1984): 37.
8. D. Seiler, "Speech Anxiety: A Block to Effective Speaking," Speech presented in district 4-H contest, Lancaster County, Nebraska, 1989.
9. L. Johnson, "Where There's a Will There's a Way," *Winning Orations* (Mankato, Minn.: Interstate Oratorical Association, 1986), 59.
10. B. Gerlach, "America—The Land of the Free?" *Winning Orations* (Mankato, Minn.: Interstate Oratorical Association, 1986): 104.
11. J. Braaten, "It's English," *Winning Orations* (Mankato, Minn.: Interstate Oratorical Association, 1984): 66.

12. T. Stalnaker, "Elevation to the Beautiful Life," *Winning Orations* (Mankato, Minn.: Interstate Oratorical Association, 1984): 92–95.

13. This example is based on "A Cruel Hoax," a speech written by Mary B. Trauba for the 1987 oratory contest competition. Permission to use "A Cruel Hoax," which has won several national oratory contests, was acquired from Mary B. Trauba, a student at the University of Nebraska, and Jack Kay, Past Chair and Director of Forensics at the University of Nebraska, Lincoln; Department of Communication Head, Wayne State University, Detroit, Michigan.

Answers for Exercise on page 265
I. (2), A. (4), B (8), II. (9), A. (1), B. (5), III. (7), A. (3), B (6)

Chapter 10

Managing Anxiety and Delivering Your Speech

LEARNING OBJECTIVES

After studying this chapter, you should be able to:

1. Describe the roles of ethics, knowledge, preparation, and self-confidence in effective speech making.

2. Discuss the symptoms and causes of speech anxiety and suggest five methods of controlling this problem.

3. Analyze the pros and cons of the four basic methods of speech delivery.

4. Identify the vocal and physical factors that contribute to an effective delivery.

5. Tell how each of the most commonly used visual aids can enhance a speech presentation.

6. Specify how speakers can polish their delivery.

Dionne:	*(seeing Gregg standing in an empty room, talking) What are you doing?*
Gregg:	*I'm practicing my speech.*
Dionne:	*Do you always practice by talking in an empty room?*
Gregg:	*No, not all the time, but it helps me feel more at ease.*
Dionne:	*Don't you get nervous when you have to give a speech?*
Gregg:	*A little, I guess. But if I'm prepared and I've practiced enough, it's a piece of cake. I really like speaking in front of others.*
Dionne:	*You've got to be kidding.*

You may find it hard to believe, but the most enjoyable part of the speech making process is the presenting of the speech to the audience. The hard part is behind you; you've done your researching and organizing, so now you can focus on the last step—delivery. An important part of preparation is practice (See Figure 10.1.) Gregg, in the scenario above, is doing what every speaker should do in preparation for giving a speech. While it is not always possible to rehearse in the room where the presentation is to be given, it is important to practice your speech in advance. Practicing the delivery will help you know what the speech will sound like and whether there need to be wording changes, as well as help to ensure your confidence about giving the speech.

Figure 10.1:

An important part of speech preparation is practicing your delivery. After you have done all your research and organizing of the speech's content, it is important that you rehearse your speech. If possible, present it to a friend or group of friends. Practicing aloud will aid you in making the necessary changes to make the speech more effective.

Richard Hutchings/Photo Edit

QUALITIES OF EFFECTIVE SPEAKERS

By cultivating certain personal qualities, you as a speaker can enhance the likelihood that your listeners will accept your message. The most effective speakers are ethical, knowledgeable, prepared, and self-confident.

Ethics

Ethics, an individual's system of moral principles, plays a key role in communication. As speakers, we are responsible for what we tell others. We should always hold the highest ethical standards. We must communicate to our audience honesty, sincerity, and integrity.

Ethical speakers do not distort or falsify evidence to misrepresent information, do not make unsupported attacks on opponents in order to discredit them, do not deceive an audience about their intention or objective in an attempt to persuade or take advantage, do not use irrelevant emotional appeals to sensationalize their message, thus diverting attention from the facts, and do not pose as an authority when they are not.[1]

Ethical speakers always cite the sources of their information. Any time you use information and ideas that are not your own, you are obligated to cite their originator or source. The use of another person's information, language, or ideas without citing the originator or author, thus making it appear that you are the originator, is referred to as **plagiarism.** For example, using statistical data, direct quotes, or any information that you did not originate without giving credit to the originator is unethical. Most speeches, unless otherwise specified, require that you as the speaker be the originator of the speech's content. Of course, it is perfectly legitimate to use a reasonable amount of information and ideas from others as long as you cite your sources.

The following are some suggestions for avoiding plagiarism:

Do not rely on a single article summary for a speech

Avoid using other people's language and ideas

Get information and ideas from a variety of sources and integrate the information into your own thoughts

Cite sources prior to any quoted material—Dr. Smith, in her 1993 article on exercise, stated "The best. . . "

Always identify your sources—*Newsweek* last week indicated that Clinton's health plan is.   .   ; According to Robert Jones, a leading economist, in the January 15, 1993, *Wallstreet Journal, "Our economy is. . . "*

Give credit to the originator of the ideas you use—Fred Keller, an educational psychologist, created the instructional program that we now use in . . .

Similar to speakers, we as listeners need to be responsible for what is truth. We should expect speakers to be ethical, but as a listener we must be willing to verify the information we receive to ensure that it is accurate and valid. (See Chapter 6 for a discussion of listening and the responsibilities of the listener.)

Knowledge

Knowledge is a speaker's greatest asset. Knowing your subject is essential if you plan to reach your listeners. Those who have become noted speakers are almost always avid readers. To enhance your understanding of events, people, and values, you must read and observe things around you. From experience, you know that it is easier to talk about things you are familiar with than those you are not. As an educated person, you should not only know about past international, national, regional, and local events, but also keep abreast of current events. You should read all kinds of books, at least one trade (professional) magazine, and one daily newspaper in addition to listening to news broadcasts and documentaries.

Preparation

People rarely make speeches without some preparation, and the most successful speakers are those who are well prepared. Imagine what went through President Clinton's mind as he was delivering his health plan speech to Congress and the American people, when he discovered that the words on the TelePrompTer were from his State of the Union speech given several months earlier. Yet for almost six minutes, he spoke with little if any hesitation, presenting the correct speech to his audience. President Clinton was able to do this because he practiced and knew the content of his speech.

A successful speech is somewhat like a successful business meeting or athletic event—both require planning, preparation, and work. Wil Linkugel, a professor of speech communication and a good friend at the University of Kansas, told this story which illustrates the importance of practice.

A student athlete was delivering a speech to the class. The student, speaking in a monotone voice, kept reading from a prepared script. Finally, Professor Linkugel interrupted the student.

Professor: Why don't you put down your notes and just tell us what your notes say?

Student: I can't do that. I'll never get it right.

Professor: Let's see what you can do.

The student tried speaking without his notes, but the result, although greatly improved, left much to be desired.

Student:	I'll never do this right!
Professor:	In practice, if you were running a pass pattern and you didn't do it right, what would your coach make you do?
Student:	We'd run it over again.
Professor:	How many times would you run it over?
Student:	As many times as it would take to get it right.

What message was Professor Linkugel trying to get across to the student? Is there a message in the story for you? Whether playing football or delivering a speech, for the beginner as well as the experienced speaker, preparation, practice, and knowledge of the fundamentals are important.

Self-Confidence

Self-confidence is so essential to becoming an effective speaker that most of this book's content is aimed at helping you strengthen this quality. Because self-confidence is so strongly influenced by anxiety, we will discuss this problem in detail.

MANAGING THE ANXIETY OF SPEECH MAKING

If you experience the fear of speaking before an audience—a condition known as **speech anxiety,** or stage fright—it may help to know that you are not alone. It is perfectly normal to encounter some anxiety before, during, and sometimes even after a speech. In fact, even the most experienced speakers confess to having some anxiety about speaking before a group. What should you know about stage fright? This question, for some teachers of public speaking, is controversial. If the subject is presented, will the mere mention of anxiety produce it unnecessarily? That is, will discussing stage fright bring out more fear in speakers than if it were never mentioned at all? There is no evidence to suggest that discussing stage fright increases or decreases it, but it is commonly accepted that the more we know about stage fright and how to cope with it, the better able we are to control it.

Understanding a particular fear is difficult unless you have personally experienced it. The following story illustrates this point. Mary's brother-in-law's back bothers him when he lifts heavy objects. She used to think that he was making excuses for being lazy, until she pinched a nerve in her back and experienced the pain her brother-in-law has long suffered.

The message was clear to her: It isn't easy to understand someone else's problem unless you have experienced it yourself. The next time her brother-in-law complained about his back, Mary was more sympathetic.

If you have had to speak before a group, you probably know a little about speech anxiety, one fear that many Americans concede is high on their list of fears, according to surveys.[2] The important thing to remember is that having some anxiety about giving a speech before a group is normal. Anxiety becomes a serious problem only when you cannot control it or choose not to communicate because of it.

Communication Apprehension

Communication apprehension, the severest form of speech anxiety, was defined in Chapter 3 as an anxiety syndrome associated with either real or anticipated communication with another person or persons.[3] Communication apprehension can be seen in individuals who either consciously or subconsciously have decided to remain silent. They perceive that their silence offers them greater advantages than speaking out, or that the disadvantages of communicating outweigh any potential gains they might receive. Communication apprehensive individuals fear speaking in all contexts, including one-on-one and in small groups. Among the fears of those with communication apprehension is the fear of speaking before a group. However, everyone who fears speaking before a group does not necessarily suffer from communication apprehension. That term refers to the much deeper problem of virtually cutting oneself off from most, if not all, communication with others.

Symptoms of Speech Anxiety

Anxiety is a condition during which our bodies secrete hormones and adrenaline that eventually overload our physical and emotional responses. These chemical reactions are the same as those you might experience when you are waiting to see a friend you haven't seen in years or going to your first job interview. Your heart begins to beat faster and your blood pressure begins to rise. More sugar is pumped into your system, and your stomach may begin to churn. When you experience these reactions, you may feel as if your body is operating in high gear and that little or nothing can be done about it. You have to realize that some of these feelings are perfectly normal, and for most us, they will not interfere with our speech performance.

Speakers who experience speech anxiety often display these visible signs:

Voice	Quivering
	Too soft
	Monotonous, nonemphatic
	Too fast
Fluency	Stammering, halting
	Awkward pauses
	Hunting for words, speech blocks
Mouth and Throat	Swallowing repeatedly
	Clearing throat repeatedly
	Breathing heavily
Facial Expressions	No eye contact, rolling eyes
	Tense face muscles, grimaces, twitches
Arms and Hands	Rigid and tense
	Fidgeting, waving hands about
Body Movement	Swaying, pacing; shuffling feet[4]

These behaviors can occur separately or in any combination, depending on the degree of anxiety the speaker is experiencing.

Speakers who experience speech anxiety may also make telling statements. For example, they may offer self-critical excuses or apologies such as "I'm not any good at this anyway," "I didn't really prepare for this because I didn't have enough time," or "I never was able to say this correctly." Instead of improving the situation, these comments tend to draw more attention to speakers' nervousness and thus magnify the problem.

Speakers who have speech anxiety often overestimate how much the audience notices about their behavior. The audience, on the other hand, tends to underestimate a speaker's anxiety. Audiences cannot detect, for example, a speaker who is experiencing butterflies unless the "butterflies" cause an observable reaction or the speaker's voice sounds nervous.

Causes of Speech Anxiety

Just as physicians can better treat an illness if they know its cause, so people can better reduce and control speech anxiety if they can determine the underlying problem. Many people with speech anxiety treat only the symptoms and tend to ignore the causes, but trying to remove the symptoms without understanding the causes is usually a losing battle.

Most speech anxiety begins at an early age as a result of negative feedback in the home. For example, children who are not encouraged to communicate or are punished for doing so are likely to learn that communicating is undesirable and that silence is beneficial. As these children avoid communicating, others may unknowingly contribute further to their fear by asking questions such as "Cat got your tongue?" or "You're afraid to talk, aren't you?" thus making them feel inadequate and perpetuating the fear and anxiety associated with communicating.

People may also develop speech anxiety if they constantly hear that speaking in front of others can be a terrible experience. Being told immediately before giving a speech, "Don't worry about it—you'll do fine," reinforces the notion that something can go wrong. If speakers believe that something can go wrong and that they might make fools of themselves, they are apt to lose confidence and develop speech anxiety.

In our society, success, winning, and "being number one" are too often considered all-important. When we can't be the most successful, we sometimes consider ourselves failures. No one likes a failure. Thus, we are apt to feel that success brings rewards and failure brings punishment. If you are a winner, you are praised, and if you are a loser, you are ridiculed. As a result, we place tremendous pressure on ourselves and others to be successful.

When we haven't been successful at something, we are often told to try again. But if the consequences of the failure are dramatic and the payoff for success doesn't seem worth the effort, we may prefer to avoid the situation. Avoidance may result in punishment, but we may perceive that as better than trying to do something and failing. Sometimes society is more lenient. For example, in a competition we assume that there will be a winner and a loser. No one likes to lose, but playing your best and losing is often acceptable. When someone makes a mistake in a speech, however, we may be more critical. Rather than acknowledge that the person is making an honest effort, we may perceive him or her as inadequate or unskilled. Consequently, the stress created by fear of making mistakes in front of others may be so great that it produces anxiety, and sometimes complete avoidance of a speaking situation.

Among the other most common causes of speech anxiety are:

Fear of physical unattractiveness

Fear of social inadequacy

Fear of criticism

Fear of the unknown

Fear of speech anxiety

Conflicting emotions

Excitement from anticipation[5]

Note that each of these reactions to a speech-making situation is *learned*. Because speech anxiety is a learned behavior, the only solution for its sufferers is to examine the potential reasons for their anxiety and learn how to use this knowledge to manage their discomfort.

Speech Anxiety and Other Cultures

Every year increasing numbers of international students and Americans whose first language is not English enter higher education in the United States. In spite of their differences, most of these students do not ask to be treated any differently than anyone else. Because of the language and cultural differences these students have experienced, they do require understanding and patience with their communication. Ester Yook and Bill Seiler, for example, in a study of Asian students, found that most Asian students were anxious about presenting a speech. They were concerned about whether they would be understood by their audience because of their accent, tone, and pronunciation.[6] They were also concerned that if they were unable to "think in English" that they might not be able to find the right word or expression they wanted, resulting in "humiliation."

Another source of anxiety for Asian students, according to Yook and Seiler, occurs because they sometimes have difficulty understanding the speech assignment fully. The potential for misunderstanding the assignment and their perceived lack of English fluency lead many Asian students to memorization of their speech. The memorization of their speech, however, prevents many of the Asian students from being conversational in style and adds to their perceived ineffectiveness and anxiety as communicators. Communicating in front of others creates some anxiety for almost all of us, but being from a different culture and speaking English as a second language can create additional anxiety. Those students from different cultural and language backgrounds don't want sympathy, but they do want their situation to be understood.

Treating Speech Anxiety

While speaking before a group may produce stress and anxiety, few people allow their nervousness to prevent them from trying and succeeding.[7] In fact, as mentioned earlier, even well-known speakers feel some nervousness before giving a speech, but they have learned to control it. The key to successful control of your anxiety is the desire to control it. To cope with speech anxiety, we must realize that the potential for failure always exists, but that we can't let it stop us from trying. If we allowed the possibility of failure to overwhelm us, we probably would never do or learn anything. A child beginning to walk is a prime example of how most of our learning occurs. At first, the child wobbles, takes a small step, and falls. But when the child falls, someone is usually there to offer help, support, and encouragement to continue. In addition, the child usually is determined to walk regardless of the difficulties. Speech making, like learning to walk, involves many of the same processes. Help, support, and encouragement are important, but the essential ingredient is determination to succeed.

Most successful people will tell you that before they were successful, they had some failures and moments of embarrassment. But their drive and self-confidence pushed them to try again. Some of my first speeches were not very good, and I was quite nervous about speaking in front of my classmates. However, it didn't take me long to realize that even the best speakers in the class felt the same way I did. The only difference was that they weren't afraid to make a mistake.

Many of us are too hard on ourselves. Some students, after giving a speech, will say that they were extremely nervous, but in fact the audience never detected any sign of nervousness whatsoever. To the audience the speaker appeared relaxed and in control.

There are no cures for speech anxiety—only ways to reduce, manage, or control it so that it does not interfere with your presentation. Experts suggest that *selecting a topic you know about* and enjoy helps to reduce anxiety, since the more you know about a subject, the easier it is for you to talk about it. According to one research study, people who are highly anxious tend to be more negative in their assessments of themselves and more concerned with what others think of them. In addition, they tend to choose unfamiliar speech topics, which compounds their problem.[8]

Being prepared can also reduce anxiety. Because anxious people are more negative in their self-assessments, they tend to spend less time preparing, convinced they are not going to succeed no matter what they do. Thus, they set themselves up for failure, which perpetuates the cycle. Preparation can break the cycle. For example, know your audience and become familiar with the physical surroundings where you are going to speak (such as the room size, lighting, placement of microphone, and audiovisual equipment). This will help create confidence by reducing the unknown.

Confidence plays a key role in controlling anxiety. I am often amazed at how many students sell themselves short. I have heard many student speakers over the past years, and every one of them had the ability and potential skill to be an effective speaker. Students who didn't believe that they could be successful seemed to have the most difficulty giving speeches. I have also had students who were extremely quiet in class, but when it came to speaking, they were exceptional. I asked one student who seldom talked in class how she felt after her speech, and she indicated that she was surprised at how good she felt. The first minute or so she was nervous, but once she realized that she knew what she was talking about and the audience appeared to be listening, she completely forgot about her nervousness and concentrated on informing her audience. You only have to try. Even if you do not do as well as you'd like, the instructor is there to help you and your classmates, and wants you to do well.

Think positively by visualizing yourself giving a successful speech. Some students tell me it is easy to think positively, but that doesn't help them give a successful speech. But it does! There is ample proof to suggest that those who think positively and visualize themselves doing well, often do. On the other hand, thinking that you are going to do poorly is a sure path of failure.

Practice is another good way to ease anxiety. The better you know the content of your speech and your delivery plan, the more comfortable you will feel about your presentation. Few things are done without some practice. For example, the quarterback who executes a perfect touchdown pass, the gymnast who scores a 10 in floor exercise, the actress who presents a flawless performance, the student who draws beautiful pictures, the person who passes the road test for a driver's license, and the person who gives a polished and interesting speech have spent hours—and sometimes years—in practice. Knowing that you don't have weeks, months, or years to practice your speech, you must practice as much as you can with the realization that you may not be perfect in all aspects of your speech. Remember that almost all speakers are somewhat nervous before a speech, and that being nervous is perfectly normal.

Giving a speech and completing a pass play in a football game are not exactly the same thing, but both require similar preparation. The successful pass play requires research, organization, learning, observation, practice, willingness to work hard, ability to perform, confidence, knowing your opponent's defenses (or knowing your audience), and timing. A successful speech presentation requires all of the aforementioned factors in addition to selecting an appropriate topic.[9]

CONTROLLING SPEECH ANXIETY

Realize that almost everyone has some anxiety about presenting a speech. You are not alone.

Select a topic that you are familiar with and that you enjoy.

Know your audience and the surroundings where your presentation will take place.

Think positively. Prepare yourself mentally for success. Believe that you are going to be successful, and you probably will be. Practice!

Ask your instructor for additional advice and other possible treatment programs that may be available.

Don't give up. Others want you to succeed, and you can if you want to.

If none of the above techniques help to reduce your anxiousness, then you should probably seek professional help. Individuals who suffer from abnormal levels of speech anxiety should know that the negative feelings associated with communicating in front of others do not just occur; they develop over a long period of time. Thus, these negative feelings do not always disappear easily. But speech anxiety is a problem that something can be done about, with help. Most university settings have psychologists or counselors who are trained to reduce the fear of speaking in public.

If your school does offer help in reducing speech anxiety, there is another alternative, called systematic desensitization.* **Systematic desensitization** is a technique where relaxation is associated with an anxiety-producing situation. For example, a student who suffers from public speaking anxiety might be asked to visualize speaking in front of a class, and then immediately associate the frightening experience with thoughts of relaxation. The theory behind systematic desensitization is that a mental rehearsal will associate relaxation with situations that create tension. Repetition of the association may help those suffering from anxiety learn that relaxation can replace tension and thus reduce their fear of speaking in public.

Overcoming anxiousness in public speaking situations is not easy, but you must remember that some anxiety can be helpful and is a normal reaction to speaking in public. When I asked students in one of my classes how they dealt with their fear of speaking, they suggested the following:

1. Practice and have your introduction, main points, and conclusion clearly in your head. Students feel that once they know their introduction, main points, and conclusion, it is a lot easier to remember the details.
2. Walk confidently to the speaking area. Students feel this helps to create more confidence. If you're confident, it is more likely you will feel relaxed. In other words, positive behavior results in positive outcomes.
3. Do not start your speech until you are ready. The students suggest that having everything under control before you start to speak makes it easier to relax and concentrate on the speech rather than themselves.
4. Look at your audience and focus most of the time on friendly faces. Students feel that if you concentrate on those who are likely to give you positive feedback, this will help make you feel good about speaking.

*If your school does not have a systematic desensitization program, write to the Speech Communication Association, 5105 Backlick Rd., Building #E, Annandale, VA 22003 for information on how to reduce stage fright. Also, see J. Ayres and T. Hoft, *Coping with Speech Anxiety* (Norwood, NJ: Ablex, 1994).

These suggestions are probably not surprising, but they are helpful in your quest to be a more successful speaker. The best thing you can do is continue giving speeches in your class and take more classes which provide you with opportunities to speak under the supervision of a trained instructor. You can reduce and control your fear of speaking, but it won't happen until you take action to do so.

METHODS OF DELIVERY

An effective delivery conveys the speaker's purpose and ideas clearly and interestingly so that the audience attends to and retains what was said as it was intended by the speaker. The effectiveness of a speech, therefore, depends both on what is said and how it is conveyed. No two speakers are alike. For example, it is unlikely that anyone could deliver Martin Luther King, Jr.'s "I Have a Dream" speech as effectively as he did. This speech, widely regarded as a masterpiece, was delivered on August 28, 1963, to over 200,000 people gathered in Washington, D.C., to participate in a peaceful demonstration furthering the cause of equal rights for black Americans. If you ever heard a recording of this speech, you know how his delivery affected his audience. King had a rich baritone voice modulated by the cadence of a Southern Baptist preacher and the fervor of a crusader. Although the words of the speech can be repeated and King's style can be imitated, the setting, timing, and circumstances cannot be reconstructed. Thus, the effect that King had on that day can never be repeated.

A poorly written speech can be improved by effective delivery, and a well-written speech can be ruined by ineffective delivery. No set of rules will guarantee an effective delivery in every situation. The only consistent rule is that you must be yourself! Of course, as a beginning speaker, you probably have many questions about how to deliver a speech: "How many notes should I use?" "Will I need a microphone?" "Where and how should I stand?" "Where or at whom should I look?" "How many and what kinds of gestures should I use?" "How and when should I use my visual aids?" "How loud should I speak?" "How fast or slow should I speak?"

Such questions are valid, but the answers will vary from person to person and from situation to situation. In the end, effective delivery comes from practice under the direction of a competent instructor. An awareness of self and knowledge of what effective delivery is also helps to improve your delivery. Although a speech may be delivered in many different ways, the four most common methods of delivery are impromptu, memorized, manuscript, and extemporaneous.

Impromptu Delivery

Impromptu delivery is the delivery of a speech without any planning or preparation. You have used this method many times, perhaps without even realizing it. Whenever you speak without prior preparation, whether in response to a question in class, to a sudden request at a business meeting, or to a comment made by a friend, you are using the impromptu method of delivery. The more formal or demanding the situation, the more most speakers prefer to avoid this approach. At times, however, you have no choice. In such cases, muster your self-control, relax, and concentrate on what you wish to say. The lack of preparation time distinguishes the impromptu method from other methods of delivery and forces speakers to depend solely on their ability to think on their feet.

Memorized Delivery

Memorized delivery requires that you memorize your speech in its entirety, usually from a word-for word script. This kind of delivery is used for short presentations, such as toasts, acceptance speeches, and introductions, and is also commonly used by speakers in contests and on lecture circuits. Speakers frequently memorize certain parts of their speeches, including examples, short stories, statistics, quotations, and other materials that they can call up at the appropriate time. Politicians, salespeople, tour guides, and others often have a memorized "pitch" or speech to fit their needs.

Memorizing has one advantage. You can concentrate less on what you have to say and focus more on your delivery. Of course, this is only true if you are extremely confident and have memorized your speech so completely that you don't need to think about each word. One disadvantage of memorized delivery is its lack of flexibility—it doesn't allow for much, if any, adaptation to your audience. Beginning speakers face another disadvantage: They may forget what they want to say and become embarrassed. In addition, it is difficult to deliver a memorized speech without sounding mechanical. To present an effective memorized address requires a great deal of practice and confidence.

Manuscript Delivery

Manuscript delivery is a method of delivery in which the speaker reads the speech word for word. As a result, such a speaker is never at a loss for words. A speaker should use a manuscript when every word, phrase, and sentence must be stated precisely. Using a manuscript is not uncommon for politicians, clergy, teachers, and others who need to present information completely and accurately or who are likely to be quoted after their presentations. In learning how to give a speech, use of the manuscript speech is often discouraged because it invites the speaker to concentrate more on the script than the audience, reducing eye contact with the audience. Also, speakers who work from manuscripts are less able to adapt to the reactions of the audience and thus may sound mechanical.

GUIDELINES FOR MANUSCRIPT SPEAKING

If you plan to speak from a manuscript, keep the following in mind.

1. WRITE YOUR MANUSCRIPT FOR THE EAR. There is a difference between content written to be read silently and to be read aloud. The silent reader can go back to a previous sentence for reference and can reread a passage if it is unclear the first time, but a person listening to a speech cannot.

2. PREPARE YOUR MANUSCRIPT IN AN EASY-TO-READ FORMAT. Type it triple-spaced. Use special marks and comments to note points you plan to emphasize.

3. THINK ABOUT WHAT YOU ARE SAYING. The presence of a manuscript often tempts a speaker to read words instead of thoughts. Try to sound spontaneous and give meaning to the manuscript.

4. READ WITH EXPRESSION AND VOCAL EMPHASIS. Remember, your voice can add meaning to the words. Thus, the use of your voice becomes an added dimension to the reading of the words.

5. PRACTICE READING OUT LOUD, preferably with a tape recorder. The key to success is to sound as if the thoughts you are reading are fresh. The manuscript should be presented with enthusiasm, vigor, and interest.[10]

Extemporaneous Delivery

Extemporaneous delivery is a method in which the speaker uses a carefully prepared and researched speech, but delivers it from notes, with a high degree of spontaneity. Extemporaneous delivery is the method most commonly used in speech classrooms. Somewhere between memorized or manuscript delivery and impromptu delivery is the extemporaneous delivery. Speakers depend on a brief presentational outline or notes and choose the actual wording of their speech at the time of delivery.

An extemporaneous speech may at first seem as difficult as an impromptu speech, but in fact it is much easier. Because it eliminates memorization and manuscript writing, it leaves more time for preparation and practice. Thus, once you have prepared your outline, you can begin to practice your delivery. The goal of the extemporaneous method is a conversational and spontaneous quality. Each time you practice your speech, the wording should be somewhat different, although the content remains the same.

Methods of Delivery: Advantages and Disadvantages		
	Advantages	**Disadvantages**
Impromptu	Spontaneous	No time for preparation
	Flexible	Can be inaccurate
	Conversational	Difficult to organize
		Can be stressful
Memorized	Good for short speeches	Inflexible
	Speaker can concentrate on delivery	Requires practice and repetition
	Easier to maintain eye contact	Speaker can forget or lose place
	Prepared	Difficult to adapt to audience response
		May sound mechanical

Manuscript	Good for material that is technical or detailed or that requires complete preciseness	No flexibility
		May sound mechanical
		Difficult to adapt to audience response
	High accuracy	
	Can be timed to the second	
	Prepared	
Extemporaneous	Flexible	May be intimidating to inexperienced speakers
	Conversational	
	Prepared	
	Organized	

The advantages of extemporaneous delivery are that it gives you better control of your presentation than the impromptu method, it allows more spontaneity and directness than the memorized and manuscript methods of delivery, and it is more adaptable to a variety of speaking situations than the other methods. Most teachers, as well as professional speakers, prefer to use the extemporaneous method because it allows them to adjust to the situation moment by moment.

VOCAL AND PHYSICAL ASPECTS OF DELIVERY

Without solid content and valid sources, nothing is worth communicating, but without effective delivery, information cannot be clearly and vividly presented. Because the audience is the ultimate judge of effectiveness, you must use your delivery to involve them in your speech. Each audience member likes to feel as if he or she is being addressed personally. Therefore, try to think of your presentation as a conversation and your audience as your partners in dialogue. Then use your voice and body to create this impression.

Vocal Aspects

Many beginning speakers overlook the important role that voice plays in delivery. As you speak, your voice should be pleasant to listen to, relate easily and clearly to your thoughts, and express a range of emotions. Your voice should convey the meaning to your listeners that you wish to convey. Thus, the more natural, spontaneous, and effortless you appear to be, regardless of how hard you are working, the more your listener can focus on what you are saying rather than how you are saying it. Three aspects of voice that determine the effectiveness of delivery are vocal quality, intelligibility, and vocal variety.

Vocal Quality   **Vocal quality** is the overall impression a speaker's voice makes on his or her listeners. Voices may be harsh, nasal, thin, mellow, resonant, or full-bodied. Attitude can affect the quality of the voice and tell listeners whether the speaker is happy, confident, angry, fearful, or sad. Vocal quality is also a highly accurate indicator of the presenter's sincerity.

Intelligibility   A speaker's **intelligibility**, the degree to which an audience can learn and understand the words he or she says, is determined by vocal volume, distinctiveness of sound, accuracy of pronunciation, articulation, and stress placed on syllables, words, and phrases. The keys to high intelligibility are self-awareness and consideration for your listeners.

To determine the proper volume, you must consider the size of the room and observe listeners' reactions. Do listeners look as if they're straining to hear you, for example? Or is your voice too loud or booming for the size of room?

We have all been known to mispronounce words. Sometimes we mispronounce words out of habit. For example, many people pronounce *realtor* as *re-la-tor* instead of *real-tor*. When we mispronounce words, we lower our intelligibility and also run the risk of lowering our credibility. This suggests that before we present a speech, we should practice it before a friend or colleague who might detect our mispronunciations. Always check any pronunciation you are not sure of in a dictionary.

There is a difference, however, between mispronounced words and regional and ethnic dialects that affect pronunciation. The effect dialect has on an audience depends a great deal on the makeup of the audience and whether they understand the difference between dialect usage and standard pronunciation of words.

Articulation is saying words clearly and distinctly. Physical problems, such as cleft palate, difficulty controlling the tongue, or misaligned jaw, may create articulation problems that require specialized help, but most articulation problems are the results of laziness. We sometimes chop, slur, or mumble words because we do not take the time to say the words correctly. People say "gonna" instead of "going to," "didja" instead of "did you," or "dunno" instead of "don't know." Such articulation errors are often the result of habit and sloppiness rather than ignorance of what is correct.

Unfortunately, many people don't realize that their articulation is incorrect unless someone points it out to them. Listen to what you say and how you sound. Concentrate on identifying and eliminating your most common articulation errors. Correcting articulation errors can be well worth the effort, making you sound more professional and intelligent and helping establish your credibility as an educated person.

EXERCISE

Professional television or radio announcers often practice their articulation by saying tongue twisters, such as the ones below. Begin by saying each word slowly and distinctly and then increase your rate to a normal speaking speed.

> **Rubber baby buggy bumpers**
> **The sixth sick sheik's sheep is sick.**
> **She sells sea shells by the sea shore.**

Vocal Variety   **Vocal variety** is the combination of rate, force, and pitch variations that add to a speaker's overall vocal quality. Such variety gives feeling to your delivery and adds emphasis to what you say. Your voice allow listeners to perceive subtle differences in the intent of your messages by altering rate, force, and pitch, coming closer to a genuine understanding between you and your audience.

Rate is the speed at which a speaker speaks—usually between 120 and 150 words per minute. Speaking at the appropriate rate requires self-awareness. A rate that is too fast, too slow, or that never changes can detract from the impact of your message. Pauses are important to consider when discussing rate. A pause can be an effective means of gaining attention, adding emphasis to an important point, and enabling listeners to follow shifts in ideas. Pauses punctuate and emphasize thoughts.

Force is the intensity and volume level of the voice. You must choose a volume level that is comfortable for your audience. However, you can use force to communicate your ideas with confidence and vigor, to emphasize an important point, and to regain lagging interest. By learning how to use force, you can greatly increase your effectiveness as a speaker.

Pitch refers to how low or high the voice is on a tonal scale. Variety in pitch can eliminate monotony and add emphasis to key words.

EXERCISE

Try reading the following sentence first without and then with pauses.

The little boy and his dog having tired of fishing wandered slowly along the dusty path in the late afternoon.
The little boy and his dog, having tired of fishing, wandered slowly along the dusty path in the late afternoon.

Do you hear the difference in emphasis and note the shift in ideas when pauses are included?

E. C. Glenn, P. J. Glenn, and S. H. Forman, *Your Voice and Articulation,* 2d ed. Englewood Cliffs, NJ: Prentice-Hall, 1989, 234.

Obviously, any change in rate, force, or pitch makes a word, phrase, or sentence stand out. The greater the amount of change or the more sudden the change is, the more emphatic the word or statement will be. So remember, the keys to vocal variety and effective delivery are contrasts a speaker uses to make selected ideas seem more important than they would seem otherwise.

EXERCISE

Read the following excerpt from Lewis Carroll's "The Walrus and the Carpenter" with no vocal variety—that is, don't vary your rate, force, or pitch. Then read it using vocal variety—that is, vary your rate, force, and pitch in order to put more meaning into the poem.

> **The sun was shining on the sea,**
> **Shining with all his might**
> **He did his very best to make**
> **The billows smooth and bright—**
> **And this was odd, because it was**
> **The middle of the night.**

What effect does vocal variety have on the poem? What effect does the use of vocal variety have on listeners?

Physical Aspects

In Chapter 5 we discussed nonverbal communication in depth. You are encouraged to review the chapter, as much of the information about nonverbal communication will aid you in your speaking performances. Among the physical factors that can affect delivery are personal appearance, body movement, gestures, facial expressions, and eye contact. All of these must be well coordinated and relevant to the purpose of your speech.

Personal Appearance   Personal appearance—what a speaker looks like and the way a speaker dresses, grooms, and presents himself or herself to others—is an extremely important consideration. Typical student attire is not always acceptable. The general rule is to use common sense in dressing for the occasion. For example, large, dangly earrings, a printed T-shirt, and a cap may distract your audience from what you are saying. First impressions are based mainly on appearance. Your audience may form quick and hard-to-change opinions about your attitude toward them and yourself. In this way, appearance can affect your credibility.

Although we do not know much about the exact role of personal appearance in communication, we do know that it influences interpersonal responses. In some situations, appearance can have a profound impact on a speaker's self-image and, therefore, affect how he or she communicates with others.[11] As simple and even superficial as it may seem, looking your best does help you convey your message. In addition, looking good makes you feel good, which ultimately will have a positive effect on your performance.

Body Movement   Body movement is closely related to personal appearance. This includes posture, which should be relaxed and natural; avoid slouching. Because an audience's attention instinctively follows moving objects, your motions should be easy and purposeful. The use of movement—stepping to the side, forward, or backward—can aid in holding attention and communicating ideas more clearly. Purposeful movement, along with posture, can indicate confidence and convey a positive self-image.

Gestures   Gestures are movements of the head, arms, and hands that help illustrate, emphasize, or clarify a point. Gestures should be spontaneous, not forced. For example, when you are talking to acquaintances about something you have strong feelings about, your gestures come naturally. If you are sad, angry, or happy, you automatically make gestures that express your emotions. To obtain equally natural gestures when giving a speech, you need to be equally involved in what you are saying. If you concentrate on getting your message across, rather than on your gestures, you will find yourself moving more freely and naturally.

When you are first learning how to give a speech, using gestures may seem a bit uncomfortable. To overcome this problem, practice using gestures in front of others who are willing to make positive suggestions to help you improve. Be assured that as you give more and more speeches, you will find that gesturing becomes more natural and easier to do. Soon, without even thinking, you'll be using strong and smooth-flowing gestures that help hold your audience's attention and add meaning to your message. (See Figure 10.2.)

Figure 10.2:

Nonverbal delivery is important. Using gestures, facial expressions and eye contact can add meaning and interest to your speech delivery.

Charles Gupton/Uniphoto

Facial Expressions **Facial expressions,** as defined in Chapter 5, are configurations of the face that can reflect, augment, contradict, or be unrelated to a speaker's vocal delivery. They account for much of the emotional impact of a speaker's message. Your face is a very expressive part of your body. Facial expressions quickly and accurately tell your audience a lot about you. For example, whether you are serious, happy, worried, or angry, the audience will be able to "read" your face. Because your audience will read a great deal into your facial expression, it is important to look warm and friendly. Such an expression will inform your listeners that you are interested in them and in what you are saying. Of course, your topic, your purpose, the situation, and your audience will all determine exactly what facial expressions are appropriate as you progress through your speech.

Eye Contact **Eye contact,** the extent to which a speaker looks directly at audience members, is associated with facial expression. Facial expressions indicate a speaker's feelings about the message, but eye contact seems more related to a speaker's feelings about the listeners. Eye contact is the most important physical aspect of delivery, as it indicates interest and concern for others and implies self-confidence. Most speech communication teachers recommend that you look at your audience while you are speaking.

Looking at members of the audience establishes a communicative bond between them and you. Failure to make eye contact is the quickest way to lose listeners. Speakers who ignore their audiences are often perceived as tentative, ill at ease, insincere, or dishonest.

Your eye contact with your audience should be pleasant and personal. Give your listeners the feeling that you are talking to them as individuals in a casual conversation. When speaking to a small audience (five to thirty people), try to look at each individual for a few seconds at a time. To avoid looking shifty, move your eyes gradually and smoothly from one person to another. For larger groups, it is best to scan the audience and occasionally talk to a specific member or members. Do not look over people's heads, and avoid staring, which can give the impression that you're angry or hostile. Try not to make your listeners uncomfortable. A colleague of mine once had students fill out peer evaluations for each speaker. One student wrote "He stared at me. I felt like he was drilling a hole through my head. It made me very nervous." The speaker in this instance would want to distribute his eye contact among more audience members.

Your eyes should convey that you are confident and sincere and are speaking with conviction. The message your audience should get from your eye contact is that you care about them and about what you are saying. At first, establishing eye contact with an audience may make you feel uncomfortable, but as you gain experience, you will begin to feel more at ease. You will soon find that making eye contact puts you in control of the situation and helps you to answer such questions as "Can they hear?" "Do they understand?" "Are they listening?"

BEHAVIORS THAT CAN DETRACT FROM YOUR DELIVERY

General Delivery
Speaking too fast
Speaking too slow
Sighing
Nervous smiling or laughing
Choppy pacing
Awkward pausing

Voice
Sing-song speech pattern
Monotone voice
Nasal twang
Mumbling
Speaking too softly
Speaking too loudly
High pitch
Shrillness, stridency
Lack of variety in pace, volume

Face
Deadpan or serious look
Facial contortions (such as scowling)
Listless or apathetic look

Body
Tense, stiff posture
Sloppy posture
Hunched shoulders
Wiggling
Swaying

Hands
Fidgeting, waving, or other
   meaningless motions
Hand in pocket
Playing with hair

Feet
Shuffling
Shifting weight
Crossing legs

Eyes
Shifty glances
Rolling movements
Looking at the floor
Looking at one side of the room
Looking at the ceiling
Staring
Lack of sustained eye contact

VISUAL AIDS

Visual aids are materials and equipment, such as key words, diagrams, models, real objects, photographs, tables, charts, and graphs, that speakers may use to enhance the speech's content as well as their delivery. Students often think that the only time they will be required to use visual aids is in classroom speech assignments. In reality, however, speeches using visual materials are presented quite frequently, and many speeches depend on them. For example, imagine an architect explaining the floor plans for a new high-rise office building without a drawing, model, or photograph; a company executive explaining this year's annual profits and losses compared to last year's without a chart or graph; a coach explaining a play without a diagram; a teacher telling the class where Athens, Greece, is located without a map or globe; or a salesperson selling a product without showing it.

Choosing and Using Visual Aids

When planning to use visual aids, keep the following hints in mind.

1. VISUAL AIDS SHOULD SERVE A NEED. They should never be used for the sake of using them. In some cases visuals are not appropriate, but in others they can get a point across better than words alone. For example, it is easier to show an audience how to tie shoes than it is to tell them. Furthermore, it is easier to tell *and* show them.

2. VISUAL AIDS SHOULD BE PLANNED AND ADAPTED TO THE AUDIENCE AND THE SITUATION. For example, the size of the visual aid and the distance between you and your audience should be considered. The visual material should be kept simple and free from too much detail.

3. VISUAL AIDS SHOULD NOT DOMINATE OR TAKE OVER A SPEAKER'S JOB. Visuals should supplement, but never replace, the speaker. Do not rely too heavily on visual aids, but instead use them to help elaborate or explain a point or idea. In a speech, visual aids always require explanation by the speaker in order to make them meaningful.

4. VISUAL AIDS SHOULD LOOK AS PROFESSIONALLY PREPARED AS POSSIBLE. Accurate and neat materials will create a positive impression on the audience and reflect favorably on the competence of the speaker. Visuals should be free from factual and spelling errors. They should also be bright, attractive, and legible.

5. VISUAL AIDS SHOULD BE PRACTICAL. Visual aids should be easy to prepare, use, and transport.

6. VISUAL AIDS THAT ARE NOT ORIGINAL OR THAT CONTAIN INFORMATION THAT IS NOT YOURS REQUIRE DOCUMENTATION. Cite your source eithdirectly on the visual where your audience can see it or in the context of speech.

7. VISUAL AIDS SHOULD CONTAIN ONLY ONE IDEA. For example, each poster should contain only one graph.

Advantages of Visual Aids

If "a picture is worth a thousand words," then visual aids are an excellent way to strengthen and reinforce the development and proof of a point.

Such aids are a special form of supporting and clarifying materials because they combine both verbal and visual modes of presentation. When carefully designed and used, visual aids can help a speaker to:

Save time

Gain attention and hold interest

Clarify and support main points

Reinforce or emphasize main points

Improve retention (See Figure 10.3)

Research has shown that audiences remember information longer when it is accompanied by visual aids.[12]

Kinds of Visual Aids

There are many different kinds of visual aids. The most frequently used visual aids are key words, real objects, models, photographs, diagrams, tables, and graphs.

Key Words   Displaying key words in writing is a simple way to highlight main points and important ideas. This approach helps the audience to focus on the most significant words and concepts being presented and, therefore, to understand and recall them more easily. Key word visuals can be easily prepared in advance. When designing them, use contrasting colors so that the lettering stands out from the background as vividly as possible. The lettering should be neat and large enough to be easily seen and

Figure 10.3:

Visuals can enhance your speech. There are many different types of visual aids that can be used to enhance a speech's content as well as the delivery of a speech. Visuals can save time, gain attention, clarify, reinforce or emphasize main points, and improve retention.

Jeffrey W. Myers/Uniphoto

understood. Figure 10.4 that follows, is an example of a key word visual representing how public school teachers rated the top disciplinary problems of the 1940s and of today.

Illustration of Key Word Visual

How Times Have Changed	
1940	**1990**
Talking out of turn	Drug abuse
Chewing gum	Alcohol abuse
Cutting in line	Rape
Running in halls	Suicide
Making noise	Pregnancy
Dress-code violations	Robbery

Figure 10.4:

Each word is used to help explain and emphasize the point the speaker is making. The visual also helps the audience remember the significant words or concepts because they see them.

Source: U.S. News & Report (November 8, 1993) p. 34–Basic Data Congressional Quarterly Researcher

Real Objects   A real object is any article related to the speech topic that a speaker displays or demonstrates, such as a musical instrument, piece of sporting equipment, or kind of food. Using a real object can make your topic more immediate and interesting, but it can also create problems if the object is too large, too small, or too impractical. Pets, for example, are often unpredictable and can be distracting before, during, and after a speech.

Models   When displaying the actual article is not practical because of size or cost, a model should be considered. A model—or representation of a real object—allows a speaker to enlarge or shrink an object to a convenient size for display. For example, it would be impractical to show the actual circuitry of a computer microchip, which is no larger than a pinhead, or the inside of an actual space shuttle, which is enormous (and also inaccessible to most people).

Models can also be life-size. Currently, cardiopulmonary resuscitation (CPR) is a popular and important subject. To demonstrate this procedure, speakers often use life-size dummies of humans.

Photographs and Prints   When models are neither available nor practical, a photograph may be used. A photograph is an excellent device for explaining details and surroundings. One student, speaking on artistic style, brought prints of several paintings to illustrate their differences. A student who spoke on the construction of the Egyptian pyramids showed photos that she had taken on a vacation trip. She realized that the original photos were too small, so she had them enlarged for effective use in the classroom. The typical photograph is usually too small to be seen clearly unless the speaker moves through the audience or passes it around. In both instances, the advantage of using photos is somewhat diminished because the audience tends to pay more attention to the pictures than to what is being said.

Drawings, Sketches, and Diagrams When photographs or prints are unavailable, too small, or lack adequate detail, a drawing, sketch, or diagram may be used. Don't worry if you're not artistic, because most drawings used in classroom speeches are relatively simple. For example, Figure 10.5 is a line drawing used to describe how a classroom can be divided in a beginning speech communication course. The diagram simply shows the division of the room for various functions and makes a professor's explanation of a seating arrangement much easier for students to comprehend.

Simple Line Drawing

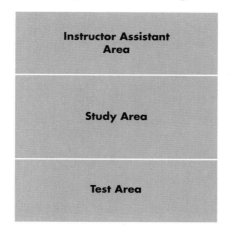

Figure 10.5:

Line drawings do not need to be elaborate or complex. In fact, line drawings, sketches, or diagrams can be rather simple.

Similarly, a speaker might use an architect's blueprint, a chart illustrating a company's organizational structure, a sketch of the basic positions of water-skiing, or a map of various segments of land. Virtually anything can be diagrammed or sketched.

In technical presentations, a diagram may be used to illustrate three-dimensional relationships. The two most common types of three-dimensional diagrams are the cutaway view and the exploded view, as illustrated in Figures 10.6 and 10.7. The cutaway allows an observer to see the inner structure

Cutaway Diagram

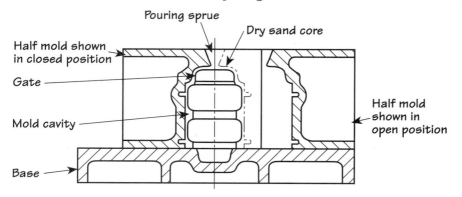

Figure 10.6:

The cutaway diagram provides a three-dimensional view of the inner structure of an object.

Exploded Diagram

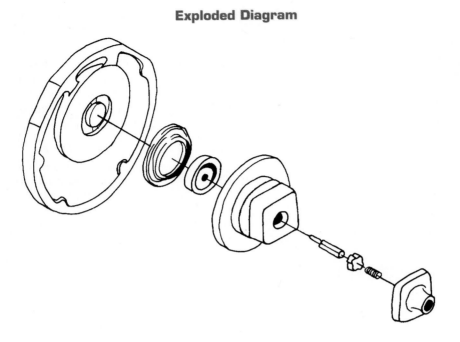

Figure 10.7:

The exploded diagram shows a three-dimensional view of the relationship between the separate parts of an object.

of an object, and the exploded view shows the systematic relationship of separate parts to the whole object. The most effective diagrams are drawn to scale and represent the real object or process as accurately as possible.

Tables and Graphs   Tables and graphs are used mainly to display statistics. A table is an orderly arrangement of data in columns to highlight similarities and differences, as shown in Table 10.1.

Tables conveniently display large amounts of data in a relatively small space, but remember that a complex or lengthy (and perhaps boring) table will require an equally complex and lengthy explanation. As with any

Table 10.1   Tables display large amounts of data in a relatively small space. The more complex the data, the more explanation is required to make the table meaningful to your audience.

Rank 1993	Rank 1992	Team	Payroll 1993	Payroll 1992
1	1	Toronto	$51,575,034	$49,427,166
2	9	NY Yankees	$46,563,791	$34,902,292
3	4	Boston	$46,164,788	$42,524,012
4	7	Atlanta	$44,856,416	$35,853,321
5	16	Chicago W. Sox	$43,765,634	$29,982,605

visual aid you decide to use, a table must be concise, simple, and clear so that the important information is easy to spot. Complex data are often better illustrated by a graph.

Graphs help to make statistical data vivid and illustrate relationships among data in ways that are easy for your audience to grasp. Line graphs, as illustrated in Figure 10.8, are particularly helpful for clarifying comparative data over time. Such graphs can help you trace trends and show increases and decreases over a span of days, months, or years. Note in Figure 10.8, for example, that the sharp downward slope of the line strongly emphasizes how dramatically farm population dropped between 1920 and 1990.

Bar graphs are another simple way to show comparisons. Note how much easier it is to compare the data depicted in the bar graph in Figure 10.9 than the data in Table 10.2. Whenever possible, your visual aids should present only one or two basic relationships so that your audience can quickly grasp your point.

Pie graphs are used to illustrate proportional divisions of a whole set of data. Each wedge of the pie represents a percentage of the whole. Pie graphs are often used to show distribution patterns and to illustrate national, state, or local budgets. Note in Figure 10.10 that the pie graph starts with a radius drawn vertically from the center to the twelve o'clock position. Each segment is then drawn in clockwise, beginning with the largest and continuing down to the smallest. A pie graph should be divided into no less than two and no more than eight segments.

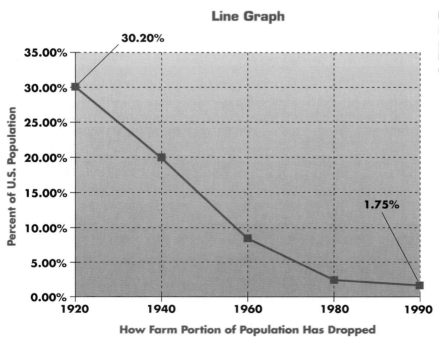

Line Graph

Figure 10.8
Line graphs are particularly helpful in clarifying comparative data over time.

How Farm Portion of Population Has Dropped

(Adapted from Census Bureau)

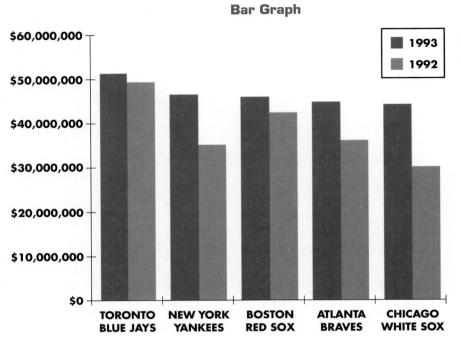

Bar Graph

Figure 10.9:
Bar graphs show
comparative data
much more clearly
than does, for
example, Table 10.1.

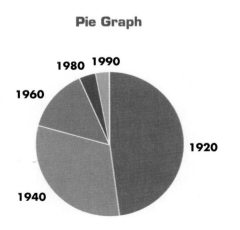

Pie Graph

How Farm Portion of Population Has Dropped

Figure 10.10:
Pie graphs illustrate
proportional divisions
of a whole set of data.
Each wedge represents
a percentage of the whole.

Methods of Presenting Visual Aids

The most frequently used methods of presentation are chalkboards, posters, projections, and handouts.

Chalkboard   The chalkboard is the most readily available method of presenting visual aids, at least in most classroomsHere are several things to consider when you are plag to use a chalkboard.

1. WHEN SHOULD YOU PUT INFORMATION ON THE BOARD? Preferences vary from speaker to speaker and from instructor to instructor. Some speakers write on the board before they speak. If putting the information on the board before you speak will not interfere with other presentations, and if you can cover what you have written (so as not to distract from other presentations), preparing the board in advance can simplify your deliveryTo be safe, ask your instructor which way he she prefers you to do it.

2. HOW SHOULD YOU WRITE ON THE BOARD? This, of course, depends on the size of the room and your writing skills. Your writing should always be large enough and neat enough for everyone in the room to reaThe appearance of your writing on the board communicates a message about you and your speech. Thus, you want what you write create a positive impression.

3. HOW SHOULD YOU USE THE BOARD WHEN DELIVERING YOUR SPEECH? Even when reading from the board, you should always try to face your audience. Use a pointer, a ruler, or your outstretched arm to help guide your listeners to the information you want them to focus on with you. Whether writing on the board or reading from it, avoid talking to the chalkboard rather than your audience.

The chalkboard is a convenient visual device, but do not be fooled by its conveniences. If it is not used properly, it can be more of a distraction than a help. Practice writing on the board before your speech. This will give you an idea of how it feels. You will also be able to determine how large to write so that those sitting in the back row can see the information.

Posters   Posters are another commonly used method of presenting information visually. The greatest advantage of posters is that they can be prepared in advance, which makes the speaker seem more efficient and professional. Many of the guidelines for writing on the chalkboard also apply to using posters. On page xx are general guidelines for using visual aids. Here are two specific suggestions for using posters:

1. If an easel is not available, check to see if there are clips on the board for hanging posters or if you will need to use masking tape. If you must use masking tape, make large loops of tape and place them on the back of the poster in advance. Then, when you are ready to display the poster, merely place it on the board, pressing firmly on the tape loops to secure it. If you have more than one poster, you can place several of them on the board at once, or you can display each individually as you need it.

2. Make sure the poster is made of firm cardboard so that it will support itself if you have to stand it in a chalk tray or on a table.

Projected Visuals The most common projected materials are slides, movies, overhead transparencies, and videotapes. The projection of such visuals requires planning and familiarity with the mechanical equipment. Each form has advantages and disadvantages, so knowing what each can and cannot do is vital. For example, showing slides and movies requires a totally darkened room, and the projectors may be noisy. Yet both enable you to show places and things that you could not show any other way. Films and videos add motion, color, and sound. But they can be costly and often tend to dominate a presentation by replacing the speaker for a period of time.

The most popular projected visual is the overhead transparency. These materials can be prepared in advance or created during a presentation, and whether prepared by the speaker or a professional, they are relatively inexpensive. In addition, overhead projectors are easy to use and do not require a darkened room. When using an overhead projector, consider the following:

Make sure the projector is focused correctly so that everyone in the room can read what is on the transparency.

Cover information on the transparency until it is needed.

Use a pointer (pencil or pen) to direct the audience's attention to what is being discussed.

Practice using the overhead. Check it beforehand to make sure that everything is working correctly.

Mechanical devices, because of their potential for breakdown, require a backup method. It is a good idea to carry a spare bulb in case one burns out and to bring copies of visual aids in handout form.

Handouts Handouts can be a useful means of presenting information to your audience. They are particularly helpful if you are unable to use any other method. Among their advantages are that they can be prepared in advance and that each audience member gets his or her own copy. Their main disadvantage is that they can become a distraction. Passing them out can interrupt the flow of your presentation, and audience members may pay more attention to the handouts than to the speech itself. As a result, you should use handouts only when you have no other alternatives or when you have a creative reason for doing so. In addition, you should wait until the end of the presentation to use them, if possible.

Developing Visual Aids

Today there are many computer programs and technologies that can help you develop visual aids. If your university or college has a media center, and most do, check with the center or your instructor to learn about the most modern and easiest methods for developing visuals and what is available to you. There are programs and techniques that will allow you to make graphics, charts, custom-made diagrams, and many other types of visuals. Making professional-looking visuals is often quite simple and may require only that you become familiar with what your campus has available.

TIPS ON USING VISUAL AIDS

Display visual materials only while you are using them. Do not distract your audience by showing your visuals too early or by leaving them on display after you've finished talking about them.

Ensure that everyone can see your visual aids by making them neat, simple, large, bright, and readable.

Do not talk to your displayed objects. Discuss them while maintaining eye contact with your audience. Use a pointer to aid you in maintaining eye contact.

Keep your visual aids on display long enough to give everyone ample opportunity to absorb the information.

Do not stand in front of your visual aids. Plan where you will place or show your visual aids and use a pointer to avoid blocking your audience's view.

Practice using your visual aids until you feel comfortable with them.

POLISHING YOUR DELIVERY

The best way to polish your delivery is to practice, practice, practice. Practice early and often until you feel comfortable with your speech's content. Exactly how much practice you will need depends on a number of considerations, including how much experience you have had speaking before audiences, how familiar you are with your subject, and how long your speech is. There is no magic amount of time that will make your delivery perfect.

If your speech is not to be memorized, make sure to use slightly different wording in each run-through. When you memorize a speech, it's possible to master the words without mastering the content. Your goal should be to learn your speech, which will mean that you have mastered its ideas.

In practicing your delivery, it is important to start with small segments. For example, practice the introduction, then one main point at a time, and then the conclusion. After you have rehearsed each small segment several times in isolation, practice the entire speech until you feel that you have mastered the content and the ideas flow smoothly.

If possible, practice in the same room where you will speak or under similar conditions. This helps you to see how things look from the front of the class and to plan where you should place your visual aids. Your last practice session should leave you with a sense of confidence and a desire to present your speech. Finally, concentrate on what you are saying and to whom you are saying it. Above all, be yourself.

SUMMARY

Ethics, an individual's system of moral principles, plays a key role in communication. Ethical speakers always cite the sources of their information. The use of another person's information, language, or ideas without citing the originator or author, thus making it appear that you are the originator, is referred to as *plagiarism.* Effective speakers, besides being ethical, are also knowledgeable, prepared, and self-confident. *Speech anxiety,* the fear of speaking before an audience, can severely undermine a speaker's self-confidence. Speech anxiety is quite common; almost everyone who speaks before a group experiences it to some extent. The important thing is to be able to control it. Speech anxiety can be reduced by selecting a topic that you know and enjoy, preparing, practicing, and knowing the surroundings in which your presentation will take place.

Communication apprehension, an anxiety syndrome associated with either real or anticipated communication with another person or persons, is the severest form of speech anxiety. An individual who suffers from communication apprehension will actually remain silent rather than risk communicating. Everyone who fears speaking before a group does not necessarily suffer from communication apprehension. Some nervousness is natural, and if controlled, can energize your presentation. If your anxiety is such that you can not present, seek the help of your instructor or a school counselor, or use *systematic desensitization,* which is a technique where relaxation is associated with an anxiety producing situation. The theory behind systematic desensitization is a mental rehearsal which associates relaxation to situations that create tension. The effectiveness of your speech presentation depends not only on what you say, but also on how you say it. Appearance, body movement, gestures, facial expressions, eye contact, and vocal characteristics all contribute to an effective speech delivery. Speakers who successfully combine all of these factors convey their purpose and ideas clearly and interestingly, so that their audience attends to and retains the intended message.

A poorly written speech can be improved by effective delivery, and a well-written speech can be ruined by an ineffective delivery. Yet there are no rules that will guarantee every speaker an effective delivery in every situation. The only consistent rule is that you must be yourself.

Although a speech may be delivered in many different ways, the four most common methods of delivery are impromptu, memorized, manuscript, and extemporaneous. An *impromptu* speech is delivered without planning or preparation. A *memorized* speech is presented from memory, usually based on a word-for-word script. A *manuscript* speech is read word for word from a script. An *extemporaneous* speech is a carefully prepared and researched presentation for which the speaker uses few notes and tries to be spontaneous.

Many beginning speakers overlook the important role that voice plays in delivery. The three essential aspects of voice are *vocal quality,* the overall impression of the voice; *intelligibility,* the clarity of the sounds and the pronunciation and articulation of the words; and *vocal variety,* the *rate* (speed at which the speaker speaks), *force* (intensity and volume level of voice), and *pitch* (how low or high the voice is on a tonal scale) variations that add life to a speaker's voice. In addition, many physical factors contribute to the success of a presentation. These include body movements such as stepping to the side, forward, or backward; *gestures,* the movements of head, arms, and hands to help illustrate, emphasize, or make a point; *facial expressions,* the configurations of the face that can reflect, augment, contradict, or be unrelated to a speaker's vocal delivery; and *eye contact,* the extent to which a speaker looks directly at audience members. Effective eye contact establishes a bond between the speaker and the audience and makes each listener feel as if he or she is being addressed personally.

Many different kinds of visual aids can be used to enhance a speaker's words. *Visual aids* are materials and equipment, such as key words, diagrams, models, real objects, photographs, tables, charts, and graphs, that speakers may use to enhance the speech's content as well as their delivery. When visual aids are used as supporting and clarifying materials, they save time, gain attention, reinforce or emphasize main points, and improve retention. The most frequently used visual aids are key words, real objects, models, diagrams, pictures, tables, and graphs.

The most common methods of presenting visuals are chalkboards, posters, projections, and handouts. The projection of visual aids requires planning and familiarity with the mechanical device to be used. The most common projected visuals are slides, overhead transparencies, movies, and videotapes.

The best way to polish your delivery is to practice, practice, practice. The amount of time spent rehearsing a speech will determine how effective your delivery will be.

KEY TERMS

Communication Apprehension: Anxiety syndrome associated with either real or anticipated communication with another person or persons.
Ethics: Individual's system of moral principles.

Extemporaneous Delivery: Delivery style in which the speaker carefully prepares the speech in advance, but delivers it with only a few notes and with a high degree of spontaneity.

Eye Contact: Extent to which a speaker looks directly at audience members.

Facial Expression: Configuration of the face that can reflect, augment, contradict, or be unrelated to a speaker's vocal delivery.

Force: Intensity and volume level of the voice.

Gesture: Movement of the head, arms, or hands that helps illustrate, emphasize, or clarify an idea.

Impromptu Delivery: Delivery style in which a speaker delivers a speech without any planning or preparation whatsoever.

Intelligibility: Speaker's vocal volume, distinctiveness of sound, clarity of pronunciation, articulation, and the stress placed on syllables, words, and phrases.

Manuscript Delivery: Delivery style in which a speaker writes the speech in its entirety and then reads it word-for-word.

Memorized Delivery: Delivery style in which a speaker memorizes a speech in its entirety from a word-for-word script.

Pitch: How low or high the voice is on a tonal scale.

Plagiarism: Use of another person's information, language, or ideas without citing the originator, making it appear that the user is the originator.

Rate: Speed at which a speaker speaks, normally between 120 words and 150 words per minute.

Speech Anxiety: Fear of speaking before an audience.

Systematic Desensitization: Technique where relaxation is associated with an anxiety producing situation.

Visual Aids: Materials and equipment, such as key words, diagrams, models, real objects, photographs, tables, charts, and graphs, that speakers use to enhance the speech's content as well as the speaker's delivery.

Vocal Quality: Overall impression that a speaker's voice makes on his or her listeners.

Vocal Variety: Variations in rate, force, and pitch.

DISCUSSION STARTERS

1. Which quality of an effective speaker–ethics, knowledge, preparation, or self-confidence–would you say is the most important? Why?

2. Why do you think most people are so fearful of speaking before an audience?

3. Your best friend must give a speech and is frightened about it. What advice would you give to help him or her manage this fear?

4. What are the vocal characteristics that distinguish an effective from an ineffective speech delivery?

5. Why is the way a speech sounds to a listener more important than its content?

6. On what basis should a speaker select one method of delivery over another?
7. If you were to develop an evaluation form to assess a speaker's vocal delivery, what factors would you include and how would you evaluate them?
8. What nonverbal behaviors distinguish effective speakers from ineffective speakers?
9. When should a speaker use visual aids in a speech?
10. If you were advising beginning speakers, what would you tell them about using notes in their first speech?
11. Based on the information you learned in this chapter, what advice would you give to a beginning speaker about delivery?

NOTES

1. J. Wenburg and W. W. Wilmot, *The Personal Communication Process* (New York: Wiley, 1973) and R. L. Johannesen, *Ethics in Human Communication,* 2d ed. (Prospect Heights, Ill.: Waveland Press, 1983).
2. Bruskin Associates, "What Are Americans Afraid Of?" *The Bruskin Report,* no. 53 (1973); D. Goleman, "Social Anxiety: New Focus Leads to Insights and Therapy," *New York Times* 18 December 1984, C. J. Solomon, "Executives Who Dread Public Speaking Learn to Keep Their Cool in the Spotlight," *Wall Street Journal* 4 May 1990; and a 1993 segment of ABC's *20/20* pointed out that the most common situation in which people are likely to experience anxiety is giving a speech.
3. J. C. McCroskey, "The Communication Apprehension Perspective," in J. A. Daly and J. C. McCroskey (eds.), *Avoiding Communication: Shyness, Reticence and Communication Apprehension* (Beverly Hills, CA: Sage, 1984): 13.
4. A. Mulac and A. R. Sherman, "Behavior Assessment of Speech Anxiety," *Quarterly Journal of Speech* 60, no. 2 (April 1974): 138.
5. E. C. Buehler and W. Linkugel, *Speech: A First Course* (New York: HarperCollins, 1962)
6. E. Yook and W. J. Seiler, "An Investigation into the Communication Needs and Concerns of Asian Students in Speech Communication Performance Classes," *Basic Communication Course Annual* 2 (November, 1990): 47–75.
7. D. W. Staacks and J. D. Stone, "An Examination of the Effect of Basic Speech Courses, Self-concept, and Self-disclosure on Communication Apprehension," *Communication Education* 33 (1984): 317–332; R. S. Lifflefield and T. L. Sellnow, "The Use of Self-disclosure as a Means for Reducing Stage Fright in Beginning Speakers," *Communication Education* 36 (1987): 62–64.
8. J. A. Daly, A. L. Vangelisti, H. L. Neel, and P. D. Cavanaugh, "Preperformance Concerns Associated with Public Speaking Anxiety," *Communication Quarterly* 37 (1989): 39–53.

9. S. R. Glaser, "Oral Communication Apprehension and Avoidance: The Current Status of Treatment Research," *Communication Education* 30 (1981): 321–341; J. Ayres and T. S. Hopf, "Visualization: A Means of Reducing Speech Anxiety," *Communication Education* 30 (1985): 318–323; A. M. Rossi and W. J. Seiler, "The Comparative Effectiveness of Systematic Desensitization and an Integrative Approach in Treating Public Speaking Anxiety: A Literature Review and Preliminary Investigation," *Imagination, Cognition and Personality* 9 (1989–1990): 49–66.

10. J. C. Humes, "Read a Speech Like a Pro," in *Talk Your Way to the Top* (New York: McGraw-Hill, 1980): 125–135; J. Venlenti, *Speak Up with Confidence: How to Prepare, Learn, and Deliver Effective Speeches* (New York: Morrow, 1982): 23–26.

11. S. Chaiken, "Communicator Physical Attractiveness and Persuasion," *Journal of Personality and Social Psychology* 37 (1979): 1387–1397.

12. E. P. Zayas-Baya, "Instructional Media in the Total Language Picture," *International Journal of Instructional Media* 5 (1977–1978): 145–150.

Chapter 11

Informative Speaking

LEARNING OBJECTIVES

After studying this chapter, you should be able to:

1. Tell why information is powerful.

2. Select an informative speech topic that focuses on objects, processes, events, or concepts.

3. Gain an audience's attention by generating a need for your information and showing its relevance to their needs and interests.

4. Demonstrate how to use organization and language to increase your audience's understanding of your topic.

5. Explain how avoiding assumptions and personalizing information can contribute to the success of an informative speech.

6. Deliver an effective informative speech.

Julie:	Ethan, do you know where the 501 Building is?
Ethan:	Sure. Do you know where the Big Red Shop is located?
Julie:	Yes.
Ethan:	It's one block south of the Big Red Shop on the same side of the street. It's the only building on that block. You can't miss it.
Julie:	Thanks.
Heather:	Can you help me with my chemistry?
Rick:	Sure. What do you need help with?
Heather:	The problems on pages 55 and 60 in the workbook. I just don't understand them.
Rick:	Okay. Let's start with the problem on page 55.
Dave:	Professor Jones, would you please explain the difference between homophily and heterophily?
Prof. Jones:	Of course. Homophily refers to the degree to which interacting individuals are similar in certain attitudes. Heterophily is the opposite of Homophily—it is the degree to which someone is different from us in various attributes. Let me give you some examples. . . .

In each of the preceding examples, someone wants information and someone gives it. The *American Heritage Dictionary of the English Language* defines **information** as "knowledge derived from study, experience or instruction." This definition makes the act of informing seem fairly simple. Yet, when you think about the amount and kinds of knowledge that you send and receive in a single day, providing information really isn't simple at all. Have you ever tried to teach someone how to perform CPR (cardiopulmonary resuscitation), use a word processor, or play a card game? If you have, you know it takes time and care to present information in proper sequence and in amounts small enough to ensure that the listener understands correctly.

Teaching or informing others can be a rewarding and satisfying experience, but if you lack the required skills, it can also be frustrating. To help you in this area, we will discuss how to present knowledge by means of the informative speech. This type of speech is one of the most often assigned in the speech communication classroom because of its far-reaching practicality. You will find that knowing how to present information clearly and systematically will be of great benefit to you both personally and professionally throughout your life.

Instructors vary in their style of presenting information to their classes. Observe carefully several of your instructors, and note what they do to ensure their message is received and understood by their students. What makes one instructor more effective than another? Be prepared to discuss what makes an effective instructor and how effective instruction relates to the informative speech.

INFORMATION AND POWER

Being informed helps reduce our uncertainty of things we know little about. Thus, it is logical that the person who possesses and controls information has power. When people need information about something they know little about, they tend to turn to those who can provide the necessary information. For example, in the dialogues at the beginning of this chapter, the person who has the desired information has the power to share it or not to share it. The greater your desire to have important information, the more valuable that information is to you. Thus, the person who has the information you want gains control over you because of his or her power to give or withhold the knowledge you seek.

The ability to communicate information is essential in our society and plays an increasingly important role in our future. In fact, over the years we have moved from an economy based on agriculture and heavy industries, such as steel, machinery, and automobile manufacturing, to an economy based on knowledge industries, such as research, health services, banking, training, and communications. During the 1950s, only about 17 percent of our labor force held information-related jobs. This figure has now increased to about 60 percent. This demand puts even more emphasis on workers' needs for greater skills in producing, storing, and delivering information. Much of the information we send and receive is written, but most is spoken. For example, teachers, trainers, consultants, media specialists, salespersons, technicians, doctors, nurses, lawyers, elected officials, and managers all depend on oral communication.

THINK ABOUT IT

Imagine a clock face to visualize our place in history.
Let the clock stand for the amount of time humans have had access to writing systems. Our clock would thus represent some 3,000 years, and

each minute would stand for 50 years. On this scale, there were no significant media changes until about nine minutes ago. At that time, the Western culture developed the printing press. About three minutes ago, the telegraph, the photograph, and the locomotive arrived. Two minutes ago we invented the telephone, the rotary press, motion pictures, the automobile, the airplane, and the radio. And one minute ago, we developed the talking picture.*

Television has appeared in the last 30 seconds, the computer in the last 15, and communication satellites even more recently. Crammed into the last 10 seconds are not only several hundred thousand new books, but low-cost electronic and laser technologies that promise almost unlimited opportunity to produce, store, retrieve, and deliver messages.** We've come a long way since the paper containing this analogy was written some thirteen years ago. Today, information is instantaneously sent around the world.*

How has technology changed the way we communicate with each other?

What changes do you see coming in the way we communicate?

*B. C. Gilliam and A. Zimmer, *ITV: Promise into Practice* (Columbus, Ohio: Department of Education, 1972), 36.

**G. C. Elmore, "Integrating Video Technology and Organizational Communication" (Paper presented at the Indiana Speech Association Convention, Indianapolis, Ind., 1981), 1.

GOAL OF INFORMATIVE SPEAKING

The general goal of informative speakers is to increase the knowledge of their listeners. There is a fine distinction between informing and persuading. The informative speech is meant to increase knowledge, whereas the purpose of the persuasive speech is to alter attitudes and behavior. Information can be presented without any attempt at persuasion, but persuasion cannot be accomplished without attempting to inform.

The difference between the two is best explained through examples. A car salesperson must rely on persuasion to sell cars. However, to persuade someone to buy a car, the salesperson will probably spend a lot of time informing the customer about the advantages of buying a specific model. The salesperson might succeed in increasing the customer's knowledge and understanding of the car (informing), yet he or she may fail in inducing the customer to buy the car (persuading). Persuasion takes place when a person stops presenting information to increase understanding and begins to present information to alter behavior.

A math professor, in explaining a complex problem, is attempting to help students understand how the problem can be solved. The professor is not hoping to persuade the students of how it should be done, but is trying to help them gain the knowledge and understanding they need to find the solution on their own. Of course, the professor could add an element of persuasion if he or she tried to show that one way of solving the problem was better than another, but that would probably be less important than teaching the basic problem solving skills.

The key to understanding the difference between information and persuasion lies in recognizing that although *information may contain some elements of persuasion, all persuasion must provide information*. Therefore, what separates an informative speech from a persuasive one is the goal of the speaker. Persuasion will be discussed in more detail in the next chapter.

STEPS IN DEVELOPING AN INFORMATIVE SPEECH

Although the steps in preparing and developing an informative speech may not always follow the same order or require the same amount of detail and involvement, the following is a typical sequence.

1. Select the topic.
2. Research the topic.
3. Analyze the audience.
4. Determine the specific purpose.
5. Organize the speech.
6. Develop the supporting materials.
7. Practice the delivery.
8. Deliver the speech.
9. Analyze the effectiveness of the speech.

Always remember that each step depends on the others and sometimes you may have to redo a step several times in order to accomplish your specific purpose.

TOPICS FOR INFORMATIVE SPEECHES

Surprisingly, some students believe they have little to inform others about. In actuality, most students have a wealth of information and a vast list of potential topics based on what they have learned from classes, readings, and other experiences. For example, geography, agriculture, computer science, social science, sex education, driver education, first aid, art, music, physical education, political science, sociology, chemistry, health, and on-the-job experiences can all offer potential topics for an informative speech.

The topic potential for an informative speech is virtually limitless. There are, however, some guidelines (suggested in Chapter 7) for selecting a speech topic that you should not ignore. They are:

1. Choose a topic that will allow you to convey an important thought or action to your audience.
2. Choose a topic that is familiar and interesting to you.
3. Choose a topic that is important to you.
4. Choose a topic that will be or can be made interesting to your audience.

Communicating with others is easier when they see value and use for the information being presented. Most audiences want the information they receive to be important and useful to them. Thus, it is necessary to select a topic that will allow you to provide benefits to your audience for listening to what you have to say. Sometimes a topic will speak for itself, such as, "How to Make Extra Money in an Innovative and Challenging Career Field" or "Five Ways to Make Your College Life Easier." Both of these topics, at least in title, provide incentives for a typical college audience to accept them as potentially beneficial. Other topics may require you to provide more incentives to your audience in order for them to want to listen to what you have to say.

If something interests you, chances are it will also interest others. Roland, for example, has been involved with computers ever since he can remember, first with video games and then with his own personal computer. In high school he took a few programming classes, and now, as a college major in computer science, he has learned much about the most recent technological advances in the field of graphic arts and design programming. This specialized knowledge made a natural topic for his informative speech. Yet, at the time of the assignment, Roland never even thought of it. Only after his speech professor spent some time asking him about his interests did he decide to speak on graphic design. The assignment required the use of visual aids. Roland already had many available aids to choose from, including flow charts of his computer programs and the graphics that he and others had designed. He was also able to expand his experiences and knowledge by interviewing professors and doing more research on a subject that he really cared about.

For the past semester Cindy has been an intern volunteer for a local family crisis line. Her responsibilities include answering phone calls from troubled people and referring them to experts and organizations that can help them with their problems. Given this experience and her major in clinical psychology, Cindy wisely chose to give her informative speech on the growing role of crisis lines in serving the mental health needs of local communities.

Roland and Cindy are probably no different from most of you. At first they doubted that they had anything worthwhile to speak about. Like them, if you stop to think about your past experiences and interests, you will probably discover that you, too, have a great deal to share with others.

Successful speakers consider their audience first. They communicate information accurately and clearly, but most importantly they make the information they present meaningful and interesting to their audience by providing new information or correcting misinformation.

Informative speech topics can be classified in many different ways. One scheme divides them into speeches about objects, processes, events, and concepts.[1]

Objects

Speeches about objects examine concrete subjects, such as people, animals, structures, and places (See Figure 11.1.) Here is a list of some possible object topics.

Ronald Reagan	Martin Luther King, Jr.
Barney the dinosaur	Compact discs
Alaska as the last frontier	Nontraditional students
Haiti	Single parents
Hillary Clinton	The Soviet people
Musical instrument	Electronic score board

Figure 11.1:

Selecting and demonstrating an object can be an excellent speech topic. For example, you can discuss its development, uses, or, in this case, its layout.

M. Siluk/The Image Works

These topics are quite general and must be narrowed in order to meet the guidelines of most classroom speaking situations. Here are some specific purpose statements for some of the topics, following the guidelines suggested in Chapter 7.

To inform the audience why Ronald Reagan was considered "The Great Communicator"

To inform the audience about the Soviet people's reactions to the changes in their political structure

To inform the audience about the latest innovations in compact disc technology

To inform the audience about the important contributions that the non-traditional student makes in the college classroom

Each of the above topic areas is tailor-made for the informative speech.

Processes

A process topic usually focuses on a demonstration in which the speaker explains how something is done or how it takes place. Here are a few sample specific purpose statements.

To inform the audience how to invest in the stock market to ensure a financially secure future

To inform the audience how to write a résumé

To inform the audience how to invest in a hose while in college

To inform the audience hoow to diet with low-fat foods

To inform the audience how to help someone who is having a heart attack

Speeches about processes generally serve two purposes: to increase understanding and to teach someone *how to do something.* This could involve anything from how to do CPR to how to buy the right car.

Process speeches are usually organized in time-sequence (chronological) order, meaning they proceed step-by-step from the beginning of the process to its end. For example, if you were to explain to your audience how to sky-dive, you would take them through all the necessary steps and procedures so that they would understand what a person had to do in order to sky-dive.

The demonstration of a process usually lends itself to the use of a visual aid. Getting your audience to understand how some things are done may require an actual demonstration. For example, informing listeners how to fold napkins may require you to do the folding during the speech presentation.

Events

Informative speeches about events discuss happenings or occasions. Among the many possibilities are:

Nuclear accidents	Hurricane Andrew
LA riots	Rose Bowl parades
Somalia	Marathons
Cancer	The fall of Communism
Baseball's moral decline	The assassination of Martin
The 1993 floods	Luther King, Jr.

Appropriate specific purposes for some of the above topics might be:

To inform the audience about the meaning and impact of the fall of Communism

To inform the audience about the latest developments in curing cancer

To inform the audience about the media's impact on major sporting events, such as the World Series

To inform the audience about the economic impact of the floods of 1993

Concepts

Speeches about concepts deal with abstract topics such as beliefs, theories, ideas, and principles. The challenge is to make the subject matter concrete so that the audience can more easily understand it. Concept-based topics include:

Relationship development	Learning theory
Principles of reading	Liberalism
Computer theory	Philosophy of sport
Love	Theory of rap music

These topics are too vague to be meaningful. If you were to ask a dozen people what each term means, you would probably receive a dozen different answers. Thus, the speaker is responsible for narrowing and focusing the subject so the audience understands the intended meaning. Here are specific purpose statements based on some of the general abstract topics.

To inform the audience about some common misconceptions regarding relationship development

To inform the audience about the two most common principles in learning theory

To inform the audience about the latest sports philosophy

To inform the audience about the theory of rap music as a specific form of social communication

Speeches about concepts take extra time and effort to develop because of their abstract nature. These topics require the use of concrete examples, definitions, and clear language.

Whether a speech is about an object, a process, an event, or a concept is not always clear because a subject may cross from one category to another. Often the differences rest with the specific purpose that the speaker chooses to emphasize. Therefore, it is important to decide how you want to treat your subject and then develop your speech accordingly. If you are unsure of your approach, you may want to review Chapter 7 for more specific information about topic selection and how to determine which topics may be best suited for you and your audience. (See the Appendix at the end of the chapter for a list of more topics.)

EXERCISE

Select one or two specific purpose statements from each of the categories presented above. Indicate what pattern of organization would be best suited for those you have selected and if visuals would be appropriate. What would you use to help make your presentation clearer to your audience, and how would you relate the subject to your audience?

PREPARING AND DEVELOPING AN INFORMATIVE SPEECH

The previous chapters on public communication relate directly to the principles and skills of informative speaking. All aspects of topic selection, audience analysis, information gathering, preparation of supporting and clarifying materials, and organizing, outlining, and delivering a speech are crucial to the effectiveness and eventual success of your informative presentation. In addition, you should know the goals and strategies involved in a presentation, including how to compete with distractions and noises such as students coming in late, an airplane overhead, a lawn mower outside the window, and whispering in the audience. Such interferences cannot be ignored if you want to be successful in transmitting information to others. To achieve your main goal of increasing knowledge, you must strive to attain two subgoals: gaining attention and increasing understanding.

Gaining and Maintaining Audience Attention

Motivating the audience to pay attention is critical to the success of any speech. (See Chapter 9 for more on motivating your audience to listen.) To accomplish this, you should generate a need for the information and show its *relevance* to the listeners. One student wondered why the audience had not paid attention to his informative speech on the harmful effects of smoking. He had failed to consider two things when selecting and preparing his speech: No one in the class smoked and everyone already knew, or at least thought they knew, the harmful effects of smoking. As a result, the audience felt it was unnecessary to pay attention. If the speaker had analyzed the audience, he could have made the appropriate adjustments. Then he might have started his speech by saying:

> I realize that none of you smoke, and that's good. I also realize that you probably know a lot about the harmful effects of smoking. But did you know that smoke from other people's cigarettes can be just as harmful to you, or even more harmful, than smoking yourself? Let me explain.

This opening attempts to pique the audience's curiosity and their need to know by asking a rhetorical question. Here are some other examples of rhetorical questions used to open speeches:

> Scientists have been working for years on the cure for the common cold, and I believe that I have found it. Do you know what I discovered?
>
> Do you want to know a sure way to get a job?
>
> Do you know why the number of suicides among college students is on the rise?
>
> Why is being thin so important in our society?
>
> What do you think is the most important skill you can learn in college?
>
> Why is there so much violence in our society?

People are also more likely to pay attention when they feel that a speech relates directly to them. A speaker who gives an audience a reason to listen by relating his or her topic to their needs and interests creates **information relevance.** Ask yourself if the information you intend to present is relevant to your listeners and, if it is not, how you are going to make it so. One student presented an extremely well researched speech on air pollution and its effects on people. He used several excellent examples about pollution on the East and West coasts, but never related them to his listeners, who were from the Midwest. To make his speech more relevant, he needed to relate the information to Midwesterners and explain why they should be concerned about the effects of pollution.

Another speaker, talking about space technology and its contributions to our daily lives, used several examples to make her topic relevant and useful to her audience. In discussing products that were specifically developed for use in space but now have become part of our everyday lives, she mentioned Velcro. She pointed out that Velcro is now commonly used in clothing, shoes, handbags, and many other items. She then held up a jacket to illustrate how Velcro works. The audience immediately recognized the relevance of her topic.

Information that is perceived as *new* also attracts the attention of an audience. Whenever the preceding statement is mentioned, some students immediately respond, "But there isn't anything new to present." Actually, "new" does not necessarily mean that you have to present something that the audience has never heard of before. It does mean that you need to devise a new view or angle. There are subjects that we have heard about many times, such as AIDS, abortion, capital punishment, gun control, pollution, smoking, drugs, safe sex, and the use of seat belts. But a speaker who provides a fresh perspective on a familiar topic makes it more interesting, and thus increases the chances of holding the audience's attention. One speaker informed the audience about illegal drugs that are medically helpful for certain diseases. She began her speech in the following manner:

> You have read and heard so much about cocaine, crack, heroin, and other illegal drugs that you are probably sick of the subject, but these drugs are not all bad. You may, at first, think that I am too liberal, but my mother is on drugs and I am glad of it. You see, my mother is suffering from cancer, and the only relief she can get is from the small doses of heroin she receives each day to ease the pain. Today, I am going to inform you about illegal drugs that actually aid our sick and dying.

This approach is not necessarily new, but it is different. Rather than taking a stand either for or against the banning of illegal drugs, the speaker focused on certain instances in which the use of illegal drugs can be beneficial. This also helped her to stay within the guidelines of the informative speech.

Sometimes focusing on an unusual aspect of a topic helps a speaker maintain the attention of the audience. Another speaker began her speech as follows:

> One summer day in 1948, Earle Smith borrowed $150.00 from the director of Harvard's Botanical Museum in order to join his friend in an archaeological dig in the highlands of Mexico.
>
> But these adventurers didn't discover the gold or jewels that we would associate with a great find. Instead they found 914 specimens of corn. Some of these kernels, perhaps two or three millennia old, were eventually put in hot oil, and amazingly, the oldest known corn in the world still popped. The director later wrote, "Seldom in Harvard's history has so small an investment paid so large a return."
>
> Admittedly, few of us consider corn to be anything more than a food to be eaten in the theater or at family picnics. However, the 1992 book *The Story of Corn* states that the average American ingests three pounds of corn in various forms every day. In one year, this adds up to 1,095 pounds of corn per person. That's almost 43 tons if we live to be 78.
>
> So lend me an ear, and we'll explore corn and its relevance to human culture. To do so, we will first examine the history of corn and its importance to those who planted it. Second, we'll discover the diverse roles corn plays today.[2]

Gaining and maintaining the attention of the audience is extremely important in presenting information. Audience members must see a benefit to receiving the information, see it as relevant to their lives, and find it interesting enough to want to listen. All of this can be quite challenging to the beginning speaker, but by making your audience the central focus of the speech and using a little creativity, you can easily gain and hold the attention of your audience.

Increasing Understanding

Once you have gained your listeners' attention, you have created the opportunity to increase their understanding. Understanding is the ability to interpret, grasp, or assign meaning to an idea. You can increase your audience's understanding by organizing your presentation systematically, choosing appropriate language, and providing clear definitions.

Organizing In a well-organized speech, ideas are managed in a clear and orderly sequence that makes the material easier to follow and understand. Effective organization helps increase the speaker's credibility and improves the audience's comprehension and retention of information. Two organizational techniques that aid listeners' understanding are planned repetition and advance organizers.

Planned Repetition **Planned repetition** is the deliberate repeating of a thought in order to increase the likelihood that the audience will understand and remember it. The repetition of information generally helps us remember things more completely. For example, we often repeat a new acquaintance's name several times to make sure that we will remember it later.

The power of repetition is so great that it is the guiding principle behind most television commercials. Although we may find it bothersome, the constant repetition of the same commercial reminds us of the product, and thus increases the chances of our purchasing it. You can use this same principle in an informative speech to get your audience to remember key ideas. For example, you might say:

> The relationship among thought, language, and reality is called linguistic relativity—the relationship is called linguistic relativity. Once again, linguistic relativity is the relationship between thought, language, and reality.
> The combination is 37-45-72-6. That's 37-45-72-6.

You could also show the combination on a visual or write it on the board for additional repetition and emphasis.

Advance Organizers **Advance organizers** are similar to signposts in that they signal what is coming, but they also warn that the information coming is significant. They signal the listener to pay attention.

This is very important.

Now get this:. . .

You will need to know the following:. . .

These warnings get the attention of your audience and emphasize that the forthcoming information is both necessary and important. Teachers use advance organizers to make sure that students know what is essential. Some examples include:

This will probably be included on your next test.

The following is vital if you are going to understand the overall concept.

The next three points are crucial to your understanding of the problem.

Advance organizers also serve as previews of main points. Using advance organizers in an informative speech introduction helps your audience concentrate and focus on what is coming in the speech. For example, one speaker said the following in her introduction to let the audience know what was coming and what was important to meet her specific purpose.

Let's first define critical thinking, then let's examine its decline, and finally, let's learn how we can develop our own critical thinking philosophy.

Choosing Language   It is extremely important to match your level of language to the knowledge your audience already possesses about your topic. If you are speaking with experts or with people who are familiar with your topic, you will be free to use technical terms, but if your audience is unfamiliar with your subject, you will need to choose your words carefully and define any special terms. In some cases, you will want to avoid technical terms altogether. This may be necessary when such terms would only confuse your audience or when your audience lacks the ability or background to understand them. Sometimes a speaker's use of too many technical terms will turn an audience off or even create hostility. A speaker should choose his or her language carefully to avoid creating unnecessary problems. When possible, choose words that are concrete over words that are abstract and use descriptions to make your points clearer.

ABSTRACT VERSUS CONCRETE WORDS   To increase your audience's understanding, try to use as many concrete words as possible. As discussed in Chapter 4, **concrete words** are symbols for specific things that can be pointed to or physically experienced (seen or touched). Thus, concrete words stand for specific places, objects, or acts: Howard Smith, Omaha, a personal computer, writing a letter to a friend. When you use concrete language that is familiar to your listeners, they will form mental pictures that are similar to your own. For example, if you say that something is the size of a dime, all your listeners should form a fairly accurate picture of the size you have in mind. Because of their specificity, concrete words leave less room for misinterpretation and misunderstanding.

In contrast, **abstract words** refer to ideas, qualities, or relationships, such as democracy, evil, and love. Their meanings depend on the experiences and intentions of the persons using them. A speaker who says that "the local food program is good for the people" may mean either that the food in the program is nutritious or that the program as a whole is beneficial. Because of its lack of precision, abstract language may leave listeners confused about the speaker's true intent.

In her speech, one student stated, "There are many things I don't like about our defense spending." Because this statement is too general and vague, it had little impact on her audience. A more precise statement would have been "There are two things I don't like about our defense spending. It costs taxpayers $200 billion each year and it takes money from desperately needed education and health programs." The second statement is concrete and specific, and thus more forceful and clear.

Abstract words allow listeners to choose from a wide range of personal images, while concrete words help listeners focus on the specific image that the speaker has in mind. Thus, as you prepare an informative speech, you should try to choose the most concrete words possible.

EXERCISE

Make the following statements more concrete so they become meaningful and better understood.

1. **We finally were free from the burdens that held us back.**
2. **The bridge was constructed of masses of steel which ran for a great distance.**
3. **The university provides access to all students regardless of background or origin.**
4. **Sex on campus has declined dramatically for quite some time.**

DESCRIPTION To make something more concrete, a speaker will often describe its size, quantity, shape, weight, composition, texture, color, age, strength, or fit. Words used to describe something are called **descriptors.** The more descriptors a speaker uses that relate to the listeners' experiences, the greater the likelihood that the message will be understood. Here is how Jim used descriptors in talking about the construction of a building:

> The first requirement when constructing a building is a sturdy foundation. The underlying groundwork for the foundation are called footings. Footings are usually made of concrete and range from about 1 foot in depth for a house to 10 feet in depth for a building with 20 floors. The width of footings ranges from 1 foot to the width of an entire building, depending on the soil's composition and its ability to support construction. Concrete, the result of

mixing lime, cement, stone, sand, and water, is prepared for use. This mixture is gray, has the consistency of cake batter, and pours like lava coming down the side of a volcano. When concrete dries, it becomes as hard as steel.

Through his explanation, Jim gave meaning to the word *footing* by using size, quantity, color, composition, texture, and strength descriptors. His vivid, colorful language appeals to the senses, thus making a meaningful and lively presentation for his audience.

EXERCISE

How would you make the following more meaningful and vivid to your listeners through the language you used?

The football stadium   The city in which the campus is located
The library on campus   The students in your speech class
The campus   The main street of the city

DEFINING One way to ensure your audience's understanding is to define all potentially unfamiliar and complex words. Consider the importance of definitions in the following cases: Jane had been involved in computer programming and in her speech discussed flow sheets and GIGO; Dana spoke on communication apprehension, Sally on the squeal rule, and Jim on the problem of ethnocentrism. In each situation, many in the audience may not have understood the speaker's subject unless the basic terms were explained. For example, Jane defined *flow sheets* as written instructions that programmers use to set up the step-by-step operations to be performed by the computer and *GIGO* as computer jargon meaning "garbage in, garbage out," or you get out of the computer what you put into it. Dana in her speech defined *communication apprehension* as the fear of communicating with others. Sally, in her speech, explained that a doctor uses the *squeal rule* when he or she tells the parents of a teenage girl that she is using birth control pills. *Ethnocentrism* was defined in Jim's speech as the belief in the inherent superiority of one's own group and culture over another.

As you probably recall from Chapter 8, the most common form of definition used by speakers, the logical definition, usually contains two parts: the dictionary definition and the characteristics that distinguish the term from other members of the same category. You most likely remember that an operational definition explains how an object or concept works and that a definition by example explains a term or a concept by using examples, either verbal or actual, to illustrate a point. In addition, there are four other methods of clearly defining a term for your listeners: contrast, synonym, antonym, and etymology.

CONTRASTS A **contrast definition** is used to show or emphasize differences. This type of definition is helpful when you want to distinguish between similar terms. For example, a speaker discussing communication apprehension and speech anxiety differentiated one term from the other by stating that communication apprehension is a trait or global anxiety, while speech anxiety is a state or situational anxiety. A person suffering from communication apprehension may also have speech anxiety, but a person with speech anxiety may not have communication apprehension. A contrast definition may also point out differences in causes and effects. Thus, the speaker might point out that people with communication apprehension actively avoid all interaction with others, while people with speech anxiety merely feel a bit of controllable discomfort when addressing an audience.

SYNONYMS   The use of synonyms can also help clarify the meaning of a word. A **synonym** is a word, phrase, or concept that has exactly the same or nearly the same meaning as another word, phrase, or concept. In describing a communicative extrovert, a speaker referred to "willingness to talk openly," "uninhibited speech," and "ability to speak in any situation without reservation." Each phrase describes the behavior that might be exhibited by a person who is a communicative extrovert.

ANTONYMS   In contrast, an **antonym** is a word, phrase, or concept that has the opposite meaning of another word, phrase, or concept. For example, a communicative extrovert is the opposite of someone with communication apprehension. Such a person is not shy, reserved, unwilling to talk, or afraid to speak. On the contrary, he or she greatly enjoys talking with others. Using an antonym helps the audience compare differences as well as leaving them with a memorable definition of an unfamiliar term.

ETYMOLOGIES   An **etymology** is a form of definition that traces the origin and development of a word. One student used etymology to explain how the Olympic Games got their name. In the Greek system of telling time, an Olympiad was the period of four years that elapsed between two successive celebrations of the Olympian. This method of figuring time became common about 300 B.C., and all events were dated from 776 B.C., the beginning of the first known Olympic Games. Such a definition provides the audience with a novel way to remember key information. The *Oxford English Dictionary* and the *Etymological Dictionary of Modern English* are excellent sources of word etymologies.

Whenever there is any possibility that your audience may not understand a term or concept, select the kind of definition that will provide the clearest explanation. In some instances, more than one kind of definition may be necessary. To err by overdefining is better than providing an inadequate definition that leaves your audience wondering what you are talking about.

HINTS FOR EFFECTIVE INFORMATIVE SPEAKING

Almost everything covered in the text to this point is relevant to informative speaking and audience participation. Adhering to the following two

additional guidelines should be particularly helpful in ensuring your success: Avoid assumptions and personalize information.

Avoid Assumptions

A student began speaking on CPR by emphasizing how important it is in
saving lives. However, she failed to explain that the acronym CPR stands for
cardiopulmonary resuscitation; she assumed that everyone already knew
that. Most of the audience did understand, but a number of people did not.
In addition, some knew what the acronym meant but did not know how the
technique worked. Because at least half of the class was unfamiliar with the
technique, they found the speaker's presentation confusing and frustrating.
One mistaken assumption undercut all the work she had put into her speech.

To avoid making assumptions:

1. Ask yourself if your listeners will already know what you are talking
   about. Here is where an audience analysis may be appropriate. If you
   are addressing your class, randomly select some of your classmates and
   ask them what they know about your topic and its related terminology.

2. If you believe that even one audience member may not understand,
   take the time to define and explain your topic.

3. If you believe that a majority of your audience already knows what you
   mean, say something like, "Many of you probably know what euthanasia is, but for those who don't,.   .   ". In this way you acknowledge
   those who already know and help those who do not.

4. Do not make the assumption that your audience needs no introductory
   information, especially if you have any doubts about what they know.
   You can always move through your basic definitions and explanations
   quickly if your audience seems to understand, but it is difficult to regain
   their interest and attention once you start talking over their heads.

Personalize Information

When you relate your topic to your listeners so they can see its relevance to
themselves, you are personalizing your information. Judy presented a
speech about nutrition and the eating habits of people in the United States.
It was an interesting speech, but the audience didn't understand what it
had to do with them. In revising her speech, Judy surveyed students in her
dorm and class about their eating habits. Then she personalized the information for her audience as follows.

> Bad eating habits can cause problems that you may not be aware of. In a sur-
> vey I took, I found that many college students like you fail to eat a variety of
> foods from the necessary basic food groups every day. In fact, my data indi-
> cate that 61 percent of you—that is more than half of you—do not eat bal-
> anced meals. Furthermore, I found that 50 percent of you skip breakfast at
> least five times a week.

What does this mean to you? According to nutrition experts, people who eat balanced meals are more motivated and less tired than people who don't eat balanced meals. In fact, those of you who drink a can of pop and eat a candy bar for breakfast—and you know who you are—are more likely to have high blood pressure, lack ambition, feel highly stressed, and fall prone to chronic diseases later in life.

Information that is personalized not only holds attention, but also gains interest. For example, think of your most effective instructors. Chances are that they take ordinary material and personalize it into meaningful, interesting knowledge. Listening to a string of facts can be boring and frustrating, but a speech comes to life when it contains personal illustrations.

People are also interested in others. If they were not, there would be no *National Enquirer, Star,* and *People* and no programs like "Life Styles of the Rich and Famous," "The Tonight Show," and talk shows such as "Oprah." Stories about human events are much more likely to touch listeners than are cold, harsh statistics. Thus, whenever possible, try to personalize your information and dramatize it in human terms. Relate it to specific people or situations that your audience members know and care about.

One student began an informative speech about the Heimlich maneuver, a technique used to clear the throat of someone who is choking, by relating the story of a 4-year-old boy who saved his 3-year-old friend. The boy, who had watched a television show in which the maneuver was used to save the life of one of the main characters, simply reenacted what he saw. By using this dramatic, real-life episode, the student was able to grab his audience's attention and prepare them for his discussion of who developed the technique, how it works, and how many lives it has saved.

The following guidelines should help you to personalize information in your speech presentations:

1. Use examples and information that specifically relate to your audience.

2. Draw conclusions that your audience can identify with and explain what the conclusions may mean to them.

3. Refer to people who are similar to your audience members, for example, student athletes, nontraditional students, minority students, foreign students, or engineering students.

4. Refer to topics and events that affect your listeners, such as campus activities, local laws, athletic and social events, cultural programs, and career decisions.

CHECKLIST FOR PREPARING AN INFORMATIVE SPEECH

1. Have you selected a topic that is appropriate for an informative speech?

2. Is the topic one in which you are interested?

3. Have you chosen a topic that will allow you to inform your audience about something they do not already know?

4. Will you be able to cover your topic adequately in the given time limit?

5. Have you worded your specific purpose to ensure that it meets the objective of the informative speech?

6. Have you selected and worded your main points so that they are clear and meet your specific purpose?

7. Have you provided adequate clarifying and supporting material to ensure that your audience will understand everything you are talking about?

8. Have you organized your speech according to the guidelines of effective organization specified in Chapter 9?

9. Have you avoided assumptions and personalized the information as much as possible?

10. Have you sufficiently practiced your delivery?

The successful informative speech always considers the listeners. The speaker carefully thinks about the following questions: What do I want my listeners to learn from my speech? What will be the best way to deliver my speech so my listeners will understand and retain the information? How will I know if I was successful in accomplishing my purpose?

EVALUATING THE INFORMATIVE SPEECH

Here are some of the criteria used to evaluate the competence of a speaker and the effectiveness of an informative speech. You should be aware of them when preparing an informative speech presentation.

Topic

The topic should merit the attention of your audience.

You need to consider what the audience already knows about the topic.

The audience should be able to see the relationship between the topic and you, and between the topic and themselves.

The specific purpose of the speech must be accomplished in the time available.

You may need to do some speculating as to how you will respond to the above criteria, but it is worth having an idea about what you are going to do, so that you can make adjustments in your speech's content and specific purpose in order too meet the criteria for a successful speech.

General Requirements

The following represent general requirements of most informative speech presentations:

Speech's purpose is clearly to inform and is stated as such.

Speech meets the time requirements set by the assignment.

Visual aids are used if required and add to the content by making the information presented more understandable.

Speaker cites sources of information that is not his or her own.

Speech purpose is relevant to the assignment and relates to the audience.

Analysis

Analysis includes both the choices the speaker makes with regard to the audience's interest in the material (for example, demographics, past experiences, beliefs, attitudes, values) and the choices the speaker makes in regard to content and the development of ideas in the speech.

Speaker sticks to informative purpose of the speech.

Speech reflects appropriate audience analysis, relating well to the audience members.

Speech topic is narrow enough to be fully developed and adequately handled in the time allotted.

Speech shows evidence of careful preparation.

Supporting Materials

Supporting materials supply documented evidence that what the speaker says is accurate and credible.

Speech is well documented.

Sources are cited completely and correctly.

Research is up-to-date.

Speaker uses adequate and sufficient clarifying materials.

Visual aids, if used, are appropriate and add to the audience's understanding of the speech's content.

Visual aids, if used, follow the guidelines established by the assignment.

Organization

When making judgments about the organization of an informative speech, the evaluator looks for a carefully planned, well-developed speech that has a unified approach to the material being presented.

I.   Introduction (overall) is properly developed.
  A.   It orients the audience to the topic.
      1.   It gains audience's attention and arouses interest.
      2.   It includes a specific purpose and thesis statement.
      3.   It defines terms (if necessary).
  B.   It motivates the audience to listen.
      1.   It is relevant.
      2.   It establishes credibility.
II. Organization of the body (overall) is clear and easy to follow.
  A.   The main points are clear and parallel in structure.
  B.   The main points are related to the purpose of the speech.
  C.   Transitions provide appropriate links between ideas.
  D.   The organizational pattern is appropriate.
III. Conclusion (overall) is properly developed.
  A.   It reinforces your purpose by reviewing the main points.
  B.   It ends with a memorable thought.

Delivery

The delivery techniques show evidence that you are aware of what the audience is interested in hearing, that you are involved in and enthusiastic about the topic, and that you are interested in sharing the material with the listeners.

Speakers' stance and posture are appropriate.

Speaker's eye contact with the audience is appropriate.

Speaker follows assignment in method of delivery (use of notes and number of note cards).

Speaker's facial expressions help convey and clarify his or her thoughts.

Speaker's body movements are appropriate and effective.

Speaker's vocal delivery (overall) enhances the speech with:

Appropriate volume	Appropriate rate
Conversational quality	Enthusiastic tone
Clear enunciation	Appropriate pauses
Appropriate vocal variety	

Language

You are aware of acceptable language and use it to enhance and clarify ideas.

Language (overall) is appropriate to the assignment and audience.

Word choice is appropriate for college level.

Grammar is appropriate and shows college-level competence.

Word pronunciations are correct.

A SAMPLE INFORMATIVE SPEECH WITH COMMENTARY

The following adaptation of a speech written by James Kimble, a University of Nebraska student, illustrates many of the strategies discussed in this chapter.[3]

I Forgot

Specific Purpose

To inform the audience about how memory affects what we do.

Thesis Statement

Today we'll examine what memory is, the different types of memory, and how it affects everything we do.

Jim begins with humor that ties in well with his speech topic. He also begins to establish relevancy of his topic to his audience and uses a rhetorical question to gain his audience's attention. This is very nicely done. his use of the naming of teachers brings immediate audience involvement. the opening paragraph lets the audience know the speaker is interested in them.

As the old saying goes, "Education is what you have left over after you have forgotten everything you have learned." Unfortunately, I can't seem to remember who first told me that. And that's not a rare occurrence. In fact, we all lose the ability to retain over 95 percent of what we experience in our day-to-day lives. For instance, how many of you can remember the names of all your teachers, from kindergarten all the way through high school? Though you probably knew them quite well at one time, they've begun to fade away, just like other things that have happened to you in your past.

Jim includes a planned repetition of his statistics about the loss of memory, emphasizing the positive side of it. This is an excellent way to help the audience see the value of listening to what he has to say. He also compares the human mind to the computer to make an abstract notion more concrete. This helps his listeners understand the point he is making.

Although 95 percent of what we experience is filed away in our subconscious, defying all effort at retrieving it, the 5 percent that we do retain helps our mind to exceed the best and most modern computers in capacity, flexibility, and speed. Our conscious memory span reaches back almost as far as our life span. For some of us, this will someday exceed eighty or ninety years. Memory is something that we use every second that we are alive and, therefore, is important to each one of us.

Jim states his thesis clearly. then he provides an advance organizer of the main points. Finally, he makes a strong case for why his audience should listen to what he has to say. In one short paragraph he has made it clear what his speech is about and what the audience will learn from listening to it. Jim has done a nice job here!

Today we'll examine what memory is, the different types of memory, and how it affects everything we do. To begin with, I'll pose the question "What is memory?" Then I'll examine three types of memory: sensory, motor skill, and semantic or verbal memory. My goal is to help us understand more about ourselves, because when we understand how we think, we can understand how other people think.

Jim begins his first main point and establishes its relevance to his audience. He

By the time you die, your brain will have processed and absorbed billions of items—words, faces, objects, scenes, *then asks a series of rhetorical questions. Next, he points out that defining memory is not easy and that the audience should not expect a simple answer. He keeps the audience in suspense, waiting to hear what he has to say.*

He begins his explanation of what is known about memory. He defines it clearly and effectively leaving no doubt as to The term's meaning. his last two sentences provide an advance organizer and transition to what is to follow. These provide links for the listener and help set up the organization of what is coming next.

In this paragraph Jim cites his first source. Edson is an excellent source, but Jim could have told a little about him so the audience would recognize his expertise. He involves the audience by using vivid examples that his listeners can identify with easily. The last sentence also employs a play on words to help the audience get the point a second time.

Here Jim refers to the audience and keeps them involved in the topic. Jim points out that each of us has some special sense and provides examples of well-known people who had special memory skills. Jim then uses a technical term and quickly defines it by a term that is familiar to everyone. He again relates to the audience by referring directly to them. He now cites his second source. Here again he might have told of the author's expertise to establish the author's credibility. He continually relates to his audience through examples.

Jim now moves into the second type of memory. He compares it to the first type of memory and defines it. He explains it through examples. This is an excellent device to gain audience comprehension as well as attention. He repeats the definition, and he relates the notion directly to his audience to maintain the subject's relevance.

facts, images, concepts, verbal expressions—all contained within the gray matter inside your head. How is this possible? Just what is memory? Well, what is love? What is time? Do we exist? The answer to all of these questions is the same. It is, we don't know! All we can do at this time is theorize. And theorize we have.

Scientists inform us that anything and everything we experience causes a physical change within the structure of our brains called an *engram.* Engram means "written on"—in this case, written on the brain. How we can selectively take these engrams from our subconscious thought into our conscious and why we sometimes can't still aren't clear. But what has become clear is that there are three distinct types of memory. Let's examine the first of them.

Sensory memory, as Lee Edson describes in his book *How We Learn,* is memory that we associate with the senses. Most of you can visualize President Reagan's face and voice, even though he's not here. Or perhaps you can imagine my fingernails scratching along a chalkboard—some of you can even hear it— now. These are both examples of our sensory memory—experiences that our minds "chalk up" to one of our senses.

Each of us has one particular sense that plays a larger role in helping us with our memories. Some notable examples are Beethoven, Mozart, and Wagner, who had incredible auditory memories. Napoleon and da Vinci were both blessed with incredible visual memories—in more familiar terms, photographic memory. Most of us do have strong visual recall, but as Allan Baddely tells us in his book *Your Memory: A User's Guide,* our auditory recall, in most cases, is even stronger. For instance, shortly after loved ones die, we often have trouble visualizing their faces, yet for many years afterwards, we can often hear their voices in our heads. Unfortunately, for some people, hearing a dead person's voice every time they look at his or her picture can become a little unsettling. So sensory memory isn't necessarily a good thing. Although it may be incredibly helpful for retention, it is not always pleasant.

More vital than sensory memory is motor skill memory. This is the retention and recall, even after long periods of nonuse, of our physical movements. Imagine if you couldn't remember how to walk or how to move your jaw up and down to eat. These are both very important motor skills. If you didn't have motor skill memory, which enables you to recall how to make various physical movements when you want to, life would be pretty miserable.

Here Jim uses some excellent examples to clarify his point. Note that all of his examples are common and easy for his audience to picture. He then cites his third source; again he might have told how the authors relate to the topic. His use of sources is excellent, however. Jim makes excellent use of an example to clarify terms. Again he directly relates the point to his audience.

All humans have the unique ability to bring back motor skills learned decades earlier. Once you've learned to ride a bike or swim, you'll be able to do these activities for the rest of your life. In the same way, we never forget how to grasp objects or how to control our eyelid movement. Forgetting how to move the muscles that perform such operations is generally unheard of, except in cases of some mental or physical illness. Our motor skill memory is nearly all-pervasive. In fact, Donald and Eleanor Lair, in their book *Techniques for Efficient Remembering,* claim that motor skill functions do not involve memory. They are reactions, like sneezing, or physiological processes, such as digestion. Obviously, our motor skill memory is important to each one of us.

Jim describes the third type of memory. Again he relates it to his audience and uses familiar terms and examples to make sure his terms are clearly understood.

The third type of memory is semantic or verbal memory. What we remember in this area are things that we've heard, read, or thought. If you know the capital of France or if you can recite the chemical formula for salt, then you know how to use your semantic memory.

Jim does a good job here of using more examples to show the relevance of the topic to the audience. These personal and practical examples keep the audience's attention. His use of comparison to make his point is well done.

For most of us, skill or deficiency in semantic memory determines whether or not we do well in school. For those of you with strong semantic memory, school is relatively easy because you remember most things you've learned in the past and have little or no trouble assimilating new knowledge into that framework. But for people who have a weak verbal memory, learning probably isn't so easy because such people have not developed the framework in which to store verbal information.

Jim qualifies his use of certain terminology and then cites his fourth source. To make his use of the source more effective, he could have said, "Weinland is a psychologist and a noted expert on memory." This would have established the source's credibility.

Our descriptions of semantic aptitude are too general when we say "strong" or "weak." James D. Weinland explains in his book How to Improve Your Memory that semantic aptitude can be further divided into two major areas: recall and recognition.

Here Jim does a good job of giving an explicit definition of a key term and clarifying it for easy comprehension. He also provides examples that the audience can identify with. Thus, he maintains their attention.

Recall is the actual production of entire thoughts pulled at will from our memory banks with little or no cue. If I asked you to recite the Pledge of Allegiance, you probably wouldn't have much trouble, even though it's not written down for you. The point is that you can recite an entire passage that is familiar to you just from its title. This is based upon semantic recall.

Jim uses a contrast definition to distinguish between recall and selective recall. He also provides an excellent practical illustration of selective recall that is directly related to something all students are familiar with and can benefit them.

Recall is a bit easier when there is a cue. Selective recall is another form of semantic memory, but it needs a larger cue to bring forth stored knowledge. An example of this occurs during a multiple-choice test. You may not always recall the correct answer, but you can sometimes recognize the incorrect answers through the process of elimination. This type of memory can be extremely helpful when other recall attempts do not work.

Before ending the speech, Jim provides one more good reason why his audience should listen to what he has to say. He emphasizes it with humor.

Now, obviously, since we are all in college, semantic memory is the area in which we want to excel because it helps us to remember facts. While this is important, you should also realize that semantic memory does even more. For example, it helps us to learn, think, read, and remember bits of information, without which we would be unable to play such games as Trivial Pursuit.

Jim's conclusion provides an overview of what he has said and some thoughts about what we have learned from the past and still need to learn in the future.

Jim repeats the three main ideas of his speech to reinforce them. In his last sentence Jim emphasizes his specific purpose one more time.

To the ancient Greeks, memory was an actual place where all human thoughts went—an area controlled by the gods. Remembering was the simple process of retrieving those thoughts from the mysterious region. Today, we have progressed in leaps and bounds in many areas of science, but when we discuss memory, we have not come much further than the Greeks. To be sure, we have managed to differentiate between the three types of memory: sensory, motor skill, and semantic. Yet, this is the major portion of our progress. The research hasn't stopped—scientists are still looking for ways to understand the human brain in order to uncover its mysteries. In addition, they are looking for ways to help us improve our memories. Memory—it is not something we should forget because it affects what we do.

Jim's speech is clearly organized and well supported. He uses a good number of sources and provides many practical examples to make his ideas and terms clear to his audience. He also uses a good amount of repetition of key points to help his audience remember them. Another thing he does well is constantly relating the subject matter to his audience. The only area where Jim might improve is in giving more information about who his sources are and how they relate to the topic. Do you recognize parts of the speech introduced in previous chapters?

SUMMARY

Information is "knowledge derived from study, experience, or instruction." The ability to present and receive information is vital for anyone who wants to be successful. Those who possess information and can communicate it effectively possess power and command respect.

The goal of an informative speech is to increase understanding, whereas the goal of a persuasive speech is to change attitudes and behaviors. Information can be presented without attempting to persuade, but persuasion cannot be accomplished without attempting to inform.

The topic for an informative speech should be something that interests you and that you know something about, and it should be something that will interest your audience. You may talk about objects (people, animals, structures, places), processes (how something is put together, works, is done), events, (happenings, occasions), or concepts (beliefs, theories, ideas, principles).

To achieve the main goal of increasing knowledge, a speaker must focus on two subgoals: gaining the audience's attention and increasing the audience's understanding. Listeners are more likely to pay attention to information that is relevant, useful, or novel. Or speakers may rely on *information relevance,* relating their information directly to the audience and thus giving them a reason to listen.

A speaker can increase an audience's understanding by organizing the presentation systematically, choosing appropriate language, and providing clear definitions. Two organizational techniques that aid listeners' understanding are *planned repetition,* the deliberate repeating of a thought, and *advance organizers,* statements that warn the listener that significant information is coming.

Speakers should avoid technical language that might be unfamiliar to the audience. In addition, they should choose words that are concrete rather than abstract and use descriptors to provide even greater clarification. *Concrete words* stand for specific things that can be pointed to or physically experienced. *Abstract words* refer to ideas, qualities, or relationships. *Descriptors* are words that are used to describe something.

Another way to aid understanding is to define all terms that might be unfamiliar to the audience. Contrasts, synonyms, antonyms, and etymologies can all clarify meanings. A *contrast* points out differences between two objects or concepts. A *synonym* is a word, phrase, or concept that is the same or nearly the same in meaning as another word, phrase, or concept. An *antonym* is a word, phrase, or concept that is opposite in meaning to another word, phrase, or concept. An *etymology* traces the origin and development of a word.

In developing an effective informative speech, you should not assume that your audience is already familiar with your topic and its special terminology, and when possible, you should personalize your speech by providing examples that touch your listeners' needs and interests.

KEY TERMS

Abstract word: Symbol for an idea, quality, or relationship.

Advance organizer: Statement that warns listeners that significant information is coming.

Antonym: Word, phrase, or concept that is opposite in meaning to another word, phrase, or concept.

Concrete Word: Symbol for a specific thing that can be pointed to or physically experienced.

Contrast: Definition that shows or emphasizes differences.
Descriptors: Words used to describe something.
Etymology: Definition that traces the origin and development of a word.
Information: Knowledge derived from study, experience, or instruction.
Information Relevance: Relation of information to an audience that gives them a reason to listen.
Planned repetition: Deliberate repetition of a thought in order to increase the likelihood that the audience will understand and remember it.
Synonym: Word, phrase, or concept that is the same or nearly the same in meaning as another word, phrase, or concept.

DISCUSSION STARTERS

1. Explain why information is so important in our society.
2. Why does having information give a person power?
3. In what ways have you used information to gain power?
4. What should be the prerequisites for selecting an informative speech topic?
5. What two or three informative speech topics interest you the most? Why?
6. In planning your informative speech, what should you take into consideration to ensure that you will be as effective as possible?
7. What criteria do you think are the most important in evaluating the competence of speakers delivering an informative speech?

NOTES

1. This section is based on S. E. Lucas, *The Art of Public Speaking,* 3rd ed. (New York: Random House, 1989): 275–283. The categories as cited in Lucas were described first by J. H. Bryns, in *Speak for Yourself: An Introduction to Public Speaking* (New York: Random House, 1981), chaps. 10–15.
2. Adapted from a speech developed by Janet Richards, a student at the University of Nebraska–Lincoln, 1993.
3. Speech written by James Kimble, a University of Nebraska debate and forensics student. Permission to reprint this speech was given by Dr. Jack Kay, Past Chair and Director of Forensics at the University of Nebraska, Lincoln; Department of Communication Head, Wayne State University, Detroit, Michigan.

APPENDIX: INFORMATIVE SPEECH TOPICS— A SAMPLE LIST

Here are some possible topics for informative speeches. The items listed are not necessarily the titles of speeches and may be broad areas that would need to be narrowed to fit specific purposes, time limits, or other requirements set by your instructor.

New Approaches to Instruction: The Technology of Education
Investment: The Stock Market Game
Television Tabloids: Their Effect on Viewers
Lasers in the Operating Room
Library Technology: Save Time and Energy
Sexual Practices in the 1990s
Students at Risk: A Local Tragedy
Pedology: An Increasing Concern
Colors Communicate Emotions
Rudeness: A National Trend
Homelessness: Someone Else's Problem
What is Binge Drinking?
How to Determine Your Career Field
Women Communicate Differently?
Agriculture's Newest Technologies
Animal Rights and Scientific Research
DNA: The Ultimate Fingerprint

New Telephone Technology
The Effects of Street Language on Society
The United States and Cultural Diversity
Native Americans: Our Real Heritage
Global Warming: Fact or Fiction
Rejection and Its Impact on our Psyche
Software of the Future
Gangs: A Social Phenomenon
Country Western Music
Embryo Cloning
Communication Apprehension
How to Prepare for Retirement
Healthcare
Adoption and the Law
How to Choose an Apartment
How to Control Stress
Advances in Automobile Safety
Videodisc Technology

Chapter 12

Persuasive Speaking

LEARNING OBJECTIVES

After studying this chapter, you should be able to:

1. Define persuasion and its four action goals.

2. Explain what constitutes an appropriate topic for a persuasive speech.

3. Discuss how questions of fact, value, and policy may serve as the basis of a persuasive speech.

4. Tell why credibility is important in persuasive speaking.

5. Differentiate among appeals to needs, logical appeals, and emotional appeals.

6. Develop a persuasive speech that demonstrates your ability to research, organize, and support your action goal.

If you were to analyze the communication you were involved in during the past week, you would probably discover that you have been in a variety of persuasive situations. In order to prove this point to some doubtful students, a professor asked his entire class to record their communication activities for a period of one week. Here are some of the activities they reported.

Called parents for additional money

Discussed who should be elected the next student representative

Asked a person for a date

Discussed with a professor why I turned in a paper late

Talked about last week's game and how well the team was playing

Asked to borrow a fraternity brother's car to go on date

Returned a pair of running shoes to a sporting goods shop because they were defective

Called my sister to say hello, found out she had the flu, and told her she needed to see a doctor

Asked several friends to join our organization

Asked my roommate for a small loan

Tried to talk a police officer out of giving me a traffic ticket

Partied instead of studying for a test

Talked a friend into going to church

Although not every situation that the students reported involved the use of persuasion, class members were surprised to discover the amount of persuasion they had used.

When you think about it, you will find that you, too, are involved in some form of persuasion much of the time. If you are not trying to persuade someone, someone is probably trying to persuade you. For example, you are involved in persuasion every time you ask or are asked to do or not do something or to believe or not believe something. To be more specific, some form of persuasion takes place when you convince your professor to excuse you from an exam, when you coax an employer to hire you, when you ask a friend for a loan, when someone recommends you see a certain movie, when someone urges you to vote for him or her in the school election, and when you talk yourself into staying home to study even though you'd rather go out with your friends.

EXERCISE

Keep a journal or list of your communication activities over a week's period of time. Label each communication event in which you used persuasion. Discuss your list in class.

Since persuasion is so much a part of our everyday activities, it is important to understand it and its goal. In this chapter, we will discuss how to select a persuasive speech topic, how to establish credibility, how to prepare and develop a persuasive speech, and how to persuade others effectively.

GOALS OF PERSUASIVE SPEAKING

Persuasion is a communication process, involving both verbal and nonverbal messages, that attempts to reinforce or change listeners' attitudes, beliefs, values, or behavior. Is it possible to change a person's attitudes, beliefs, or values without changing his or her behavior? The answer is yes, it is. For example, you may skillfully argue that your friend should wear a seat belt and convince him that seat belts are smart to use. However, despite your friend's new attitude toward seat belts, he may still never put one on. Have you used persuasion effectively? This is a debatable question. You have changed your friend's attitude, but not his behavior. Which is more important?

The ultimate goal of all persuasion is action; that is, successful persuasion reinforces existing behavior, changes existing behavior, or leads to new behavior. When you want to convince someone not to change a behavior, you try to reinforce the existing behavior. At other times, you may want a person to do something different. When a speaker's main goal is to achieve action, he or she will also seek one of four subgoals: adoption, discontinuance, deterrence, or continuance of a particular behavior.[1]

Adoption is an action goal that asks listeners to demonstrate their acceptance of an attitude, belief, or value by performing the action suggested by the speaker. For example, assume you had never liked the thought of donating blood, but one day you saw a television commercial pleading for blood to help the victims of a recent disaster. If the next day you donated blood, you would be displaying adoption. You still may not like the thought of giving blood, but the commercial would have persuaded you to do so. Of course, the fact that you gave blood once does not mean that you will continue to give it whenever you are asked. Your adoption of the persuasive message may be only temporary and may stop until you receive another persuasive message that convinces you to take action again.

Discontinuance is the opposite of adoption. If your action goal is discontinuance, you want your listeners to stop doing something—running, drinking alcohol, using illegal drugs, paying high tuition, discriminating against others, eating junk food, avoiding difficult courses. You are trying to alter what you believe is a negative behavior rather than encouraging others to do something that you believe is a positive behavior.

Deterrence is an action goal that asks listeners to demonstrate their acceptance of an attitude, belief, or value by avoiding a certain behavior. Sample deterrent messages include: if you don't eat junk food, don't start now; if you don't own a gun, don't buy one; if you support busing to promote school integration, don't vote to eliminate the law. This action goal is similar to discontinuance in that you do not want a negative behavior to occur; but in deterrence, you are trying to *prevent* its occurrence rather than *end* its occurrence.

Continuance is an action goal that asks listeners to demonstrate their acceptance of an attitude, belief, or value by continuing to perform a certain behavior. For example: if you jog, don't stop; keep reading for pleasure; stay involved in extracurricular activities; keep buying from your locally owned store. This action goal is similar to adoption because you want a positive behavior to occur; but in continuance, you are trying to *keep* an existing behavior rather than *begin* a new behavior.

Note that the first two action goals, adoption and discontinuance, ask people to *change* their behavior, while the last two, deterrence and continuance, ask people *not to change,* but to continue doing what they are already doing or not change to something new.

Getting others to change or not to change their behaviors is not always easy. (See Figure 12.1). Therefore, a speaker may have to settle for a

Figure 12.1:

Not all persuasion leads to change. It is not always easy to get people to take action even though they may agree with the idea behind the persuasive message. Sometimes getting people to listen and to consider a particular point of view is all that can be expected. For example, many smokers continue to smoke even though they know it is harmful. Can you think of other instances where persuasion does not always lead to change?

James D. Wilson/Woodfin Camp, Inc.

change in attitudes, beliefs, or values, as in the seat belt example. A change in attitudes, beliefs, or values, such as accepting the idea of wearing seat belts, is part of the persuasive process and must almost always occur before a change in behavior can take place. Not all persuasive speaking will lead to action, nor should persuasive speakers consider themselves failures if they do not obtain behavior change. Especially as a beginner, you should not always expect to obtain a change in action or behavior, but you should be able to get others to listen to what you have to say and to consider your point of view.

TOPICS FOR PERSUASIVE SPEECHES

Some themes lend themselves more readily to persuasive speaking than others. Especially adaptable are current and controversial subjects. You will increase your likelihood of success if you:

1. Select a topic that you are interested in, know something about, want to speak about, need to speak about, or are personally concerned about.
2. Select a subject that is worthwhile and of potential concern to your audience.
3. Select a topic with an action goal. For example, the notion that exercise and eating well are good for your health may be a good persuasive theme, but if everyone in your audience is physically in good shape and healthy, could you come up with a strong action goal?
4. Select an issue that is current, but avoid one that is common knowledge or that has been discussed widely, unless you plan to add a new perspective to it. (See Chapter 7 for more on selecting a topic and the Appendix at the end of this chapter for a list of persuasive topics.)

Persuasive speeches are often, but not always, given in situations where there are two or more opposing viewpoints and the speaker's point of view differs from that of the audience. For example, the speaker may want the audience to support higher tuition because it will lead to better quality instruction, but most of the audience may believe that tuition is already too high. Especially when a speaker's goal is adoption or discontinuance, there must be some difference between the speaker's view and that of the audience, or there is no need for persuasion. On the other hand, when the speaker's goal is deterrence or avoidance, the speaker's and the audience's points of view may be more closely united. Thus, the speaker's goal is to reinforce behaviors that are similar to those proposed in the speech.

Persuasive speech topics may also center around questions of fact, questions of value, questions of policy, or any combination of the three types of questions.

Questions of Fact

A **question of fact** asks what is true and what is false. Consider these questions: Which building is the tallest in the world? Who is the richest person in the United States? Which basketball player scored the most points last season? Which university was the first to be established in the United States? Note that these questions can be answered with a fact that can be verified in reference books. Because they are so cut-and-dried, there can be little debate about them, making them weak topics for a persuasive speech.

In contrast, persuasive speeches may be built on predictions of future events that will eventually become matters of fact. Consider these: Who will be the next president of the United States? Which college football team will win the national championship next year? Will there be a third world war in the next five years? Although none of these questions can be answered with certainty, a persuasive speaker could build an effective case predicting the answer to each.

Persuasive speeches may also be based on complicated answers to questions of fact or justifications for answers that are unclear. Why did so many tragic air disasters occur during the past decade? Was it because of drugs? Poorly trained air traffic controllers? Overworked controllers? Outdated equipment? Insufficient rules for the use of air space near airports? Although no one answer covers the entire situation, a speaker could build a strong argument to show that one of these factors is the primary cause of air accidents.

Finally, some persuasive speeches may attempt to answer questions of fact that are not completely verifiable; for example, Do unidentified flying objects really exist? Can hypnotism enable a person to relive past lives? Is there intelligent life in outer space? A speech on the existence of intelligent life in outer space might be planned something like this:

Specific Purpose   To persuade the audience that there is intelligent life in outer space.

Thesis   There have been numerous signs of intelligent life in outer space, and our universe size provides us with sufficient reason to believe other intelligent life exists.

Main Points

I.   There have been numerous signs that there is intelligent life in outer space.

 A. The National Science Foundation, in a 1991 report, indicates that radio signals are being received from outer space.

 B. Recent sightings of UFOs by military and commercial pilots strongly suggest life in other solar systems.

II. The size of the universe allows sufficient reason to believe that there is some form of intelligent life in outer space.

 A. Scientists suggest that we have only begun to learn about what exists beyond our solar system.

 B. There is an infinite number of solar systems beyond ours, which leaves a strong possibility for other intelligent life.

On the surface, questions of fact may appear more appropriate for an informative speech than for a persuasive one, but if you consider the difficulty of persuading an audience that college athletics are big business and should be banned, that an earthquake will destroy the western part of the United States, or that the pyramids of Egypt were designed by an intelligence far superior to ours today, you can see that questions of fact can offer rich possibilities for persuasion.

Questions of Value

A **question of value** asks whether something is good or bad, desirable or undesirable. Value was defined in Chapter 3 as "a general, relatively long lasting ideal that guides behavior." A value is something that requires a more judgmental response than does a question of fact. Some typical questions of value are: Who was the most effective political speaker during the twentieth century? Have American businesses lost their will to compete in the world market? Are today's college students better educated than college students were ten years ago? Does a college athletics program promote sexism on campus? Are professional athletes the best role models for our youth? Does sex education belong in our schools? The answers to these questions are not based solely on fact, but on what each individual considers to be right or wrong, ethical or unethical, acceptable or unacceptable.

The answers to questions of value may seem to be based solely on personal opinion and subjectivity rather than on objective evidence, but this is not the case. Effective persuasive speakers will have evidence to support their positions and will be able to justify their opinions. For example, suppose a speaker contends that the social use of drugs is harmful. She might plan her speech as follows:

Specific Purpose   To persuade the audience that the social use of drugs is harmful.

Thesis   Social drug use is harmful because it affects personal relationships and interferes with work.

Main Points
I. Social use of drugs affects personal relationships.
   A. According to a national survey, social drug users are involved in twice as many divorces as nonusers.
   B. Researchers have shown that the children of social drug users are more likely to be loners, have fewer friends, and eventually use drugs themselves.
II. Social use of drugs interferes with work.
   A. The rate of absenteeism from work of social drug users is four times that of nonusers.
   B. The job turnover rate of social drug users is at least double that of nonusers.

C. Social drug users are 30 percent less productive than nonusers doing the same job.

Values vary dramatically from one person to the next. Person A may think that rap music is bad for society and Person B may think it is good for society; A may think that alcohol should be illegal on campus and B may think it should be legal; A may believe that college sports are not necessary and B may think that they are absolutely necessary. When it comes to questions of value, one person's judgment is no better or worse than another's. People's values are usually more complicated because they are rooted in emotion rather than reason, and it is often extremely difficult to get people to change their values. A speaker's position on a question of value may be difficult to defend. Therefore, you will need to do a great deal of research and gather evidence to build a strong case supporting one value over another, even though you believe your values are right—because so are your listeners'. (See Figure 12.2).

Questions of Policy

A **question of policy** goes beyond seeking judgmental responses to seeking courses of action. Whereas a question of value asks if something is right or wrong, a question of policy asks if something should or should not be done. Should student parking on campus be more accessible? Should universities provide birth control to students? Should student athletes be given special treatment over nonathletes? Should all students be tested for drugs before entering college? Should students be tested for basic English competencies before they graduate? Should the government provide basic health care for every American citizen? Should all those working in jobs that involve the safety of others be tested for drugs? Questions of policy involve both facts and values and are therefore never simple. Neither are the answers to questions of policy agreed upon by everyone.

Persuasive speakers can defend an existing policy, suggest modifications of an existing policy, suggest a new policy to replace an old one, or

Calvin and Hobbes

by Bill Watterson

Figure 12.2:

Values are complicated. The cartoon illustrates the point that values are often based on emotion and personal views and thus, are difficult to change.

create a policy where none exists. If you defend an existing policy, you must persuade your listeners that what exists is the best for the situation. If you want to modify or replace an existing policy, you must persuade your listeners that the old policy does not work and that your new one will. If you hope to create a new policy, you must persuade your audience that a policy is needed and that yours is the right one for the situation.

When discussing questions of policy, persuasive speakers usually focus on three considerations: need, plan, and suitability. If you believe that things are not fine as they are, then you must argue that there is a *need* for change. When you advocate change, you must provide a *plan*, or solution. The plan tells the audience what you think should be done. Finally, you must defend your plan by explaining its *suitability* for the situation. Examine how student Mary Trouba used need, plan, and suitability in her persuasive speech.[2]

Specific Purpose	To persuade the audience that radical right-wing hate groups are a danger to society.
Thesis	Radical right-wing hate groups are a danger to society because they flagrantly violate the American ideals of equality and religious tolerance.

Need

I. Right-wing religious groups flagrantly violate the American ideals of equality and religious tolerance.

    A. Right-wing hate groups are growing at a alarming rate.

    B. Right-wing hate groups are employing criminal means to achieve their ends.

    C. Right-wing hate groups are building a frightening capacity to inflict moral damage on society.

Plan

II. We must enact a twofold solution that includes legal and attitudinal components.

    A. The first step is to take legal action to crack down these groups.

    B. The second step is to educate people about these groups.

Suitability

III. The two-step plan will control these groups and help to reduce their negative impact on society.

    A. Laws can prevent paramilitary groups from forming and thus reduce their impact.

    B. Research has shown that people who are educated about extremist groups are less likely to join them.

PERSUASIVE CLAIMS

When attempting to answer questions of fact, value, and policy, we cannot always develop a formal logical response or answer to meet the objections of others. Not everything we argue can be approached with a set of formalized rules; the evidence is not always so clear-cut that it leaves no question that what you claim is true.

Stephen Toulmin, a British philosopher, developed a model which helps us understand everyday persuasive arguments.[3] Toulmin's approach to supporting a persuasion position or argument involves three basic parts: claim, data, and warrant. The *claim* is what the persuader wants or hopes will be believed, accepted, or done. Claims, however, require evidence, or what Toulmin refers to as *data*. Data are the supporting materials or evidence that should allow the listener of the claim to accept it as stated. Unfortunately, there is not always a clear or irrefutable relationship between the claim and the data. Thus, the persuader must provide an explanation of the relationship between the claim and the data. Toulmin refers to this as the *warrant*.

The following represents a possible application of Toulmin:

Claim	Adventure activities, such as skydiving and bungee jumping, often result in tragedy due to lack of safety precautions.
Data	The July 2, 1993, *New York Times* reported a Colorado man was killed after bungee jumping 190 feet from a hot-air balloon . . . while using a 260-foot cord.
Warrant	The jump company, Bungee America, was neither licensed nor insured by the State of Colorado. If safety regulations were required, perhaps this tragedy could have been prevented.[4]

If you apply Toulmin's model, listeners can usually respond to the claim in one of three ways.

1. They can accept the claim at face value. This is usually the case when there is common knowledge that the claim is probably true, for example, the claim that our country's educational programs need improvement.
2. They can reject the claim outright. This usually happens when the claim is clearly false, such as the claim that there is no pollution in our country's lakes and streams. It also occurs when listeners are biased against the claim or see no relationship between the claim and themselves. For example, if a claim that the forests of this country are not being depleted is made to a group trying to preserve our environment, it is unlikely they would accept this claim because of their biased views.
3. They can accept or reject the claim according to their evaluation of data and warrant. That is, the person making the claim must be able to provide evidence to support or demonstrate that the claim is true.

When speakers provide evidence to support their claims, it is still up to listeners to accept the claim based on the evidence presented. Listeners essentially have three options:

1. They can accept the claim as supported by the evidence.
2. They can reject the claim as not supported by the evidence.
3. They can request that the speaker provide more evidence to support the claim.

Competent speakers consider all the options in developing their arguments so as to make their claim and the evidence they use stand on their own merits. They realize that not everyone will interpret the evidence in the same way they do, nor will everyone be convinced, even though the evidence they present may be, in their opinion, the best there is.

FALLACIES OR ERRORS IN ARGUMENT DEVELOPMENT

As both creators and consumers of persuasive messages, we must be able to analyze and evaluate others' as well as our own use of reasoning to support persuasive messages. It is especially important to use reasoning that does not cause our listeners to question are credibility by presenting flawed arguments. Arguments that are flawed because they do not follow the rules of logic and therefore are not believable are called **fallacies.** Flawed reasoning occurs all the time and often without people realizing that they are guilty of it. As a critical thinker, however, it is important that you understand what fallacies are, how to recognize them, and why you should not use them or let others use them in their communication.

There are many different types of fallacies used in our communication, but only the commonly used or major errors in reasoning will be presented here to help you guard against them.

One major misuse of information involves fact and opinion. When speakers state opinions as if they are facts, this can be misleading and result in fallacious argument. For example, "Our university's policy on drinking is too stringent" and "Our university is short 250 parking spaces" are both statements of information. Which is fact and which is opinion? The first statement is opinion and the second is fact. How do you know which is which? Facts can be verified—thus, if the university is 250 parking spaces short, that can be verified, while the university's policy on drinking may be considered stringent or it may not—that is a matter of opinion. Opinions can be helpful in persuasive speeches or in arguments we develop, but to treat an opinion as if it were fact, or a fact as though it were an opinion, can lead to an error in critical thinking. In either case, you will appear to claim too little or too much and thus raise questions about your competence and ethics.

Another misuse of facts is the use of irrelevevant information to divert attention from the real issue. This occurs when a speaker wishes to draw attention away from an issue on which he or she is being questioned or challenged. For example, have you ever questioned someone about something he or she did wrong and received a response that isn't relevant to what you are referring to? In fact, the person you are questioning or challenging changes the subject to something entirely different or may even attack your credibility to avoid discussing the issue. Using irrelevant information to divert attention away from the real issue is referred to as a **red herring** fallacy.

Questionable cause, another common fallacy, occurs when a speaker alleges something that does not relate to, or produce, the outcome cliamed in the argument. Wanting to know what has caused certain events to occur is part of our nature. If cheating on campus is increasing, enrollment on campus is increasing or decreasing, or courses are to be eliminated from the curriculum, we want to know why. In our desire to know the cause of certain events or behaviors, we sometimes attribute what has happened to something that is not relevant or even related to the situation. For example, claiming that the drinking of alcohol on campus has increased this year because there is nothing else to do is a questionable cause, especially if there are the same number of activities on campus now as there have been in the past.

Another common critical thinking fallacy is the hasty generalization. **Hasty generalization** is a type of fallacy that occurs when a speaker doesn't have sufficient data and thus argues or reasons from specific example. The problem occurs because conclusions are drawn from insufficient data or cases to support an argument. It is not uncommon to find people making generalizations based on only one, or at most a few, examples. For instance, to argue that male students think date rape is not a problem on their campus, a speaker might cite the opinions of two or three close friends. The speaker might state, "In surveying people I know, they do not believe that date rape is a problem on our campus." The argument that date rape is not a problem may sound impressive, but it is not based on a large or representative enough sample of students to make the claim. Thus, the argument can be refuted as a hasty generalization.

When someone attacks a person rather than the argument being made, this fallacy is called an **ad hominem.** This is also referred to as "name calling." If you call someone a geek or a jerk in response to an argument being made in order to diminish the relevance or significance of the argument, you are using name calling as a means of refuting the argument. What is wrong with this? Such an approach is a smokescreen to cover your inability to provide good counter-arguments or evidence to challenge what the other person is claiming. Sidestepping the issue by name calling, ridiculing, or other personal attacks can be a successful means of diffusing an argument, but doing so results in a fallacious argument.

When you develop or encounter arguments or reasoning that do not fit any of the fallacies described above, but you suspect the argument's validity, put the argument to the following test: Can the argument be outlined, does the data support the claim, and is there a solid relationship between the data and the claim? It is not always important to know the name of a specific type of fallacy, but it is important that you analyze how arguments are developed and used in order to determine if they are valid.

ESTABLISHING CREDIBILITY

The most valuable tool that you, as a persuasive speaker, can posses is **credibility** or believability based on the audience's evaluation of your competence, knowledge, experience, and character. The audience is the ultimate judge of credibility, but there is much you can do to influence their opinion. The key is to establish your competence and character right from the beginning of your speech.

Competence

An audience will judge your competence by the amount of knowledge, degree of involvement, and extent of experience you display. The more expertise you show in your subject, the more likely it is that your audience will accept what you have to say. You can establish your expertise in several ways.

1. DEMONSTRATE INVOLVEMENT. One student, in urging action to avoid chemical pollution of water, described her mother's death as a result of drinking contaminated water. Although her firsthand experiences did not in themselves make her an expert environmentalist, they clearly established her involvement in the issue.

2. RELATE EXPERIENCE. One student chose to speak on the value of internships. Because he had participated in the internship program, his audience accepted him as knowledgeable and committed.

3. CITE RESEARCH. Quoting information from written sources and interviews with experts can add weight and objectivity to your arguments. Mentioning sources that are respected by your audience adds to your credibility and indicates that you are well-read. One student, who tried to persuade her audience that many cesarian sections as a means of child birth are necessary, used the following research to develop her credibility.

> According to the Journal of the American Medical Association of January 2, 1991, "967,000 Cesarean sections are currently performed in the United States each year, representing approximately 25% of all births." Yet, this is nothing of which to be proud since it is only necessary 12–14% of the time, contributes to increased health care costs, and may often be clinically unnecessary. It is for this reason that we need to end this proliferation.[5]

Each time you cite a valid source, you add to your credibility by demonstrating that you have done your research and know what you are talking about.

Character

An audience's judgment of your character is based on their perceptions of your trustworthiness and ethics. The best way to establish your character is to be honest and fair.

Trustworthiness   A speaker's **trustworthiness** is the audience's perception of his or her reliability and dependability. Others attribute trustworthiness to us based on their past experiences with us. For example, they may judge our reliability according to whether we come to class every time it meets. They may evaluate our dependability according to how we have followed through on our promises. People who have had positive experiences with what we have done are more apt to see us as trustworthy.

Ethics   In Chapter 10 we defined **ethics** as an individual's system of moral principles and stated that ethics play a key role in communication. While this is certainly true in communication in general, it is especially true in persuasion. Persuasive speakers who are known to be unethical or dishonest are less likely to be successful in achieving their persuasive purpose than are people who are recognized as ethical and honest. You must earn your reputation as an ethical person through your actions. The best way to establish your ethicalness is to do the following.

1. CITE SOURCES WHEN INFORMATION IS NOT YOUR OWN, AND CITE YOUR SOURCES ACCURATELY. As you develop your speech, be sure you give credit to your sources of information and to ideas that are not your own. If you do not cite the sources of your information, you are guilty of plagiarism, as indicated in Chapter 10. Provide the audience with an oral footnote such as "The following was taken from. . . " or "The following is a quotation from. . . ". Be specific about who and where your information came from.

2. DO NOT FALSIFY OR DISTORT INFORMATION IN ORDER TO MAKE YOUR POINT. Never make up information, attribute information to a source that is not responsible for it, take quotation out of context, or distort information to meet your purpose.

3. SHOW RESPECT FOR YOUR AUDIENCE. When audience members perceive that you are being respectful, even though they may not agree with your point of view, they are more likely to listen. And when they listen, you have at least a chance of persuading them. Do not try to trick audience members into accepting your point of view or ridicule them for not agreeing with you.

Your audience's evaluation of your credibility will ultimately determine whether they accept or reject your persuasive goals. You should remember that credibility is earned, that it depends on others' perceptions, and that it is not permanent. Credibility changes from topic to topic, from situation to situation, and from audience to audience, and so you must establish your credibility each time you speak.

EXERCISE

List five well-known individuals whom you believe to be highly credible, and briefly describe what makes them credible. Compare your names and opinions with those of your classmates. What did you learn about credibility in making the comparisons?

PREPARING AND DEVELOPING A PERSUASIVE SPEECH

In a classroom situation, you will usually have only one opportunity to convince your audience to accept your persuasive purpose. Therefore, it is important to set realistic persuasive goals and to give some special thought to how you research, organize, and support your topic.

Researching the Topic

Your research for a persuasive speech must be especially thorough. You'll need to gather as much information as possible about your topic, because the more you know, the better equipped you will be to support your position. When doing your research, look primarily for evidence that supports and clarifies your views. If, in the process, you discover information that contradicts your stand, make note of it and look for material that you can use to refute such information. Such anticipation of possible objections is especially helpful when your position is controversial and when your audience's opinions are likely to be split. If you know the arguments that may be used against you, you will be better able to support and defend your position.

Organizing the Topic

A persuasive speech requires several special decisions that will affect organization, for example:

1. SHOULD YOU PRESENT ONE SIDE OR BOTH SIDES OF AN ISSUE? The answer to this question depends on your audience. If your listeners basically support your position, then presenting one side may be sufficient. If their views are divided or opposed to your position, it may be more effective to present both sides. This decision also depends on your audience's knowledge of the topic and their evaluation of your credibility. If audience members are well informed and educated, presenting both sides of an argument helps minimize the effect that counterarguments can have on your audience.

2. WHEN SHOULD YOU PRESENT YOUR STRONGEST ARGUMENTS? Presenting your strongest arguments at either the beginning or the end of your speech is more effective than presenting them in the middle. A good strategy is to state your strongest arguments early and then repeat them toward the end. Because audience attention is most likely to wander in the middle

of a speech, that is a good time to present a personal examples supporting your position.

3. WHAT IS THE BEST WAY TO ORGANIZE YOUR PERSUASIVE SPEECH? The most effective sequence of presentation depends on your topic, specific purpose, and audience. Among the patterns of organization that work well for persuasive speeches are problem-solution, cause-effect, and motivated sequence. Each has been discussed in Chapter 9.

Supporting the Topic

In persuasive speeches, speakers try to influence their audience through the impressiveness of their supporting materials. Thus, they choose their supporting materials carefully to build the kind of appeal that is most likely to sway their listeners. Based on their topic and their audience analysis, persuasive speakers will try to appeal to their listeners' needs, to their logic, or to their emotions.

Appeals to Needs **Appeals to needs** attempt to move people to action by calling on physical and psychological requirements and desires. Of course, different people have different needs, but most of us want to protect or enhance factors that affect our physical, safety, social, and self-esteem needs.[6]

Physical needs are our most basic physiological requirements, such as the needs for food, water, sleep, sex, and other physical comforts. *Safety needs* pertain to our desires for stability, order, protection from violence, freedom from stress and disease, security, and structure. *Social needs* relate to our hopes to be loved and to belong, our needs for affection from family and friends, for membership in groups, and for the acceptance and approval of others. *Self-esteem needs* reflect our desires for recognition, respect from others, and self-respect.

Speakers can appeal to any of these needs to motivate listeners to take action. For example, a speaker trying to sell individual retirement accounts would aim his or her appeal at our needs for security and stability; a speaker who hoped to persuade listeners to lose weight would call on their needs for physical comfort, acceptance by others, and self-esteem. Our readiness to accept ideas or to take action depends heavily on the speaker's ability to relate his or her message to our needs.

Logical Appeals Attempts to move people to action through the use of evidence and proof are called **logical appeals.** When speakers lead their listeners to think "Yes, that's logical" or "That makes sense," they are building their case by calling on their audience's ability to reason. To accomplish this, competent persuasive speakers use evidence such as statistics, examples, and testimony and any other supporting materials that will sway their listeners.

A logical appeal requires an ability to argue for your point of view. When you argue in persuasive speaking, you usually state a *proposition,* which is what you want your listeners to do after you have completed your speech. A proposition usually assumes that there is more than one way to do things; for example, abortion should be illegal or abortion should be legal, college athletes should be paid or college athletes should not be paid. You usually try to justify your position with reasons and evidence. The *justification* is the use of all the supporting materials you can find to support your proposition, including statistics, facts, examples, testimony, pictures, objects, and so on.

In presenting their evidence, persuasive speakers guide their listeners through a carefully planned sequence of thought that clearly leads to the desired conclusion. This train of logic may fall into one of four categories: deductive reasoning, inductive reasoning, causal reasoning, or reasoning by analogy.

Deductive reasoning is a sequence of thought that moves from general information to a specific conclusion. It presents a general premise (a generalization) and a minor premise (a specific instance) that leads to a precise deduction (a conclusion about the instance). One student set up his argument as follows.

General Premise	Heart disease is a major health concern in the Midwest.
Minor Premise	Nebraska is a part of the Midwest.
Conclusion	Therefore, heart disease is a major health concern in Nebraska.

Great care must be taken that the premises are accurate, because faulty premises can only lead to a faulty conclusion. For example:

General Premise	All car salespersons are crooks.
Minor Premise	Carolyn is a car salesperson.
Conclusion	Therefore, Carolyn is a crook.

The general premise must be both accurate and defensible before deductive reasoning can be used effectively as evidence to support a position.

Inductive reasoning is the opposite of deductive reasoning—it is a sequence of thought that moves from the specific to the general. An argument based on induction usually progresses from a series of related facts or situations to a general conclusion. A student discussing university teaching evaluations wants her listeners to agree that the speech professors at her university are excellent teachers. She therefore leads them through the following sequence of inductive reasoning.

Facts

1. My speech communication professor is an excellent classroom teacher.
2. The speech professor I had last semester was also an excellent classroom teacher.

3. My roommate's speech professor is an excellent classroom teacher.

4. My roommate has a friend whose speech professor is an excellent classroom teacher.

Conclusion   Speech professors at the University of Nebraska are, in general, excellent classroom teachers.

When your facts can be verified, when there are a sufficient number of facts, and when there are sufficient links between the facts and the conclusion, inductive reasoning can be an excellent way to persuade an audience of the validity of your argument.

Of course, inductive reasoning can also be misused. For example, how often have you heard such general statements as "Football players are intellectually void," "Politicians are crooks," "Farmers are hard-working," "College students are elitists," "Single parents are hurting their children," or "The middle class is going broke"? Each of these generalizations is usually based on some past experience, but the problem is that such experiences are not always sufficient to support the conclusion.

To avoid problems when using inductive reasoning, make sure your facts are accurate and that they support your conclusion. Also, make sure your conclusion does not extend beyond the facts you have presented. You will undermine your own case if your conclusion is so general that someone can point out its exceptions.

Causal reasoning is a sequence of thought that links causes with effects. Thus, it always implies or includes the word *because:* "The earth's temperature is turning colder *because* the ozone layer is thinning." As in any form of reasoning, it is necessary to support the conclusion with evidence. In the above example, the speaker would go on to cite some scientific evidence linking thinning ozone to falling temperatures. The more verifiable and valid the evidence is, the more defensible the conclusion about the cause-and-effect relationship between ozone and temperature will be. Even though other factors may also be causes of the earth's cooling, the speaker's argument can be considered reasonable if he or she can produce scientific evidence to support this point of view.

Reasoning by analogy is a sequence of thought that compares similar things or circumstances in order to draw a conclusion. It says, in effect, that what holds true in one case will also hold true in a similar case. Thus, in arguing that American auto manufacturers should change their approach to production, you might use the following reasoning.

General Premise   American automobile production must improve.

Minor Premise   The Japanese method of auto production has been extremely successful.

Conclusion   American auto manufacturers should adopt the Japanese method if they wish to be successful.

Analogy can be a useful reasoning tool when it is used wisely and with appropriate support for its conclusion. The relationship in the analogy must be valid, and the conclusion should be based on the assumption that all other factors are equal. For instance, our example is based on the assumption that the Japanese method is a good way to manufacture cars and that American manufacturers could be just as successful as the Japanese. On the other hand, if the argument implied that the Japanese method's success could be traced to the worker's pride, dedication, and involvement in the production process, then similar factors would have to be applied to the American work force. Thus, to avoid problems in drawing analogies, it is crucial to consider any dissimilarities that may refute your point.

You may wish to base your speech on a single form of reasoning, of you may prefer a combination of types of reasoning. Whatever your choice, you must remember that your argument is only as good as the evidence you use to support it.

Emotional Appeals   Attempts to move people to action by playing on their feelings—for example, by making them feel guilty, unhappy, afraid, happy, proud, sympathetic, or nostalgic—are known as **emotional appeals.** Because emotions are extremely strong motivators, this form for appeal can be highly effective. Note how the following introduction to a persuasive speech appeals to the emotions.

> It is 1968, Tamaqua, Pennsylvania, where a little baby girl has just breathed her first breath. Her name is Kim. It is 1978, and ten-year-old Kim moves with her mom and dad to Florida and is enrolled in a Catholic school. It is 1985, and Kim enrolls in college. A picture-perfect all-American girl—Kim never used drugs, she studied hard, and she made the decision to remain a virgin until marriage. It is 1987, and Kim has two wisdom teeth extracted. It is 1989, and Kim is diagnosed with AIDS. It is 1990, and Kim lies on her living room sofa, her skin chalky, her body frail, and her weight 101 pounds. It is 1991; now she resembles a skeleton, her weight 65 pounds, struggling to breathe what might be her last breath. "See you tomorrow?" her father says as he carries her to bed. "Hopefully not," she replies. It's December, 1991, and Kim is dead.
>
>   Kimberly Bergalis became the first ever documented case of AIDS transmission from a health care worker to patient in 1989, but she wasn't the last. . . .[7]

Emotional appeals can be so powerful that they sway people to do things that might not be logical. A student's cheating on an exam, for example, can by no means by justified through logical thought, but the student may believe that she is justified from an emotional viewpoint because of parental pressure to get good grades. In fact, persuasive speakers often mix both logical and emotional appeals to achieve the strongest effect.

EXERCISE

Analyze several advertisements in a national magazine. What appeals did the advertisers use? Did the ads appeal to you? Why or why not? Were the ads ethical? Why or why not?

Supporting materials help make the audience believe in the information.

Supporting materials appeal to the audience's needs, logic, and emotions.

Supporting materials include such things as factual statements, statistical data, personal experiences, analogies, contrast, examples and illustrations, expert testimony, value appeals, and eye-witness accounts.

Visual aids are used where appropriate and helpful.

Supporting materials are documented, cited correctly, and up-to-date.

Supporting materials help the speaker establish and confirm credibility.

Organization

When making judgments about the organization of a persuasive speech, the evaluator looks for a carefully planned, well-developed speech that has a unified approach to the material being presented.

I. Introduction (overall) is properly developed.
   A. It orients the audience to the topic.
      1. It gains the audience's attention and arouses interest.
      2. It includes a specific purpose and thesis statement.
      3. It defines terms (if necessary).
   B. It motivates the audience to listen.
      1. It is relevant.
      2. It establishes credibility.
   C. Organization of the body (overall) is clear and easy to follow.
      1. The main points are clear and parallel in structure.
      2. The main points are related to the purpose of the speech.
      3. Transitions provide appropriate links between ideas.
      4. The organizational pattern is appropriate.
   D. Conclusion (overall) is properly developed.
      1. It reinforces the purpose by reviewing the main points.
      2. It ends with a memorable thought, and the audience knows what is expected of them.

Delivery

The delivery techniques show evidence that you are aware of what the audience is interested in hearing, that you are involved in and enthusiastic about the topic, and that you are interested in sharing the material with the listeners.

Speaker is enthusiastic.

Nonverbal communication (gestures, movements, eye contact, posture, facial expression) enhances and clarifies the verbal delivery.

Speaker shows an awareness of the audience and adjusts delivery to meet audience needs.

Speaker is confident and poised.

Speaker's vocal delivery (overall) enhances the speech with:

Appropriate volume	Appropriate rate
Conversational quality	Enthusiastic tone
Clear enunciation	Appropriate pauses
Appropriate vocal variety	

Language

You are aware of acceptable language and use it to enhance and clarify ideas.

Language (overall) is appropriate to the assignment and audience.

Word choice is appropriate for college level.

Grammar is appropriate and shows college-level competence.

Word pronunciations are correct.

A PERSUASIVE SPEECH WITH COMMENTARY

The following adaptation of a speech written by Tim Borchers, a University of Nebraska student and now graduate student at Wayne State University in Detroit, illustrates many of the strategies discussed in this chapter.[8]

The Invisible Killer

Specific Purpose

To persuade listeners that radon gas is harmful and to take action to protect their home from it.

Thesis Statement

Radon gas exists, is a killer and we need to do something about it.

To get his audience's attention and involvement, Tim begins by using suspense and emotionally loaded statements that are tied directly to his audience. In addition, he appeals to their need for safety and ties it all to his thesis. He should be very careful that his delivery is sincere and convincing, but not too dramatic. Tim provides testimony to support his opening statements, but also to add to his credibility.

It sneaks into your home at anytime. In broad daylight or under cover of darkness—silently it sneaks up on you and your family. Slowly, but surely, it kills you and the ones you love. This inhuman silent killer is radon, a colorless, odorless gas generated by the decay of radium in the soil. As a gas, radon moves along for miles underground, seeping into buildings primarily through cracks in basements and sewer pipes. According to the EPA (Environmental Protection Agency), each year this killer strikes up to 30,000 innocent victims by infecting them with lung cancer.

He provides an example about a family's discovery of the gas to substantiate his

After hearing this warning, Donna and Steve Fairbanks of Leeds, Maine, had their home tested for radon. When they *claim and an analogy to cigarette smoking to illustrate the potency of the gas.*

Tim points out that even though this is a serious problem, few people know about it and thus the public needs to be informed. His delivery is fluent. He uses his voice and body to give more meaning to what he is saying and to keep his audience's attention. Tim at this point forecasts what is to follow and states his persuasive purpose. He keeps the audience's attention by not directly telling them what his specific solution is. He does an excellent job of always relating his message directly to the audience.

Tim begins his first main point. He uses credible neutral sources as well as statistics to develop and support the need and show how serious the problem is.

Continuing to use his vopice and body language effectively, Tim does a good job of making it easy for his audience to listen to him. Give credibility to sources and what they represent.

In order to give his statistics impact, TIim provides specific examples of people who were directly affected by Radon. The examples certainly make his point that Radon is in homes. To make this information even more credible, he should have cited the sources of this information.

Tim does a nice job with this example because it brings out the emotional impact of the problem on people.

Tim provides more dataon how widespread the problem is and how it could affect everyone in the audience. He again does an excellent job of relating the problem to his audience. Tim shows that even though the problem has been known to many, it continues and is being ignored. He relates the point to his

got the results, they learned that the radon levels were so high in their home, it was as if they had been smoking seven packs of cigarettes every day.

Yet efforts to stop radon have been unsuccessful because the general public is uninformed about the problem and because the government is not adequately addressing this killer. In order to halt this deadly attack of radon, we must first understand radon's reach, then see why our defenses against radon are weak, and then find ways in which we can defend ourselves from radon's killing potential.

What makes radon so deadly is that is kills silently and slowly. Silently, the gas sneaks into our homes and workplaces without notice. Once there, says Dr. Glen Lykken, Professor of Physics at the University of North Dakota, the gas attaches to smoke or dust particles in the air and is inhaled. Once in the lungs, the gas emits energy, killing the lung cells.

Dr. Lykken says there is a 20-year period between exposure to the radon and the detection of lung cancer. Slowly, the gas kills its victim. According to Bill Brink, of the Region 7 EPA office in Kansas City, Missouri, the gas is responsible for between 5,000 and 30,000 deaths from lung cancer each year, making it the second leading cause of lung cancer next to cigarette smoking.

This news was especially alarming to Stanley Watras and his wife Diane. Watras, a nuclear power plant worker, set off radiation detectors on his way into work one morning at the Limerick Nuclear Plant in Boyerton, Pennsylvania. It was discovered that Watras and his family had been exposed to more radiation at home than he had ever been at work in the nuclear power plant. Their neighbors across the street also live with the killer.

Kay Jones listened with tears in her eyes as officials told her the radon levels in her home were 780 times higher than those allowable by federal law in uranium mines.

But radon is not isolated to that small Boyerton, Pennsylvania, neighborhood. According to the EPA radon levels above the national safety standard have documented in almost every state. While radon is a problem that many of us have been aware of for several years, a study conducted by the EPA in 1988 showed that the radon risk continues to climb. Another study that examined homes in 10 states found radon danger in one of five homes. Extrapolating *audience by reminding them they need to be concerned because the Radon problem is growing and is a threat to everyone. He also uses vivid language to be convincing.*

Tim does a nice job of reemphasizing the problem as he continues to develop it. He forecasts what is to follow, providing the audience with reasons why the problem still exists.

Tim provides documentation to support his three assertions. The use of supporting material is important to making his case. Had he not supported the assertions, they would have been much less effective. But he should be careful not to just provide a string of facts. To help reinforce his argument, Tim quotes additional testimony and uses a military metaphor, referring to Radon as the "enemy." He does a good job in drawing a specific conclusion for the audience.

Here Tim uses a transition and signpost to let the audience know that he has moved to the next point. He continues the military metaphor with the word "combat." He returns to the analogy of smoking. The analogy is excellent because it is something familiar to everyone in the audience. Tim uses vocal variety, pauses, and sufficient eye contact to communicate directly with his listeners. He cites a source from Nebraska, which is directly relevant to his audience. This might not have been the best source if Tim was in another state. The use of suspense is an excellent device to kerep the audience involved as well as to let them know they may have a problem and not even know it.

Tim does a nice job of describing why there is a problem and what has and has not been done. This lets the listeners know that something needs to be done. He also provides data to support why not much is being done. Tim uses his vopice well to express this information clearly and directly. His use of testimony is ex-

from these two surveys, the EPA now estimates that some 3 million homes in those 17 states alone have radon levels above the national safety standard. Even when you leave your home, you still may be threatened. Every building, including offices, schools, apartments and homes, is vulnerable to radon's deadly attack.

Since radon is so dangerous, it is doubly troubling that our defenses against it are so weak. Three advantages radon has on us are: (1) the trapping of radon in buildings, (2) the lack of public awareness of the problem, and (3) the lack of governmental action.

Ironically, steps taken by homeowners to make their homes more energy efficient actually end up trapping the deadly gas in their homes. John A. Paul and Andrew P. Linstrom of the Regional Air Pollution Control Clinic of Dayton, Ohio, state that most indoor radon problems are aggravated by effective use of insulation to make homes energy efficient. The insulating of buildings and homes restricts the air flow and allows the buildup of the deadly gas. Richard Guimond, director of the EPA's Radon Action Program, says, "The more you try to button down a house, the higher the pollution levels become." So by insulating our homes, we are actually aiding the enemy.

Further, we as individuals are not sufficiently prepared to combat radon. For example, some people in New Jersey, New York, and Pennsylvania are living in homes that have radon levels so high, it is as if they were smoking five packs of cigarettes each day. Yet, *Newsweek*, September 26, 1988, points out that only 10 to 15 percent of these residents have had their homes tested for radon. Further, those who have heard of the problem are confused about what exactly to do to solve the problem. According to Harold Borchert, of the Nebraska Department of Health's Division of Radiological Health, "The real danger is that people become confused about the conflicting details of the problem and give up trying to understand the problem." Finally, it is impossible to determine which homes have radon and which do not. The EPA says tests are are currently being conducted to pinpoint radon plagued homes, but early results have been inconclusive.

One reason the public is uninformed about the problem is that the government is a weak police force against radon's threat. Put simply, the EPA lacks the money to carry out its war on radon. While the Indoor Radon Abatement Act of 1988 calls for annual federal spending of $15 million for radon, only $7 to 8 million of this has been appropriated to the EPA. According to Bill Brink of the Kansas City EPA office, this amount is nowhere near enough money. Even the

cellent. All of this establishes the prob-
lem the listeners face and helps build his
credibility.

Tim begins to move toward the solution
and what he wants his listeners to do—
his persuasive goal. He is telling his lis-
teners what they need to do in order to
help make their world safer to live in.
Tim might have used an analogy or
other device to help explain the terminol-
ogy. Tim uses testimony to support his
assertion that something can be done to
reduce the risk from Radon. He is also
providing his listeners with steps they
can take to help themselves.

Again Tim relies on testimony to sup-
port the actions he wants his listeners to
take. He does this clearly and directly,
leaving no doubt what needs to be done.

Tim makes an emotional appeal to im-
press his audience again with the serious
health risks involved.

Tim offers hope that the problem can be
solved if the listeners take action. His sin-
cerity and his use of testimony here en-
hance his credibility and persuasiveness.

full amount of $15 million wouldn't be sufficient to fund EPA's radon program. "We could use ten times that amount," says Brink. Currently, he says, only twenty states have been tested for radon, a process that could be accelerated. Also, the EPA would like to test 3 out of every 100 schools for radon, but now can only afford to test only 1 out of every 100. Overall, says Brink, the EPA's radon program, including training, research, and a public information campaign, is "grossly underfunded."

But still, defending against radon is possible and inexpensive and can be carried out on two levels, the personal and the governmental. The first step on the personal level is training. We should all have our houses or apartments tested so they are within the advisable guideline of 4 picocuries per liter of air. The EPA has two booklets available, "A Citizen's Guide to Radon" and "Radon Reduction Methods." Both are available from area health offices and describe ways we can protect ourselves from radon's killing potential. Area health offices also have lists of companies who do radon testing. According to the Omaha *World Herald* of September 25, 1988, there are over 1,200 companies nationwide who do radon testing for less than $25.

If your house or apartment is found to have a high level of radon, you can take several steps to reduce the level. According to Dana K. Mount, North Dakota State Department of Health, short-term defenses included discouraging smoking in homes, spending less time in the basement, keeping crawl spaces open, and opening windows when possible. We should also inform our neighbors or local health officials if we have a problem, so they can take appropriate action. Long-term solutions include changing air ventilation in the house, soil ventilation around the house, and sealing off entry routes where the gas can sweep into the house. We must remember that any step we take to reduce the amount of radon in our homes also reduces our immediate risk of getting lung cancer.

But we can't solve the problem by ourselves. Federal, state, and local governments also need to address this killer. First, the EPA must receive all funding allocated to it by the Indoor Radon Abatement Act of 1988. Next, this amount should be increased so the EPA can provide a full arsenal of defense against radon. State and local governments, too, need to become involved. State governments should circulate radon information, test homes for radon, and provide low interest loans to homeowners who implement radon reduction devices. Finally, local governments need to work with contractors and realtors to amend building codes and make homes safer.

Tim's comment about moving to another planet makes vivid his closing point that something has to be done. He continues to involve his audience by providing them with specific actions they can take. In his final statement, he again points to the seriousness of the problem, but also to the possibility of a solution if the audience is willing to act: "It's not too late." His final sentence provides a view of what the world would be like without Radon. This vision is extremely important and should be emphasized throughout the speech.

While the only way we could totally escape radon would be to move to another planet, we can and should make our own planet safer for us to live on. First by informing each other and then by taking steps to reduce the level of radon in our homes, we can make our houses and apartments safer. By making our homes safer today, we help alleviate the problem of radon in our atmosphere tomorrow. It's not too late to secure our homes and to protect ourselves and our loved ones from radon's killing potential. After all, our homes should be a place of rest, not our final resting place.

SUMMARY

Persuasion affects us every day of our lives. If we are not attempting to persuade others, they are attempting to persuade us. An understanding of persuasion and its strategies can help us create effective persuasive messages and prepare us to analyze and comprehend the persuasive messages that we receive.

Persuasion is a process, involving both verbal and nonverbal messages, that attempts to reinforce or change attitudes, beliefs, values, or behavior. The difference between a persuasive and an informative speech is the purpose of the speaker. The purpose of the informative speech is to have listeners understand and learn, whereas the purpose of the persuasive speech is to change the behavior of the listeners.

There are four action goals in persuasive speaking: (1) *Adoption* asks listeners to demonstrate their acceptance of an idea, belief, or value by performing the desired behavior, (2) *discontinuance* asks listeners to stop doing something, (3) *deterrence* asks listeners to avoid certain behaviors, and (4) *continuance* asks listeners to continue certain behaviors.

In selecting a persuasive topic, you should consider your interest in the subject, its value and concern to your audience, its potential as an action goal, and its currentness. Persuasive speech topics, may center around a *question of fact,* what is true and what is false; a *question of value,* whether something is good or bad, desirable or undesirable; or a *question of policy,* what actions should be taken. When attempting to answer questions of fact, value, and policy, you cannot always develop a formal logical response or answer to meet the objections of others. Toulmin's model can help meet objections of others with its three basic parts: claim, data, and warrant.

Arguments that are flawed because they do not follow the rules of logic and therefore are not believed are called *fallacies.* One major misuse of information involves fact and opinion. When speakers state opinions as if they are facts, this can be misleading and result in fallacious arguments. A *red herring* fallacy is when irrelevant information is used to divert attention away from the real issue. Another common fallacy, *questionable cause,* occurs when a speaker alleges something that does not relate to, or produce, the outcome cliamed in the argument. *Hasty generalization,* another type of fallacy, occurs when a speaker doesn't have sufficient data and thus argues or reasons from specific example. Finally, *ad hominem* is when someone attacks a person rather than the argument itself. This is also referred to as "name calling."

Credibility, a speaker's believability based on the audience's evaluation of his or her competence and character, is critical to the success of any persuasive speech. Competence is our perception of a speaker's knowledge, and character is our perception of his or her *trustworthiness* (reliability and dependability) and *ethics* (moral principles).

Preparing and developing a persuasive speech requires special attention to research, organization, and supporting materials. Your research must be particularly thorough and accurate. Your method of organization must be carefully matched to your topic, specific purpose, and audience.

Like an informative speech, the persuasive speech may follow a problem-solution, cause-and-effect, or motivated sequence pattern.

Persuasive speakers use supporting materials to build the kind of appeal that is most likely to sway their listeners. *Appeals to needs* attempt to move people to action by calling on their physical and psychological requirements and desires. *Logical appeals* use evidence and proof to support the speaker's views. In presenting a logical appeal, a speaker may use *deductive reasoning,* a sequence of thought that moves from general information to a specific conclusion; *inductive reasoning,* a sequence of thought that moves from the specific to the general; *causal reasoning,* a sequence of thought that links causes with effects and implies or includes the word "because"; and *reasoning by analogy,* a sequence of thought that compares similar things or circumstances in order to draw a conclusion. *Emotional appeals* attempt to move people to action by playing on their feelings. Emotional appeals, if properly selected, can be a powerful way to sway people to do things that may not necessarily be logical. It is not unusual for persuasive speakers to mix both logical and emotional appeals to achieve the strongest effect.

KEY TERMS

Ad Hominem: Fallacy which the person rather than his or her argument is attacked. This is also referred to as "name calling."

Adoption: Action goal that asks listeners to demonstrate their acceptance of an attitude, belief, or value by performing the behavior suggested by the speaker.

Appeal to Needs: Attempt to move people to action by calling on their physical and psychological requirements and desires.

Causal Reasoning: Sequence of thought that links causes with effects; it either implies or explicitly states the word *because.*

Continuance: Action goal that asks listeners to demonstrate their acceptance of an attitude, belief, or value by continuing to perform the behavior suggested by the speaker.

Credibility: Speaker's believability based on the audience's evaluation of the speaker's competence, experience, and character.

Deductive reasoning: Sequence of thought that moves from general information to a specific conclusion; it consists of a general premise, a minor premise, and a conclusion.

Deterrence: Action goal that asks listeners to demonstrate their acceptance of an attitude, belief, or value by avoiding certain behavior.

Discontinuance: Action goal that asks listeners to demonstrate their acceptance of an attitude, belief, or value by avoiding certain behaviors; the opposite of Adoption.

Emotional Appeal: Attempt to move people to action by playing on their feelings.

Ethics: Individual's system of moral principles.

Fallacy: Argument that is flawed because it does not follow the rules of logic.

Hasty Generalization: Fallacy that occurs when a speaker doesn't have sufficient data, and thus argues or reasons from specific example.

Inductive Reasoning: Sequence of thought that moves from specific facts to a general conclusion.

Logical Appeal: Attempt to move people to action through the use of evidence and proof.

Persuasion: Communication process, involving both verbal and nonverbal messages, that attempts to reinforce or change listeners' attitudes, beliefs, values, or behavior.

Question of Fact: Question that asks what is true and what is false.

Question of Policy: Question that asks what actions should be taken.

Question of Value: Question that asks whether something is good or bad, desirable or undesirable.

Questionable Cause: Fallacy which occurs when a speaker alleges something that does not relate to, or produce, the outcome cliamed in the argument.

Reasoning by Analogy: Sequence of thought that compares similar things or circumstances in order to draw a conclusion.

Red herring: Fallacy that uses irrelevant information to divert attention away from the real issue.

Trustworthiness: Speaker's reliability and dependability, as perceived by the audience.

DISCUSSION STARTERS

1. In what ways does persuasion affect your daily life?
2. Why is behavioral change the ultimate goal of persuasion?

3. What advice would you give to someone who was assigned to give a persuasive speech and needed to select a topic?
4. What determines whether a topic is appropriate for a persuasive speech?
5. Do you have credibility? Explain your response.
6. If a person has lost credibility, what can he or she do to regain it?
7. How can you establish credibility in a persuasive speech?
8. In what ways does organizing a persuasive speech differ from organizing an informative speech?
9. Are supporting materials in a persuasive speech used differently from the way they are used in an informative speech? Explain your response.
10. How do you know if a speaker is being ethical in what he or she tells you?
11. What criteria would you use to judge the effectiveness of a persuasive speech?

NOTES

1. Adapted from W. Fotheringham, *Perspectives on Persuasion* (Boston: Allyn & Bacon, 1966): 33.
2. Adapted from a speech presented by Mary B. Trouba, reprinted from *Winning Orations:* Interstate Oratorical Association, 1986, with permission.
3. S. Toulmin, *The Uses of Argument* (Cambridge, England: Cambridge University Press, 1969): 94–145.
4. Adapted from a persuasive speech written by Melissa Nicholas, University of Nebraska student, entitled "Unnecessary Risk," 1993.
5. Taken from a speech presented by Whitney Sugarman, reprinted with permission from *Winning Orations* (Mankato, Minn.: Interstate Oratorical Association, 1992).
6. A. H. Maslow, *Motivation and Personality*, 2d ed. (New York: Harper-Collins, 1970). Maslow in this edition includes two additional desires or needs—need to know and understand and aesthetic desire—as higher stages of his hierarchy. These are often associated with subcategories of self-actualization, which is not included here.
7. Speech presented by Heather Jamison, reprinted with permission from *Winning Orations* (Mankato, Minn.: Interstate Oratorical Association, 1992).
8. Speech reprinted and modified with permission of Tim Borchers, a student, and Dr. Ann Pettus, Director of Forensics at the University of Nebraska, Lincoln, 1990.

APPENDIX: PERSUASIVE SPEECH TOPICS—A SAMPLE LIST

Here are some possible topics for persuasive speeches. The items listed are not necessarily titles of speeches and may be broad areas that would need to be narrowed to fit specific purposes, time limits, or other requirements set by your instructor.

Increasing Aid to Farmers

Children at Risk in Our Society

Internships Are Beneficial

Helping the Homeless

Sex Education Is Still Needed

Elderly Abuse on the Rise

Poaching of Animals

Teenage Pregnancies Increase

Control of Acid Rain

Tabloids Are Nothing But Rumor

Tanning Beds Can Be Fatal

Women Need Not Be Second

The Best Vacation You Can Take

All College Instructors Must Speak English Clearly

Recycling to Save the Environment

The Impact of Video

Majoring in Communication

Sexual Assaults Are Increasing

Teacher Certification

Professional Athletes Are Too Greedy

Youth Programs

Teacher Competencies

Americans Lack Discipline

Dumping of Nuclear Waste

The United States Is No Longer a World Competitor

Rap Music Can Send Important Messages

Sexual Abuse of Children

Biking: An Excellent Form of Transportation

Sunscreen Lotions and Skin Cancer

The Best Way to Make a Buck While in College

Spring Break: Do It the Inexpensive Way

Fast Food Is Harmful

College Athletics Is Big Business

Improving Our Prisons

Political Involvement

Athletes and Winning

Pornographic Films

Ban Small Cars

Corruption in Sports

Traditional Family Values

Plan For Your Retirement Now

The Impact of the Brady Bill

Gay Rights

INTERPERSONAL COMMUNICATION

Chapter 13

Interpersonal Communication

LEARNING OBJECTIVES

After studying this chapter, you should be able to:

1. Distinguish between intrapersonal and interpersonal communication.

2. Analyze how motivation affects relationships, using Maslow's hierarchy of individual needs and Schutz's theory of interpersonal needs.

3. Understand the importance of small talk in the development of relationships.

4. Explain the role of self-disclosure in relationships.

5. Describe how the Johari Window illustrates the process of awareness and self-disclosure in interpersonal relationships.

6. Cite guidelines for more effective self-disclosure.

Adrienne says she and Carl are strong-willed and independent, and their friendship took time to stabilize: "Our childhood relationship was always to the extreme. We were either the best of friends or the worst of enemies. We played together a lot and were neighborhood ringleaders. While he was the little brother and I often played the protector, we also knew how to hit each other's hot button, and did."

Barbara J. Eckl, "Siblings," *Wisconsin: The Milwaukee Journal Magazine,* September 5, 1993, 20

• •

Kathy Jo,

So this is the end, eh? Thank you for always being there for me and listening to me blab. You're going to be great! I am so proud of you! I Love you,

Steve

Personal Ad—*Daily Nebraskan,* December 13, 1993, 18

• •

So while Sunday morning services and age-divided Bible studies remain the basis of church community, specialized groups are taking shape: grief support, children of divorce, homosexuals, rape survivors, single parents, parents of teens, parents of preschoolers, stress reduction, and more.

Adeana Leftin, "Churches Develop Small Groups to Address Members' Needs," *Lincoln Journal Star,* September 4, 1993, 1

• •

Interviews are like blind dates and they are just as unpopular. They involve two strangers with an eye toward a future relationship and only the most basic information to work with. It's no wonder then that most blind dates, and quite a few interviews, end with frozen smiles and limp handshakes.

Kate Tyndall, "The Interview: The Right Strategy, The Best Questions," *Hemispheres,* October, 1992, 32.

• •

Dear Beth:

I'm 18 and was going with a guy who's 28. We had a great relationship and all. Last time I saw him, he said, "See you tomorrow." Well, tomorrow came, and he didn't. That was three weeks ago. I really loved him, and I know he loved me. I don't know his phone number or exactly where he lives.

Deserted

Deserted:

I'm afraid your idea of a great relationship was different from his. It's hard to imagine how you could feel you know a person well enough to have a relationship when you don't even know his phone number or address. You've been used.

Beth Winship, "Teens,"*Detroit Free Press,* 29 December, 1980, 2C.

You have only to examine your community or school newspaper to see the importance of interpersonal communication. The interpersonal situations described above indicate why relationships are essential in helping us learn who we are, what we mean to others, and how to be ourselves. This chapter focuses on concepts and issues relevant to interpersonal communication. Although the only way to create, continue, and end relationships is through interpersonal communication, a relationship always begins and ends with intrapersonal communication.

EXERCISE

Take a few minutes and look through your local or school newspaper or current contemporary magazines for articles related to interpersonal communication. What kind of articles relating to interpersonal communication did you find? Why do think there are so many articles in newspapers and magazines related to our relationships with others?

INTRAPERSONAL COMMUNICATION

In order to communicate well with others, we must first understand how we communicate with ourselves. As defined in Chapter 1, the process of understanding information within oneself is called **intrapersonal communication.** Although such communication begins and ends within ourselves and no one else need be involved, intrapersonal communication affects how we communicate and, ultimately, our relationships with others.

Because all messages that we create first occur within us, we can never separate ourselves from our interaction with others, no matter how neutral or empathetic we may think we are. We say "I understand your feelings" to someone, but we can only understand another's feelings after they are filtered through our own feelings and perceptions. Our feelings and perceptions ultimately become what we communicate to others and what allows us to establish relationships. (See Chapter 1 for more on intrapersonal communication.)

INTERPERSONAL COMMUNICATION

In Chapter 1, **interpersonal communication** was defined as the informal exchange of information between two or more people. Interpersonal communication allows us to establish relationships with others. A **relationship** is an association between at least two people and may be described in terms of intimacy or kinship—for example, acquaintance, girlfriend, boyfriend, lover, wife, husband, mother, father, child, uncle, or cousin. Sometimes relationships are based on roles—for example, two roommates, neighbors or, partner's, or boss and employee, teacher and student, doctor and patient, minister and church members. Relationships can also be described in terms of time, as in, 'I knew her in high school" or "They just met him the other day." Finally, relationships may be based on activities or participation in events, for example, "We play softball together," "We go to the same church," "He is in my class," "She works with me," or "We belong to the same fraternity."[1] Through our many different kinds of relationships, we satisfy our desire to be with others and to communicate with them.

THE MOTIVATION TO COMMUNICATE AND FORM RELATIONSHIPS

Interpersonal relationships help us understand ourselves as well as understand others. The quotations in the beginning of the chapter suggest the need people have for meaningful relationships and the importance people place on them. The relationships described in each of the opening situations imply that people make many judgments, draw many inferences, and reach many conclusions about others through their communication or lack of it. In the interview and the "Dear Beth" scenarios, at least one person involved desired to know more about the other person. The interpersonal phenomenon of wanting to know more about others is referred to as the uncertainty principle.[2] The **uncertainty principle** suggests that when we initially meet others to whom we are attracted, our need to know about them tends to make us draw inferences from the physical data that is observed. There is an urge or need to lessen our uncertainty about those individuals, which can motivate a desire for further communication with them.

Each of us has many different physical and emotional needs that we wish to fulfill. Usually, our most significant communication with others is about some interpersonal need we have or the other person has. The more we understand about our needs and the needs of others, the more effective we can become at interpersonal communication. Our interpersonal needs and the needs of others are what drive us to be the individuals we are when we are by ourselves or with others. Two approaches that can help us better understand our motivation to communicate with others are Abraham Maslow's hierarchy of individual needs and William Schutz's theory of interpersonal needs.

Maslow's Hierarchy of Individual Needs

According to Maslow's **Hierarchy of Individual Needs,** human needs can be classified into seven categories—physiological, safety, social, self-esteem, self-actualization, knowing and understanding, and aesthetics. The categories can be ranked in order of priority.[3] According to Maslow, our lower-order needs must be satisfied before higher-order needs can be met. Maslow uses a pyramid, shown in Figure 13.1, to demonstrate how one category builds onto the other.

Physiological Needs   The first level, physiological needs, includes the most basic biological needs necessary to maintain life, such as food, water, sleep, sex, and physical comfort. According to Maslow, we must satisfy most of these basic needs to some degree before we can focus on other needs.

Safety Needs   Once we have satisfied our physiological needs, safety needs gain importance. Among these are our needs for stability, order, freedom from violence and disease, and security. According to Maslow, physiological and safety needs form the basis for most human motivation. People who can satisfy these two lower-order categories can then consider the higher-order categories.

Need for Belonging and Love   Our need for belonging and love includes needs for friendship, acceptance, approval, and the giving and re-

Aesthetic needs

Need to experience and understand beauty for its own sake

Needs to know

Curiosity, need to learn about the world to satisfy the basic growth urge of human beings

Needs for self-actualization

Fulfillment of all lower needs and realization of potential

Needs for esteem

Need for self-respect, feeling of adequacy, competence, mastery

Needs for love and belongingness

Need for affection, feeling wanted, giving, and receiving

Needs for safety

Avoidance of danger and anxiety, need for security

Physiological needs

Needs for food, drink, sleep, sex, physical comfort, and so on

This hierarchy illustrates how needs build upon each other. The lower needs in the hierarchy begin with physical needs and move to higher, more abstract needs, which depend more heavily upon our interaction with others.

ceiving of affection. Such needs are so strong that Maslow considers them to be the foundation for all other higher-order desires. The high priority we place on belonging and love is why interpersonal communication and relationships are important to us.

Need for Self-Esteem   Maslow defines the next highest need—self-esteem—as self-respect; feelings of adequacy, competence, and mastery; respect from others; and recognition from others. Because we judge ourselves by how we believe others see us, our needs for self-esteem strongly motivate us to seek out positive relationships (see Chapter 3 for a more thorough discussion of self-esteem).

Need for Self-Actualization   This need represents the desire for self-fulfillment, the need to live up to our fullest potential. This need stems from the desire to be the very best we can be and to do our very best given what we have. To be satisfied with who we are and what we can do is an achievement that ordinarily requires strong interpersonal communication skills and positive relationships.

Need for Knowing and Understanding   We are extremely curious beings and it is our motivation to know about and understand the unknown that drives us to learn more about the world around us and its effects on us. To satisfy our need for knowledge and to reduce uncertainty, we must communicate in some form with the world around us.

Aesthetic Needs   The highest-level need, according to Maslow, is the need to experience and understand beauty for its own sake. Our need to observe and absorb the world around us is reflected in this need. To fulfill our aesthetic need does not require that we judge our surroundings all the time, but that we take them in for what they are and how they relate to us. The fulfillment of this need requires a deep sense of intrapersonal communication and a high self-esteem.

According to Maslow, all people attempt to fulfill the above needs to one degree or another. If a need is blocked or unfulfilled, there is a drive to achieve it. If Maslow's theory represents our needs accurately, the desire to fulfill them helps to explain why we communicate with others. Each need, to one degree or another, requires communication in order to be fulfilled.

Schutz's Theory of Interpersonal Needs

According to Schutz's **Theory of Interpersonal Needs,** three needs—the needs for affection, inclusion, and control—determine our communication behaviors with others.[4] Because most communication takes place at the interpersonal level, it is essential to recognize the interpersonal needs that we all possess regardless of our background or culture. Although each need can differ from person to person, from situation to situation, and from culture to culture, understanding interpersonal needs can help us understand our reasons for entering or not entering into relationships with others.

Need for Affection   Our need for affection is the need we have to feel likable or lovable. This need for affection is comparable to Maslow's need for belonging and love. Every day we see people striving to fulfill this need; for example, people who join dating services or call 900 phone numbers to talk to others are all searching to fill their needs of belonging and love. According to Schutz's theory, a person who seems to be liked by many and therefore has adequately fulfilled this need is referred to as "personal." Someone who is unable to fulfill this need is labeled either "underpersonal" or "overpersonal."

Underpersonal people are those who avoid emotional commitments or involvement with others. If we examine these individuals, we often find that they are hiding their true selves because they fear that others may not like them as they are. These people, like all other human beings, have a need for affection, but they have learned to cover it by not letting others get close to them. Some underpersonals find numerous excuses for not developing close personal relationships. Others may be friendly to everyone, but keep their friendships on a superficial level. Do you know someone who may fit this category? Why do you think they are unwilling to get close to others?

Overpersonal individuals are the opposite of underpersonals. They need affection so badly that they often go to extremes to assure themselves of their acceptance by others. They frequently seek approval by being extremely intimate in what they communicate to others. They may even attempt to pay for friendship, for example, by always buying things for others but never letting others buy anything for them. These individuals may be possessive and get jealous when others talk to their friends. They may even attempt to block their friends from establishing new friendships by finding fault with every new acquaintance.

Personal people tend to be poised, confident, and mature and able to deal with almost everyone with whom they come in contact. Personal people want to be liked, but they do not consider being liked by everyone essential for happiness. They are easy to talk with and are at ease with themselves.

THINK ABOUT IT

"How does one person go about 'proving' that he or she loves another person?"

It's a lot easier to prove that you don't love someone than it is to prove that you do, but one of the best "proofs" I know in everyday life is the desire to devote time to the person with no expectation of any sort of compensation, including gratitude.

How does the above statement relate to what has been discussed in the chapter so far?

Marilyn Vossavant, "Ask Marilyn," *Parade Magazine*, 21 January 1990, 17.

Need for Inclusion   The interpersonal need for inclusion encompasses our needs to feel significant and worthwhile. Schutz describes individuals in terms of this need as "social," "undersocial," or "oversocial." Undersocial people do not like being around other people because, like underpersonal individuals, they find communicating with others threatening. They tend to be shy and find initiating conversation with others difficult. Although often intelligent, undersocials are loners who prefer to do things by themselves or in large groups where they can hide in the crowd. Typically, undersocials find it difficult to speak out and generally avoid saying anything for fear of drawing attention to themselves.

Oversocial people cannot stop themselves from getting involved and communicating with others. They attempt to dominate conversations, often speak out of turn and find it hard to keep quiet. They prefer situations where they can take over relationships by dominating the flow of communication. The oversocial person fears being ignored by others. Sometimes oversocial people tend to be overbearing. Can you think of people you know who have the tendency to be oversocial? How do you react to them when they are being oversocial or overbearing?

Social people have satisfied their needs for inclusion. They are capable of handling situations with or without others, and few, if any, situations make them feel uncomfortable. They have confidence in themselves and are assertive enough to speak when they feel it is necessary to do so.

Need for Control   Schutz's third need is for control, which is derived from responsibility and leadership. Almost all of us have some need to control others and our surroundings. On the other hand, some individuals wish to be controlled by others. The strength of this need and the way we manifest it determines whether we are "abdicrats," "autocrats," or "democrats."

Abdicrats are extremely submissive to others. They have little or no self-confidence, often perceive themselves as incompetent, take few risks, rarely make decisions on their own, and need much reinforcement to see themselves as useful and capable.

Autocrats never have enough control. They try to dominate others. In a group, they are always willing to make the decisions or at least voice strong opinions about what decision ought to be made. Because autocrats have a strong need for power, they may not care whom they hurt in their search for control. They are also somewhat closed-minded, seeing their own positions as the only correct ones. And they show little, if any, respect for others.

Democrats have their control needs basically satisfied. They feel comfortable as either leaders or followers, do not exaggerate either the leader's or the follower's role, and are open-minded and willing to accept others' suggestions for the good of the group. They like to get things done, but not at the expense of someone else.

Schultz's theory of needs clearly illustrates the reasons that motivate us to communicate with others. We develop relationships with others for many reasons. The social needs we have just discussed explain a great deal about our motivation to form relationships, but there are also three additional reasons to develop relationships: avoidance or lessening of loneliness, learning about ourselves, and sharing.

Avoidance or Lessening of Loneliness

Social relationships are at the core of human life. In a society that promotes the joys of independence, living alone, and being your own best friend, it may seem out of place to speak of loneliness. Yet loneliness is a fact of modern life, as undeniable as the divorce and suicide statistics. Our need to avoid or at least lessen this feeling causes us to develop relationships. (See Figure 13.2).

There is a difference between being alone and being lonely. A person can be alone but not lonely, and a person can be lonely but not alone. Two forms of loneliness are apparent: emotional and social. Although their

Figure 13.2:

Social relationships are at the core of human life. Our desire to avoid the feeling of being alone causes us to develop relationships with others.

Tony Freeman/Photo Edit

symptoms differ, the causes appear to be the same: the inability to form relationships. Emotional loneliness is based on our need for intimacy with a spouse, a lover, or a best friend. The symptoms of emotional loneliness include feelings of tension, restlessness, loss of appetite (or overeating), inability to sleep (or oversleeping), and anxiety. In social loneliness, a sense of detachment from others prevails. There are many individuals who have emotional relationships with others but still feel socially alone. This feeling occurs because meaningful relationships have not developed in their lives.

Learning About Ourselves

Through contact with others, we learn about ourselves. In Chapter 3 we defined self-concept as what we perceive ourselves to be and the mental picture we have of our physical, social, and psychological selves. We develop our self-concept based on the wide range of interactions that take place in our lives. The primary contributor to our self-concept is the reactions others have to us. We seek out both supportive and nonsupportive reactions in order to see ourselves in as many different ways as possible and thus gain a better understanding of who we are. The most enduring relationships are those that are supportive and reinforcing in developing our self-concept. Each relationship we form becomes a source of information that tells us who we are. The relationships that are important to us become the most influential in determining how we see ourselves.

Sharing

The most obvious reason for needing and establishing relationships with others is to share ourselves with them. We need to share our feelings—our successes, in order to gain rewards or positive reactions, and our sorrows and failures, in order to gain reassurance that we are still all right. Relationships that are built on trust and caring are the main sources of such rewards and reassurances.

INTERPERSONAL ATTRACTION: GETTING TO KNOW OTHERS

One of the most interesting aspects of being a human being is the way we react to other people—making acquaintances, becoming friends with a few of those acquaintances, and sometimes actively disliking others. Each of us tends to evaluate others in positive and negative terms, and they, of course, evaluate us in return.[5]

There are some very specific and increasingly predictable factors that determine who we will get to know and how well we will get to know them. Interpersonal attraction ranges from love to hate and all the possibilities in between. There are more than five billion people living, and any one of us will come into contact with only a very small percentage of them. Within this small percentage, there remain hundreds of potential friends, enemies, and lovers. We, however, tend to form meaningful relationships with only a small number of individuals at any given time. A question often asked by researchers is: On what basis do we decide which acquaintances will become meaningful and lasting? How would you answer this question?

Getting to know others may have little or nothing to do with their specific characteristics, or with ours, either. Usually, the likelihood of two people becoming acquainted has to do with contact through physical proximity and a positive rather than negative experience at the time of contact. Usually, the contact is not planned but occurs out of circumstance—for example, a person may sit next to us on an airplane, stand next to us in line at the cafeteria, or be a neighbor, a classmate, a co-worker, a member of our church, a player on our softball team, and so on. Of all the individuals we come into contact with, we will get to know some of them better than others. If we encounter a person more than once and the person becomes recognizable, we are more likely to be comfortable interacting with them or at least making small talk with them. **Small talk** is casual conversation that is often impersonal and superficial, including a greeting and some comments about the weather, or a trivial or newsworthy event. The ability to engage in small talk, however, is a very important social skill (see Figure 13.3).

Most relationships begin with small talk, and many depend upon small talk to continue. Small talk provides an avenue for getting to know another person by exchanging thoughts about non-threatening, impersonal, and safe subjects. Some people, however, believe small talk is a

Figure 13.3:

Small talk is important to relationship development. Without small talk many relationships would probably not develop. Even though conversation may sometimes seem impersonal and superficial, it is an important social skill in relationship development.

David Young-Wolff/Photo Edit

waste of their time because it involves only trivial and unimportant information. Most communication scholars, on the other hand, believe that new relationships develop mainly through the exchange of small talk.

Those who are skilled at social interaction are those who are perceived as friendly, who think well of themselves, who are not easily provoked to anger, and who find it easy to engage in small talk.[6] It is not completely clear why some people find carrying on conversations with others easy while others do not. Birth order may be one factor: according to one research study, younger siblings seem to be much more socially skilled than firstborns. It was also found that those with older, opposite-sex siblings interact more easily with members of the opposite sex.[7] It appears that one's family, in particular one's siblings, may play a large role in the development of one's interpersonal communication skills.

In meeting people for the first time, opening lines play a crucial role in establishing relationships. Kleinke, Meeker, and Staneski, three social psychologists, conducted a survey on lines males and females use when making an initial contact with someone of the opposite sex to indicate an interest in them and how the person is hearing the lines responded.[8] The results of the survey showed that most initial reactions involve one of three message categories: cute-flippant, innoccuous, and direct. Listed below are the categories and some sample lines that were used by people who were surveyed:

Cute-Flippant (males) Isn't it cold? Let's make some body heat.
(females) Hey baby, you've got a gorgeous chassis.
Mind if I look under the hood?

Innocuous (males) Where are you from?
(females) Could you tell me what time it is?

Direct (males) Hi. I like you.
(females) I don't have anybody to introduce me, but I'd really like to get to know you.

The study's findings conclude that most males and females prefer opening lines that are innocuous or direct over cute-flippant. Some women, however, were more positive about innocuous lines than men. Women also tended to be much more negative about cute-flippant lines than men. Thus, for most first-time encounters with a person, a cute-flippant opening line is more likely to create a negative impression, especially if the target is a female. The safest strategy for either sex is to use an innocuous line—it will usually receive a positive response and you will avoid offending anyone.

According to the research by Kleine, Meeker, and Staneski, when starting a conversation with someone of the opposite sex, opening remarks should be innoccuous or direct rather than cute-flippant. Given the settings listed below write opening lines that youmight use under preferred opening lines and then list lines you have heard others use that were least preferred by you. If time permits discuss with others.

Setting	Preferred Opening Lines	Least Preferred Opening lines
Sample:		
General Situation:	*Hi.*	*Your place or mine?*
Bar:		
Restaurant:		
Supermarket:		
Laundromat:		
Beach:		
Classroom		

If you feel you need to improve your small-talk skills, here are a few more suggestions to consider:[9]

1. Use the other person's name several times in your conversations with him or her. Knowing and recalling a person's name creates the impression that the person matters to you. To remember a person's name, you have to listen to it, rehearse it in your mind, and, if necessary, have the person restate it or spell it for you. Think about how you feel when others remember your name—you probably feel good, and this is the same feeling others will have when you remember their names. Besides, using someone's name helps make small talk more comfortable.

2. As discussed in Chapters 6 and 10, eye contact is extremely important in order to effectively initiate and maintain interaction with others. When you look at another person you are indicating that you are interested in them. Of course, you don't want to stare, nor do you want to avoid looking at the other person altogether. There should be a balance and comfortableness in the eye relationship when conversing with others. There are some cultural groups—for example, some Hispanics and Japanese—that believe that staring or looking into someone's eyes is disrespectful. When you communicate with people from these cultures, you might focus your eyes less directly or on the lower part of the face.

3. To be effective in encounters in which you are involved in small talk, your nonverbal behaviors—such as your smile, your facial expressions, and your body position—should indicate that you are open, positive, and interested in the other person. Giving positive cues by leaning forward, smiling, and nodding your head are signs of caring about the other person and will help to improve your small-talk conversations. It is also important to know cultural differences related to the use of nonverbal communication when you are involved in small talk with individuals who come from different backgrounds and cultures than yours. See Chapter 5 for more on nonverbal communication and cultural differences.

4. People usually like to talk about themselves. If you can get the other person to talk about himself or herself, that can be a strong motivator for continuing the conversation. This is especially true if you listen care-

fully and ask questions such as "Where are you from?" "Where did you go high school?" or "Tell me about yourself." You must listen at all times and use follow-up questions to keep the person talking.

The most important thing to remember about small talk is to keep it casual, light, and positive. You don't want to move too quickly to disclosing very personal information, because that can be threatening and a real conversation-stopper. Also try not to be negative or a whiner. If you are always negative in your comments and come to be seen as a griper, you are likely to reduce opportunities for future interaction. Use small talk to help decrease the uncertainty between yourself and others. By doing so, you will increase your chances for initiating and developing lasting relationships.

THINK ABOUT IT

A survey of married couples points to the importance of small talk.

Small talk may save marriages, according to the findings of two social scientists. As reported in the University of California at Berkeley Wellness Letter, a survey of 31 married couples (average age, early 40s; average length of marriage, 20 years) showed that the communication valued most did not consist of evening-long sessions hashing out their differences, but of easygoing, pleasant conversations about everyday events.

Wives, in particular, interpreted this kind of open, informal chatting as an indication of mutual affection. Husbands, however, valued empathetic listening on the part of their wives give-and-take more than discussion, interpreting attentive listening as a sign of affection in their wives.

Why do you think that men and women take these two different perspectives on the type of communication they exchange?

Are there any assumptions that may have to be taken into account when examining the survey's findings?

Think about your friends and how you met them. Most of the initial contact you had with them was probably due to physical proximity. That is, the more convenient people are to us, the more likely our chances are of becoming close friends with them. If two people find themselves in proximity and their interactions are positive, they are likely to become friends. As an acquaintanceship evolves from first encounter to a more engaged relationship, there are two additional contributing factors—our need to associate with someone and our reactions to their observable physical attributes.

Need to Associate

There is no question that most of us feel it is very important in our lives to make new friends, spend time with existing friends, and share personal feelings with those with whom we feel close.[10] Most of us would probably agree that we would prefer relationships that are enjoyable over those that are not. Males who have a strong need to be with others are also relatively high in self-esteem, and they spend more time talking to attractive females than do males who have less of a need to be with others.[11] For example, in the typical college classroom, male or female students who have a strong need to associate with others make more friends than do those who are more independent.[12] Of course, success in developing a relationship also depends on one's social skills and on one's motivation to continue the relationship.

Physical Attributes

Most of us have learned that "beauty is only skin-deep," and most of us know that reacting to stereotypes based on appearance is meaningless. But as discussed in Chapter 5, physical characteristics do play a significant role in communication as well as in relationship development. In the early stages of interpersonal contact, some people hold a positive stereotype about physically attractive people and a negative stereotype about those who are not physically attractive.[13] In our society we commonly accept or reject people based on such observable characteristics as skin color, sex, height, weight, accent, and hair color.

In our culture, both males and females are strongly influenced by attractiveness.[14] However, males are generally more responsive to females' appearance than females are to males'.[15] In most cultures at any given time, there is general agreement as to what constitutes attractiveness and what does not.[16] For example, most of us would find it difficult to express what attractiveness is. However, we "know it when we see it."

How does attractiveness affect relationships and interpersonal communication? Most people, according to one research study, are afraid of being rejected by those who are more attractive than they are.[17] There is also a tendency by many to reject others who are far less attractive than they believe themselves to be; in other words, they are saying, "I can do better than that." As a result, people tend to pair off, especially in romantic relationships, by selecting individuals who are at a similar level of attractiveness.[18] "Mismatches" do occur, such as that portrayed by the characters of Catherine (an attractive woman) and Vincent (an unattractive, disfigured man) in the story of "Beauty and the Beast." More recently, in real life, the conventionally attractive actress Julia Roberts married the eccentric-looking musician and actor Lyle Lovett. Why do these exceptions occur, and how do people explain them? If one person in a relationship seems more attractive than another, people tend to infer that the less attractive person offers something to balance the mismatch—he or she must be rich, powerful, intelligent, sexy, or famous. (For example, in "Beauty and the Beast," Vincent's appearance is unattractive, but his kindness, gentleness, and bravery makes Catherine's love for him believable. (See Figure 13.4). Whether we wish to accept it or not, physical appearance does play a role in determining relationships. Although this attractiveness may not always predict the outcome of a relationship, research has shown that physical attractiveness is important in getting our attention.[19]

SELF-DISCLOSURE IN RELATIONSHIPS

Relationships are built on interaction. The more sincere, honest, and open the interactions between individuals, the stronger and more lasting their relationship. Much of our interpersonal communication, however, is small talk—talk about the weather, sports, class assignments, television programs, movies. Such light conversation usually does not provide a means for us to learn who we are, fulfill our interpersonal needs, or allow for growth in our relationships. Nonetheless, it does maintain an important opening to further interaction.

In order to reduce uncertainty and to meet our physical and emotional needs, we must communicate who we are: we must disclose information about ourselves. **Self-disclosure,** or the voluntary sharing of information about ourselves that another person is not likely to know, can be as

Figure 13.4:

When couples differ in attractiveness, how do you explain the relationship? People usually select partners who they perceive to be similar in physical attractiveness or who are more attractive themselves. In what cases might there be exceptions to this rule?

Jeff Christensen/Gamma-Liaison

simple and unthreatening as telling our name, as seen in Figure 13.5, or as complex and threatening as revealing deep feelings.

When self-disclosure occurs in caring relationships, it usually results in greater self-understanding and in self-improvement. The principal benefit of self-disclosure should be personal growth. In addition, when we disclose ourselves to others, it encourages them to do the same with us, and it creates an atmosphere that fosters interpersonal communication and meaningful relationships.

To benefit from disclosure, we must realize that it is an ongoing process that should be incorporated into our daily behavior. Ultimately, disclosure is a prerequisite for personal as well as interpersonal growth.

Process of Self-Disclosure

One of the best ways to gain an understanding of how the self-disclosure process increases our knowledge of others is by examining the Johari Window (Figure 13.6). The graphic model of the **Johari Window** depicts the process of increasing awareness of information about others in interpersonal relationships. The model was developed to illustrate four kinds of in-

Figure 13.5:

Self-disclosure is the voluntary sharing of information about ourselves that another person is not likely to know about us. It can also be simple and non-threatening information which helps to create a more meaningful relationship.

Drawing by Maslin; © 1992 The New Yorker Magazine, Inc.

"There's something you should know about me, Carla—I never had a favorite Beatle."

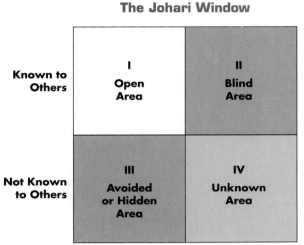

The Johari Window

	Known to Others	Not Known to Others
	I **Open Area**	**II** **Blind Area**
	III **Avoided or Hidden Area**	**IV** **Unknown Area**

Figure 13.6:

This figure illustrates four kinds of information that exists or that is not known about a person: the open area, blind area, hidden area, and unknown area. What we know about others is primarily through self-disclosure and interpersonal communication.

J. Luft, *Group Processes: An Introduction to Group Dynamics,* Palo Alto, Calif.: National Press, 1970.

formation about a person.[20] They are the open area, the blind area, the avoided or hidden area, and the unknown area. The areas expand and contract depending on the relationship and the amount and type of information that has been exchanged.

Area I: Open Area   The **open area,** or area of information that is known to self and others, includes information that is readily available to others through observation or willingness to share. For example, when people meet for the first time, they undoubtedly note each other's height, weight, color of skin, and sex. They may freely share their names, home towns, schools, and majors, and the courses they are taking.

During the first meeting, individuals usually disclose minimal information about themselves. Thus, the open area is relatively small, but as people get to know each other through their interactions, this area becomes much larger, as shown in Figure 13.7.

Area II: Blind Area   The **blind area** includes information that others perceive about us but that we do not recognize or acknowledge about ourselves. For example, instructors who show favoritism to certain students may not realize that their behavior is being interpreted in that way. In fact, when confronted by student evaluations that point out the problem, they often deny such a practice and argue that they treat everyone equally.

Area III: Hidden Area   The **hidden area** includes personal and private information about ourselves that we choose not to disclose to others.

The Johari Window

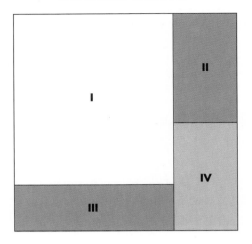

Figure 13.7:

**As we communicate
with others and
self-disclose more,
the larger the *open
area* becomes.
The open area
represents what is
known about self
and others in
a relationship.**

J. Luft, *Group Processes:
An Introduction to
Group Dynamics,*
Palo Alto, Calif.:
National Press, 1970.

Personal information cannot be known to others unless we choose to disclose it, while private information is information that we are even more selective about disclosing. If a relationship is to grow, the hidden area must eventually shrink as its information is shared with the other person.

Area IV: Unknown Area   The fourth window is the **unknown area,** which contains information that is not known either to us or to others. Because we are human, there are aspects of ourselves that we may submerge or repress into our subconscious indefinitely; for example, a part of our personality, a sexual preference, or the harm a drug is having on us physically or mentally. These aspects may never become known to us, or they could emerge through therapy, hypnosis, or another mind-altering experience which brings out aspects of ourselves that were previously unknown to us. Another example of something unknown to us might be an event that we think we recall but cannot be sure actually happened. Finally, there are aspects of ourselves we don't know about because they haven't had the opportunity to surface. For example, can you give artificial respiration to someone if you have never done it before? You may think you can, but you don't really know if you can until you actually have the occasion to try it.

Generally, the more closed you are or defensive you tend to be, the more likely you are to keep information about yourself from others, and therefore the smaller your open area will be. The more willing you are to communicate with others and to allow feedback from others, the more comfortable you will be letting others know you, and the larger your open area will be.

EXERCISE

Draw Johari Windows that you feel represent you in the following situations.

1. **The way in which you relate to people in general.**
2. **Your relationship with someone to whom you are very close—a boyfriend, girlfriend, spouse, or parent.**

How do the windows differ, and why do they differ?

The Johari Window provides an interesting explanation of how the information we share with others allows us to get to know ourselves and others. It doesn't, however, explain why some people tend to disclose more than others. Researchers have found that women are more likely to disclose than men, although that is not always true in all situations. For example, one research study suggests that women are more likely than men to disclose to intimate friends, and men are more likely than women to disclose to strangers or casual acquaintances.[21] What is self-disclosed is equally as important as to whom you self-disclose.

Social Penetration Theory   Social penetration theory, which was developed by social psychologists Irwin Altman and Dalmas Taylor, provides another view of how people enter relationships and how their communication moves from superficial levels or small talk to more intimate and self-revealing talk. **Social penetration,** according to Altman and Taylor, is the process of increasing disclosure and intimacy in a relationship.[22] Figure 13.8 illustrates the view that self-disclosure moves gradually along with the

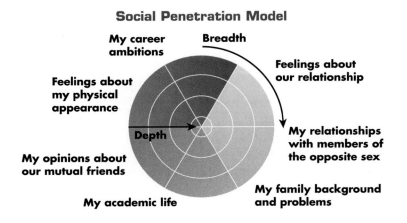

Social Penetration Model

My career ambitions

Breadth

Feelings about our relationship

Feelings about my physical appearance

Depth

My relationships with members of the opposite sex

My opinions about our mutual friends

My academic life

My family background and problems

Figure 13.8:

The social penetration model portrays relationship development starting with factual information and small talk, but as the relationship develops, conversation becomes more personal, including feelings about self and values.

From *Social Penetration: The Development of Interpersonal Relationships.* Copyright © 1973 by Irwin Altman and Dalmas Taylor.

developmental process of the relationship. The model is easier to understand when it is thought of as a dartboard, with the outer ring representing superficial communication and the innermost circle, or bull's eye, representing the intimacy and depth of interaction in a close relationship. As we begin new relationships, we tend to provide information such as "Hi, I'm Bill, and I love to watch basketball." As the relationship develops and moves from a casual acquaintanceship to a friendship, the conversations move to more intimate topics about ourselves. When you first meet someone, the information exchanged mostly consists of biographical facts, such as your name and interests. The first levels of a casual interaction involve more breadth of information, but as the relationship becomes more intimate it involves more depth of information. The depth represents the penetration from external (factual) information to inner feelings, which reveal more information about self-concepts and values.

The movement, or penetration, depicted in the model progresses through the different types of interpersonal communication that we exchange with others. For example, "My name is Bill" and "I love you with all my heart" are two very different levels of exchange in the development of a relationship. One is factual and the other is a sharing of emotions and personal feelings. Once deeper levels are reached, the participants increasingly share more breadth and depth of personal information. The depth represents the greater "interpersonalness" that occurs as the relationship develops from a casual to a more intimate relationship.

People from many cultural backgrounds tend to follow similar movement in their interactions. For example, other cultures are also likely to begin with "small talk" and progress to more intimate levels of interaction as the relationship continues. Of course, there are differences in some cultures, especially in the initial contact stage, but in general, as human beings make friends, those differences seem to diminish. No matter what interaction level is obtained in a relationship, there are research findings that provide general conclusions about self-disclosure:

1. Disclosure increases with increased intimacy.

2. Disclosure increases when rewarded—if the reward outweighs the risk of disclosing.

3. Disclosure increases with the need to reduce uncertainty in a relationship.

4. Disclosure tends to be reciprocal—when one person in a relationship discloses, it increases the likelihood that the other person will also disclose.

5. Women tend to disclose more often than men.

6. Women seem to disclose more with those they feel close to, whereas men seem to disclose more with those they trust.

7. Disclosure is culturally regulated by norms of appropriateness.

Self-disclosure research is helpful to our understanding of human communication. A review of self-disclosure research by Arthur Bochner, a communication scholar, found that people self-disclose to people they like; they do, however, overestimate the amount they actually do self-disclose; self-disclosure does not automatically mean attraction and in fact, if inappropriate, can cause negative reactions; and finally, liking someone and wanting a relationship to continue may, in fact, discourage self-disclosing because doing so may risk damaging the relationship.[23] Because self-disclosure is not always wise or appropriate, some scholars suggest that another way of moving relationships from casual to more intimate requires "rhetorical sensitivity."

Rhetorical Sensitivity   A different approach to self-disclosure in gaining information and developing relationships with other people is **rhetorical sensitivity.**[24] Rhetorical sensitivity, according Roderick Hart and Don Burks, is an alternative form of communication that can be applied to interpersonal communication situations where wide open self-disclosure could be harmful to those involved. Rhetorically sensitive people are adaptive to others and are able to balance their self-interests with the interests of others. They are effective interpersonal communicators because they can adjust their communication by taking into account the beliefs, values, and mood of the other person. Taking into account the other person's views or feelings does not mean changing your own view or position, but it does mean you are able to find an effective way to communicate your thoughts without offending or hurting the other person.

Rhetorically sensitive individuals generally display the following attributes:

1. They accept personal complexity; they understand that every person is made up of many selves. For example, one person may be a mother, a daughter, a Republican, an abuse victim, a physician, and a consumer.

2. They are flexible and avoid rigidity in communicating with others.

3. They do not change their own values, but they can communicate them in a variety of ways so not to offend others.

4. They are aware of when the time is appropriate to communicate something and when it is not.[25]

Rhetorically sensitive people are people who know and understand self-disclosure, and know how to adapt their message to an audience and situation.

Guidelines for Self-disclosure

The open and honest sharing of our feelings, concerns, and secrets with others is what self-disclosure is all about. This does not mean, however, that we must disclose everything or that we cannot withhold information if it is likely to hurt us or someone else. The goal is to match the amount and kind of self-disclosure to the situation. Here are a few guidelines that should help you in your self-disclosure.

1. Use *reasoned self-disclosure.* Although open and honest relationships are desirable, it is important to recognize situational constraints. For example, suppose that as a youngster, you were caught shoplifting from a local store. You only shoplifted that one time, and since that time you have not done anything similar. However, now you are planning on running for the office of treasurer of an organization and you must decide whether you should disclose the fact that you once stole something. This disclosure, however, more than likely would hurt your chances of winning the election. Thus, you choose not to bring up your shoplifting experience during the election. Not revealing something does not mean that you are being dishonest, but merely that in some situations and with certain individuals, not revealing a particular past behavior may be a sensible alternative.

2. *Make self-disclosure a two-way process.* Relationships built on one-sided exchanges are generally not very enduring, meaningful, or healthy. People are more likely to disclose information when they feel safe and when their openness is positively received. It follows, therefore, that each party will feel safer if both are involved in the self-disclosure process. Once an atmosphere of give-and-take is established, if one person increases self-disclosure, the other person will usually follow suit. In this way, trust builds, self-disclosure continues to increase, and the relationship grows steadily deeper.

3. *Match self-disclosure to the situation and to the person to whom the information is disclosed.* When we self-disclose, we run the risk of being rejected. We can minimize this risk somewhat if we carefully match the disclosure to the person and the situation. Self-disclosure should be a slow process, because rushing to reveal personal information can increase vulnerability. In addition, it is safest to disclose only to truly caring people and to be sensitive to both their verbal and their nonverbal cues. Disclosing too much too soon or disclosing to the wrong person can lead to embarrassment, pain, and, sometimes, serious harm.

Ultimately, self-disclosure must be based on personal judgment rather than rigid rules. The key should always be concern for both self and others. Self-disclosure is the most sensitive and beautiful form of communication that we can engage in as we develop and maintain lasting relationships. There are many reasons why we sometimes find it difficult to open ourselves to others. However, when a relationship is based on mutual feelings and genuine communication, it cannot help but grow and mature.

SUMMARY

Interpersonal communication, the informal exchange of information between two or more people, cannot exist without *intrapersonal communication,* the process of understanding information within oneself. A *relationship* is an association between at least two people and may be described in terms of intimacy or kinship. Interpersonal communication allows relationships to become established and to grow. Continual communication allows relationships to develop and to satisfy our social needs.

The interpersonal phenomenon of wanting to know more about others is referred to as the uncertainty principle. The *uncertainty principle* suggests that when we initially meet others to whom we are attracted, our need to know about them tends to make us draw inferences from the physical data that is observed. Many needs that we have as humans can be satisfied through communication. Two approaches that attempt to explain needs are Maslow's *Hierarchy of Individual Needs* and Schutz's *Theory of Interpersonal Needs.* Maslow's hierarchy is based on the idea that lower-order physical and safety needs must be satisfied before higher-order needs can be fulfilled. Each category of need is a stepping-stone to the next. According to Schutz, needs for affection, inclusion, and control determine how we communicate with others. People who have satisfied their need for affection are referred to as personal, and those who have not satisfied this need are classified as either underpersonal or overpersonal. People who have satisfied their need for inclusion are social, and those who have not are either undersocial or oversocial. People who have satisfied their need for control are called democrats, and those who have not are either abdicrats or autocrats. Both theories explain why relationships are so important to us.

If we encounter a person more than once and the person becomes recognizable, we are more likely to comfortable interacting with him or her or at least making small talk. *Small talk* is casual conversation that is often impersonal and superficial; it includes a greeting and perhaps comments about the weather, newsworthy events, or trivial events. The ability to engage in small talk, however, is a very important social skill.

Most relationships begin with small talk and often depend upon small talk to continue. Small talk provides an avenue for getting to know another person by talking about non-threatening, impersonal, and safe subjects. Some people, however, believe small talk is a waste of time because for them it communicates only trivial or unimportant information. On the other hand, most communication scholars believe that relationships develop through the exchange of small talk.

We develop relationships to avoid or lessen loneliness, to learn about ourselves, and to share. Lasting relationships are open—that is, they allow for relatively free *self-disclosure,* the volunteering of information about ourselves that another person is not likely to know. The more information people reveal about themselves within a relationship, the more likely the relationship is to grow and mature into a healthy and satisfying experience.

The *Johari Window* is a graphic model that depicts the process of awareness and self-disclosure in interpersonal relations. It illustrates four kinds of information about a person. (1) The *open area* represents information that is known to the self and to others; (2) the *blind area* represents information that others perceive about us but that we do not know, (3) the *hidden area* represents information about ourselves that we choose not to share with others, and (4) the *unknown area* represents information that is not known to us or to others. The four areas expand and contract in relationships over time and from situation to situation.

Social penetration theory provides another view of how people enter relationships and how their communicationes from superficial levels, or small talk, to more intimate and self-revealinlk. *Social penetration* is the process of increasing disclosure and intimacy in a relationship.

Rhetorical senstivity is a different approach to self-disclosure that can be applied to interpersonal communication situations where wide open self-disclosure could be harmful to those involved. Because frankness creates vulnerability, each participant must consider situational constraints when deciding what should or should not be disclosed. This considered restraint is referred to as reasoned self-disclosure. Self-disclosure should be built on mutual sharing and should be engaged in only when individuals feel safe and believe that their confidences will be received positively. For relationships to grow, there must be self-disclosure.

KEY TERMS

Blind Area: Quadrant of the Johari Window that represents information that others perceive about us, but that we do not recognize or acknowledge about ourselves.

Hidden Area: Quadrant of the Johari Window that represents personal and private information about ourselves that we choose not to disclose to others.

Hierarchy of Individual Needs: Theory developed by Abraham Maslow that rank-orders physical, safety, social, self-esteem, and self-actualization needs in order, and states that the lower-order needs must be satisfied before the higher-order needs.

Interpersonal Communication: Informal exchange of information between two or more people.

Intrapersonal Communication: Process of understanding information within oneself.

Johari Window: Graphic model that depicts awareness and self-disclosure in interpersonal relations by illustrating the proportion of information about oneself that is known to oneself and to others.

Open Area: Quadrant of the Johari Window that represents information that is known to self and others through observation or a willingness to share.

Relationship: An association between at least two people, it may be described in terms of intimacy or of kinship.

Rhetorical Sensitivity: A different approach to self-disclosure in gaining information and developing relationships with other people.

Self-Disclosure: Voluntary sharing of information about ourselves that another person is not likely to know.

Small Talk: Casual conversation that is often impersonal and superficial; many include a greeting and/or comments about the weather, newsworthy events, or other impersonal events.

Social Penetration: The process of increasing disclosure and intimacy in a relationship.

Theory of Interpersonal Needs: Theory developed by William Schutz contending that three basic needs—affection, inclusion, and control—determine our communication behaviors with others.

Uncertainty Principle: A principle that suggests that when we initially meet others to whom we are attracted, our need to know about them tends to make us draw inferences from the physical data that is observed.

Unknown Area: Quadrant of the Johari Window that represents information not known either to oneself or others.

DISCUSSION STARTERS

1. What does intrapersonal communication have to do with interpersonal communication? With relationships?
2. What are the similarities and differences between the hierarchy of needs and the theory of interpersonal needs?
3. In what ways do our needs affect our communication?
4. How would you describe an undersocial person? What could you do to help this type of individual?
5. In your opinion, which factor plays the strongest role in people's development in relationships? Explain.
6. Why is small talk important in relationship development?
7. Do we place too much value on physical appearance when we establish relationships?
8. What is an ideal intimate relationship? An ideal friendship? An ideal business relationship? An ideal student-teacher relationship?
9. Why is it so difficult for most of us to self-disclose to those whom we love and who love us?
10. Why is reasoned self-disclosure so important?

NOTES

1. M. L. Knapp, *Interpersonal Communication and Human Relationships* (Boston: Allyn & Bacon, 1984), 30.
2. C. R. Berger and R. J. Calabrese, "Some Explorations in Initial Interactions and Beyond: Toward a Developmental Theory of Interpersonal Communication," *Human Communication Research* 1 (1975): 98–112.

3. A. H. Maslow, *Motivation and Personality,* 2nd ed. (New York: Harper & Row, 1970), 35–150.

4. W. C. Schutz, *The Interpersonal Underworld* (Palo Alto, CA: Science and Behavior Books, 1966), 13–20.

5. B. Park and C. Flink, "A Social Relations Analysis of Agreement in Liking Judgments," *Journal of Personality and Social Psychology* 56 (1989): 506–518.

6. J. M. Reisman, "Friendliness and Its Correlates," *Journal of Social and Clinical Psychology* 2 (1984):143–155.

7. W. Ickes and M. Turner, "On the Social Advantages of having an Older, Opposite-Sex Sibling: Birth Order Influences in Mixed-Sex Dyads," *Journal of Personality and Social Psychology* 45 (1983): 210–222.

8. C. L. Kleinke, F. B. Meeker, and R. A. Staneski, "Preference for Opening Lines: Comparing Ratings by Men and Women," *Sex Roles* 15 (1986): 585–600.

9. J. S. Caputo, H. C. Hazel, and C. McMahon, *Interpersonal Communication: Competency Through Critical Thinking* (Boston: Allyn and Bacon, 1994), 98–99.

10. Research and Forecasts, Inc., *"The Connecticut Mutual Life Report on American Values in the '80s: The Impact of Belief,"* Hartford: Connecticut Mutual Life Insurance, 1981).

11. B. B. Crouse and A. Mehrabian, "Affiliation of Opposite-sexed Strangers," *Journal of Research in Personality* 11 (1977): 38–47.

12. D. Bryne and V. Greedlinger, "Need for Affiliation as a Predictor of Classroom Friendships" (unpublished manuscript, State University of New York at Albany, 1989).

13. L. Albright, D. A. Kenny, and T. E. Malloy, "Consensus in Personality Judgments at Zero Acquaintance," *Journal of Personality and Social Psychology* 55 (1988): 387–395; C. S. Fichten and R. Amsel, "Trait Attributions About College Students with a Physical Disability: Circumplex Analysis and Methodological Issues," *Journal of Applied Social Psychology* 16 (1986): 410–427.

14. T. F. Cash and R. N. Kilcullen, The Eye of the Beholder: Susceptibility to Sexism and Beautyism in the Evaluation of Managerial Applicants," *Journal of Applied Social Psychology* 15 (1985): 591–605; V. S. Folkes, "Forming Relationships and the Matching Hypothesis," *Journal of Personality and Social Psychology* 8 (1982): 631-636; E. Hatfield and S. Sprecher, *Mirror, Mirror . . . The Importance of Looks in Everyday Life* (Albany, NY: SUNY Press, 1986).

15. A. Feingold, *Good-looking People Are Not What We Think: An Integration of the Experimental Literature on Physical Attractiveness Stereotyping with the Literature on Correlates of Physical Attractiveness* (unpublished manuscript, Yale University, New Haven, CT.: 1990).

16. L. Banner, *American Beauty* (New York: Knopf, 1983).

17. W. M. Bernstein, B. O. Stephenson, M. L. Snyder, and R. A. Wicklund, "Causal Ambiguity and Heterosexual Affiliation," *Journal of Experimental Social Psychology* 19 (1983): 78–92.

18. K. H. Price and S. G. Vandenberg, "Matching for Physical Attractiveness in Married Couples," *Personality and Social Psychology* 5 (1979): 398–400.

19. M. Lea, "Factors Underlying Friendship: An Analysis of Responses on the Acquaintance Description Form in Relation to Wright's Friendship Model," *Journal of Social and Personal Relationships* 6 (1989): 275–292.

20. J. Luft, *Group Processes: An Introduction to Group Dynamics* (Palo Alto, CA.: National Press, 1970), 11–14.

21. J. Stokes, A. Fuehrer, and L. Childs, " Gender Differences in Self-Disclosure to Various Target Persons," *Journal of Counseling Psychology* 27 (1980): 192–198.

22. I. Altman and D. Taylor, Social Penetration: *The Development of Interpersonal Relationships* (New York: Holt, Rinehart & Winston, 1973); S. W. Littlejohn, *Theories of Human Communication* 4th Ed. (Belmont, CA: Wadsworth, 1992), 274.

23. A. P. Bochner, "The Functions of Human Communicating in Interpersonal Bonding," in *Handbook of Rhetorical and Communication Theory*, eds. C. C. Arnold and J. W. Bowers, (Boston: Allyn and Bacon, 1984): 554–621.

24. R. P. Hart and D. M. Burks, "Rhetorical Sensitivity and Social Interaction," *Speech Monographs* 39 (1972): 75–91.

25. S. W. Littlejohn, *Theories of Human Communication* 4th Ed. (Belmont, CA: Wadsworth, 1992), 112.

Chapter 14

Developing Relationships

LEARNING OBJECTIVES

After studying this chapter, you should be able to:

1. Trace the development of a relationship through various stages of development.

2. Explain what interpersonal conflict is and discuss the differences between constructive and destructive outcomes of conflict.

3. Demonstrate how to improve interpersonal communication by encouraging more communication and active listening.

Thursday: It's the one free day Sam has during the week to do what he wants. He usually likes to spend part of the day relaxing, either by sleeping in or playing racquetball. Sam is a good student and is sure that he did very well on his midterm in calculus. Given that he has had a good night's sleep for a change, he decides to go to the racquetball courts to see if there is anybody there to play with.

On his way to the courts, he picks up his mail and discovers that he has received an award for his excellent grades. Sam is so pleased that he can't help but begin to hum out loud as he continues his walk to the racquetball courts.

When he gets there, Sam notices a student from his calculus class sitting outside. Sam isn't sure of her name, but she smiles and says hello. "Hi," says Sam. "My name is Sam Jackson. You're in my calculus class, aren't you?"

"Yes, you're the guy who always gets the top score on every test. I wonder if you're as good on the racquetball court as you are in calculus. Would you like to play? By the way, my name is Marie."

Sam smiles and thinks to himself as they walk onto the court, "I wonder if she might be willing to go out for lunch and a beer after the game. I'd like to make some new friends on campus."

FORMING AND DISSOLVING RELATIONSHIPS

A relationship has the potential to form any time two people make contact with each other. The above scenario between Sam and Marie is similar to the way many relationships begin. Whether Sam and Marie's relationship evolves into any kind of ongoing or lasting relationship depends upon many factors, such as attraction, proximity, motivation, and need. Communication, however, is the overriding factor that will determine the kind of relationship Sam and Marie may develop and how long it may last.

How we progress as individuals, survive, develop intimacy, and make sense of our world depends on how we relate to others. As explained in Chapter 13, the depth and quality of our relationships depend on the kind, amount, and effectiveness of the communication that takes place. Many relationships go through predictable stages of growth and deterioration. This chapter examines two theories of relationship development and dissolution: Mark Knapp's theory of relationship stages and Steve Duck's theory of dissolution stages. Also discussed are interpersonal conflict, conflict resolution, and how to improve your interpersonal communication.

KNAPP'S RELATIONSHIP STAGES[1]

For most of us, relationships form and develop quite routinely, although the process is easier for some people than it is for others. Initially, people come together because of mutual attraction based on either physical appeal or personality. In our everyday life, we are enormously influenced by first impressions. In our society we tend to make many snap judgments about people and form instant likes and dislikes. Most of us are aware that not all of our first impressions are completely rational—for example, sudden lust, love at first sight, or the immediate intense dislike of someone with whom we have had no previous contact. Many social psychologists suggest that relationship development has a lot to do with the "chemistry" between the individuals in the relationship. Either the chemistry is right and the relationship develops, or it's not right and the relationship never quite clicks or never moves beyond the initial stages. The "chemistry" explanation probably has some truth to it, but there are also many other variables that influence the development of a relationship.[1]

We are most often attracted to individuals who support us and have similar interests, attitudes, likes, and dislikes. In fact, when asked to characterize their ideal friend, people often describe someone who is similar to their perceptions of themselves. For example, those who are religious tend to seek other religious people; those who like sports tend to seek other sports fans; and those who like children tend to seek others who like children. Of course, opposites sometimes do attract, but relationships in which there are significant differences in important attitudes or behaviors are often strained and are more likely to deteriorate than are those without significant disparities.

Coming Together

Theorists such as Knapp believe that if relationships are to develop into something more than a brief encounter, they must go through different stages of growth. Although not all relationships go through the stages at the same rate or in the same way, the coming-together sequence usually progresses from initiating to experimenting, intensifying, integrating, and, ultimately bonding.[2]

Initiating   This is the stage during which individuals meet and interact for the first time. The initial interaction may be a brief exchange of words or eye contact during which the two individuals recognize each other's existence and potential interest to meet and begin a conversation. If conversation does not begin, the initiating stage may end and the potential relationship may not progress any further (see Figure 14.1). Whether the interaction continues depends on various assessments that the individuals make; for example, whether the other person is attractive or unattractive and ap-

Figure 14.1:

Initial interaction is a brief exchange of words or eye contact in which individuals recognize each other's existence and possess a potential interest to continue the relationship. Whether there is further interaction depends on various assessments that are made and depends on whether both parties are open to the encounter.

Reprinted by permission of United Feature Syndicate, Inc.

UNITED FEATURE SYNDICATE, 200 Park Avenue, New York, N.Y. 10166 (212) 692-3700

proachable or unapproachable. The decision to pursue the relationship also depends on whether the other person is open to the encounter: for example, whether she or he is in a hurry, too busy, or too involved with others.

During the initiating stage we mentally process many impressions that lead to a key decision: "Yes, I do want to meet you" or "No, I am not interested in you." It may take less than fifteen seconds to determine whether a relationship will progress or not. At this stage, most people feel a similar sense of extreme vulnerability and caution, even though there is considerable variance among people's initiating behaviors.

Experimenting This stage of coming together requires risk-taking, because little is known as yet about the other person. We attempt to answer the question "Who is this person?" This phase can be extremely awkward, consisting mainly of small talk: "What's your name?" "Where are you from?" What's your major?" "Do you know so-and-so?" Such conversation serves several important functions in the development of a relationship: (1) it uncovers similarities and interests that may lead to deeper conversation; (2) it serves as an audition for the potential friend; (3) it lets the other person know who we are and provides clues as to how he or she can get to know us better; and (4) it establishes the common ground we share with the other person.

The experimenting stage, although involving some risk, is usually pleasant, relaxed, and uncritical. Involvement and commitment are limited, and often remain that way through the duration of the relationship. In fact, most relationships do not go beyond this stage. This is not to imply that such relationships are meaningless or useless.

Intensifying   This stage marks an increase in the participants' commitment and involvement in the relationship. Simply put, the two people become close friends. The commitment is typified by an increased sharing of more personal and private information about oneself and one's family. For example, at this stage, it would not be out of line to share such confidences as "My mother and father are affectionate people," "I love you," "I am a sensitive person," "I once cheated on an exam," "My father is having another relationship," "I was promoted," "I drink too heavily," "I don't use drugs," and "I really enjoy sex."

Although a deepening of the relationship occurs at this stage, there is still a sense of caution and testing to gain approval before continuing. In typical romantic relationships, we see much testing of commitment—sitting close together, for instance, may occur before holding hands, hugging, or kissing. Each behavior in the relationship is engaged in to seek approval. The relationship is beginning to mature and the participants are more sensitive to each other's needs.

During this phase many things happen verbally.

1. Forms of address become informal—first name, nickname, or some term of endearment.

2. Use of the first-person plural becomes more common—"We should do this" or "Let's do this."

3. Private symbols begin to develop—special slang or jargon or conventional language forms with understood, private meanings.

4. Verbal shortcuts built on a backlog of accumulated and shared assumptions, knowledge, and experiences appear more often. For instance, your friend needs be told that he or she is loved; you say that the person is important to you, but you never say you love him or her.

5. More direct expressions of commitment may appear—"We really have a good thing going" or "I don't know who I'd talk to if you weren't around." Sometimes such expressions receive an echo—"I really like you a lot" or "I really like you, too, Elmer."

6. Each partner acts increasingly as a helper in the other's daily process of understanding what he or she is all about—"In other words, you mean you're. . . " or "But yesterday, you said you were. . . "

Integrating   At this point the relationship conveys a sense of togetherness. Others expect to see the individuals together, and when they do not, they often ask about the other person. The two people have established a deep commitment and the relationship has become extremely important to them. Many assumptions take place between the individuals. For example, sharing is expected, and borrowing from the other person usually needs no formal request because it is assumed to be all right.

Although a strong mutual commitment characterizes this stage of a relationship, it does not mean a total giving of oneself to the other. The verbal and nonverbal expressions of the integrating stage take many forms. For example, the individuals see themselves as something special or unique. The sharing of rings, pins, pictures, and other artifacts illustrates to themselves and others their commitment to each other. They may behave in similar ways or speak of common sharing—our account, our apartment, our stereo.

Bonding   The final stage in a relationship's development and growth is bonding, the public announcement of the commitment—as when a couple announces that they are going steady, engaged, or getting married. Bonding is the understanding that the commitment has progressed from private knowledge to public knowledge, thus making a breakup of the relationship more difficult. (See Figure 14.2).

The relationship at this stage is contractual in nature, even though a formal contract, such as a marriage license, is not required. What is required is an agreement that the relationship exists and that explicit and implicit agreements hold the relationship together. The commitment implies the relationship is "for better or for worse" and is defined according to established norms, policies, or laws of the culture and society in which it exists.

Figure 14.2:

Bonding is the final stage of relationship development. Bonding involves the public announcement of the partners' commitment to the relationship. It is in this stage that the relationship is formalized and there are agreements both explicit and implicit that hold the relationship together.

John Henley/The Stock Market

Coming Apart

In our society, there are no guarantees that a formal commitment will create a lasting relationship. When a relationship stops growing and differences begin to emerge, the coming-apart process begins. Some relationships may go through some or all of the stages in this process and emerge stronger than before, but when the forces that pull a relationship apart are stronger than the forces that hold it together, the alliance ends. As with the coming-together process, Knapp's coming-apart process has five stages—differentiating, circumscribing, stagnating, avoiding, and terminating.[3]

Differentiating   In differentiating, the first stage of coming apart, the differences between the individuals are highlighted and become forces that slow or limit the growth of the relationship. The pair's communication tends to focus on how each differs from the other and there is less tolerance of these differences. Indeed, differences that were once overlooked or negotiated now become the center of attention, putting stress on the relationship and its existence. Typically, things that were once described as "ours" now become "mine": "This is my apartment," "These are my books," and "They are my friends."

Conversations often move from mild disagreement to heated anger: "Do I have to do all the work around here? You don't do a darn thing." "Why is it that your so-called friends never clean up after themselves?" "I pay the phone bill, but you're the one who uses it the most." Conflict begins to overshadow the more positive aspects of the relationship and the partners may become cruel to one another.

Circumscribing   In this stage, information exchange is reduced and some areas of difference are completely avoided because conversation would only lead to a deepening of the conflict. Comments during this stage may include "I don't want to talk about it," "Can't you see that I'm busy?" "Why do you keep bringing up the past?" "Let's just be friends and forget it." Communication loses some of its personal qualities and becomes increasingly superficial as the relationship becomes more strained. Interactions, in their amount and depth of disclosure, resemble those of the initiating and experimenting stages of coming together: "Have you eaten?" "Did I get any calls today?" "I saw Joe and he said to say "Hi."

People in the circumscribing stage often conceal their faltering relationship in public. For example, driving to a party, a couple may sit in cold silence, staring stonily into space. But once they arrive at their destination, they put on their party personalities—smiling, telling jokes, not disagreeing with one another. When they return to the privacy of their car, they résumé their cold behavior.

Stagnating   At this stage the relationship reaches a standstill. The participants avoid interaction and take care to sidestep controversy. Some people feel this is the "boring" stage of a relationship, yet there is no active move to do anything about it. Little hope remains for the relationship once it has deteriorated to this stage, yet one of the partners may still want it to be revived.

During stagnation, both verbal and nonverbal communication are more thoroughly thought out, and the partners plan what to say, making interactions stylized and cold. Both persons are apt to reflect unhappiness and to act as if each is a stranger to the other.

Often the stagnation stage is relatively brief, but when it is extended it is usually because of complications. For example, some people may be seriously distressed by the loss of their relationship even though they know that parting is the right decision. Others may prolong the situation in fear of additional pain, in hopes of getting the relationship back on track, or in an attempt to punish the other person.

Avoiding   Up to this point the participants in the relationship are still seeing each other or sharing the same living quarters. But the fourth stage, the avoiding stage, is marked by physical distancing and eventual separation. The basic message is "I am not interested in being with you anymore." As far as the participants are concerned, the relationship is over and they have no interest in reestablishing it.

At times the interaction in this stage is brief, direct, unfriendly, and even antagonistic: "I really don't care to see you," "Don't call me; we have nothing to discuss," "I'm busy tonight and, for that matter, I'm going to be busy for quite some time."

Terminating   The last stage in the breaking up of a relationship occurs when the individuals take the necessary steps to end it. Termination can be early, that is, when the relationship has barely begun, or it can occur after many years. When relationships that break up in the early stages of development, such as during initiating or experimenting, the feelings of parting are usually not complex or lasting.

The interaction during this stage is self-centered and seeks to justify the termination: "I need to do something for myself—I've always put more into the relationship than I've gotten out of it," "We just have too many differences that I didn't know existed until now," "I found out that we just weren't meant for each other."

When both individuals know that the relationship is ending, they say good-bye to each other in three ways—in a summary statement, in behaviors signaling the termination or limited contact, and in comments establishing what the relationship will be like in the future, if there is to be any relationship at all.[4]

Summary statements review the relationship in the past and provide a rationale for its termination: "While our love used to be very special, we both have changed over the years. We are not the same couple that we were when we first met." Ending behaviors reflect new rules of contact: "It would be good for both of us not to see so much of each other," "I wish you would stop coming over all the time." Finally, when the relationship is over, the participants state their preferences for how to deal with each other in the future: "I don't want to see you anymore," "We can get together once in a while, but I only want us to be friends and nothing more."

The process of coming together and coming apart are complex and continuous as we move in, through, and out of relationships. See Figure 14.3 for a review of Knapp's stages. Knapp acknowledges that not all relationships move through each of the escalating and de-escalating stages at the same pace, but he states that most relationships do go through the interaction stages systematically and sequentially. Of course, not all relationships that we are involved in are destined for termination, but most relationships do go through some of the "coming apart" stages from time to time. He also suggests that relationships can move forward and backward from one stage to the next. There are at least three reasons, according to Knapp and Vangelisti, why relationships move through the stages sequentially: each stage provides information that allows movement to the next; each stage enables the participants to predict what may or may not occur in the next stage; and skipping a stage creates risk and uncertainty in the relationship.[5] Lasting relationships that are happy and satisfying are that way because the participants have learned to satisfy each other through their communication.

EXERCISE

You have been reading about how relationships develop, and it should be clear that no two relationships are alike nor do they evolve in the same way. Consider a relationship that is important to you. Record and label the stages from the time of the first meeting to the present.

After you have completed the labeling of the stages, imagine that your relationship is a book and that each stage or period in the relationship's history is a chapter. Create a title for each chapter that captures the essence of the relationship during that period. You can include as many chapters as you find necessary in chronicling the relationship.

After you have finished titling of each chapter, write a brief explanation of what the title means. Do the chapters follow any particular pattern of development? What are the similarities and differences between your chapters and the stages described above?

Reprinted by permission from author. *Journal of Social and Personal Relationships*, 7: 1990, by permission of Sage Publications Ltd.

DUCK'S DISSOLUTION STAGES

Communications scholar Steve Duck theorizes that dissolving relationships go through a rather complex decision-making process that does not always follow a specific order or a series of stages.[6] According to Duck,

Knapp's Stages of Development

Stages of Relationship Development: A Review		
Process	**Stage**	**Representative Dialogue**
Coming together	Initiating	"Hi, how ya doin'?" "Fine. You?"
	Experimenting	"Oh, so you like to ski... so do I." "You do? Great. Where do you go?"
	Intensifying	"I...think I love you." "I love you too."
	Integrating	"I feel so much a part of you." "Yeah, we are like one person." "What happens to you happens to me."
	Bonding	"I want to be with you always." "Let's get married."
Coming apart	Differentiating	"I just don't like big social gatherings." "Sometimes I don't understand you. This is one area where I'm certainly not like you at all."
	Circumscribing	"Did you have a good time on your trip?" "What time will dinner be ready?"
	Stagnating	"What's there to talk about?" "Right. I know what you're going to say and you know what I'm going to say."
	Avoiding	"I'm so busy, I just don't know when I'll be able to see you." "If I'm not around when you try, you'll understand."
	Terminating	"I'm leaving you...and don't bother trying to contact me." "Don't worry."

Figure 14.3:

The stages of development in any relationship are complex and continuous. Although most relationships move through the stages sequentially, there are no predictable patterns of movement or that every relationship will move to termination. Every relationship, however, goes through some of the coming together and coming apart stages as the relationship either grows or dissolves.

Taken from Mark L. Knapp and Anita L. Vangelisti. *Interpersonal Communication and Human Relationships*, 2nd ed (Boston: Allyn & Bacon, 1992), 33. Reprinted by permission.

breakups of relationships often occur sporadically, inconsistently, and with uncertainty over a period of time, but a person deciding what to do about a relationship can proceed through the following four phases: the intrapyschic, dyadic, social, and grave-dressing (See Figure 14.4.) The "on again, off again" form that some relationships take follows the phases of Duck's approach.[7]

Intrapsychic   The *intrapsychic* phase is where a person begins to internally assess his or her dissatisfaction with a relationship. This phase involves perception, assessments, and decision-making about what to do in regard to the relationship. In this phase, communication may actually decrease at times while each of the partners may seek comfort from others outside the relationship.

Dyadic   In the *dyadic* phase, the persons in the relationship discuss the status of their relationship. The interactions vary from cooperative to uncooperative in discussing the partner's unsatisfying traits or behaviors, and whether to solve the problem or to separate. There is much negotiation, persuasion, and argument during this period, during which each person is trying to get the other to comply or change in some fashion. Sometimes the dyadic phase ends with an agreement to repair the relationship, but if it doesn't, the relationship may eventually move on to the next phase.

Social   In the *social* phase the relationship difficulties become more public within the context of family, friends, co-workers, or other acquaintances. Most relationships that break up, except possibly secret love affairs, do not stand completely alone and usually impact on others outside the dissolving relationship. For example there is usually an effect on children if their parents separate. During the social phase, the opinions and feelings of others are often taken into account and sometimes have an impact on what the couple eventually does. For example, the children of a married couple may influence the couple to stay together in spite of their differences. The concern may become "What kind of relationship should be continued, if any? How should it be presented to others?" Other issues that evolve include where to place blame, how to save face, how to explain of what has happened, and who should be sought out for support or to provide approval for the decision.

Grave Dressing   Duck names the final phase *grave dressing*, because after the breakup, each partner gives his or her account of why the relationship ended. These explanations aid in the healing process of coping and in

Duck's Dissolution Stages

Breakdown: Dissatisfaction with relationship

Threshold: I can't stand this any more.

Intrapsychic Phase

- Focus on partner's behavior
- Assess adequacy of partner's role performances
- Depict and evaluate negative aspects of being in the relationship
- Consider costs of withdrawal
- Assess positive aspects of alternative relationships
- Face the dilemma of expressing or repressing feelings

Threshold: I'd be justified in withdrawing.

Dyadic Phase

- Face the dilemma of choosing between confrontation and avoidance
- Confront partner
- Negotiate in relationship talks
- Attempt repair and reconciliation
- Assess joint costs of withdrawal or reduced intimacy

Threshold: I mean it.

Social Phase

- Negotiate postdissolution state with partner
- Initiate gossip or discussion network
- Create publicly negotiable face-saving and blame-placing stories and accounts
- Consider and face up to implied social network effects, if any
- Call in intervention teams

Threshold: It's now inevitable.

Grave-dressing Phase

- Heal wounded emotions
- Reformulate postmortems
- Circulate own version of breakup

Figure 14.4:

When relationships break up they go through a rather complex decision making process that, according to Steve Duck, includes four phases of disengagement: intrapsychic, dyadic, social, and grave dressing.

Adapted from *Personal Relationships,* by Steve Duck. Copyright © 1982 by Academic Press, Inc. Reprinted with permission of Academic Press, Inc., and the author.

the recovery from the breakup. It is not unusual for one or both individuals in the relationship to explain to others why the relationship dissolved. For example, if the relationship ended on friendly terms, you might hear such things as "It just didn't work—we were too different," or "We needed time to grow, so we decided not to see each other for awhile." If, on the other hand, the relationship ended on unfriendly terms, you might hear such explanations as "He always wanted things for himself—he was selfish," or "She never seemed to be satisfied with what I'd do for her." Not all relationships, however, end with mutual agreement that the relationship should end. You are probably aware of situations in which one partner didn't want to lose the other but the person ending the relationship simply saw no reason to continue it. In such a case, the grave-dressing phase is usually one-sided; where the person ending he relationship might say, "It just wasn't working" or "I have found someone new." Meanwhile, the person who does not want the relationship to end is looking for a way to keep the relationship going, and cannot face the fact that it is over. In this situation, the person is trying to justify to him- or herself and others that the termination is only temporary and that the other person will come to his/her senses and return.

Each phase requires certain communication challenges that Duck refers to as "social management problems." For example, in the intrapsychic phase, one must have the ability to discuss the perceived differences with one's partner. In the social phase, one must be able to discuss the breakup with others outside of the relationship. Clearly, as relationships move in and out of various phases or stages of termination, communication plays a role. The more skilled we are at communicating, the more likely we will be to move through the stages smoothly (that is, if terminating a relationship can ever be easy).

Leslie Baxter, in her research supporting some of Duck's explanations regarding dissolving relationships, believes that disengagement often involves repeated attempts to limit or end relationships. Attempts to end relationships are cyclical and involve different communication strategies. Moreover, the communication strategies used during the breakup of relationships involve varying degrees of *directness* and *concern* for the other person.[8] The direct strategies are explicit statements stating the desire to end the relationship, while indirect strategies are more subtle in their design. For example, an indirect strategy might involve using excuses such as "I have too much homework," thus, implying, "I cannot see you now."

Someone with concern for the other person is more likely to use the indirect approach; the direct approach is much more expedient, and may show little or no concern about hurting the other person. Baxter implies that strategies used in ending a relationship depend greatly on whether the breakup is one-sided or agreed upon by both parties. As suggested earlier, agreed-upon breakups usually involve some negotiation and face-saving on behalf of both parties involved. All relationships move through various stages and often move between various levels of tension or conflict. Conflict can lead to better relationships, if the nature of the conflict is understood by both parties in the relationship.

INTERPERSONAL CONFLICT

Conflict in relationships may occur for a number of reasons, including differences in the individuals' ability to self-disclose and differences in the individuals' view of a situation. Many scholars agree that conflict is inevitable in all relationships and that conflict need not be destructive (see Figure 14.5). Conflict often results in stronger and more durable relationships. Conflict in itself should not be considered negative or destructive, but a natural part of any relationship. However, conflict does become destructive when the parties involved are unwilling to negotiate their differences and instead engage in personal attacks on one another.

Interpersonal conflict occurs when incompatible goals are perceived between two individuals and one individual is not able to gain acceptance of his or her goals by the other. In other words, conflict results when two individuals perceive they have incompatible goals and they cannot achieve their individual goals unless one or both of them lose something. For example, suppose you want to go to a dance and your friend wants to go to a movie. It is impossible to go to both events in the same evening and you and your friend cannot agree which to attend. You have incompatible goals, and one must lose in order for the other to win.

Figure 14.5:

Conflict in relationships is inevitable and occurs for a variety of reasons, including differences in ability to self-disclose or differences in how a situation is viewed. Conflict is expected, to some degree, in every relationship; it should not be considered negative or destructive, but a natural part of any relationship. If the parties involved are unwilling to negotiate differences and engage in personal attacks, it can become destructive.

Bob Daemmrich/Tony Stone Images

Conflict is destructive when the resolution of the conflict ends with a winner and a loser. Conflict can also be destructive if the individuals involved act too aggressively, if they withdraw from each other, if they withhold their feelings from each other, or if they accuse each other for what is happening. Conflict is destructive in proportion to the importance of the goals to the individuals. Conflict becomes dysfunctional when it prevents us from doing our work or feeling good about ourselves. Conflict motivates behaviors, and when it forces us to do things that we don't want to do, it is destructive. An example that conflict can be destructive is the statistic that shows the divorce rate in our society to be over 50 percent. In addition, the rate of divorce has increased 700 percent since 1900.[9] Of course, not all divorces or separations are the result of conflict, nor is all conflict necessarily destructive. In fact, some people thrive on conflict—it is conflict that allows them to perform at extremely high levels. However when conflict results in the termination of a relationship and leaves one or both of the parties feeling foolish, inadequate, or angry, it is usually destructive.

A number of conflict management skills can be used to help resolve interpersonal conflict. *Self-regulation* is learning to control your emotions and thus keep in check what you say. In order to keep conflict minimal, it is best not to say things that will be hurtful to another. *Self-expression* is controlling what you do say, being descriptive rather than accusatory or defensive in what you communicate. *Negotiation* is the skill of compromise that allows the conflict to be resolved with both parties getting something they want. This is not always easy, especially if you approach conflict with the idea that you must win and the other person must lose. Negotiation requires give-and-take and the attitude that the relationship is more important than winning or losing. When appropriate, the importance of the relationship should be discussed or brought out during the negotiation process. In effect, the negotiators say to one another, "We have a definite disagreement here but, no matter what, our relationship is more important than the disagreement. We are confirming the importance of the relationship when we put it above winning the conflict." In order to reduce conflict and build relationships, we need to learn how to communicate effectively with each other.[10]

EXERCISE

As women contribute more to family income, they expect in return that the household responsibilities will be divided more equitably according to a Roper organization survey. While many men acknowledge responsibility for part of the household work, it added, women report that men are failing to live up to this ideal, and that their failure to do so is a major source of irritation to women.

1. **How can the above conflict be avoided?**
2. **Are there always going to be inequities between men and women regarding household responsibilities?**
3. **Form groups and negotiate the responsibilities of individuals who share living space.**

Was there any conflict within your group? If so, how did the group deal with it?

(Lincoln Journal-Star, "Women Growing Increasing Dissatisfied With Men," 26 April 1990, 1)

COMMUNICATING IN RELATIONSHIPS

Our ability to communicate interpersonally will to a large degree determine our success in forming and stabilizing relationships. Those who are skilled at social interaction are perceived to be friendly; think well of themselves; are not easily provoked to anger; and find it easy to engage in small talk.[11] Why some people find carrying on conversations easy and others do not is not fully understood by communication scholars. Birth order may be one factor, according to one research study. Younger siblings seem to be much more socially skilled than firstborns. Researchers also found that those with older, opposite-sex siblings interact more easily with members of the opposite sex.[12] Families, and in particular, siblings, may play a large role in the development of our interpersonal communication skills.

For most of us, the family is the main source of our identity formation. As discussed in Chapter 3, our self-concept is made up of our self-image (what we perceive ourselves to be) and our self-esteem (our feelings and attitudes toward ourselves). There is little question that our family—whether it is a single- or two-parent family, or whether you are an only child or one of many siblings—has a strong influence on our feelings about ourselves. If the communication environment is positive and supportive, chances are our self-concept will also be positive.

Establishing supportive and caring relationships is important to our well-being, and this process is generally easier when communication is both positive and supportive.[13] In other words, as the cliché goes, "If you can't say something nice, don't say anything at all." A recent research study discusses actions and verbal and nonverbal assurances that may affect commitment and satisfaction in romantic relationships.[14]

Romantic exchanges included such things as:

1. Act cheerful and positive when talking to the other.
2. Do favors for the other or help him/her out with tasks.
3. Initiate celebrations of special events from the couple's past, for example, the day we met.
4. Do things to surprise the other.

5. Suggest going out to eat at a favorite or special restaurant.
6. Create a romantic environment, for example, candlelight and flowers.
7. Give the other person items of sentimental value, such as gifts or cards.
8. Suggest ways to spend time doing things with each other.

Assurances include the following verbal and nonverbal actions:

1. Physically display affection through kisses and hugs.
2. Express aloud to the other what it would be like without him/her.
3. Reminisce aloud with the other about good times enjoyed together in the past.
4. Verbally express love for the person, explicitly.
5. Express long-term commitment to the relationship's future.
6. Act in playful ways toward the other.

The research findings suggest that behaviors such as those listed above do increase relationship commitment and satisfaction. However, it is interesting that females were more likely than males to report use of these strategies, which suggests that females undertake more relationship maintenance activity than their male partners.

Positive and supportive communication occurs in environments that are caring, open, flexible, warm, animated, and receptive. In such environments, communication is constructive and centers on the individuals and their relationship. Here are some expressions of how people feel when constructive communication is at the center of their relationship.

I feel that I can talk and that there is someone who will listen to me.

I feel accepted and supported.

I feel there is a willingness to see my point of view.

I don't feel a need or pressure to change—I am accepted for who I am.

I don't feel that I am constantly being judged or evaluated.

I feel that I am trusted.

I feel that I am treated with respect as a person.

I feel that I am treated fairly.

I feel good about myself and about us.

I feel like a responsible person.

I feel that I have control over myself.

I feel that someone is interested in me and cares about me.

I don't feel as if I have to justify everything that I do.

Two of the most effective and constructive means of demonstrating care and support for someone are to invite more communication and to listen actively.

Inviting More Communication

Many of us listen to others express their feelings and then immediately express our own. This gives the impression that we do not even acknowledge the other person's existence, let alone what he or she has just said. In contrast, skilled and caring communicators usually do not respond immediately with ideas, judgments, or feelings that express their own views. Instead, they invite others to express more of their thoughts by responding with such noncommittal responses as:

Interesting	I see.
Uh-huh.	Oh.
You did, huh?	Really?

Or, they may be more direct in asking the other person to continue by saying, for example:

That's interesting. Go on.

Tell me about it.

Let's discuss it.

Tell me everything.

I understand. What else happened?

Such invitations to talk can contribute much to the development of a meaningful relationship. The willingness to listen and reserve judgment creates a positive and supportive environment that in effect tells people they are valuable, they are loved, and they have control over their own behavior.

Active Listening

Probably the most effective way to indicate to others that they should continue to communicate is to respond to them with active listening. **Active listening** involves the process of analyzing and evaluating what others say in an effort to understand their feelings or the true meaning of their message. To check their understanding, active listeners may restate the message as they hear it in their own words and ask the sender for verification. Active listeners are never judgmental. Neither do they give advice, state opinions, or ask question in a negative or patronizing tone. They focus only on understanding the speaker's message. Examine the following conversation:

John: I wish I had a different instructor for speech this semester. Sam's instructor doesn't require many speeches, but mine requires one almost every week.

Jane: You feel that you're being put upon because of the instructor you have?

John:	Yes. Sam gets to go out more often, but I have to stay home to prepare my dumb speeches.
Jane:	You'd really like to have Sam's teacher rather than yours, huh?
John:	Yes, I don't like giving speeches, plus I hate spending the time it takes to prepare them.
Jane:	So, you hate giving speeches.
John:	Yeah! Especially when I have to stay home and Sam gets to go out.
Jane:	So, you don't hate it all the time.
John:	No, not all the time, but it's that the teacher is so demanding.
Jane:	What do you mean, "demanding"?
John:	She expects so much of us.
Jane:	Is that bad?
John:	No, I guess not.

In this short interaction, Jane listened thoughtfully and invited John to voice his feelings and frustrations. She did not express judgment nor did she agree or disagree. She showed that she understood and empathized with John's problem, but she did not try to present a solution to the problem—she left that up to John. Her active listening helped him understand and deal with his feelings.

Active listening promotes a number of positive feelings within a relationship:

1. It helps a person overcome the fear of expressing negative feelings.
2. It fosters an atmosphere of warmth and caring.
3. It helps to facilitate problem solving.

Active listening is not easy. It requires skill and a positive attitude toward the person who is talking. To be an effective active listener, you must:

1. want to hear what the other person has to say and be willing to take time to listen.
2. be receptive to the other person's feelings, whatever they are and however different they may be from your own.
3. place trust in the other person and avoid being judgmental or evaluative.
4. recognize that feelings change and that a situation that seems desperate or insurmountable one day may seem much more manageable the next day.
5. recognize that the other person is an individual separate from you, and that he or she has the same needs for affection, inclusion, and control that you have.
6. be willing to suspend your own thoughts and feelings, at least initially, in order to attend to the other person.

7. use feedback to ensure that you understand the other person. The more accurate your understanding, the greater the likelihood that you can be of help.

Communicating within relationships requires an understanding of the other person. Successful relationships are those in which each partner is open, flexible, and willing to listen to the other person. In order to improve your interpersonal communication skills, you must be committed to doing so. You must be willing to share yourself with others through self-disclosure, and you must be willing to attempt to understand the other person through active listening. Communicating in a relationship is a mutual responsibility, and one person can not guarantee its success. Interpersonal relationships are constantly moving from stage to stage and back and forth, and individuals who are successful in maintaining as well as deepening relationships are sensitive to the needs of the other person.

THINK ABOUT IT

A mother writes her least unfavorite lines used by her children:

"*Not now; I'll do it later.*"

"*How come I always have to do everything?*"

"*You just don't understand.*"

"*Nothing.*"

"*Everybody is doing it.*"

"*Get real.*"

The mother calls this "smart-mouthing," the father calls it "talking back," and the child calls it "communication." What do you call these lines? What are some of your least favorite lines used by your parents?

SUMMARY

Relationships—which occur whenever two people interact, whether for a moment or for a lifetime—go through a series of stages of development and deterioration. The five stages of the coming-together phase are initiating, experimenting, intensifying, integrating, and bonding; the five stages of coming apart are differentiating, circumscribing, stagnating, avoiding, and terminating. All relationships move through at least some of these stages, but not all relationships move through them in the same order or with the same intensity. Superficial relationships go through only the first one or two stages of development and terminate without going through the entire coming-apart series. There are three reasons for the sequence followed during the complex and continuous processes of coming together and coming apart: each stage provides information for the next, each stage helps predict what may or may not occur in the next stage, and skipping a stage creates risk and uncertainty in a relationship.

Dissolving relationships go through a rather complex decision-making process that does not always follow a specific order or series of stages. Breakups of relationships often occur sporadically, inconsistently, and with uncertainty over a period of time, but a person making decisions about what to do at the end of a relationship can proceed through the following four phases: intrapyschic, dyadic, social, and grave-dressing.

In the intrapsychic phase, a person begins to internally assess his or her dissatisfaction with a relationship. In the dyadic phase, the persons in the relationship discuss the status of their relationship. During the social phase, the relationship's difficulties become more public within the context of family, friends, co-workers, or other acquaintances. In the final phase, grave dressing. Each partner gives his or her account of why the relationship has ended. Each phase requires certain communication abilities, referred to as "social management abilities."

Conflict appears to be inevitable in all relationships. *Interpersonal conflict* occurs when individuals perceive that they have incompatible goals as a result of at least one of the individuals not being able to gain acceptance of his or her goals by the other. Conflict can be destructive if it can be resolved only by one party winning and the other losing. Interpersonal conflict can be resolved and can be constructive through self-regulation, self-expression, negotiation, and reaffirmation of the relationship.

In a positive and supportive environment, communication between individuals usually reflects caring, openness, flexibility, warmth, animation, and receptivity. The two best ways to develop and maintain relationships are to invite more communication and to be an active listener. *Active listening* is the process of analyzing and evaluating what another person is saying in an effort to understand the feelings in and meaning of the speaker's message.

KEY TERMS

Active Listening: Process of analyzing and evaluating what others say in an effort to understand their feelings or the true meaning of their message.

Interpersonal Conflict: Opposition of individuals who perceive incompatible goals as a result of at least one individuals not being able to gain acceptance of his or her goals by the other.

Discussion Starters

1. In your opinion, which reason plays the strongest role in people's development in relationships? Explain.
2. What did you agree with and disagree with in the explanation of the stages of relationship development?
3. Compare and contrast Knapp's "coming apart" with Duck's dissolution stages.
4. What is an ideal intimate relationship? An ideal friendship? An ideal business relationship? An ideal student-teacher relationship?
5. Describe what it takes to have a lasting relationship.
6. What happens when a relationship begins to come apart?
7. In what ways can conflict be constructive? Destructive?
8. What advice would you give to someone who wanted to improve his or her interpersonal communication?

Notes

1. M. L. Knapp and A. L. Vangelisti, *Interpersonal Communication and Human Relationships,* 2nd ed. (Boston: Allyn & Bacon, 1992): 29–63.
2. Knapp and Vangelisti: 52–56.
3. Knapp and Vangelisti: 40–45.
4. M. L. Knapp, R. P. Hart, G. W. Friedrich, et al., "The Rhetoric of Goodbye: Verbal and Nonverbal Correlates of Human Leave-Taking," *Speech Monographs* 40 (1973): 182–198.
5. Knapp and Vangelisti: 52–53.
6. S. Duck (ed.), *Personal Relationships 4: Dissolving Personal Relationships* (London: Academic Press, 1982; L. A. Baxter, "Accomplishing Relationship Disengagement," in *Understanding Personal Relationships: An Interdisciplinary Approach*, eds. S. Duck, and D. Perlman (Beverly Hills, Calif.: Sage, 1985): 243–266; S. Duck, *Human Relationships: An Introduction to Social Psychology* (Beverly Hills, Calif.: Sage, 1986).
7. S. Duck (ed.), "A Topography of Relationship Disengagement and Dissolution," in *Personal Relationships* (London: Academic Press, 1982): 1–30.
8. L. A. Baxter, Trajectories of Relationships Disengagement," *Journal of Social and Personal Relationship* 1 (1984): 29–48; L. A. Baxter, "Strategies for Ending Relationships: Two Studies," *Western Journal of Speech Communication* 46 (1982): 223–241.
9. K. M. Galvin and B. J. Brommel, *Family Communication: Cohesion and Change,* 3rd Ed. (Glenview, Ill: Scott, Foresman, 1991), 7
10. W. W. Wilmot, *Dyadic Communication*, 3rd ed. (New York: Random House, 1987), 230.

11. J. M. Reisman, "Friendliness and Its Correlates," *Journal of Social and Clinical Psychology* 2 (1984): 143–155.
12. W. Ickes and M. Turner, "On the Social Advantages of Having an Older, Opposite- Sex Sibling: Birth Order Influences in Mixed-Sex Dyads," *Journal of Personality and Social Psychology* 45 (1983): 210–22.
13. Ideas for this section came from a Parent Effectiveness Training workshop and from T. Gordon, P.E.T.: *Parent Effectiveness Training* (New York: Wyden, 1970).
14. E. P. Simon and L. A. Baxter, "Attachment-Style Differences in Relationship Maintenance Strategies," *Western Journal of Communication* 57 (Fall 1993): 416–430.

Chapter 15

Small Group Communication

LEARNING OBJECTIVES

After studying this chapter, you should be able to:

1. Define a group.

2. Distinguish between the personal and task-related purposes of small group communication.

3. Identify the characteristics that distinguish small group communication from other forms of communication.

4. Describe the roles and responsibilities of small group leaders.

5. Specify the responsibilities of a small group participant.

6. Describe group-centered and self-centered behaviors by group members.

7. Outline the steps in problem-solving and decision-making.

8. Develop criteria for evaluating a small group discussion.

The assignment is over, and group X has accomplished its goal. Each member is satisfied not only with his or her own work, but also with the performance of the group as a whole. The meetings ran smoothly, and little, if any, time was wasted. Group Y also attained the same goal, but no one seems satisfied either with what was achieved or with the group itself. In fact, group Y's members feel that their working together as a group was a complete waste of time. How is it possible that two groups could perform the same task and yet have such different reactions?

The answer to the above question lies in the fact that many variables contribute to a group's success or failure. No two groups will produce identical results, because no two groups are identical in their makeup. Furthermore, prior success cannot guarantee that a group will be successful in every problem or situation that it confronts. Nonetheless, group members' understanding of some key factors can increase a group's chances of success. To help you become a more effective group member and to improve your group communication skills, this chapter explains the purposes and characteristics of small groups. The chapter then explores four crucial aspects of small group communication: leadership, member participation, methods of group problem-solving and decision-making, and evaluation.

If you listed all the times you participated in group discussions over the past month, you would have evidence of how common small group activities and meetings are in our lives. The family is probably the most common small group, but we also participate in work groups and social groups. Many of you are members of service or professional groups, such as the Agronomy Club, Geology Club, Theater Club, Association for Computing Machinery, African People's Union, Native American Student Congress, Young Democrats, College Republicans, or Feminist Action Alliance. Even if you do not belong to such formal organizations, any time you get together with people and talk about issues or problems, you are involved in small group communication. **Small group communication** is the exchange of information among a relatively small number of persons (usually three to thirteen persons) who share a common purpose, such as doing a job or solving a problem.

Classroom discussion, the most widely used instructional method in our educational system today, is another form of small group communication. Small group communication is so common in business, industry, and government that the average worker with a position in middle or higher management in any profession spends one-fourth to one-third of each working day in such discussions. It is not surprising, therefore, that the ability to use small group communication to accomplish a task and establish an atmosphere of cooperation is essential to success in virtually every career.

THINK ABOUT IT

Here is a riddle: What is more boring than a droning professor, more tedious than peeling potatoes, and more frustrating than a perpetual busy signal when you need to reach someone by phone?

The answer, according to many business people, is a meeting.

Cox News Service, 1990

Why is this so? Do you think meetings have to be boring and tedious? What does this tell you about the success of some groups?

WHAT IS A GROUP?

A group is not just a number of people who happen to be in the same place. To qualify as a group, a collection of people must be related in six ways:

1. Perceptions. Do the members make an impression on one another?
2. Motivation. Are there rewards for being together?
3. Goals. Do the persons have a common purpose?
4. Organization. Does each person have some role or task?
5. Interdependency. Must each person depend on the others for his or her efforts to be successful?
6. Interaction. Is the number of persons small enough so that each person can communicate face to face with every other person?[1]

For our purposes, a **group** is a collection of individuals who influence one another, derive mutual satisfaction from one another, have a common purpose, take on roles, are interdependent, and interact face-to-face. If any element is left out, what exists is a collection of independent people, not a group. People standing at a corner waiting for a bus, for example, meet some of the criteria of a group. They have a common purpose (transportation), they may interact in some face-to-face communication, they may make an impression on one another, and they may even get some satisfaction from the fact that they do not have to stand alone. But they do not constitute a group according to our definition, because they are not interdependent and they do not take on roles.

One author defines "groupness"—the necessary property that groups possess but that collections of individuals do not—as follows.

"Groupness" emerges from the relationship among the people involved, just as "cubeness" emerges from the image of a set of planes, intersects and angles in specific relationships to each other. One can draw a cube with twelve lines, but only if they are assembled in a definite way. Any other arrangement of the lines gives something other than a cube. Likewise, one can have a collection or set of people without having a group.[2]

The point here is that a group exists as something apart from the individuals who belong to it. Just as twelve lines, when arranged in the proper relationship, form a cube, several individuals, when they develop proper relationships, form a group. And just as the lines that form a cube lose their individual identity, the members of a group lose their individual identities when "groupness" is developed.

Small groups can take irrational risks as a result of shared responsibilities. In the mob hangings of the Old West, people who were considered rational and conservative found themselves caught up in a group frenzy when peer pressure took over. The 1992 Los Angeles street rioting is another example of irrational behavior performed by groups. The tendency for groups to take actions that a lone, rational individual wouldn't take is called the **risky shift phenomenon.** Can you cite some modern examples of the risky shift phenomenon at work? Have you ever personally witnessed an event that resulted from this phenomenon? How would you explain it?

PURPOSES OF SMALL GROUP COMMUNICATION

Small groups may perform many tasks and solve many problems, but all the purposes they serve can be grouped into two general categories: social purposes and task-related purposes.[3]

Social Purposes

Social reasons for participating in groups fall into four main categories: socialization, catharsis, therapy, and learning.

Socialization   We engage in small group communication when socializing with others, such as during coffee breaks, at parties, or at any event where people share time and conversation. When we gather in small groups for social purposes, our goals are to strengthen our interpersonal relationships and to promote our own well-being. Such groups fulfill our interpersonal needs for inclusion and affection.

Catharsis   Small group communication allows us to vent our emotions, including frustrations, fears, and complaints, as well as our hopes and desires. When we have a chance to let others know how we feel about something, we often experience a catharsis, or release from tension. This purpose is usually accomplished in the supportive atmosphere of bull sessions or family discussions, where self-disclosure is appropriate. Cathartic group communication tends to focus on personal problems rather than on inter-personal needs.

Therapy   Therapeutic small group communication sessions are used pri-marily to help people alter their attitudes, feelings, or behaviors in regard to some aspect of their personal life. For example, a therapeutic group might include people who have a drinking problem, a drug problem, or an-other specific problem such as difficulty in coping with the loss of a loved one. Usually, a therapeutic group is led by a professional trained in group psychotherapy or counseling.

Learning   The most common reason that people join small groups is to learn from one another. Learning occurs in all kinds of settings, but the one you are probably most familiar with is the classroom (see Figure 15.1). The underlying assumption of learning groups is that the sharing of informa-tion will enable the individual to increase knowledge more and make bet-ter decisions than he or she could if working alone.

Task-Related Purposes

Small group communication is frequently used to accomplish two general tasks: decision-making and problem-solving.

Decision-Making   People come together in groups to make decisions, such as determining which spring vacation trip to take, where to hold a dance, which play to stage, or which computer is the most practical for stu-dent use. Discussing alternatives with others helps people decide which

Figure 15.1:

Learning in small groups. The use of small groups in educa-tion is extremely popular. Working in groups is effective for increasing knowledge and helping individuals make better decisions.

Richard Biegun/Gamma-Liaison

choice is the best, not only for themselves, but for the group as a whole. In addition, when people participate in the decision-making process, they are more likely to accept the final outcome and to help carry it out. Most of us resent being told what to do, but we are more tolerant of a decision if we help shape it.

A classic research study by Coch and French, Jr. demonstrated the value of group decision-making. The study focused on a garment factory where managers had always made decisions without seeking input from their workers. The managers decided to update some of their production techniques, but the workers were resisting the changes.

To analyze the problem, an experiment was set up in which workers were divided into groups that would operate using different procedures: (1) no-participation procedure, which was essentially the way things had always been done—employees had no voice in planning and change; (2) participation-through-representation procedures, in which a few employee representatives were involved in the decision-making process; and (3) total-participation procedure, in which all the employees were involved. In each case, whether the workers contributed or not, the final decision was up to management.

The results revealed that:

1. The no-participation group continued to resist changes.
2. Both participation groups relearned their jobs significantly faster and surpassed the previous average production levels much sooner.
3. The total-participation group performed slightly better than the partic-ipation-through-representation group.[4]

What conclusion can you draw from these results regarding decision-making and groups?

Problem-Solving   Working in small groups is also an excellent way to solve problems. People form problem-solving groups in almost every imaginable context—in the workplace, in government, in school, and at home. The huge variety of problems they attempt to solve include how to improve health care, how to stop violence in on our streets, how to resolve the problem of parking on campus, and how to improve a faltering relationship.

CHARACTERISTICS OF SMALL GROUPS

Small groups have a number of characteristics that make them a unique and specialized context for communication. These characteristics, which include interdependence, a common goal, group personality, commitment, cohesiveness, group conflict, social facilitation, gender differences, group size, and norms, determine who will join the group, how well the group will function, and how the members will interact.

Interdependence

Probably the most essential characteristic of a small group is **interdependence**—the mutual dependence of group members on one another. Interdependence is reflected in all the other group characteristics, because without it there would be no group. To a large extent, interdependence is built on each member's willingness to subordinate his or her individual desires and goals in order to accomplish the group's goal. One example is the class assignment in which a group of students are expected to produce a joint project. Invariably, at least one member is not motivated, will not conform, or is not committed to the task, and thus tries to avoid doing his or her share of the work. Usually, these projects are evaluated so that all group members receive the same grade. Since each individual's grade depends on the others' contributions, either the group will have to pressure the nonperforming member to produce his or her share, or each member will have to work harder to make up for the nonperformer's failure.

Groups function best and are most satisfying for their members when each individual recognizes and respects the crucial role that interdependence plays in group processes. Such members can appreciate that the group's success is based on each member's cooperation and willingness to work toward a common goal.

Common Goal

The driving force that brings people together to form groups is a **common goal.** Examples of common goals may include protesting a change in dormitory visitation rules, lobbying for more student parking, working for equal campus access to physically impaired students, or supporting a charity. The goal itself draws people into a group, even though their approaches to the goal may differ.

Group Personality

When people come together in a group, they form a collective identity that becomes the **group personality.** Some examples might be: Fraternity Z is very conservative; the debate team is quite intelligent; and sorority Y is very social.

Each member's personality influences every other member's personality, which, in turn, determines the collective temperament. Of course, there are exceptions. For example, a group that is generally conservative may have some liberal members. The presence of these others can influence each individual so that the separate personalities blend into a single group personality.

Commitment

Another important characteristic of a group is commitment—to the task, to the group, and to the other individuals in the group. **Commitment** is the desire of group members to work together to complete their task to the satisfaction of the entire group. Members' commitment to their group stems from their interpersonal attraction; their commonality of attitudes, beliefs, and values; the fulfillment of their interpersonal needs; and the rewards that the group can offer.

Commitment is important to a group's effectiveness and ultimate success. For example, how often have you been in a group where one or two of the members did most of the work and the others did little or nothing? Those who do little or nothing to help the group accomplish its task are not committed to the group or the task and ultimately impact negatively on the group's cohesiveness and effectiveness. Working in a group to accomplish a difficult task—and contributing to the accomplishment of the task when other group members are not doing so—is commitment. For a group to be truly effective, all of its members must be committed to the group, to the other group members, and to the successful completion of the task. To be Committed means that the desire to remain in the group is greater than the desire to leave.

Cohesiveness

Cohesiveness, an extention of commitment, is the attraction that group members feel for each other and their willingness to stick together. Cohesiveness is based on each member's need to remain in the group and the group's ability to provide members with rewards, making it worthwhile for them to give time and energy to the group. In a sense, cohesiveness is a form of loyalty or commitment.

Sometimes individuals will stick with a group even when it is not in their best interest to do so. Groups can become too cohesive or committed, resulting in **groupthink**—a dysfunction in which group members see the harmony of the group as being more important than the consideration of new ideas, the critical examination of ideas, the willingness to change flawed decisions, or the willingness to allow new members to participate.[5] To illustrate groupthink, consider the following situation. Students are asked to choose one of three solutions to a certain social problem. The class divides fairly equally into three groups. Each group is asked to defend its selection and to persuade the instructor that its solution is the best one. As an incentive for preparing a sound argument, students are told that only one of the solutions will be accepted.

As the groups begin to organize, their members make a modest effort to pull together. Each group selects a representative to present its argument. After hearing each representative, the instructor announces that he or she is undecided. Therefore, all groups have one more chance to develop their arguments. The instructor also announces that students who do not like their group's solution are welcome to join another group. No one switches groups, even though some are tempted.

To raise the stakes, the instructor states that the two losing groups will be assigned a research project over the weekend, while the winning group will be exempt from this assignment. In response, the intensity within each group builds. Members pull their chairs closer together and talk more forcibly about their solution. They support each other's views more openly. The common objective has now become quite clear: The students must persuade their instructor that their group's solution is the best one, whether it is or it isn't, or else they will have to do the research project. Groupthink is more likely to occur when a group's cohesiveness and commitment are too high and when the group is under pressure to achieve consensus at the expense of having the best possible solution.

Cohesiveness is an important characteristic of every group, even when members are joined by chance rather than by choice. Cohesiveness, however, does not mean conformity. Cohesiveness is a positive force or "chemistry" that attracts members of the group toward one another and increases effective group interaction.

Group Conflict

Conflict, in our culture, is often defined as a clash; a fight; or the existence of incompatible desires, ideas, or opinions that result in a negative occurrence. We are often told to avoid conflict at all costs. You can pick up any contemporary popular magazine today and you will probably find articles on how to avoid conflict with friends, family, and co-workers. The implication in the articles is that conflict is unusual, undesirable, abnormal, and unpleasant and that it should be avoided at all costs. However, the truth of the matter is that whenever people come together in any communicative context there is bound to be conflict of some sort. Conflict, however, does not always have to be harmful. Conflict can be productive and can result in better decisions and solutions to problems.

Effective group decision-making and problem-solving often depends on conflict and open disagreement. Of course, too much conflict can create undue tension, and the kind of conflict that results from personal attacks on individual group members is often the least productive and usually leads to hurt feelings, withdrawal, and eventually to the disbanding of the group.

The benefits of group conflict, when it is understood and controlled, include better understanding of group members and issues, better involvement, increased motivation, better decisions, and greater group cohesiveness. These benefits are more likely to occur when groups open themselves to collaboration or compromise.

In collaboration, negotiating and problem solving is used to find a solution that fully meets the needs of all parties involved in a group conflict.

In other words, each party gets what he or she wants. For example, you're serving on a college curriculum committee. The student members think that the general education course should be practical, and the faculty believes it should be more theoretical. There is much discussion, but eventually both sides see the benefits of each view and agree that all the general education courses should include both practice and theory. The result is an ideal solution that both students and faculty members believe they have won without the other group's having lost. The collaboration between the students and faculty generated by the conflict between practice and theory in the curriculum has resulted in a superior, integrated general education curriculum.

Compromise is a shared outcome. Compromise occurs when conflicting parties are willing to give up part of their goal to arrive at an alternative solution that provides parts of both parties' original goals. Compromise implies giving up something to gain something more important, so that both parties involved gain from the compromise. For example, a grading appeals committee composed of two students and four faculty members has been presented with an appeal in which a student believes he should have gotten an "A" and the professor of the course, insists the student got what he earned—a "C." After hearing both sides, one student and two faculty members on the committee believe that the student should have received an "A," whereas the other student and the other two faculty members believe that the "C" grade was appropriate. There is a deadlock, that must be resolved. Through a compromise, the conflicting parties agree that the student should receive a "B" grade. The result is that neither party got all of what it wanted, but both got part of what they wanted.

Social Facilitation and Gender Differences

In a group, each individual's behavior is affected by the presence of the other members. Each person derives energy from the presence of the others that must then be released. This tendency for a person to release energy that would not be released if the individual were acting alone is called **social facilitation.** Social facilitation can commonly be seen in people's tendency to compete with each other in group settings. For example, the vying of students for their teacher's attention is a form of social facilitation.

Social facilitation is something akin to running a race with an audience as opposed to running a race with no one present. The runner will try harder in front of the audience than he or she would if no one were watching. Furthermore, if there were both an audience and other runners, all of the runners would put forth even more effort, which would give the group a sense of energy that is greater than the sum of its parts. Thus, competition can be healthy in a group if it is carried out in the spirit of cooperation.

The differences between the way men communicate in groups and the way women communicate in groups are not clear, nor are the results of research always accurate or fair to one gender or the other. We could probably agree that most men are physically stronger than most women, but some women are stronger than some men. To say, however, that men on average are physically stronger than women is a reasonable statement to make. To say that all men are stronger than all women is not accurate, nor is it fair. Much of the research examining women and men is done by comparing averages. Thus, particular individual behaviors are usually not allowed for, leaving only averages for our consideration.

Research shows that groups consisting of both men and women are more likely to be dominated by men talking than by women talking. Men tend to demonstrate more task-related behavior than do women—that is, men tend to be more impatient and more goal-oriented than women in order to move on to the next issue or problem. Women tend toward offering positive responses to others' comments, and in general, tend to express their subjective opinions more readily than men. On the other hand, men tend to be more objective in their comments than women.[6]

Because of stereotypical beliefs that exist in our society, women are sometimes perceived as being less competent than men in solving problems or in making small group decisions. However, little, if any, difference has been found by researchers between men and women in problem-solving abilities. The research does suggest that men appear to be better at certain kinds of problem-solving tasks than women but that the difference is reduced or eliminated when men and women work together and when both are highly motivated to solve the problem. (See Figure 15.2).[7]

When groups are in competition with one another, it appears that women are more cooperative with their opponents than are men. Women are more likely to share resources with their opponents and are more interested in fairness than in winning. Men are more willing to engage in aggressive behavior and to gain their way through deception and deceit than

Figure 15.2:

Research suggests that men and women differ in their interaction within small groups, but the differences are reduced or eliminated when men and women work together and when both are highly motivated to solve the problem.

Tom Stwart/The Stock Market

are women. Also, men are more likely to be anti-social, using revenge, verbal aggression, and even physical violence, while women are more likely to use socially acceptable behavior, such as reasoning and understanding, to solve conflict.[8]

When groups are small in size, women prefer to work with other women, while men don't have a gender preference. It is much more difficult to achieve cohesiveness in all-male groups than in mixed-gender groups or all-female groups. As our culture continues to change, so will our stereotypes of men and women. When comparing the research on men and women based on gender rather than on biological sex, we are beginning to find that differences are not so much based on biological sex as on masculine and feminine traits. That is, individuals who have masculine traits, whether they are male or female, are more likely to be competitive and to attempt to dominate and control interactions, while individuals with more feminine traits are less likely to display those behaviors.[9] It is important that both men and women understand the existing stereotypes and make sure that each participatant in a group is provided an equal opportunity to participate.

Group Size

Group Size   The number of participants in the group, has important ramifications for the group's effectiveness. Although there is no perfect number of members for a group, there are some indications that groups of certain sizes are more appropriate for certain kinds of tasks. For example, five-member groups are the most effective for dealing with intellectual tasks: coordinating, analyzing, evaluating information, and making administrative decisions. Many small group textbooks recommend that committees have no fewer than three and no more than nine members.

A group that is too small may limit the information and ideas that are generated, while a group that is too large may limit the contribution that each person can make. As a group increases in size, the number of possible interactions increases dramatically. (See Figure 15.3). The possible interactions include all of the possible combinations of members. For example, in a three-person group, Person A could interact with Person B and Person C separately, or with Persons B and C simultaneously. Person B and C would have similar interaction possibilities, resulting in nine possible interactions.[10]

An important consideration in deciding group size is that the larger the group, the greater the variety of skills and information possessed by its members. On the other hand, the advantages gained when a group has more than seven members seem to be outweighed by potential disadvantages. For example, ten opinions may seem to be superior to five and twenty opinions may seem to be superior to ten, but in reality having twice

Group Size and Potential Interactions

Number in Group	Interactions Possible
2	2
3	9
4	28
5	75
6	186
7	411
8	1,056

Figure 15.3:

This figure illustrates that as the number of members in the group increases, the number of interactions increases dramatically. The possible interactions include each group member as well as every combination of members within the group. As the group grows in size past seven, the advantages gained in potential interaction may be offset by the potential for conflict and an inability to reach consensus.

as many opinions can create twice as much potential for conflict and make consensus at least twice as difficult to reach. In addition, some consideration should be given to the balance of men and women in the group. As indicated earlier, stereotypical differences between men and women do exist in our society; thus, when possible, it is best to form either groups that consists of an equal number of men and women, or groups where women are slightly in the majority. These two arrangements tend to discourage stereotypical behavior and create a more balanced group perspective.

When deciding on the most effective size for a group, remember the following points:

1. Large groups limit the time for and the amount of individual interaction.

2. Large groups provide a greater opportunity for aggressive members to assert their dominance. As a result, less-assertive members may feel isolated and may withdraw from the group altogether.

3. Large groups make it difficult to follow a set agenda. It is easy for someone in a large group to switch topics or introduce subjects unrelated to the group's original priorities.

Norms

Norms are the expected and shared ways in which group members behave. Both informal and formal guidelines determine which behaviors are acceptable and which are not. In most group situations, the norms are informal and unwritten. In your speech class, for example, you know that certain behaviors are expected of you. At a minimum, it is informally assumed that you will read your assignments, respect others' rights to speak, do your own work, and be on time for class. However, there may also be formal written rules, such as specific dates for the completion of assignments; attendance requirements; and guidelines for achieving specific grades.

For a group to function effectively, its members must agree on how things are to be done. Therefore, groups, no matter what their size or task, establish norms. This is done for a variety of reasons, but the strongest one is that shared ways of behaving enable members to attain group goals and to satisfy interpersonal needs. If there were no guidelines for behavior, most groups would be ineffective and disorganized.

Norms also help give a group structure. If members know what is expected of them, they are more likely to act accordingly and function more efficiently. Sometimes the norms are as simple as getting the task done, or as involved as participating in complex rituals and ceremonies that must be respected if a member is to remain in the group.

In more formal situations, to increase efficiency and order, many groups use preestablished rules to guide their interaction. *Robert's Rules of Order* is the most widely used authority on conducting social, business, and government meetings. Such formal rules specify the roles of members, how meetings are to be conducted, and how topics for discussion are to be introduced, discussed, and accepted or rejected by the group's members. When it is important to maintain formal order, a group may appoint a parliamentarian to ensure that its rules are correctly interpreted and followed.

Leadership

A significant factor in the success of every small group is **leadership,** which is any behavior that helps clarify or guide the group to achieve its goals. It is also the ability to exert influence over others. A **leader** is a person assigned or selected, or who emerges from a group, to guide or provide direction toward reaching the group's goals. In most cases, only one person serves as leader, although sometimes two or more persons may share the responsibility. Leadership is a role that can only be given by the group, and a leader can lead only with the group's permission. (See Figure 15.4.)

Leading a Group

A leader is the person at the center of a group's attention, or the person to whom the group members address their messages. For example, in class-

Figure 15.4:

Leaders implement task needs and help maintain the personal needs of the members with the group.

Billy E. Barnes/Tony Stone Images

rooms, the teacher is the leader and the students usually center their attention on the teacher, addressing their communications to him or her. At times, students may address messages to other students, or one student may hold the attention of the class, but in neither situation does a student actually become the leader of the class.

Another way to identify a leader is by the behaviors that a person displays in guiding a group to their specific goal. If a person communicates a direction and the group members follow that direction to reach their goal, then that person is demonstrating leadership.

Finally, a leader can be identified by his or her position or title, such as student council president, chairperson of the committee, boss, teacher, captain, father, mother, and so on. But this method of identification requires caution. Even though a title signifies that a person is a nominal leader, it does not mean that he or she has leadership skills.

In most cases, a leader's ability to manage determines the success or failure of a group. Granted, not all successes or failures can be traced directly to the person in charge, because the participants, the nature of the task to be accomplished, and the information available for completing the task also contribute to the outcome. The role of the leader in small group projects is to get the task done. To do this, he or she must be objective enough to determine how the group is functioning and whether it is progressing toward its goal. At times, this requires the ability to "step back" and examine the group from an objective point of view.

Leaders must help meet two sets of needs found in all groups. **Task needs** are related to the content of the task and to all behaviors that lead to the completion of the task, including defining and assessing the task, gathering information, studying the problem, and solving the problem. **Maintenance needs** are related to the personal satisfaction that the group members receive from working together. Maintenance needs pertain to such intangibles as atmosphere, structure, role responsibility, praise, and social-emotional control.

To meet maintenance needs, leaders in small groups must carry out a number of functions:

Initiating—preparing members for the discussion

Organizing—keeping members on track

Maintaining effective interaction—spreading participation

Ensuring member satisfaction—promoting interpersonal relationships

Facilitating understanding—encouraging effective listening

Stimulating creativity and critical thinking—encouraging evaluation and improvement

EXERCISE

List the characteristics and skills you believe a good leader should possess. Then rank-order them, with 1 being the most important, 2 being the second most important, and so on. Form small groups (of three to seven people) to discuss each member's rankings and to create a new rank-order list of leadership qualities or characteristics. Place the group's top five qualities on the board and compare them with the qualities of the other groups in the class. How do the lists compare? How do people acquire the characteristics and skills you listed?

List five people you believe to be leaders, and list the characteristics and skills you believe each possesses. Do all have the same qualities, or are there differences? Is there a quality that is universal among all five? Discuss your answers with your classmates.

Leadership Styles

In dealing with group members, most leaders fall into one of two categories: **Task-oriented leaders,** who gain satisfaction from performing the task, and **relationship-oriented leaders,** who attempt to obtain a position of prominence and to establish good interpersonal relationships.[11]

Task-oriented leaders are mainly concerned with completing the job or solving the problem. Such leaders spend little time developing relationships unless doing so will help get the task completed more quickly. Relationship-oriented leaders, on the other hand, emphasize people rather than the task and focus on attending to the interpersonal needs of their group's members.

Leaders may also be classified as autocratic, democratic, and laissez-faire.[12]

Autocratic leaders keep complete control and make all decisions for the group. They decide what will be talked about, when it will be talked about, who may speak, and who may not. They often make decisions that affect the group without consulting the other members. Autocratic leaders are able to tell others what to do, either because their position gives them the power or because the group allows them to do so.

Democratic leaders guide and direct the group, but share control and remain open to all views. This leadership style allows the will of the majority to prevail even when the majority's view differs from the leader's. Because democratic leaders guide and suggest rather than prescribe and require, they make a final decision only after consulting all group members. Interaction among group members and democratic leaders is usually quite open and subject only to the constraints established by the group.

Laissez-faire leaders give complete decision-making freedom to the group or to individual members and often become figureheads who remain only minimally involved. They do not believe in taking charge and may actually feel uncomfortable in such a role. As a result, the group receives little or no direction. Some experts feel that the laissez-faire style of leadership is a contradiction in terms. It implies that a leader is in control without leading at all.

In theory, the differences among the three styles of leadership are clear. The autocratic leader has complete control, the democratic leader shares control, and the laissez-faire leader gives up control. In practice, though, the three styles are not always so clear-cut. Most leaders do not use the same style all the time but vary their style to match each situation. Certain circumstances, group members, and group purposes call for direct control, while others require little or no control. For example, a military leader in combat and a doctor in a medical emergency will of necessity be autocratic leaders. Such situations require immediate action, and putting decisions to a vote could create great problems. The democratic-leadership style is most often used when a leader has been elected. For example, the president of the student government or the chair of a committee would probably use a democratic style. This style is most common when the leader is both a representative and a member of the group. The laissez-faire leadership style is often used when group members do not want or need a rigid structure to accomplish their goal, such as a group conducting a study session. If such a group decided that they needed a leader, they would take appropriate action, but in most cases this kind of group does not desire or require any management and so it remains leaderless.

Leaders are not always free to follow the leadership style they prefer. For example, persons who would rather be democratic or laissez-faire leaders might discover that pressure from others, the need to get things done in a certain way, or the desire to save time and energy require them to be more autocratic than they would like. On other occasions, when it is important for members to agree with a decision, leaders are more likely to use a democratic style. No single leadership style is perfect for all situations.

Research, although not conclusive, suggests that the democratic leadership style is superior to the autocratic style in getting a task done and at the same time satisfying group members.[13] Autocratic leaders are likely to get more done, but member satisfaction is considerably lower. Probably the most significant finding of the research is that autocratic leaders generate more hostility and aggression among group members, whereas democratic leaders facilitate more originality, individuality, and independence. Groups with laissez-faire leaders accomplish less, produce work of lower quality, and waste more time. Although it is impossible to say exactly when one

Leadership Styles		
Autocratic	**Democratic**	**Laissez-Faire**
Keeps complete control	Shares control	Gives up control
Makes all policy and decisions for the group	Involves members in all policy- and decision-making; does not make any decisions without consulting group members	Gives total freedom to group members to make policies and decisions; gets involved only when called upon
Defines tasks and assigns them to members	May guide task assignment to be sure work is accomplished, but allows members to divide work	Completely avoids participation

style will be better than another, common sense tells us that a leader needs to be flexible in order to obtain the best balance of production and satisfaction from a group.

Leadership and Gender Differences

A question that researchers have long been trying to answer is "Do male leaders and female leaders differ in their leadership style or approach to leadership?" What do you think? Social scientist, Marilyn Loden, in her book *Feminine Leadership, or How to Succeed in Business Without Being One of the Boys* contends that the sexes do indeed differ in leadership style.[14] It is Loden's belief that female leaders often adopt a less directive style emphasizing cooperativeness, whereas males tend to exhibit a more directive, "take-charge" strategy. Research on male and female leadership by social scientists has generally found that there is no consistent or significant difference between the sexes in terms of leadership style. The question is—who is right?

Because of the complexity of the subject, the answer to the above question is not a simple one. A review of 150 research studies related to male and female leadership were analyzed by Alice Eagly and Blair Johnson.[15] Eagly and Johnson found that potential differences between males and females were examined on two dimensions in the existing research: (1) task accomplishment versus maintenance of interpersonal relationships, and (2) participative (democratic) versus directive (autocratic) leardership style. Sex-role stereotypes suggest that female leaders might show more concern for interpersonal relations and tend to be more democratic in their leadership style than male leaders. Results of the Eagly and Johnson study, however, did not support these stereotypes. Their results suggest there is no evidence of any substantial difference between males and females regarding the first dimension (task accomplishment versus maintenance of interpersonal relationships). There is, however, a significant difference between males and females regarding the second dimension (participative versus directive leadership style). Here, Eagly and Johnson found that females were more democratic or participative than males. What do you think accounts for this difference?

According to Eagly and Johnson, the difference in leadership styles may exist because—as evidence suggests—women possess better interpersonal skills than men. However, this cause-and-effect connection is still only speculation. Much more research must be done before a definitive conclusion can be drawn about gender differences in leadership style—and whether (and in what situations) those differences might be to a leader's advantage or disadvantage.

CONDUCTING A MEETING

When a group meets for the first time, the members usually begin by introducing themselves and briefly telling their reasons for joining the group or what they hope to accomplish as a member.

After introductions, and depending on the nature of the group and its assigned task, members may appoint or elect a recording secretary. This person keeps a written account of the meeting's discussions, including topics and general comments. This record can be referred to later, if necessary.

To ensure efficiency, procedures must be established, and meetings must be conducted according to a well-organized plan. The best way to accomplish this is by creating an **agenda,** a list of all topics to be discussed during a meeting. The agenda is usually determined by the leader, either alone or in consultation with the group before each meeting. Sometimes, at the end of a meeting, the agenda for the next meeting is established.

A typical meeting agenda might look like this:

1. Call to order
2. Introduction of new members
3. Reading, correction, and approval of minutes from previous meeting, if any
4. Unfinished business
5. New business
6. Announcements
7. Adjournment

Not all meetings operate in exactly the same way, but having an agenda should make any meeting run smoother. Classroom groups may not follow a formalized structure, but in general, they do need a sense of organization and an informal agenda.

GUIDE TO A SUCCESSFUL MEETING

Do

Identify a purpose; plan an agenda and disseminate it in advance.

Invite only people who need to be present.

Establish start, break, and stop times, and stick to them.

Have a moderator (leader) to keep discussion on track.

Decide what follow-up actions are needed, and set deadlines for them.

Don't

Hold unnecessary meetings.

Invite everyone who might have an opinion on the subject being discussed.

Let people drone on, dominate, or avoid participation in discussions.

Allow conversations to wander off the subject.

Fail to act on decisions made.[16]

MEMBER PARTICIPATION

For a group to be successful, all its members must be actively involved. Just as leaders have certain responsibilities to their groups, so do members. The more the members know about their leader's role, the better equipped they will be to perform their own roles. Furthermore, leadership changes from time to time, so members should be ready to assume greater responsibility if doing so will benefit the group.

Another responsibility of group participants is knowing what is on the agenda, so they can come to meetings prepared to contribute. Meaningful input often calls for research, so each participant should be willing to spend time and energy in advance preparation. Probably one of the greatest weaknesses of beginning group participants is their tendency to arrive at meetings unprepared. The group must then either spend time helping them to catch up or do without their contributions. Either way, valuable time, effort, and input are lost. Successful group outcomes depend upon group-centered behaviors, which enhance participation and member satisfaction, as opposed to self-centered behaviors, which hinder or disrupt participation and lead to member dissatisfaction.

Group-Centered Behaviors

Small group discussions are enhanced when participants exercise group-centered behaviors such as the following:

1. Attitudes of respect and open-mindedness toward others in the group
2. Favorable attitude toward flexible, permissive interaction
3. Awareness of communication barriers and desire to overcome them
4. Awareness of the need for understanding group processes
5. Ability and desire to speak clearly and to the point
6. Understanding of the need for attentive listening
7. Ability to think logically and analytically
8. Desire to cooperate and compromise in order to reach group goals.[17]

Group discussions usually include questions, statements, and exclamations that may be either long or short, and focus on one purpose or many. To be group-centered and to contribute to the group's productivity, all comments should be relevant, related, timely, sufficiently long, clear, informative, open to evaluation, and provocative.[18]

Relevance   Members' comments should pertain to the topic and goals of the discussion at hand and should deviate only when tension needs to be released. All contributions should be relevant either to the task or to some interpersonal need.

Relatedness   A comment cannot be relevant to a task or an interpersonal need without being related to the comments that precede or follow it. A speaker should be able to make an explicit transitional statement, such as "Joe suggested that we change our policy. I agree. Let me provide some additional reasons why we should change," or "Jane indicated that we are in deep financial trouble. That may be so, but before we examine that possibility we should look at the latest data, which suggest that our membership fees are coming in at a much faster rate than last year." The goal of such comments is to make sure that contributions tie in with what has been said before and what is apt to be said next.

Timeliness   Because good ideas can come up at any time, it is helpful to record those that are not appropriate at the moment and then introduce them later, when the timing is right. To give more impact to a good idea you should, introduce it at a favorable time so that it gets the group's full attention and consideration.

Sufficient Length   Choosing the best length for a comment requires good judgment. The goal is to make sure that the comment you contribute is long enough to make your point. Observe the group's reaction to your statements and then act accordingly. Basically, your comments should present your view on a single point, give your reasons for holding that view, and express your judgment of its significance. If you think before you speak, you are more likely to select the most appropriate information and present it clearly and concisely.

Clarity   Always remember that meanings are in people, not in words. Thus, you cannot assume that everyone in the group will understand your idea in the same way that you do. To avoid misunderstandings, define your terms and provide examples to ensure a common ground.

Informativeness   Make sure that your statements are accurate and objective. This requires having a good understanding of the topic and doing prior research. Cite sources of information when appropriate, and select sources that are not biased.

Openness to Evaluation   One of the greatest anxieties group members face is opening their ideas to the group's evaluation. Group discussion can lead to the best possible information and the best possible decision, but this will happen only if members open their comments to evaluation. Criticism should not be ignored or avoided. At the same time, members must remember that evaluations can be constructive only when they focus on the contribution and not on the person. It is one thing to find fault with certain data, and it is quite another thing to find fault with the member who presented the data. Criticism should be based on what was said, not on who said it. To give effective analyses, members should describe and clarify rather than just find fault.

Provocativeness   Comments should be made not only to bring the group closer to its goal, but also to fuel thought for further contributions. Time is important, and we know that one of the disadvantages of small group discussion is that it takes time. However, lack of time should never be the sole reason for closing off discussion if an idea has not been fully discussed and evaluated. Asking questions, challenging ideas, and disagreeing can be valuable contributions as long as their goal is to make the final group product the best one possible.

Self-Centered Behaviors

In most groups, members are eager to make constructive contributions. From time to time, however, you will encounter individuals whose attitudes are not so positive. For the good of the group, it is important to recognize such people and learn how to cope with them. Here are some common self-centered behaviors.

Being Aggressive   Individuals use aggressiveness to deflate the status of others in order to make themselves look better. The aggressor disapproves of the ideas or values of others, attacks the group as a whole, or declares the problem a waste of time.

Blocking   In this role, participants resist, disagree with, and oppose issues beyond reasonableness. They tend to hang onto ideas even after they have been rejected or ruled out by the rest of the group.

Recognition Seeking   People with this attitude must be the center of attention or they are not happy. They are egotistical and try to gain attention by bragging about themselves or their achievements. They want to be the focus of the discussion and believe that everything must be approved by them before it can possibly be accepted by the group.

Self-Confessing Individuals with this trait often contribute irrelevant information about themselves. They frequently recite their past experiences as a means of gaining attention: "When I was in high school, the teachers wanted everyone to be involved in student activities. I didn't think activities were important then, and I certainly don't think they are now."

Acting the Buffoon Some people are constantly joking or engaging in other kinds of horseplay, which is disruptive to the group's accomplishing its goal. Such individuals often show a lack of involvement in what the group is trying to accomplish. Of course, occasional humor may be helpful to release tension or stress in the group. However humor becomes disruptive when it is used to belittle group members or otherwise interferes with the accomplishment of the group's task.

Dominating This kind of conduct is found in persons who want to be in charge of everything. They try to control others through manipulation, flattery, status, constant interruptions, and other means. They enjoy telling other people what to do, but dislike being told what to do by others.

Help-Seeking Some people join groups to satisfy their own personal needs. They try to get sympathy from other group members by expressing their insecurities or by constantly belittling themselves. They may say, "I don't know what to do. I guess I'm not much help to this group" or "I really would like to help, but I'm having so much trouble in my other classes that I haven't had time to do my research on this problem."

Withdrawing Some group members prefer not to participate at all. They choose not to say anything, and so can hardly be considered members of the group. If they are asked for an opinion, they usually say that they do not have one. Whatever the reason—shyness, boredom, failure to prepare, or lack of interest—the withdrawer does little to contribute to the group's success.[19]

Being able to recognize and handle counterproductive contributions is the responsibility not only of the leader, but of each group member. Sometimes the best approach to these situations is to discuss them openly: "John, you sure have been quiet about this problem. What do you think?" "Sally, your jokes seem to indicate that you don't see the issues as very serious. Why?" Sometimes conflict needs to be resolved with a vote by the group. This lets individuals know what the position of the majority is so that discussion can move along.

PROBLEM-SOLVING AND DECISION-MAKING

Although the goal of some discussions, such as those in classrooms, is to share information, the goal of most is to solve problems and make decisions. How can we raise more money for the band to go on a tour? What can we do about the number of uninvited people who are coming into our dorm? Who should be held responsible for date rape? What can be done to eliminate violence from our schools?

When solving problems and making decisions, a group must consider the alternatives and arrive at a joint conclusion. To do this most effectively, they must take an organized and thorough approach to determining the exact nature of the problem and discussing its many aspects and potential solutions.

Determining the Problem

Let us assume that a group has been formed to do a speech classroom assignment. The first step is to select a problem or topic for discussion. This is not always easy—after all, the topic has to be both important and interesting to everyone in the group. A good place to look for ideas might be in areas that need improvement on your own campus: What should be the role of athletics on the campus? Should better protection be provided for students who attend evening classes? The surrounding community is also a source for discussion topics: What can be done about public parking in the downtown area? What does the business community do to help college students get jobs?

State, regional, and national issues can provide a still broader base for topics: Can the state provide sufficient funding to the university? What should be the role of the federal government in providing loans to students? Selecting from thousands of topics and problems takes time. However, if the group does its homework, picking a topic that is agreeable to all members should not be difficult.

After a topic or problem is selected, it should be stated in the form of a question. There are four types of discussion questions: questions of fact, interpretation, value, and policy. A **question of fact** asks whether something is true or false; its answer can be verified. What is the present cost of tuition? How many students are enrolled in each of the various colleges? A **question of interpretation** asks for the meaning or explanation of something. How does the economy of the state affect tuition? How can athletics contribute to a better education? A **question of value** asks whether something is good or bad, desirable or undesirable. Which college offers the best education for its students? Do coeducational dormitories provide satisfactory living conditions? A **question of policy** asks what actions should be taken. What restrictions should be placed on alcohol on campus? What role should students have in evaluating instruction on campus?

Questions of fact leave little room for discussion. The answer can usually be found through research, and unless there are discrepancies in the data, no discussion is required. In contrast, questions of interpretation, value, and policy are not easily answered, and thus make for good discussions.

When phrasing discussion questions, keep the following guidelines in mind:

1. The wording should reflect the discussion purpose.
2. The wording should focus attention on the real problem.
3. The wording should specify whose behavior is subject to change.
4. The wording should not suggest possible solutions.
5. The wording should avoid emotional language.[20]

Procedures for Discussing the Problem

The second step in group problem-solving and decision-making is to determine the plan for discussing the topic as it is specified. The agenda for discussing a problem usually includes five specific steps: definition of the problem, analysis of the problem, suggestions of possible solutions, selection of the best solution, and putting the best solution into operation.[21] Here is an outline of a typical problem-solving discussion.

I. Definition of the problem
   A. *Symptoms.* How does the problem show itself, or what are the difficulties?
   B. *Size.* How large is the problem? Is it increasing or decreasing? What results can be expected if the problem is not solved?
   C. *Goal.* What general state of affairs is desired (in contrast to the present unsatisfactory one)?

II. Analysis of the problem.
   A. *Causes of the problem.* What causes or conditions underlie the difficulties?
   B. *Present efforts to solve the problem.* What is being done now to deal with the problem? In what ways are these efforts unsuccessful? What hints do these efforts provide for further attacks on the problem?

    C. Requirements of a solution

        1. *Direction.* Where shall we attack the problem?

            a. Would an attack on some outstanding symptom be the most fruitful approach?

            b. Is there a cause that would be worthwhile to attack, a cause with these two essential characteristics:

                (1) Would its removal substantially eliminate or greatly modify the problem?

                (2) Could its removal be accomplished with facilities—personnel, equipment, finances—that are (or can be made) available?

    D. *Boundaries.* What other values—social customs, laws, institutions—must not be harmed in attempting to solve this problem?

III. Suggestions of possible solutions

    A. *One possible solution*

        1. *Nature.* What, specifically, is the plan?

        2. *Strengths.* In what ways would this plan effectively fulfill the requirements of a solution, that is, make notable progress in the right direction and stay satisfactorily within the boundaries of a solution?

        3. *Weaknesses.* In what ways would this plan fall short of effectively fulfilling these requirements?

    B. *Another possible solution*

    C. *Another possible solution*

    D. *Another possible solution*

IV. Selection of the best solution

    A. *Best solution (or solution with modifications).* How does this solution excel over others?

    B. *Part of problem unsolved.* If solution leaves any part unsolved, why is it still considered the best?

V. Putting the best solution into operation

    A. *Major difficulties to be faced*

    B. *Possible ways of overcoming difficulties*

    C. *Best way to overcome difficulties*

This approach is widely accepted for more formal problem-solving discussions, such as those you may be required to develop for ideas. A more informal way of discussing a problem—one that might be appropriate for other school, work, and social groups—included the following steps.[22]

1. Ventilation. Group members come together and vent their feelings and beliefs about the problem or task.

2. Clarification. After venting their feelings, group members identify the exact problem and try to express it so that all members have the same understanding of it.

3. Fact-finding. Group members collect all the information they can on the problem. The information should help them identify the cause(s) of the problem.

4. Discovery. Group develops possible solutions for the problem under discussion.

5. Evaluation. Group assesses the solutions it has generated. Groups commonly have difficulty in holding off the evaluation process, but it is wise to keep from evaluating too early in the process.

6. Decision-making. Group makes its decision, based on its evaluation of what would be the best possible solution.

EXERCISE

In your opinion, is each of the following an advantage or a disadvantage of small group communication? Justify your responses.

1. **Two heads are frequently better than one.**
2. **Small group communication requires interpersonal communication skills.**
3. **Working in a small group limits individual responsibility.**
4. **People are more likely to carry out decisions that they have helped to make.**
5. **Group decision-making and problem-solving takes time.**
6. **Working in a group can help to satisfy social needs.**
7. **Membership in a group can change individual attitudes and behavior.**

Sometimes groups find themselves unable to generate new ideas or to be creative in solving a particular aspect of a problem. In such cases, they may find brainstorming (also discussed in Chapter 7) helpful. **Brainstorming,** a technique used to generate as many ideas as possible within a limited amount of time, can be used during any phase of the group discussion process to produce topics, information, or solutions to problems. Whenever a group stops progressing because it is unable to generate new ideas, it should consider brainstorming. During the brainstorming session, group members throw out as many ideas as possible pertaining to their discussion, no matter how farfetched they might seem. One person records the ideas for later analysis. The leader lets the comments flow freely. Once the group has freed itself from stale thinking and gained a new perspective, it should continue its discussion as planned.

GUIDELINES FOR PRODUCTIVE BRAINSTORMING

1. Don't criticize any idea.
2. No idea is too wild.
3. Quantity is important.
4. Seize opportunities to improve on or to add to ideas suggested by others.[23]

EXERCISE

Divide into small groups and brainstorm the following problem: There are only 500 parking places on campus but there are 1,000 requests for parking.

Limit the brainstorming session to 10 minutes. Share your group's ideas with the rest of the class.

EVALUATING SMALL GROUP PERFORMANCE

To ensure its success, every group must periodically evaluate itself. Here are some questions that every group leader and every group member should ask.

1. Are we using our time efficiently? If not, why not?
2. Does everyone have an opportunity to participate?
3. Are some people dominating the discussion?
4. Are people listening to what others are saying?
5. Is each person bringing adequate information and research to the discussion?
6. Is the atmosphere free from personal conflict?
7. Does the group's communication stay within the agenda?
8. Are the members happy about what is taking place in the discussion? If not, why not?
9. Do we set realistic goals for our meetings?
10. Do we get things accomplished? If not, why not?

For an evaluation to produce results, its findings must be made known to all the members of the group. A crucial requirement for such sharing is a nonthreatening atmosphere. The leader and all the members must be willing to examine what is going on without becoming defensive. The group's success is related to each member's willingness to work and to cooperate with the others. If the group is not getting its job done, or if some or all members are unhappy, corrective steps must be taken. Otherwise people will lose interest in the group and it will disintegrate.

SUMMARY

Small group communication is the exchange of information that occurs among a relatively small number of persons (usually three to thirteen persons) who share a common purpose, such as doing a job or solving a problem. Small group communication serves a wide range of purposes that can be arranged in two categories: personal purposes and task-related purposes. Personal purposes include socialization, catharsis, therapy, and learning; task-related purposes include decision-making and problem-solving.

A *group* is a collection of individuals whose members influence one another, derive mutual satisfaction from one another, have a common purpose, take on roles, are interdependent, and interact face-to-face. Some groups may take on irrational actions or risks that a lone, rational individual wouldn't take is referred to as a *risky shift phenomenon.*

Several characteristics make the small group a unique context for communication. They are *interdependence* (mutual dependence), *common goal* (a driving force), *group personality* (a collective identity), *commitment* (the desire to work together), *cohesiveness* (attraction/commitment)—groups sometimes can become too cohesive, resulting in *groupthink* (a dysfunction in which the harmony of the group is more important than other considerations), *conflict:* (a clash or fight, or incompatable desires, ideas, or opinions), *social facilitation* (release of energy), *group size* (the number of participants), and *norms* (expected and shared behavior).

Leadership is any behavior that helps to clarify, guide, or achieve the goals of a group. A *leader* is a person assigned or selected to guide the group or provide direction towards the group's goal. There is a body of research related to gender differences and leadership which provides no definitive answers, but does suggest potential differences between male and female leaders. The research indicates that female leaders might show more concern for interpersonal relations and tend to be more democratic in their style than men. Further, women may possess better interpersonal skills than men, but the advantages and disadvantages of any of the research findings might not necessarily mean better leadership. When conducting a meeting, the leader is often responsible for setting as well as carrying out the *agenda,* which is a list of all the topics to be discussed during a meeting.

The leader's approach affects the atmosphere within the group as well as its effectiveness and efficiency in making decisions. Research indicates that the democratic leadership style is superior to the autocratic style in getting the task done and satisfying the group members. Autocratic leaders are able to produce more, but also seem to generate more hostility and aggression among group members. Laissez-faire groups tend to accomplish less, produce work of lower quality, and waste more time. To be most effective, a leader must know how to use all three leadership styles and know how to match the appropriate style to the individual situation.

Leaders are responsible for keeping things going, organizing discussion, promoting interpersonal relationships, facilitating understanding, and stimulating creativity. In addition, they must be able to meet group members' *task needs* (needs related to getting the task completed), and *maintenance needs* (needs related to the personal satisfaction of working together). The leader is also responsible for setting and carrying out the *agenda,* which is a list of all the topics to be discussed during a meeting.

Group-centered behaviors are critical to the success of any group. To obtain the best results, participants should possess specific traits: open-mindedness toward others, flexibility, awareness of communication barriers, understanding of the group process, ability to speak clearly and to point, willingness to listen attentively, capacity to think logically and analytically, and readiness to cooperate and compromise. Members' comments should be relevant, related, timely, sufficiently long, clear, informative, open to evaluation, and provocative.

Self-centered behaviors can interfere with a group's productivity and effectiveness. They are: being aggressive, blocking, seeking recognition, self-confessing, acting the buffoon, dominating, seeking help, and withdrawing. Group members should recognize such behaviors and help the leader to control them.

Problem-solving and decision-making require a systematic approach if the best conclusions are to be reached. The first step in the process of decision-making is to determine the problem or topic, which should then be stated in the form of a question. Questions are of four types: a *question of fact* asks whether something is true or false; a *question of interpretation* asks for the meaning or understanding of something; a *question of value* asks whether something is good or bad, desirable or undesirable; and a *question of policy* asks what actions should be taken.

Once the discussion question is clearly formulated, it is time to select a procedure for discussing the problem. There are two common methods of solving problems and making decisions. The first and more formal approach includes five steps: (1) definition of the problem, (2) analysis of the problem, (3) suggestions of possible solutions, (4) selection of the best solution, and (5) putting the best solution into operation. The second and more informal approach includes six steps: (1) ventilation, (2) clarification, (3) fact finding, (4) discovery, (5) evaluation, and (6) decision making.

When a group hits a snag in the problem-solving or decision-making process, *brainstorming* can help them generate new ideas. The keys to productive brainstorming are openness and creativity.

Evaluation is a key step in ensuring a group's progress and success. For an evaluation to accomplish its purpose, the leader and all group members must be willing to accept its findings and then to take the appropriate corrective steps.

KEY TERMS

Agenda: List of all topics to be discussed during a meeting.
Autocratic leader: Leader who keeps complete control and makes all the decisions for the group.

Brainstorming: Technique for generating as many ideas as possible within a limited amount of time.

Cohesiveness: Attraction that group members feel for each other and their willingness to stick together; a form of loyalty.

Commitment: Desire of group members to work together to get their task completed to the satisfaction of the entire group.

Common goal: The driving force that brings people together to form a group.

Conflict: A clash or fight, or incompatable desires, ideas, or opinions.

Democratic Leader: Leader who guides and directs, but shares control and remains open to all views.

Group: Collection of individuals who form a system in which members influence one another, derive mutual satisfaction from one another, have a common purpose, take on roles, are interdependent, and interact face-to-face.

Group personality: Collective identity that members of a group form when they come together.

Group Size: Number of participants involved in a given group communication.

Groupthink: A dysfunction in which group members see the harmony of the group as being more important than new ideas, the critical examination of ideas, the willingness to change decisions, or the willingness to allow new members to participate.

Interdependence: Mutual dependence of group members up on one another.

Laissez-faire Leader: Leader who gives complete decision-making freedom to the group or to individual members.

Leader: Person assigned or selected to lead or provide direction in order to reach a group's goals.

Leadership: Any behavior that helps to clarify, guide, or achieve a group's goals; the ability to exert influence over others.

Maintenance need: Need related to organizing and developing a group so that the members can realize personal satisfaction from working together.

Norms: Expected and shared ways in which group members behave.

Question of Fact: Question that asks what is true or false.

Question of Interpretation: Question that asks for the meaning or explanation of something.

Question of Policy: Question that asks what actions should be taken.

Question of Value: Question that asks whether something is good or bad, desirable or undesirable.

Relationship-oriented Leader: Leader who attempts to obtain a position of prominence and create good interpersonal relationships.

Risky shift phenomenon: Tendency for groups to take action that alone, rational individual wouldn't take.

Small group communication: Exchange of information among a relatively small number of persons (usually three to thirteen person), who share a common purpose, such as doing a job or solving a problem.

Social facilitation: Tendency for a person acting in a group to release energy which would not be released if the person were acting alone.

Task Needs: Needs related to the content of a task and all behaviors that lead to the completion of the task.

Task-oriented leader: Leader who gains satisfaction from performing the task.

DISCUSSION STARTERS

1. Why is it important to have good group communication skills?
2. What are the relationships between personal and task-related purposes in small group communication?
3. What are some personal goals that would not permit you to accept conflicting group goals under certain circumstances?
4. What makes a group?
5. Which group characteristic do you think is the most important? Why?
6. Describe a group in which you have participated that illustrates the characteristic of cohesiveness.
7. What are the effects of group size?
8. Describe at least two norms that are operating in your class.
9. What role does small group communication play in your daily activities?
10. Do the advantages of a group outweigh the disadvantages? Explain.
11. Why is leadership so important to the success of small groups?
12. Are leadership and leader the same? Explain.
13. Do you think there are differences between male and female leadership styles? Explain.
14. What is the best way to identify a leader?
15. Which leadership style is the most appropriate for small group discussions? Why?
16. In what ways can leadership affect small group communication?
17. What are the functions of a leader in a small group?
18. What are the responsibilities of a group participant?
19. Explain the differences between constructive and counterproductive contributions by group members.
20. Who is responsible for handling counterproductive contributions?
21. How specifically would you handle a group member who was acting the role of a buffoon?
22. How would you lead withdrawn group members back into a discussion without embarrassing them?
23. How would you organize a discussion on the following topic: What should be the role and responsibility of students in monitoring drug use on campus?

24. Describe a situation in which the use of brainstorming would be appropriate.
25. How would you go about evaluating a small group discussion?

NOTES

1. M. E. Shaw, *Group Dynamics: The Psychology of Small Group Behavior*, 2d ed. (New York: McGraw-Hill, 1976): 6–10.
2. J. K. Brilhart, *Effective Group Discussion*, 5th ed. (Dubuque, IA: Wm. C. Brown, 1986): 21.
3. R. V. Harnack, T. B. Fest, and B. S. Jones, *Group Discussion Theory and Technique*, 2d ed. (Englewood Cliffs, NJ.: Prentice-Hall, 1977) 25–28; and J. K. Brilhart and G. J. Galanes, *Effective Group Discussion*, 7th ed. (Dubuque, IA: Wm. C. Brown, 1992): 10, 169–171.
4. L. Coch and J.R.P. French, Jr., "Overcoming Resistance to Change," in *Group Dynamics: Research and Theory*, ed. D. Cartwright and A. Zander, 2d ed. (Evanston, Ill.: Row Peterson, 1960): 319–341.
5. I. L. Janis, Groupthink: Psychological Studies of Policy Decisions and Fiascoes, 2d ed. (Boston: Houghton Mifflin, 1983).
6. L. P. Stewart, A. D. Stewart, S. A. Friedley, and P. J. Cooper, Communication *Between the Sexes: Sex Differences and Sex Role Stereotypes*, 2d ed. (Scottsdale, AZ: Gorsuch Scarisbrick, 1990): 43–114; D. N. Maltz and R. A. Borker, "A Cultural Approach to Male-Female Miscommunication," in *Language and Social Identity*, ed. J. J. Gumperz (Cambridge: Cambridge University Press, 1982): 195–216; E. Baird, "Sex Differences in Group Communication: A Review of Relevant Research," *Quarterly Journal of Speech* 62 (1976): 179–92.
7. F. B. Meeker and P. A. Weitzel-O'Neil, "Sex Roles and Interpersonal Behavior in Task-Oriented Groups," *American Sociological Review* 42 (1977): 91–105; R. L. Hoffman and N. K. V. Maier, "Quality and Acceptance of Problem Solutions by Members of Homogeneous and Heterogeneous Groups," *Journal of Abnormaland Social Psychology* 62 (1961): 401–7.
8. J. C. McCroskey, V. P. Richmond, and R. A. Stewart, *One on One: The Foundations of Interpersonal Communication* (Englewood Cliffs, NJ: Prentice-Hall, 1986): 244–47; M. E. Roloff, "The Impact of Socialization on Sex Differences in Conflict Resolution" (paper presented at the Annual Convention of the International Communication Association, Acapulco, Mexico, May, 1980); E. A. Mabry, "Some Theoretical Implications of Female and Male Interaction in Unstructured Small Groups," *Small Group Behavior* 20 (1989): 536–50; W. E. Jurma and B. C. Wright, "Follower Reactions to Male and Female Leaders Who Maintain or Lose Reward Power," *Small Group Research* 21 (1990): 97–112.
9. J. Bond and W. Vinacke, "Coalition in Mixed Sex Triads," *Sociometry* 24 (1961): 61–65; B. A. Fisher, "Differential Effects of Sexual Composi-

tion Interaction Patterns in Dyads," *Human Communication Research* 9 (1983): 225–38; W. E. Jurma and B. C. Wright, "Follower Reactions to Male and Female Leaders Who Maintain or Lose Reward Power," *Small Group Research* 21 (1990): 97–112; D. J. Canary and Brian H. Spitzberg, "Appropriateness and Effectiveness Perceptions of Conflict Strategies," *Human Communication Research* 14 (1987): 93–118.

10. R. Bostrum, "Patterns of Communicative Interaction in Small Groups," *Speech Monographs* 37 (1970): 257–263.

11. F. E. Fiedler, *A Theory of Leadership Effectiveness* (New York: McGraw-Hill, 1967).

12. R. K. White and R. Lippitt, *Autocracy and Democracy: An Experimental Inquiry* (New York: Harper & Row, 1960): 26–27.

13. R. K. White and R. Lippitt, "Leader Behavior and Member Reaction in Three 'Social Climates,'" in *Group Dynamics: Research and Theory,* ed. Dorwin Cartwright and Alvin Zarda, 2d ed. (New York: Harper & Row, 1960): 527–553; L. P. Bradford and R. Lippitt, "Building a Democratic Work Group, *Personnel* 22 (1945) 142–152; and W. M. Fox, "Group Reaction to Two Types of Conference Leadership," *Human Relations* 10 (1957): 279–289.

14. M. Loden, *Feminine Leadership, or How to Succeed in Business Without Being One of the Boys,* (New York: Times Books, 1985).

15. A. H. Eagly and R. T. Johnson, "Gender and Leadership Style: A Meta-Analysis," *Psychological Bulletin* 108 (1990): 233–256.

16. Harrison Conference Services, business schools at University of Georgia, Georgia State University.

17. M. H. Farwell, "An Explanation of a Televised Method of Teaching Group Process" (Unpublished master's thesis, The Pennsylvania State University, University Park, 1964).

18. R. V. Harnack, T. B. Fest, and B. S. Jones, *Group Discussion: Theory and Technique,* 2d ed. (Englewood Cliffs, NJ: Prentice-Hall, 1977): 202–203.

19. K. D. Benne and P. Sheats, "Functional Roles of Group Members," *Journal of Social Issues* 4 (1948): 41–49.

20. Harnack, Fest, and Jones, *Group Discussion,* 153–154.

21. Dewey, *How We Think* (Lexington, MA: Heath, 1933).

22. D. Barnlund and F. S. Haiman, *The Dynamics of Discussion* (Boston: Houghton Mifflin, 1960): 86–91.

23. A. Osborn, *Applied Imagination: Principles and Procedures of Creative Thinking* (New York: Scribner, 1953): 300–301.

Chapter 16

Employment Interviewing: Preparing for Your Future

LEARNING OBJECTIVES

After studying this chapter, you should be able to:

1. Describe the qualities that employers seek in applicants.

2. Develop a résumé that will make a good impression on prospective employers.

3. Research a company to determine its background, products, location, and future.

4. Conduct yourself effectively in an employment interview.

*B*ill, *who is graduating in May, is looking for a public relations position with a major corporation. He has called Mr. Muller, the personnel director of S & S Enterprises, to discuss his chances of being hired by that firm.*

Liz is looking for an internship in marketing in order to get some experience before she goes into the real job hunt. She has contacted several marketing firms through her university internship office and is ready to be interviewed.

Sam needs to earn a few dollars in order to make it through college. He decides to get a part-time job and is scheduled to interview with a local clothing store.

The students in these examples will participate in interviews that will impact the rest of their lives. In this chapter, we will look at the employment interview—what you as a job hunter can expect to encounter and how you can prepare to make the best impression.[1]

PREPARING FOR JOB HUNTING

The purpose of this book is to help you with the following skills: speaking, organizing, critical thinking, researching, persuading, informing, listening, discussing, making decisions, solving problems, and using verbal and nonverbal language. Another purpose is to help you develop your leadership and interpersonal skills. After you have completed this course, it will then be up to you to continue developing each skill throughout your education and your lifetime. Because employment interviews are among the most important interpersonal communication events of your life, an entire chapter has been devoted to them.

THINK ABOUT IT ▮▮▮▮▮

SKILLS! That one word means a lot to your future. The experts we surveyed repeatedly emphasized "skills" and "competencies" rather than specific studies.

Your major alone may not make a decisive difference in your future, but the skills you master and the way you communicate them to others can carry you through a lifetime of careers.[2]

In your opinion, what is the message embedded in the above statements?

Most of you taking this course are probably just beginning your college education. Whether you are a recent high school graduate or someone who has returned to school after pursuing other interests, the following pages about employment interviews will give you important information that will aid you in preparing for your future after graduation. Although graduation and hunting for a full-time job may seem far away, your preparation for them should begin now. You can begin by attending your university's or community's career day programs. Such programs bring undergraduates, graduate students, and alumni/alumnal together with employers from government, private enterprise, and nonprofit organizations. It is a time for even freshmen to find out what organizations in various fields are looking for in potential employees. Don't wait until you are a senior to begin researching this information.

Choosing a career may be the most important decision you will ever make. (See Figure 16.1) An estimated 10,000 days of your lifetime are at stake—that's about how much time the average person spends on the job. According to some experts, there are a minimum of 42,000 career options for college students to choose from. However, today's college graduates are finding that the number of job candidates often exceeds the number of professional openings available in many career fields. The prediction by *Ford's Insider Newspaper* is that employment opportunities are expected to increase 15 percent by the year 2000 but the number of college graduates entering the labor force will continue to exceed the number of openings. Most jobs through the year 2000 will become available as a result of replacing existing workers.[3] Thus, even occupations with little or no employment growth, or slower than average employment growth, still have many job openings and will continue to have openings for the right individuals.

Studying the following pages will not guarantee you the perfect job after graduation, but it should improve your chances of landing it. Approximately 150 million employment interviews are conducted in the United

Figure 16.1:

The employment interview is one of the most important communication events in most people's lives. It is important that you are prepared to discuss your goals and skills.

Barbara Filet/Tony Stone Images

States each year. To compete successfully for available jobs requires planning and preparation—now, rather than at the time of graduation.

In order to learn first-hand what corporations are looking for today when they hire a college graduate, I interviewed Gary Danek, a Unit Manager at Proctor and Gamble, a "Fortune 500" corporation. We spoke for the first time in the fall of 1991 and then again, to update our first interview, in November of 1994. Danek has been with Proctor and Gamble for more than twenty-five years and has interviewed hundreds of college students. Here are some excepts from both of our conversations:

Dr. S.: What advice would you give to first- or second-year students to help them prepare for an employment interview after they have graduated?

Mr. D.: I would suggest students, besides getting good grades, should participate in as many activities as time will allow. Activities are important because they create a much more rounded individual who is interested in working with others. Students should try to get into leadership positions whenever possible. This will show they have an ability to take charge of things and to influence others which is critical for success in most careers. The key here is that students get involved in activities early and often. I realize that some students must work full- or part-time and that's okay. But even then, they should be more than just someone putting time in on the job. They should take initiative and begin to show their leadership and decision making potential.

I also would highly recommend that they take both oral and written communication courses, because, in order to succeed, students must be able to communicate effectively.

Students need to be able to demonstrate that they can set specific goals that can be measured within a particular time frame. This is often done via leadership roles or personal motivation to get things done. The goal should be more than just getting a college degree. Getting a degree should be a goal of everyone who enters college. Most employers will look at the quantity and quality of the students' experiences.

Dr. S.: Can you give me some examples of specific goals that can be measured within a time frame?

Mr. D.: Yes. For example, a student may work for a school newspaper and be responsible for getting businesses to buy advertising space in the paper. The job might require the student to get ten ads per semester. The student sets her goal to get fifteen ads. Here the student has taken initiative and set her own goal. Naturally, any thing above the ten required is going beyond the newspaper's expectation. By setting realistic goals and accomplishing them, this student is showing that she is motivated. She is also demonstrating that she can influence people by getting them to buy ads in the school paper. Accomplishing her goal shows employers some very important behaviors that they look for in potential employees: goal setting, going beyond what everyone else is expected to accomplish, and an ability to influence others in order to reach her goal.

Dr. S.: What are the specific criteria or qualities employers look for in those they hire?

Mr. D.: The selection criteria differ from company to company, but his company criteria are based upon the same factors they use for job performance reviews. For example, initiative and follow-through, leadership, thinking and problem solving, communication, working effectively with others, creativity and innovation, and priority setting are important skills.

Dr. S.: Of the criteria you describe which do you believe to be the most important?

Mr. D.: Communication—without effective communication a person would not be able to meet all the other criteria.

Dr. S.: What is the typical first interview like?

Mr. D.: The first interview often takes place on campus and lasts about twenty to thirty minutes. Most employers are usually interested in learning if the applicant (student) has the qualities and skills to be successful.

Dr. S.: What are some typical questions you might ask in the first interview?

Mr. D.: To determine whether an applicant (student) meets the criteria I described earlier. For example, to explore *initiative and follow-through* (achieving goals) I would ask: Give me an example of a situation where you had to overcome major obstacles to achieve your objective. Or, tell me about a goal you set that took a long time to achieve or that you're still working towards. For *leadership* I might ask: Tell me about a time when you were able to step into a situation, take charge, muster support, and bring about excellent results. Or, tell me about a time when you accomplished something significant that wouldn't have happened if you hadn't been there to make it happen. For *thinking and problem solving,* I might ask: Tell me about a time when you had to analyze facts quickly, define the key issues, and develop a plan which produced good results. Or, tell me about a complex problem you solved, and, if you had to do that activity over again, how you would do it differently. For *communication* (selling or motivating, listening and speaking), I might ask: Tell me about a situation where you had to be persuasive and sell your idea to someone else. Or, tell me about a time when you had to present a proposal to a person in authority and were able to do this successfully. For *working effectively with others* (teamwork), I might ask: Can you give me an example which would show you've been able to develop and maintain productive relations with others, even though they may have different points of view? Or, tell me about a time when you were able to motivate others to get the desired results. For *creativity and innovation* (improving productivity, using resources), I might ask: Tell me about a situation in which you were able to find a new and better way of doing something significant. Or, describe a time when you were able to come up with a new idea that was the key to the success of some activity or project. For *priority setting,* I might ask: Tell me about a time when you had to balance many competing priorities and did so successfully. Or, tell me about a time when you had to pick out the most important things in some activity and make sure those got done.

Dr. S.: How important is the résumé?

Mr. D.: Very important! It should be done neatly and should clearly state the applicant's (student's) work experiences as well as the activities he or she has participated in while in school.

Dr. S.: What are the major reasons for rejecting an applicant?

Mr. D.: Usually it is because the applicant (student) hasn't met any of the selection criteria, lacks organizational skills, cannot communicate effectively, or lacks self-confidence.

Dr. S.: What, if any, questions should an applicant avoid asking during the first interview?

Mr. D.: An applicant should not ask about salary, how many hours will I work, how many sick days are there, is there an expense account, or how much vacation time will I get? These questions indicate the person is not interested in working but in what he or she can get from the job or how he or she can get out of work.

Dr. S.: What are some appropriate questions for the applicant to ask?

Mr. D.: What is the typical day like for a person who has this job, how do you get people to do what you want, are there opportunities for training or additional schooling, why is the company moving into this market, and so on. All of these questions indicate an interest in the company and the job.

Dr. S.: Finally, what specifically are you looking for in an applicant?

Mr. D.: A person who can juggle many balls at one time and do it well. That is, most companies need individuals who are able to address many issues and deal with a variety of people and to it successfully.

It should be clear from what Danek says that there is great deal that you can do to prepare yourself for the employment interview. No matter if you are a first year student or a graduating senior, it is important that you start preparing today for the interview.

Dr. Larry Routh, Director of Career Services at the University of Nebraska-Lincoln, suggests that students get as much experience in team-building and working in teams as possible. Companies are no longer looking exclusively for people with supervisory skills, increasingly they are looking for individuals who can work with others. One company recruiter asks students the following question: "When you work as a part of a team, what unique role do you play?" One senior student answered this question by indicating that she was the person who brought the group back to task by clarifying and pulling the group ideas to the objective. Routh suggested that his own strength is the ability to transform ideas when working on a team. Routh's strength is quite different from the senior student's, but both are important to team success. "Hiring people who are team players is important to many companies who have downsized said Dr. Routh "They have fewer management openings because they are becoming more team-oriented."

What is your role when working with others? Is it leading, organizing, brainstorming, or something else? You need to identify what your strengths are.

Internships are also important. Dr. Routh suggests that as soon as possible, students should get involved in internships related to the jobs they will seek after graduation. He says that students who can say that they have done the same or similar work will have a better chance of getting the job than those with no experience.

QUALITIES EMPLOYERS SEEK

Demographics of our nation's workplace are changing rapidly as we move into the next century. Women now make up 50 percent of the workforce, and there has also been significant growth in Hispanic and Asian working populations. In addition, people are living longer and working longer. What does this mean to you? It means that you will be facing increased competition because there will be more applicants for the jobs available. Because many organizations are reducing management positions, advancement positions are going to be fewer and much more difficult to get. In the past, college graduates who started on the ground floor of an organization were almost guaranteed that by working hard they could move up the corporate ladder to higher management positions. Now, higher management jobs are fewer and there is keen competition for those that are available.

The typical employee of the '60s, '70, and 80s stayed with the same company for 20, 30, or 40 years. During this period, individuals made career changes only two or three times. Today, however, a typical college graduate can expect to change jobs, from five to seven times. These trends are causing organizations to rethink how—and who—they are going to hire. Employers are increasingly concerned with their organizational culture and with hiring someone who is right, not for a specific position but for the organization in general.[4]

Listed below are qualities today's employers are looking for in prospective employees.

1. You must not only have specific job skills but be able to handle rapid change and periods of job ambiguity.

2. You must have computer literacy that enables you to enter, extract, and input data using common computer systems.

3. You must have a global perspective and understand other cultures.

4. You must have interpersonal skills, both to secure a position and to move up in an organization.[5]

Almost every career requires such skills as writing, speaking, reading, listening, decision-making, organizing researching, reasoning, creativity, persuasiveness and, leadership. In addition, certain other characteristics may be important in all careers: desire to achieve, aggressiveness, ambition, dependability, discipline, honesty, initiative, motivation, orientation to people, persistence, responsibility, self-confidence, ability to be a self-starter, sensitivity, sincerity, tenacity, and tough-mindedness.[6] The way you acquire the necessary skills, traits, and behaviors is largely up to you. Without them, no matter how bright and knowledgeable you may be, landing a job is extremely difficult, if not impossible. The most likely ways of obtaining these skills and behaviors are through courses, reading, internships, part-time or full-time employment, extracurricular activities, and participation in communication functions. Acquiring most of them requires training and practice under a qualified instructor.

Knowing what an employer is looking for in a potential employee can help an applicant prepare for an interview. Most employers that I have talked with emphasize the ability to communicate. Can people speak clearly? Can they articulate what kind of person they believe themselves to be? In what kinds of work situations do they perform well? What are their strengths and weaknesses? Employers want to know about the personal qualities of the individual, so they ask questions designed to draw him or her out and reveal whether the applicant has a sense of himself or herself. One thing they look for is the ability to verbalize an idea in clear, simple, understandable language. They also look for the ability to listen attentively and then respond to the idea or thought presented to them.

They also look for creativity. Is the applicant spontaneous? Some recruiters will ask a few "off-the-wall" questions just to see if this "throws" an applicant. How does an applicant respond in these tough situations? Can the applicant be creative in his or her answers? This, is very important to most employers, because in business situations with customers, employees often have to respond to sudden changes and problems that they may not be familiar with. Employers need to know whether an applicant can handle such situations.

What employers look for most are personal qualities—assertiveness, self-motivation, drive, ambition, and a competitive instinct. Applicants should be high achievers and should want to work hard. Employers say they can usually tell about these qualities from how the person presents himself or herself and from reviewing the activities he or she has engaged in. Much of this information can be found right on the job application and résumé.

How the applicant has written his or her résumé is very important.

PREPARATION FOR AN INTERVIEW

Preparation for a job interview takes planning; it also takes thought about what will be expected of you as an applicant. Initial job interviews average only twenty to thirty minutes—a short time in comparison to the time spent earning a college degree. Yet these are probably the most important minutes you will spend in determining your job future. You would be surprised to learn how many applicants fail to plan adequately. Instead, many enter the interview essentially saying, "Here I am. Now what?" This gives the just impression that they are indifferent—an impression that can seldom be dispelled in the course of the interview. Ensuring that an impression of indifference isn't left with the interviewer is up to you. Make sure that you are prepared and that you present a positive picture of yourself.

Writing a Résumé

A **résumé** (sometimes referred to as a vitae) is a written document that briefly and accurately describes an individual's personal, educational, and professional qualifications and experiences (See Figure 16.2). A well written résumé increases a person's chances of making a good impression. A poorly written résumé can seriously jeopardize a person's chances, even though he or she may be well qualified. The résumé should clearly detail the experiences the applicant has had and demomstrate that he or she is an individual who takes action. For example, an assertive person might say, "I can do these things" and "I decided on this course of action," whereas a more passive person might say, "These are the experiences I have had." Employers are looking for people who demonstrate that they can do things and get them done.

Many companies are now requesting that résumés be written in such a way that they can be scanned and placed into a computer database. This means that résumés must include key words that describe your competencies and skills. The employer is then able quickly and efficiently to search thousands of résumés for certain key words and narrow down a long list of potentially qualified applicants for a specific job. So that it can be scanned, a résumé must be typed neatly on a high-quality white bond paper. Some applicants have their résumé reproduced at a local print shop or create on a word processor to obtain an even more professional look.

There are two kinds of résumés: the standard data sheet used by most placement and employment services (See Figure 16.3) and the self-prepared, or personal, résumé. The personal résumé may highlight work experience (See Figure 16.4) or skills (See Figure 16.5.) In addition, many employment agencies and companies also require applicants to complete an application form, which requests personal data (name, address, phone number, social security number, citizenship, and whether you have ever been convicted of a felony), job interests (position desired, date available, and salary desired), educational training (high school, college, or graduate school), references (name of reference and person's occupation, phone

THE WIZARD OF ID   Brant parker and Johnny hart

By permission of Johnny Hart and Creators Syndicate, Inc.

Figure 16.2:

Résumés reflect who you are and your qualifications for the job. Employers want to know a person's qualifications and the résumé, if done concisely and accurately, is an invaluable tool for creating a favorable impression.

Standard Data Sheet

PERSONAL DATA FORM

Name _____   Social Security Number _____
        Last   First   Middle

Present Mailing Address _____   _____
        Street / Box   City   State   Zip   (Area Code)   Phone Number

Permanent Address _____   _____
        Street / Box   City   State   Zip   (Area Code)   Phone Number

CAREER OBJECTIVE _____

EDUCATION

    University   Major   Degree   Date

Areas Of Concentration And/Or Certification _____

Percent Of College Expenses Earned By: Working _____ Scholarships _____ Other _____
                                              (Specify)

Citizen _____ Non-Citizen _____ Type Of Visa _____

Position (Include Student Teaching Experience If Applicable) Acquired Skills   Dates   Employer/Organization

EXPERIENCE

LOCATION PREFERENCES: Flexible _____ Restricted _____ Location _____

ACTIVITIES, HONORS, AND OTHER INFORMATION:

I hereby authorize the CPPC to release this data sheet and related information including references, to any and all prospective employers and/or institutions of higher learning.

_____   _____
            Signature   Date

number, and address), employment history (name and address of business, dates of employment, salary received, position held, and reason for leaving), and possibly voluntary information (sex, race, or ethnic identification; military service; whether you are a veteran or disabled veteran; and whether you are handicapped). Computer database approaches can match your qualifications and interests with the requirements of companies and businesses nationwide.

A résumé is an extremely powerful form of communication. Because it represents the applicant, it must be accurate, complete, and neat. The contents and layouts of résumés vary almost as widely as the number of individuals who apply for jobs. The safest general rules, are *to keep it simple, to limit it to one or two pages, and to list items within each section, beginning with most recent.* Employers are busy and do not have time to read lengthy, involved reports.

Most résumés include the following sections: introductory information, career objective, educational training, work experiences, extracurricular activities, and references. The *introductory information* section should include the applicant's name, address, and phone number. As an applicant, you are not required to provide information that might lead to discrimination. Such information includes your age, sex, marital status, race, religion, and other data set forth in The Title VII Equal Employment Opportunity Act of 1972 and other affirmative-action laws. Including such facts in a résumé is up to the applicant, but it is generally advised that they be omitted.

Many placement-service directors recommend that a brief *career objective* be stated on the résumé immediately following the introductory information. This objective should be as specific as possible. For example:

> My long-term objective is to become a public relations director in either a major corporation or a recognized agency. My immediate goal is to obtain experience in sales, advertising, or marketing related to that long-term objective.

Such a statement can help a potential employer understand the applicant's goals and assess how those goals can be met by the company.

In the *educational training* section of the résumé, the applicant should list colleges and universities attended, degrees conferred, dates of degrees, majors, minors, and special major subjects. Scholarships should be listed, and a statement about grade achievement may be included, although it is not required.

The *work experience* section should include all paid and unpaid jobs held, the dates they were held, and their locations. If the applicant has held numerous part-time jobs, only a few of the most important, most recent, and most relevant jobs should be listed. Other job experience can always be discussed at the interview, if it is appropriate to do so.

In the *extracurricular activities* section the applicant should list all offices held, all social and professional organizations that he or she has been involved in, and any athletic participation. The purpose of this section is to demonstrate the applicant's outside interests, well-roundedness, and social, leadership, and organizational skills. Such information is less important for experienced or older applicants who have demonstrated similar skills in other areas.

The *reference* section should simply state that the applicant will provide references upon request. In preparation, you might make a list of persons who are familiar with your work experience and professors in your major field or with whom you have taken several courses. Even though you may not be planning to apply for a job now, it is wise to get to know your professors and to make sure that they get to know you. Find an

Self-prepared or Personal Résumé Emphasizing Work Experience

Jo Ann Doe
712 Garfield Street, Apt. 2-A
Lincoln, Nebraska 68508
402/484-9797

OBJECTIVE

An administrative assistant position in a federal, state, or city government agency where I can utilize my public relations skills.

EXPERIENCE

<u>Assistant Campaign Manager:</u> Senator Jack Kay, Lincoln, Nebraska (July 1992-November 1994).

Responsible for directing and coordinating all publicity activities.
Arranged and scheduled personal appearances, debates, and media releases.
Purchased, designed, and supervised the development of campaign materials.
Recruited, trained, and supervised community volunteer groups.
Supervised a staff of 16 community volunteers.

<u>Staff Assistant as an Intern:</u> United Volunteer Agency, Lincoln, Nebraska (December 1991-June 1992).

Responsible for communicating the scope of Agency programs to Lincoln area businesses and community groups.
Prepared Agency filmstrips, brochures, and news releases.
Conducted public relations information sessions.

<u>Legislative Assistant:</u> Nebraska Legislative Session, Lincoln, Nebraska (June 1990-December 1991).

Responsible for the collection, compilation, and release of information briefs and legislative action profiles to public news media.
Typed and edited legislative bills.

EDUCATION

The University of Nebraska, Lincoln, Nebraska (1990-1994)
Bachelor of Arts Degree. Speech Communication and Journalism. Grade Point Average: 3.75/4.00.

EDUCATIONAL HIGHLIGHTS

Outstanding Senior Award, Creative Writing Award. Speech Club Secretary, Phi Delta Kappa Vice-President.

Related Course Work
Public Relations and Publicity	Survey of Mass Media
Social Political Communication	Interviewing
Public Speaking	Advertising Principles
Federal Grant Development	Public Opinion

Available: Immediately

References: Upon request

Figure 16.4:

This figure illustrates a résumé that is used by many students. The résumé layout is fairly standard, but may vary depending upon the work experiences of the individual.

Self-prepared or Personal Résumé Emphasizing Skills

Figure 16.5:

This figure illustrates a résumé that emphasizes a person's skills. The résumé layout is fairly standard, but may vary depending upon the work experiences and skills of the individual.

Adapted from *Introducing Résumé Expert Computer Software for Writing Your Résumé*, Kansas City, Mo.: Business Technology, 1990, 31.

Robert L. Smith
1525 East Center Street   Los Angeles, California 90008
213/674-9797

OBJECTIVE	To help a retail company provide high customer satisfaction while managing merchandise efficiently in an entry level management position
SKILLS	• Resolved customer problems in retail merchandising • Organized product floor for customer convenience • Experienced in dealing with wholesalers • Organized and maintained inventories • College courses in management, personnel, finance, statistics, and marketing
EDUCATION	University of Southern California, Los Angeles, California Bachelor of Science Degree Business, May 1991, Management
HONORS	Academic Scholarships, Delta Mu Delta (Business Honorary)
ACTIVITIES and MEMBERSHIPS	President of Delta Mu Delta; Student Senator; Youth Leader of 30 member church youth group.
EXPERIENCE **February 89– Present**	B. C. PRINTING, Los Angeles *Graphic Arts–Delivery Person* • Mastered all aspects of pre-press operations • Effectively dealt with and resolved conflicts • Oversaw various camera procedures including working with numerous types of film and preparing press plates
January 88–89	QUALITY PRESS, INC., Los Angeles *Internship Graphic Arts–Delivery Person* • Demonstrated ability to serve and communicate with customers in a diverse office supply operation • Organized and maintained product floor and inventory
Additional Information	Paid 100% of college expenses Worked to support wife and child while attending college Computer training includes Basic, Cobol, Assembler, and Pascal
Available	Immediately
References	Available on request

appropriate time (for example, during their office hours) and reason (for example, discussing a paper or an assignment) to visit with your professors so they become acquainted with you. Most professors enjoy meeting with their students. Use common sense and don't overstay your visits. A professor will find it easier to write a letter of recommendation for you, and the letter will be more personal and believable, if he or she knows who you are.

Never put a person's name on a reference list unless you have his or her permission to do so. When asking individuals to write references for you, be prepared to hand them a copy of your résumé and to tell them what kind of job you are seeking. Contacting people to write letters of recommendation should be done as professionally and efficiently as possible. Remember that, you are requesting someone to take time to help you. However, since most people enjoy helping others, you should never be afraid to ask for a reference.

After you write your résumé, proofread it carefully for errors and omissions. Then ask a counselor in the placement office or a professor to suggest improvements. If you follow the simple guidelines and examples in this chapter, your completed résumé should be acceptable.

EXERCISE

List at least three people who could write a letter of recommendation for you. Do not include relatives or friends. After each name, describe what you think that individual knows about you as a person, your competencies, and your ability to succeed.

Searching the Job Market

Getting a job requires motivation, energy, hard work, and preparation. Even an applicant with superb qualifications faces tremendous competition for the best positions. According to placement service records, the average applicant spends only about three to ten hours a week searching for employment. However, the person who is highly motivated will treat the search as if it were a job itself. The more time a person spends searching, the sooner and more likely he or she will be hired.

Newspaper want ads, professional magazines, placement services, former teachers, and people working in jobs you are interested in can all be good sources of job leads. However, the most productive approach to locating jobs is networking. **Networking** is the systematic contacting of people who can provide information about available jobs or who can offer jobs. Relatives, friends, classmates, colleagues, and people at social and professional gatherings are all potential sources of information. If someone does not know of any job openings him or herself, ask if he or she knows of anyone who might. Then contact that person. In this way, your network expands from one person to another and you gain additional names and/or job information from each new contact. The more people you know, the better your chances of being interviewed and the greater your opportunity for employment.

THINK ABOUT IT ▬▬▬▬▬▬▬▬▬▬▬▬▬

Twenty years from now, the typical American worker will have changed jobs four times and careers twice, and will be employed in an occupation that does not exist today.

Jeffrey Hallet, *Worklife Visions,* 1990

What does this tell you about your employment search? How does that make you feel? How can you prepare?

Researching the Company

Before arriving for an interview, you should know the full name of the company; how old it is; where its headquarters, plants, offices, or stores are located; what its products or services are, what its economic growth has been; and how its prospects look for the future. Such knowledge demonstrates your initiative and interest to the interviewer and can serve as a springboard for discussions. This also shows that you have a particular interest in the company, rather than giving the impression that you're "settling" for whatever job you can find.

An applicant can find out about almost any business or professional organization by sending for its annual report and/or recruiting materials and by looking through some of the following publications.[7] Such resources are available in libraries and placement offices.

Dun and Bradstreet's Reference Book contains a virtually complete listing of all types of business organizations, arranged geographically and coded as to product or service. Included is an evaluation of each firm's reliability.

MacRea's Blue Book consists of four volumes listing the names and addresses of companies, classified by product and trade name. Included in the listing are the locations of branches and the capital rating of the company.

Moody's Manuals are individual volumes on different industries: banking and finance, manufacturing (domestic and foreign), public utilities, and transportation.

Standard and Poor's Corporation Records lists thousands of leading business firms, and identifies their products, number of employees, and names and positions of key employees.

Thomas's Register of American Manufacturers, consisting of seven volumes plus an index, contains detailed information on leading manufacturing organizations throughout the country. Names and addresses of companies are listed under product headings and are classified by state and city.

Careers in Business lists companies interested in hiring business and liberal arts graduates. Included in the listings are the name of the person to contact, the type and size of the business, and the majors they normally hire.

There are also specialized directories.

Standard Directory of Advertising Agencies lists 4,000 leading advertising agencies in the United States, giving their key executives, major accounts, and geographical location.

Polk's Bank Directory lists the names, addresses, and directors of banks.

American Register of Importers and Exporters lists 30,000 importers and exporters classified by product, with names of executives.

Management Consulting lists 2,600 consulting firms, arranged by type of consulting and location, with principals' and officers' names.

Handbook of Independent Marketing/Advertising Services lists 200 consulting firms in the fields of marketing, advertising, packaging, media, and new products.

PR Blue Book lists public relations consulting firms with owners' names plus 5,000 public relations directors of major organizations.

EXERCISE

Go to your college or university placement office and find out what services it offers. What publications and guidance are available? Can it help you research a company? If so, how?

KEY FACTS TO KNOW ABOUT AN ORGANIZATION

Statistics	Geographical location
	Location of corporate headquarters
	Size of organization in industry
Financial stability	Bond ratings
	Growth in sales and profits
	View of stock analysis
Growth plans	New plants, stores, offices
Research and development programs	Investments for the future
Product development and manufacturing	Emerging products and services
	Uses of new technologies
	Competition
Marketing and distribution methods	In-house sales force
	Advertising methods
	Service centers
	Computerized communication with customers

Employee benefits	Wealth-building benefit plans
	Tuition reimbursement
	Pension plan
	Health programs
	Child Care
	Product discounts
Quality of work factors	Continuing training
	Relocation policies
	Promotion-from-within
	Performance reviews[8]

Developing Questions for the Interviewer

In preparation for your meeting, you should think about possible questions to ask the interviewer. Sometimes an interviewer may choose to say little or to stop talking altogether, in which case it becomes your responsibility to carry on the conversation by asking questions and continuing to emphasize your qualifications for the job. Whether or not the interviewer stops talking, you should have a list of questions to ask. This does not mean coming to the interview with a written list of questions, but it does mean coming prepared to ask questions such as, "What are the duties and responsibilities of the job? Does the company provide training programs? How much traveling is involved in the job? What's the next step up from the starting position? Would I be able to continue my education?"

Other Considerations

As a job applicant, you are expected to show good judgment and common sense about appearance, assertiveness, being on time, and being at the right place. If you plan ahead and follow these simple suggestions, you should be able to avoid any serious problems.

How to Dress for an Interview

Your primary goal in dressing for an interview is to feel great about the way you look, while projecting an image that matches the requirements of the job and the company.

Go for perfection. Wear professionally pressed clothing in natural fabrics. Spend as much as you can possibly afford on your interview clothes. Don't make a fashion statement. Conservative is the watchword. The interview is usually not the time to make a personal statement of nonconformity or disagreement with society's concept of professional image.[9]

THE INTERVIEW

Much of the responsibility for a successful interview rests with the interviewer, but this doesn't mean that you can merely relax and let things happen. On the contrary, research suggests that most interviewers develop a strong opinion about a job applicant in the first thirty seconds. If you do poorly at the opening, your chances of getting the job are slim, no matter how brilliantly you handle the rest of the interview. It may seem unfair or superficial, but people do judge others on the basis of first impressions, and such impressions can be long-lasting. Whatever you do, be on time for the interview.

Frequently Asked Questions

One expert states that most applicants make two devastating mistakes when they are being questioned. First, they fail to listen to the question; in consequence, they answer a question that was not asked or give superfluous information. Second, they attempt to answer questions with virtually no preparation. Lack of preparation will reduce the chances of success even for skillful communicators. You should always take a moment to think about your answer before you respond to each question, unless it is something that you have already thought through.

Here are some of the most common questions interviewers ask and some possible responses to them.

1. *"What can you tell me about yourself?"*
   This is not an invitation to give your life history. The interviewer is looking for clues about your character, qualifications, ambitions, and motivations. The following is a good example of a positive response. "In high school I was involved in competitive sports and I always tried to improve in each sport I participated in. As a college student, I worked in a clothing store part-time and found that I could sell things easily. The sale was important, but for me, it was even more important to make sure that the customer was satisfied. It wasn't long before customers came back to the store and specifically asked for me to help them. I'm very competitive and it means a lot to me to be the best."

2. *"Why do you want to work for us?"*
   This is an obvious question and, if you have done research on the company, you should be able to give a good reason. Organize your reasons into several short sentences that clearly spell out your interest. "You are a leader in the field of electronics. Your company is a Fortune 500 company. Your management is very progressive."

3. *"Why should I hire you?"*
   Once again, you should not be long-winded, but you should provide a summary of your qualifications. Be positive and show that you are capable of doing the job. "Based on the internships that I have participated in and the related part-time experiences I have had, I can do the job."

4. *"How do you feel about your progress to date?"*

    Never apologize for what you have done. Be prepared with at least one positive assessment of your accomplishments that you have not already mentioned. "I think I did well in school. In fact, in a number of courses I received the highest exam scores in the class." "As an intern for the X Company, I received some of the highest evaluations that had been given in years." "Considering that I played on the university's volleyball team and worked part time, I think you'll agree that I accomplished quite a bit during my four years in school."

5. *"What would you like to be doing five years from now?"*

    Know what you can realistically accomplish. You can find out by talking to others about what they accomplished in their first five years with a particular company. "I hope to be the best I can be at my job, and, because many in this line of work are promoted to area manager, I am planning on that also."

6. *"What is your greatest weakness?"*

    You cannot avoid this question by saying that you do not have any; everyone has weaknesses. The best approach is to admit a weakness, but show that you are working on it and have a plan to overcome it. If possible, cite a weakness that will work to the company's advantage. "I'm not very good at detail work, but I have been working on it and I've improved dramatically over the past several years." "I'm such a perfectionist that I won't stop until a report is written just right."

7. *"What is your greatest strength?"*

    This is a real opportunity to "toot your own horn." Do not brag or get too egotistical, but let the employer know that you believe in yourself and that you know your strengths. "I feel that my strongest asset is my ability to stick to things to get them done. I feel a real sense of accomplishment when I finish a job and it turns out just as I'd planned. I've set some high goals for myself. For example, I want to graduate with highest distinction. And even though I had a slow start in my freshman year, I made up for it by doing an honors thesis."

8. *"What goals have you set and how did you meet them?"*

    This question examines your ability to plan ahead and meet your plan with specific actions. "Last year, during a magazine drive to raise money for our band trip, I set my goal at raising 20 percent more than I had the year before. I knew the drive was going to begin in September, so I started contacting people in August. I asked each of my customers from last year to give me the name of one or two new people who might also buy a magazine. I not only met my goal, but also I was the top salesperson on the drive."

No matter what question you are asked, answer it honestly and succinctly. Most interviewers are looking for positive statements, well-expressed ideas, persuasiveness, and clear thinking under pressure.

In the unlikely event that you are asked a question that violates the affirmative action laws, you can decline to answer. You might say, "I'm sorry, but I don't find that question relevant to the position being offered and it is against affirmative action laws to ask it." You may simply ask the interviewer why he or she is asking you that question. Make sure that you are tactful, but be firm in letting the interviewer know that he or she is doing something illegal.

If an interviewer were to ask you any of the eight frequently-asked questions given above, do you know how you would answer them? The key to formulating your response is to understand why a particular question is being asked. Remember the purpose of the employment interview is to identify the best-qualified person for the job. The more often you can demonstrate, through your response to the questions asked, that you are the best qualified, the more likely you are to get the job offer.

Other Considerations

Always maintain eye contact with the interviewer. Show that you are confident by looking straight at the speaker. Making eye contact may not get you the job, but the absence of eye contact can reduce your chances dramatically.

Most interviewers greet the applicant with a handshake. Make sure that your clasp is firm. Being jittery about the interview can result in your having cold, clammy hands, which creates a negative impression. Therefore, try to make sure your hands are warm and dry. If this is not possible, your firm handshake will help you show more confidence.

When the interviewer asks you to sit down, if you have a choice, take a chair beside the desk rather than one in front. This helps eliminate any physical barriers between you and the interviewer and also makes you seem a little more equal, for which the interviewer will unconsciously respect you.

Before leaving, try to find out exactly what action will follow the interview (for example; a telephone call or a letter) and when it will happen. Shake hands as you say good-bye, and thank the interviewer for spending time with you.

FACTORS LEADING TO REJECTION

Rejection is difficult for all of us to accept, but you should never give up. Being rejected by employers eight or nine times before receiving a job offer is not unusual in the recent job market.[10]

Employers from numerous companies were recently asked, "What negative factors most often lead to the rejection of an applicant?" Here are their responses in order of frequency:

1. Negative personality or poor impression—more specifically, lack of motivation, ambition, maturity, aggressiveness, or enthusiasm

2. Inability to communicate; poor communication skills

3. Lack of competence; inadequate training

4. Low grades; poor grades in major field

5. Lack of specific goals

6. Unrealistic expectations

7. Lack of interest in type of work

8. Unwillingness to travel or relocate

9. Poor preparation for the interview

10. Lack of experience.[11]

You must realize that the likelihood of not receiving a job offer is influenced by the number of people seeking the job and the number of jobs available. Of course, you can enhance your chances of getting job offers by being prepared and by presenting yourself in a positive and energetic way.

OTHER FACTORS LEADING TO JOB OFFERS

An applicant who is well-rounded, has earned good grades, has some relevant work experience, has participated in a variety of extracurricular activities, projects an all-around, pleasant personality, and has effective written and oral communication skills is more likely to get job offers than one who does not possess these qualities, according to Jason Meyers of *Collegiate Employment Institute Newsletter*.[12] Meyers says, A candidate who strives to attain these qualities and who comes across as a hard-working, mature individual should have a promising career outlook."[13]

A research study cited by Meyers in his article asked recruiters to describe what they believed to be the qualities of a well-rounded individual. They characterized a well-rounded person as having maturity, the ability to be part of a team, a good work ethic, good decision-making skills, superior work habits, and good judgment. Another study cited by Meyers found that the characteristics recruiters most often sought in job applicants were divided into two categories: *quantifiable* characteristics, such as grade point average, education, and work experience; and *interpersonal* characteristics, such as communication skills, personality, and career and management skills. This study suggests that a balance between quantifiable characteristics and interpersonal characteristics is what makes an ideal job candidate.[14]

It seems that those who are well-prepared; have effective communication skills; are mature, motivated, hard-working team players; and can make good decisions will always be in demand. You must just ask yourself how you match up to these qualities now, and then try to improve in those areas in which you are not strong. You must also be able to demonstrate that you actually possess these qualities through the actions you have taken.

SUMMARY

Choosing a career is one of the most important decisions a person can make, and a successful job interview is a crucial step in achieving that end. Planning and preparation are critical to a successful employment interview. Applicants must know their strengths and weaknesses and be able to communicate effectively with the interviewer. Getting a job requires motivation, energy, hard work, and research, as well as knowing where to look and whom to contact in order to obtain the necessary information.

An effective *résumé* (a written document describing professional, educational, and personal qualifications and experience) can pave the way for a productive interview. In judging a résumé, employers look for accuracy and neatness. The two most common kinds of résumés are the standard data sheet used by most placement and employment services, and the self-prepared résumé. Both formats summarize basic information about the applicant's career objective, educational training, work experience, extracurricular activities, and references.

Searching the job market requires motivation, energy, hard work, and preparation. Sources for job openings include newspaper want ads, professional magazines, placement services, former teachers, and friends or others who work in companies that have jobs that interest you. *Networking* is the systematic contacting of people who can provide information about available jobs or who can offer jobs. The more people you know, the better your chances for employment.

Before an interview, an applicant should find out about a company's background, location, products or services, growth, and prospects for the future. Using such information, the applicant can prepare questions to ask the interviewer.

Applicants must create a strong positive impression from the moment they meet the interviewer. They should prepare responses to commonly asked questions, show confidence, maintain eye contact with the interviewer, give a firm handshake, and if given a choice, sit in a chair at the side of the desk or table rather than in front.

Job applicants who prepare carefully and present themselves well can avoid some of the most common reasons for rejection.

KEY TERMS

Networking: Systematic contacting of people who can give information about or offer jobs or who can provide information about others who can.

Résumé: Written document that briefly describes a person's professional, educational, and personal qualifications and experiences.

DISCUSSION STARTERS

1. Why is the choice of a career field so important?
2. What can people do to increase their chances of getting a job?
3. If you were an employer, what would you look for in a job applicant?
4. What advice would you give fellow students about writing résumés?
5. Why should personal data such as age, gender, marital status, and religion be omitted from a résumé?
6. How should you go about getting references? Whom should you ask?
7. What is the best approach to a job search? Why?
8. What should you know about a company before you are interviewed?
9. Why is it important for an applicant to ask questions of the interviewer?
10. What questions does an interviewer usually ask an applicant?
11. What can someone do to lessen the chances of being rejected?

NOTES

1. A special thanks to Dr. Larry R. Routh, Director of Career Planning and Placement Center, University of Nebraska at, Lincoln, for his review, information, and suggestions.
2. J. Meyers, "The Ideal Job Candidate," *Collegiate Employment Institute Newsletter,* July 15, 1989, 6.; *Ford's Insider: Continuing Series of College Newspaper Supplements* (Knoxville, Tenn.: 13–30 Corporation, 1980): 14.
3. Ford's Insider, 4.
4. C. J. Stewart and W. B. Cash, Jr., *Interviewing Principles and Practices,* 7th ed. (Dubuque, Iowa: Brown, 1993), 163; D. E. Bowen, G. E. Ledford, and B. R. Nathan, "Hiring for the Organization, Not the Job," *Academy of Management Executive* 5 (November 1991): 35–51.
5. C. J. Stewart and W. B. Cash, Jr., 164.
6. Ibid., 146.
7. From *Researching an Organization,* pamphlet printed by Placement Service, University of Nebraska at Lincoln 1993.
8. Ibid.
9. J. LaFevre, "How You Really Get Hired," *CPC Annual 1990/91,* 34th ed. (Bethlehem, Pa.: College Placement Council).
10. Interview with Dr. Larry R. Routh, Director of Career Planning, December, 1993.
11. *The Endicott Report: Trends in the Employment of College and University Graduates in Business and Industry* (Evanston, Ill.: The Placement Center, Northwestern University, 1980), 8. Dr. Routh (in our December, 1993 interview) told me that the rejection reasons companies give today are no different from those given in 1980.
12. J. Meyers, 6.
13. Ibid., 6.
14. Ibid, 6.

GLOSSARY

A

Abstract word: Symbol for an idea, quality, or relationship. [Chapters 4 & 11]

Active Listening: Process of analyzing and evaluating what others say in an effort to understand their feelings or the true meaning of their message. [Chapter 14]

Adaptor: Body motion to increase feeling at ease in communication situations. [Chapter 5]

Ad Hominen: Fallacy in which a person is attacked, rather than his or her argument; also referred to as "name calling" [Chapter 12]

Adoption: Action goal that asks listeners to demonstrate their acceptance of an attitude, belief, or value by performing the behavior suggested by the speaker. [Chapter 12]

Advance Organizer: Statement that warns listener that significant information is coming. [Chapter 11]

Affect Display: Body motion that expresses emotions and feelings. [Chapter 5]

Agenda: List of all topics to be discussed during a meeting. [Chapter 15]

Alter-Adaptors: Body motion directed at others that is learned from past experience and from the manipulation of objects. [Chapter 5]

Analogy: Comparison of two things that are similar in certain essential characteristics. [Chapter 8]

Androgynous: A term describing a person with both masculine and feminine traits. [Chapter 3]

Antonym: Word, phrase, or concept that is opposite in meaning to another word, phrase, or concept. [Chapter 11]

Appeal to Needs: Attempt to move people to action by calling on their physical and psychological requirements and desires. [Chapter 12]

Artifact: Ornament or possession that communicates information about a person. [Chapter 5]

Attending: Focusing on specific stimuli while ignoring or downplaying other stimuli. [Chapter 6]

Attitude: Evaluative disposition, feeling, or position about oneself, others, events, ideas, or objects. [Chapter 3]

Audience: Collection of individuals who have come together to watch or listen to someone or something, such as to listen to a speech. [Chapter 7]

Audience Analysis: Collection and interpretation of data about characteristics, attitudes, values, and beliefs of an audience. [Chapter 7]

Autocratic Leader: Leader who keeps complete control and makes all the decisions for the group. [Chapter 15]

B

Belief: Conviction or confidence in the truth of something that is not based on absolute proof. [Chapter 3]

Bipolar Question: Question that demands a single-word answer (yes-no, true-false); extreme form of closed question that allows no freedom of expression. [Chapter 8]

Blind Area: Quadrant of the Johari Window that represents information that others perceive about us, but that we do not recognize or acknowledge about ourselves. [Chapter 13]

Body: Main section of a speech that develops the speaker's general and specific purposes. [Chapter 9]

Body Motion: Any movement of the face or body that communicates a message. [Chapter 5]

Brainstorming: Technique used to generate as many ideas as possible in a limited amount of time. [Chapters 7 & 15]

Brief Example: Specific instance that is used to introduce a topic, drive home a point, or create a desired response. [Chapter 8]

Bypassing: Misunderstanding that occurs between a sender and a receiver because of the symbolic nature of language. [Chapter 4]

C

Captive Participant: Person who is required to hear a particular speech. [Chapter 7]

Cause-Effect Pattern: Order of presentation in which the speaker first explains the causes of an event, problem, or issue and then discusses their consequences. [Chapter 9]

Causal Reasoning: Sequence of thought that links causes with effects; it either implies or explicitly states the word *because.* [Chapter 12]

Channel: Route by which messages flow between the source and the receiver; for example, light waves and sound waves. [Chapter 1]

Chronemics: Study of how people perceive time, and how they structure and use time as communication. [Chapter 5]

Closed Question: Question that calls for a restricted or short response from the interviewee. [Chapter 8]

Closure: Filling in of details by a perceiver so that whatever is perceived appears to be completed. [Chapter 2]

Cohesiveness: Attraction that group members feel for each other; their willingness to stick together; a form of loyalty. [Chapter 15]

Commitment: Desire of group members to work together to get their task completed to the satisfaction of the entire group. [Chapter 15]

Common Goal: The driving force that brings people together to form a group. [Chapter 15]

Communication: The simultaneous sharing and creating of meaning through human symbolic action. [Chapter 1]

Communication Apprehension: Anxiety syndrome associated with real or anticipated communication with other persons. [Chapters 3 & 10]

Complementing: Use of nonverbal cues to complete, describe, or accent verbal cues. [Chapter 5]

Conclusion: Closing statements that focus the audience's thoughts on the specific purpose of a speech and bring the most important points together in a condensed and uniform way. [Chapter 9]

Concrete Word: Symbol for a specific thing that can be pointed to or physically experienced. [Chapters 4 & 11]

Conflict: A clash or fight; incompatible desires, ideas, or opinions. [Chapter 15]

Connotation: Subjective meaning of a word; what a word suggests because of feelings or associations it evokes. [Chapter 4]

Context: Circumstances or situation in which communication occurs. [Chapter 1]

Continuance: Action goal that asks listeners to demonstrate their acceptance of an attitude, belief, or value by continuing to perform the behavior suggested by the speaker. [Chapter 12]

Contrast: Definition that shows or emphasizes differences. [Chapter 11]

Credibility: Speaker's believability based on the audience's evaluation of the speaker's competence, knowledge, experience, and character. [Chapters 9 & 12]

Critical Listening: Listening that judges the accuracy of the infpresented, determines the reasonableness of its conclusions, and evaluates its presenter. [Chapter 6]

Critical Thinking: The ability to analyze and assess information. [Chapter 6]

Culture: Patterns of values and traditions which are symbolically communicated through objects, behaviors, and utterances. [Chapter 2]

D

Dating: Form of indexing that sorts people, events, ideas, and objects according to time. [Chapter 4]

Deceiving: Use of nonverbal cues to present a false appearance or incorrect information in order to mislead others. [Chapter 5]

Deductive Reasoning: Sequence of thought that moves from general information to a specific conclusion; it consists of a general premise, a minor premise, and a conclusion. [Chapter 12]

Deintensifying: Facial behavior response that understates reactions and emotions in order to create or maintain a favorable relationship with another person. [Chapter 5]

Decoding: Process of translating a message into the thoughts or feelings that were communicated. [Chapter 1]

Definition by Example: Clarifying a term not by describing it or giving its meaning, but by describing or showing an example. [Chapter 8]

Demographic Analysis: Collection and interpretation of data characteristics (age, gender, religion, occupation, and so on), of individuals, excluding values, attitudes, and beliefs. [Chapter 7]

Democratic Leader: Leader who guides and directs, but shares control and remains open to all views. [Chapter 15]

Denotation: Objective meaning of a word, or standard dictionary definition. [Chapter 4]

Descriptive Feedback: Receiver's checking of his or her understanding of a sender's nonverbal behavior by describing his or her interpretation of it to the sender. [Chapter 5]

Descriptors: Words used to describe something. [Chapter 11]

Deterrence: Action goal that asks listeners to demonstrate their acceptance of an attitude, belief, or value by avoiding certain behavior. [Chapter 12]

Discontinuance: Action goal that asks listeners to demonstrate their acceptance of an attitude, belief, or value by avoiding a certain behavior; the opposite of Adoption. [Chapter 12]

Doublespeak: The deliberate misuse of language to distort meaning. [Chapter 4]

Dyadic Communication: Exchange of information between two people. [Chapter 1]

E

Emblem: Body motion that can be translated directly into words or phrases. [Chapter 5]

Emotional Appeal: Attempt to move people to action by playing on their feelings. [Chapter 12]

Empathic Listening: Listening to understand what another person is thinking and feeling. [Chapter 6]

Empathy: Identification with another person, or vicarious experiencing of his or her feelings, thoughts, and attitudes. [Chapter 1]

Encoding: Process by which the source changes thoughts or feelings into the words, sounds, and physical expressions that make up the actual message to be sent. [Chapter 1]

Entertainment Speech: Speech that provides enjoyment and amusement. [Chapter 7]

Environment: Psychological and physical surroundings in which communication occurs, encompassing the attitudes, feelings, perceptions, and relationships of the communicators as well as thecharacteristics of the location in which communication takes place. [Chapters 1 & 5]

Ethics: Individuals' system of moral principles. [Chapters 10 & 12]

Ethnocentric: Term describing a person who notices differences that go beyond pride in his or her heritage or background to the conviction that he or she knows more and is better than those who are different. [Chapter 2]

Etymology: Definition that traces the origin and development of a word. [Chapter 11]

Euphemism: Use of an inoffensive or mild expression for one that may offend, cause embarrassment, or suggest something unpleasant. [Chapter 4]

Evaluative listening: Listening to judge or analyze information. [Chapter 6]

Example: Simple, representative incident or model that clarifies a point. [Chapter 8]

Expert Opinion: Opinions, testimony, or conclusions of witnesses or recognized authorities. [Chapter 8]

Extemporaneous Delivery: Delivery style in which the speaker carefully prepares the speech in advance, but delivers it with only a few notes and with a high degree of spontaneity. [Chapter 10]

Eye Contact: Extent to which a speaker looks directly at audience members. [Chapter 10]

F

Facial Expression: Configuration of the face that can reflect, augment, contradict, or be unrelated to a speaker's vocal delivery. [Chapters 5 & 10]

Facial Management Techniques: Control of facial muscles in order to conceal inappropriate or unacceptable responses. [Chapter 5]

Factual Illustration: Report of something that exists or actually happened. [Chapter 8]

Fallacy: Argument that is flawed because it does not follow the rules of logic.

Feedback: Response or reaction that the receiver gives to a source in message. [Chapter 1]

Figurative Analogy: Comparison of things in different categories. [Chapter 8]

Figure and Ground Organization: Ordering of perceptions so that some stimuli are in focus and others become the background. [Chapter 2]

Force: Intensity and volume level of the voice. [Chapter 10]

Friendship-Warmth Touch: Touch that communicates appreciation of the special attributes of another person. [Chapter 5]

Full-Content Outline: Detailed skeleton of a speech with all main and secondary points written in complete sentences. [Chapter 9]

Functional Approach: Examination of nonverbal behavior not by looking at each nonverbal cue separately, but by looking at how they all interact to perform various communicative functions. [Chapter 5]

Functional-Professional Touch: Unsympathetic, impersonal, cold, or businesslike touch. [Chapter 5]

G

Gender: A social construct related to masculine and feminine behaviors which are learned. [Chapter 2]

Gender-Inclusive Language: Language that does not discriminate against males or females. [Chapter 4]

General Purpose: Overall goal of a speech, usually one of three overlapping functions—to inform, to persuade, or to entertain. [Chapter 7]

Gesture: Movement of the head, arms, or hands that helps illustrate, emphasize, or clarify an idea. [Chapter 10]

Grammar: Rules that govern how words are put together to form phrases and sentences. [Chapter 4]

Group: Collection of individuals who form a system in which members influence one another, derive mutual satisfaction from one another, have a common purpose, take on roles, are interdependent, and interact face-to-face. [Chapter 15]

Group Personality: Collective identity that members of a group form when they come together. [Chapter 15]

Group Size: Number of participants in the group. [Chapter 15]

Groupthink: A dysfunction in which group members see the harmony of the group as being more important than new ideas, the critical examination of ideas, the willingness to change decisions, or the willingness to allow new members to participate. [Chapter 15]

H

Hastly Generalization: Fallacy that occurs when a speaker doesn't have sufficient data, and thus argues or reasons from specific example. [Chapter 12]

Hearing: Passive physiological process in which sound is received by the ear. [Chapter 6]

Hidden Area: Quadrant of the Johari Window that represents personal and private information about ourselves that we choose not to disclose to others. [Chapter 13]

Hierarchy of Individual Needs: Theory developed by Abraham Maslow that rank-orders physical, safety, social, self-esteem, and self-actualization needs, and states that the lower-order needs must be satisfied before the higher-order needs. [Chapter 13]

Hypothetical Illustration: Report of something that could or probably would happen given a specific set of circumstances. [Chapter 8]

I

Identification Theory: Asserts that a child learns his or her sex role and behaviors through intimate and ongoing interaction with a parent or caretaker. [Chapter 2]

Illustration: Extended example, narrative, case history, or anecdote that is striking and memorable. [Chapter 8]

Illustrator: Body motion that accents, reinforces, or emphasizes an accompanying verbal message. [Chapter 5]

Impromptu Delivery: Delivery style in which a speaker delivers a speech without any planning or preparation whatsoever. [Chapter 10]

Indexing: Technique to reduce indiscrimination by identifying the specific persons, ideas, events, or objects a statement refers to.

Indiscrimination: Neglect of individual differences and overemphasis of similarities. [Chapter 4]

Inductive Reasoning: Sequence of thought that moves from specific facts to a general conclusion. [Chapter 12]

Information: Knowledge derived from study, experience, or instruction. [Chapter 11]

Information Relevance: Relation of information to an audience that gives them a reason to listen. [Chapter 11]

Informative Speech: Speech that enhances an audience's knowledge and understanding by explaining what something means, how something works, or how something is done. [Chapter 7]

Intelligibility: Speaker's vocal volume, distinctiveness of sound, clarity of pronunciation, articulation, and the stress placed on syllables, words, and phrases. [Chapter 10]

Intensifying: Facial behavior response that exaggerates expressions in order to meet the expectation of others. [Chapter 5]

Intentional Communication: Message that is purposely send to a specific receiver. [Chapter 1]

Interaction: Exchange of communication in which communicators take turns sending and receiving messages. [Chapter 1]

Intercultural Communication: The study of communication between different cultures. [Chapter 2]

Interdependence: Mutual dependence of group members on one another. [Chapter 15]

Interference: Anything that changes the meaning of an intended message. [Chapter 1]

Internal Summary: Short review statement given at the end of a main point. [Chapter 9]

International Phonetic Alphabet (IPA): Alphabet of sounds devised to provide a consistent and universal system for transcribing speech sounds of all languages. [Chapter 4]

Interpersonal Communication: Informal exchange of information between two or more people. [Chapters 1 & 13]

Interpersonal Conflict: Opposition of individuals who perceive incompatible goals as a result of at least one individual not being able to gain acceptance of his or her goals by the other. [Chapter 14]

Interpretation: Assigning of meaning to stimuli. [Chapter 2]

Interview: Carefully planned and executed question-and-answer session designed to exchange desired information between two parties. [Chapters 1 & 8]

Intrapersonal Communication: Process of understanding information within oneself. [Chapters 1 & 13]

Introduction: Opening statement that orients the audience to the subject and motivates them to listen. [Chapter 9]

J

Johari Window: Graphic model that depicts awareness and self- disclosure in interpersonal relations by illustrating the proportion of information about oneself that is known to oneself and to others. [Chapter 13]

L

Laissez-faire Leader: Leader who gives complete decision-making freedom to the group or to individual members. [Chapter 15]

Language: Structured system of signs, sounds, gestures, and marks used and understood to express ideas and feelings among people within a community, nation, geographical area, or cultural tradition. [Chapter 4]

Leader: Person assigned or selected to lead or provide direction in order to reach a group's goals. [Chapter 15]

Leadership: Any behavior that helps to clarify, guide, or achieve a group's goals; the ability to exert influence over others. [Chapter 15]

Leading Question: Question that explicitly or implicitly guides the interviewee to an expected or desired response. [Chapter 8]

Listening: Active process of receiving aural stimuli by hearing, selecting, attending, understanding, evaluating, and remembering. [Chapter 6]

Listening for Enjoyment: Listening for pleasure, personal satisfaction, or appreciation. [Chapter 6]

Listening for Information: Listening to gain comprehension. [Chapter 6]

Literal Analogy: Comparison of members of the same category. [Chapter 8]

Logical Appeal: Attempt to move people to action through the use of evidence and proof. [Chapter 12]

Logical Definition: Definition consisting of a term's dictionary definition and the characteristics that distinguish the term from other members of the same category. [Chapter 8]

Love-Intimacy Touch: Touch usually occurring in romantic relationships; which includes kissing, stroking, and other forms of highly communicative touch. [Chapter 5]

M

Main Points: Principal subdivisions of a speech. [Chapter 9]

Maintenance Need: Need related to organizing and developing a group so that the members can realize personal satisfaction from working together. [Chapter 15]

Manuscript Delivery: Delivery style in which a speaker writes the speech in its entirety and then reads it word-for-word. [Chapter 10]

Masking: Facial behavior response that replaces an expression of emotion with another thought to be more appropriate for the situation. [Chapter 5]

Mean: Arithmetic value, often referred to as the average, that is the sum of all the values in a set divided by the number of values in the set. [Chapter 8]

Median: The middle value in a series of numbers, with half the values above it and half below it. [Chapter 8]

Memorized Delivery: Delivery style in which a speaker memorizes a speech in its entirety from a word-for-word script. [Chapter 10]

Metaphor: Figure of speech in which a word or phrase relates one object or idea to another object or idea that is not commonly linked together. [Chapter 4]

Message: Stimulus that is produced by the source. [Chapter 1]

Mode: The most frequent value in a series of numbers. [Chapter 8]

Moderately Scheduled Interview: Interview format in which the interviewer follows a list of basic questions or topics and possible probes under each question or topic. [Chapter 8]

Motivated Sequence: Pattern of organization specifically developed for persuasive speaking that combines logic and practical psychology. Five steps are involved: attention, need, satisfaction, visualization, and action. [Chapter 9]

N

Networking: Systematic contacting of people who can either give information about or offer jobs or provide information about others who can do so. [Chapter 16]

Neutral Question: Question that avoids implying an expected or desired response. [Chapter 8]

Neutralizing: Facial behavior response that avoids showing any emotional expression in a given situation. [Chapter 5]

Nonscheduled Interview: Interview format in which the interviewer follows a central objective or a list of possible topics and subtopics, with no formalized order of questions and no anticipated responses. [Chapter 8]

Nonverbal Communication: Any information that is expressed without words. [Chapters 1 & 5]

Norms: Expected and shared ways in which group members behave. [Chapter 15]

O

Object-Adaptor: Body motion that involves the use of an object (such as a pencil, a paper clip, or keys) for something other than its intended function. [Chapter 5]

Observation: Method of collecting information about an audience in which the speaker watches audience members and notes their behaviors and characteristics. [Chapter 7]

Open Area: Quadrant of the Johari Window that represents information that is known to self and others through observation or a willingness to share. [Chapter 13]

Open Question: Question that evokes a response of more than just a few words. [Chapter 8]

Operational Definition: Definition that explains how an object or concept works or lists the steps that make up a process. [Chapter 8]

Organization: Categorizing of stimuli in our environment in order to make sense of them. [Chapter 2]

Organizing: Arranging of ideas and elements into a systematic and meaningful whole. [Chapter 9]

Outlining: Arranging materials in a logical sequence (often referred to as the blueprint or skeleton of a speech) and writing out that sequence in a standardized form. [Chapter 9]

P

Paralanguage: The way we vocalize, or say, the words we speak, rather than the words themselves. [Chapter 5]

Pendulum Effect: Escalating conflict between two persons or groups that results from their use of polar terms to describe and defend their perceptions of reality. [Chapter 4]

Perception: Process of selecting, organizing, and interpreting information in order to give it personal meaning. [Chapter 2]

Perceptual Set: Fixed, previously determined view of events, objects, or people. [Chapter 2]

Persuasion: Communication process, involving both verbal and nonverbal messages, that attempts to reinforce or change listeners' attitudes, beliefs, values, or behavior. [Chapter 12]

Persuasive Speech: Speech that attempts to change listeners' attitudes or behaviors by advocating or trying to gain acceptance of the speaker's point of view. [Chapter 7]

Phoneme: Smallest distinctive and functional unit of sound in a language. [Chapter 4]

Pitch: How low or high the voice is on a tonal scale. [Chapter 10]

Plagiarism: Use of another person's information, language, or ideas without citing the originator and making it appear that the user is the originator. [Chapter 10]

Planned Repetition: Deliberate repetition of a thought in order to increase the likelihood that the audience will understand and remember it. [Chapter 11]

Polarization: endency to view things in terms of extremes. [Chapter 4]

Preliminary Outline: List of all the main points that may be used in a speech. [Chapter 9]

Presentational Outline: Condensation of the full-content outline that aids delivery by minimizing detail and listing key words and phrases in place of full sentences. [Chapter 9]

Primary Question: Question that introduces a new topic or a new area within a topic. [Chapter 8]

Problem-Solution Pattern: Order of presentation that first discusses a problem and then suggests solutions. [Chapter 9]

Proxemics: Study of the use of space and of distance between individuals when they are communicating. [Chapter 5]

Proximity: Grouping of stimuli that are physically close to one another. [Chapter 2]

Process: Series of actions that has no beginning or end and is constantly changing. [Chapter 1]

Psychological Analysis: Collection and interpretation of data about audience members' values, attitudes, and beliefs. [Chapter 7]

Public Communication: Transmission of a message from one person who speaks to a number of individuals who listen. [Chapter 1]

Public Speaking: Presentation of a speech, usually prepared in advance, during which the speaker is the central focus of an audience's attention. [Chapter 7]

Q

Questionable Cause: Fallacy which occurs when a speaker alleges something that does not relate to or produce the outcome claimed in the argument. [Chapter 12]

Question of Fact: Question that asks what is true and what is false. [Chapters 12 & 15]

Question of Interpretation: Question that asks for the meaning or explanation of something. [Chapter 15]

Question of Policy: Question that asks what actions should be taken. [Chapters 12 & 15]

Question of Value: Question that asks whether something is good or bad, desirable or undesirable. [Chapters 12 & 15]

Questionnaire: Set of written questions that is distributed to respondents to gather desired information. [Chapter 7]

R

Random Sampling: Method of selecting a small number of interviewees from a larger group so that every individual has an equal chance of being selected. [Chapter 7]

Range: The lowest to highest numbers, or vice versa, in a series of numbers. [Chapter 8]

Rate: Speed at which a speaker speaks, normally between 120 words and 150 words per minute. [Chapter 10]

Reasoning by Analogy: Sequence of thought that compares similar things or circumstances in order to draw a conclusion. [Chapter 12]

Receiver: Individual who analyzes and interprets the message. [Chapter 1]

Red Herring: Fallacy that uses irrelevant information to divert attention away from th real issue.

Regulating: Use of nonverbal cues to control the flow of communication. [Chapter 5]

Regulator: Body motion that controls, monitors, or maintains the interaction between speaker and listener. [Chapter 5]

Relationship: Association between at least two people. [Chapter 13]

Relationship-oriented Leader: Leader who attempts to obtain a position of prominence and create good interpersonal relationships. [Chapter 15]

Reliability: In relation to an interview, the extent to which the same information could be obtained from the same interviewee in a different interview. [Chapter 8]

Remembering: Recalling something from stored memory; thinking of something again. [Chapter 6]

Repeating: Use of nonverbal cues to repeat what is expressed verbally. [Chapter 5]

Responding: Overt verbal and nonverbal behavior by the listener indicating to the speaker what has and has not been received. [Chapter 6]

Restatement: Expression of the same idea, using different words. [Chapter 8]

Résumé: Written document that briefly describes a person's professional, personal, and educational qualifications and experiences. [Chapter 16]

Reviewing the Current Media: Technique for developing a list of possible topics by looking at current publications, television, movies, and other forms of communicating to the public. [Chapter 7]

Rhetorical Sensitivity: A different approach to self-disclosure in gaining information and developing relationships with other people. [Chapter 13]

S

Secondary or Probing Question: Question used to encourage the interviewee to expand on replies that may have been incomplete, unresponsive, unclear, or inaccurate. [Chapter 8]

Selecting: In the process of listening, the stage of choosing the stimul that will be listened to. [Chapter 6]

Selection: Sorting of one stimulus from another. [Chapter 2]

Selective Attention: Focusing on specific stimuli while ignoring or downplaying other stimuli. [Chapter 2]

Selective Retention: Processing, storage, and retrieval of information that we have already selected, organized, and interpreted. [Chapter 2]

Self-Adaptor: Body motion that is not directed at others but serves some personal need. [Chapter 5]

Self-Concept: Person's mental picture and evaluation of his or her physical, social, and psychological attributes. [Chapter 3]

Self-Disclosure: Voluntary sharing of information about ourselves that another person is not likely to know. [Chapter 13]

Self-Esteem: A person's feelings and attitudes toward himself or herself. [Chapter 3]

Self-Fulfilling Prophecy: Molding of behavior by expectations so that what was expected does indeed happen. [Chapter 3]

Self-Image: Person's mental picture of himself or herself. [Chapter 3]

Self-Inventory: Technique for developing a list of possible topics by listing one's own interests. [Chapter 7]

Semantics: The study of meaning, or the association of words with ideas, feelings, and contexts. [Chapter 4]

Sexist Language: Language that creates sexual stereotypes or implies that one gender is superior to the other. [Chapter 4]

Sexual-Arousal Touch: Most intimate level of personal contact with another. [Chapter 5]

Signpost: Word, phrase, or short statement that indicates to an audience the direction a speaker will take next. [Chapter 9]

Similarity: Grouping of stimuli that resemble one another in size, shape, color, or another trait. [Chapter 2]

Small Group Communication: Exchange of information among a relatively small number of persons (usually three to thirteen) who share a common purpose, such as doing a job or solving a problem. [Chapters 1 & 15]

Small Talk: Casual conversation that is often impersonal and superficial; may include a greeting and/or comments about the weather, newsworthy events, or other unimportant events. [Chapter 13]

Social-Cognitive Theory: Theory that early behaviors are learned from same-sex models and serve as foundations for other types of behavior. [Chapter 2]

Social Facilitation: Tendency for a person acting in a group to release energy that would not be released if the person were acting alone. [Chapter 15]

Social Penetration: The process of increasing disclosure and intimacy in a relationship. [Chapter 13]

Social-Polite Touch: Touch that acknowledges another person according to the norms or rules of a society. [Chapter 5]

Source: Creator of messages. [Chapter 1]

Spatial Pattern: Order of presentation in which the content of a speech is organized according to relationships in space. [Chapter 9]

Specific Purpose Statement: Single phrase that defines precisely what is to be accomplished in a speech. [Chapter 7]

Speech Anxiety: Fear of speaking before an audience. [Chapter 10]

Speech Communication: A humanistic and scientific field of study, research, and application, focusing on how, why, and with what effects people communicate through language and nonverbal behaviors. [Chapter 1]

Statistics: Numerical data that show relationships, summarize, or interpret many instances. [Chapter 8]

Stereotyping: Categorizing of events, objects, and people without regard to unique individual characteristics and qualities. [Chapter 2]

Stimulus: Something that incites or quickens action, feeling, or thought. [Chapter 2]

Style of Communication: Way a person interacts verbally and nonverbally with others. [Chapter 3]

Substituting: Use of nonverbal cues in place of verbal messages when speaking is impossible, undesirable, or inappropriate. [Chapter 5]

Survey Interview: Series of carefully planned and executed person-to-person, question-and-answer sessions during which the speaker tries to discover specific information that will help in the preparation of a speech. [Chapter 7]

Synonym: Word, term, or concept that is the same or nearly the same in meaning as another word, phrase, or concept. [Chapter 11]

System: Combination of parts interdependently acting to form a whole. [Chapter 1]

Systematic Desensitization: Technique where relaxation is associated with an anxiety-producing situation. [Chapter 10]

T

Task Need: Need related to the content of a task and all behaviors that lead to the completion of the task. [Chapter 15]

Task-oriented Leader: Leader who gains satisfaction from performing the task. [Chapter 15]

Territoriality: Need to identify certain areas of space as our own. [Chapter 5]

Theory of Interpersonal Needs: Theory developed by William Schutz contending that three basic needs—affection, inclusion, and control—determine our communication behaviors with others. [Chapter 13]

Thesis Statement: Sentence that states specifically what is going to be discussed in a speech. [Chapter 7]

Time-Sequence (Chronological) Pattern: Order of presentation that begins at a particular point in time and continues either forward or backward. [Chapter 9]

Topical Pattern: Order of presentation in which the main topic is divided into a series of related subtopics. [Chapter 9]

Transaction: Exchange of communication in which the communicators engage in actions simultaneously; that is, encoding and decoding go on at the same time. [Chapter 1]

Transition: Phrase or word used to link ideas. [Chapter 9]

Trustworthiness: Speaker's reliability and dependability, as perceived by audience. [Chapter 12]

U

Uncertainty Principle: A principle that suggests that when we initially meet others to whom we are attracted, our need to know about them tends to make us draw inferences from the physical data we observe. [Chapter 13]

Understanding: Assigning meaning to the stimuli that have been selected and attended to. [Chapter 6]

Unknown Area: Quadrant of the Johari Window that represents information not known either to oneself or others. [Chapter 13]

Unintentional Communication: Message that is either not intended to be sent or not intended for the person who receives it. [Chapter 1]

V

Validity: In relation to an interview, the extent to which both the interviewer and the interviewee accomplish the purpose of the interview. [Chapter 8]

Value: General, relatively long-lasting ideal that guides behavior. [Chapter 3]

Verbal Immediacy: Use of language that identifies and projects the speaker's feelings and makes the message more relevant to the listener. [Chapter 4]

Visual Aids: Materials and equipment, such as key words diagrams, models, real objects, photographs, tables, charts, and graphs, that speakers use to enhance. [Chapter 10]

Vividness: Active, direct, and fresh language that brings a sense of excitement and urgency to a message. [Chapter 4]

Vocal Quality: Overall impression that a speaker's voice makes on his or her listeners. [Chapter 10]

Vocal Variety: Variations in rate, force, and pitch. [Chapter 10]

Voluntary Participant: Person who chooses to listen to a particular speech. [Chapter 7]

W

Word: Symbol that stands for the object or concept that it names. [Chapter 4]

SUBJECT INDEX